Between Paris and Fresno

Armenian Studies in Honor of Dickran Kouymjian

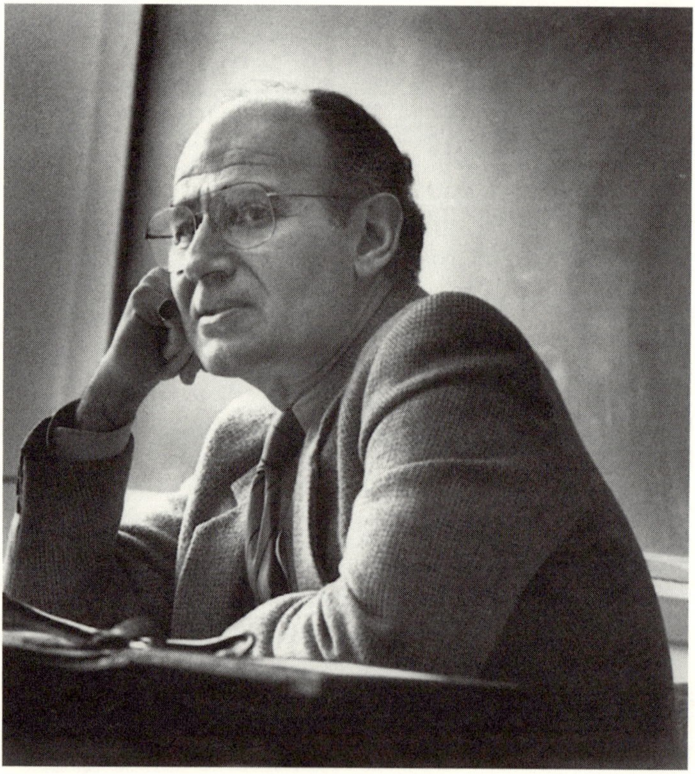

Dickran Kouymjian

Armenian Studies Series, No. 13

Between Paris and Fresno

Armenian Studies in Honor of Dickran Kouymjian

Edited by
Barlow Der Mugrdechian

MAZDA PUBLISHERS, Inc. ♦ Costa Mesa, California ♦ 2008

Mazda Publishers, Inc.
Academic Publishers Since 1980
P.O. Box 2603, Costa Mesa, California 92628 U.S.A.
www.mazdapub.com
A. K. Jabbari, Publisher.

Library of Congress Cataloging-in-Publication Data

Between Paris and Fresno: Armenian studies in honor of
Dickran Kouymjian / edited by Barlow Der Mugrdechian.
p. cm. — (Armenian studies series ; no. 13)
Includes bibliographical references.

ISBN 13: 978-1-56859-168-1 (alk. paper)
ISBN: 1-56859-168-3

1. Armenians. 2. Armenia—History. 3. Armenian philology. 4. Art, Armenian.
I. Kouymjian, Dickran.
DS176.B48 2008
956.6'2—dc22
2008010714

انتشارات مزدا

This Publication Was Made Possible
By A Generous Grant From
The Dolores Zohrab Liebmann Fund.

CONTENTS

History

Preface

Professor Dickran Kouymjian is a true Renaissance man. For the last forty-five years he has been busy producing books and articles on such diverse fields as history, numismatics, art, philology, and literature. In addition, he has a superb knowledge of music, film, theater, antiques, and rare books. Under his tutelage, the Armenian Studies Program at California State University, Fresno has instructed more undergraduate students in various fields of Armenology than any other program in the United States. Furthermore, his research on William Saroyan has revived interest in this great Armenian-American writer. The large number of well-known contributors to this *Festschrift* clearly indicates the high regard in which he is held by scholars from various disciplines. It is my pleasure, therefore, to include this volume, in our Armenian Studies Series.

GEORGE A. BOURNOUTIAN
General Editor

DICKRAN KOUYMJIAN-SCHOLAR AND TEACHER

Barlow Der Mugrdechian

Between Paris and Fresno: Armenian Studies in Honor of Dickran Kouymjian pays tribute to the productive career of a scholar, teacher, mentor, and public speaker. The articles included in this *Festschrift* underline the broad spectrum of his interests in Armenian, Islamic, Classical, and Byzantine history and art, the humanities, literature, film, genocide, and Saroyan studies.

The title reflects Dickran Kouymjian's comings and goings for thirty years between the cities where he has made his home, but it also relates to a biography that he started after the death, in 1981, of his friend, the famous Armenian-American writer William Saroyan. One can read on the liner notes of his book *William Saroyan: An Armenian Trilogy* (1986): "[Dickran Kouymjian] is preparing a book on the author's last years entitled: *Between Paris and Fresno: William Saroyan after Fifty*. Like Saroyan, he shares his time between those cities." I thought it fitting to use Professor Kouymjian's title to describe his own journey during the past decades, rather than one trying to encompass the diverse areas of his research and publishing, or of the essays of his colleagues and friends, as he had done for the *Festschrift* in homage to his mentor, George C. Miles (1974).

The idea of preparing a *Festschrift* was formulated in late 2003 and a first announcement and solicitation for articles began early in 2004, coinciding with several significant milestones in Dr. Kouymjian's life: his seventieth birthday (1934-2004); his forty-fifth year as a university teacher (1959-2004); and his fifteenth year as holder of the Haig and Isabel Berberian Chair of Armenian Studies (1989-2004). Its completion coincides with another milestone—his thirtieth year of teaching at California State University, Fresno (1977-2007).

Son of Armenian Genocide survivors, Toros Kouymjian and Zabelle Calusdian, Dickran was born an American in Tulcea, Romania, where he lived until the age of five, when his family returned to the United States upon the outbreak of World War II, in 1939. His parents met and married in 1926, in Chicago.

Professor Kouymjian attended the University of Wisconsin, Madison, and his interests varied from physical chemistry, to engineering, and finally to European cultural history. He felt fortunate to have studied under Professors George Mosse for European cultural history and Michael Petrovich for Russian intellectual history. After graduating in January 1957, he served for six months as an officer in the United States Corps of Engineers, and then went to Brussels to cover the World's Fair (Expo 58) for *Down Beat Jazz* magazine. Afterward, he headed for Beirut as a correspondent for the International Press Service to cover the revolution in Iraq and the civil war in Beirut. While there, he enrolled in the M.A. program in Arabic Studies at the American University of Beirut (AUB). In the following year, after a summer spent in Anatolia, Iran, Pakistan, Afghanistan, and India, where he interviewed the Dalai Lama (just after his escape from Tibet), and President Nehru, he was invited to teach full-time at AUB.

Professor Kouymjian's Master's thesis (1961) was on "The Crisis in the Armenian Church," under the direction of Karekin vardapet Sarkissian, later Catholicos, who remained a life-long friend. It was then he decided to pursue a Ph.D. in Oriental studies and was accepted in the doctoral program in Near Eastern Languages and Literature at Columbia University. He was simultaneously offered a teaching fellowship in the Columbia Humanities Program. By 1967, he had completed most of the work on his dissertation "A Numismatic History of Southeastern Caucasia and Adharbayjan Based on the Islamic Coinage of the 5th/11th to the 7th/13th Centuries" (defended in 1969). In that last New York year, Dr. Kouymjian married Angèle Kapoïan, a Parisian-Armenian who was teaching French language and literature at the Chapin School in Manhattan. Her parents, also survivors of the Armenian Genocide, had married and settled in Paris. Angèle Kapoïan is also a scholar and teacher who shares Dr. Kouymjian's love of research and travel. They have been a constant source of inspiration for each other.

After completing what was probably the first American doctorate in Armenian Studies at Columbia University, under the direction of Professors Nina Garsöian, Tibor Halasi-Kun, and George C. Miles, Professor Kouymjian embarked on a varied and interesting career. He was hired by the American University in Cairo as Assistant Professor of Middle Eastern History and Assistant Director of the Center for Arabic Studies (1967-1971), then back to Beirut, both at Haigazian College as Professor and Chair of Armenian Studies (1971-1972) and again at the American University of Beirut as Associate Professor of Armenian and Near Eastern History (1971-1976).

With the onset of the civil war, the Kouymjians settled in the French capital. Dickran began teaching at the American University in Paris (Near Eastern and Classical History and Art), before finally settling into his permanent position, since 1977, at Fresno State. He has also taught elsewhere: the University of Paris III as Professor, Chairholder of Armenian and Director of the Armenian Section, Institut National des Langues et Civilisations Orientales (INALCO) (1988-1991), as well as in visiting positions, as a Fulbright Senior Lecturer at Yerevan State University, Department of Foreign Languages and Literature (1987), as William Saroyan Visiting Professor of Armenian Studies at the University of California, Berkeley (1996-1997), and as Visiting Professor at the University of Louvain-la-Neuve, Belgium. This cosmopolitan experience has given Professor Kouymjian a unique insight into Armenian Studies, as he has been able to live and work in Armenian communities throughout the world.

In addition to being a scholar and teacher, Dr. Kouymjian is an avid collector of books and art, reflecting his broader interests outside of academe. His love of music, theater, and travel reflect his zest for life and love of classical culture.

Professor Kouymjian entered graduate studies in 1958; thus, his career spans the period during which the discipline of Armenian Studies developed and matured in the United States. The founding of the first endowed chair of Armenian Studies at Harvard University in 1959, where graduate students could receive doctoral training in the field, began a new phase in the development of the discipline. Since then, many universities in the United States have established endowed chairs in Armenian Studies and many other universities and colleges now also offer coursework in the specialty, both at the undergraduate and graduate levels. Dr. Kouymjian has played an instrumental part in the development of the discipline at virtually every step.

That same period of growth in Armenian Studies saw the proliferation of a variety of new publications, especially in the areas of Armenian history, literature, art, language, and linguistics, expanding the field considerably. New periodicals, such as the *Journal of the Society for Armenian Studies (JSAS)* (1974) and the *Journal of Armenian Studies (JAS)* (1975), were established, providing fresh venues for the publication of armenological articles. Professor Kouymjian serves on their editorial boards as well as those of the *Revue des études arméniennes*, *The Armenian Review*, and *Ararat Quarterly*.

Throughout his career, Dr. Kouymjian has interacted with several generations of scholars and teachers, always willing to share his insight and advice on a variety of issues and answering any questions posed. He has freely shared his professional opinions and knowledge with any who have asked and has a particular fondness for assisting graduate students, encouraging them to complete their studies.

Dickran Kouymjian, along with Richard Hovannisian, Robert Thomson, Nina Garsoïan, and Avedis Sanjian, was one of the founding members of the Society for Armenian Studies (SAS), established in Boston in 1974; today it is an international organization with more than 230 members. The Society was started to promote the academic study of Armenian culture and civilization, including history, language, literature, and social, political, and economic questions; to facilitate the exchange of scholarly information pertaining to Armenian Studies around the world; and to sponsor panels and conferences on Armenian Studies. He has served on the SAS Executive Council as President for four terms, and has been an active member of the Society, making a significant contribution to its development. His thoughtful and insightful articles on Armenian Studies as a discipline, which have appeared in various publications, have engendered a healthy discussion on the current and future status of the field.

Dr. Kouymjian is a founding member of and has also served on the Executive Committee of the Association internationale des études arméniennes (AIEA), a European-based association with goals similar to the SAS. He was also a charter member of the Middle East Studies Association (1968). His broad network of contacts with scholars in Europe and Armenia has helped strengthen communications among specialists.

In addition to serving as Coordinator-Director of the Armenian Studies Program at California State University, Fresno, for the last thirty years, Professor Kouymjian has, since 1989, been the holder of the Berberian Chair of Armenian Studies, the first endowed Chair established at Fresno State and in the entire California State University system. Upon his arrival in Fresno, he reorganized Armenian Studies as it is today and succeeded in institutionalizing the Program, developing a variety of courses, some of which were accepted in the university's General Education program, while at the same time making them appealing and accessible to all.

Prof. Kouymjian also promoted an outreach program that brought community members on campus, establishing a closer bond with the University. He developed numerous popular weekend classes, open to all, to explore specific contemporary topics in depth. With the addition of a second full-time lecturer, Barlow Der Mugrdechian, in 1985, the Program continued to develop, becoming the most active undergraduate Armenian curriculum in the United States. In its scope, its academic rigor, and in the number of students enrolled, the Program has become nationally and internationally recognized. The flagship *Hye Sharzhoom/Armenian Action* newspaper conceived and launched by Professor Kouymjian in 1979 and later continued by Barlow Der Mugrdechian, has served as the local, national, and international voice of the faculty and the Armenian Students Organization for nearly three decades. Today it reaches a worldwide audience of close to 8,000.

Dr. Kouymjian's remarkably productive career is reflected in the scope of articles contained in this volume. His broad interests led to research in nearly all of the areas represented in the volume. In particular, his contributions to medieval and early modern history and art history have been substantial through articles, book chapters, and communications at major international conferences. He has authored or edited some fifteen books and monographs and more than 250 academic articles. (A bibliography of his publications is included in this volume.) He has presented papers at more than 100 national and international conferences and has himself organized a number of them: "David of Sasun, the Armenian Folk Epic" (1979), "Armenian Architecture" (1980), "William Saroyan" (1981, 1996, 1999), "Movsēs Xorenac'i et l'historiographie arménienne des origines" (1991), and more recently "The Massacres of Adana of 1909" (1999). He is a member of ten professional societies, a Fellow of the American Numismatic Society, and has served on the Board of Scholars of the Zoryan Institute, NAASR, the Armenian Film Foundation, and for a time the William Saroyan Foundation.

Professor Kouymjian developed the study of the arts of Armenia, as a regularly offered course at Fresno State, based on his landmark text, *The Arts of Armenia*, accompanied with 300 slides commissioned and published by the Calouste Gulbenkian Foundation. The heavily illustrated survey course introduces students to architecture, manuscript painting, and the minor arts (sculpture, metalwork, frescoes, ceramics, etc.). This popular class, part of the General Education option, now attracts as many non-Armenians as Armenians.

Dickran Kouymjian's innovative academic efforts include projects to digitalize and make accessible Armenian miniature paintings and to teach Armenian art courses completely on-line, the first time that this has been done anywhere in the world. The digitalized images are freely available through an important database for Armenian manuscript illuminations, housed on the Armenian Studies Program website, armenianstudies.csufresno.edu, under the Index of Armenian Art (IAA) heading. A similar database for Armenian architecture has also been placed on the website, again under Dr. Kouymjian's direction. He earlier compiled the two issues of the *Index of Armenian Art*, the first attempt to catalogue all illustrated Armenian manuscripts from inception through the eleventh century; it was the direct forerunner of the current digital database.

Research on William Saroyan has occupied a significant portion of Professor Kouymjian's career. Having known Saroyan well during the decade before the latter's death, he strove to make Fresno State an important center for the study of the internationally recognized author. He edited two volumes of unpublished Saroyan plays,

William Saroyan: An Armenian Trilogy (1986) and *Warsaw Visitor & Tales from the Vienna Streets: The Last Two Plays of William Saroyan* (1991), both issued by The Press at California State University, Fresno. He has written, taught, and spoken many times on this most famous of local-born Armenians and his efforts have contributed to the revival of Saroyan studies.

The Armenian Genocide has been another major area of interest for Dr. Kouymjian. In 1984, he testified before the Permanent Peoples' Tribunal in France, which formally confirmed the facts of the Genocide. More recently he and his wife compiled the section on Armenian artists and the Genocide for the online *The Legacy Project*. He has advised countless numbers of scholars on issues relating to the Armenian Genocide, especially the destruction of Armenian cultural monuments as a continuation of the genocidal process.

Professor Kouymjian has also been repeatedly recognized for his teaching skills, devotion to students, and leadership roles. Over the past fifty years, he has taught thousands of students on three continents, usually leaving a lasting and personal legacy. Students have been attracted to his broad knowledge, charisma, and ability to engender interest in the subject matter. He is able to engage students directly and to work with them closely in writing and research, encouraging them to delve deeper into the subject. Anyone who has ever taken a course with "Dr. K," as he is affectionately called, finds it an unforgettable experience.

In 1969, and again in 1970, the Student Council of the American University in Cairo gave him an Outstanding Professor Award and in 1986, he was elected "Outstanding Professor of the Year," by the Faculty Senate at California State University, Fresno. In 1996, he was elected to Phi Kappa Phi, the professional honor society, with special recognition. In 1998, he was the nominee of the Fresno State chapter of Phi Kappa Phi in the triennial national competition for the outstanding scholar of the United States; he was among the top five nation-wide. In 1999, Phi Kappa Phi chose Professor Kouymjian as the "University Scholar of the Year." Again in 1999, he was the recipient of the Provost's Award for Excellence in Teaching in the newly established category of "Outstanding Achievements in Research." Furthermore, in that same year, 1999-2000, he was chosen "Man of the Year" by the Armenian National Committee,

Central Valley. In 2001, he was invited to serve on the selection committee of the prestigious Francqui Fund Prize (the Belgian Nobel Prize as it is sometimes called). In 2003, he received the Arthur H. Dadian Armenian Heritage Award, bestowed by the Armenian Students Association of America.

Other distinctions include being chosen the sixth recipient of the Hagop Kevorkian Lectureship in Near Eastern Civilization at New York University in 1979; his distinguished lectures were on the topic "The Iconography of Armenian Pentecost." In 1996, he received encyclicals from both His Holiness Aram I, Catholicos of the Great House of Cilicia, and the late Karekin I, Catholicos of All Armenians, for his work in Armenian Studies. The latter also honored him with the St. Sahag and St. Mesrob medal, the highest honor bestowed by the Armenian Church to scholars and writers. In the same year he was made an Honorary Lifetime member of the National Association for Armenian Studies and Research.

In 1996, the two Catholicoses appointed him as one of the Chairmen of the International Conferences Committee for the 1700th anniversary celebration of Armenian Christianity. In 1997, he served as one of two Americans on the International Advisory Board of the 35th International Orientalist Congress held in Budapest. In the Spring of 2001, he was invited to give a series of ten seminars to doctoral students at the Oriental Institute of the Catholic University of Louvain-la-Neuve on "Armenian History and Art: The Search for an Identity." In 2005, he was awarded an honorary doctorate degree by the National Academy of Sciences of the Republic of Armenia.

In October 2006, Prof. Kouymjian was invited to Etchmiadzin by His Holiness Karekin II, Catholicos of All Armenians, to be honored on the occasion of the Armenian translation and publication of the *Album of Armenian Paleography*. The *Album*, prepared by Michael Stone, Dickran Kouymjian, and Henning Lehmann, is a comprehensive and groundbreaking study of the history of Armenian writing and utilizes modern scientific methods to elucidate the development of Armenian scripts. At the request of Catholicos Aram I, Dr. Kouymjian is currently preparing, with several other specialists, a master catalogue of the objects in the Cilician Museum of the Catholicosate in Antelias.

For the past year and a half, Dickran and Angèle Kouymjian were actively involved in *"Arménie mon amie, l'Année de l'Arménie en France* [The Year of Armenia in France]," which started Sept. 21, 2006, Armenian Independence Day, and ended July 14, 2007, Bastille Day. It is significant that Armenia was honored with hundreds of museum exhibits, concerts, theatrical performances and film festivals, conferences, etc., in forty French cities. Two of the largest and most splendid exhibitions ever of medieval Armenian Christian art were held: the first, *Armenia Sacra*, at the Louvre (February-April) with 210 objects, including about forty massive *khatchkars* (cross-stones, unique to Armenia) and a catalogue of 470 pages, for which Dr. Kouymjian participated from the beginning, writing two chapters and describing and analyzing seventeen liturgical objects from the Treasury of Holy Etchmiadzin; the second, *Arménie. La magie de l'écrit*, at the Vielle Charité in Marseille (April-July) presented nearly 400 inscribed objects in all artistic media with another massive catalogue for which he wrote five chapters and many notices. He also contributed significantly to two major exhibits on the great Armenian-Georgian filmmaker and artist Sergei Paradjanov, with whom he had a very warm and personal relationship. Dr. Kouymjian lent literally hundreds of documents and photos from his personal archives, including the first publication of a detailed journal he kept of Paradjanov working on a film (1987), commissioned by Catholicos Vazken I about the Treasures of Etchmiadzin, but which was never completed. Dr. Kouymjian also contributed to the organization and catalogue of an exhibit devoted to Armenian textiles, especially Armenian altar curtains, for the Textile Museum in Lyon and with Angèle Kouymjian on the immediate post-Genocide Armenian embroidery crafts for the Muséon Arlaten in Arles. Further details on these and a half dozen other exhibits that he actively participated in are found in his complete bibliography in this volume.

A nearly fifty-year career and an entire lifetime are difficult to capture in the few words I have written here. This introduction and appreciation for Prof. Kouymjian gives only a summary of the more outstanding moments in his very productive life.

Tireless researcher, enthusiastic teacher, demanding mentor, are among the terms which best describe Dickran Kouymjian, whose impact on Armenian Studies, as well as on the community-at-large, has been great and enduring.

It has been a pleasure and a privilege to have had the opportunity to work with a professor, a sometimes mentor, a colleague, and a warm and generous human being such as Dickran Kouymjian.

The official languages of *Between Paris and Fresno: Armenian Studies in Honor of Dickran Kouymjian* are English and French, with thirty-seven articles in English and nine in French. The forty-six contributors are from such diverse countries as Armenia, Austria, Belgium, Canada, Denmark, England, France, Ireland, Israel, Italy, the Netherlands, Switzerland, and the United States.

Another group of scholars, close friends, and colleagues, expressed a desire to participate and communicated titles in response to the original announcement of the *Festschrift*. For a variety of reasons they were not able to submit their studies. They are listed in alphabetical order for the record: Sylvia Agémian (Beirut) "Un Évangile arménien illustré du XVe siècle au Musée Cilicie (ancienne collection Kaloust et Emma Sogoian); Anny Bakalian (New York) "The Centenary of Armenians in America: A Review of the Field"; Michael Bates (New York) "The Governor Bakkar b. Muslim of Armenia and the Caucasus in the Eight Century"; Eva de Vries (Netherlands) "Michel Psellos sur l'art de la peinture"; Ara Dostourian (Rhode Island) "The Chronicle of Matthew of Edessa"; Valentina Calzolari (Geneva) "Sur un Évangile du XVIIe siècle conserve à la Bibliothèque Bodmer de Genève"; Hervé Georgelin (Paris) "Armenian Education in a Non-Armenian Environment: The Case of Late Ottoman Smyrna"; John Greppin (Cleveland) "A Newly Rediscovered Manuscript of the Baṙk‘ Gaghianosi"; Anahid Kassabian (New York) "What Is Armenian Film, and How Do We Know One When We See One?"; David Kertmenjian (Yerevan) "The Medieval School in Architecture of the Lake Van Region"; Christel Kessler (Cambridge, England) "The Crux of Building Mecca Oriented in the Highstreet of Fatimid Cairo and Its Central Square—1125-1502"; Robert Krikorian (Maryland) "The Destruction of Memory: Armenians and Ottoman Historiography"; Bernard Outtier (Saint-Martin-de-la-Mer, France) "Quelques nouveaux manuscrits arméniens entrevus à Paris"; Dennis Papazian (New Jersey) "Religious and Secular Nationalism"; R. P. Athanase Renoux (Abbaye d'en Calcat, France) "Le 15 Nawasard: L'annonciation à la Mère de Dieu"; Thomas Sinclair (Cyprus) "The History of Arjēsh/Erciş in the Late Middle Ages and Early Period of

Ottoman Rule"; Theo Maarten van Lint (Oxford) "On Some Poems by Grigor Tghay"; and Zaven Yegavian (Lisbon) "Lexicography in the Twentieth Century."

Many scholars expressed to the editor their good wishes and congratulations to Prof. Kouymjian for his numerous contributions to the field of Armenian Studies. Their names are listed in the *Tabula Gratulatoria*, which appears in the *Festschrift*.

The format of *Between Paris and Fresno: Armenian Studies in Honor of Dickran Kouymjian* follows in general that of two such volumes edited by Dr. Kouymjian, *Studies in Honor of George C. Miles* (Beirut, 1974) and *Armenian Studies/Études arméniennes*: *In Memoriam Haïg Berbérian* (Lisbon, 1986).

I wish to thank all of the contributors for their participation and patience in the production of the volume. It has been a pleasure to have worked with such a group of colleagues. Any editorial errors or inconsistencies that appear in the volume are the final responsibility of the editor. Special thanks to Avo Arikian for his assistance in preparing some of the Armenian language text, Ali Peyvandi for assisting in various tasks, Alina Melkonian for her assistance with French texts, Hazel Antaramian Hofman for her careful reading of the manuscript, and George Bournoutian, director of the Armenian Series at Mazda Press, for his support and encouragement during the preparation of this volume.

Finally, I would like to express my profound gratitude to The Dolores Zohrab Liebmann Fund (New York) for its subvention, which made publication of this *Festschrift* possible.

TRANSLITERATION SYSTEM

The transliteration system for Armenian used in this volume is a scheme adapted for desktop publishing from the Library of Congress' *Cataloguing Service*, *Bulletin* 121, Spring 1977. It is based on the phonetic values of Classical and Eastern Armenian. The transliteration system used in the French articles maintains the phonetic rules for French, except for common place names.

Աա	Aa	Կկ	Kk	Սս	Ss
Բբ	Bb	Հհ	Hh	Վվ	Vv
Գգ	Gg	Ձձ	Dz	Տտ	Tt
Դդ	Dd	Ղղ	Gh	Րր	Rr
Եե[1]	Ee	Ճճ	Ch	Ցց	Ts‘ ts‘
	Yy[2]	Մմ	Mm	Ււ	Ww
Զզ	Zz	Յյ[1]	Yy	Ու	Uu
Էէ	Ēē		Hh[4]	Փփ	P‘p‘
Ըը	Ĕĕ	Նն	Nn	Քք	K‘k‘
Թթ	T‘t‘	Շշ	Sh sh[3]	Եւ	Ew ew
Ժժ	Zh zh[3]	Ոո	Oo	In classical orth.	
Իի	Ii	Չչ	Ch‘ ch‘	Եւ	Ev ev
Լլ	Ll	Պպ	Pp	In reformed orth.	
Խխ	Kh kh[3]	Ջջ	Jj	Օօ	Ōō
Ծծ	Ts ts[3]	Ռռ	Ṙṙ[5]	Ֆֆ	Ff

[1] Armenian names ending in –եան (in Classical orthography), or –յան (in Reformed orthography) may be Romanized –ian, save for Armenians in Armenia and other successor states of the Soviet Union. In that case, those may be Romanized –yan, save for common conventions such as Ter Petrossian.

[2] This value is only used when the letter is in the initial position of a name and followed by a vowel in Classical Orthography.

[3] The acute accent is placed between the letters representing two different sounds when the combination might otherwise be read as a diagraph.

[4] This value is used when the letter is in the initial position of a word or of a stem in a compound in Classical orthography.

[5] This derivation from the Library of Congress scheme was necessitated by the needs of desktop publishing.

Bibliography of Dickran Kouymjian
1958-2007

1958

1. "Cardinal Agajanian Holds Services at Brussels World's Fair," *The Hairenik Weekly*, vol. XXIV, no. 29 (August 28, 1958), pp. 1, 5.
2. Review of John Carswell, *Coptic Tattoo Designs* (Beirut: American University of Beirut Press, 1957), *Beirut Weekly*, vol. I, no. 1 (1958), p. 38.
3. "Forster's 1927 Lectures Serve as Critic's Approach to Novels," review of several books in World of Books, *AUB Collegian* (November 1, 1958).
4. "The Short Story Fills Twentieth-century Man's Need for Easy Reading in a Fast-paced World," several book reviews, *AUB Collegian* (November 15, 1958).
5. "Ten Little Indians," theater review, *Beirut Weekly*, vol. 1, no. 3 (December 6, 1958), pp. 13, 37.
6. "Jazz in Beirut," *Beirut Weekly*, vol. 1, no. 3 (December 6, 1958), pp. 14-15.
7. "Mainardi-Zecchei Recital," *Beirut Weekly*, vol. 1, no. 3 (December 6, 1958), p. 33.
8. "The Stereophonic Disc," *Beirut Weekly*, vol. 1, no. 3 (December 6, 1958), p. 39.
9. "Sonnet of Innocence," under pseudonym S. Armen, *Beirut Weekly*, vol. 1, no. 4 (December 13, 1958), p. 7.
10. "Novello Recital," *Beirut Weekly*, vol. 1, no. 4 (December 13, 1958), p. 277.

1961

11. *The Crisis in the Armenian Church*, M.A. thesis, American University of Beirut (196l), unpublished.

1965

12. "The Ethos of a People," Artin K. Shalian, *David of Sassoun. The Armenian Folk Epic in Four Cycles* (Athens, Ohio, 1964), *Ararat*, vol. VI, no. 3 (1965), pp. 55-58.
13. "A Rare Example of Medieval Art: The Church of Aght'amar," review article of Sirarpie Der Nersessian, *Aght'amar, Church of the Holy Cross* (Cambridge: Harvard University Press, 1965), and M. S. Ipşiroglu, *Die Kirche von Achtamar* (Berlin & Mainz, 1963), *Ararat*, vol. VI, no. 4 (1965), pp. 83-88.

1967-1968

14. Reviews and abstracts in *Numismatic Literature*, American Numismatic Society.

1969

15. *A Numismatic History of Southeastern Caucasia and Adharbayjan Based on the Islamic Coinage of the 5th/11th to the 7th/13th Centuries*, doctoral dissertation, Armenian Studies Program, Near and Middle Eastern Languages and Civilization (Columbia University, New York, 1969), iii, xii, 466 pages, Ann Arbor: University Microfilms, no. 70-17,025.
16. "Mxit'ar of Ani on the Rise of the Seljuqs," *Revue des études arméniennes*, vol. VI (1969), pp. 331-353.
17. Review of John A. Boyle, "Kirakos of Ganjak on the Mongols," *Central Asiatic Journal*, VII/3 (1963), *Revue des études arméniennes*, vol. VI (1969), p. 441.
18. Short reviews and abstracts in *Numismatic Literature*, American Numismatic Society.

1970

19. "A Numismatic History of Southeastern Caucasia and Adharbayjan Based on the Islamic Coinage of the 5th/11th to the 7th/13th Centuries," *Dissertation Abstracts International*, vol. XXXI, no. 3 (1970), p. 1175A.
20. "Letter to Editor in Reply to an Article in *Hairenik Daily* on Armenian Schools," by Mesrob Janashian, English translation by A. Kapoïan and D. Kouymjian, five parts, *Hay Endanik* (October, 1970) and other Armenian journals.

21. Short reviews and abstracts in *Numismatic Literature*, American Numismatic Society.
22. Short reviews and abstracts in *Journal of Ecumenical Studies.*

1971

23. "An Historical and Dynastic Survey of Caucasia, Eastern Anatolia and Adharbayjan from the XIth to the XIIIth Century," *Haigazian Armenological Review,* vol. II (1971), pp. 99-122.
24. Review article, Avedis K. Sanjian, *Colophons of Armenian Manuscripts, 1301-1480. A Source for Middle Eastern History* (Cambridge: Harvard University Press, 1969), *International Journal of Middle East Studies*, Cambridge, vol. 3, no. 1 (1971), pp. 81-89; reply by Sanjian in vol. 3, no. 3 (1971), pp. 365-371; my reply to Sanjian, vol. 4, no. 2 (1972), pp. 238-239.
25. Reviews and abstracts in *Numismatic Literature*, American Numismatic Society.
26. Reviews and abstracts in *Journal of Ecumenical Studies.*

1972

27. "The Status of Armenian Studies in the Diaspora," *Shirak*, Beirut, vol. XV, no. 10 (1972), pp. 29-58 (in Armenian).
28. "Mxit'ar of Ani on the Ghaznavids," *Lraber*, Bulletin of the Armenian Academy of Sciences, no. 4 (1972), pp. 74-84 (in Armenian with résumé in Russian).
29. "To the Editor," reply to A. Sanjian (see no. 24), *International Journal of Middle East Studies*, vol. 4, no. 2 (1972), pp. 238-239.
30. Review of Henry Field, ed., *Contributions to the Archaeology of Armenia* (Cambridge: Harvard University, 1968), *Haigazian Armenological Review*, vol. III (1972), pp. 295-297.
31. Review of Robert W. Thomson, *The Teachings of Saint Gregory: An Early Armenian Catechism* (Cambridge: Harvard University Press, 1970), *Haigazian Armenological Review*, vol. III (1972), pp. 297-299.
32. Reviews and abstracts in *Numismatic Literature*, American Numismatic Society.

1973

33. "Armenian Architecture (IVth-VIIth Centuries): A Reassessment on the Occasion of an Exhibition," *al-Kulliyah*, Beirut (Spring, 1973), pp. 14-19, reprinted in *The Armenian Reporter* (August 30, 1973), pp. 6-7, 12; Armenian trans., *Banber* (Beirut, 1973) vol. I, no. 2.
34. "La Cathédrale d'Etchmiadzin et l'architecture arménienne du IVe-VIIe siècle," *Samedi*, no. 208 (August, 1973), pp. 11-12.
35. "Problems of Medieval Armenian and Muslim Historiography: The Mxit'ar of Ani Fragment," *International Journal of Middle Eastern Studies*, vol. 4, no. 4 (1973), pp. 461-471.
36. Review of C. E. Bosworth, ed., *Iran and Islam in Memory of the Late Vladimir Minorsky* (Edinburgh University Press, 1972), *Islamic Culture* (1973), pp. 134-141.
37. Reviews and abstracts in *Numismatic Literature*, American Numismatic Society
38. Twelfth Annual Research Report, AUB (March, 1973), pp. 41-42.

1974

39. *Near Eastern Numismatics, Iconography, Epigraphy and History: Studies in Honor of George C. Miles*, ed., (Beirut: American University of Beirut Press, 1974), 4°, xxv, 478 pages.
40. "A Bibliography of the Works of George C. Miles," *Studies in Honor of George C. Miles* (Beirut, 1974), pp. xvii-xxv.
41. "A Unique Coin of the Shirvânshâh Minûchihr II Dated A.H. 555/1160 A.D.," *Studies in Honor of George C. Miles* (Beirut, 1974), pp. 339-346.
42. "On the Historical Tracks of the Ererouk Basilica," *Hask*, Antelias, vol. XLIII, nos. 7-8 (1974), pp. 296-310 (in Armenian).
43. "The Museum Calouste Built: Islamic Art in the Gulbenkian Art Museum in Lisbon," with Angèle Kapoïan, *Aramco World Magazine*, vol. 25, no. 5 (1974), pp. 6-11; Armenian trans. *Patanekan ardzagang*, vol. 39 (Beirut, 1974), pp. 266-274.

T

1975

44. *The Splendor of Egypt. A Commentary on Napoleon Bonaparte's Expedition (1798-1801) and the* Description de l'Égypte, with Angèle Kapoïan (Delmar, N.Y.: Caravan Books, 1975), in-folio, 212 pages, 100 plates.
45. "The Canons Dated 1280 A.D. of the Armenian Akhî-type Brotherhood of Erzinjan," *Actes du XXIXe congrès international des orientalistes*, Paris, 1973 (Paris, 1975), part I, vol. 2, pp. 107-115.
46. "The Art of Oil," with Angèle Kapoïan, *Ararat*, vol. XVI, no. 2 (1975), pp. 14-19.
47. "IIAA: The Iconographical Index of Armenian Art," *Journal of Armenian Studies*, vol. I, no. 1 (1975), pp. 65-67.

1976

48. "Three Unique Coins of the Eldiguzid Atabegs of Northwestern Iran," *Actes du 8ème congrès international de numismatique* (Paris-Basel, 1976), pp. 527-541.

1977

49. *Index of Armenian Art (IAA)*, fascicle I. *Armenian Manuscript Illumination to the Year 1000 A.D.* (Fresno-Paris, 1977), xiii, 36 pages.
50. *The Conservation and Preservation of Ancient Coins*, Technical Report RP/1975-76/3.421.5, UNESCO Mission to the Department of Antiquities, Libyan Arab Republic, UNESCO (Paris, 1977), 46 pages.
51. *The Ererouk Basilica*, *Documents of Armenian Architecture/Documenti di Architetura Armena*, vol. 9, with A. Alpago-Novello and P. Papoudjian (Milan: Polytechnic of Milan and the Armenian Academy of Sciences, 1977).
52. "Traccie storiche della basilica di Ererouk," *Ricerca sull' Architettura Armena*, vol. 15, *Fonti*, II (Milan, 1977), pp. 57-72.
53. "Armenian Participation in the XVth International Congress of Byzantines Studies," *Society for Armenian Studies Newsletter*, vol. 2, no. 1/2 (Winter, 1977), p. 5.

54. "Far Eastern Influences in Armenian Miniature Painting in the Mongol Period," *Armenian Post*, 3 parts (December 6, 13, 20, 1977).

1978

55. "The Armenians in Lebanon: Their Cultural Accomplishments," editor with J. Munro, special supplement, *Ararat* (Summer, 1978), pp. 17-41.
56. "The Formative Period of Armenian Architecture: The IVth to the VIIth Century," *The Armenian Review*, vol. XXXI, no. 1 (Spring, 1978), pp. 17-41.
57. "The Problem of the Zoomorphic Figure in the Iconography of Armenian Pentecost: A Preliminary Report," *Atti del Primo Simposio Internazionale de Arte Armena, Bergamo, 1975* (Venice, 1978), pp. 403-413.
58. "Second International Symposium on Armenian Art," *Armenian Observer* (October 4, 1978), pp. 2, 8.

1979

59. *Index of Armenian Art (IAA)*, fascicle II. *Illuminated Armenian Manuscripts of the 11th Century, Preliminary Report and Checklist* (Fresno, 1979).
60. "Illustrated Armenian Manuscripts to the Year 1000 A.D.," *Arkheion Pontou*, vol. 36 (Athens, 1979), pp. 249-252.
61. "Introduction to the Armenian Community in Lebanon," *The Armenian Review*, vol. XXXII, no. 2 (1979), pp. 115-118.
62. "In Memoriam Haig Berbérian (1887-1978)," *Society for Armenian Studies Newsletter*, vol. IV, no. 1 (Winter, 1979), p. 3.
63. "Society for Armenian Studies (A Short History)," *Bulletin of the Middle East Studies Association*, vol. XIII, no. 1 (1979), pp. 81-82.

1980

64. *Essays on Armenian Numismatics in Honor of Fr. Clement Sibilian*, ed., with Y. Nercessian (Los Angeles: Armenian Numismatic Society, 1980), 4°, 168 pages, 21 plates.
65. "The Iconography of the 'Coronation' Trams of King Levon II," *Essays on Armenian Numismatics in Honor of Fr. Clement*

Sibilian (Los Angeles: Armenian Numismatic Society, 1980), pp. 67-74.

66. "Necrology: Haïg Berbérian (April 18, 1887-October 3, 1978)," *The Armenian Review*, vol. XXXIII, no. 2 (1980), pp. 249-252.
67. Review of Yves Ternon & Jean-Claude Kebabdjian, *Arménie 1900* (Paris: Edition Astrid, 1980), *Society for Armenian Studies Newsletter*, vol. V, no. 2 (Spring, 1980), p. 6.
68. Review of Bezalel Narkiss, ed., with Michael Stone and Avedis Sanjian, *Armenian Art Treasures of Jerusalem* (New Rochelle: Caratzas Brothers, 1979), *Society for Armenian Studies Newsletter*, vol. V, no. 2 (Spring, 1980), p. 6.

1981

69. *Armenian Architecture, an Exhibition*, Armenian Studies Program, California State University, Fresno, Occasional Papers, no. 1 (Fresno, 1981), 16 pages.
70. "Exhibition of Armenian Architecture," *April*, vol. 5, no. 8 (1981), pp. 40-44 (in Armenian).
71. "The *Scaenae Frons* in Armenian Art: The Classical Tradition in the East," *Byzantium and the Classical Tradition,* A. Bryer, ed. (Birmingham, England, 1981), pp. 155-171.
72. "A Letter from Paris to William Saroyan," *International Herald Tribune* (June 5, 1981); reprinted in the *Fresno Bee* (July 5, 1981), pp. 1, 8; French trans. "Lettre à Saroyan," *L'Arménie aujourd'hui*, nos. 4-6, (1988), pp. 40-42; reprinted in *Armenia Today* (Yerevan, 1988), no. 4-6.
73. "The Purpose and Direction of Armenian Studies in the Diaspora," *La Struttura Negata, Cultura Armena nella Diaspora* (Milan, 1981), pp. 97-104, reprinted in *Hay Endanik*, no. 1-2 (1981), pp. 42-47; reprinted in the *Zoryan Institute Newsletter*, vol. VI, no. 3, pp. 3, 6, 8; reprinted in *Society for Armenian Studies Newsletter*, vol. VI, no. 3, pp. 6, 8-9.
74. "The Classical Tradition in Armenian Art," *Revue des études arméniennes*, vol. XV (1981), pp. 263-288.
75. "Saroyan and 'Haratch' or William Saroyan's Last Armenian-Theme Play," *Haratch, Art and Thought* (July, 1981), pp. 2-4, reprinted in *Haratch 60* (1986), pp. 247-256 (in Armenian).
76. "Paul Zareh Bedoukian," *Selected Numismatic Studies of Paul Z. Bedoukian* (Los Angeles, 1981), pp. xv-xix.

77. "Preface," *William Saroyan Festival Program* (Fresno: California State University, 1981), pp. 1-2.
78. "Saroyan on the Armenians: *Haratch* and Other Unpublished Plays," *William Saroyan Festival Program* (Fresno: California State University, 1981), pp. 3-11.
79. "A Note on the Background of *Haratch* and Saroyan's Writing Technique," *William Saroyan Festival Program* (Fresno, 1981), pp. 12-13.
80. "The Armenian Diaspora in France: *Hay Baykar* and the ICOM Phenomenon," *Armenians in the Eighties, Prospects and Challenges, a Symposium* (Berkeley, 1981), pp. 90-95.

1982

81. "Sous le joug des Turcomans et des Turcs ottomans (XVe-XVIe siècles)," *Histoire des Arméniens,* Gérard Dédéyan, ed. (Toulouse: Privat, 1982), pp. 341-376.
82. "The Armenian Inscriptions," Annex II, A. S. Melikian-Chirvani, *Islamic Metalwork from the Iranian World, 8th-18th Century* (London: Victoria & Albert Museum, 1982), pp. 403-406.
83. "Computerization of Manuscript Illuminations: The Index of Armenian Art," *Actes du XVIe congrès international d'études byzantines* (Vienna, 1982), 10 pages.
84. *I.A.A. Index of Armenian Art*, brochure, Armenian Studies Program (Fresno: California State University, 1982), 8 pages.
85. "Monetary Circulation in Southeastern Caucasia and Azerbaijan in the 12th-13th Centuries," *Actes du 9ème congrès international de numismatique,* Berne, September 1979 (Louvain-la-Neuve and Luxembourg, 1982), pp. 883-884.
86. "Reflections on an Exhibit," *The Armenian Review*, vol. 35, no. 2 (1982), pp. 200-207.
87. "Report," National Endowment for the Humanities Grant for William Saroyan Paris Archives (1982), *Armenian Assembly Newsletter.*
88. "Preface," reprint edition of Edwin M. Bliss, *Turkey and the Armenian Atrocities* (Fresno: Meshag Press, 1982), pp. i-iv.

1983

89. "Dated Armenian Manuscripts as a Statistical Tool for Armenian History," *Medieval Armenian Culture*, T. Samuelian and M.

Stone, eds., University of Pennsylvania Armenian Texts and Studies, vol. 6 (Chico, CA, 1983, published 1984), pp. 425-439.

90. "Ethnic Origins and the 'Armenian' Policy of Emperor Heraclius," *Revue des études arméniennes*, vol. XVII (1983), pp. 635-642.
91. "Preface," *William Saroyan: My Real Work is Being* by David Stephen Calonne (Chapel Hill, NC: North Carolina University Press, 1983), pp. 2-4.
92. "Reflections on Armenian Painting on the Occasion of an Exhibit," *Five West Coast Artists of Armenian Ancestry* (Fresno Arts Center, Fresno, 1983), pp. 6-10.
93. "Foreword," *Armenian Needlelace and Embroidery* by Alice Odian Kasparian (McLean, Virginia, 1983), pp. 13-14.

1984

94. "Destruction des monuments historiques arméniens, poursuite de la politique de génocide," *Le Crime de Silence* (Flammarion, Paris, 1984), pp. 295-310; English trans., "The Destruction of Armenian Historical Monuments as a Continuation of the Turkish Policy of Genocide," *The Crime of Silence, Permanent Peoples' Tribunal* (London: Zed, 1985), pp. 173-185; German trans., "Die Zerstörung armenischer Kulturdenkmäler-eine Forsetzung der türkischen Völkermord-Politik," *Das Verbrechen des Schweigens, Die Verhandlung des türkischen Völkermords an den Armeniern vor dem Ständigen Tribunal der Völker*, Gesellschaft für bedrohte Völker (Göttingen, n.d. [1985]), pp. 155-162; reprinted in English, *The Zoryan Bulletin*, vol. II, no. 2 (Summer, 1984), pp. 4-5, 8; reprinted in French, *Abaka* (Nov. 11, 1985), p. 7; extracts translated into Armenian, *Hayrenik'i dzayn*, no. 30 (1990), pp. 2, 3, 7.
95. "Le cinéma arménien aux États-Unis," *Armenia* (June 1984), pp. 44-48.
96. "The Good Job de William Saroyan," *Armenia* (June, 1984), pp. 48-49.
97. "The Last of the Armenian Plays (of William Saroyan)," *Ararat*, vol. XXV, no. 2 (Spring, 1984), pp. 24-28, for revised version (see no. 114).

98. "L'importance des centres de documentation arméniens," *Bulletin de la documentation arménienne*, CRDA, Paris, no. 1 (June, 1984), p. 2.
99. Review of Lawrence Lee & Barry Gifford, *Saroyan: A Biography* (New York: Harper & Row, 1984); *San Diego Union* (December 26, 1984); reprinted in *Asbarez* (January 26, 1985); *The Armenian Reporter* (January 31, 1985).

1985

100. *Lazar P'arpets'i, 'History of the Armenians' and the 'Letter' to Vahan Mamikonean, A Photographic Reproduction of the 1904 Tiflis Edition*, with introduction and bibliography, Classical Armenian Text Reprint Series (Caravan Books, Delmar, N.Y., 1985), xl, xvi, 211 pages.
101. "Ghazar P'arpets'i on Nvarsak and Vahan Mamikonian," *The Armenian Review*, vol. 38, no. 3 (1985), pp. 14-28.

1986

102. *Armenian Studies/Études arméniennes: In Memoriam Haïg Berbérian*, editor (Lisbon: Calouste Gulbenkian Foundation, 1986), xli, 883 pages.
102a. Review by Peter Cowe, *Journal of the Society for Armenian Studies*, vol. 5, pp. 227-230.
102b. Review by J.-P. Mahé, *Revue des études arméniennes*, vol. XXII (1988-89), pp. 554-559.
103. "Bibliography of Haïg Berbérian," with Angèle Kapoïan, *Armenian Studies/Études arméniennes: In Memoriam Haïg Berbérian* (Lisbon: Calouste Gulbenkian Foundation, 1986), pp. xxix-xli.
104. "Julfa on the Arax and Its Funerary Monuments," with Jurgis Baltrušaitis, *Armenian Studies/Études arméniennes: In Memoriam Haïg Berbérian* (Lisbon: Calouste Gulbenkian Foundation, 1986), pp. 9-53.
105. "Chinese Influences on Armenian Miniature Painting in the Mongol Period," *Armenian Studies/Études arméniennes: In Memoriam Haïg Berbérian* (Lisbon: Calouste Gulbenkian Foundation, 1986), pp. 415-468.

106. *William Saroyan: An Armenian Trilogy*, edited with an introduction and glossary (Fresno: The Press at California State University, 1986), 195 pages, 57 illustrations.
106a. Review by Nubar Agishian, *Navasart* (Los Angeles, 1986).
106b. Review by Lemyel Amirian, *Armenian Observer*, part I (January 7, 1987), part II (January 14, 1987), p. 27, and *The California Courier* (January 8, 1987), p. 11 (part I).
106c. Review by Ara Baliozian, *Armenian Life* (January 9, 1987), p. 26.
106d. Review by K. Tölölyan, *Choice* (March, 1987).
106e. Review by Aram Veeser, *Ararat*, vol. XXXIV, no. 134 (Spring, 1993), pp. 67-72; reprinted in *Critical Essays on William Saroyan,* Harry Keyishian, ed. (New York: Simon & Schuster Macmillan, 1995).
107. *Ptghni/Arudch*, vol. 16, *Documents of Armenian Architecture/ Documenti di Architettura Armena*, bilingual publication, English editor (Milan, 1986).
108. *Lazar P'arpets'i, The Historian of the Wars of Vardan and Letter of Vahan Mamikonean* (Delmar, 1986), xl pages (see no. 100).
108a. Review by Levon A. Saryan, *Ararat*, vol. 33 (Summer, 1992), pp. 62-63.
109. "From the Society" (Annual Report of the Society for Armenian Studies), *Society for Armenian Studies Newsletter*, vol. X, no. 3-XI, no. 1 (March, 1986), pp. 1-4.
110. Review of Richard G. Hovannisian, *The Armenian Image in History and Literature*, Studies in Near Eastern Culture and Society, vol. 3 (Malibu, 1981), *Middle East Studies Association Bulletin*, no. 20 (1986), pp. 109-110.

1987

111. *Gandzasar*, vol. 17, *Documents of Armenian Architecture/ Documenti di Architettura Armena*, bilingual publication, English editor (Milan, 1987).
112. "William Saroyan and the Armenian Ethnic Experience in America," *Journal of Armenian Studies*, vol. III, nos. 1-2 (1986-87), pp. 161-174.
113. "William Saroyan, Filmmaker," *Ekran* (Yerevan, 1987), no. 7 (July, 1987), pp. 12-14 (in Armenian).

114. "Saroyan Shoots a Film," *William Saroyan: The Man and the Writer Remembered*, Leo Hamalian, ed. (Rutherford, Madison, Teaneck, New Jersey, London & Toronto: Associated University Presses, 1987), pp. 77-83.
115. Review of Frédéric Feydit, *Amulettes de l'Arménie chrétienne* (Venice, 1986), *Journal of the Society for Armenian Studies*, vol. 3 (1987), pp. 173-174.
116. Review of Gilles Hennequin, *Catalogue des monnaies musulmanes de la Bibliothèque nationale*, [Tome V], *Asie pré-mongole, les Seljuqs et leurs successeurs*, xi, 932 pages (Paris: Bibliothèque nationale de France, 1985), *Middle East Studies Association Bulletin*, no. 21 (1987), pp. 93-94.

1988

117. *Sevan*, vol. 18, *Documents of Armenian Architecture/ Documenti di Architettura Armena*, bilingual publication, English editor (Milan, 1988).
118. "A Critical Bibliography for the History of Armenia from 1375 to 1605," *The Armenian Review*, vol. 41, no. 1 (Spring, 1988), pp. 39-45.
119. "William Saroyan and the Armenian Ethnic Experience in America" (Armenian translation of no. 112 with Russian résumé), *Banber*, quarterly of Yerevan State University, no. 1/64, (1988), pp. 94-101.
120. "Saroyan gira un film," *Nuovo Cinema qoutidiano, Publicato per la XXIV Mostra Internazionale del Nuovo Cinema*, Pesaro, no. 4 (June 14, 1988), p. 3.
121. "Paradzanov, Pelesjan e gli altri," *Nuovo Cinema qoutidiano, Publicato per la XXIV Mostra Internazionale del Nuovo Cinema,* Pesaro, no. 8 (June 18, 1988), p. 1.

1989

122. *Gharabagh*, vol. 19, *Documents of Armenian Architecture/ Documenti di Architettura Armena*, bilingual publication, English editor (Milan, 1989).
123. *Sorhul*, vol. 20, *Documents of Armenian Architecture/ Documenti di Architettura Armena*, bilingual publication, English editor (Milan, 1989).

124. "The Status of Artists and Intellectuals in Soviet Armenia," *The Armenian Review*, vol. 42, no. 3 (Autumn, 1989, published 1990), pp. 53-62.

125. Review of Robert W. Edwards, *The Fortifications of Armenian Cilicia*, Dumbarton Oaks Studies, vol. XXIII (Washington, D.C.: Dumbarton Oaks Research Library and Collection, 1987), *Revue des études arméniennes*, vol. XXI (1988-1989), pp. 540-546.

126. Review of V. Nersessian, *Armenian Illuminated Gospel-Books* (London: The British Library, 1987), *Revue des études arméniennes*, vol. XXI (1990), pp. 546-548.

1990

127. "Les XVe et XVIe siècles: l'Arménie sans état et sans espoir," chap. V of *Les Arméniens. Histoire d'une chrétienté*, G. Dédéyan, ed. (Toulouse: Privat, 1990), pp. 40-43.

128. "Le sort des monuments architecturaux arméniens depuis les voyages de H. F. B. Lynch," *Fragments d'un discours d'Arménie: photographies originales de H. F. B. Lynch*, Artémis and Berdj Achdjian, eds. (Paris, 1990), pp. 3-7.

129. "Requiem pour Paradjanov. Réflexions à propos d'un collage," *Haratch, Art and Thought* (October, 1990), p. 3.

1991

130. *Warsaw Visitor & Tales from the Vienna Streets, The Last Two Plays of William Saroyan*, edited with an introduction (Fresno: The Press at California State University, 1991), ix, 212 pages, 43 illustrations.

130a. Review by Nubar Agishian, *Navasart*, Los Angeles, vol. X, no. 117 (April, 1992), pp. 6-12.

130b. Review by Aram Veeser, *Ararat*, vol. XXXIV, no. 134 (Spring, 1993), pp. 67-72; reprinted in *Critical Essays on William Saroyan,* edited by Harry Keyishian (New York: Simon & Schuster Macmillan, 1995).

130c. Review by Arby Ovannesian, *Haratch*, *Art and Thought* (May, 1994), pp. 3-4.

130d. Review by Aram Veeser, *Journal of Armenian Studies*, vol. V, no. 2 (Winter/Spring, 1995-1996), pp. 99-110.

131. "Les tapis à inscriptions arméniennes," R. H. Kévorkian and Berdj Achdjian, *Tapis et textiles arméniens* (Marseille, 1991), pp. 67-72.
132. "Requiem for Paradjanov," (in Armenian), *Hnch'ak hayastani*, vol. I (Yerevan, October 15, 1991), p. 6 (translation of no. 129).
133. "Identifying the Apostles in Armenian Narrative Miniatures," *Abstracts of Lectures, Fifth Biennial Conference, Association internationale des études arméniennes* (Bologna, 1990; Leiden, 1991), pp. 29-30.
134. Résumé, "Le livre manuscrit arménien et sa décoration," *Program* of "Le livre et la mémoire dans la tradition arménienne," a conference at the Fondation Léa et Napoléon Bullukian, Champagne au Mont d'Or (Lyon, March 16, 1991).

1992

135. *The Arts of Armenia (Accompanied by a Collection of 300 Slides in Color)* (Lisbon: Calouste Gulbenkian Foundation, 1992), 85 pages, 300 slides.
136. *Nor Djulfa*, vol. 21, *Documents of Armenian Architecture/ Documenti di Architettura Armena*, bilingual publication, English editor (Venice: OEMMA Edizioni, 1992), 123 pages.
137. "Simple Mechanical-Chemical Cleaning of Ancient Coins," *Armenian Numismatic Journal*, vol. XVIII, no. 3 (September, 1992), pp. 55-58 (abridged version of no. 50).
138. "Dated Armenian Manuscript Bindings from the Mekhitarist Library, Venice," *Atti del Quinto Simposio Internazionale di Arte Armena–1988* (Venice: San Lazzaro, 1992), pp. 403-412.
139. "Whitman and Saroyan: Singing the Song of America," *Walt Whitman Quarterly Review*, vol. 10, no. 1 (Summer, 1992), pp. 16-24.
140. "Les Arméniens aux États-Unis," special issue *Arménie: 3000 ans d'histoire*, *Les Dossiers d'archéologie*, no. 177 (Paris, December, 1992), pp. 136-138.
141. "A Tribute to a Scholar," *Father Levon Zekiyan, Commemorative Booklet* (Los Angeles, 1992), p. 13.
142. "April 24, 1992 Armenian Genocide Address," *The Armenian Reporter International* (May 23, 1992), pp. 14, 24.

143. Review of Kevork Gulian's *Elementary Modern Armenian Grammar* (New York: Hippocrene Books, 1990), *Modern Language Journal*, vol. 76/1 (1992), pp. 82-83.

1993

144. "Inscribed Armenian Manuscript Bindings: A Preliminary General Survey," *Armenian Texts, Tasks and Tools. Papers of an Association internationale des études arméniennes Workshop on Priorities, Problems and Techniques of Text Editions*, Henning Lehmann and J. J. S. Weitenberg, eds. (Aarhus, 1993), pp. 101-109, pls. 1-5.
145. "Les Arméniens et le cinéma américain," *Le cinéma arménien* (Paris: Centre Georges Pompidou, 1993), pp. 104-122.
146. "The Evolution of Armenian Gospel Illumination: The Formative Period (9th-11th Centuries)," *Armenia and the Bible*, Christoph Burchard, ed. (Atlanta: Scholars Press, 1993), pp. 125-142.
147. Review article "New Publications in French on Armenian Subjects," *Society for Armenian Studies Newsletter*, vol. XVII, no. 2 (Autumn, 1993), pp. 10-12.

1994

148. "The Genocide and Armenian Political Violence: Attitudes of Armenian Militants to the Genocide," *Genocide & Human Rights*, a special issue, *Journal of Armenian Studies*, vol. IV, nos. 1 and 2 (1992, pub. 1994), pp. 187-198.
149. "From Disintegration to Reintegration: Armenians at the Start of the Modern Era, XVIth-XVIIth Centuries," *Revue du monde arménien*, vol. I (1994), pp. 9-18.
150. "Lazar Parpetzi," *Studies in Classical Armenian Literature*, John Greppin, ed. (Delmar, N.Y.: Caravan Books, 1994), pp. 152-192.
151. Review of Robert Thomson, translator, *The History of Lazar P'arpets'i*, *The Armenian Review*, vol. 45, no. 3 (Autumn, 1992, published April, 1994), pp. 72-74.

1995

152. "[Armenischen] Künstler in der Diaspora," *Armenien, Wiederentdeckung einer alten Kulturlandschaft*, exhibition

catalogue, 14 January—17 April 1995 (Bochum: Bochum Museum, 1995), pp. 363-366, illustrated.

153. "Armenian Gospel Illumination and the Classical Tradition," *Text and Context. Studies in the Armenian New Testament, Papers Presented to the Conference on the Armenian New Testament, May 22-28, 1992*, S. Ajamian and M. E. Stone, eds., University of Pennsylvania Armenian Texts and Studies, vol. 13 (Atlanta: Scholars Press, 1995), pp. 59-73, with 6 figs.

154. "Survival of an Independent Armenia in a Hostile Environment," *The Armenian Reporter International*, vol. 28, no. 29 (1995), pp. 5, 30.

155. "A Unique Armenian Papyrus," *Vth International Conference on Armenian Linguistics*, Abstracts (Montreal, 1995), pp. 10-11.

156. "The Album of Armenian Paleography: Report on a Workshop of January 20-24, 1994 in Aarhus," *Revue des études arméniennes*, vol. 25 (1994-5), pp. 483-494.

157. "Armenian Iconography: A New Approach," *Journal of the Society for Armenian Studies*, vol. 6 (1992, 1993, issued 1995), pp. 201-222.

158. "Armenia at the Start of the Modern Era, XVIth-XVIIth Centuries," *Bazmavep*, vol. 153 (1995), pp. 218-229.

159. "Whitman and Saroyan: Singing the Song of America," *Critical Essays on William Saroyan,* Harry Keyishian, ed. (New York: Simon & Schuster Macmillan, 1995), pp. 72-80, originally published in the *Walt Whitman Quarterly Review* (no. 139).

160. Reviews of Bernard Coulie, *Répertoire des bibliothèques et des catalogues de manuscrits arméniens* (Turnhout, 1992), and *idem*, *Répertoire des manuscrits arméniens/Census of Armenian Manuscripts, Liste des sigles utilisés pour désigner les manuscrits* (Leiden, 1994), *Journal of the Society for Armenian Studies*, vol. 6 (1992-1993, issued 1995), pp. 255-258.

1996

161. "A Unique Armenian Papyrus," *Acts of the Vth International Conference on Armenian Linguistics*, D. Sakayan, ed. (Delmar, N.Y.: Caravan Books, 1996), pp. 381-386.

162. "Armenia. VI. Other arts. 1. Ceramics. 2. Jewellery. 3. Metalwork. 4. Textiles, embroidery, and lace," *The Dictionary of Art* (New York & London: Macmillan-Grove, 1996), vol. 2, pp. 439-443.
163. "Major Exhibit on Armenia in Paris," *Armenian Reporter International* (June 29, 1996), p. 20, 23.
164. "Treasures of Ancient Armenia from the Beginning to the 4th Century," *Armenian Observer* (September, 1996).
165. "Two Major Exhibits in France," *Society for Armenian Studies Newsletter*, vol. XX, no. 1/45 (November, 1996), p. 1.
166. "Armenian Manuscript Illumination in the Formative Period: Text Groups, Eusebian Apparatus, Evangelists' Portraits," *Settimnane di studio del Centro italiano di studi sull'alto medioevo* (Spoleto, Italy 1996), pp. 1015-1051, 20 plates.

1997

167. "Identifying the Apostles in Armenian Narrative Miniatures," *From Byzantium to Iran: Armenian Studies in Honour of Nina G. Garsoïan*, Jean-Pierre Mahé and Robert W. Thomson, eds. (Atlanta: Scholars Press, 1997), pp. 453-474.
168. "Armenian Paleography: A Reassessment," *Scribes et manuscrits du Moyen-Orient*, François Déroche and Francis Richard, eds. (Paris: Bibliothèque nationale de France, 1997), pp. 177-188.
169. Review article, "A Final Look at Eastern Asia Minor," *Journal of the Society for Armenian Studies*, vol. 7 (1994, pub. 1997), pp. 1-8.
170. "Armenia: A Decade of Turmoil," *The Armenian Reporter International* (March 16, 1997), pp. 14-16, and *Armenian Observer* (March 26, 1997), pp. 8-9.
171. "The New Julfa Style of Armenian Manuscript Binding," *Journal of the Society for Armenian Studies*, vol. 8 (1995, pub. 1997), pp. 13-36.
172. "Armenia from the Fall of the Cilician Kingdom (1375) to the Forced Emigration under Shah Abbas (1604)," *The Armenian People from Ancient to Modern Times,* Richard Hovannisian, ed. (New York: St. Martin's Press, 1997), vol. 2, pp. 1-50.
173. "Response to 'Modern Armenian Culture': The Distinguished Lecture of Levon Zekiyan," *Armenian Perspectives: 10th*

Anniversary Conference of the Association International des Études Arméniennes, edited by Nicholas Awde, Caucasus World Series (Richmond, Surrey: Curzon Press, 1997), pp. 355-361, notes pp. 430-431.

1998

174. "Paris and the Arts," *The Armenian Reporter International* (January 24, 1998), pp. 17, 19.
175. "Les reliures de manuscrits arméniens à inscriptions," *Recherches de codicologie comparée. La composition du codex au Moyen Âge, en Orient et en Occident*, Philippe Hoffman, ed. (Paris: Presses de l'École normale supérieure, 1998), pp. 259-274.
176. "Armenia in the Age of Columbus," *Armenian Mind*, vol. II, no. 1 (Yerevan, 1998), pp. 109-126.
177. Reprint of "Armenia from the Fall of the Cilician Kingdom (1375) to the Forced Emigration under Shah Abbas (1604)," (no. 172) and "A Critical Bibliography for the History of Armenia from 1375 to 1605" (no. 118) (Fresno: California State University, Fresno, Armenian Studies Program, 1998), ii, 50, 7 pages.
178. "A Unique Armeno-Greek Papyrus," *Études coptes,* vol. V, M. Rassart-Debergh, ed. (Paris, Louvain: Editions Peeters, 1998), pp. 165-169.
179. "Der Kuenstler William Saroyan," *ADK (Armenisch-Deutsche Korrespondenz)* (1998), no. 4, pp. 32-33.
180. "Confiscation and Destruction: A Manifestation of the Genocidal Process," *Armenian Forum*, vol. 1, no. 3 (Autumn, 1998), pp. 1-12.
181. "The Miniature Cycle in the Armenian Version of the History of Alexander the Great," *Twenty-Fourth Annual Byzantine Studies Conference Abstracts* (Lexington: University of Kentucky, 1998), p. 96.

1999

182. *Ghazar P'arpec'i matenagitut'yun* [Bibliography of Ghazar P'arpec'i], publication of the St. Mesrop Mashtots' College, vol. 4 (Yerevan, 1999), 24 pages.

183. "L'iconographie de l'Histoire d'Alexandre le Grand dans les manuscrits arméniens," *Alexandre le Grand dans les littératures occidentales et proche-orientales. Actes du Colloque de Paris, 27-29 novembre 1997*, Laurence Harf-Lancner, Claire Kappler et François Suard, eds. (Nanterre: Université Paris X, 1999), pp. 95-112, with six color plates.

184. "Letter to the Editor," *Armenian Numismatic Journal*, vol. xxv/2 (June, 1999), p. 20, on Kh. Musheghian.

185. "Sirarpie Der Nersessian, A Pioneer of Armenian Studies," *Ararat Literary Quarterly*, vol. XL, no. 157 (Winter, 1999), pp. 2-7.

186. "La confiscation des biens et la destruction des monuments historiques comme manifestations du processus génocidaire," *L'actualité du Génocide des Arméniens* (Paris, 1999), pp. 213-224.

2000

187. *Moïse de Khorène et l'historiographie arménienne des origines*, editor (Antelias, Lebanon: Press of the Catholicosate of Cilicia, 2000), 223 pages.

188. "Moïse de Khorène: le témoignage des scribes," *Moïse de Khorène et l'historiographie arménienne des origines* (Antelias, Lebanon: Press of the Catholicosate of Cilicia, 2000), pp. 93-102.

189. "Kai Armenikos Xrusos," *Istorika* (Athens, April 2000), pp. 14-24, illustrated, in Greek (translation of no. 186).

190. "Van under the Mongol, Turkmen, Persian, and Ottoman Domination," *Van,* vol. 1, Historic Armenian Cities and Provinces, Richard Hovannisian, ed. (Costa Mesa: Mazda, 2000), pp. 78-93.

191. "Visual Perceptions of Van through Nineteenth and Early Twentieth Century Travel Accounts," *Van,* vol. 1, Historic Armenian Cities and Provinces, Richard Hovannisian, ed. (Costa Mesa: Mazda, 2000), pp. 108-122.

2001

192. "Armenian Town. Foreword," *Armenian Town. Poetry by: P. Aloojian, J. Baloian. Y. S. Bulbulian, R. Dzerigian, M.*

Krekorian, B. Najimian-Magarity (Fresno: The William Saroyan Society, 2001), pp. ix-x.

193. "Preface," exhibition catalogue of the exhibit *Modern Icons: Contemporary Artists and the Legacy of the Armenian Illuminated Manuscripts*, Brand Library and Art Center, Glendale Library (September 15-October 20, 2001), pp. 2-3.
194. "Preface," Berge Bulbulian, *The Fresno Armenians*, 2nd edition (Fresno, 2001), pp. xiii-xvii.
195. "Tribute," *40th Anniversary of Professor Richard G. Hovannisian's Contribution to Armenian Studies*, banquet book (n. p. [Los Angeles, UCLA], 2001), p. 80.
196. "Confiscation of Armenian Property and the Destruction of Armenian Historical Monuments as a Manifestation of the Genocidal Process," *Anatomy of Genocide: State-Sponsored Mass-Killings in the Twentieth Century*, Alexandre Kimenyi and Otis L. Scott, eds. (Lewiston, N.Y.: Edwin Mellen Press, 2001), pp. 307-319.

2002

197. *Album of Armenian Paleography,* with Michael Stone and Henning Lehmann, sponsored by the Armenian Academy of Sciences (Aarhus: Aarhus University Press, 2002), in-folio, 556 pages, 220 color plates.

197a. Review by Patrick Donabedian, *Haratch, Art and Thought* (October 5, 2003), pp. 1, 4.

197b. Review by Vrej Nersessian, *Journal of the Society for Armenian Studies,* vol. 13 (2003, 2004), pp. 147-156.

197c. Review by Giusto Traina, *Litterae Caelestes. rivista annuale internazionale de paleografia, codicologia, diplomatica e storia delle testimonianze scritte*, vol. 1 (2005), pp. 218-220.

197d. Review by Peter Cowe, *Journal of the Society for Armenian Studies,* vol. 14 (2005), pp. 175-180.

198. "History of Armenian Paleography," special extract, Michael Stone, Dickran Kouymjian, Henning Lehmann, *Album of Armenian Paleography* (Aarhus: Aarhus University Press, 2002), pp. 5-75.
199. Review of Robert Thomson, *The Lawcode [Datastanagirk'] of Mxit'ar Goš* (Amsterdam & Atlanta, 2000), *Speculum*, vol. 77/3 (July, 2002), pp. 1026-27.

2003

200. *La Storia di Alessandro il Macedone, Codice miniato armeno del secolo XIV* (Venezia, ms. San Lazzaro 424), editor in chief Giusto Traina, with the collaboration of Carlo Franco, Dickran Kouymjian, Cecilia Veronese Arslan, "Helios" Collana editoriale del Centro Veneto Studi e Ricerche sulle Civiltà Classiche e Orientali, no. 5, 2 vols., I, Introduction, study of the miniatures, translation, bibliography, index, 194 pages; II, *Le miniature*, facsimile of 254 folios (Padua, 2003).
201. "When Does Genocide End? The Armenian Case," *The Armenian Weekly*, vol. 69, no. 15 (April 12, 2003), pp. 8-9.
202. "Introduction to Warsaw Visitor [and] Tales from the Vienna Streets: The Last Two Plays of William Saroyan," (see no. 130), *Twentieth-Century Literary Criticism*, vol. 137 (New York, Gale, 2003), pp. 172-186.
203. "The Role of University Chairs," *Journal of Armenian Studies*, vol. VII, no. 2 (Summer, 2003), pp. 31-35.
204. "The Future of Armenian Studies," *Journal of Armenian Studies*, vol. VII, no. 2 (Summer, 2003), pp. 185-190.
205. "Entretien avec Jean-Pierre Péroncel-Hugoz, grand reporter au *Monde*, de retour d'Azerbaïdjan," *Haratch* (September 2, 2003), p. 2; partially reprinted with photos as "Entretien avec J.-P. Péroncel-Hugoz: Ces chrétiens du Caucase, massacrés et vainqueurs…," *Le Libre Journal*, no. 305 (October, 2003), pp. 8-9, and again as "On dirait qu'il n'y a jamais eu d'Arméniens à Bakou," *Nouvelles d'Arménie*, no. 91 (November, 2003), pp. 36-37.
206. "The Anatolia College Gospels," American College in Thessaloniki, *Anatolia Alumnus* (October, 2003), no. 90, pp. 84-95, with a Greek translation.
207. "When Does Genocide End? The Armenian Case," *Avarayr*, Official Chronicle of the Knights of Vartan Brotherhood, (March-April 2003), p. 3 (May-June 2003), p. 4 (see no. 201).
208. "The Decline and Revival of Erzerum: Sixteenth-Eighteenth Centuries," *Armenian Karin/Erzerum*, vol. 4, Historic Armenian Cities and Provinces, Richard Hovannisian, ed. (Costa Mesa, CA: Mazda Publishers, 2003), pp. 123-134.
209. "Picasso Museum in Antibes Features Sarian and Sarkis," *The Armenian Reporter International* (June 28, 2003), pp. 1-2; *The*

Armenian Mirror Spectator (June 28, 2003); *Nor Gyank* (July 3, 2003).

210. Review of S. Peter Cowe, *Ani. World Architectural Heritage of a Medieval Armenian Capital* (Louvain: Peters, 2001), *Journal of the Society for Armenian Studies*, vol. 12 (2001, 2002, pub. 2003), pp. 75-77.
211. Review of Garo Kürkman, *Ottoman Silver Marks* (Istanbul: Mathusalem Publications, 1996), *Journal of the Society for Armenian Studies*, vol. 12 (2001, 2002, pub. 2003), pp. 86-88.

2004

212. "A Journey to Greece and Anatolia," *The Anatolian* (Spring, 2004), p. 7.
213. Review of Robert W. Thomson, *The Armenian History Attributed to Sebeos*, 2 vols. (Liverpool: Liverpool University Press, 1999), *Speculum*, vol. 79/2 (April, 2004), pp. 566-568.

2005

214. "The Right Hand of St. Gregory and other Armenian Arm Relics," *Les objets de la mémoire. Pour une approche comparatiste des reliques et de leur culte*, Philippe Borgeaud and Youri Volokhine, eds. (Geneva: Peter Lang, 2005), pp. 215-240.
215. "Sirarpie Der Nersessian (1896-1989). Pioneer of Armenian Art History," *Women Medievalists and the Academy*, Jane Chance, ed. (Madison: University of Wisconsin Press, 2005), pp. 482-493.
216. "The Legacy of the Indjoudjians," with Berdj Achdjian, *Hali*, no. 142 (2005), pp. 68-73.

2006

217. *Album of Armenian Paleography,* with Michael Stone and Henning Lehmann, sponsored by the Armenian Academy of Sciences (see no. 197), Armenian translation by Aram Topchyan and Gohar Muradyan, Mother See of Holy Etchmiadzin (Yerevan: Tigran Medzn Press, 2006), in-folio, 556 pages, 220 color plates.
218. "Chinese Motifs in Thirteenth-Century Armenian Art: The Mongol Connection," *Beyond the Legacy of Genghis Khan*,

Linda Komaroff, ed. (Leiden: Brill, 2006), pp. 303-324, pls. 23-25, figs. 58-67.

219. "Foreword," Hrayr S. Karaguezian, *Genocide and Life Insurance. The Armenian Case* (La Verne, CA: University of La Verne Press, 2006), pp. ix-xiii.

220. "Armenian Binding from Manuscript to Printed Book (16th–19th cent.)," *Gazette du livre médiéval*, no. 49 (Autumn, 2006), pp. 1-14.

2007

221. "Paradjanov: un artiste qui faisait des films," *Paradjanov le magnifique*, 13 February—2 April 2007, catalogue (Paris: École nationale supérieure des beaux-arts, 2007), pp. 35-51.

222. "Requiem pour Paradjanov, réflexion à propos d'un collage," *Paradjanov le magnifique*, 13 February—2 April 2007, catalogue (Paris: École nationale supérieure des beaux-arts, 2007), pp. 156-159 (reprint of no. 129).

223. "Portrait de l'artiste en cinéaste. Journal d'un tournage manqué," *À la recherche de Serguei Paradjanov*, Dominique Bax and Cyril Béghin, eds., Théâtre au cinéma, vol. 18 (Bobigny: Magic Cinéma, 2007), pp. 146-161.

224. "L'architecture en Grande Arménie (milieu XIIIe- milieu XVe siècle)," *Armenia sacra : Mémoire chrétienne des Arméniens (IVe–XVIIIe siècle)*, Le Louvre, 21 February–21 May 2007, catalogue Jannic Durand, Ioanna Rapti, Dorota Giovannoni eds. (Paris: Somogy, 2007), pp. 300-305.

225. "Architecture et sculpture, les derniers feux," *Armenia sacra : Mémoire chrétienne des Arméniens (IVe–XVIIIe siècle),* Le Louvre, 21 February–21 May 2007, catalogue Jannic Durand, Ioanna Rapti, Dorota Giovannoni eds. (Paris: Somogy, 2007) pp. 366-371.

226. 17 descriptive notices of liturgical objects from Etchmiadzin, *Armenia sacra : Mémoire chrétienne des Arméniens (IVe–XVIIIe siècle),* Le Louvre, 21 February–21 May 2007, catalogue Jannic Durand, Ioanna Rapti, Dorota Giovannoni eds. (Paris: Somogy, 2007), p. 34, 276-277, 279-280, 404, 414-415, 417, 418-419, 420, 421, 422, 423, 424-425, 426-427, 431, 442, 443, 444.

227. "L'art des tentures de chœur arméniennes," *Ors et trésors d'Arménie*, Musée des tissus et des Arts décoratifs and Musée d'art religieux de Fourvière, 22 March—15 July, catalogue Maria-Anne Privat-Savigny and Bernard Berthod, eds. (Lyon, 2007), pp. 30-35.
228. "L'orfèverie liturgique en Arménie," *Ors et trésors d'Arménie*, Musée des tissus et des Arts décoratifs and Musée d'art religieux de Fourvière, 22 March—15 July, catalogue Maria-Anne Privat-Savigny and Bernard Berthod, eds. (Lyon, 2007), pp. 78-89.
229. 39 descriptive notices of altar curtains and liturgical objects from Etchmiadzin *Ors et trésors d'Arménie*, Musée des tissus et des Arts décoratifs and Musée d'art religieux de Fourvière, 22 March—15 July, catalogue Maria-Anne Privat-Savigny and Bernard Berthod, eds. (Lyon, 2007), pp. 65-66, 67-68, 68-69, 70-71, 72, 73-74, 74, 92, 93, 95, 94-95, 95, 99, 99-100, 100, 100-101, 101, 102, 103, 105-106, 107-108, 109, 116, 117-118, 121, 122, 123, 125, 126-127, 127-8, 131-132, 134.
230. "Profession photographe : les photographes arméniens dans l'Empire ottoman," *Qantara*, Institut du monde arabe, no. 63 (2007), pp. 44-47.
231. "Les différents types d'écriture arménienne (V^{e}-XIXe siècle)," *Arménie : la magie de l'écrit,* La Vieille Charité, Marseille, 27 April–22 July, catalogue, Claude Mutafian, ed. (Paris-Marseille: Somogy, 2007), pp. 52-67.
232. "La structure et l'illustration des manuscrits arméniens," *Arménie : la magie de l'écrit,* La Vieille Charité, Marseille, 27 April–22 July, catalogue, Claude Mutafian, ed. (Paris-Marseille: Somogy, 2007), pp. 82-93.
233. "Les illustrations du Roman d'Alexandre et autres textes profanes," *Arménie : la magie de l'écrit,* La Vieille Charité, Marseille, 27 April–22 July, catalogue, Claude Mutafian, ed. (Paris-Marseille: Somogy, 2007), pp. 164-172.
234. "Le manuscrit arménien après l'imprimerie (XVIe-XIXe siècles)," *Arménie : la magie de l'écrit,* La Vieille Charité, Marseille, 27 April–22 July, catalogue, Claude Mutafian, ed. (Paris-Marseille: Somogy, 2007), pp. 173-177.
235. "Les reliures à inscriptions des manuscrits arméniens," *Arménie: la magie de l'écrit,* La Vieille Charité, Marseille, 27

April–22 July, catalogue, Claude Mutafian, ed. (Paris-Marseille: Somogy, 2007), pp. 236-247.

236. "Les fiancés de Kütahya," *Arménie : la magie de l'écrit,* La Vieille Charité, Marseille, 27 April–22 July, catalogue, Claude Mutafian, ed. (Paris-Marseille: Somogy, 2007), p. 256.

237. 13 descriptive notices of manuscripts, inscribed stones, ceramics and textiles, *Arménie : la magie de l'écrit,* La Vieille Charité, Marseille, 27 April–22 July, catalogue, Claude Mutafian, ed. (Paris-Marseille: Somogy, 2007), pp. 55, 90, 165-171, 175, 190, 256, 259, 278, 280, 357.

238. "Textiles arméniens: une riche palette," *Trames d'Arménie : tapis et broderies sur les chemins de l'exil (1900-1940),* Muséon Arlaten, 16 June 2007–6 January 2008, catalogue Dominique Serena, ed. (Arles, 2007), pp. 29-35.

239. 3 descriptive notices with Angèle Kapoïan, *Trames d'Arménie : tapis et broderies sur les chemins de l'exil (1900-1940),* Muséon Arlaten, 16 June 2007–6 January 2008, catalogue Dominique Serena, ed. (Arles, 2007), pp. 96-99.

240. "Sous le joug des Turcomans et des Turcs ottomans (XVe-XVIe siècle)," *Histoire du peuple arménien,* Gérard Dédéyan, ed. (Toulouse: Privat, 2007), pp. 377-411, augmented and revised edition of the 1982 volume *Histoire des Arméniens* (see no. 81*)*.

241. "L'image de l'Arménie et des Arméniens en Occident," *Loin de l'Ararat : les petites Arménies de l'Europe et de la Méditerranée. Les Arméniens de Marseille*, Musée des civilisations de l'Europe et de la Méditerranée (MUCEM, virtual exhibition) et Musée d'Histoire de la Ville de Marseille, under the direction of Myriame Morel-Deledalle, Claire Mouradian, Florence Pizzorni-Itié, 22 June–29 September 2007 (Paris: Hazan, 2007), pp. 42-44.

242. "Évolution de la paléographie arménienne," *Illuminations d'Arménie. Arts du livre et de la pierre dans l'Arménie ancienne et médiévale*, Fondation Martin Bodmer, Geneva, 15 September–30 December 2007, catalogue Valentina Calzolari, ed. (Geneva: Fondation Martin Bodmer, 2007), pp. 27-33.

243. "La structure et l'illustration des manuscrits arméniens," *Illuminations d'Arménie. Arts du livre et de la pierre dans l'Arménie ancienne et médiévale*, Fondation Martin Bodmer,

Geneva, 15 September–30 December 2007, catalogue Valentina Calzolari, ed. (Geneva: Fondation Martin Bodmer, 2007), pp. 41-59.

244. 4 descriptive notices of manuscripts, *Illuminations d'Arménie. Arts du livre et de la pierre dans l'Arménie ancienne et médiévale*, Fondation Martin Bodmer, Geneva, 15 September–30 December 2007, catalogue Valentina Calzolari, ed. (Geneva: Fondation Martin Bodmer, 2007), pp. 126-128, 164-171, 172-177, 226-229.

245. "Armenians in Constantinople 1453-1600," proceedings of the conference *Constantinopla. 550 años desde su caida*, vol. III, *Constantinopla Otomana*, Spain, December 4-6, 2003, E. Motos Guirao, M. Morfakidis Filactós, eds. (Granada, 2006, published 2007, vol. III, pp. 35-41.

In Press

246. "Cilicia and Its Catholicosate from the Fall of the Kingdom, 1375-1915," *Armenian Cilicia*, proceedings of the conference, in the series Historic Armenian Cities and Provinces, UCLA, October 18-20, 2000, Richard Hovannisian and Simon Payaslian, eds. (Costa Mesa: Mazda), in press.

247. "The Decoration of Medieval Armenian Manuscript Bindings," proceedings of the conference, *Le reliure médiévale,* Institut de France, Paris, May 22-24, 2003, pp. 209-218, in press.

248. "The Intrusion of East Asian Imagery in Thirteenth Century Armenia: Political and Cultural Exchange along the Silk Road," *The Journey of Maps and Images on the Silk Road,* Andreas Kaplony and Philippe Forêt, eds. (Leiden: E. J. Brill), pp. 188-214, in press.

249. "From Manuscript to Printed Book: Armenian Bookbinding from the Sixteenth to the Nineteenth Century," Second International Symposium on *The History of Printing and Publishing in the Languages and Countries of the Middle East*, Paris, Bibliothèque nationale de France, November 2005, *Journal of Semitic Studies*, in press.

250. "Post-Byzantine Armenian Bookbinding and Its Relationship to the Greek Tradition," proceedings of an international conference *The Book in Byzantium: Byzantine and Post-*

Byzantine Bookbinding, Athens, Greece, October 13-16, 2005, in press.

251. "Christian Iconographic Motifs in the Armenian Alexander Romance," *Jos Weitenberg Festschrift*, Hebrew University Armenian Studies series (Louvain: Peeters), in press.
252. "Sources and Specificity of Armenian Spirituality," Proceedings of the International Symposium on Armenian Spirituality, Ecumenical Institute, Bossey, Switzerland, 25 June-1 July 2001, in preparation.
253. "Armenian Spirituality and the Arts: Architecture, Painting, and Liturgical Metalwork," Proceedings of the International Symposium on Armenian Spirituality, Ecumenical Institute, Bossey, Switzerland, 25 June-1 July 2001, in preparation.
254. "Armenian Miniature Painting in Asia Minor in the Eleventh Century: The Melitene Group," *The Armenian Communities of the Region of Kesaria (Gesaria/Caesarea)*, proceedings of the conference, in the series Historic Armenian Cities and Provinces, UCLA, May 17, 2003, Richard Hovannisian, ed., in preparation.
255. "Armenian Illuminated Manuscripts," proceedings of the conference, *Where the Only-Begotten Descended: The Church of Armenia through the Ages*, University of Michigan, Ann Arbor, April 1-4, 2004, in preparation.
256. "Reliques et reliquaires. Comment les Arméniens honorent leurs saints," *ARMENIACA : La culture arménienne hier et aujourd'hui, 1600 ans après la création de l'écriture*, proceedings of a conference on the occasion of the Année de l'Arménie en France, Aix-en-Provence, March 16-17, 2007, in preparation.
257. "La conquête de Constantinople et l'Église arménienne, 1453-1600," proceedings of an international congress, *L'Église arménienne entre Grecs et Latins (fin XIe–milieu XVe s.)*, Montpellier, June 12-13, 2007, in preparation.

Tabula Gratulatoria

Margaret Lavinia Anderson
Professor of History
University of California, Berkeley
Berkeley, California

Aram Arkun
Historian
New York, New York

Jere L. Bacharach
Professor Emeritus
Department of History
University of Washington
Seattle, Washington

Kevork B. Bardakjian
Marie Manoogian Professor of Armenian Language & Literature
Director, Armenian Studies Program (1995-2007)
University of Michigan, Ann Arbor
Ann Arbor, Michigan

Eileen Barker
Professor Emeritus of Sociology with Special Reference
to the Study of Religion
London School of Economics
London, England

Houri Berberian
Associate Professor of History
Director of Middle Eastern Studies
California State University, Long Beach
Long Beach, California

Aida Boudjikanian
Montreal, Canada

Anthony A. M. Bryer
Emeritus Professor of Byzantine Studies
University of Birmingham
Birmingham, England

Christoph Burchard
Emeritus Professor of New Testament Theology
University of Heidelberg, Faculty of Theology
Heidelberg, Germany

Valentina Calzolari
Professor of Armenian Language and Literature
Université de Genève
Geneva, Switzerland

John Carswell
London and Malaga, Spain

Bernard Coulie
Rector, Université catholique de Louvain
Louvain-la-Neuve, Belgium

Anthony Cutler
Evan Pugh Professor of Art History
Penn State University
Union Park, Pennsylvania

R. Hrair Dekmejian
Professor of Political Science
Director, Institute of Armenian Studies
University of Southern California
Los Angeles, California

Walter B. Denny
Professor of Art History
University of Massachusetts at Amherst
Amherst, Massachusetts

Robert Der Merguerian
Emeritus Professor
Université de Provence
Aix-en-Provence, France

Patrick Donabedian
Maître de conférences d'Etudes arméniennes
Université de Provence
Aix-en-Provence, France

Bill Erysian
Coordinator, Grants and International Projects
California State University, Fresno
Fresno, California

Clive Foss
Professor of History
Georgetown University
Washington, D.C.

Armen Garabedian
Tadeh-Barth Publications
New York, New York

Nina Garsöian
Emerita Professor of Armenian Studies
Avedissian Chair of Armenian Studies
Columbia University
New York, New York

Oleg Grabar
Aga Khan Professor of Islamic Art and Architecture
Professor Emeritus
Harvard University
Boston, Massachusetts

Vartan Gregorian
Carnegie Endowment
New York, New York

Arpi Hamalian
Education Department
Concordia University
Montreal, Quebec, Canada

Christian Hannick
Professor of Slavic Philology
University of Würzburg
Germany

Margit A. Hazarabedian
Comparative Epic, Folklore, and Armenian Studies
University of California, Berkeley
Berkeley, California

David G. Hirsch
Librarian for Middle Eastern Studies
Charles E. Young Research Library
University of California, Los Angeles
Los Angeles, California

Matthew Ari Jendian
Associate Professor of Sociology
Director, American Humanics Program
California State University, Fresno
Fresno, California

Marilyn Jenkins-Madina
Research Curator
Department of Islamic Art
Metropolitan Museum of Art
New York, New York

Séta Kapoïan
Geneva, Switzerland

Hrayr Karaguezian
Los Angeles, California

Joseph A. Kéchichian
Editor, *Journal of the Society for Armenian Studies* (2008-2010)
Honorary Consul of the Sultanate of Oman
Los Angeles, California

Robert O. Krikorian
Institute for European, Russian and Eurasian Studies
George Washington University
Washington, D.C.

Gerard Jirair Libaridian
Alex Manoogian Professor of Modern Armenian History
Director, Armenian Studies Program (2007-present)
University of Michigan, Ann Arbor
Ann Arbor, Michigan

Ann Lousin
Professor of Law
The John Marshall Law School
Chicago, Illinois

Sylva Natalie Manoogian
Ph.D. Candidate, Department of Information Studies
University of California, Los Angeles
Los Angeles, California

Lucy Der Manuelian
Arthur H. Dadian and Ara Oztemel Professor of
Armenian Art and Architectural History
Tufts University
Medford, Massachusetts

Otto Meinardus (†)
Professor of Philosophy and Coptic Studies
Egypt and Germany

Robert Mirak
Boston, Massachusetts

Anahit Musheghyan
Armenian National Academy of Sciences
Institute of History
Yerevan, Armenia

Dennis R. Papazian
Professor Emeritus
University of Michigan-Dearborn
Founding Director, Armenian Research Center
Dearborn, Michigan

Nishan Parlakian
Professor Emeritus
John Jay College
City University of New York

Simon Payaslian
Charles K. and Elisabeth M. Kenosian Professor of
Modern Armenian History and Literature
Boston University
Boston, Massachusetts

James Russell
Mashtots Chair of Armenian Studies
Harvard University
Boston, Massachusetts

Ara Sanjian
Associate Professor of Armenian and Middle Eastern History
University of Michigan-Dearborn
Director, Armenian Research Center
Dearborn, Michigan

Ara Sarafian
Gomidas Institute
London, England

Levon A. Saryan
Technical Director, Industrial Toxicology
Aurora Health Care
Milwaukee, Wisconsin

Andrea Schmidt
Professor, Institut Orientaliste
Université catholique de Louvain
Belgium

George Shirinian
Zoryan Institute
Toronto, Canada

Hovann H. Simonian
Ph.D. Candidate, Department of Political Science
University of Southern California
Los Angeles, California

Thomas A. Sinclair
Department of Turkish Studies
University of Cyprus
Cyprus

Alice-Mary Talbot
Director of Byzantine Studies
Dumbarton Oaks
Washington, D.C.

Levon K. Topouzian
Emeritus Assistant Professor
Northwestern University
Associate Professor University of Illinois
Chicago, Illinois

Theo Maarten van Lint
Calouste Gulbenkian Professor of Armenian Studies
University of Oxford
Oxford, England

1

For Dickran Kouymjian

Peter Balakian

As Dickran Kouymjian retires from his long and distinguished position as director of Armenian Studies at California State University, Fresno, all of us both in the Armenian community and in higher education reflect on his career with gratitude. He has been an originator, a creative force in the academy for almost a half-century. As the Haig and Isabel Berberian Professor of Armenian Studies at California State University, Fresno, for the past twenty years, and Director of the Program for thirty years, Dickran has created a new template for Armenian studies, and he has brought the study of Armenian art and architecture and artifacts into the mainstream of Western civilization and art history. His courses and his scholarship have opened up new vistas for several generations of students and fellow scholars.

All of Dickran's work is marked by a cosmopolitanism that has defined his career from the start. Having taught at American University of Beirut, American University in Cairo, American University in Paris, Haigazian University, and Yerevan State University, as well as Berkeley and Fresno, he has brought an enormously international sensibility to his scholarship and teaching and has exemplified an interdisciplinary vision of scholarship. His work as scholar, teacher, and educational leader has been exemplary. He has been a force in the pioneering of Armenian Studies not only in the United States, but in Europe and the Middle East as well.

I salute you Dickran for all you have done. Your work on the destruction of Armenian material culture in Turkey helped me further grasp the meaning of the Armenian Genocide and I found it most useful in writing *The Burning Tigris*. But don't disappear in Paris, you are needed always by the culture you have served so well.

But I hope you can disappear just enough, so you can keep your important scholarly work alive and well. Congratulations.

2

Dickran Kouymjian à la Sorbonne (1984)

Yves Ternon

Du 13 au 16 avril 1984 s'est tenu à Paris, dans le grand amphithéâtre de la Sorbonne, une session du Tribunal permanent des peuples consacrée au génocide des Arméniens. Le tribunal, fondé par le sénateur et juriste italien Lelio Basso, était présidé par François Rigaux, professeur de droit à l'université catholique de Louvain. Parmi les douze autres membres du tribunal, trois avaient reçu un prix Nobel : Sean Mac Bride, Adolfo Perez Esquivel, George Wald. Pendant les deux jours d'audience publique, le tribunal entendit les rapports d'historiens et de juristes venus des Etats-Unis, de Grande-Bretagne, d'Allemagne, de Belgique et de France. Dickran Kouymjian, professeur à l'université d'État de Californie, Fresno, lut, en français, un rapport sur la *Destruction des monuments historiques arméniens, poursuite de la politique turque de génocide*. Cette contribution apportait un éclairage singulier sur la volonté des Jeunes-Turcs, puis de la République de Turquie d'effacer toute trace de présence arménienne sur le territoire historique de ce peuple. La communication de Dickran Kouymjian faisait le lien entre le génocide perpétré par le Comité Union et Progrès en 1915-1916 et la captation des bénéfices de ce crime par le mouvement kémaliste dès 1919. Le sort réservé aux monuments arméniens met en évidence la continuité idéologique entre la purification ethnique réalisée par la suppression de toute vie arménienne, en Anatolie orientale singulièrement, et le nettoyage méticuleux opéré après 1919 afin d'effacer les références à une présence arménienne en Turquie. Cette opération est une des composantes du négationnisme d'État lequel est la marque spécifique du déni du génocide arménien. Non seulement le nom d'Arménie est rayé des cartes et documents turcs, mais il est interdit d'introduire en Turquie des cartes étrangères portant cette mention. A la fin des années 50, le gouvernement turc change le nom de 90% des lieux des provinces orientales, des villes jusqu'aux hameaux, à l'exception des villes les plus importantes. Dans les six provinces qui forment le berceau historique du peuple arménien, il n'y a plus d'Arméniens que des crypto-Arméniens, descendants de ces femmes et enfants prélevés sur les convois de déportés et islamisés de force.

Le rapport de Dickran Kouymjian se concentre sur le soin méticuleux apporté tout au long du XXe siècle – donc de 1915 à 1984, date de ce rapport – par les gouvernements qui se sont succédé à la tête de l'État ottoman, puis de l'État turc pour détruire les monuments arméniens. L'inventaire réalisé en 1914 par le patriarcat arménien de Constantinople dénombrait 210 monastères, 700 églises monastiques, 1,639 églises paroissiales dans l'Empire ottoman. Cet inventaire était en fait incomplet. Kouymjian distingue huit formes de destruction de ces monuments :

1. Destruction intentionnelle d'églises, de bâtiments à usage civil et d'habitations par le feu et l'explosif, entre 1915 et 1922. En 1915, dans la région située entre Van et Mouch, l'artillerie ottomane a détruit quelques trente monastères. De 1915 à 1922, 1036 églises et monastères arméniens ont été rasés et 691 autres institutions religieuses en partie détruites.
2. Destruction plus tardive de monuments au canon. Les églises ont servi de cible à des exercices d'artillerie pratiqués au cours de manœuvres de l'armée turque en Anatolie orientale.
3. Destruction par les paysans qui, incités par les autorités, utilisent les pierres des églises arméniennes comme matériaux de construction de leurs maisons.
4. Transformation des églises arméniennes en mosquées, prisons, greniers, étables, fermes.
5. Destruction due à l'absence de tout entretien. Toutes les églises arméniennes existant encore en Turquie sont menacées. Depuis vingt ans, le patriarcat d'Istanbul sollicite l'autorisation de procéder à des réparations de bâtiments dans la capitale, et il se heurte à une fin de non-recevoir.
6. Démolition pour construction de routes, de barrages ou d'autres travaux publics.
7. Effacement des inscriptions en langue arménienne sur les bâtiments encore existants.

8. Enfin, réattribution des monuments, surtout des plus connus, à l'architecture médiévale turque des Seldjoukides. Cette manipulation intentionnelle pratiquée par des historiens d'art au service du gouvernement est d'autant plus absurde que les monuments concernés, comme les églises de Kars et d'Aghtamar, ont été construits au Xe siècle, donc avant l'arrivée des Seldjoukides en Anatolie.

Ces destructions, souligne Dickran Kouymjian, sont faites en violation des dispositions des articles 38 à 44 du traité de Lausanne signé par la Turquie en 1923. Des experts avaient proposé que l'UNESCO joue un rôle actif dans la sauvegarde de certains édifices, comme la cathédrale d'Ani et l'église d'Aght'amar, qui occupent une place importante dans l'histoire de l'art. Mais les statuts de l'UNESCO ne lui permettent de consacrer des fonds à une œuvre de conservation que si le gouvernement concerné lui adresse une invitation à le faire. Il y a donc lieu de craindre qu'une demande de cet organisme ne fasse qu'accélérer la destruction des monuments encore existants. Le gouvernement turc a le cynisme d'adhérer aux accords internationaux qui protègent les monuments des minorités dans un État – traité de La Haye de 1945 sur la conservation des monuments culturels en temps de guerre ; traité international de 1969 pour la conservation des monuments culturels des minorités – tout en poursuivant son programme de destruction intentionnelle.

Cette communication est accompagnée de la projection de trente-neuf diapositives, propriété pour la plupart de l'auteur, montrant des monuments détruits ou gravement endommagés, en particulier la vieille ville de Van, la basilique de Tekor, le monastère de Khts'konk, la cathédrale d'Ani, les églises de la Sainte-Mère de Dieu, du Saint-Sauveur, de Saint-Grégoire à Ani, la cathédrale de Kars.

En 1998, au cours du colloque organisé à la Sorbonne, du 16 au 18 avril, par le Comité de défense de la cause arménienne, Dickran Kouymjian a présenté une communication sur un thème plus large, puisqu'il étudiait l'ensemble de la spoliation de la richesse arménienne. Non seulement il reprenait le contenu de sa communication de 1984, mais il examinait le vol de l'or arménien déposé dans les banques ottomanes, la question des assurances-vie, la saisie des biens immobiliers et leur confiscation. Il soulignait la responsabilité de la République de Turquie : elle achève le travail commencé par le gouvernement « ajoutant à l'horreur du premier génocide du siècle les touches finales de l'une des plus grandes spoliations de biens et de terres de notre époque ».

Le rapport de Dickran Kouymjian devant le Tribunal permanent des peuples est publié en français dans *Le Crime de silence. Le Génocide des Arméniens* (Paris : Champs Flammarion, 1984), pp. 295-310. Il a été traduit en anglais : "The Destruction of Armenian Historical Monuments as a Continuation of the Turkish Policy of Genocide," *A Crime of Silence. The Armenian Genocide* (Londres : Zed Books, 1985), pp. 173-185, et allemand : "Die Zerstörung armenischer Kulturdenkmäler – eine Forsetzung der türkischen Völkermord-Politik," *Das Verbrechen des Schweigens, Die Verhandlung des türkischen Völkermords an den Armeniern vor dem Ständigen Tribunal der Völker* (Göttingen : Geselleschaft für bedrohte Völker [1985]), pp. 155-162.

La communication faite au colloque de 1998 est intitulée : « La Confiscation des biens et la destruction des monuments historiques comme manifestations du processus génocidaire », (*L'Actualité du génocide des Arméniens* [Paris : Edipol, 1999], pp. 218-230).

3

Berkeley Visitor: Tales from Telegraph Avenue

Michael Kovacs

It's 1996. Search engine company Yahoo! goes public. Despite having only sixty-eight employees, Yahoo! is valued at approximately $850 million.[1] In the first four months of 1996 alone, American households deposit approximately $100 billion in stock mutual funds as enthusiasm for the "New Economy" and the "Information Superhighway" captures the imaginations and checkbooks of middle-class Americans.[2] Technology is booming. Life in America is good.

I'm twenty-two years old on a foggy morning in Berkeley, California, in late August, walking up Telegraph Avenue and through Sather Gate and onto the UC Berkeley Campus where I'm greeted by the great white marble Doe Library and the Campanile Tower. It's my final semester before I graduate and receive a degree in English, with an emphasis in American literature. Who knows what's next, once I leave this little Athens in the hills.

* * *

Fiction is the most fundamental human art. Fiction is storytelling, and through the stories told we arguably construct our realities and define our dreams. Fiction is also conservative and conventional, something that can be studied, taught, criticized and sold, and in certain times in history, banned and burned. Difficult and obscure novels sit on shelves unread – until an English professor puts one of these books in his or her course syllabus, in which case

---

[1] John Cassidy, *dot.con: How America Lost Its Mind and Money in the Internet Era* (New York: HarperCollins, 2002), p. 100.
[2] Ibid., p. 110.

the student is "forced" to turn the pages of Joyce or Wolfe or Kerouac or Saroyan.

* * *

It's 1:50 p.m. I take my seat in 155 Kreber Hall and sip at a double latte. The class: English 166, Section 2, William Saroyan. The instructor: Dr. Dickran Kouymjian, William Saroyan Visiting Professor of Armenian Studies. "Visiting professor," I note. I attempt to say the last name a couple times – "Ku – yum – gin" – unsure of the correct pronunciation and ethnicity. Japanese, perhaps?

But I'm certain I want to be a writer. What that means exactly, I don't know. I have recently completed my senior honors thesis on Jack Kerouac and his method of writing known as spontaneous prose. "An obscure topic," I was told by my faculty advisor. "Are you sure? We have experts in almost every other topic?" she advised. I received a B+ after a full year of research and laborious hours writing. It's my first taste of rejection. It's a bitter taste, but I learn it certainly won't kill you.

A man appears in the lecture hall. He's professorial, dressed in white shirt and tie, wool brown vest sweater, and grey tweed jacket. He looks up from the lecture floor through his silver-rimmed glasses. He is balding, with thick grey hair trimmed on the side. His eyes are bright and hard, he is not angry but serious. He is not Japanese.

The man greets us: "Afternoon. My name is Dickran. Dickran Kouymjian. You may call me Dr. K, if you'd like."

I feel oddly buzzed, almost happy, as I read the course description from the syllabus:

> The course is devoted to Fresno born writer William Saroyan (1908-1981); the course focuses on creative activity through books, films, and voice recordings. William Saroyan was for a time (1935-1945) one of the three or four most famous writers in the English language. After the Second World War, his fame began to decline, but he kept writing and publishing at an unbelievable rate. Saroyan always had trouble with the critics, especially those connected to the academic world. He is also considered by some to be the first genuine ethnic writer in American literature. The course will explore two major

> themes: 1) Saroyan and the Critics, 2) Was Saroyan an Ethnic Writer?[3]

I am familiar with the writing of Saroyan, particularly two works – a short story called "The Daring Young Man on the Flying Trapeze" and a novel titled, *The Human Comedy*. I suddenly remember my high school English teacher Ms. Macias, and silently thank her for introducing Saroyan to our senior class. Again and again, I find myself giving thanks to the teachers who have come into my life, who have had the foresight and rigor to stand outside the halls of academia, distance themselves from the preference for lofty intellectual theorems, who have come to appreciate creative human growth for the sake of growth itself.

My odd buzz heightens as I listen to Dr. Kouymjian's introduction to Saroyan, that after the publication of the "Daring Young Man" in *Story* magazine, Saroyan would write a story a day for thirty-three days and publish his first book, *The Daring Young Man on the Flying Trapeze and Other Stories*; that the career of William Saroyan marched forward more than fifty years, and included an enormous amount of work in every arena of writing, bringing him countless awards including the Pulitzer Prize for his Broadway play, *The Time of Your Life*. From a scholarly and personal perspective, Dr. Kouymjian would later remark in an interview:

> At the end of his [William Saroyan's] life, those last years, he entrusted me with a good deal of responsibility, and I still feel that I have a mission to carry out in the best way I can.[4]

In these first moments with Dr. Kouymjian, I can sense his admiration for Saroyan, both as an artist and Armenian. Even more, I am delighted to have the rare opportunity to learn about this prolific

---

[3] Dickran Kouymjian, English 166, Section 2, Course Syllabus (UC Berkeley, 1996).

[4] Matthew Maroot, Staff Writer, *Hye Sharzhoom*, interview with Dickran Kouymjian titled, "Saroyan Conference Attracts Large Audience," vol. 20, no. 4 (May, 1999).
http://armenianstudies.csufresno.edu/hye_sharzhoom/vol20/may66/saroyan.html.

American writer, an obscure American writer whose name and works I have not once heard spoken within the halls of the Berkeley English Department.

More significantly, through my research and writing on Kerouac, time and again I came upon references to William Saroyan's influence on Jack Kerouac and the Beat Writers of the 1940s and 1950s. In an October 8, 1941, letter to best friend Sebastian Sampas, a nineteen-year-old Kerouac writes, "Got the following writers from Hartford Library – Wolfe, Saroyan, Halper, Dos Passos, William James (Psychology). What men!"[5] Indeed, Kerouac studied the works of Saroyan, as did a group of young contemporaries later to be called the "Beat Generation." Pete Hamill, a Saroyan scholar, perceptively points out the need to explore Saroyan's work and its importance to the writers of the following generation:

> There appears to be a lot of Saroyan in Jack Kerouac and the other beat writers. The critics now ignore him. But my sense is that Saroyan's achievement will be recognized eventually for what it is: a large, almost Balzacian attempt to turn one man's experience of the world into literature.[6]

Yes, there is a Saroyan connection to Kerouac and the Beats. Yes, the critics and universities do ignore Saroyan and his achievements. But then there are scholars and educators such as Dr. Kouymjian who points out in his essay, "Who Reads Saroyan Today?":

> Literary criticism in America has been dominated by the universities. It was and is the college educated writer, or failed writer, the M.F.A. in English literature, and increasingly the Ph.D. who decided and decides what gets into the "canon," that is the accepted tradition.[7]

---

[5] Anne Charter, *Selected Letters of Jack Kerouac, 1940-1956* (New York: Viking, 1995), p. 18.

[6] Peter Hamill, "Under Saroyan's Spell," in *William Saroyan: The Man and Writer Remembered,* Leo Hamalian, ed. (Rutherford [NJ]: Fairleigh Dickinson University Press, 1987), p. 194.

[7] Dickran Kouymjian, from an unpublished essay, *Who Reads Saroyan Today?* (Pasadena: December 6, 1998).

I don't realize that, for this one semester in 1996, during these final days on the UC Berkeley campus, that I am about to embark on a great adventure, an adventure with Dr. Kouymjian at the helm, with William Saroyan novels and shorts stories and plays in my book bag, and a transfer of knowledge about a particular man and writer and spirit that will help shape the rest of my life. I continue to follow my own path, study writers who are "obscure," those left on shelves, labeled and tossed to the margins as insignificant by literary scholars who comfortably quantify creativity in intellectual terms.

Dr. Kouymjian is our Berkeley Visitor, years into his own great adventure as scholar, professor, writer, student, husband, and friend. As Dr. Kouymjian notes in *An Armenian Trilogy*, "Saroyan wanted the plays to be studied and published; that is why he passed them on to me in use in my classes."[8] By "studied," it is my belief Saroyan wanted students to learn not how to take something apart, but how to assemble it, live it, breathe it, enjoy it, and express it. Saroyan never abandoned his own energies, he never quit. All along he kept creating and writing, and like his protagonist in his first short story, "The Daring Young Man on the Flying Trapeze," Saroyan at the end dies in a world callously indifferent to the sacrifice of creation.

Yet, Saroyan knew how to save the writer. At the end he passed on his energy and works to individuals such as Dr. Kouymjian who understand "salvation comes through art which immortalizes being."[9]

* * *

Ironically, at UC Berkeley, where the Saroyan archives had been deposited for 15 years after his death, and where a major endowment named the William Saroyan Chair of Armenian Studies had been in place for some years, no Saroyan course was taught until 1996, this one fall semester in 155 Kreber Hall, by Dr. Dickran Kouymjian, a visiting professor from California State University, Fresno. There were 24 students in all, mostly English majors, and only four were

---

[8] *William Saroyan: An Armenian Trilogy,* Dickran Kouymjian, ed. (Fresno: The Press at California State University, Fresno, 1986) p. x.

[9] Dickran Kouymjian, Contributing Writer, *Hye Sharzhoom*, "A Semester at Berkeley," vol. 18, no. 3 (March, 1997). http://armenianstudies.csufresno.edu/hye_sharzhoom/vol18/march57/berkeley.html.

Armenian. Most had never heard of Saroyan. But as the next dot.com went public and another senior thesis written on Shakespeare, the students in 155 Kreber Hall began preparations to commemorate the 15th anniversary of the death of William Saroyan. The conference would be entitled, "Saroyan Plus Fifteen."

* * *

Dr. Kouymjian was like no other professor I had at Berkeley. Indeed, I studied under some of the most respected literary scholars and writers of our day; yet, after years of study and research at Berkeley, and even as a graduate student at Stanford University, it is Dr. Kouymjian whom I continue to single out as an exemplary scholar, writer, professor, mentor, and friend.

That fall semester in 1996, Dr. Kouymjian would invite myself and another graduating senior, Michael Kloster, to join leading Saroyan scholars from around the world to present papers at "Saroyan Plus Fifteen." With the support of classmates and our professor, we researched, wrote, edited, practiced, and presented our papers. Dr. Kouymjian recounts this experience in his essay, "A Semester at Berkeley":

> Certainly this was one of the most positive experiences during my Berkeley stay. All the students were behind their classmates, who, apprehensive about being on the same platform with the very experts whose books they were quoting, wrote and rewrote their essays. They had a dry run in class with heavy questioning and criticism. I assured them continually that the work they were doing was as good as the experts and that the level of their own preparation would be on par with that of the scholars present.[10]

The all-day conference held on the Berkeley campus would draw over 100 people to Wheeler Hall, including famed and distinguished poet and City Lights publisher, Lawrence Ferlinghetti. Dr. Kouymjian's vision was to bring together those interested in Saroyan's literary achievement, as well as writers who knew him from California and Paris. Like the writing of Saroyan, "Saroyan

[10] Kouymjian, *Who Reads Saroyan Today?*.

Plus Fifteen" turned out to be a marathon lecture session with three panels that lasted over 12 hours, with an extraordinary film segment at the end. It was alive and spontaneous, structured when required, and touched on subjects typically ignored by the world of academia – most predominately, why is Saroyan not taught? Ferlinghetti even posed the question, "How much of Saroyan's writing had not been published?" One scholar replied, "10,000 letters and 200 plays." Of course, there is much more.

* * *

After the 1996 fall semester, the next time I would cross paths with Dr. Kouymjian would be at Stanford University on May 10, 1997, at an event entitled, "The Spirit of Saroyan." Presented by The Stanford University Libraries and The Associates of the Stanford University Libraries, "The Spirit of Saroyan" honored the recent acquisition of The William Saroyan Collection that was given to the Stanford University Libraries by the William Saroyan Foundation. The collection at Stanford fills hundreds of boxes containing manuscripts, journals, correspondence, photographs, contracts, and personal items such as soup labels, paper clips, hotel stationary, and hair shavings. As fate would have it, I would attend Stanford University as a graduate student in the fall of 1997, studying American literature with full access to The William Saroyan Collection.

Accessing Saroyan's place in American literature, Dr. Kouymjian presented a paper at "The Spirit of Saroyan" event entitled, "Who Reads Saroyan Today?," commenting:

> In order for the mini-revival which started after his death to continue, Saroyan has to get back into the canon, has to become once again a subject for M.A. and doctoral theses, and has to reappear in survey courses of twentieth century American fiction. Can this happen and will it happen? It certainly can happen.[11]

To ensure Saroyan's legacy, Dr. Kouymjian would champion Saroyan even further two years later, in March 1999, by organizing an international conference and celebration entitled, "Saroyan at

---

[11] Maroot, interview with Dickran Kouymjian.

Ninety." Organized by the Armenian Studies Program at Fresno State and the William Saroyan Society, the event attracted scholars, writers, friends, and relatives of the writer to the Fresno State campus. Now, a Lecturer of English at a state university, I once again presented a paper on Saroyan.

"The idea of celebrating Saroyan is linked closely with the need to keep his image alive and up-to-date,"[12] Dr. Kouymjian remarks in an interview after the event. Once again, Dr. Kouymjian demonstrates his seriousness and dedication to Saroyan's work, and quest to keep his writing and image alive.

* * *

It's 2004. Today's Yahoo! news section reads: Gunmen strike U.S. Consulate in Saudi City – Bush links Saudi attack to Iraq election – Ukraine's outgoing president won't halt vote – Lawmakers enter fray on drug use in baseball.

* * *

I'm thirty-years-old on a rainy evening in San Jose, California, in early December, sitting in my study writing about William Saroyan and Dr. Dickran Kouymjian's contributions to the field of Saroyan research and studies. Who reads Saroyan today? Well, I certainly do. In the years that I have taught at the college level, I have assigned Saroyan short stories, novels, and plays. As I complete my first novel, I stand on the shoulders of Saroyan and his incredible body of work. In spring 2004, the American Conservatory Theater (A.C.T.) in San Francisco presented a production of *The Time of Your Life*, billing the author as "one of San Francisco's greatest writers, born to Armenian immigrants in Fresno, California."[13] *The Time of Your Life* is a play that reflects a city and nation on the edge, balancing on a fault line between hope and despair. More than 60 years later, we are once again a nation teetering somewhere between hope and

---

[12] Ibid.

[13] American Conservatory Theater, Press Release: *A.C.T. Announces Casting for the Time of Your Life* (February 27, 2004, San Francisco, California).

despair, unsure where our answers lie. Saroyan's writing came from deep within his spirit, autobiographical and often capturing the bittersweet loneliness of lost and suffering souls. His characters are often consumed by dreams of happiness, who never give up the struggle to fulfill those dreams. Even more, his characters call for hope, honesty, brotherly love, and compassion. Understanding these motifs is where the value of Saroyan will be found. Saroyan lived as a great writer. Dr. Kouymjian lives as a significant scholar and educator. I live giving thanks to the courage and devotion of both men, never forgetting this particular Berkeley Visitor, always happy to share my Tales from Telegraph Avenue.

4

Remarks on the *Album of Armenian Paleography*

Michael E. Stone

It gives me great pleasure to dedicate the following remarks to Dickran Kouymjian, a distinguished scholar, a fine human being, and a close friend. I hope that these memories of the creation and gestation of the *Album of Armenian Paleography* will give insight into the book, into its genesis, and into its authors. It was a labour that Dickran and I shared, and his individual contribution was stamped with the special lines of his personality and the impress of his scholarship.

In July 16-20, 1989, the Association internationale des études arméniennes (AIEA) initiated a workshop on "Priorities, Problems and Techniques of Text Editions." It was organized most graciously by Henning Lehmann at Aarhus University's Conference Center in Sandbjerg in Denmark. The beautiful surroundings of the Sandbjerg Conference Center and the sunny weather that prevailed doubtless contributed to making this a pleasant gathering. However, it was the combination of people present and their interaction that made it a milestone event. The intellectual challenges of the workshop were quite remarkable and the problems discussed engendered and stimulated a number of systematic scholarly projects. Such were Bernard Coulie's *Catalogus Catalogorum*, as we called it;[1] Michel Thierry's repertoire of Armenian monasteries and scriptoria[2] and the *Album of Armenian Paleography*. In more general terms, the AIEA's decision to concentrate its publications program on *instruments de travail* had major impact on the tools available to those interested in

---

[1] B. Coulie, *Répertoire des bibliothèques et des catalogues de manuscrits arméniens,* Corpus Christianorum (Turnhout, Belgium: Brepols, 1992).

[2] M. Thierry, *Répertoire des monastères arméniens,* Corpus Christianorum (Turnhout, Belgium: Brepols, 1993).

Armenian texts and philology.[3] I could reminisce at length about this workshop, which as I look back over the first two decades of AIEA's history, stands out in my mind as most remarkable.

In the opening remarks for the Sandbjerg workshop, which I had the privilege of making, I talked of the needs of scholars of Armenian manuscripts. I said that "[t]here is a need for a more securely based palaeographic typology of the Armenian scripts. A first step might be the publication of an album of dated Armenian scripts."[4] In retrospect, I claim no prophetic powers, and this observation was a fairly obvious one to anybody working on Armenian manuscripts at that time. The concluding session of the workshop, after a stimulating three full days of discussion, addressed the needs that had been defined more distinctly as a result of the workshop's deliberations. Ways were sought to stimulate the creation of the *instruments de travail* that would fill those *lacunae*. I was so brash as to undertake the preparation of an album of Armenian manuscript writing. As I made this offer during that rather down-to-earth concluding session, Henning Lehmann was signalling that he would join me in the endeavour. We agreed and, within an hour had decided to ask Dickran Kouymjian to join us, and obtained his assent. Thus began a cooperative saga that ended with the publication more than a decade later of the *Album of Armenian Paleography*, edited by the three of us.

I wanted Dickran Kouymjian to join the team because of his broad and detailed knowledge of Armenian manuscripts. We had first met in Cambridge, MA in June 1964. There I gave my first lecture at a conference sponsored by NAASR. In those days, Dickran had a notable handlebar mustache and was studying with Nina Garsoïan at Columbia. It was a long time before we met again, and I do not remember where that was, but we quickly discovered a common interest in Armenian manuscripts in all their aspects, as

---

[3] Robert Thomson's *A Bibliography of Classical Armenian Literature to 1500 A.D.*, Corpus Christianorum (Turnhout, Belgium: Brepols, 1995) was another work published in the same program, as well as Coulie's *Répertoire de manuscrits arméniens* (Leiden: AIEA, 1994).

[4] M. E. Stone, "Priorities, Problems and Techniques of Text Editions," *Armenian Texts, Tasks and Tools,* H. Lehmann and J. J. S. Weitenberg, eds. *Acta Jutlandica* LXIX:1, Humanities Series 68 (Aarhus: Aarhus University Press, 1993), p. 14.

well as a distinct personal compatibility. Of course, I had seen his articles over the years and was well aware of the range and detail of his knowledge. His writing encompassed projects such as his lecture at the Sandbjerg Workshop, or his earlier pioneering volume on Armenian iconography.[5] So, when the idea of the *Album* came up in 1989, I was determined that Dickran should be involved and he, equally enthusiastically, joined the team.

The process of selecting the manuscripts and the discussion of the development of Armenian writing were the two first substantive aspects of the job in which we cooperated. We traveled, together with Nira Stone, to Armenia to ask the cooperation of the Matenadaran in our work (Fig. 1).[6]

---

[5] Dickran Kouymjian, "Inscribed Armenian Manuscript Bindings: A Preliminary General Survey," *Armenian Texts, Tasks and Tools,* H. Lehmann and J. J. S. Weitenberg, eds., *Acta Jutlandica* LXIX:1, Humanities Series 68 (Aarhus: Aarhus University Press, 1993), pp. 101-109; Dickran Kouymjian, *Index of Armenian Art* (Fresno: Armenian Studies Program, 1982.)

[6] A listing of the editorial team consultations and of the expeditions made for purposes of examination of manuscripts and photography is given in the *Album*, p. 7: "Four major joint consultative and planning sessions were held: two in Leiden-Wassenaar (1991 and 1998) and two in Aarhus (1994 and 1998). Campaigns for selection of manuscripts and photography were mounted as follows: in Yerevan once by Kouymjian and Stone, and a second and third times by Stone; in Jerusalem by Stone; in Venice by Lehmann, Kouymjian, and Stone, and a second time by Kouymjian; and in London, Dublin, Leiden and the East Coast of the United States by Stone." The Preface of the *Album* contains some further details relating to these matters.

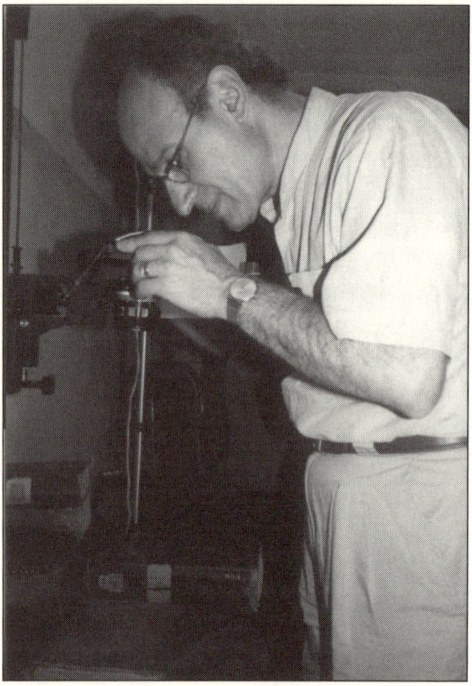

Fig. 1-Dickran Kouymjian photographing manuscripts in the Matenadaran, 1991.

Immediately it became clear to us that the process of selection of manuscripts was a most complex one. First, from collections in Armenia, in Europe, in Britain, in North America, and in Jerusalem, we prepared black and white photographs of many hundreds of manuscripts, more than 600. We selected the broad group of manuscripts for photography by preliminary study of the catalogues of the various manuscript libraries and from personal knowledge. We examined these initial selections by autopsy and photographed many of them. This process was aided and the selection broadened and focused by Dickran's insights. It was he who insisted that well-known or famous manuscripts be included, naturally provided they were of paleographic significance. It was he who followed up hints by Dashian and others with Holmesian persistence and finally located the "lost" Armenian papyrus in the Louvre.[7] He also introduced into our purview Armenian inscriptions on monastery frescos in Egypt[8] and he insisted on the importance of the chancellery documents from Cilicia.[9]

After the manuscripts had been assembled in black and white photos, there came a weekend in 1994 when Dickran, Nira, and I went to Aarhus as guests of Henning and Else Lehmann.[10] This was the time of winnowing and the selection of the pages to be featured in the *Album*, a crucial stage in our work. On a very long table we laid out all the black and white pictures arranged by date and started eliminating manuscripts and pages — one because the page was not clean, another since a different contemporary manuscript was a better example of a sub-type of script, a third for another reason. Dickran's discriminating eye and almost eidetic memory played a major role in this task. It was time-consuming but, at its end we had reduced the total to the just under two hundred manuscript pages, which formed the body of the *Album.*

At a third juncture, Dickran again made a major contribution, this time to the presentation of the material. This was the major thrust of the 1998 workshops (Figs. 2 and 3).

---

[7] See Dickran Kouymjian, "Unique Armenian Papyrus," *Acts of the Vth International Conference on Armenian Linguistics*, Dora Sakayan, ed. (Delmar, NY: Caravan Books, 1996), pp. 381-386. An edition was given by James Clackson, "A Greek Papyrus in Armenian Script" *Zeitschrift für Papyrologie und Epigraphik* 129 (2000), pp. 223-258. See Kouymjian's discussion in *Album of Armenian Paleography*, pp. 59-63 and further bibliography there.

[8] *Album of Armenian Paleography*, illustration 19, p. 71.

[9] Claude Mutafian had assembled interesting examples of these for the exhibit he organized in Paris in 1993. See his work, *Le Royaume arménien de Cilicie XII*[e]*-XIV*[e] *siècle* (Paris: CNRS Editions, 1993).

[10] Dickran Kouymjian, "Album of Armenian Paleography: Report on a Workshop of January 20-24, 1994 in Aarhus," *Revue des études arméniennes* 25 (1994-1995), pp. 483-494.

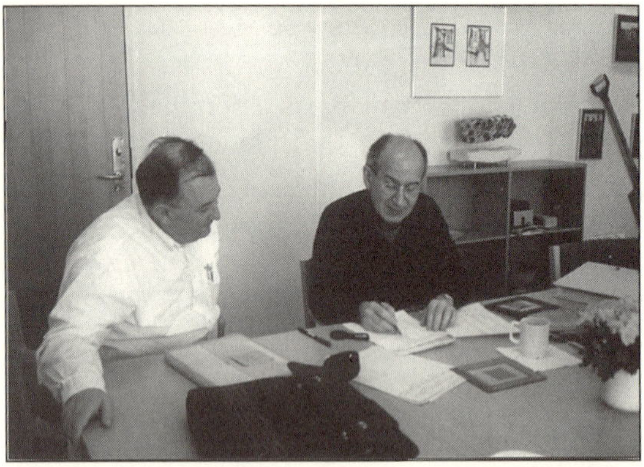

Fig. 2-Dickran Kouymjian and Michael Stone at working meeting, Wassenaar, 1998.

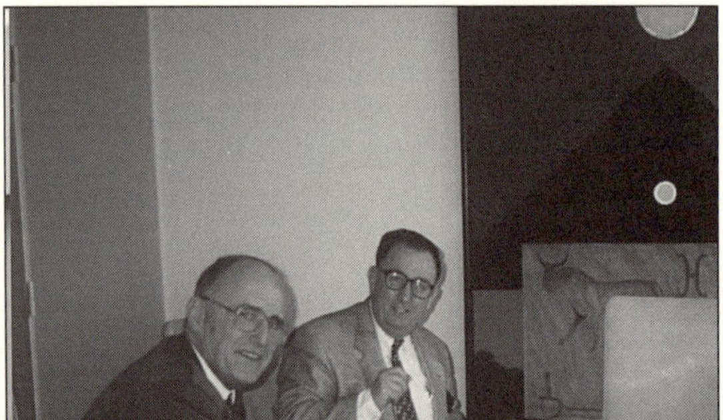

Fig. 3-Henning Lehmann and Michael Stone at working meeting, Aarhus, 1998.

He invested a great deal of time and energy in the documentation of the manuscripts which had been selected, enriching the bibliographical notes on individual manuscripts, as well as insisting vehemently on certain features of the layout and format, at points where I might have conceded. His insistence was all to the good. The voluminous correspondence between Dickran, the Press, and myself would fill an archive were it on paper. Fortunately for my storage area, it is nearly all on computer.

In addition to these matters and, of course, in addition to the chapter he himself wrote, it was the scholarly discussions that made joint work so exciting. I suppose our chief points of disagreement were two. I wanted to write the introductory chapters without using the traditionally accepted technical terms. Dickran fought like a lion for the traditional terms. In the end, we used both, in carefully distinguished parts of the introduction. The traditional terminology was discussed and analyzed in presenting the history of Armenian paleography (Kouymjian) but neutral terminology served in the analysis of the typology of the scripts (Stone). We thus avoided prejudging the stages of development of the script, yet could put what we were doing into the context of previous analyses of Armenian book-hands. The book is better for facing this issue head-on.

The other matter on which we differed, and still do, is that of the origin of the *bolorgir* script. My own tendency is to put the origin of this script before the tenth century and to regard it as developing from the later forms of the uncial (*erkat'agir*) script. Dickran holds that it is older, being an invention by Mesrob Mashtots' himself, and that both script forms had existed from the very origins of Armenian writing. This argument probably cannot be resolved definitively at the present stage of knowledge.

Of course, there were many other incidents, meetings, wonderful discussions, amicable disagreements, travels, and adventures on the way from idea to the *Album*. But, above all there was an amity and collegiality enhanced by a rich and caring friendship. Indeed, it was a great pleasure to work together with this distinguished scholar. I must add also that Henning Lehmann was a wonderful friend and colleague and his contribution to the work, despite the burdens of his long rectorship of Aarhus University, was truly substantial. The *Album* is dedicated to St. Mesrob Mashtots', but it is also a monument to collegiality and friendship.

Art and Archaeology

5

"Hands On" Dvin: Reflections on the Dvin Capital

Hilary Richardson

The well known capital from Dvin is the starting point for a small meandering trail of research which demonstrates, en route, the generosity of Armenian scholars who have always given me so much support.

It began with a drawing. Sometimes when studying an object or building, it can be practical to draw it, in order to find out how it was made or designed. There is an element of discovery. In the course of observing the subject for depiction, the eye concentrates in a more searching way than a mere look or glance requires. By making a drawing the subject can become fixed in the memory to some extent, so that it leaves a more permanent impression. In addition, on a rare occasion, a feature may emerge that had not previously been perceived and had escaped notice altogether.

This is what happened to me a long time ago when I made a drawing of the broken capital, dating to the sixth century, found in the excavations at Dvin in the nineteen forties, and now preserved in the State History Museum in Yerevan. The capital (or possible base) is well known because of its remarkable subject, clearly linking Christian Armenian themes with those of early Palestine. The carving is stylised ornamentally, and while the left front section is missing, there is reason to believe that it must have corresponded with the surviving portion on the right, and balanced it.

Two scenes are partially preserved, one on the front face and the other on the right side. They share the same sculptural style as other reliefs of the period, carved with vigour and a strong feeling for decoration. The front design is centred on a large leaved cross and above it a bust of Christ that fills the upper part, resting on the horizontal arms of the cross, with an angel alongside at the right. The curves of Christ's halo, inset with another cross, align with the upward curving extremities of the cross arm. One must presume that the missing portion on the left repeated this motif. Christ's hair is abundant, falling on either side and framing a long face. The features are stylised in the tradition of the region at the time, with the raised line of the nose and eyebrows forming a single, well-defined unit. The eyes are large and clearly delineated. The face of the angel to the right of Christ is treated in the same way, but here the halo is plain. (Fig. 1)

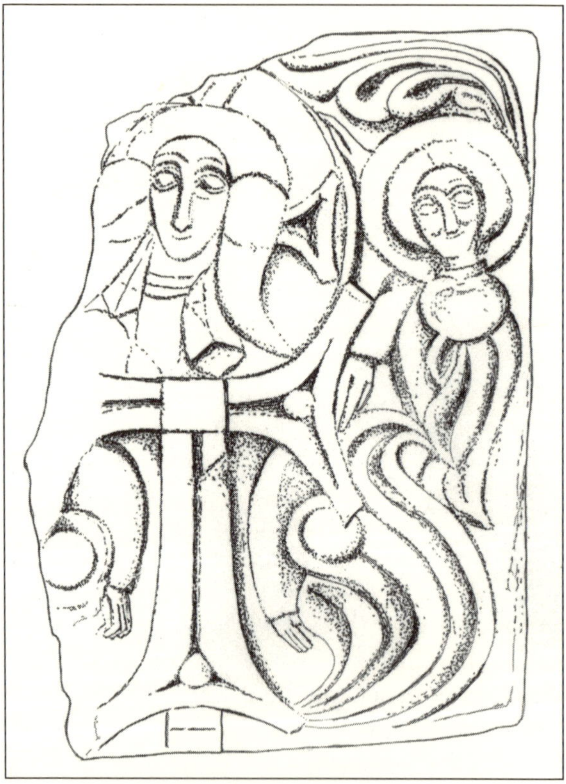

Fig. 1- Dvin, fragment of capital, front.

The angel in all probability was one of a pair, each supporting the image of Christ between them. The curve of the angel's arm follows the arc that forms the end of the cross-arm, matching the curve of the halo and cross already noted. The long fingers of the hand are notable. Everything is simplified and expressive. The angel's upper hand holds the top of Christ's halo and is seen from the side. One of the angel's wings is like a leafy canopy above, echoing the pattern of foliage springing from the base of the cross. The wings and leaves seem to merge, while the angel's body looks circular, rather like a pomegranate. Discs are found elsewhere in the design, decorating the cross, where they may denote jewels, and in the foliage. The whole interlocking composition has been organised and worked out with great care.

A surprising detail appeared in my drawing of the capital: two curving shoulders and arms are visible below the arms of the cross on either side of the upright. They are not attached to any body. They belong to two separate individuals, who are otherwise not represented. Their shapes blend with the foliage also, like the angel's wings, but there is no ambivalence about their presence, which is quite definite with the hands clearly depicted. Again, this is part of an exact integration of the different elements of the theme to produce a decorative result.

A striking relief of a horseman existed on the side of the capital, though only a fragment remains. (Fig. 2) A hand holding the reins is all that survives of the rider. The forequarters of a fine horse, its mane ornamented in curls, is shown in profile as it crushes the head of a monster or vishap with its hooves. The scene represents a mounted saint whose identity is hard to establish definitely.

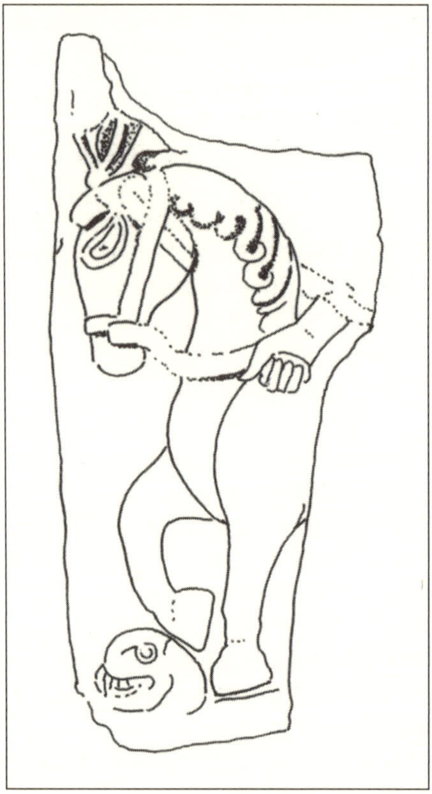

Fig. 2- Dvin, fragment of capital, right side.

In terms of design, the capital compares closely with the lintel from Dvin, only half of which is left. (Fig. 3) Again, at the centre there is a decorative leaved cross, now with a vine sprouting from the base whose branches spread out into a vine harvest scene, implying biblical symbolism. The bunches of grapes, exotic leaves and twining stems are interwoven in a dense pattern from which a basket and two human figures have to be extricated by the viewer or they might go unnoticed. The sculptor has turned the subject into something like a tapestry in low relief. The carving on the Dvin capital is slightly more three dimensional in treatment than the lintel, but has much the same approach.

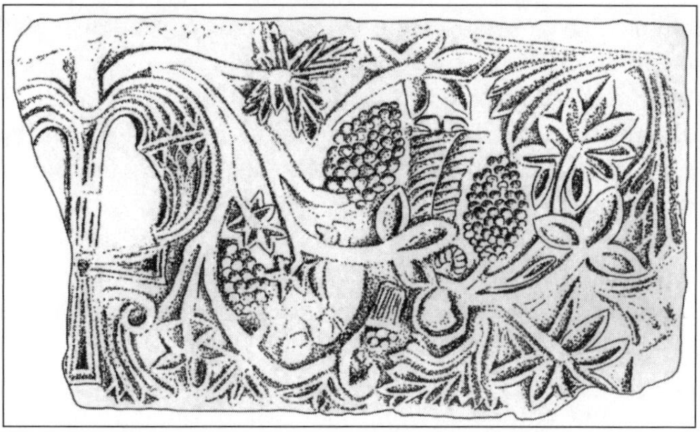

Fig. 3-Dvin, lintel.

Interpretation and study

The Dvin capital was recognised for its importance in the whole perspective of early Christian art. The theme of the bust of Christ in a medallion above the cross links it to Syro-Palestinian iconography, particularly to scenes on the pilgrim ampullae from the Holy Land of sixth century date, which were made to contain sanctified oil from the sacred sites at Jerusalem and Bethlehem.[1]

The collections of these ampullae in the north of Italy, at Monza and Bobbio, go back to around 600, to Theodelinda, the Lombard Queen, during the time of Gregory the Great (d. 604). Bobbio was the last of the monasteries founded by the Irish missionary, Saint Columbanus, a few years before his death there on 23 November 615. He had been welcomed by King Agilulf and Theodelinda, who granted him the land for a monastery which became celebrated for its library and learning. *Peregrinatio* was a special feature of Irish monasticism, and Columbanus, along with his followers, had given the movement an immense impetus.[2] The Monza and Bobbio ampullae supply a great amount of information and witness direct contact with the Holy Land. Their significance and their early

---

[1] André Grabar, *Ampoules de Terre Sainte* (Paris: C. Klincksieck, 1958).
[2] G. S. M. Walker, ed., *Sancti Columbani Opera* (Dublin: Dublin Institute for Advanced Studies, 1970).

connections have been discussed by many scholars, including memorable observations by Ainalov.[3]

Armenian art-historians, such as N. Stepanian and S. Der Nersessian, have placed the Dvin capital in this setting. At first there had been a suggestion that the angel on the right was the figure of St. John the Baptist. Stepanian points out that it was precisely at this epoch, from the fifth to the seventh centuries, that the long-lasting characteristics of Armenian medieval work were elaborated.[4]

The concept of a cross surmounted by the head of Christ is also found in early Ireland in a few examples, such as the stone pillar from Clogher, Co. Tyrone, which dates to the seventh century.[5] Although quite different from the eastern models, and a very disparate group, the same basic idea is present. The Syro-Palestinian type of iconography appeared in Ireland because Ireland remained in touch with other Christian centres, in spite of its situation so far away on the extreme west of Europe.

It was research on the Irish high crosses that had brought me to Armenia and Georgia thirty years ago, for comparative purposes. The setting up of crosses was an essential factor in the evangelisation of both Armenia and Georgia. Carved stelae from the early centuries of Christianity survive there in considerable numbers, at a time when free-standing stone monuments are difficult to find elsewhere. On my first visit in 1974 my introduction was brilliant: on arrival at the Matenadaran I was given every facility by Dr Babken Chookaszian, whose help was invaluable. Later, Levon Chookaszian, knowing my interests, introduced me to Patrick Donabédian in spring 1982. I remember vividly the last evening of my stay then, when Patrick arrived in freezing weather at my hotel, bringing an enormous collection of photographs, all his research material on early stone carvings. He shared his knowledge with great generosity. These are a

---

[3] D. V. Ainalov, *The Hellenistic Origins of Byzantine Art* (New Brunswick, NJ: Rutgers University Press, 1961).

[4] N. (Nonna) Stepanian, *L'Art décoratif de l'Arménie médiévale* (Leningrad: Aurore, 1971), pp. 14-15; Sirarpie Der Nersessian, *Armenian Art* (London: Thames and Hudson, 1978), pp. 52-53.

[5] Helen M. Roe, "A Stone Cross at Clogher, Co. Tyrone," *Journal of the Royal Society of Antiquaries of Ireland,* vol. XC, part II (1960), pp. 191-206.

few of the names, among many Armenian scholars, who have gone out of their way to assist me.

Further questions

It was hard to find an explanation for the two single arms carved on the Dvin capital. Do they stand for the two thieves? In this case each arm could be a short-hand device for representing the whole body. The careful lay-out of the design militates against any accidental inclusion, mistakes or changes in the work as it progressed.

I wrote to Professor Der Nersessian for her opinion. I had attended a course of lectures she had given at the centre for medieval studies (C.E.S.C.M.) 1967 session at Poitiers on *"La miniature arménienne sur X^e^ et XIe siècles"* and I had heard about her from Dr Françoise Henry, the authority on early Irish art, who had studied in Paris in the twenties at the same time as she was there. She kindly replied to me.

August 23, 1982 — 120 Avenue de Versailles,
75016 Paris

Dear Miss Richardson,

I am sorry to be so late in answering your letter but as you know – due to circumstances – I have very little free time. Moreover your question is difficult to answer for I am as baffled as you are by the two hands on the capital of Dvin which I had not noticed before – the one on the left is particularly clear. I doubt however that they indicate the two thieves for there is no room for their crosses and on the ampullae they are usually on the same level as that of Christ. One might also think of the two adoring figures so often figured on the ampullae, kneeling at the foot of the cross but their hands are raised in prayer. The whole composition is intriguing, for I do not recall another example with an angel next to the cross, although angels flying toward the cross are frequently represented on compositions of later date.

I am afraid this letter does not help you much. I was interested to hear you had been to Armenia – I hope you were pleased with your visit.

Sincerely,
Sirarpie Der Nersessian

Some years later I approached her again as I had been asked to write an appreciation of Françoise Henry and thought she might remember her from student days at the Sorbonne. I had studied the History of European Painting with Françoise Henry (1902-1982) at University College Dublin and had worked as her assistant in the Department of Archaeology. She was some years younger than Sirarpie Der Nersessian, who was a post-graduate, when she was a student, but she knew her by appearance and had the highest regard for her. Mlle. Henry's teachers in Paris had included Emile Mâle and Henri Focillon, and it was the latter who directed her principal thesis for her *doctorat d'état* which was published in two volumes in 1933 as *La sculpture irlandaises pendant les douze premiers siècles de l'ère Chrétienne*. She dedicated it to Focillon.[6]

In the same letter I asked about another scholar who had done major work on sculpture (including the Irish high crosses) – Arthur Kingsley Porter, the first holder of the William Dorr Boardman chair of Fine Arts at Harvard, who had been a friend of Focillon as well.[7] Professor Der Nersessian patiently filled me in on these queries even though there was little to report, but her description of her own experiences is interesting; and then her mind went back again to the Dvin puzzle which seemed to fascinate her. She had forgotten that she had replied to me in 1982, when she was preoccupied with her sister's illness. Her letters are a model of good scholarship, both precise and helpful.

September 21st, 1987 120 Avenue de Versailles
75016 Paris

Dear Miss Richardson,

I thank you for your letter of 29.8.87 and I apologize for my delay in answering it. I am sorry that I cannot be of any assistance in regard to Françoise Henry and the Focillon group. I never met Mlle.

---

[6] Hilary Richardson, "Preface" in *Studies in Early Christian and Medieval Irish Art* by Françoise Henry, vol III, Sculpture and Architecture (London: Pindar, 1985).

[7] Hilary Richardson, "The Fate of Kingsley Porter," *Donegal Annual* No. 45 (1993), pp. 83-87.

Henry, though of course I am familiar with her work. When I was in Dublin studying the Chester Beatty manuscripts, she was out of town and our paths did not cross in Paris. I belong to an older generation than the Focillon group; when I was preparing my licence at the Sorbonne, Emile Mâle was the professor of Medieval art and when Focillon came I already had my licence and diplome d'etudes superieres and I was working primarily with Gabriel Millet, the professor of Byzantine Art at the Ecole des Hautes Etudes. Officially Focillon was the director of my thèse complémentaire (we had to have two theses in those days for the Doctorat ès Lettres) but our contacts were limited to a formal visit once a year. I came to know Focillon well only during the war years when he was in the United States. I did not know Kingsley Porter either, I believe I met him only a couple of times for, here again, my contacts were with Rufus Morey and the Princeton group who were interested in Byzantine Art. In fact it was through the contacts I had with them when they came to consult the photographic collection of Byzantine art at the Ecole des Hautes Etudes (the only one at that time) that I happened to be invited to the United States.

I found in my files a letter you had written on April 20, 1982. I am afraid I did not answer it for it came at a time when my sister – whom I have lost since – was very ill and I had to neglect everything else. My answer would have been very much what it is now: in spite of your comparisons I am very skeptical about any direct connections between Irish and Armenian sculpture. But I should like to discuss the question with you if you ever come to Paris. My telephone number is 45272894.

I am very much intrigued by the two hands on the capital of Dvin – which no one else had noticed. Can they belong to an earlier scene – are there any signs that the capital may have been recarved?

May I say again that I should be very happy to meet you.

Sincerely yours,
Sirarpie Der Nersessian

The arms remain an enigma, but as regards the remarkable similarities that exist between features of Armenian art and early Irish art, the topic is too big to be discussed here, and alas, the opportunity to hear Sirarpie Der Nersessian's views never came.

Nevertheless there is a simple and reasonable explanation for the similarities, which grows more convincing as more evidence has emerged in recent years. The most persuasive solution to the resemblances (such as the use in the early Irish church of the liturgical fan, long since obsolete and totally forgotten, unlike the *k'shots'* in the Armenian church) is that fundamental themes were commonly shared throughout the early Christian world, and were able to survive best on the peripheries.[8] Here original traits were retained; on the other hand, radical changes and major upsets to established ways and customs were more easily avoided in peripheral situations.

In the case of Ireland, as a Christian country, it was isolated from its immediate neighbours for over a hundred years when they reverted to paganism following the barbarian invasions and the settlement of the Anglo-Saxon peoples. Ireland was able to hold on to the same values as Christians in the east Mediterranean region and beyond, and managed to pursue its own course for a number of centuries. At the same time, there is no doubt that monks, in particular, were great travellers, not to mention pilgrims, and that sea routes and waterways were used with an ease that is often not fully appreciated. Records of certain contacts do exist. However it seems more than likely that a common underlying stratum of culture is the main answer to the problem; a culture that was preserved among Christian communities at great distances from each other and that linked their ways of thinking; and a culture that went far back to the victory of the faith and early celebrations of the Triumph of the Cross. The presence of this partially buried layer is tangible and can be recognised, in spite of differences in style, inevitable changes, and the growth of new developments in the course of time.[9] Richard Harries, Bishop of Oxford, in his recent book *The Passion in Art* "considers the Passion as portrayed in the whole sweep of Christian history" and vindicates the view expressed here on early Armenian

[8] Hilary Richardson, "Remarks on the liturgical fan, flabellum or rhipidion" in *The Age of Migrating Ideas: Early Medieval Art in Britain and Ireland,* R. M. Spearman and J. Higgitt, eds. (Edinburgh: A. Sutton Pub., 1993), pp. 27-34.

[9] Hilary Richardson, "The Jewelled Cross and Its Canopy" in *From the Isles of the North,* ed. C. Bourke (Belfast: HMSO, 1995), pp. 177-186.

and Irish work in a section entitled "On the Edges of Empire – Signs in Stone from the Seventh Century."[10]

[10] Richard Harries, *The Passion in Art* (Aldershot and Vermont: Ashgate, 2004), pp. 22-27.

6

Trusting Architecture: Inscribed Churches and Their Function on the Eastern Frontier[1]

Christina Maranci

In late summer, the sun parches the high plain of Ararat. The town of T'alin, southwest of the Aragats mountains, becomes a stretch of dusty earth, fieldstone, and steppe grasses. Traveling by road from Yerevan, modern buildings of concrete and aluminum give way to a fenced precinct. Within lies an open field, punctured here and there by building debris, tilted steles, and dry brush. At opposite ends stand two structures: a small chapel and a large basilica, each capped with a dome and fitted with lateral arms. The diminutive chapel stands erect, perched above the pavement on a stepped foundation. Chunky denticulations mask its rooflines, creating a play of classical shadows on the upper reaches of wall. Below the gable of the west façade an inscribed message declares:

> I Nersēs, aphipat, patrik, lord of Shirak and Arsharunik,
> built this church in the name of the holy Mother of God,
> for the intercession
> of myself and my wife Shushan, and
> for our son Hrahat

Such messages marked the landscape of early medieval Armenia. From around 630 to 680 AD, over two dozen domed structures rose up from the semi-desert highlands between Byzantium and Persia, and thirteen of them are inscribed. Texts in *erkat'agir* extend along façades, girdle perimeter walls, or appear in

---

[1] This brief essay forms part of my forthcoming book *The Geometry of Power: The Role of the Monument in Early Medieval Armenia*, which explores Armenian architecture, epigraphy, decoration, and ritual in the seventh century.

framed panels. Most often foundation records, the inscriptions announce the names of patrons, construction dates, and the purpose and circumstances of the commission. In this sense, they belong to a longstanding tradition of architectural epigraphy.

For a number of reasons, however, the inscribed monuments of Armenia hold special value. Rich in prosopographical, topographical, and chronological information, they throw open a window onto the landscape of the Christian East during an era of obscurity. In a period from which chronicles are few, and not one dated Byzantine monument survives, Caucasian epigraphy emerges as a critical primary source for the history of the Mediterranean and Near East. As Timothy Greenwood has shown, many of the texts either constitute exclusive sources of information about contemporary events, or function as independent controls of other primary evidence. The inscriptions thus provide rare insight into seventh-century Armenia, Byzantium, Persia, and the early Umayyad empire.[2]

Yet their potential has only been partially realized. Focusing on textual analysis and the gathering of facts, students of history, epigraphy, and philology have too often sundered the inscription from the monument on which it is engraved. This process, encouraged by professional specializations and models of publication, often obscures the physical reality of the message. Set in uniform printed characters on a white page, the monumental inscription is, as Amy Papalexandrou recently put it, "reduced to the level of pure text."[3] Historians of architecture are often equally perfunctory: texts first harvested for information about donors and dates are then dropped from discussion. Both practices obscure the medieval relationship between viewer, building, and inscribed message. They also veil a number of critical questions: Who were the intended and actual audiences of the texts? How was information transmitted to them and under what circumstances? The former is of particular importance, as the seventh-century eastern frontier hosted

---

[2] Timothy Greenwood, "A Corpus of Early Armenian Inscriptions," *Dumbarton Oaks Papers*, 58 (2004), pp. 27-91.

[3] Amy Papalexandrou: "Text in Context: Eloquent Monuments and the Byzantine Beholder," *Word and Image* 17, no. 3 (2001), pp. 259-283.

heterogeneous and shifting groups of diverse ethnicities, social backgrounds, linguistic knowledge, and levels of literacy.

The central question, also yet unanswered, regards the act of inscribing exterior surfaces. Perhaps owing to a historicist bias towards "loquacious" monuments, few have been sensitive to fluctuations in the production of inscribed buildings, and what those fluctuations might signify. In this context, it is important to note that exterior inscriptions were by no means commonplace in the early medieval Mediterranean. As Irene Bierman recently observed, inscriptions on surviving monuments from the sixth to tenth centuries were most often confined to interior spaces.[4] While acknowledging the uneven nature of the material, one may note that the surviving epigraphy of early Byzantine, Umayyad, Abbasid, and early Fatimid buildings most often occurs within the spatial envelope. A survey of the architecture thus suggests that the Armenian inscriptions deserve careful attention, not only for the factual data they provide, but also as an unusually substantial corpus of exterior epigraphy in the early medieval Near East.

They compel us to probe the very nature of inscribing. What does a "written" building mean? How does it work? To paraphrase Oleg Grabar, why write on buildings at all?[5] These questions have been explored in studies of Islamic architecture, a ninth-century church in Greece, and the building façades of Romanesque Europe. In each case, scholars have focused on relations between inscriptions and their publics. They have shown how texts gave voice to monuments, and how monuments, in turn, controlled and shaped the reception of texts. In this light, the Armenian case is again of crucial importance. More robust than the early Byzantine material, and earlier than both the Fatimid and Romanesque data, Armenia offers extraordinarily fertile ground to study the medieval function and experience of the inscribed building.

As part of a larger study of the function of architecture on the eastern frontier, this brief essay offers some preliminary and general

---

4 Irene Bierman, *Writing Signs: The Fatimid Public Text* (Berkeley: University of California Press, 1998), p. 59.

5 Oleg Grabar, "Graffiti or Proclamations: Why Write on Buildings?" Paper delivered at the Annual Meeting of the College Art Association, Philadelphia, 1983.

thoughts on the desire to inscribe. It will be suggested that the churches functioned not only as congregational spaces, but also as documents in masonry. Significantly, the number of surviving inscribed monuments in the Caucasus dated to the seventh century is dramatically higher than that of the previous century. Based on the corpus compiled by Greenwood, two inscribed monuments survive from the fifth and sixth centuries.[6] Even allowing for accidents of survival, it remains striking that the seventh century produced at least six times this number. It will be suggested that this phenomenon is linked to the immediate political world of the seventh-century frontier, an era characterized by dramatic change.

Historical studies of early medieval Armenia often focus on themes of internal continuity from the pre-Arab era to the seventh century, stressing a robust economy and tenacious social structure. Yet these points should not obscure the larger and more pressing reality of political upheaval. During the first half of the seventh century, Armenia became a militarized zone, the theatre for conflicts between Byzantine and Persian forces, and an early target of the Arab invasions. Planted at the epicenter, the Armenian nobility engaged in a breathless series of diplomatic dances. Brokering deals and switching sides, by an aristocratic collective or by single agents, became something of a national pastime. It is perhaps not surprising, particularly to modern eyes, that in such a climate should arise a concern for the production, delivery, storage, and retrieval of written documents. As in Norman England, one may argue that rise of documentation in Armenia seems linked to distrust rather than social progress.[7]

Yet while written documents were often held in archives, the monumental inscriptions of Armenia are much more accessible, almost always exhibited on exterior walls. As physical documents of ephemeral events, they rendered permanent the rank, jurisdiction, and allegiances of their patrons. Thus the churches functioned as much more than houses of God: they were markers of power, loci of local and dynastic memory, and pacts of alliance. Packed with

---

[6] Greenwood catalogues the portal inscription at Tekor and the Greek inscription at Ereruk'.

[7] Paraphrased from Michael T. Clanchy, *From Memory to Written Record: England 1066-1307* (London: Edward Arnold Ltd., 1979), p. 7.

names, titles, jurisdictions, and unusually precise chronologies, the monuments formed the material nexus of a community, "gathering the universe in and around themselves."[8] Like stone pages set upright, the churches imprinted the complicated and shifting landscape of the eastern frontier with the authority of the text.

The Rise of the Written

To understand the rise and function of inscribed buildings in seventh-century Armenia, it is critical to explore the role of contemporary written documents on the eastern frontier. The paucity of original evidence renders this task difficult; nevertheless, a close reading of the chronicle attributed to Sebēos offers insight into the problem. Written communications figure largely in the narrative, as affirmations of all kinds are sought and executed on parchment. Moreover, numerous copies of correspondence are included within the text.

Appointments were often made through writing, as when the Persian king Khosrov promoted the Armenian Smbat to the position of governor (*marzpan*).[9]

The same tradition is also practiced by the Byzantines: the emperor Maurice promises Smbat honors, rewards, and gifts through "letters and trustworthy messengers."[10] Constans also elects a certain Varaztirots' to the position of *curopalates* using a writ.[11] Unfortunately, "when the edict giving [the aspet Varaztirots'] the rank… was on its way, suddenly an illness struck him and he died."[12] Summons to court were similarly made in writing. When Smbat is requested by Khosrov, "the messengers arrived with letters and summoned him with great splendour."[13] The author of the chronicle also reports penned warrants (*hrovatark*), complaints, and accusations. After an argument with his uncle Sahak, the noble

---

[8] Gaston Bachelard, *The Poetics of Space. The Classic Look at How We Experience Intimate Places* (Boston: Beacon Press, 1994).

[9] *The Armenian History Attributed to Sebēos*, trans. and comm. Robert Thomson with James Howard-Johnston and Timothy Greenwood (Liverpool: Liverpool University Press, 1999), p. 47.

[10] Ibid., p. 38.

[11] Ibid., p. 109.

[12] Ibid.

[13] Ibid., p. 49.

Step'anos Siwni wrote him a letter of condemnation "and sealed it with his own seal, that of the bishop of his house, and also with the seals of the other princes of Siwnik'."[14]

Written documents play the most critical role in the brokering of alliances. In the 590s, Khosrov sends a letter-patent to the Byzantine emperor Maurice, requesting that they "observe a pact of peace between us" and that this oath (*ukht*) "be secure between us and between our sons who will reign after us."[15] Newly elected to the throne in c. 610, Heraclius sends to king Khosrov an envoy of "messengers with splendid treasures and letters to [the king] to request peace."[16] (Khosrov takes the gifts, kills the messengers, and writes no thank-you notes.) When the Persians initiate attacks on Byzantine territory, Heraclius tries again, issuing the king "a letter with gifts, to seek from him reconciliation and peace with me." This time, the Persian king responds with a letter addressed to "Heraclius, our senseless and insignificant servant."[17] In 628, however, rapprochement is made between the two sides. Kawat (Khosrov's son) gives up his territory, and orders a letter of greeting to be written to Heraclius. "He had an oath taken to him, salt-sealed and brought with the letter, and he sent …magnificent presents to confirm this agreement with him. Heraclius likewise "wrote a solemn covenant and confirmed peace with an oath" which was also sent with gifts and treasures.[18] Arab rulers seem to continue the tradition. Sebēos reports that the Umayyads also used official writing in diplomatic negotiations, as in the threatening letter of caliph Othman (644-656) to Constans. According to the copy included in the chronicle, the Arab orders the emperor to submit, in return for some dubious honors: the rank of "great prince," and a share of war booty- "three for me, and one for you."[19]

Documents were no less instrumental in negotiations with the Armenian Church. Sebēos reports that the Greek general Mzhēzh Gnuni ordered the Armenian patriarch Ezr to accompany him to

---

[14] Ibid., p. 43.
[15] Ibid., p. 19.
[16] Ibid., p. 66.
[17] Ibid., p. 79.
[18] Ibid., p. 86.
[19] Ibid., p. 144.

Byzantine territory and to take the eucharist with the emperor. The catholicos leery of entering Greek territory "requested a statement of faith from the king. Immediately a document was sent to him written in the king's hand..."[20] Written statements and defenses of Armenian orthodoxy are also included in Sebēos' chronicle, as in the correspondence between the Armenian patriarch Komitas and Modestos, patriarch of Jerusalem.[21] Chapter 46, moreover, consists of a copy of the letter from Constans to the Armenians, "The True and Orthodox Letter of Nicaea."[22]

Another such statement is featured in the account of the patriarch Nersēs. When he attempted to humor the emperor Constans and profess his faith in Byzantine Chalcedonianism, his fellow Armenian clergy, incensed at his betrayal, revealed to Constans that Nersēs could not be trusted. They informed the emperor that Nersēs had recently convened a council condemning Chalcedonianism, and contended that Nersēs had composed a "document... concerning the faith, and sealed it with his own ring, and then with ours, and then with the rings of all the princes." "That document is with him," they told him. "Order a search made to see."[23] Similarly, the Persian king Khosrov III, unpersuaded of the authenticity of Armenian Christianity, demanded that a document articulating this faith to be brought before him. It was found in the treasury, sealed with the rings of previous Persian rulers. Assured of Armenia's religious position, the king ordered a copy of the letter, sealed with his own ring, to be deposited in the royal treasury.[24] It is interesting that in both cases, the dispute was resolved with the retrieval of a document; no further investigation was apparently needed to establish truth.[25]

These observations by no means should suggest that documents were invented in the seventh century. To be sure, edicts, letters-patent, and written oaths were long important in political

---

[20] Ibid., p. 91.

[21] Ibid., pp. 70-77.

[22] Ibid., p. 114.

[23] Ibid., p. 142.

[24] Ibid., p. 118.

[25] In the above examples, along with many others, the medium of writing is identified specifically in the chronicle. In many other instances, however, oaths are mentioned but not specified as written. Yet, as they often involve the oath being "sent" we may assume they took some kind of physical form.

negotiations, and form a standard theme in ancient and medieval literature. As Robert Thomson has pointed out, Sebēos' own discussion of documents at times borrows from biblical sources.[26] In the fifth-century *Epic Histories* and *History of Ghazar P'arpets'i*, documents are mentioned with some frequency. In Sebēos' narrative, however, we may note a surge in their number and role as a ratifying agent. Allowing for accidents of survival, differing external circumstances, and authorial aims, it is still interesting to quantify the mention of written documents in each text. In Ghazar's *History*, they occur in twenty-three instances; in the *Epic Histories*, only fourteen. The chronicle of Sebēos, however, contains over thirty-seven separate episodes involving written documentation.

Another comparison between Armenian histories of the fifth century may be instructive here. As recounted in the *Epic Histories*, the Persian king demands that Arshak, king of Armenia swear an oath of allegiance: "They brought the holy gospels and Shapuh king of Persia made Arshak king of Armenia take an oath, swearing on the divine gospels that he would never again be false to him, but that he would keep his oath and maintain his alliance with him."[27] The gospel book was then sealed and stored in the royal treasury. In the seventh-century chronicle, a similar expression of alliance is requested by Heraclius of Khoream. In this case, however, a similar agreement concluded with a pact and an oath in writing with a seal. Thus the transaction was rendered legitimate through documentary means, in which the terms of the agreement were set down in writing.

Taken as a whole, the textual evidence thus suggests that the seventh-century frontier was a world of documents: of couriers, copyists, and witnesses; of salt, seals, and archives. Yet it is dangerous to interpret such evidence as indicating a transition from oral to written culture, or an increase in levels of literacy. While these questions drive lively discussion regarding other medieval cultures, the evidence for early medieval Armenia remains too slight

---

[26] In his reception of a particularly nasty letter from the Persian king, Heraclius, weeping bitterly, spreads the document on a church altar, as did Hezekiah upon reception of a similar note from Sennacherib, King of the Assyrians (Isaiah 37 1 14). Ibid., p. 80.

[27] *The Epic Histories Attributed to P'awstos Buzand*, trans. and comm. by Nina G. Garsoïan (Cambridge Mass: Harvard University, 1989), p. 147.

and restricted to a narrow segment of the population. In any event, such issues are perhaps less important than probing the nature of the document as a physical symbol. Whether read silently (or more likely) performed, whether received with total, partial, or even a lack of comprehension by its audiences, the written contract functioned as currency in political negotiations, as a marker of authenticity, and an invitation to mutual agreement and trust. In view of the rise in documents reported and the concomitant increase in inscribed architecture, one may suggest that writing, or more precisely *the written*, assumed a central role in the political and social landscape of the seventh-century Caucasus.

Conclusion

As a stone repository of texts, accessible to multiple audiences, the inscribed churches of Armenia can be situated within a much broader tradition of building and writing in the Middle Ages. In her recent essay on the portal of St.-Lazare, Autun, Linda Seidel has suggested that the inscribed name of Gislebertus does not denote an itinerant sculptor, as commonly believed, but an eponymous duke who donated relics to the church, thus conveying an important message of local power and legitimacy in twelfth-century Burgundy.[28] Rendered in visible and material terms, she argues, this message was critical in the midst of territorial battles between the clergy and the local duchies. In both Romanesque France and seventh-century Armenia, the building inscription responded to an unstable climate by "publishing" and storing data in an archive of masonry.

In this sense, inscriptions could inspire more trust than written documents. Unlike the more vulnerable media of parchment and papyri, engraved messages were virtually indestructible. Barring the collapse of the building, the deeply-incised texts of the seventh-century were more difficult to efface. It is their seemingly permanent character that is noted by the monk Khuzhik in the *History* of Ghazar P'arpets'i. Observing the trial of the Armenians by the Persians, he wishes to make account of the event:

---

[28] Linda Seidel, *Legends in Limestone: Lazarus, Gislebertus, and the Cathedral of Autun* (Chicago and London: The University of Chicago Press, 1999), p. 78.

> to write faithfully on the tablets of his mind, as in an inscription... to describe ...truthfully and coherently as a record for all faithful hearers in succeeding generations for ever.[29]

A sense of permanence may also be associated with the very term for the engraving style used in the inscriptions. The script's name is generally thought to be based on the Armenian word for iron (*erkat'*), from the metal chisel used to cut the lapidary inscriptions. One is thus tempted to agree with Kouymjian's comments regarding the derivation of the term *erkat'agir*. He writes of the "instantly perceptible monumentality in early inscriptions. It as though the letters were fashioned from iron and would, thus, endure forever."[30]

The accessibility of the texts is equally significant. Sebēos mentions several instances in which written documents were stored out of sight in royal archives and treasuries, to be retrieved only by specific order. That the monuments exhibited the texts "for all faithful hearers in succeeding generations forever" is thus crucial; rendering it impossible to lie about their existence (or absence). It is also important that monumental epigraphy, more than written documents, operates in the realm of the three-dimensional. The object-like quality of the texts allowed that density of data was matched by density of mass. Enveloping a sacred core, finally, could only further affirm their authenticity, like oaths sworn on the Gospel.

If writing took on a sense of three-dimensionality in the inscribed monuments, the converse also happened: the buildings became nearer to text on a page. This "textuality," moreover, may be evoked by the philological associations of the Armenian term for oath, *ukht*. By the fifth century, the word referred not only to covenants or pacts, but also carried an additional range of meanings, including "congregation of clergy" and built structures. Churches and monasteries were referred to sometimes as "places of oath" (*ukhti tegh*), or, more tellingly, simply as "oaths."[31] It is thus

---

[29] *The History of Ghazar P'arpets'i,* trans. and comm. by Robert W. Thomson (Atlanta, Georgia: Scholars Press, 1991), p. 145.

[30] Michael E. Stone, Dickran Kouymjian, Henning Lehmann, *Album of Armenian Paleography* (Aarhus: Aarhus University Press, 2002), p. 69.

[31] *Nor Baṙgirk' Haykazian Lezui* (Yerevan: Yerevani Hamalsarani Hratarakch'ut'yun, 1981), vol. 2, p. 542.

tempting to imagine the performance of oaths at church buildings, which were transformed, through their inscribed surfaces, into spatial documents of events. Regardless, by the seventh century in Armenia, oaths were inextricably linked with buildings. The churches of Armenia, perhaps more than any other early medieval tradition, show how inscribed monuments could function in an era of conflict: as assertions of legitimacy, gestures of diplomacy, invitations to trust, and exhortations to loyalty. They served to fix the fluid and changeful, like molten iron cooled to its solid state.

7

The Church of Surb Astuatsatsin in Shiraz

Marco Brambilla

The city of Shiraz in southern Iran is a vibrant, historical tapestry – home to the ruins of Persepolis, and the birthplace of the beloved Persian poets Hafez and Saadi, its place as a cultural treasure of Iran cannot be undermined. Against this decidedly Persian backdrop, there exists an equally remarkable jewel, all but hidden from sight – an Armenian church, built in 1664, that encapsulates the cosmopolitan dynamism of seventeenth century Persia. Dedicated to St. Mary, Mother of God, the Church of Surb Astuatsatsin is situated in the modern-day province of Fars, and represents a noteworthy departure from the normative conception of Armenian architecture. (Fig. 1)

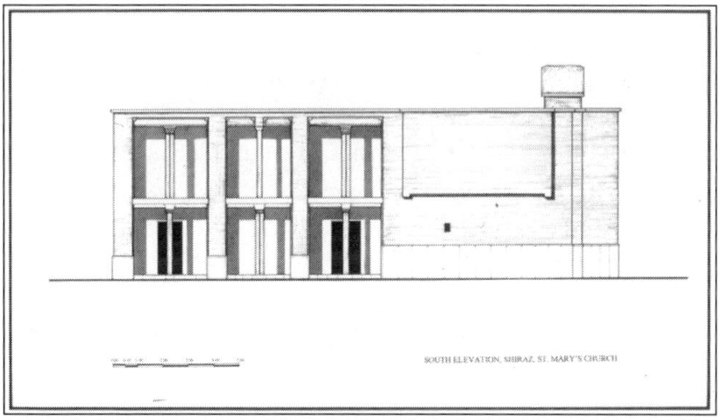

Fig. 1-Elevation. Surb Astuatsatsin. Shiraz.

Historically, the presence of Armenians in Shiraz has not been well documented, both too far from the Armenian heartland and too insignificant a colony to have been chronicled on a regular basis.

Between 1603 and 1607, over one hundred thousand Armenians emigrated to Isfahan from Armenia under orders from Shah Abbas the Great, giving rise to a small Armenian community within Iran.

Even before the relocation directive was issued by Shah Abbas, there existed thriving Armenian enclaves within Iran – notably, in Isfahan, where Armenian merchants enjoyed special concessions granted by the Shah as early as 1592. Similarly, by 1607, letters written by merchants mention Shiraz as a center of international trade, and home to a flourishing, if small, Armenian community.

The Armenian community of Isfahan grew in numbers significantly as newly-arrived Armenians settled in the vicinity, distinguishing themselves as a prosperous, wealthy, and successful minority engaged heavily in international trade. Over time, this success gave rise to an increasing need to develop and expand upon additional satellite support stations to improve existing trade routes.

It should be noted that Armenians played a key role in the reorganization of the Safavid Empire, and their fate was closely linked to the political and economic developments in Iran.

By 1456, Sultan Mehmet II already had conquered Constantinople, and had established the Ottoman Empire as the most formidable military power in the Middle East. Following the Battle of Chaldiran, Armenia was divided between Turkey and Iran, and struggling desperately to survive.

In 1587, Shah Abbas the First ascended to the throne of an empire in disarray – important cities such as Tabriz were given away to the Ottoman Turks, while many of the eastern provinces, including Herat, suffered encroachment from Uzbeks, Afghans, and the Mughal Empire of India.

But within only a few years, this charismatic and visionary ruler established the Safavid Empire as the "other" leading force in the region, reclaiming Tabriz and many other territories lost in prior years. Shah Abbas moved the capital to Isfahan, the geographical center of the Empire, and reestablished Persia as one of the most powerful and wealthy nations of the world. With this relocation, a renaissance came to Isfahan, witnessing its development and expansion, and establishing it as one of the largest cities in the world, after Paris and London.

A cosmopolitan, colorful, and efficient city, Isfahan possessed all the necessary infrastructure essential to becoming a center of international trade and culture. Simultaneously, Shah Abbas implemented a series of significant political reforms, affecting Iran, and to a great extent, the Armenian residents in Iran until the present day. Chief amongst these was the establishment of the Twelve Saint Shia as the state religion. This centrally enforced state religion had a unifying effect on the country, which while leading to forced conversion, often by the sword, also created a bulwark against encroachments from the surrounding power centers – the Uzbeks to the East, and the Ottoman Empire in the West.

Pursued rigorously and continuously, this state religion gave rise to a renewed interest in the establishment and restoration of several shrines of Shia saints, notably the cities of Najaf, Karbala, and Mashad, which became popular destinations for pilgrims, as well as focal points for the faithful.

In addition to the initiatives to unify the religious identity of the Safavid dynasty, Shah Abbas also implemented numerous social and economic reforms. Chief amongst these were improvements to the infrastructure supporting communication, travel, and trade, making the roads safe for commerce, and thus hospitable to economic growth. For European travelers approaching Persia from the west, this was of crucial importance, and gave rise to increased, meaningful contact between East and West.

Special tax exemptions were granted to trade representatives from Europe, beginning with the Dutch and British, and later expanded to include the French and Russians. At the same time, the export of gold and other hard currency was prohibited, ensuring that Persia's wealth remained within her borders.

Thus, in a relatively short time, the Safavid Empire of the early seventeenth century amassed a considerable fortune – daily utensils of the court were cast in pure gold, studded with jewels, while saddles for royal horses were adorned with diamonds, emeralds, rubies, and pearls. This luxury was owed in no small part to the Armenian enclave in Isfahan. In fact, Armenians were the primary point of contact in trade relationships with the European powers.

Although small in number, Armenians were a multilingual, Christian people, possessing the fortitude necessary to endure the hardships of long journeys, well-established relationships with different countries, solid experience in national and international commerce, and an acumen for managing profitable businesses. As a result of these factors, considerable wealth developed within the Armenian community in Persia, helping its development as an integral component of the imperial economy.

In 1606, the Armenian residents of Iran were granted the status of "royal privileged person" – an exclusive status not unlike the "Most Favored Nation" designation granted by the United States today. The distinction was not without its benefits – four years later, Shah Abbas granted permission to the Armenians of Isfahan to build a church, and in 1615, ceded a tract of royal land, already partly inhabited by Armenians, theretofore known as *New Julfa*, to the Armenian community. In 1617, the Shah stripped the East Indian Company of their monopoly to trade in silk, granting it to the Armenians, and giving rise to two Armenian companies: the Julfa Armenian Trading Company, and the Suratum, which obtained exclusive rights to trade with Russia.

By 1630, several Armenian schools and an Armenian university had been built in New Julfa, engaged in the training of multilingual, capable business people for the numerous commercial opportunities of this new, cosmopolitan world.

The chief exports of the time were silk, pearls from the Persian Gulf, precious gems, dried fruits, camel hair, carpets and other handicrafts. Armenians, however, imported various goods from India, Russia, and later, from Europe, which they sold within the Empire, or exported to other countries.

Trade occurred primarily along two major export routes – in the north, through the Caucasus and Russia, and through the Persian Gulf – particularly the Ports of Hormuz and Abbas – in the south. Encouraging trade routes outside the traditional passage through Turkey and Constantinople to Europe was an integral part of the political and economic reforms of Shah Abbas. As a result, taxes and tolls were not paid to the Ottoman Empire, as well as significantly diminishing the dependency upon Turkish trade roads, where kidnappings and brigandage was not an uncommon event.

During this time, the city of Shiraz developed into an important center of trade and commerce, strategically situated between the Empire's economic heart in Isfahan, and the ports along the Persian Gulf. Among the several major merchant families of Isfahan, an Armenian who had been given the title of Allah Verdi Khan, asked permission to relocate five hundred Armenian families to Shiraz.

This influx of Armenians gave new momentum to life in this Diaspora. The Armenians, who apparently had some sort of a chapel in this location, demolished the old church and built the new one dedicating it to St. Mary, Mother of God. Of course, there is nothing strange to the fact that they built a church. The church itself is located in the *Bazarche-ye Armaniha* [Armenian bazaar] district. It is directly accessible from Gha'ani Street in Durban-e Moshir, in a quarter that is still known by its historical appellation *Sar'e Juyeh-e Armaniha* [at the Armenian water canal]. A door at the end of a long, thirty-foot corridor guards access to the premises, ultimately leading into a courtyard. This layout is not unusual amongst many of the Armenian churches in Isfahan, owing to the fact that such structures often were used as places of refuge in dire times, and as such, were designed to be well-protected and easily defendable.

The courtyard is sunken some five feet lower than street level, and is accessible through a series of stairs. In the past, several rooms and facilities provided habitable space, kitchens, and storage areas in the courtyard around the main church. Today, little of the original structures survives, while the courtyard itself is only a fraction of its original dimensions. As was common at the time of its construction, the entire courtyard is paved, save for a few trees and flower beds. The courtyard also features a small water basin, and numerous tombstones of varying age.

The church proper is built upon a small platform, elevated some 10 inches above the surrounding ground. Constructed entirely of bricks and wooden beams, the structure recalls the techniques typical of seventeenth century Persian architecture. It has a cruciform floor plan that is well hidden within the exterior walls. Its orientation is, of course, east-west, with the altar (bema) on the east and two lateral apses on the sides. The main entrance is in the west with two additional doors providing access to the church from north and south. (Fig. 2)

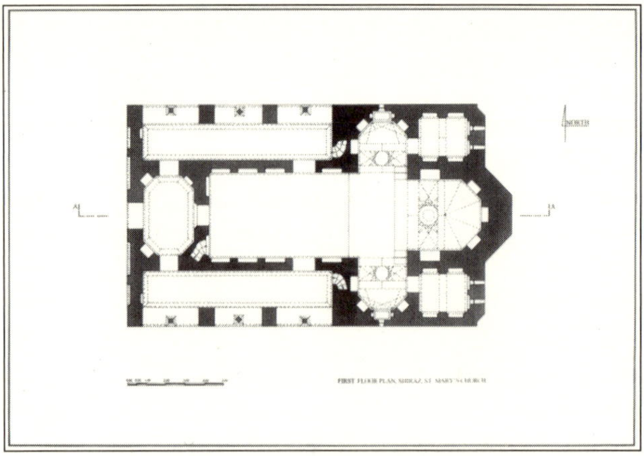

Fig. 2-Floor Plan. Surb Astuatsatsin.

An octagonal portico is set in the west of the structure, situated just before the main door of the church – a feature uncommon in Armenian architecture. This space has two relatively deep niches, which are generally used to light candles; additionally, a number of tombstones are incorporated into its various walls.

For the most part, the majority of these belong to Armenians who passed away in Shiraz, at one time or another. True to its cosmopolitan nature, however, there are tombstones in English, and perhaps more surprisingly, in Persian. The remains therein belonged primarily to British and Portuguese dignitaries that did not make it back to their countries of origin, and were ultimately buried in the only spot related to the Christian faith for many miles.

Two corridors extend to the north and south, delineated by a series of subtle columns. This motif is repeated on the second floor, where a corridor forms an upper gallery to the church at this level. In the interior the cruciform plan is much more evident. The altar in the East is elevated a few steps, thus responding to a liturgical need of the Armenian church but also distinguishing the area where the altar is separated from the main *sala*. Two rooms are situated on the sides of the main altar and are used as sacristies. A semi-circular dome covers the main altar, a motif mimicked in the shallow, curved domes that cover the two lateral altars. This is in stark contrast to the flat, wooden ceiling that covers the remainder of the building, entirely adorned with interior paintings. (Fig. 3)

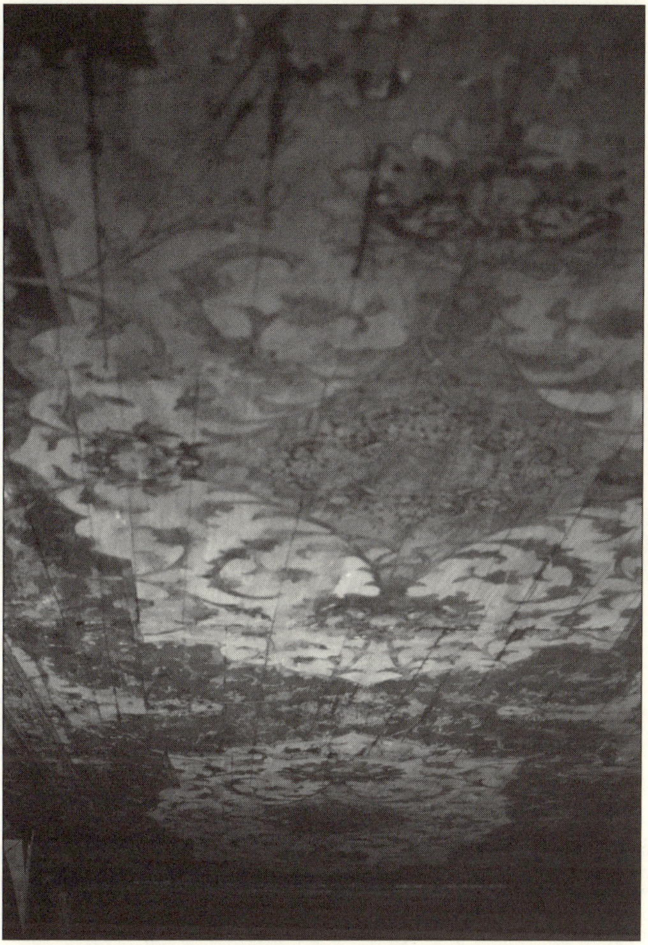

Fig. 3-Painted decoration of the ceiling with carpet motifs.

In the West, opposite the altar, a second story space recalls the *matronei* of Renaissance churches. This space, quite typical to Iranian architecture, was used also in some of the churches of Isfahan, where it would be used only by women attending the service. It is accessed through a staircase in the interior of the church, and is divided from the main room by a pair of elegant Safavid columns and a wooden balustrade. (Fig. 4)

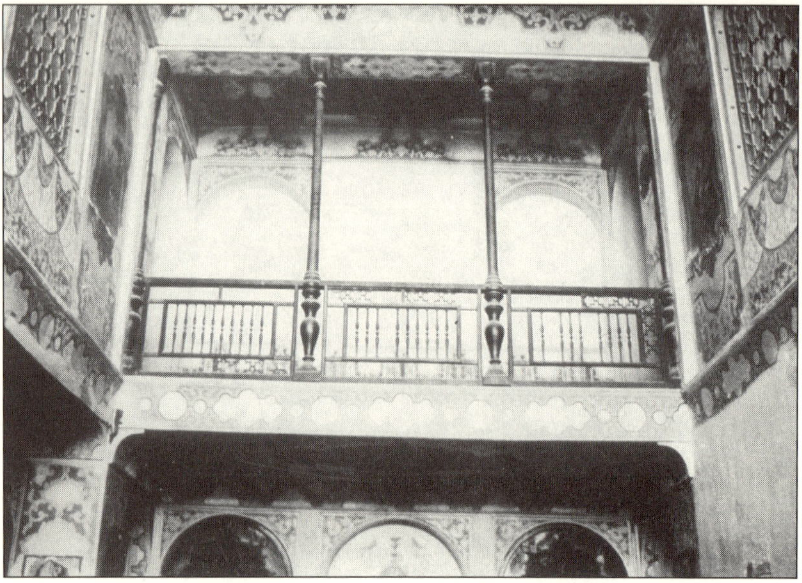

Fig. 4-Interior with *matronei* to the west.

The entire surface of both lateral walls to the north and south reflects the architectural motifs contemporary to the Safavid period. Divided into several horizontal and vertical partitions, the space consists of a series of continuous decorative bands, as well as two panels of niches, or RAF – one above the other, and ornate with *muqarnas*.

The roof of the building is an unusual departure from more commonly encountered features in Armenian architecture, in that the dome is entirely hidden within the exterior envelope of the building. The usual Armenian domes, cupolas, and belltowers are conspicuously absent, and the exterior suggests little of its intricate, interior complexities. (Fig. 5)

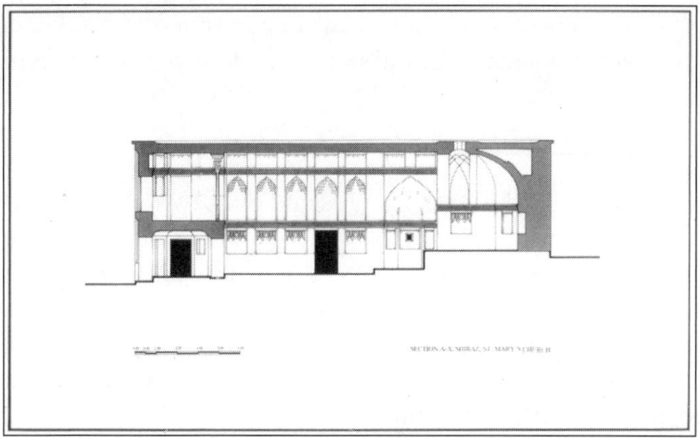

Fig. 5-Longitudinal section. Surb Astuatsatsin.

Once again, history provides an explanation for this peculiarity. By the time of the church's construction in 1664, Shah Abbas the Great was dead. With his death, many of the privileges enjoyed by the Armenian community in Persia were diminished or eliminated by his successor, Shah Abbas the Second. Notably, Armenians lost their status as "Royal Privileged Persons," and with it, the host of special allowances they had enjoyed, including special tax status, favorable consideration in matters of commerce and trade, and the access to the royal court that had historically garnered concessions from the Shah.

Between 1656 and 1662, Mohammed Beg, the Grand Vizier of the then-adolescent Shah, further exacerbated the situation by pressing for a reconsideration of the treatment of non-Muslims living within the Empire. Thus began a systematic persecution that significantly damaged the social and religious fabric of the Armenian community, precipitating an end to the "reign of the Armenian merchants." Against this backdrop, it was assumed that it would be impossible to obtain a permit to build a larger church. Moreover, in a city that housed the shrines of the venerable saints of the Shia, the construction of any religious building that might attract the attention of devout Muslims was expressly forbidden.

Thus, the church was disguised and hidden. Sunken some five feet lower than street level, the structure appears foundationally inclined to camouflage, practically invisible from the street. Its exterior is devoid of any significant decorations or ornamentation, while the western façade has a series of plain partitions, typical of Persian architecture during the period. Were it not for the recent addition of a small cross, one might never guess as to the purpose of the building.

Architecturally, the exterior presents only two elements of some interest – the elegant rotation of the columns around the church on the first and second floors, and the floral decoration of plaster in a narrow, medallion band between the columns.

The austerity of the exterior contrasts markedly with the interior of the structure. Here, hidden from prying eyes, it was possible to indulge in a magnificent explosion of colors and decorations. Gold was used extensively; dark blue, turquoise, red, and various shades of brown comprise the interior's vibrant palette, lending it a richness absent to its exterior. Geometric ornaments and floral decorations with birds and intricate patterns abound.

Clearly, the church in Shiraz is a significant departure from more-commonly encountered images of Armenian churches. It is not built in stone; it lacks the impressive volume, the dominant architectural elements, such as the domes and belltowers, and the magnificent outward projection of impressive decorations.

Yet, it recalls another type of Armenian chapel or church, more commonly encountered in rural areas, and less impressive than previous examples, but nonetheless adhering to a certain architectural expression within its limitations. In theory, the group of churches that would have been proximate to the church in Shiraz, both geographically and chronologically, are drawn from the long list of religious buildings in Isfahan.

This discussion would not be complete if reference was not made to these churches built in the same period of time in New Julfa. Between 1607 and 1705, more than thirty churches were built in Isfahan. Of these, thirteen remain today, relatively unscathed by time – others are in partial ruins, but for the most part, little record of the existence of these structures remains.

In varying degrees, all of these churches utilize Persian construction techniques and decorative elements common to Safavid Persia. Armenians adopted the new building materials – not stone, but brick – as well as the various decorative technologies developed in Persia and employed extensively during the early Safavid period.

For the first time in their history, however, it was necessary to build a decidedly Christian religious building in an overwhelmingly Muslim environment. In contrast to the churches of Isfahan, which are undeniably prominent and overtly religious structures, with their recognizable central domes and bell-towers, the Shiraz church eschews external ornamentation in favor of achieving an understated inconspicuousness.

However, virtually all Armenian churches in Isfahan have a central dome of sorts and although one may argue that the bell-towers were added at later time, the fact is these are prominent structures, recognizable from their exteriors as "religious" buildings. Contrasting the Shiraz church with contemporary Armenian churches in Isfahan yields differences that are immediate and striking. Unlike the Church of St. Nicholas (1630), the Cathedral of Surb Amenp'rkich' (1664), and the Church of Surb Astuatsatsin (1613), the Shiraz church employs a cruciform floor plan unseen elsewhere. Likewise, whereas the interiors of the Isfahan churches are brightly-lit, airy, and luminous, with large openings to allow exterior light, the Shiraz structure is decidedly dark, lacking any direct opening of considerable size to the exterior. Perhaps the only exception to this is an alabaster plate that covers a small oculus in the center of the dome over the altar, bathing the altar in a muted, almost mystical light.

As far as the decorations are concerned it must be remembered that while Armenians used decorative elements and techniques widely used in Iran, the interior perception of the space, often also influenced by resident European painters, was still "Armenian."

The interior of the churches in Isfahan are literally covered with scenes from the Bible and other religious motifs. In contrast, the church in Shiraz does not have even one permanent decoration incorporated in the structure. In fact, anything related to the Christian faith is "removable," including decorations, paintings, or liturgical artifacts.

One may argue that the Armenian churches of Isfahan are Armenian religious structures built with the tools of Iranian architecture. But can the same be said about the church in Shiraz? One can certainly understand the camouflaged exterior. One could also understand the necessity to use local technologies, but even in the interior, the architectural language is pure Safavid Persian. It is a language spoken by its structure, its brickwork and half-domes, and the treatment of its lateral walls, with their rich *rafs*, decorative bands, and *muqarnas*. It is echoed by the second floor *matronei*, and the structure's decorative elements, such as its columns – a well known typology widely used in Safavid Persia. These are seen with regional variations generally in hypostyle rooms. Most notable, these identical columns are used in the building known as *Chehel Sotun* in Isfahan. And finally there is the incredible ceiling of the church, said to mirror the magnificent Safavid carpets that once adorned the church, many centuries ago.

In fact, their spatial placement would even confirm this theory in as much as the arrangements of the ceiling decorations appear to follow a natural placement of carpets on the floor to cover the entire space. Thus, the ceiling is not treated as a continuous and homogenous panel, but rather, is subdivided into a number of rectangle-carpets, just as one might expect to find covering the floor.

Furthermore, there are different "carpets" laid in different directions, one perpendicular to the other. Each has a central medallion, rich floral art nouveau designs and borders, similar to many Persian carpets. One may look to many Safavid carpets, fabrics and other artifacts with similar decorations, but ultimately there is no denying the strong Safavid character of the entire presentation of the interior space. But ultimately, it fails to explain why the church of Shiraz is so different from all other Armenian churches, including those in Isfahan.

And maybe this can provide at least a partial explanation. One must remember that when the first generation of powerful and wealthy Armenian merchants came into being, they were following closely the customs of the Persian court and while maintaining their Christian faith. The "Iranization" of the Armenian community was nonetheless measured–while Armenian merchants from Old Julfa were well traveled and exposed to many cultures, they never enjoyed direct access to the Persian court, renowned for its formality and pomp.

While the churches of Isfahan were being built, there existed fierce competition amongst the various merchant families – the patrons of the projects – as to which church would be the most impressive, expensive, and spectacular.

Chardin, who calls New Julfa the largest suburb of the world, mentions that there were many rich people in New Julfa – of these, ten had amassed extraordinary wealth, with a net worth of 500,000 Liras.

But Shiraz was far from Isfahan. It was at best an Armenian "outpost," built by second generation Armenian-Iranians that grew up amidst the lavish, cosmopolitan environments of Isfahan. So the church is smaller, better camouflaged in a city dominated by Shia, and although well decorated, it does not use the architectural vocabulary of the churches of Isfahan. In fact, it uses the architectural tastes and elements acquired by the Armenian patrons largely used in their own homes.

Thus, while the religious requirements and traditions impose a beautifully proportioned floor plan with two lateral altars over a slightly raised platform, all other architectural elements are not bound by any liturgical or religious matters, reflecting instead what was largely used in the houses of the time.

In my opinion, it is for this reason that these Armenians, that would dress like Persians, that were given permission to use the turban, who had Persian names and indulged in many of the luxuries of their time, created something truly unique in Armenian. This dynamic intermingling of cultures led to this ecclesiastical architecture.

A church that is inspired by local residential architecture, superimposed upon the most symbolically significant floor plan that a church could ever have – that of the cross.

8

The Motif of the Sphinx in the Decoration of Manuscripts Illuminated by T'oros Ṙoslin

Levon Chookaszian

When studying the development of artistic traditions of illustrations in the manuscripts signed by T'oros Ṙoslin, or attributed to him, it is impossible to disregard the decorative motifs that play an important role. The latter often originate not only from the artworks of the preceding centuries, but also from ancient world civilization. Examples of inspiration coming down to the Armenian artist from the arsenal of antique art are so numerous and so diverse that it is not possible to examine them all within one article.

In various chapters of a monograph on T'oros Ṙoslin,[1] I have already noted the commonality of miniatures in Ṙoslin's manuscripts with works of Greco-Roman civilization. The abundance of antique memorials on the territory of Cilicia and neighboring lands facilitated Ṙoslin's and his colleagues' acquaintance, to a considerable extent, with the beauties of the ancient world.

Of the immense number of their favorite antique artistic phenomena, it is important to distinguish examples that are especially striking. They allow one to examine the development of traditions in the art of Ṙoslin and his colleagues once more, from another viewpoint. Ṙoslin's artistic orientations, weighing on the side of antique world traditions, take a far clearer shape through a close study of the decorative realm of miniatures in the manuscripts that have preserved the artist's name.

Decorative motifs interwoven into a single whole and perpetuated in the décor, distinctly reveal the antique components of

---

[1] The monograph on T'oros Ṙoslin, which is unpublished, is currently being translated into English.

Ṙoslin's taste. Among the motifs inherited from the ancient world, the sphinx is often particularly represented in Ṙoslin's heritage. This mystical creature with a human head, a quadruped's body, and a bird's wings attracted many of the artists and sculptors of the East and the West. Its name comes from the Greek word "sfingo," which means "to press," "to strangle."[2] In general, this monster was represented with a man's or woman's head. The sphinx has Egyptian, Babylonian, and Sassanid roots. In Egypt, it was endowed with a lion's body, while the Chaldeans gave it a bull's body.[3] On the territory of ancient Armenia, statuettes with human heads and bodies of wingless lions and winged bulls were found,[4] which belong to the Urartian period. Consequently, these images occupied a definite place in the mythological notions of ancient Armenians as far back as the remote past.

The ancient Greeks preferred representations of sphinxes with a woman's head, lion's body, and bird's wings.[5] This creature occupied an important place in Byzantine and Islamic arts. The first Muslim examples of the representations of the sphinx are connected with Egypt and Spain. Various specimens of comparatively primitive representations of sphinxes are found on Coptic fabrics.[6] Scholars have not clarified where they had been woven. There are doubts whether these fabrics are a primitive repetition of Iranian prototypes or are imported.[7] Before beginning a detailed examination of Muslim examples, it should be noted that these monsters often appear in Roman sculpture as well.

---

[2] Mark Naumovich Botvinnik, M. A. Kogan, M. B. Rabinovich, B. P. Seletsky, *Mythological Dictionary*, Simon M. K'rkasharian, trans. (Yerevan, 1985), pp. 224-225 (in Armenian).

[3] Louis Réau, *Iconographie de l'Art chretien*, t. 2 (Paris, 1957), p. 120.

[4] Asatur Sh. Mnats'akanian, *Armenian Ornamental Art* (Yerevan, 1955), p. 12, fig. 31, p. 122, fig. 293 (in Armenian).

[5] Botvinnik, *Mythological Dictionary*, p. 224.

[6] Eva Baer, *Sphinxes and Harpies in Medieval Islamic Art, An Iconographical Study* (Oriental Notes and Studies, N. 6) (Jerusalem: Israel Oriental Society, 1965), pp. 19-20.

[7] Ibid., p. 20.

Sphinxes with a beast's head are quite frequent among Roman examples.[8] The wingless and incomplete sphinx is known from as far back as ancient Egypt. Classifying the numerous specimens of this creature, scholars distinguish three different types: complete sphinx, incomplete sphinx, and winged quadruped,[9] which are repeatedly found in T'oros Ṙoslin's art. Of monsters belonging to the class of the winged quadruped, the winged lion is the first to appear in the miniatures of manuscripts signed by T'oros Ṙoslin.[10]

This fantastic creature was known on the territory of Armenia as early as the Urartian period;[11] thus, it is natural that the representation of a sphinx appears in the works of Armenian miniaturists so frequently, basically as the symbol of the Evangelist Mark.[12] The mythological beast appears as Mark already on the masts of the decorated initial on the title page of the Mughni Gospel (Matenadaran, Ms. 7736) of the eleventh century.[13] In the canon tables of this codex, the sphinx is for the first time represented as a decorative motif for the headpiece, i.e., exactly in that part of it, where centuries later, this creature appears in the miniatures of Ṙoslin's manuscripts. It is noteworthy that this motif is well known after the examples of decorated Byzantine fabrics of the twelfth-thirteenth centuries.[14]

Winged lions in the miniatures of manuscripts that have preserved Ṙoslin's signature, first appear in those canon tables in the Zeitun Gospel of 1256 (Matenadaran, Ms. 10450), which contain Eusebius's letter to Carpianus (folios 3v, 4). Here, these beasts are shown on the top of the columns, as capital decorations. Placing the sphinxes in that location, Ṙoslin seems to be following the principles

---

[8] Denise Jalabert, "De l'Art Oriental Antique à l'Art Roman, Recherches sur la faune et la flore Romanes, Le Sphinx," *Bulletin Monumental*, vol. 94 (Paris, 1935), p. 78.

[9] Ibid., pp. 78-79.

[10] George Wells Ferguson, *Signs and Symbols in Christian Art* (New York: Oxford University Press, 1954), p. 20.

[11] Mnats'akanian, *Armenian Ornamental Art*, pp. 177-178, fig. 431.

[12] Tatiana A. Izmailova, *Armenian Miniatures of the XIth Century* (Moscow: Iskusstvo, 1979), p. 151.

[13] Ibid., pp. 82, 85, 86.

[14] Otto von Falke, *Kunstgeschichte der Seidenweberei* (Berlin, 1936), Abb. 203, 204, 206.

of Roman sculpture, in particular the traditions of artworks in southern France. The tradition of decorating capitals with the images of ordinary lions, standing with their backs to each other, is characteristic for the buildings in Chauvigny, la Charité-sur-Loire, Lascar and many other structures.[15] This occurrence is also observed in French miniature painting.

It is interesting to note that in the second volume of the so-called Second Bible of St. Martial (Paris, Bibliothèque Nationale), the capitals are adorned with the figures of lions, one of which covers the other with its body.[16]

In the French and Armenian miniatures compared, the beasts differ (in one case we deal with an ordinary lion and in the second, with a winged lion); however, their location is similar. It is impossible to assert with certitude that Ṙoslin was familiar with the codex of St. Martial of Limoges (France), but it should be assumed that he could have seen such manuscripts.

It should be remarked that in Armenian book art, wingless lions with their backs turned to each other and looking at each other are first found in one of the canon tables of a Cilician Gospel of 1193 (Venice, Mekhitarist Congregation Library, Ms. 1635).[17] The tails of these beasts, as distinct from sphinxes, are interlaced behind their backs. This phenomenon present in French book painting could have penetrated Cilician miniatures long before Ṙoslin's works.

Images of fantastic creatures on the capitals passed from Roman art to certain Byzantine miniatures. In this respect, the canon tables in the tenth-eleventh century Gospel (Athos, Iveron Monastery Collection, Ms. 2), where the capitals are decorated with griffins and

---

[15] Emil Mâle, *L'Art Réligieux du XIIe siècle en France* (Paris, 1924), p. 347; Jurgis Baltrusaitis, *Le stylistique ornamentale dans la sculpture romane* (Paris, 1931), figs. 378, 407.

[16] Vilhelm Slomann, *Bicorporates, Studies in Revivals and Migrations of Art Motifs* (Copenhagen: Munksgaard, 1967), vol. 1, pp. 99, 203, n. 7, vol. 2, fig. 484.

[17] Sirarpie Der Nersessian, *Manuscrits arméniens illustrés des XIIe, XIIIe et XIVe siècles de la Bibliothèque des Peres Mekhitharistes des Venise* (Paris: E. du Boccard, 1937), pl. XVIII.

ordinary birds with their backs turned to each other, are noteworthy.[18]

It may be noted with certainty that on some antique artworks, the conveyance of such winged lions, as in the Zeitun Gospel, go back with their roots several millennia; ordinary lions, showing their backs to each other and facing one another exactly in the same manner, are found on the seal in Souz and are dated from about 3000 B.C. (Paris, Louvre).[19] The king of beasts with its kin is similarly represented on a Corinthian plate of the first half of the sixth century B.C. (Copenhagen, Antique Collection of the Danish National Museum) and among the reliefs of the Achaemenid mirror belonging to Norbert Schimmel (New York).[20] In Ṙoslin's epoch, this representation is encountered in the decoration of the fabrics partly woven of silk, a thirteenth century piece from Regensburg (Copenhagen, Museum of Applied Arts).[21]

The beasts shown in the Zeitun Gospel are endowed with yet another Eastern peculiarity: their tails stretch between their legs, go under their bellies and then rise up along their backs, i.e., they demonstrate a feature, which, though widely known through Roman sculptures, is of Eastern origin[22] and for centuries had been observed in numerous examples of Armenian art, in general and miniature painting, in particular. The beasts in the Zeitun Gospel touch each other with their wings, reminding one of the sphinxes in the medallion on the silk fabrics made in Egypt in the epoch of the Fatimid rule (1096-1097) and one in the Vatican Museum.[23]

Later, this peculiarity is observed in the representations of paired sphinxes on various metal objects of the twelfth century from Iran. In this connection, noteworthy are the bronze mirror, property of the Detroit Institute of Arts, and the gold necklace at the Metropolitan Museum in New York. An occurrence which is of interest is found

---

[18] Stylianos M. Pelekanidis, P. C. Christou, Ch. Tsioumis, S. N. Kadas, *The Treasures of Mount Athos, Illuminated Manuscripts*, vol. 2 (Athens: Ekdotike Athenon, 1975), figs. 7, 8.
[19] Slomann, *Bicorporates*, fig. 112.
[20] Ibid., fig. 466.
[21] Ibid., fig. 467.
[22] Jalabert, "De l'Art Oriental Antique à l'Art Roman, Recherches sur la faune et la flore Romanes, Le Sphinx," p. 83, figs. 1, 4, 5, 7, 8, 27.
[23] Baer, *Sphinxes and Harpies in Medieval Islamic Art*, p. 3, fig. 4.

on a Mamluk metal basin from the Victoria and Albert Museum in London, among the reliefs of which, paired sphinxes are represented with human faces and their backs turned to each other.[24]

These examples or their ancient prototypes might have become a source of inspiration for the miniaturist of the Zeitun Gospel, but for the appearance of winged lions in the place of capitals in the canon tables of the Gospel of 1253 (Washington, Freer Gallery, Ms. 44.17), like Ṙoslin's manuscripts, executed in Hṙomkla.[25]

In the decoration of the Gospel of 1248 (Antelias, Collection of the Catholicosate of Cilicia, Ms. 8), which has preserved the name of Kirakos, its illustrator and Ṙoslin's teacher, these beasts are shown in a somewhat different way. The winged lions with their backs turned to each other, do not look at one another, but their tails are interlaced.[26] It is not difficult to be convinced that the tastes and experience of the colleagues from the scriptorium in Hṙomkla, as well as that of Ṙoslin's teacher, played a guiding role for the miniaturist of the Gospel of Zeitun when illustrating the canon tables.

Later, in Ṙoslin's Gospel of 1262 (Jerusalem, Ms. 2660), the artist preserved the same posture of the winged lions in one of the canon tables (fol. 1v), not representing the capitals themselves.[27] In another canon table of the same manuscript (fol. 2), wingless lions with their backs turned to each other are represented in place of the capital.[28] Here, another feature, hitherto absent in earlier manuscripts, is also observed: the beasts turn and not only look at each other, but also embrace one another with their paws, exactly the same way as in the decoration of the above-mentioned Achaemenid mirror from Norbert Schimmel's collection.

---

[24] Ibid., p. 19, fig. 35.

[25] Sirarpie Der Nersessian, *Armenian Manuscripts in the Freer Gallery of Art* (Washington, 1963), figs. 33, 34.

[26] Sylvia Agémian, *Manuscrits arménien enluminés du catholicossat de Cilicie*, préface de S.S. le Catholicos Karékin II (Antelias: Editions du Catholicossate arménien, 1991), figs. 3, 4.

[27] Sirarpie Der Nersessian, *Miniature Painting in the Armenian Kingdom of Cilicia from the Twelfth to the Fourteenth Century* (Dumbarton Oaks Studies, XXXI), vol. 2 (Washington D.C., 1993), fig. 279.

[28] Ibid., fig. 280.

This version of representing paired lions was quite usual for Ṙoslin and his contemporaries and was in the field of their vision every day, as it was imprinted on the coins of the Armenian Kingdom of Cilicia.[29] This seems to have been quite sufficient for the king of beasts-single or in pair with its kin, with wings or without them, as well as other winged monsters with a lion's body with their backs turned to each other-to appear so frequently in the design of manuscripts signed by Roslin.

Interestingly, in the epoch of the great artist, fabrics with the representations of lions with their backs turned to each other and necks connected with chains were common in the territory of the Seljuk Sultanate of Konya, neighboring Cilicia.[30] The whole artistic atmosphere of the Mediterranean Sea basin seems to have promoted the spread of analogous motifs.

Before passing to the examination of the image of the complete sphinx, it should be noted that the motif of winged lions likewise undergoes other changes in the miniatures of Ṙoslinian manuscripts. For instance, in the Sebastia Gospel of 1262 (Walters Gallery, Baltimore), in the canon tables with the letter of Eusebius to Carpianus (fol. 1v, 2), the lions shown, instead of the capitals, are connected not only with their tails, but also with their wings.[31] (Fig. 1)

---

[29] Paul Bedoukian, *Coinage of Cilician Armenia* (Danbury, Conn.: Bedoukian, 1979).

[30] Heinrich Jakob Schmidt, *Alte Seidenstoffe* (Braunschweig, Klinhardt, & Biermann, 1958), Abb. 149.

[31] Sirarpie Der Nersessian, *Armenian Manuscripts in the Walters Art Gallery* (Baltimore: The Trustees, 1973), pls. 30, 31.

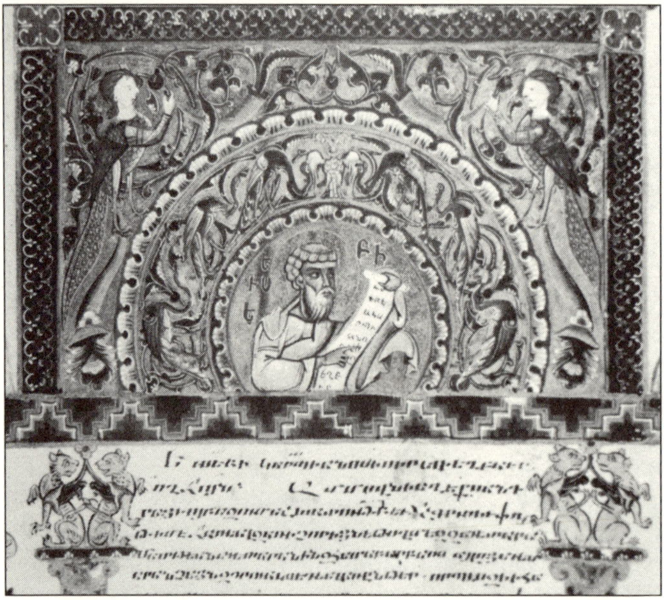

Fig. 1- Letter of Eusebius (Detail), Baltimore, Walters Art Gallery 539, Four Gospels 1262 A.D., folio 1v.

Dedicatory canon tables in the same manuscript (fol. 11v, 12) bring forth an entirely different example. Here, only one winged lion is shown frontally and in an unusual posture, with the legs crossed as a human being, instead of the capital.[32] In one of the canon tables of the Cilician Gospel of 1193 (Venice, Mekhitarist Congregation Library, Ms. 1635), an analogous peculiarity that recalls this miniature of Ṙoslin's codex is found. Again, a winged lion is represented instead of the capital; however, this time it has a halo and is shown from the side.[33]

This signifies that even if the illustrator of the dedicatory canon table in the Sebastia Gospel was familiar with the work by the artist of the manuscript of 1193, he did not however, blindly copy the artistic phenomenon seen. In the miniature of Ṙoslin's manuscript, the king of beasts seems to be pressed under some weight. Indeed (as

---

[32] Ibid., pls. 40, 41.

[33] Der Nersessian, *Manuscripts arménien illustrés*, fig. 44.

a matter of fact), he holds the architrave and the headpiece. This impression seems to be indicating that when working on this part of the decoration of the codex, Ṙoslin or his colleague could have been inspired by the sculptures of those sphinxes that served as column bases in Italian churches of the 12-13th centuries.[34]

At the same time, the frontal posture of the lion with crossed paws is surprisingly reminiscent of the image of the lion struggling with a dragon, dating from the mid-twelfth century, on the *plafond* of the Palantine Chapel in Palermo, Sicily.[35] This work is considered to have been executed by an Arab artist. Unfortunately, it is not possible to specify whether the posture of the two lions in the compared examples is an accidental coincidence. It is a fact of surprising similarity.

The circumstance of the miniature of the Sebastia Gospel, where the lion is shown winged, while in the fresco in Palermo it is wingless, is insignificant. In another Ṙoslin manuscript (Jerusalem, Ms. 2660), created in the same year as the Sebastia Gospel, another wingless lion, again with crossed paws, is represented frontally instead of the capital over the central column in one of the canon tables (fol. 7v).[36] I think that Ṙoslin illuminated the Jerusalem manuscript earlier than the Sebastia Gospel, and the innovations mentioned in the first codex were developed a bit later in the second one.

In another canon table of the Sebastia Gospel (fol. 10), a winged lion is represented in a different and unusual pose: this time it is shown standing on a bowl between peacocks placed in the upper part of the headpiece. Here, the king of beasts is shown sideways, with a paw raised, like the lions familiar from the examples of heraldics.[37]

---

[34] Hans Wentzel, *Antiken-Imitationen des 12. und 13.* Jahrhunderts in Italien.–Zeitschsift für Kunstwissenschaft, Bd. IX (Berlin, 1955), S. 41, 43, Abb. 11, 14, 15.

[35] Willy Hartner and Richard Ettinghausen, "The Conquering Lion, the Life Cycle of a Symbol," *Oriens*, vol. 17 (Leiden, 1964), fig. 3, p. 165.

[36] M. Ciucci, "Un contributo alla conoscenza di Toros Roslin: L'Evangeliario i Levon e Keran" del 1262 del patriarcato armeno di Gerusalemme (codice 2660); "Atti del Terzo Simposio Internazionale di Arte Armena" 1981, Milano-Vicenza-Castelfranco V.- Piazzola sul Brenta-Venezia, 25 Settembre – 1 Ottobre (San Lazzaro-Venezia, 1985), fig. 3.

[37] Der Nersessian, *Armenian Manuscripts in the Walters Art Gallery*, pl. 39.

It is interesting that over the headpiece of the title page of the Gospel of Matthew in Ṙoslin's manuscript of 1260 (Jerusalem, Ms. 251), the lion also stands on a bowl, but here it is shown without wings.[38] The beast is represented here between two human figures, wearing the masks of a goat and an eagle. There is no doubt that this representation served a model for the sphinx in the Sebastia Gospel.

In separate canon tables of the latter (fols. 7v, 8), the motif of the capital improves even more, owing to the appearance of a pair of crowned sphinxes. They are depicted in a manner familiar to us: with their backs turned to each other and looking at one another. Their tails come out from under their bellies and rise over their backs, as in the examples discussed above.[39]

This representation is even more closely contiguous with the already mentioned fabrics of the Fatimid epoch from the Vatican Museum and in general, with the works from Egypt of the Fatimid period, in the decoration of which the earliest examples of crowned sphinxes with human faces are apparently found.[40] The creatures in Ṙoslinian codices recall with their crowns the sphinxes on the capitals of the Cuno church (Maine-et-Loire) and from the museum in Arles,[41] thus occupying a distinctive place among these French and Egyptian examples, not repeating them.

In general, in Armenian book art, sphinxes are encountered for the first time in the eleventh century, in the Gospel of 1053, and in the Mughni Gospel (Matenadaran, Mss. 3793, 7736), where they are placed in the headpieces of canon tables.[42] Later, this image appears in the headpiece of the title page of the Mush Homiliary of 1202

---

[38] Der Nersessian, *Miniature Painting in the Armenian Kingdom of Cilicia*, fig. 289.

[39] Der Nersessian, *Armenian Manuscripts in the Walters Art Gallery*, pl. 36, 37.

[40] Baer, *Sphinxes and Harpies in Medieval Islamic Art*, figs. 4, 8.

[41] Jalabert, "De l'Art Oriental Antique à l'Art Roman, Recherches sur la faune et la flore Romanes, Le Sphinx," fig. 1, 3.

[42] See Izmailova, *Armenian Miniature Painting of the 11th Century*, pp. 56, 85; *Armenian Miniature Painting: Hovhannes Sanduhkavanets'i*, Compilation, introduction and comments by Tatiana Izmailova (Yerevan, 1986), pls. 16, 28.

(Matenadaran, Ms. 7729).[43] As for the winged and crowned sphinx with a human face, it is first found in the Gospel of 1206, not studied yet (Alex and Mary Manoogian Museum, Detroit), the illustrator of which is the well-known scribe and miniaturist Kozma. Here, the sphinx is placed over the headpiece of the title page in the Gospel of John.

The winged lion with a human face, but without a crown, appears in Ṙoslin's art in one of the dedicatory canon tables of the Zeitun Gospel (fol. 6) almost in the same part of the headpiece as in the Gospel of 1053. In the miniature of Ṙoslin's manuscript, this monster is placed in a circle, as well as the lion, the mountain goat and the two-headed eagle shown in the vicinity. It is of no less interest that the principle of representing various animals that are inscribed in circles with vegetative ornamentation characterize a number of canon tables in the Mughni Gospel.[44] As is known, this manuscript is considered one of the rarest surviving examples of the book painting of the city of Ani, and, consequently, here, we deal with a feature inherited in the decoration of the Ṙoslinian manuscript from the miniature painting of Ani.

Sphinxes in the manuscripts that have preserved the name of T'oros Ṙoslin appear in other parts of the decoration of canon tables. In one of the canon tables in the Gospel of 1260 (Jerusalem, Ms. 251), two creatures with women's faces appear in the upper part of the headpiece (fol. 14). They are depicted approaching each other on both sides of the floral pattern. Their faces are turned back which imparts something very lively and real to their images.[45] In the course of centuries, these monsters have repeatedly been depicted opposite each other. The same refers to other creatures and fantastic beasts shown on both sides of a tree or a plant. (Fig. 2)

---

[43] Emma Korkhmazian, Irina Drambian, Hravard Hakobian, *Armenian Miniatures of the 13th and 14th Centuries from the Matenadaran Collection* (Yerevan, Leningrad: Aurora, 1984), pl. 1.

[44] *Armenian Miniature Painting: Hovhannes Sanduhkavanets'i*, pls. 26, 27.

[45] Der Nersessian, *Miniature Painting in the Armenian Kingdom of Cilicia*, fig. 286.

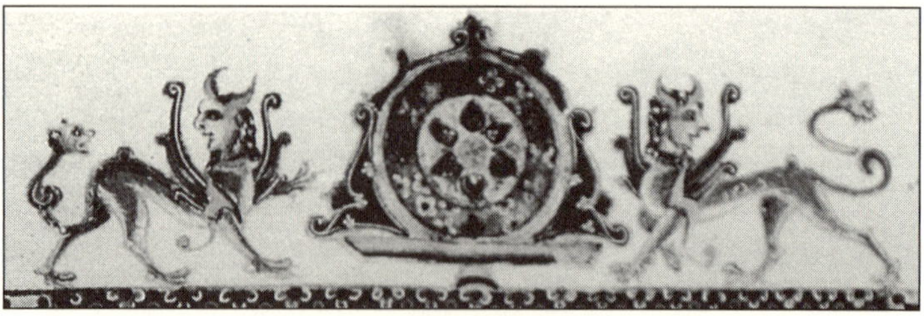

Figure 2- Dedicatory page (Detail), Jerusalem, Armenian Patriarchate 251, Four Gospels 1260 A.D., folio 14.

Examples of similar representations date back to the third millennium B.C.[46] This principle was inherited by the masters of different Eastern peoples and later it became widespread even in Roman sculpture. Specimens of early Islamic fabrics coming down from Egypt are the earliest medieval examples that represent quadrupeds with human faces on both sides of a tree.[47] In times, preceding Ṙoslin's epoch, images of sphinxes, separated from one another by a tree or a plant, are recurrent on silk fabrics coming down from Iran (twelfth century) of the period of the Seljuk conquest.[48]

Sphinxes in the last miniature of Ṙoslin's codex under consideration, greatly differ from hitherto known examples, owing to the fact that their faces that are turned back. Their bodies, with a gracefulness typical of them, recall the sphinxes that appear in the decoration of Iranian ceramics of the 12-13th centuries.[49] According to the specialists' opinion, the main influence defining the character of Islamic sphinxes is apparently linked with the Iranian tradition.[50]

Eva Bauer writes "To study the Iranian heritage… important is the way of combining the two sphinxes. These heraldic groups, sometimes in pair with each other, or with their backs turned to one another, are decorative compositions characteristic of the Islamic period. The pairs of sphinxes are physically joined with their wings

---

[46] Jalabert, "De l'Art Oriental Antique à l'Art Roman, Recherches sur la faune et la flore Romanes, Le Sphinx," pp. 95-96.
[47] Baer, *Sphinxes and Harpies in Medieval Islamic Art*, figs. 3, 5.
[48] Ibid., figs. 11, 12.
[49] Ibid., figs. 65, 74.
[50] Ibid., p. 20.

and tails, continuing the Achaemenid tradition of conveying beasts."[51] Bauer assumes that both the motif and the manner of their conveyance demonstrate the millennial existence of art forms. She also makes another interesting remark indicating that sphinxes reached Mesopotamia and Asia Minor at the beginning of the thirteenth century, i.e., the territories occupied by the Seljuks.[52]

In general, sphinxes with human faces are represented with human ears, but the creatures in the miniature under consideration in Ṙoslin's manuscript are endowed with the pointed and bent horn-like ears of a quadruped, as is observed in individual Roman sculptural examples.[53]

The images in the Ṙoslinian manuscript are not a repetition of any sphinx familiar to us and are very peculiar in appearance. Unlike the ancient Greek, Roman or Romanesque examples, certain feathers in the wings of the monsters represented by the Armenian painter bend in the form of a staff, thus recalling the analogous features of the beasts in the miniatures of the Mughni Gospel.

Jalabert who studied the iconography of these mythical creatures, marks the mentioned trait in such obviously Eastern works, as the Byzantine-Sassanid silk fabrics from the Berlin Museum or the wooden *panneau* of the end of the tenth century of the Fatimids' ancient palace in Cairo.[54]

Independent of Jalabert, Baer also pays attention to this peculiarity of the wings, ascribing a Sassanid origin to it.[55] Apparently, the frequent appearance of sphinxes with such wings is not accidental in the samples of Persian fabrics and ceramics of the twelfth-thirteenth centuries, that is, the Seljuk period.[56] It is interesting that the wing feathers bend in the form of a staff not only in the sphinxes of the Mughni Gospel, but also in the miniatures of other Armenian manuscripts, as in the Homiliary of Mush and in the above-mentioned Gospel of 1206 by the scribe Kozma.

---

[51] Ibid., p. 23.
[52] Ibid., p. 16.
[53] Jalabert, "De l'Art Oriental Antique à l'Art Roman, Recherches sur la faune et la flore Romanes, Le Sphinx," p. 75, figs. 1, 4.
[54] Ibid.
[55] Baer, *Sphinxes and Harpies in Medieval Islamic Art*, pp. 22-23, fig. 38.
[56] Ibid., figs. 11, 12, 65, 74.

To these paintings may be added an example of applied arts. The silver casket kept in the treasury of the Cathedral in Trier and dated from the mid-thirteenth century and the beginning of the fourteenth century, which was earlier considered a Syrian work,[57] was later connected with Mamluk jewellery,[58] finally was presented as an Armenian piece.[59]

The sphinxes of the miniature in Ṙoslinian codices have yet another interesting feature familiar from the design of the Mughni Gospel and the carved wooden door of 1114 in the Monastery of the Holy Apostles in Mush.[60] We deal with the monsters' tails, which end in the dragon's head. This detail also brings the miniature in Roslin's manuscript close to the panneau at the Fatimids' Palace in Cairo and the Trier casket.

It should be noted that separate sphinxes with human faces made of bronze in the twelfth century and coming from the Seljuk territories in Asia Minor are also endowed with dragon heads on their tails.[61] The same peculiarity characterizes the sphinxes in other Armenian miniatures of the Ṙoslinian epoch. Illustrations of the Gospel of 1206 by the scribe Kozma and the Miscellany [Zhoghovatsu] of 1219 (Matenadaran, Ms. 1382) from the Monastery of Hаṙij are implied.[62] It is interesting to note the usual lions, with dragon heads on their tails, are also observed in the works of Armenian art.

Among such works are the reliefs in the burial chamber of the Proshian princes at the Monastery of Geghard[63] and the title page of

---

[57] Boris Marshak, *Scan of the 13th Century in the Near East*, "Reports of the State Hermitage," Issue XLVII (Leningrad, 1982), p. 64-65, fig. 2; Mikhail Kramarovki, "Monomach's Headgear: Byzantium or the East?" *Reports of the State Hermitage*, pp. 68-70.

[58] Marilyn Jenkins, "Mamluk Jewelry: Influence and Echoes," *Muqarnas, An Annual on Islamic Art and Architecture*, vol. 5 (Leiden, 1988), pp. 29-42.

[59] Volkmar Gantzhorn, *Der christlich orientalische Teppich* (Köln, 1990), S. 97-98, Abb. 129.

[60] Izmailova, *Armenian Miniature Painting of the 11th Century*, p. 82, 173.

[61] Baer, *Sphinxes and Harpies in Medieval Islamic Art*, p. 15, fig. 29a, b, p. 60, note 41.

[62] Mnats'akanian, *Armenian Ornamental Art*, p. 346, fig. 729.

[63] "Documenti di Architettura Armena", 6, *Geghard* (Milano, 1973), fig. 17.

the Gospel of 1200 (Matenadaran Ms. 2589) copied by Sargis and illustrated by Hairapet.[64] It is remarkable that the place where this codex was created is considered the territory of the Seljuk Sultanate of Konya. According to Sirarpie Der Nersessian, the manuscript was created in the Armenian center of the Sultanate, while Tatiana Izmailova assumes that it was copied in the southern part of the Seljuk lands looking in the sea.[65] These examples clearly demonstrate the degree of vitality of analogous artistic motifs and mythological images in different Armenian regions.

Another pair of monsters placed on both sides of the bowl over the headpiece of the title-page of the Gospel of Mark (fol. 131)[66] is observed in the decoration of the Sebastia Gospel. Usually these creatures are depicted in pairs, opposite each other or with their backs turned to each other,[67] while here the monster shown on the right seems to be pursuing the other. Their motion is directed to the left. The beast represented on the right has an eagle's head, a lion's body and a bird's wings. The creature depicted on the left is a winged sphinx with a face of a youth and a lion's body and paws. (Fig. 3)

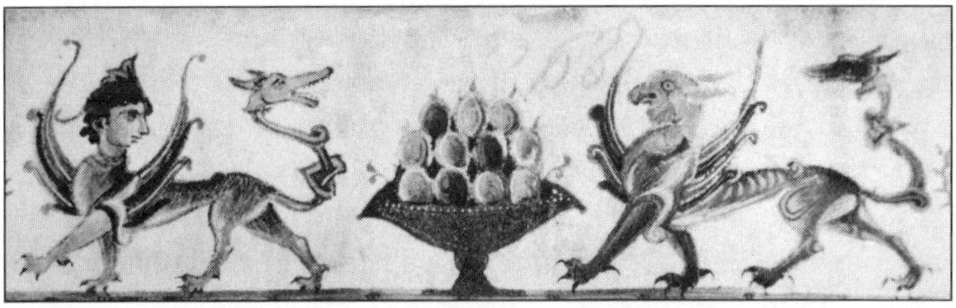

Figure 3- Headpiece of the title page of Gospel of Mark (Detail), Baltimore, Walters Art Gallery 539, Four Gospels, 1262 A.D., folio 131.

---

[64] Mnats'akanian, *Armenian Ornamental Art*, p. 580, fig. 1103.

[65] Tatiana A. Izmailova, *On the Connections of Armenian Miniature Painting with the Art of the Jerusalem Kingdom* (Matenadaran Ms. 2589). The Second International Symposium on Georgian Art (Tbilisi, 1977); Izmailova, *The Manuscript of the Year 1200* (Matenadaran, Ms. 2589) "Vyzantijskij Vremennik," (Moscow, 1981), vol. 42, pp. 136-138.

[66] Der Nersessian, *Armenian Manuscripts in the Walters Art Gallery*, pl. 62.

[67] Jalabert, "De l'Art Oriental Antique à l'Art Roman, Recherches sur la faune et la flore Romanes, Le Sphinx," p. 95, fig. 22.

These monsters are shown with dragon heads on their tails. The eagle-headed beast has horn-like, pointed ears, which allows us to finally identify it with a griffin's image. According to Herodotus and Pliny, this fantastical creature has its origins in the land of the Scythians and is indebted to Egyptian art for its birth.[68] It is also known in the art of Achaemenid Iran.

In ancient times, this beast was considered the keeper of graves and treasures. It was regarded as the symbol of science for its ability to identify hidden treasures.[69] Furthermore, the image of a griffin had different meanings contradicting each other: on the one hand, it represented the Savior, and on the other; those who oppressed and pursued the Christians.[70] Quite often this monster was regarded as one of the personifications of the devil.[71] The griffin is known according to antique Greek works, Byzantine mosaics and reliefs of early Christian sarcophagi,[72] and in later period by the decoration of textile production.

Of textile examples, noteworthy are the eighth-eleventh century fabrics found in the grave of St. Ursula in Köln,[73] the silk fragment of the tenth-twelfth centuries from the museum in Cleveland, whose Syrian origin is doubted by scholars, and the Byzantine fabrics of the eleventh century from the treasury of the Church of St. Stefan in Sance.[74] The image of this creature is familiar to the Islamic art of Egypt of the tenth-eleventh centuries.[75] Even in Ṙoslin's epoch, in the lands adjoining Cilicia (as assumed by scholars), particularly Syria, such silk fabrics as the sample with the representation of a pair of griffins at the Metropolitan Museum in New York, were commonly in use.[76]

---

[68] Réau, *Iconographie de l'Art chretien*, p. 116.

[69] Ibid., p. 117.

[70] Ferguson, *Signs and Symbols in Christian Art*, p. 18.

[71] Réau, *Iconographie de l'Art chretien*, p. 117.

[72] Ibid.

[73] David Talbot Rice, *Art of the Byzantine Era* (London: Thames and Hudson, 1963), fig. 22.

[74] David Talbot Rice, *Art Byzantin* (Paris-Bruxelles, 1959), fig. 131.

[75] Richard Ettinghausen and Oleg Grabar, *The Art and Architecture of Islam: 650-1250* (New York: Penguin, 1987), fig. 139, 175.

[76] Maurice Sven Dimand, *A Handbook of Muhammadan Art* (New York, 1947), fig. 169.

The presence of this beast was marked in eleventh century Armenian book painting, particularly in the miniatures of the city of Ani – in the headpieces of the canon tables of the Gospel of 1053 and the Mughni Gospel,[77] later in the Cilician Gospel of 1193 as well (collection of the Mekhitarists in Venice), and later in the miniature of the thirteenth century (e.g., in the collection of 1219 from the Monastery of Hařij, etc.).[78] The image of the griffin also appears on a veil of the eleventh-twelfth centuries or a later period, before 1295,[79] and on the Trier casket[80] that are considered to be Armenian works.

In the miniature of Roslin's manuscript under consideration, two circumstances should receive attention. First of all, the arrangement of the sphinx and griffin is curious. Their location over the headpiece of the canon table is observed here for the first time in Armenian miniatures. In the Gospel of the thirteenth century (Athos, Monastery of Dionysius, Ms. 4), a Byzantine miniaturist depicts two griffins jumping towards each other on both sides of the floral pattern in the same place.[81] Is it coincidental or should one see a certain connection between the illustrator of the Armenian miniature and the Byzantine master?

The second circumstance is yet more interesting. Here, we deal with the scene of a griffin pursuing a sphinx. Before a detailed consideration of this composition, it is necessary to cite a remark by Baer. She considers that among fantastic and real beasts presented on metal objects of the Ayyubid period, the sphinx most frequently is represented in a festive march or race.[82] We deal with 13th century works by Syrian-Egyptian masters on metal. In these works, as well as in Persian ceramics, there are examples decorated with friezes. Worthy of attention is the fact that friezal compositions exclusively consist of sphinxes, marching one after another, or sphinxes accompanied by fantastic, and sometimes real beasts. These

---

[77] *Armenian Miniature Painting: Hovhannes Sanduhkavanets'i*, pl. 16, 27.

[78] Der Nersessian, *Manuscrits arméniens illustrès*, fig. 49; Mnats'akanian, *Armenian Ornamental Art*, p. 346, fig. 729, p. 503, fig. 1017.

[79] Gantzhorn, *Der christlich orientalische Teppich*, S. 114, Abb. 162.

[80] Marshak, *Scan of the 13th Century in the Near East*, fig. 2.

[81] Pelekanidis et. al, *The Treasures of Mount Athos, Illuminated Manuscripts*, vol. 1 (Athens, 1973), fig. 17.

[82] Baer, *Sphinxes and Harpies in Medieval Islamic Art*, pp. 18-19.

decorative belts, as Baer states "... firmly exist in the Iranian tradition."[83]

The scholar points out that friezal compositions with sphinxes pursued by griffins, lions and other beasts are known in many art works. As in ancient times, the Syrian-Egyptian masters on metal obviously preferred those representations where a sphinx followed a griffin or vice versa. According to Baer, in the imagination of Islamic artists, both beasts were still connected with each other in an obvious way.[84]

The list of thirteenth century works brought by Baer to demonstrate the frieze belts, presenting the relation of a sphinx and a griffin, gives rise to definite ideas. Among these works are a candelabrum from Mesopotamia (London, the British Museum, 1954-2-15.1), the ceramic bowl (made in the enamel technique), the location of which is unknown, the famous Syrian basin of ca. 1300, more familiar as the Font of St. Louis (Louvre) and other pieces from the end of the thirteenth century.[85] The bronze dish from the first half of the thirteenth century found in Syria (St.-Petersburg, Hermitage Museum), may be added to these examples.[86]

The commonality of the miniature in Roslin's manuscript with the examples of Islamic artistic metalwork is not surprising. In the illustrations of the manuscripts that have preserved the name of T'oros Ṙoslin, one discovers other similar features with the works of the Ayyubid period.

The Cilician state had numerous contacts with the neighboring states and peoples, among them the Mamluks of Egypt; consequently, T'oros Ṙoslin and his colleagues had broad opportunities to get acquainted with the works of Islamic masters of metalwork. During these cultural relations, there was mutual acquaintance with the artistic achievements of the Armenian and other peoples, where exchange of artistic production and mutual spiritual enrichment took place. For this very reason, scenes with

---

[83] Ibid, p. 24.

[84] Ibid., pp. 24-25, figs. 21, 41, 42.

[85] Ibid., p. 25, note 99.

[86] Richard Ettinghausen, *The Unicorn, Studies in Muslim Iconography* (Washington: Smithsonian Institute, 1950), pl. 18 middle, p. 26.

Christian themes appear in certain samples of artistic handicrafts, particularly, in the décor of metalware.[87]

In all probability, these artworks representing New Testament compositions expressed not only Byzantine or Syrian influence, but also the influence of numerous miniaturists of Cilician Armenia.

It is interesting that in the miniature of the Ṙoslinian manuscript under consideration, the sphinx is shown with his head turned and looking at the griffin pursuing him, i.e., just the same way as it is observed in the décor of the Font of St. Louis and candelabrum from Mesopotamia.[88] Consequently, not only the theme, but also the same detail makes the works under comparison related.

The peculiarity of the sphinx's character in the Armenian miniature is partly achieved here by means of the headgear that resembles a vegetative leaf that distinguishes it from the analogous creatures in the décor of comparable pieces and from the monsters in Ṙoslin's manuscript of 1260. Like the latter, the monsters in the miniature of the Sebastia Gospel also have wings with folding feathers. It is interesting to note that the beasts in this manuscript appear almost without any change over the headpiece of a dedicatory canon table (fol. 12) in the Gospel of 1265 (Jerusalem, Ms. 1956), illuminated by Ṙoslin. They differ from the previous pair of monsters in that they do not pursue each other but move toward one another.[89] In addition, they are represented here on different sides of a gold medallion framed with floral ornamentation; the griffin is shown on the left and the sphinx, on the right. (Fig. 4)

---

[87] Ranee A. Katzenstein and Glenn D. Lowry, "Christian Themes in Thirteenth-Century Islamic Metalwork," *Muqarnas, An Annual on Islamic Art and Architecture*, vol. 1 (New Haven and London, 1983), pp. 53-68.

[88] Baer, *Sphinxes and Harpies in Medieval Islamic Art*, fig. 41, 42.

[89] Der Nersessian, *Miniature Painting in the Armenian Kingdom of Cilicia,* fig. 284.

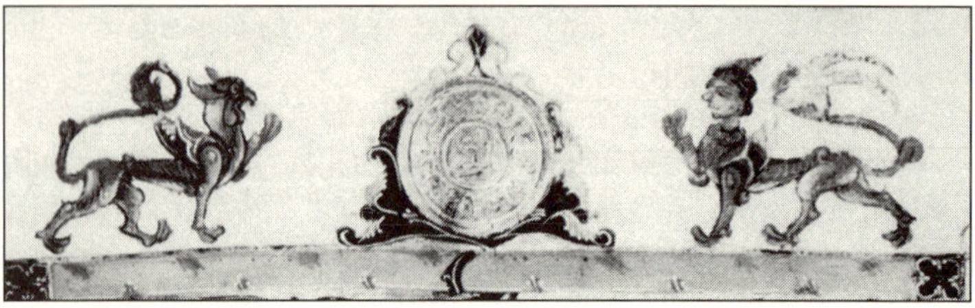

Figure 4- Dedicatory page (Detail), Jerusalem, Armenian Patriarchate 1956, Four Gospels, 1265 A.D., folio 12.

These beasts differ from the monsters examined in Ṙoslin's miniatures in their small wings, while the sphinx likewise in its tail, terminating in the head of the mountain goat that was not found in Armenian art of the previous period. The location of these creatures and the manner of their depiction opposite each other can be compared to the miniature (more than the title page in the Gospel of Mark in Ṙoslin's codex in Baltimore) close to the griffins of the mentioned canon of concordance in the thirteenth century Gospel from the Monastery of Dionysius on Athos.

The image of the griffin receives an unexpected development over the headpiece of the title page in the Gospel of John (fol. 271) in Roslin's Gospel of 1265.[90] The beast, having jumped rapidly over the sphinx's back, bites it furiously. The theme of the griffin attacking the sphinx is familiar from the décor of the Islamic metal basin of 1238-1240 (Louvre), also referring to the Ayyubid period.[91] This proves once again that such Islamic objects could have inspired the illustrators of Armenian manuscripts just the same way as Islamic masters of metalwork could have been inspired by the history of Christ's life and Christian art.

Separate examples of Byzantine textile production could have promoted the acquaintance of the Armenian miniaturist with this theme. Among the latter, one should mention the above cited fabrics of the eighth-tenth centuries from the sepulcher of St. Ursula (where

---

[90] Der Nersessian, *L'Art arménien des origins au XVIIe siecle* (Paris, 1977), fig. 99.

[91] D. S. Rice, "Inlaid Brasses from the Workshop of Ahmad Al-Mawsilt," *Ars Ortientalis*, vol. 2 (1957), p. 307.

a griffin is represented standing on an ordinary lion), or the 8th century fabric from the Textile Museum in Lyon (representing a griffin attacking a bull).[92]

Armenian artists before Ṙoslin, also revealed interest in such narratives. They were interested in the scenes of combat between a griffin and a lion. One of the canon tables of the Mughni Gospel of the eleventh century is persuasive in this (here, the composition under consideration is placed inside the headpiece). The beasts are already seized by the fit of struggle, but their confrontation has not yet entered a decisive stage.[93] The same creatures later appear in the Gospel of 1197 (which was kept previously in Lvov, and now in Gnezno, Poland), over the headpiece of the title page in the Gospel of Mark.[94] The griffin here is shown on the lion's back, locked in an embrace. These beasts are shown almost in the same way over the headpiece of the title-page in the Gospel of Luke in the codex of 1253 (Washington, Freer Gallery of Art, Ms. 44.17),[95] executed in Hṙomkla, where T'oros Ṙoslin worked at that time.

In their turn, the above-mentioned Armenian and non-Armenian examples could have promoted the illustrators of Roslin's manuscripts to advance and enrich Armenian miniature painting with a new plot–the scene of combat between a griffin and a sphinx.

Tracing the development of the sphinx motif in the decoration of Ṙoslinian codices, we find two completely different personifications of this monster in the headpiece of the title-page in the Gospel of Luke (fol. 201) in the Baltimore manuscript of 1262. Here, these beasts are depicted with their backs turned to each other, but looking at one another.[96] (Fig. 5)

---

[92] Rice, *Art of the Byzantine Era*, il. 22; Tamara Talbot Rice, "Animal Combat Scenes in Byzantine Art," *Studies in Memory of D. Talbot Rice*, G. Robertson and G. Henderson, eds. (Edinburgh, 1975), fig. 7c, 7d.

[93] *Armenian Miniature Painting: Hovhannes Sanduhkavanets'i*, pl. 32.

[94] Nerses Akinian, *The Gospel of Skevra of 1197 in the Library of the Armenian Bishopry in Lwow* (Vienna, 1930), fig. 10 (in Armenian); Günter Prinzing, "Neue Funde, Ein verschollenes Prachtwerk der armenischen Buchmalerei in Gnesen wiederentdeckt," *Kunstchronik*, Heft (6 June 1993, Munchen), S. 310-314.

[95] Der Nersessian, *Armenian Manuscripts in the Freer Gallery of Art*, fig. 50.

[96] Der Nersessian, *Armenian Manuscripts in the Walters Art Gallery*, pl. 69.

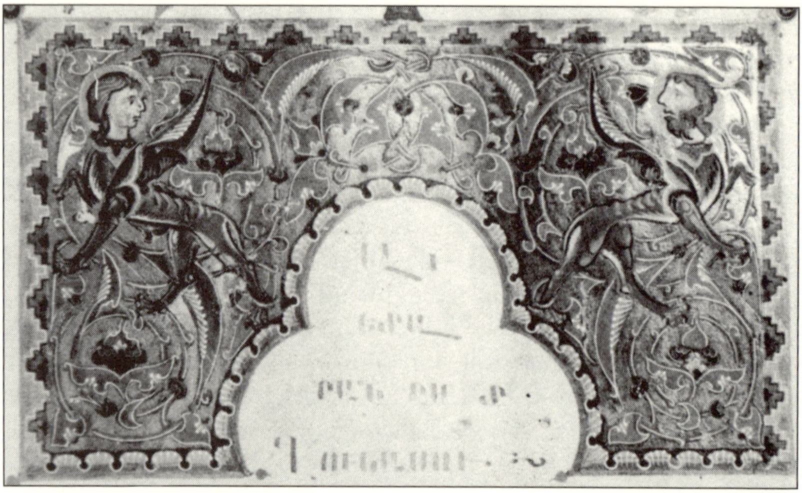

Figure 5- Headpiece of the title page of Gospel of Luke (Detail), Baltimore, Walters Art Gallery 539, Four Gospels 1262 A.D., folio 201.

The sphinxes here preserve the body of a lion and wings, but lack the dragon's heads on their tails. The first creature shown on the left has a woman's face, while the second one, placed on the right, has a man's bearded face. These monsters have *nimbs*, which is a rare feature. The sphinxes in the title page of the already mentioned Mush Homiliary also have halos. A haloed sphinx appears on a hexagonal dish (attributed to the second half of the thirteenth century) from the Metropolitan Museum of Art in New York.

Scholars are not certain about the origin of a plate from Anatolia, i.e., Western Armenia. The examined creatures of the miniature of the Sebastia Gospel stand out among the rest of the creatures mentioned above by a chevron-shaped cut on their breast, showing the beads that decorate the throats of the sphinxes. Owing to this chevron-shaped opening, an impression arises that actors are wearing the skins of fantastic beasts that are in front of us. The sphinx with a chevron-shaped opening on the breast first appears on a ceramic sphere (New York, Metropolitan Museum, 52.122 Roger's Fund), which is one part of a lamp and referring to Egypt of the Fatimid epoch.[97]

It is remarkable that these monsters from the miniature in the Sebastia Gospel have features from even more ancient times.[98] Prior to turning to them, it should be noted that the chevron-shaped opening characterizes the sphinxes in one of the canon tables of the Gospel (attributed to Kirakos, T'oros Ṙoslin's teacher) kept in Dublin (Chester Beatty Library, Ms. 558),[99] and also in the décor of the Trier casket mentioned earlier.[100]

The depiction of a bearded sphinx relates to the earliest iconography of these mythical creatures. As was previously noted, one of the beasts examined in the title page of the Sebastia Gospel is represented in this very way. It is noteworthy that two bearded sphinxes confronting each other are carved on the stone of the façade of the eastern stairs of Persepolis (Iran).[101] They are represented in exactly the same manner in a Persian silk fabric of Seljuk period, created centuries later.[102] Eva Baer points that sphinxes of such type are relatively rare in works of the Islamic period; however, they are known from the décor of artistic metalwork.[103]

In the case of the monsters examined in the miniature of the Sebastia Gospel, it should be noted that their illustrator does not copy their prototype blindly as he places a beardless beast opposite the bearded one. This is reminiscent of sphinxes of different gender on the capitals at the Museum in Arles and church of Saint-Denis Amboise, where the beasts are likewise represented with their backs turned to each other and looking at one another.[104] The reason for this coincidence is unknown to us, but the differences in the examples compared are also striking.

---

[97] Baer, *Sphinxes and Harpies in Medieval Islamic Art*, p. 5, fig. 8.

[98] Der Nersessian, *Miniature Painting in the Armenian Kingdom of Cilicia*, pp. 46-47.

[99] Der Nersessian, *The Chester Beatty Library, A Catalogue of the Armenian Manuscripts*, vol. 2 (Dublin, 1958), pl. 8.

[100] Marshak, *Scan of the 13th Century in the Near East*, fig. 2.

[101] Baer, *Sphinxes and Harpies in Medieval Islamic Art*, fig. 36, p. 21.

[102] Ibid., pp. 21-22, fig. 11.

[103] Ibid., p. 22, note 82.

[104] Jalabert, "De l'Art Oriental Antique à l'Art Roman, Recherches sur la faune et la flore Romanes, Le Sphinx," p. 75, figs. 3, 5.

Fantastic creatures in Armenian miniature painting differ from the monsters of the mentioned French reliefs in quite a real, lively character and elastic, muscled body, reminiscent of the Eastern sphinxes. There is no doubt that Eastern features prevail in the depiction of these beasts in the miniature of the Sebastia Gospel. One should not overlook the circumstance that the examined sphinxes are framed with a vegetative pattern, where the twisting stem forms circles and branch off to decorate a segment of the parchment that serves as a background for these monsters.

Jalabert finds that this occurrence is characteristic of the iconography of the sphinxes represented in all the Eastern arts, originating from the Sassanid art.[105] The described principle is even inherent in some Roman reliefs, as the latter refer to the great trend, which spread from Sassanid Iran into Asia Minor and the Byzantine Empire, Egypt, Spain and other countries.[106]

It should be added to the remarks of Jalabert that in general the depiction of fantastic beasts on the background of plants is characteristic of the examples of ceramics from Fatimid Egypt and the Persian period of Ravi.[107] As for Islamic metal objects of the thirteenth century, in their décor the sphinxes are mainly represented on this very background.[108]

As it appears from the above stated, this is one of those cases when both the East and the West offer the artist one and the same aesthetic phenomenon; consequently, the Cilician miniaturist does not remain disinterested towards the decorative motifs that came into his field of vision.

In the miniatures of Ṙoslinian manuscripts, the type of the incomplete sphinx is not forgotten either. It appears next to sirens and lions in the headpiece of one of the canon tables (fol. 2) in the Gospel of 1262 kept in Jerusalem (Ms. 2660).[109] (Fig. 6)

---

[105] Ibid., p. 96, figs. 23, 24.

[106] Ibid., p. 101.

[107] Baer, *Sphinxes and Harpies in Medieval Islamic Art*, p. 11, fig. 18.

[108] Ibid., p. 19, note 74.

[109] Der Nersessian, *Miniature Painting in the Armenian Kingdom of Cilicia*, fig. 280.

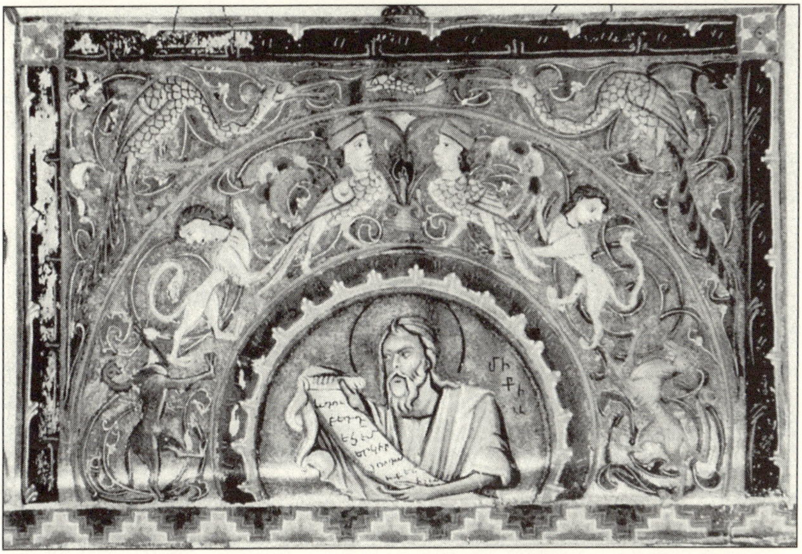

Figure 6- Letter of Eusebius (Detail), Jerusalem, Armenian Patriarchate 2660, Four Gospels, 1262 A.D., folio 2.

Here we have two wingless creatures with the face of a youth and the body of a lion that are represented symmetrically, in active motion. Having turned, they examine the dragon's heads on their tails. It should be noted that this is not the only example of the incomplete sphinx in Armenian art. Two such creatures are depicted in the reliefs of the interior in the church of the Holy Virgin at the Monastery of Makaravank (the year of 1205), but they are crowned and touch each other with their backs.[110]

Completing the study of the theme of sphinxes, we come to a conclusion that owing to this motif, the apparent hidden links between the miniatures in Ṙoslinian manuscripts and Armenian art and the book painting of the earlier times, in particular, become obvious. The examination of sphinxes in the décor of codices that have preserved the signature of T'oros Ṙoslin allows one to discover

---

[110] Patrick Donabedian, Jean Michel Thierry, Nicole Thierry, *Armenian Art* (New York: H. N. Abrams, in association with Prelacy of the Armenian Apostolic Church of America-Catholicosate of Cilicia, 1989), fig. 330.

the commonality of decoration of these manuscripts with the Cilician and, especially, Hṙomkla book painting.

Thus, peculiarities inherited by Ṙoslin and his colleagues from their teachers have been highlighted, and also it becomes clear how the masters of Ṙoslinian manuscripts outstripped their predecessors.

Comparing the works of the latter with the creations by Ṙoslin and his loyal supporters, one may become convinced that only in Ṙoslinian foliants does the depiction of sphinxes appear so frequently. There is no other Armenian miniaturist in whose decoration of codices the figures of this monster were represented in such diversity. Various forms of conveying this creature allow us to make a conclusion that the depictions of this fantastic beast had been permanently and subsequently worked out and transformed in the workshop of T'oros Ṙoslin.

It may be assumed that the motif of the sphinx had a special significance for the master. The motif of the sphinx allows one to unveil the links, which existed between Cilician manuscript painting and Persian, Arabic, Byzantine, Seljuk works, particularly, artworks that were attributed to Armenian masters or that reflected inspiration that took origin from Armenian art.

9

Un manuscrit arménien illustré du XVe siècle de la Bibliothèque nationale de France

Edda Vardanyan

Le manuscrit arménien N°18 de la Bibliothèque nationale de France (BnF, arm. 18) est un Tétraévangile copié et illustré au Vaspurakan au milieu du XVe siècle[1]. Il est un des meilleurs exemples de la production artistique des scriptoria du nord-est du Lac de Van connue, comme l'École de Van[2].

L'histoire du manuscrit figure dans son colophon principal (ff°307v°-311) écrit par le scribe Khach'atur[3]. Le manuscrit fut copié en 1456 « dans le monastère appelé Ktuts' sous la protection des églises du Saint-Précurseur [*Karapet*] et de la Sainte-Mère-de-Dieu [*Astuatsatsin*], Sainte-Croix [Surb Khach'], de Saint Grégoire l'Illuminateur, des Saintes Hripsimiennes et des autres saints rassemblés ici » (f°310).

---

1 R. H. Kévorkian, A. Ter-Stépanian, *Manuscrits arméniens de la Bibliothèque Nationale de France, Catalogue* (Paris, 1998), pp. 26-30. Les miniatures du cycle évangélique de ce manuscrit sont publiées par F. Macler, *Miniatures arméniennes, Vies du Christ* (Paris, 1913), pp. 20-21, pl. XVI-XIX.

2 F. Macler, *Miniatures arméniennes,* p. 4; S. Der Nersessian, *The Chester Beatty Library. A Catalogue of the Armenian Manuscripts,* 2 vols. (Dublin, 1958), p. XXXIII.

3 Dans le manuscrit, on dénombre trois autres colophons: du XVe s. (f°311), du XVIIe s. (f°311) et du XVIIIe s. (f°313v°), cf. Kévorkian, Ter-Stépanian, *Manuscrits arméniens*, p. 30.

L'ermitage de Ktuts' est situé sur l'île du même nom, à l'est du Lac de Van[4]. Au XVe siècle, c'est un scriptorium très actif, surtout après 1450[5]. Le scribe Khach'atur, moine de ce monastère, prie dans son colophon qu'on se souvienne de l'abbé Ewatshēn, de Step'anos K'ahanay « qui s'est donné beaucoup de peine pour affiner ce volume », de son maître le vardapet Grigor At'abekents'[6] qui lui a enseigné l'art de la calligraphie, ainsi que de ses parents et de ses frères.

Le manuscrit et copié « à la demande du bienveillant Seigneur [*tanutēr*] Yohanēs » qui n'avait pas de postérité, mais entendant la parole qui dit : « Bienheureux celui qui aura une postérité à Sion et une famille à Jérusalem » (Isaïe, 31, 9b) « il désira avoir pour postérité cette prodigieuse perle divine » et consacra sa fortune à l'acquisition de l'Évangile. Dans le colophon, on lit la demande traditionnelle de se souvenir de l'acquéreur du manuscrit et de tous ses proches (f°310).

Une grande partie du colophon est consacrée à l'enlumineur du manuscrit, le peintre Minas: « Seigneur Dieu, créateur de toutes les créatures, toi qui pares également tous les justes d'un manteau resplendissant de lumière, c'est toi qui décoreras aussi, d'une couronne d'étoiles, le peintre [Naghash] Tēr Minas, son père Makht'um, sa mère Msĕr Melik', et tous ses proches par le sang, vivants ou morts ... » (f°310v°).

Le peintre Minas est le miniaturiste le plus renommé du XVe siècle. Il a déployé une grande activité entre les années 1432 et 1483, formant des élèves et illustrant des manuscrits dans les scriptoria situés dans le bassin du Lac de Van (Aght'amar, Van, Archēsh,

---

4 Selon la tradition, l'ermitage avait été fondé par Grégoire l'Illuminateur dont les reliques étaient conservées à l'église St-Karapet du monastère, cf. H. Oskian, *Les couvents du Vaspurakan-Van,* t. 1 (Vienne, 1940), pp. 51-86 (en arménien) ; M. Thierry, *Monuments arméniens du Vaspurakan* (Paris, 1989), pp. 161-172.

5 Oskian, *Les couvents du Vaspurakan-Van* p. 58 ; *Catalogue des manuscrits du Matenadaran Mashtots' d'Erévan,* t. 1 (Erevan, 1965), p. 21 (en arménien).

6 Grigor At'abekents', moine au monastère d'Argelan, et l'un des scribes renommés du XVe s. Il travaille dans les années 1439-1478.

Argelan, Sukharavank‘, Ktuts‘, Lim)[7]. Il est le fondateur d’un nouveau style artistique d’illustration de manuscrits, qui s’implante et se développe dans la région. L’art de Minas (et par la suite des autres miniaturistes de l’École de Van), diffère à la fois des exemples antérieurs de la miniature du Vaspurakan et des manuscrits contemporains de Khizan. L’art qu’il a pratiqué peut être considéré comme une réaction contre des formes populaires en faveur d’un style plus élégant. Comparés aux critères en vigueur au Vaspurakan, ses manuscrits sont somptueux et réservés à une élite. Étroitement lié au Catholicossat d’Aght‘amar, Minas était très apprécié par ses contemporains: dans leurs colophons, les copistes font son éloge sur le plan professionnel aussi bien que personnel[8].

Dans le colophon de notre manuscrit, des paroles de louange et d’admiration sont décernées à Minas par le scribe Khach‘atur : « Je vous prie encore de vous rappeler dans vos prières le bon peintre Tēr Minas, qui est tout semblable à Beçaléel, le premier peintre de l’Arche, lui qui reçut l’Esprit. Et il est des disciples des saints vardapets T‘ovma et Mkrtich‘ Awlbekents‘. Il est compétent et inspiré, comme ses maîtres, en toute sagesse, et il est plein des grâces sept fois rayonnantes, lui qui nous a jugés dignes de le servir, qui nous a aimés d’une affection fraternelle et riche en conseils spirituels. Nous sommes restés longtemps ensemble et nous avons bénéficié de sa sagesse et de ses conseils » (ff°310v°-311).

Les vardapets susmentionnés, maîtres de Minas, sont des grands érudits de cette époque. L’une est T‘ovma Metsop‘ets‘i, éminent historiographe et pédagogue, homme de lettres, l’un des principaux initiateurs du Concile National de 1441 et du transfert du Siège

---

7 E. Vardanyan, « Catalogue des manuscrits du peintre Minas », *Revue des Études Arméniennes,* 27 (1998-1999), pp. 359-378. Parmi les élèves de Minas on trouve d’importants représentants de l’art du Vaspurakan des XVe-XVIe siècles, tels Karapet Aght‘amarats‘i, Murad *sarkawag*, Karapet Berkrets‘i.

8 L. Khach‘ikyan, *Colophons des manuscrits arméniens du XVe siècle,* vol. 2 (Erevan, 1958), pp. 135, 182, 240 (en arménien) ; E. Vardanyan, « Un *Mastoc‘* d’ordination et de sacre royal du XVe siècle », *Revue des Etudes Arméniennes*, 29 (2003-2004), pp. 210-212.

patriarcal de Sis à Etchmiadzin[9]. L'autre, Mkrtich' Ōrbēleants', est camarade d'études et compagnon de T'ovma Metsop'ets'i, prieur du monastère Tēr Yuskan Ordi. Entre 1418 et 1439, qui formé plusieurs scribes et miniaturistes, dont Grigor At'abekents' mentionné dans notre colophon. Il a lui-même copié et enluminé des manuscrits[10].

Le titre de *naghash* (Peintre) attribué à Minas dans le colophon, ainsi que la comparaison avec Beçaléel, artisan de l'Arche de l'Alliance (Exode 31, 1-11), sont conditionnés par le fait que Minas œuvre uniquement comme miniaturiste et non comme copiste[11]. Cette circonstance est soulignée dans ses signatures et dans les colophons des scribes, où il est toujours mentionné comme« « enlumineur » (*ts'aghkogh*, *nkarogh*, ou *naghash*). Ce fait le place à un niveau supérieur de la tradition arménienne de la production manuscrite et permet de qualifier Minas d'artiste « professionnel ».

L'œuvre de Minas, tout en représentant une étape nouvelle de l'enluminure du Vaspurakan, constitue le tournant qui la fait sortir des limites du style archaïsant et artisanal de l'époque précédente. L'activité de Minas est en fait l'une des expressions de l'idéologie nationale théocratique menée à cette époque par T'ovma Metsop'ets'i. Elle consiste en l'instauration de l'hégémonie ecclésiastique dans la vie arménienne par la réunification de l'Église, conditionnée également par la lutte menée contre les partisans de l'union avec l'Église catholique[12]. L'expression artistique de cette idéologie se manifeste dans le principe dogmatique de l'illustration des manuscrits avec un choix de sujets strictement défini et l'emploi de schémas iconographiques précis propres à l'art officiel. Le manuscrit BnF arm. 18 en est le meilleur exemple.

---

9 Son *Colophon* est l'unique source importante relative à ce transfert, voir T'ovma Metsop'ets'i, *Historiographie,* éd. L. Khach'ikyan (Erevan, 1999), pp. 218-275 (en arménien).

10 Le seul manuscrit à nous parvenu, enluminé par Mkrtich' Ōrbēleants', actuellement conservé au Musée d'Histoire d'Arménie (Erevan) fait l'objet d'un article en cours de préparation de l'auteur.

11 A. Mat'evosyan, *Le scriptorium de Metsop'avank aux XIIe-XVe siècles* (Etchmiadzin, 1997), p. 160 (en arménien).

12 A. Hovhannesyan, *Études de l'histoire de l'esprit d'émancipation en Arménie,* t. I (Erevan, 1957), p. 445 (en arménien).

***

Conformément à la pratique habituelle au Vaspurakan aux XIVe-XVe siècles, les treize miniatures à sujets évangéliques sont placées au début du livre, précédées par la lettre d'Eusèbe (ff°1v° - 2) et les tables de Canons décorées (ff°2v° - 6). Les miniatures de couleurs vives, dominées par le rouge et rehaussées d'or, sont entourées d'un cadre chromatique. Chaque scène s'accompagne d'une inscription contenant le titre. Elle se lit généralement en haut de la page, au-dessus du cadre des miniatures, sauf pour les scènes de la Crucifixion, de la Mise au tombeau et de la Descente aux Enfers où les inscriptions sont incluses dans le champ pictural, et occupent la partie supérieure de la composition.

Le cycle évangélique[13], où manque l'Annonciation, commence par la Nativité (f°8, Fig. 1). La miniature est accompagnée de l'inscription: «Naissance de notre Seigneur Dieu à Bethléem, ville de David ». La composition est combinée avec l'Adoration des Mages, mettant l'accent sur l'idée de la Théophanie. Par un fond doré le peintre crée l'impression de l'intérieur d'une grotte[14], dans laquelle se trouvent Marie, la mangeoire avec l'Enfant et les Mages. Le type des couronnes de ces derniers évoque les exemples ciliciens, surtout ceux du peintre Sargis Picak[15].

---

[13] La succession des scènes a été dérangée lors d'une reliure postérieure. Néanmoins, nous présentons les scènes selon la suite chronologique de la vie du Christ.

[14] La miniature des XIIIe-XIVe siècles du Vaspurakan utilise le contour dans le même but, T. Velmans, « Les miniatures inédites d'un manuscrit arménien de la région du Vaspourakan (XIVe siècle) », *Cahiers Archéologiques,* 38 (1990), p. 124.

[15] Cf. S. Der Nersessian, *Miniature Painting in the Armenian Kingdom of Cilicia (From the Twelfth to the Fourteenth Century),* 2 vols. (Washington: Dumbarton Oaks Research Library and Collection, 1993), figs. 598, 619, 623, 625, 626, 629.

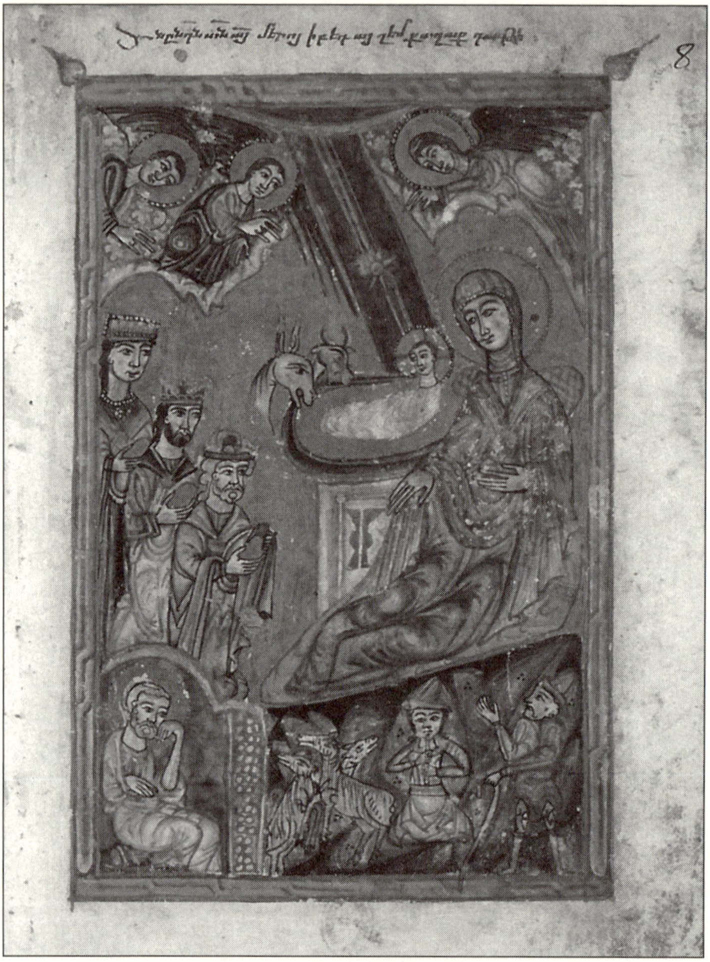

Fig. 1-Bibliothèque nationale de France.
Arm. 18, Nativité, f°8.

Les quatre personnages de la Présentation au Temple (f°11v°, Fig. 2) sont disposés symétriquement à l'intérieur du cadre, à l'exemple de l'iconographie cilicienne des XIIIe-XIVe siècles[16]. Le grand prêtre Siméon, accompagné de la prophétesse Anne, tient l'Enfant. En face de Siméon, on voit Marie et Joseph portant les

---

16 Ibid., figs. 357-361.

deux tourterelles. L'action se déroule sur un fond architectural composé de trois arcs et de colonnes, tandis qu'au-dessus de la composition trois petits édicules à toit figurent l'extérieur du temple. Entre ces éléments architecturaux se trouve l'inscription : « Venue du Seigneur Dieu dans le Temple de Salomon ».

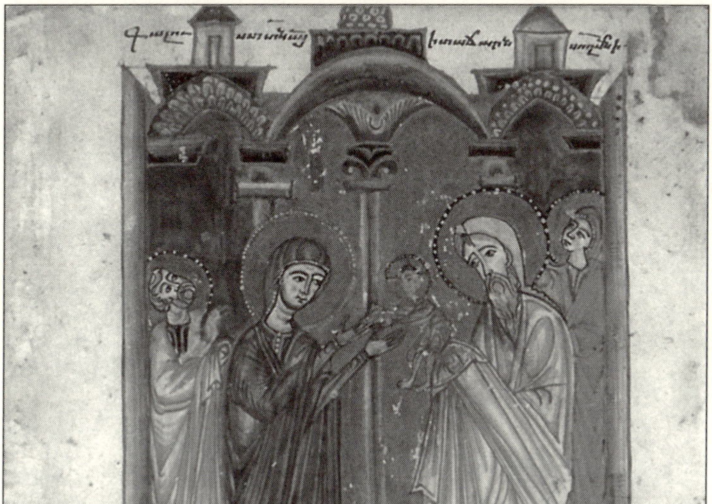

Fig. 2- Bibliothèque nationale de France.
Arm. 18, Présentation au temple, f°11v.

La scène du Baptême (f°10, Fig. 3) représente Jésus debout dans le fleuve montant jusqu'à ses épaules, formant, autour du corps, un dôme ovoïde. Cette « cloche » symbolise le Jourdain retournant en arrière[17]. Un trait arménien habituel est la représentation d'un segment de ciel avec la main de Dieu, et le Saint Esprit sous forme de colombe. La ressemblance avec les normes ciliciennes se fait jour dans l'enrichissement de la composition par le paysage, tendant ici vers la schématisation.

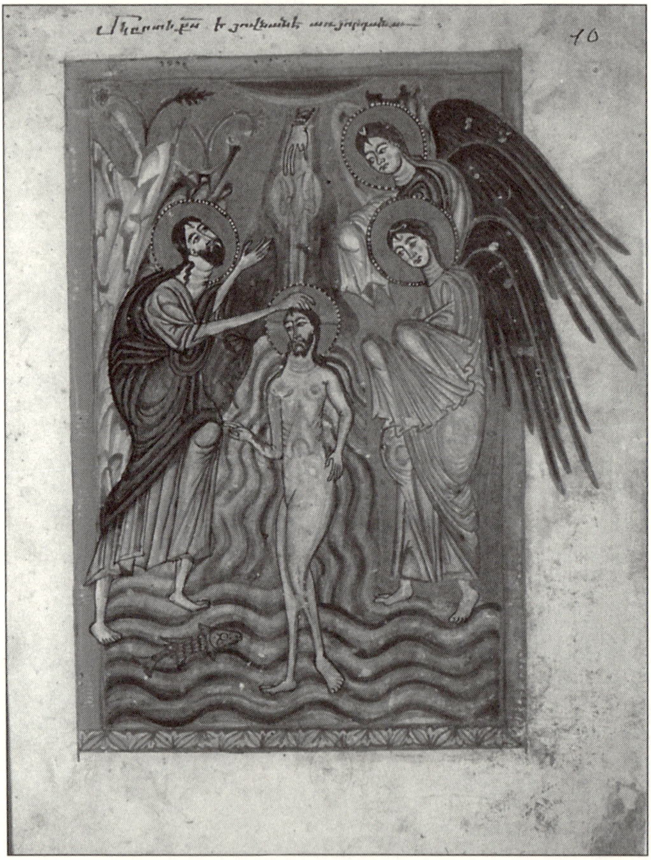

Fig. 3- Bibliothèque nationale de France.
Arm. 18, Baptême, f°10.

[17] Iconographie archaïque définie comme cappadocienne, C. Jolivet-Lévy, *Études cappadociennes* (London, 2002), pp. 186-187.

Dans la Transfiguration (f°21v°) le Christ vêtu, selon le récit évangélique, de vêtements blancs resplendissants est debout dans une mandorle ovale à fond bleu, traduisant le monde céleste. À ses côtés, les prophètes Moïse et Élie sont enveloppés aussi de deux portions d'auréoles rectangulaires d'un fond couleur feu. Dans les manuscrits de Minas, elles ont, parfois, une forme irrégulière, flamboyante[18].

La Résurrection de Lazare (f°15) représente le Christ accompagné des douze apôtres. Les Juifs sont à l'intérieur d'un petit édifice à coupole au-dessus du tombeau. La main de l'un d'entre eux sortant d'au-dessous de l'architrave est tendue vers le Christ. Ce schéma iconographique devient le trait caractéristique de l'École de Van[19].

L'Entrée à Jérusalem (f°16v°, Fig. 4), accompagnée de l'inscription « La venue du Seigneur Dieu au Temple », montre le Christ assis de face, les jambes pendant du même côté de l'âne. Ce détail rappelle singulièrement les images du caractère triomphal portant la signification symbolique d'un « avènement », caractéristiques de l'iconographie officielle[20]. Les Juifs, barbus et voilés, viennent à la rencontre de Jésus. Derrière le Christ, un rinceau réservé en blanc sur fond rouge est dessiné comme fond de la composition.

---

18 P. ex. dans le Lectionnaire de Minas de 1477, Mat 6378, f°447.

19 Dans une miniature contemporaine de 1447 d'un auteur inconnu (Nouvelle Djoulfa, Iran, ms. 559 (54), f°3), l'inscription les identifie comme étant les grands prêtres, cf. S. Der Nersessian, A. Mekhitarian, *Miniatures arméniennes d'Ispahan* (Bruxelles, 1986), fig. 88.

20 Selon André Grabar, cette attitude du Christ dans l'Entrée à Jérusalem est inspirée des formules iconographiques de l'art impérial romain, A. Grabar, *L'Empereur dans l'art byzantin* (Paris, 1936), pp. 234-236. Ce schéma iconographique figure aussi sur la reliure en ivoire de l'Évangile d'Etchmiadzin (VIe s.) et dans les manuscrits ciliciens. Au Vaspurakan, il est attesté dans les fresques d'Aght'amar.

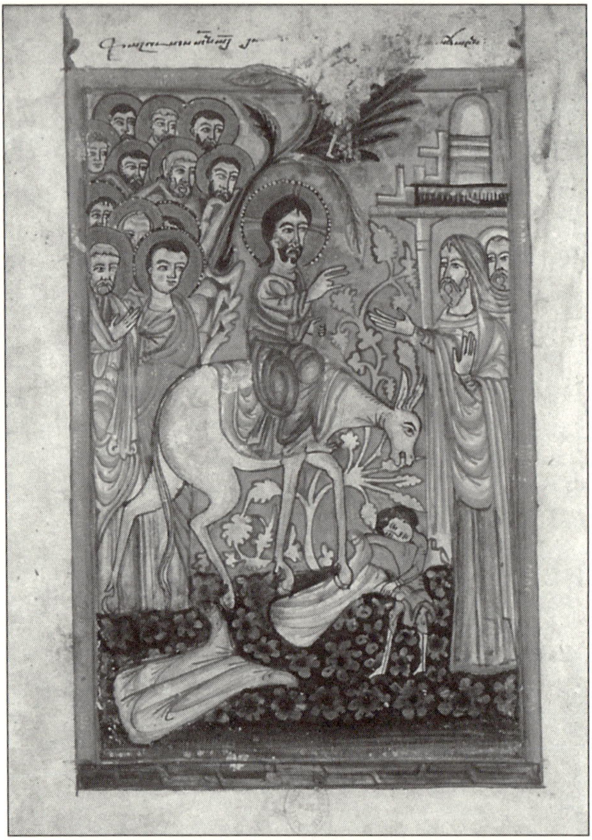

**Fig. 4- Bibliothèque nationale de France.
Arm. 18, Entrée à Jérusalem, f°18.**

Le sujet johannique du Lavement des pieds (Jean, 13, 1-17) (f°18) représente Jésus assis, en train d'essuyer le pied de Pierre. Cette iconographie, adoptée dans la miniature du Vaspurakan, remonte à la tradition orientale archaïque[21]. Au-dessus de la composition, comme dans la scène de la Présentation au Temple, deux édifices minuscules couverts de toits coniques figurent l'extérieur, tandis que l'intérieur est indiqué par un fond doré.

---

21 L. Zakaryan, *Sur l'histoire de la miniature du Vaspurakan* (Erevan, 1980), p. 52, (en russe).

La Crucifixion (f°19v°, Fig. 5) représente la variante simplifiée de la scène, avec des personnages en nombre réduit, ce qui correspond au texte de l'Évangile de Jean (Jean, 19, 25-27). Cette composition, avec la seule présence de Marie et de Jean, est spécialement caractéristique (avec des modifications insignifiantes) de l'enluminure des XVe - XVIe siècles. Pour l'illustration de notre manuscrit, Minas emprunte le type utilisé par le peintre cilicien Sargis Picak avec différentes variantes[22], où Jean est représenté sans Évangile, et où le soleil et la lune apparaissent dans le haut de la miniature. La légende, entrecoupée par le soleil et la lune, porte: « Le Dieu crucifié».

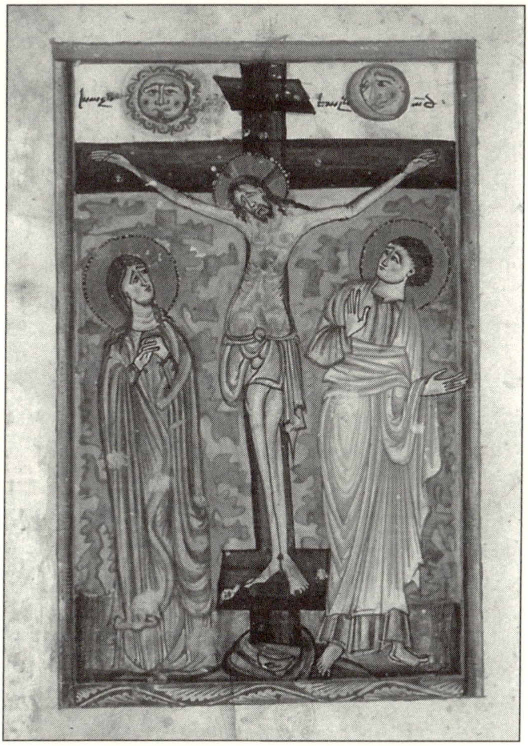

Fig. 5- Bibliothèque nationale de France.
Arm. 18, Crucifixion, f°19v°.

[22] Der Nersessian, *Miniature Painting* …, fig. 602.

La scène de la Mise au tombeau (f°13, Fig. 6) témoigne de la composition symétrique, adoptée par les peintres du Vaspurakan au XVe siècle. Joseph d'Arimathie et Nicodème, vêtus de tuniques à manches courtes, allongent le corps du Christ sur une dalle de pierre disposée devant la croix. La grande croix au fond de l'image est l'un des symboles du Second Avènement du Christ[23]. Cette scène qui remplace à la fois la Descente de la Croix et le Thrène (Lamentation sur le Christ) n'a plus de rôle narratif et représente un thème symbolique[24]. La composition de la scène est une modification du type employé au XIVe siècle par les peintres ciliciens, notamment par Sargis Picak[25]. La légende placée dans le cadre de la miniature porte la mention: « Sépulture du Seigneur Dieu dans le tombeau neuf ».

---

23 Der Nersessian, *The Chester Beatty Library,* p. 61.

24 Les deux scènes sont présentes dans les manuscrits byzantins à cycle narratif. À partir des XIe-XIIIe siècles, dans l'iconographie byzantine, la Mise au tombeau est remplacée par le Thrène. On remarque l'évolution de cette scène narrative vers une image liturgique par une tendance dont le but est de donner à la miniature la signification d'une icône, K. Weitzmann « The Origin of the Threnos, » dans *Byzantine Book Illumination and Ivories* (London, 1987), IX, pp. 476-490.

25 Dans l'Évangile de 1346 de Sargis Picak (Jérusalem, Bibliothèque Saint Jacques, ms. 1973, f°79v°), le corps du Christ est placé dans un sarcophage, Der Nersessian, *Miniature Painting ...,* fig. 603. Minas modifie ce schéma: le sarcophage a disparu et le corps du Christ est placé sur une dalle en pierre.

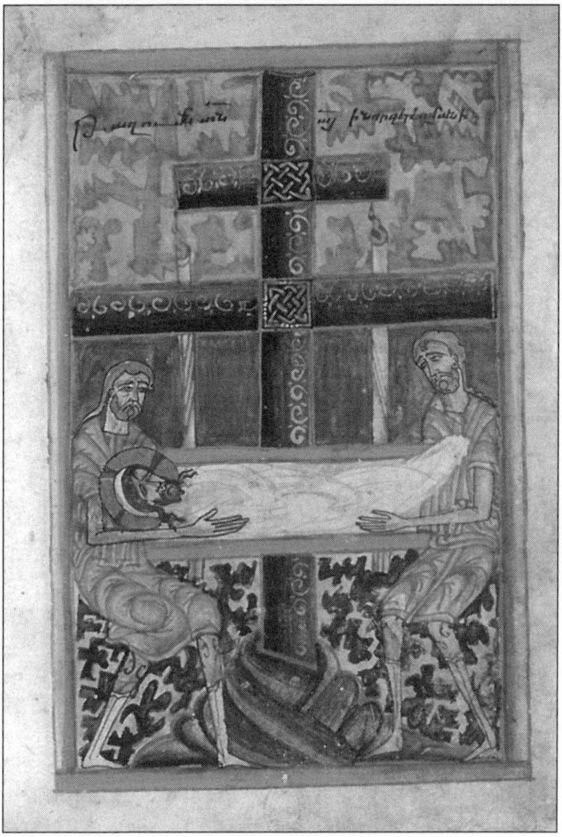

Fig. 6- Bibliothèque nationale de France.
Arm. 18, Mise au tombeau, f°13.

La Descente aux enfers (f°13v°, Fig. 7) intitulée « La destruction de l'enfers et la libération des âmes » est la plus remarquable enluminure du manuscrit. Elle représente Jésus assis, armé de la croix de la Résurrection à double traverse, au centre de la composition. Les pieds posés sur les portes brisées de l'enfer, il saisit Adam, accompagné de deux femmes dont l'une est Ève[26]. À droite,

[26] La présence de deux femmes à côté d'Adam est assez fréquente dans la miniature du Vaspurakan au XVe siècle. La femme placée derrière Ève, vêtue de la même façon qu'elle, se substitue, selon toute probabilité, à Abel, Der Nersessian, *The Chester Beatty Library*, p. 77.

Jean-Baptiste et les rois Salomon et David sont représentés dans le tombeau. La composition est intéressante en raison de l'attitude assise du Christ. Cette attitude évoque la représentation du Christ Trônant dans la scène de sa Seconde Venue. Le parallélisme du caractère triomphal des deux scènes est connu dans l'art byzantin aussi bien que dans l'art cilicien[27]. Ici, cette attitude du Christ se rencontre aussi dans la représentation des donateurs placés près du Christ, qui implique en fait le Second Avènement du Sauveur. Dans notre miniature, Minas souligne avec une force particulière le caractère triomphal de la Descente aux enfers, en lui attribuant une interprétation eschatologique.

[27] Comme exemples, on peut citer la mosaïque byzantine du XIIe siècle de la basilique de Torcello et l'Évangile de 1262 (Walters Art Gallery, ms. 539, f°109v°) enluminé par T'oros Roslin (S. Der Nersessian, *Miniature Painting ...*, fig. 222). A. Grabar considère la scène de la Descente aux enfers comme une composition symbolique, dont certains éléments reprennent des formules iconographiques de l'art impérial romain. Il note également des parallèles entre les scènes de la Descente aux enfers et du Second Avènement du Christ, Grabar, *L'Empereur dans l'art byzantin,* pp. 24, 245-250.

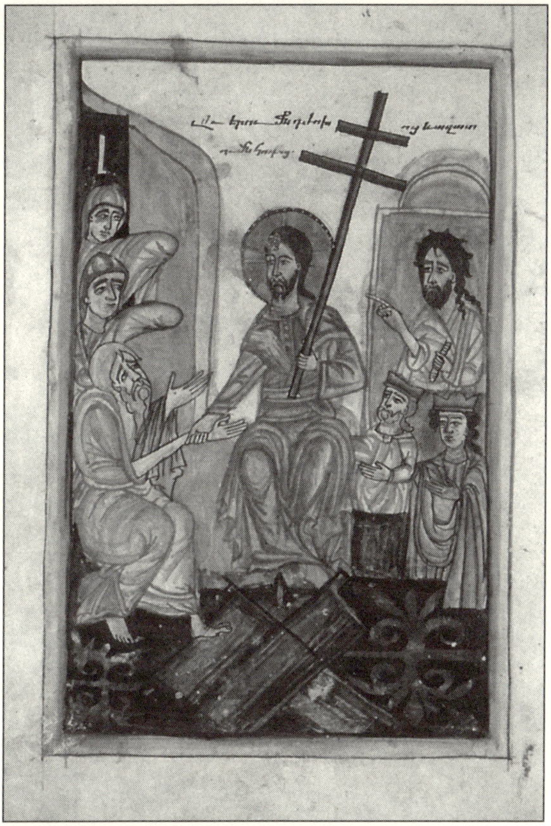

Fig. 7- Bibliothèque nationale de France.
Arm. 18, Descente aux enfers, f°13v°.

La composition habituelle de la Résurrection (f°25) avec les trois femmes *myrrophores* est enrichie par une draperie, reposant sur de fines colonnes dans la partie supérieure de la composition. Elle indique, probablement, le rideau du temple, motif courant au Vaspurakan à la période antérieure qu'on représentait sous des formes très réalistes, accompagné d'inscriptions[28]. Les soldats, coiffés de bonnets phrygiens, sont groupés en bas de la composition,

---

[28] Velmans, « Les miniatures inédites d'un manuscrit arménien de la région du Vaspourakan (XIVe siècle)», p. 137, fig. 20 ; Der Nersessian, *The Chester Beatty Library,* Pl. 35b.

très serrés, ne formant qu'un seul corps avec quatre têtes. Cette tendance à la stylisation se manifeste déjà dans la miniature cilicienne des XIIIe-XIVe siècles, conservant toutefois les traits réalistes[29]. Dans la miniature du Vaspurakan, cette formule inaugurée par Minas devient habituelle dans l'œuvre de ses élèves et successeurs. L'enluminure est accompagnée de la légende « Résurrection du Seigneur Dieu du tombeau neuf ».

La scène de l'Ascension (f°23v°, Fig. 8) porte la légende « Notre Seigneur est enlevé au ciel ». Par l'attitude du Christ, bénissant des deux mains, Minas répète, une fois de plus, le schéma utilisé par les peintres ciliciens des XIIIe-XIVe siècles, symbolisant le Second Avènement du Christ[30]. Des rinceaux fleuris à la place des arbres à côté de la Vierge distinguent notre miniature des compositions habituelles[31]. Le paysage figurant sous la forme d'un motif floral perd son sens initial et se sert d'un élément décoratif pour exprimer la joie[32].

---

[29] Der Nersessian, *Miniature Painting* ..., fig. 365.

[30] Ce geste du Christ est habituel dans les images du Jugement dernier et dans les portraits des donateurs auprès du Christ trônant, Der Nersessian, *Miniature Painting* ..., figs. 222, 641, 654.

[31] Les arbres à côté de la Vierge sont caractéristiques de l'iconographie byzantine, J. Beckwith, *Early Christian and Byzantine Art* (London: Penguin, 1970), fig. 162 ; N. Thierry, « À propos de l'Ascension d'Ayvali Kilise et de celle de Sainte-Sophie de Salonique», dans *Peintures d'Asie Mineure et de Transcaucasie aux Xe et XIe siècles* (London: Variorum Reprints, 1977), IV, p. 153.

[32] La transformation du paysage en un motif décoratif est propre à la miniature du Vaspurakan, cf. l'Évangile de 1455 (Walters Art Gallery, ms. 543) enluminé par le peintre Khach'atur à Khizan, école où cette manière de décoration est assez fréquente, S. Der Nersessian, *Armenian Manuscripts in the Walters Art Gallery* (Baltimore, 1973), pls. 86-95, 107.

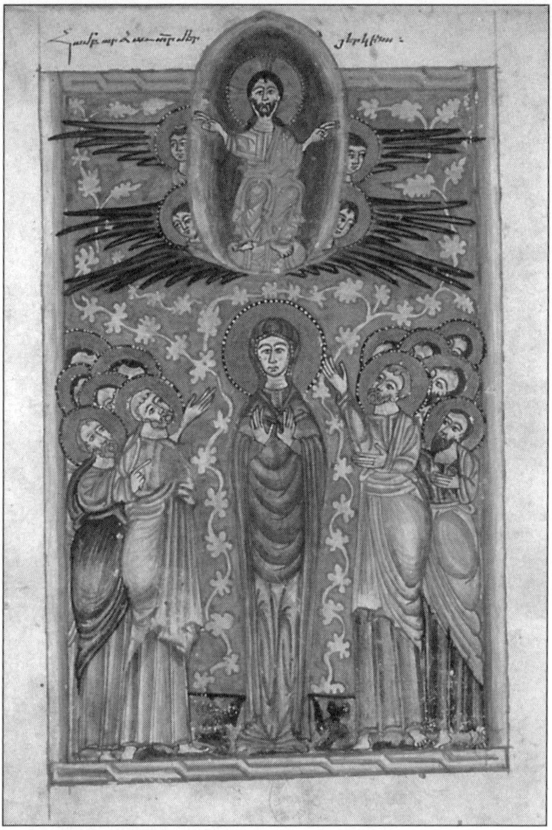

Fig. 8- Bibliothèque nationale de France.
Arm. 18, Ascension, f°23v°.

La Pentecôte (f° 27, Fig. 9) est intitulée « La venue du Saint-Esprit parmi les Saints Apôtres ». Les apôtres siègent sur deux registres horizontaux superposés[33]. La colombe du Saint-Esprit plane

[33] L'emplacement des apôtres sur deux niveaux de hauteur suit la formule courante à cette période. La miniature arménienne d'un Évangile du XVe siècle (Bibliothèque nationale de France, ms. syr. 344) est très semblable, mais elle dispose les apôtres sur deux colonnes verticales, Macler, *Miniatures arméniennes, Vies du Christ,* pl. 26, fig. 60. On rencontre le même schéma sur la porte en bois sculpté de l'église des Saints-Apôtres de Sévan, datée de 1486.

au-dessus des figures, et des rayons vont de la colombe aux apôtres. Le cynocéphale placé sous l'arc de la porte parmi les peuples venus à Jérusalem répète la variante des manuscrits ciliciens[34].

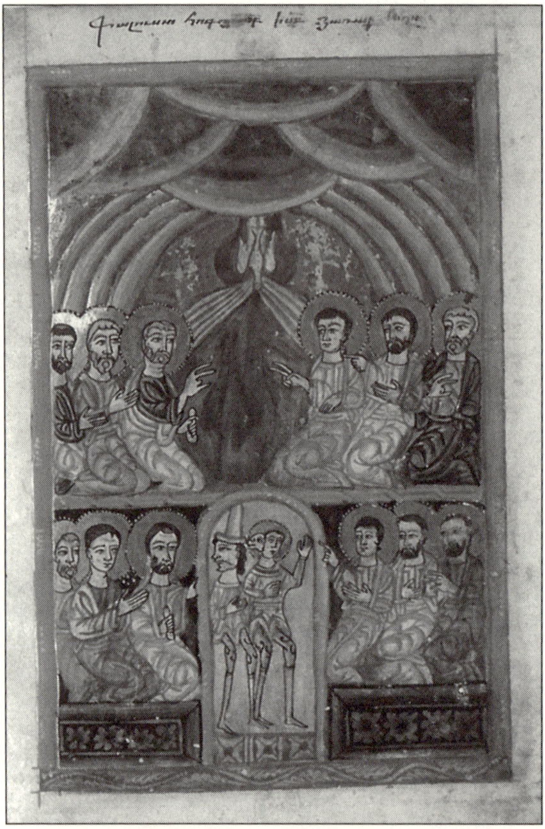

Fig. 9-Bibliothèque nationale de France.
Arm. 18, Pentecôte, f°27.

---

[34] D. Kouymjian, « The Problem of the Zoomorphic Figure in the Iconography of Armenian Pentecost: a Preliminary Report », dans *Atti del primo simposio internazionale di arte Armena* (Venise, 1978), pp. 403-413; Otto F. Meinardus, « Der Kynokephalos in der armenischen Pfingst-Ikonographie », *Revue des Études Arméniennes,* 20 (1996-1997), pp. 427-439.

Ainsi, il s'agit d'un cycle évangélique soumis à la signification dogmatique des enluminures. Cela s'exprime premièrement dans le choix des scènes évangéliques constituées par les fêtes principales. Les scènes narratives secondaires, comme les miracles et les guérisons, qui enrichissaient auparavant le cycle évangélique des manuscrits du Vaspurakan sont exclues. Les scènes de la vie du Christ sont représentées moins dans un style narratif que selon leur essence symbolique et rituelle.

Dans l'illustration du texte de l'Évangile, la préférence est donnée à Jean. Cela est attesté par la présence de Nicodème dans l'épisode de la Mise au tombeau (Jean, 19, 25-27, 38-42), et par le Lavement des pieds (Jean, 13, 1-12). C'est de là que sont empruntées les inscriptions accompagnant les scènes de la Résurrection et de la Mise au tombeau: « La Résurrection du Seigneur dans le tombeau neuf » (Jean, 19, 41). On remarque aussi l'influence du texte rituel et théologique : l'inscription « Le Dieu crucifié» qui accompagne la scène de la Crucifixion correspond aux passages des hymnes [*Sharakan*] lus pendant la messe à l'occasion de la fête de la Sainte-Croix[35].

Il faut noter que les Évangéliaires de Minas incluent souvent des sujets de l'Ancien Testament (le Sacrifice d'Abraham, l'Arbre de Jessé et la Vision d'Ézéchiel) et les scènes eschatologiques (la Seconde Venue du Christ, la Croix Triomphale et le Jugement Dernier). Bien qu'absentes dans notre manuscrit, ces scènes ont une grande place dans l'œuvre de Minas et deviennent caractéristiques de l'École de Van[36]. Exprimant les idées formant l'axe de l'Évangile, à savoir l'Incarnation, le Sacrifice et la Seconde Venue du Christ, elles servent à constituer une chaîne logique comprenant les scènes de la vie du Christ, porteuse de l'idée du Salut[37]. Ce schéma d'illustration

---

35 A. Renoux, « La croix dans le rite arménien, histoire et symbolisme », *Melto, recherches orientales* (Kaslik-Liban, 1969), N°1, pp. 123-175.

36 Edda Vardanyan, « Catalogue des manuscrits du peintre Minas ». Pour les scènes eschatologiques et vétérotestamentaires dans les manuscrits de l'École de Van, voir S. Der Nersessian, « An Armenian Gospel of the Fifteenth Century », dans *Études byzantines et arméniennes* (Louvain, 1973), pp. 683-694.

37 L'orientation liturgique des miniatures de Minas est plus accentuée dans ses illustrations des manuscrits rituels.

des manuscrits constitue le caractère dogmatique des enluminures de Minas.

Chaque évangile de notre manuscrit commence par le portrait en pleine page de son auteur: Matt'ieu f°28v°, Marc f°108v°, Luc f°160v°, Jean f°244v°. Les types des évangélistes, leurs attitudes et les accessoires sont traditionnels : Matt'ieu et Luc écrivent (Fig. 11), Marc médite, Jean dicte à Prochore (Fig. 10). Les pages de titre (ff° 30, 110, 162, 246) présentent une grande variété dans le choix et la manière de combiner les motifs, une adaptation parfaite au cadre, des compositions claires et harmonieuses, un dessin précis et une science du coloris qui fait chatoyer les couleurs sur un fond d'or. La première lettre de chaque évangile est formée par le symbole de l'évangéliste. Ainsi, l'ange de Matt'ieu tient à bras tendu un rouleau, sa main gauche retient l'extrémité de son aile, formant la lettre Գ (Fig. 12); pour Marc un lion et un bœuf nimbés, liés par la queue et tenant les livres des évangiles, dessinent la lettre Ս; le bœuf de saint Luc forme la lettre Ք; l'aigle de Jean tenant un livre dans son bec s'incline pour former la boucle de la lettre Ի. Les lettres de la première ligne sont ornithomorphes ou ornées d'entrelacs. Dans la marge droite est placé une sorte de long candélabre végétal, dont les feuilles enlacées sont surmontées d'une croix. Les initiales des chapitres représentent souvent un oiseau dans une attitude donnée, selon la forme de la lettre.

Les miniatures marginales sont très nombreuses. Monochromes et composées surtout d'éléments floraux, de sirènes et d'oiseaux, elles apparaissent en moyenne toutes les trois ou quatre pages. Il y a quelques ornements marginaux se rapportant au texte. Contrairement aux autres, ils sont colorés et rehaussés d'or. Dans les quatre Évangiles, il s'agit d'un petit ciborium qui figure le temple de Jérusalem (ff°87, 145, 227v°, 276), d'une myrophore nimbée d'or qui se tient debout, portant un vase dans ses mains tendues (ff°104, 302), et de Joseph d'Arimathie en buste sous les traits d'un vieillard, nimbé d'or, les mains voilées (ff°155v°, 238).

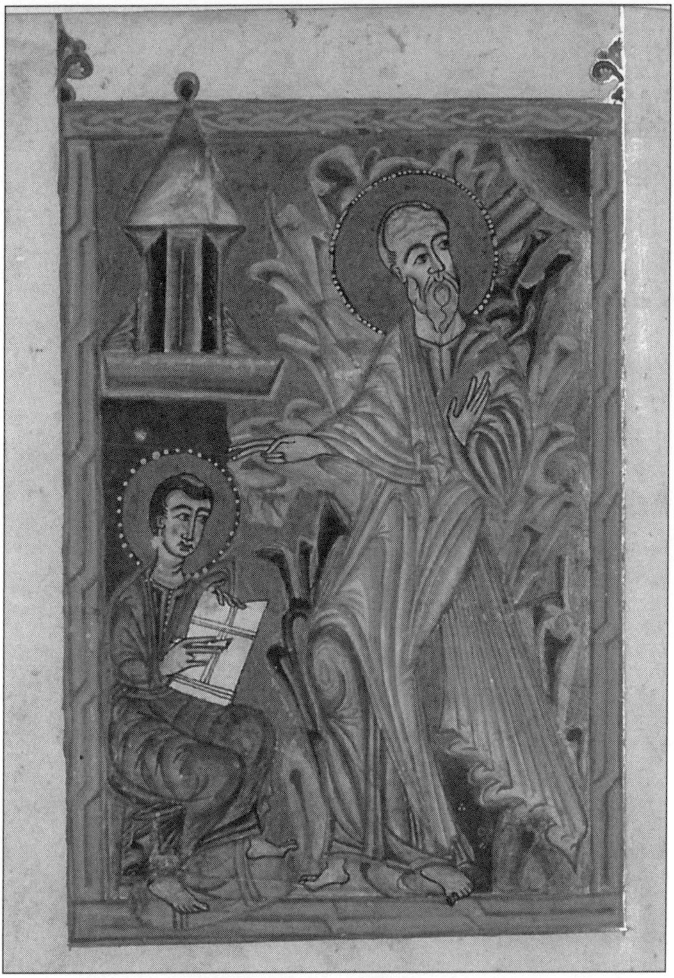

Fig. 10-Bibliothèque nationale de France.
Arm. 18, Evangéliste Jean dictant à Prochore, f°244v.

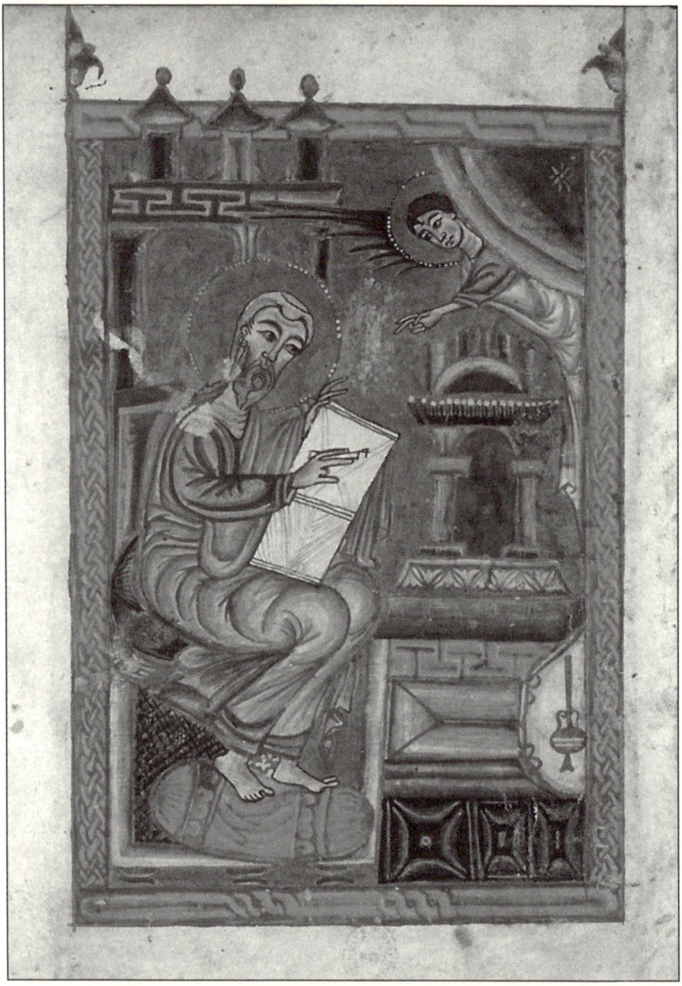

**Fig. 11-Bibliothèque nationale de France.
Arm. 18, Evangéliste Matt'ieu , f°28v°.**

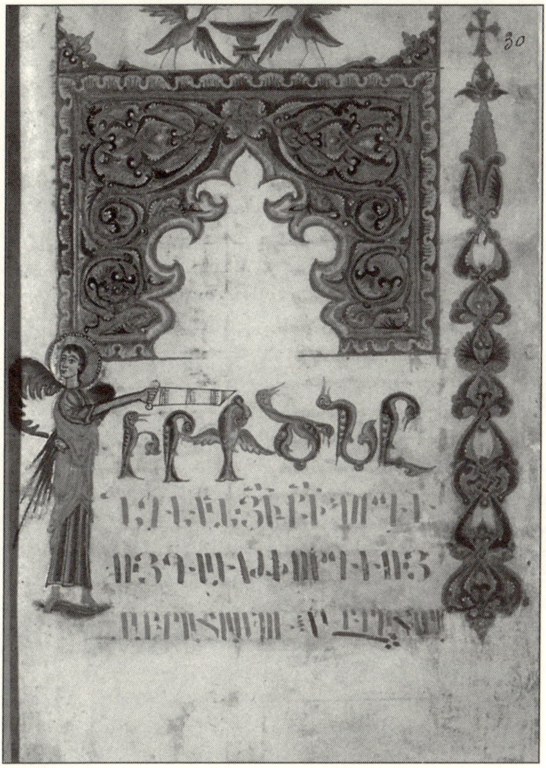

Fig. 12-Pages de titre l'Evangile de Matt'ieu , f°30.

***

L'année 1456 où Minas a enluminé ce manuscrit représente une période importante dans l'œuvre du peintre[38]. En effet cette période marque un tournant dans l'évolution et les options à venir de son style et de sa manière artistique, malgré la communauté stylistique

38 L'enluminure de notre manuscrit manifeste beaucoup d'affinités avec les autres miniatures de Minas de cette période, celles des Évangéliaires de 1455 (Jérusalem, Bibliothèque Saint Jacques, ms. 3815), de 1456 (Erevan, Maténadaran, ms. 5629), de 1461 (New York, Pierpont Morgan Library, ms. 749) et du Lectionnaire *Chashots'* de 1460 (Erevan, Maténadaran, ms. 982).

relative qui caractérise l'École de Van. À cette époque Minas est déjà célèbre au Vaspurakan. Ses manuscrits manifestant une exécution remarquablement habile, il reçoit des commandes importantes et prestigieuses[39].

Les traits individuels et les particularités d'expression de l'art de Minas sont évidents dans notre manuscrit. Les compositions sont simples et montrent un désir marqué de disposition symétrique. Dans certaines scènes, le miniaturiste abrège le groupe de personnages, souhaitant donner à sa composition un caractère équilibré et achevé. Parfois, le peintre rompt la stabilité limitée du cadre de la miniature : une partie de la composition sort dans la marge, comme les constructions architecturales voûtées des scènes de la Présentation au temple et du Lavement des pieds, la mandorle du Christ dans la Transfiguration et dans l'Ascension, l'arbre dans l'Entrée à Jérusalem et les ailes de l'ange dans le Baptême.

Les proportions des figures sont élancées, silhouettes étroites à petites têtes. Cette manière distingue Minas des autres représentants de l'École de Van. Les visages des personnages, travaillés à l'aide d'ombres, aux grands yeux en amande, ont un contour allongé et portent le sceau d'une légère mélancolie.

Les accessoires sont souvent conventionnels et stylisés, telles la table dans la Présentation au temple et les armes des soldats dans la Résurrection. Dans certains cas, ils sont à peine reconnaissables, tels les bancs sur lesquels sont assis les apôtres dans les scènes de la Pentecôte et du Lavement des pieds. Le même schématisme s'observe dans les paysages. Les stylisations sont souvent employées pour rendre les scènes plus laconiques et les compositions plus compactes. On le voit parfaitement à la manière de représenter les soldats dans la scène de la Résurrection.

Néanmoins, la tendance de l'artiste à user d'ornements est évidente. Parfois, il en couvre tout le fond de la miniature. Dans les scènes de la Crucifixion, de la Résurrection de Lazare et de la Mise

---

39 Le cercle de ses commanditaires inclut principalement des hauts dignitaires d'Église (archevêques, évêques, supérieurs de monastères, moines éminents), des représentants de la couche moyenne des citadins, qui jouent un rôle important dans la vie politique du Vaspurakan et qui constituent le soutien social du Catholicossat d'Aght'amar, E. Vardanyan, « Catalogue des manuscrits du peintre Minas ».

au tombeau, Minas emploie un ornement géométrique de forme brusque et irrégulière, qui renforce le caractère dramatique des scènes. Par contre, les floraisons de l'Entrée à Jérusalem et de l'Ascension apportent de la joie aux miniatures.

La gamme chromatique, saturée de couleurs denses et d'or, est dominée par le rouge dont les diverses nuances, harmonieusement assemblées, rendent reconnaissable le style de Minas. L'or, généralement peu fréquent dans la miniature du Vaspurakan, est utilisé ici en grande quantité comme dans les autres manuscrits de Minas.

Il faut noter l'influence fortement exprimée de l'art cilicien (principalement de Sargis Picak, comme nous l'avons vu) sur l'œuvre de Minas. Mais cette influence est loin d'être unilatérale, elle se présente comme une approche repensée de l'art cilicien, fondée sur les traditions locales. Le contact de l'art somptueux de la Cilicie adoucit le style de Minas tout en lui conférant une nuance de distinction. Il conserve une certaine sécheresse, habituelle dans l'enluminure du Vaspurakan.

On pourrait motiver cette influence par l'existence d'un grand nombre de manuscrits ciliciens au monastère d'Aght'amar, où ils étaient très appréciés[40]. Mais le fait d'être attiré par les critères ciliciens n'est pas simplement affaire de préférence artistique, mais également de situation politique créée dans le pays. À cette époque au Vaspurakan resurgit la question de la restauration de la souveraineté et de la royauté, et le Royaume arménien de Cilicie est perçu comme l'incarnation de l'auto-conscience politique[41]. En outre, l'idéologie théocratique incarnée à cette époque par Tovma Metsop'ets'i et l'activation des intérêts nationaux dans le milieu ecclésiastique, couronnées par la réinstallation du Siège patriarcal à Etchmiadzin, aboutissent à l'aspiration de l'art vers une expression nationale, « étatique », ayant une valeur officielle. Notre peintre, élève de T'. Metsop'ets'i, est l'initiateur de cette aspiration.

---

40 Mat'evosyan, *Le scriptorium de Metsop'avank,* p. 153.

41 La tentative de la restauration de la royauté des Arcrunis au Vaspurakan, conçue au sein du Catholicossat d'Aght'amar, ainsi que le rôle du peintre Minas dans cet événement historique font l'objet d'un article inédit de l'auteur.

Le caractère novateur de l'art de Minas conduit à une conception et à une interprétation originales de l'influence subie, tandis que la synthèse de diverses traditions crée une nouvelle qualité dans l'enluminure du Vaspurakan. La révélation du contexte théologique des miniatures et la continuité de ses traditions artistiques par ses successeurs, justifient le caractère « professionnel » de l'art du peintre Minas, « semblable à Beçaléel ».

A Phylactery of St. Phokas

Helmut Buschhausen

In 2006, a dealer of antiquities in Vienna offered a small phylactery of blue glass (3.7 to 4.1 cm. in diameter) with the mark of St. Phokas (Fig. 1) of Sinope, at the southern shore of the Black Sea.

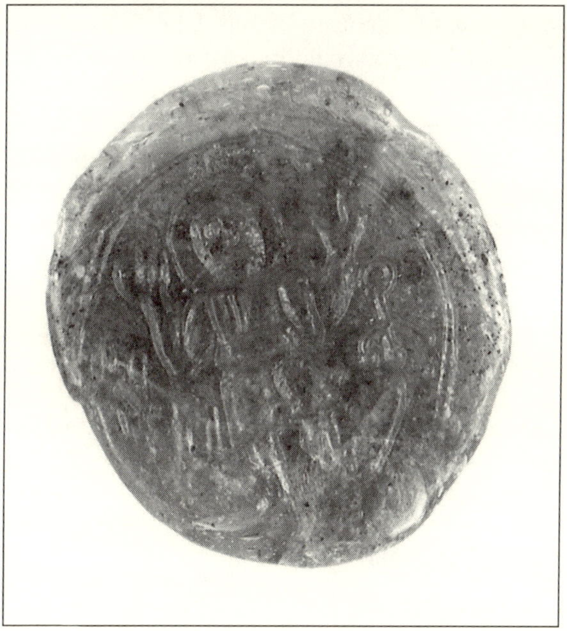

Fig. 1-Mainz, Römisch-Germanisches Zentralmuseum, Phylactery of glass with St. Phokas.

St. Phokas was the patron Saint of the Black Sea. The beardless Saint is represented in enlarged scale and standing in the pose of an

Orans in the middle of a little ship. He is dressed in a short tunic and a chlamys. The ship has rudders and oars at the after-body, beside the fore-body there is an unidentified object: a rod on three feet and a ring at the top. The object has been interpreted by G. Vikan as a lamp's pedestal on three-feet as a part of a holy shrine, but perhaps it can be seen as a spherical boy similar to the upper part of the Pharos of Alexandria in a sixth century mosaic at Qasr el Lebia.[1]

The mark of St. Phokas influenced another image on a stamp in the Walters Art Gallery in Baltimore, with the negative stamp of St. Isidor of Chios, the patron of the sailors of the Mediterranean Sea and the city of Venice. He came from Alexandria and was tortured and beheaded under the emperor Decius. St. Isidor holds in his left hand a spear and in his fullness of power with his right hand, the mast of a little ship. To the left a small sanctuary can be seen with a cross on the top and a chalice inside, determined as a sanctuary by the abbreviation of the name of Jesus Christ above the top. The stamp of St. Isidor is negative and was used for eulogia of Bread or small flasks of oil.

To my knowledge there is only one picture of St. Phokas with the same iconography.[2] In 1896 a small stamp was found in Chersonnes on the Crimea and was interpreted as a bread stamp for Eulogion (Fig. 2).

---

[1] A. Alföldi Rosenbaum, "Justinianic pavements in Cyrenaic churches," *Monografie di archeologia Libica XIV* (Rome, 1978), pl. 17, 1.

[2] O.B. Ošarina, "O simboličeskom zamlysle glinjanoj eblogii s izobraženlem sv. Foki iz sobranija Ermitaža," *Anticnaja drevnosti srednie veka*, Bypusk 34 (St. Petersburg, 2003), pp. 54-63; Cat. *Iskusstvo Vizantii v Sobrinjah SSSR* (Moscow, 1977), no. 198; André Grabar, *Martyrium: Recherches sur le culte des reliques et l'art Chrétien antique* (Paris, 1946), II, pp. 106, 344, fig. 138; G. Vikan, *Byzantine Pilgrimage Art* (Washington D.C., 1982), p. 13f., fig. 6; N. Malicki, "Glinyj Gružok is Hersonesa s Izobraženiem sv. Foki," *Materialy po Russkomu Isskustvu*, I (St. Petersburg, 1918), pp. 1-9.; M. G. Kolesnikova, "Hram v Rajone Hersonesa (raskopi 1963-1965 gg)," *Vizatijiskij Vremenik* 39 (1978), pp. 160-172, fig. 13; V. Lautšev, "Etud po vizantijskoj epigrafik," *Drevnosti južnoj Rosii* 23 (1899), 30ff.=*Vizantijskij Vremenik* 6 (1899), pp. 337-369, dort 344.

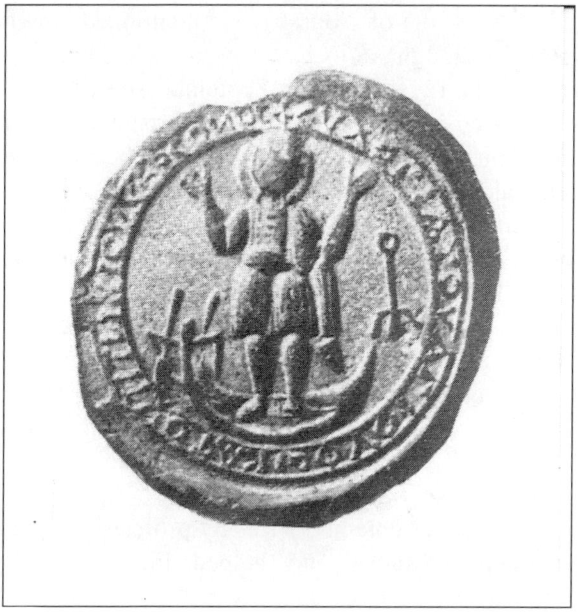

Fig. 2-Bread stamp of Chersonnes with Phokas.

Many similar but negative stamps had been discovered, one with St. George in Chersonnes, one with St. Peter and Andreas in Smyrna, now in the Kunsthistorisches Museum of Vienna, another one with St. Peter and Paul from the Basilica of St. Demetrios in Thessalonika. All of these stamps are negative and a positive of the picture was seen after use on the bread[3] or flask on tone, but the piece with St. Phokas found in Chersonnes is positive and therefore not a stamp for bread, but a model for the Eulogian stamp, which was discovered in Chersonnes in 1964.[4] The inscription on the stamp mentions the Eulogion of Phokas, the patron of the House of alms in Chersonnes:

Εὐ(λο)γία τοϋ ἁγίου Φωκᾶ τοῦ πιωχ(ε)ίου Χερσ(ῶ)υος

Three saints with the name Phokas are known to us:

---

[3] G. Galvaris, *Bread and the Liturgy* (Madison, Milwaukee, London, 1970), p. 128.

[4] L.G. Kolesnikova, "Hram v portovom rajone Xersonesa," *Vizantijskij Vremenik* 29 (1978), pp. 170, 13.

1) The first (5th of March) is mentioned in occidental martyrologies. He died in Antioch.

2) The second (21st/22nd of September) was the bishop of Sinope. He was said to be the son of a ship carpenter. On the mosaics of San Marco in Venice (thirteenth century), he is at the rudder. After a juridical examination by the praefectus Africanus, he was sent to the emperor Trajan.[5] Finally he was beheaded and the Menologion of Emperor Basil II is representing the martyrium.[6] He belonged to the canon of Byzantine saints of the city of Constantinople and was represented on ivories of the 10th to 12th centuries. The head of Phokas was transferred to the main city and he was mentioned by Ioannes Chrysostomos (PG 50, 699-706). The emperor Nikophoros Phokas built a church in honor of Phokas in Constantinople, but Herakleios dedicated the church to the Evangelist John.

3) The third (22nd September) was by profession a gardener. He had a beneficent character and helped the poor. He showed hospitality to the police spies one day before the soldiers arrested him. He was martyred, after suffering many tortures; he found his death in an overheated bathroom. At the beginning of the fifth century Asteios of Amaseia wrote a panegyric sermon on Phokas, perhaps at his anniversary in front of his tomb in Sinope. In this sermon he mentions the use of phylacteries.

In the middle-Byzantine period he is included in the canon of bishops, in the Apsis of Neredica near Novgorod from 1189. Asteios mentions in his sermon (PO 40, 303), that travelers of Phokas' ship have saved one of the daily meals to sell it to the ship's crew and afterwards to offer the income from it to the Saint. The church with its tomb was in Sinope, and was very wealthy, but a part of the income was used for the poor. Ado mentions that a part of the relic was transferred from Vienna (PL 128, 82) to France.

Van den Vorst[7] believes that the two Saints with the name of Phokas were duplicates and in reality one person only.

---

[5] T. Freudenberger, "Die Auswirkungen kaiserlicher Politik und die Ausbreitung des Christentums bis zu Diokletian," *Kirchengeschichte als Missionsgeschichte*, I (München, 1974), p. 134.

[6] Rome, Bibl. Vat., cod. gr. 1613, fol. 58r.

[7] Van der Vorst, "Saint Phokas," *Analecta Bollandiana 30* (1911), pp. 152-195. There the translation of the Armenian passio by P. Peeters, 190ff.

The church of St. Phokas had been discovered at Çiftlik, 10 km to the south of Sinope, and excavated from 1993 to 1997 (Fig. 3).[8]

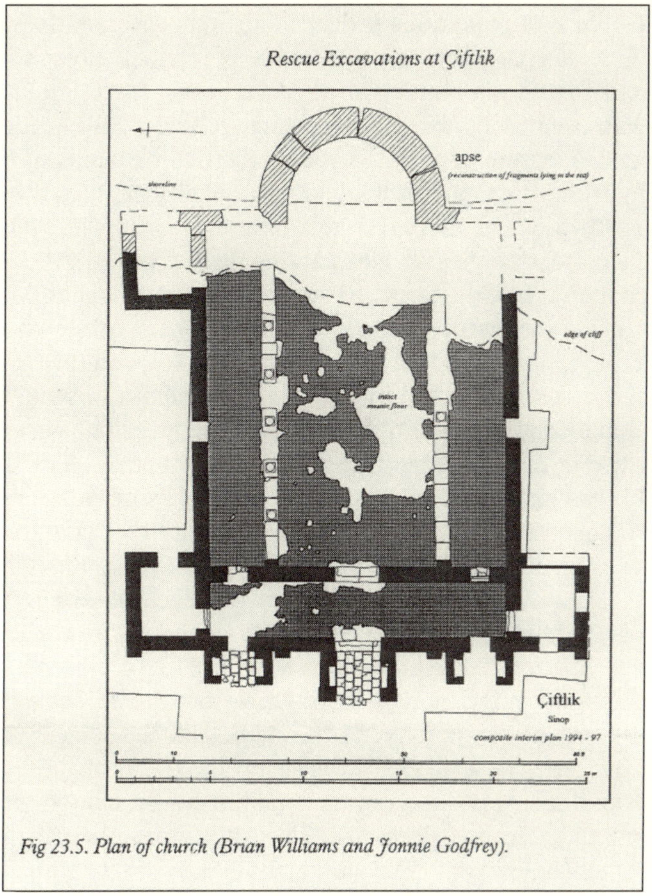

Fig. 3-Çiftlik. Basilica of the Church of Phokas.

The church was built on the shore of the Black Sea. Its eastern part with the apse was destroyed by the water of the Black Sea. Parts of the west and south are badly damaged, but some surviving

---

[8] St. Hill, "Rescue excavations at Çiftlik (Sinop)," *Ancient Anatolia: Fifty Year's Work by the British Institute of Archaeology at Ankara*, ed. R. Matthews (London, 1998), pp. 285-300. Fig. 23.2, 23.5, 23.6, 23.4.

fragments made it possible to reconstruct the apse. The entire building was damaged twice by earthquakes during the time of construction. The whole church seems to have been built on a cliff and therefore in a precarious spot. Perhaps this was the place where the Saint was martyred, but his tomb or chapel have not been discovered.

St. Hill excavated a basilica with three naves, a gallery cut out of Proconnesian marble, a mosaic with geometric ornaments of the end of the fourth century, a narthex and four-sided chambers projecting from the narthex and the naves to south and north. The whole has resemblance to churches of Constantinople and not to Asia Minor, but to Bulgaria. In Odessa, K. Škorpil excavated churches with side chambers in Djanavar-tepe and in the older phase of the church of Pirinitsch-tepe; the first has been built in the fifth century, the first phase of the second is dated by coins in the time of Constantine I.[9] A single nave church with side chambers presents Nr. 32 of Binbirkilise in Lykaonia, but the church is very narrow. The Basilica of Çiftlik has resemblances to the early churches of Constantinople of the sixth century, but unfortunately we do not have any examples of churches from the fourth century.

One or the oldest churches of Egypt was excavated at Dayr Abu Fano near al-Minya. (Fig. 4) The church was built for astronomical reasons in 350. The St. Abu Fano was born in 355 in Memphis and became a monk in the monastery of Howr, but in 375 he became ill by Morbus Bechterew and lived in a totally dark cell for 18 years. He died in 395 after he had seen in a vision the death of the Emperor Theodosios I. He was buried in the small one nave church with side chambers and after his death in 395, at the beginning of the fifth century, the whole church was enlarged.

---

[9] R. F. Hoddinor, *Bulgaria in Antiquity* (London, 1975), Fig. 104-105. A. Tschilingirow, Christliche Kunst in Bulgarian von der Spätznike bis zum Ausgang des Mittelalters (Berlin, 1978), pp. 16-18.

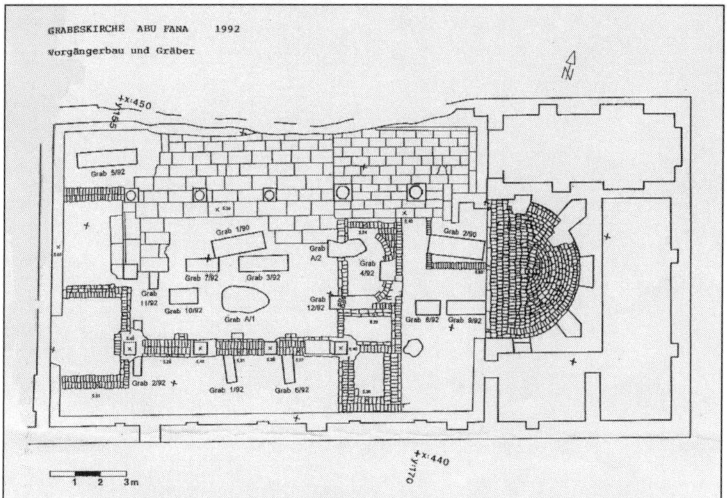

Abb. 6: Die Grabeskirche (Thomas Pertlwieser)

Fig. 4-Abu Fano. Church of the fourth century.

St. Phokas became the patron of sailors. Churches were built in Sidon, Trabizon and Sicily, and he was venerated in Armenia. P. Peeters translated the text of the Armenian passio into Latin.[10]

[10] Van den Vorst, "Saint Phokas," 1290ff.

11

Twelve Objects with Armenian Inscriptions from a Private Collection in New York

Roberta Ervine

It is a special pleasure to offer this modest tribute to Prof. Dickran Kouymjian. From his knowledge of — and contagious enthusiasm for — the history and beauty of Armenian objects we have all benefited.

The twelve household objects described here were purchased together in the 1990's. Although all of them may not have originated there, their immediate source is Istanbul.

The collection comprises four bowls, two plates, a seal, a sieve, a pen case, a four-tiered food carrying container, a cooking pot, and an ewer. While the seal and pen case are brass, the remaining objects are tinned copper of different thicknesses. The bowls, and one of the plates as well, appear to have been made in two pieces: sides and rim, in one piece, were later soldered to the disk that became their bottom.

Their inscriptions more often than not give us only the owner's name. One records a place name; it was donated to the church "of the Holy Illuminator" — but there is nothing to tell us which of the many churches by that name was the recipient of the gift.

Six of the inscriptions give dates: these range from 1747 to sometime in the 1790's. In other words, their manufacture spanned the reigns of four sultans, from Mahmoud I through Selim III, ten patriarchal reigns in Istanbul (albeit with only eight reigning patriarchs), three catholicoses, and four patriarchs of Jerusalem, beginning with that outstanding churchman, Grigor the Chainbearer. One wonders how the events of the eighteenth century's tumultuous second half affected the creators and owners of these most ordinary items.

To put everyday objects into the perspective of more memorable historical events is always a pleasurable exercise. Somehow, it lends these simple pieces more vivid color when one thinks that as some of them were created, the revolutions in America and France were taking place; that the first item of known date was manufactured while the Bourbon king Louis XV was in the middle of his sixty years on the throne, whereas the last was made during the reign of Napoleon; that they were first used in a period that saw their owners' European contemporaries reacting to Bach and Mozart, Beethoven and Paganini, Schleiermacher and Swedenborg, and buying the latest in Heppelwhite furniture. As far as Armenian developments of their time period are concerned, we will never know how much, if at all, the users of these objects participated in the growing Armenian political awareness reflected in the careers of Yovsēp' Ēmin, Catholicos Simēon Erevants'i, Abp. Yovsēp' Arghutian, Yovhannēs Lazarian and others shaping the Armenian future while these objects were first in use. Were they active participants in the movements of their time, or were they fully absorbed in the minutiae of an ordinary Ottoman Armenian life, as recounted for us in, among others, the *Chronicle* of Astuatsatur dpir, Yovhan Yerets', and Aṙakel of Akn? That at least three of the owners traveled is clear from their title *mahtesi*, or *hajji*; indicating that they had made the pilgrimage to Jerusalem. At least one, Ṙap'ayēl son of Tēr T'uma, was from the family of a priest, and one probably was a priest himself — Grigor, "Christ's servant," owner of the seal.

In a way, the objects speak for themselves. We could wish they spoke more, but are grateful for their mere physical testimony to the daily living of Ottoman Armenians in the later eighteenth century.

Below, each inscription is first transcribed as it appears on the object. When the inscriptions contain abbreviations, these are expanded in a second rendering in lower case Armenian letters, and then a third rendering is given in English letters. If more than the owner's name appears in the inscription, a translation is supplied. If the inscription consists solely of the owner's name, without abbreviations, only a transcription and a transliteration into English are given.

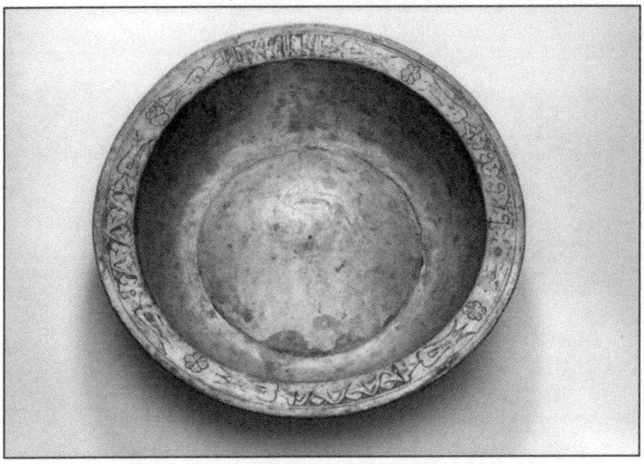

Fig. 1-Bowl I

The bowl (Fig. 1) measures 11 in. across and is 2.5 in. deep. Its 1 in. wide, flat lip bears three crudely incised cartouches of foliage, each with a stylized tulip at either end. Each patterned panel is separated from the next by a six-petalled flower. The inscription, in raised letters against a background of diagonal scratching, constitutes a fourth cartouche. It gives the owner's name, written out fully, without abbreviations or ligatures:

Խանճի Հանէս
Khanchi Hanēs

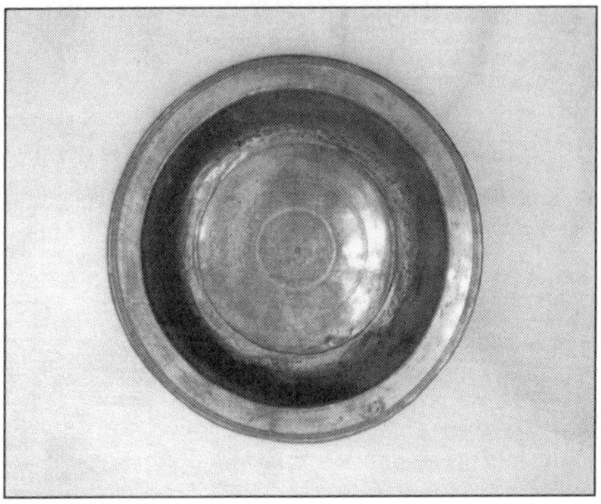

Fig. 2-Bowl II

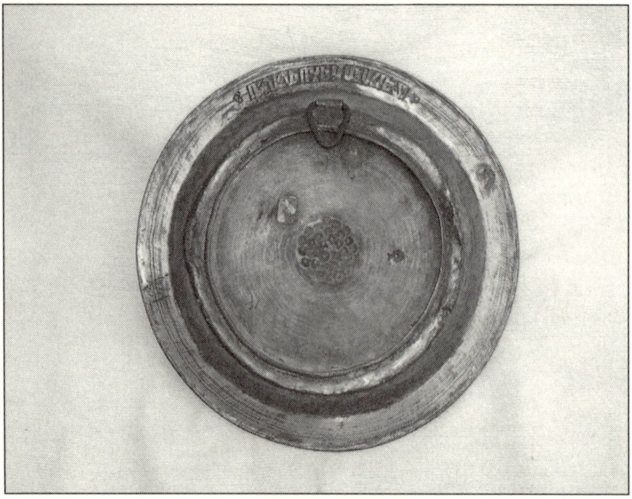

Fig. 3-Bowl II

The bowl (Fig. 2 & 3) measures 8 in. across, and is 1.5 in. deep. There is a tear along one side of the bottom, and it appears that a new piece has been inserted into the center bottom of the bowl. The upper surface of the bowl is devoid of decoration, except for a double incised line that runs round the outside of its .75 in. flat lip. There are two marks on the underside of the lip. On the bottom of the bowl, at the center, a numeral has been marked in simple chisel gouges. In the center of the bottom, there is a circular grouping of nail head imprints. An eye is attached on the underside, for hanging the bowl.

The inscription appears on the underside of the bowl's rim, in raised letters set off against a band of diagonal scratching. The band of letters terminates at either end in a tri-lobed flowerette. The letters in the inscription are all ligatured, except for the Կ and Տ of Կարապետ.

ՈւՆՆէսի որդի Կարապետ
Ownnēsi ordi Karapet
Karapet, son of Ownnēs

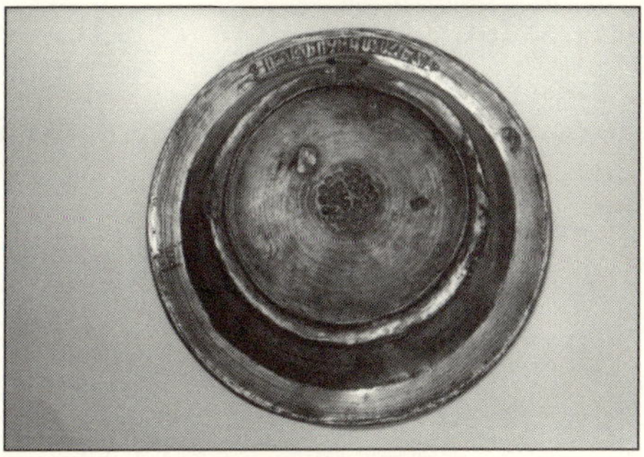

Fig. 4-Bowl III

This bowl (Fig. 4) is almost identical to the previous one, but "inside out," that is, the nailhead pattern on the disk, which comprises the bowl's bottom, is visible on the inside of the bowl, rather than on the outside. The inscription too, while identical to that on bowl II, is found on the upper surface of the rim, rather than on the underside. The bowl bears the same two maker's marks as does bowl II; both are found on the upper surface of the rim.

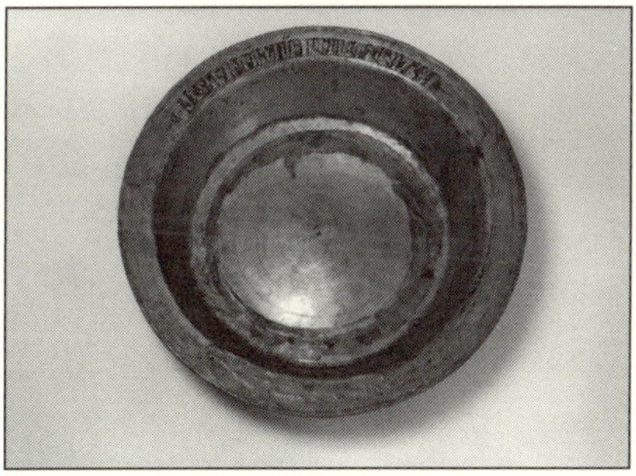

Fig. 5-Bowl IV

Slightly larger than the two previous bowls, this one (Fig. 5) measures 10 in. across and 1.8 in. deep. Its bottom shows signs of repair. The inscription, as in the previous instances, is of raised letters enclosed in a cartouche of diagonal scratching, which terminates at either end in a simple flowerette. However, in this case the inscription is divided internally into four sections, marked by plain, vertical raised bars. There are several abbreviations, and some ligatures. Line divisions below represent the sections into which the inscription is divided. Underlining indicates ligatured letters.

յՇՏԿ Է
Ի ԴՈՒՌՆ
ՍԲ
ԼՈՒՍԱՒՈՐՉԱյ 1768

Յիշատակ է
ի դուռն
սուրբ
լուսաւորչայ 1768

A memorial
to the church
of the Holy
Illuminator 1768

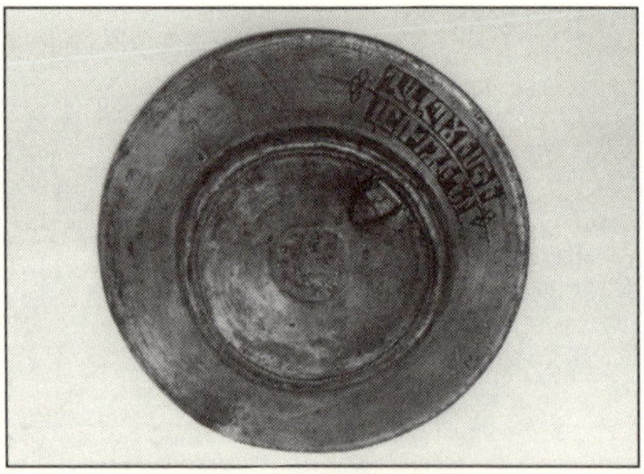

Fig. 6-Plate I

This small plate (Fig. 6) measures 6.25 in. across and is slightly concave. It has been mended on one of its edges, and as is the case with the bowls above, its bottom is welded to the rim as a separate piece. The same pattern of nail heads which appeared on bowls II-III is visible in the center underside. The initials ՆՏ or ՏԴ, depending on from which direction one views them, appear on the underside of the rim. An eye has been affixed to the plate just below the inscription, so that it can be hung.

The inscription is two lines long. It occupies a cartouche like those mentioned above, with a raised horizontal line dividing the two lines of script. As in bowl IV, the cartouche terminates in a simple, tri-lobed flowerette. The style of the inscription is similar to that of bowl IV, though its letters are slightly more angular. There are abbreviations and two ligatures, as indicated by underlining below.

ՂԱԼ ՊՃԻ ՄՀԻ
ԱՐ ՈՒԹԻՆԻ

ղալապճի մահտեսի
արութինի

Of the pilgrim ghalapchi
Arut'in

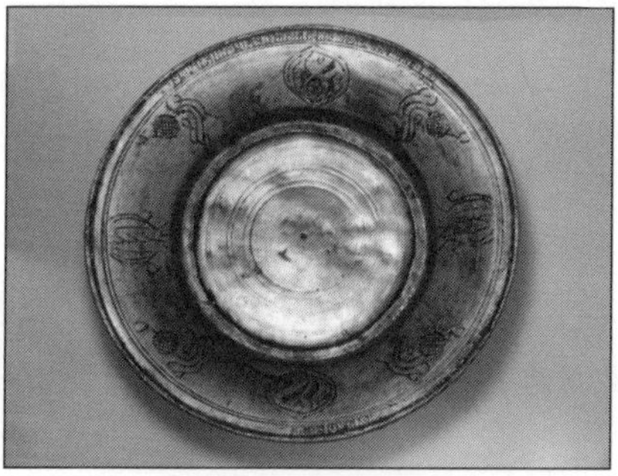

Fig. 7-Plate II

This plate (Fig. 7) measures 8.5 in. across, with a wide (2 in.) lip or flange, and a raised outer edge. It is heavy for its size. In addition to the usual incised lines around its perimeter, the flange bears a design of stylized fruits and foliage: two pomegranates, two medallions of raised foliage design, and four small round fruits attached to stems are arranged symmetrically around the flange. There are concentric circles incised on the bottom of the bowl. On the outside of the bottom, the same pattern of nailheads is visible as on bowls II-III and plate I. An eye has been attached to the plate for hanging.

There are two inscriptions on the plate, both at the outside edge of the flange, opposite one another. They are in small lettering, between the incised, decorative lines and the raised lip of the flange. The letters are raised, against a background of diagonal scratching. The date differs in style from the rest of the writing, being composed of simple, incised lines.

Inscription 1:

ՏՐ ԹՈՒՄԱ
Տէր Թումա
Lord T‘uma

Inscription 2:

ՏՐ ԹՈՒՄԱՅԻ
ՈՐԴԻ ՌԱՓԱՅԷԼԻ
ԹՎԻՆ ՋՄԼԶ
Տէր Թումայի
որդի Ռափայէլի
թվին ռմլզ

Of Ṙap‘ayēl,
son of Lord T‘uma ,
date 1236 (=1787)

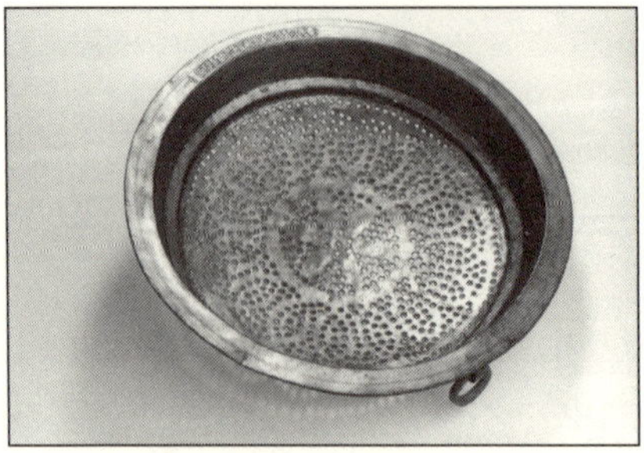

Fig. 8-Sieve

This large piece (Fig. 8) measures 14.25 in. across and is 3 in. deep. It is pierced across the whole extent of its bottom with a geometric design of holes, constituting a rosette at the center surrounded by a stylized ring of foliage, formed from overlapping circles. A single row of holes marks the outermost limit of the design. A sturdy ring is attached to one side of the sieve.

The inscription runs along one side of the 1 in. lip. As is the case with the other inscriptions in this collection, the inscription is in raised letters within a cartouche of scratching, which terminates in a simple flower at either end. There are several ligatures, as indicated below with underlining.

ԱՅՏԻՆԻ ՈՐԴԻ ԱԲՐԻՀԱՄ ԶՃՂ.Զ
Abriham son of Aytin 1196 (=1747)

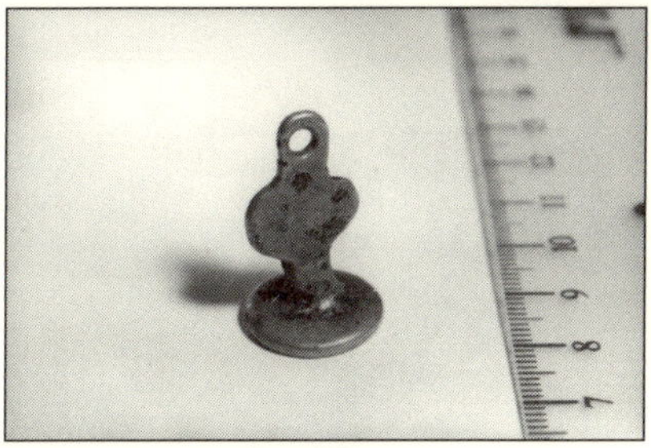

Fig. 9-Seal

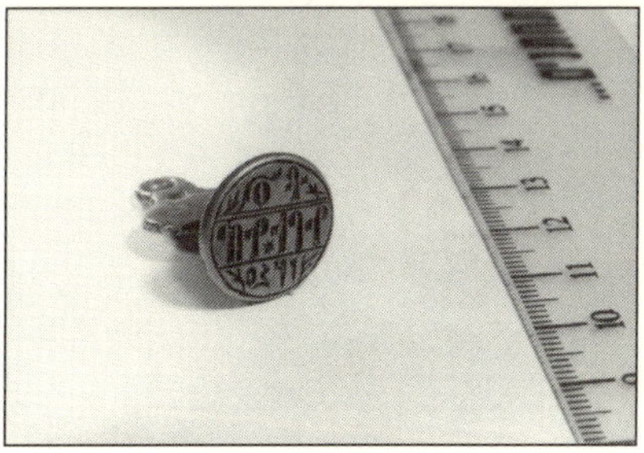

Fig. 10-Seal

Measuring just over an inch in height and .75 in. in diameter, the brass seal shows a clear inscription in three lines (Figs. 9 & 10), set within an incised circle. Between the first and second lines of the inscription a double line is drawn; between the second and third, a single line. There are two stars as well, one at the beginning of the first line, and the other in the middle of the second. Two sprigs set off the date in the third line. As is usual with seals, all the words are ligatured. The date is in arabic numbers.

ՔԻ ԾՅ
ԳՐԻԳՈՐ
1245

Քրիստոսի ծառայ
Գրիգոր
1245

Christ's servant
Grigor
1245 (=1796)

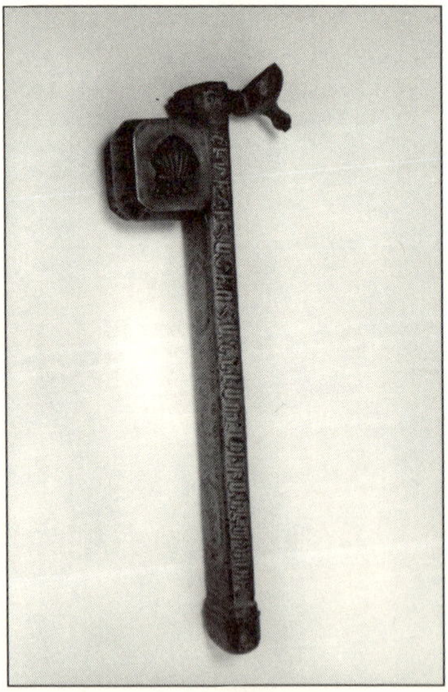

Fig. 11-Writing Case

This fine writing case (Fig. 11) measures 10 in. in length, 1 in. in depth, and .5 in. in width. It has a hinged lid and an attached inkwell with a lid in the shape of a scallop shell. The body of the case is covered in an etched floral design. There is a monogram on the bottom front of the inkwell, which appears to include the name Sargis.

The inscription runs the length of the top edge of the case. There is no background striation, and there are no ligatures or abbreviations. The date is in arabic numbers, with the final numeral missing. The execution of the letters does not show the same degree of skill as in the previous examples.

ՏԷՄԻՃԻ ՀԱՃԻ ՈՀԱՆՆԷՍՈՂԼՈՒ ԲԱՆԷՍԻՆ 124՞
Of Tēmichi Hachi Banēs Ohannēsoghlu, 124? (=179?)

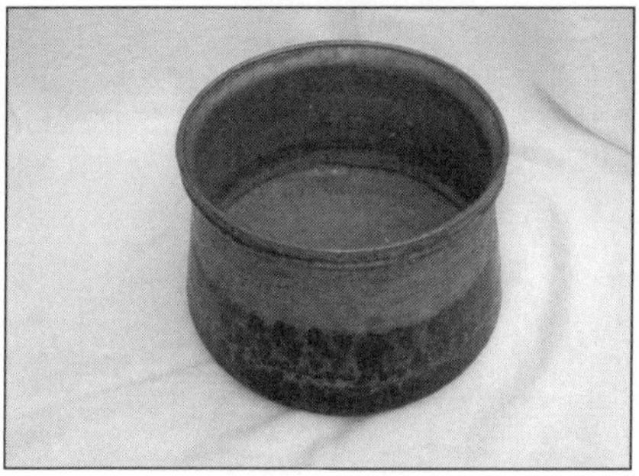

Fig. 12-Pot

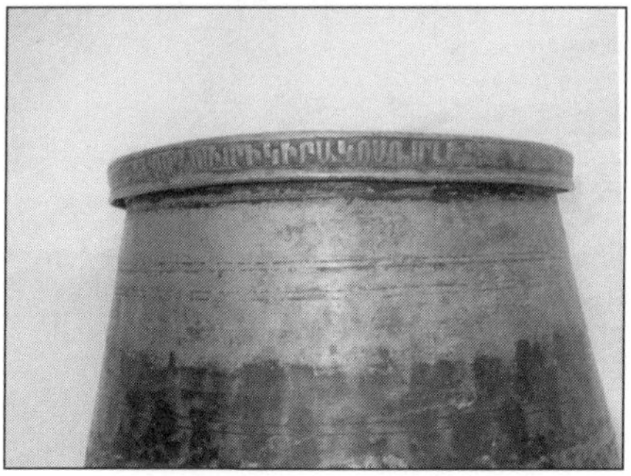

Fig. 13-Pot

Measuring 8 in. across the mouth and 9 across the base, this is a pot blackened from use (Figs. 12 & 13). It is decorated with simple, incised lines running round the exterior in three pairs. Single lines adorn the upper and lower edge of its extended lip, which is folded under to provide a space between lip and pot for the insertion of a temporary handle, or for lifting by other means.

The inscription, like most of the others in this collection, is composed of raised letters set in a band of diagonal scratching, which terminates at either end in a stylized, tri-lobed flower. The two ligatures in the inscription are indicated in the transcription by underlining.

ՊՈՂՈՍԻ ՈՐԴԻ ԿԻՐԱԿՈՍ ՌՄԼԵ
Kirakos, son of Poghos 1235 (=1786)

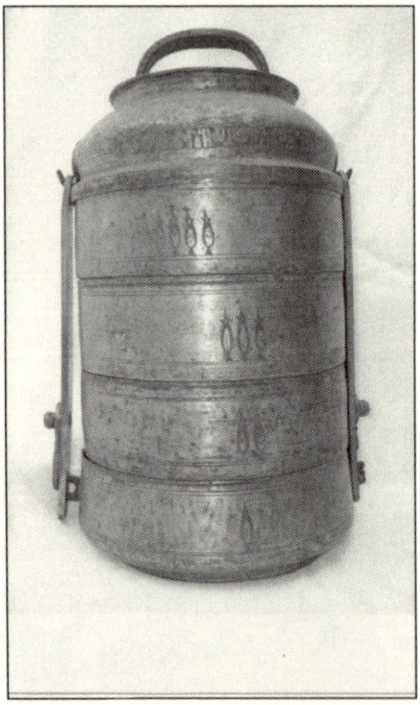

Fig. 14-Lunch Pail

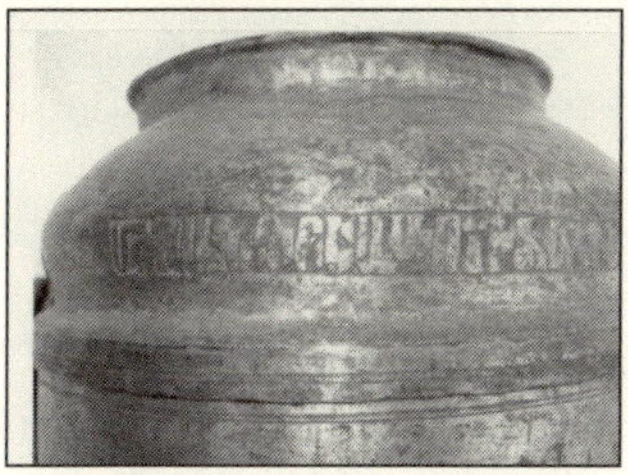

Fig. 15-Lunch Pail

This four-tiered food carrying pail measures 12 in. tall and 8 in. in diameter (Fig. 14 & 15). Each section is 2 in. deep, while the lid, which may be inverted and used as a bowl, is 3 in. deep. A raised base accounts for the remaining 1 in. of height. There is a sturdy handle fixed to the top through two eyes; the handle is formed in such a way that it lies flat when the pail is at rest, or when its top is inverted for use as a bowl. In the center of the top's upper surface, a nailhead pattern can be seen which resembles that in the center of Bowls II-III and Plate II.

The four tiers can be locked together into a single unit by a metal bar with a hole that fits over a hook at the lower edge of the lid, and an eye that accommodates a hook on the bottom tier.

In addition to simple ornamentation consisting of pairs of incised lines near the top and bottom of each section and around the lid, each section is marked with a stylized flower or flowers indicating where it should sit in the ensemble: the lowest tier bears one flower, the one above it bears two, the third bears three, and the top tier bears four.

The inscription, as in the other instances above, is set in a band of diagonal scratching, which terminates at either end in a stylized, tri-lobed flower. The inscription's ligatures are indicated below by underlining. There is a bar between the two halves of the word ՈՐԴԻ; each syllable of the word is ligatured.

ՄՀԻ ԱՆԴՐԷԱՍԻ ՈՐԴԻ ԾԵՐՈՆ
մահտեսի Անդրէասի որդի Ծերոն
The pilgrim Andreas' son Tseron

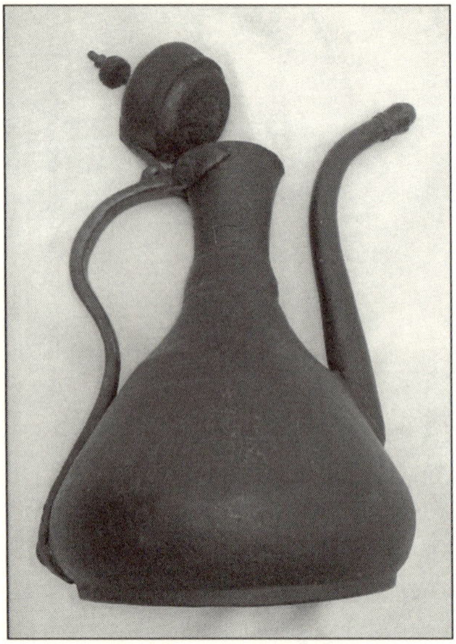

Fig. 16-Lidded Ewer

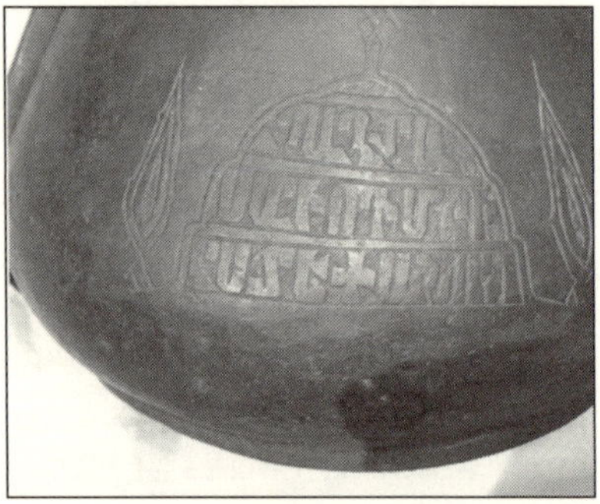

Fig. 17-Lidded Ewer

The black patina has not been removed from this 12.5 in. tall piece (Fig. 16 & 17), which measures 6.5 in. across the bottom. The lid is hinged on a pin; the eye through which the pin passes is riveted to the lid through a piece of metal in the shape of a stylized leaf. The lid is surmounted by a simple acorn; its under surface is adorned with a raised rosette. The body is ornamented simply, with incised lines running round the body. There is a raised band between the neck and the body.

The inscription fits within a dome shaped cartouche surmounted by a simple cross and flanked by two stylized trees of life. The three lines of the inscription are separated from one another by raised lines. There is a bar before and after the final word, է (though it is possible that the first bar was intended as an ի, it seems rather that the bars were intended to prevent one's reading the last two words together as one). The letter Փ is represented by a cross. Ligatures are indicated below by underlining.

ՊԱՂՏԱ
ՍԱՐԻ ՈՐԴԻ ՄՀԻ
ԸՍՏԵՓԱՆ Է
Պաղտասարի
որդի մահտեսի
Ըստեփան է

It is [of] pilgrim Step'an,
son of Paghdasar

12

Les tissus médiévaux arméniens : essai d'identification

Marielle Martiniani-Reber

A travers les représentations sculptées, la peinture des manuscrits arméniens, et les rares textiles qui ont subsisté jusqu'à nous, il est possible d'examiner quelques particularités techniques et iconographiques des étoffes présentes en Arménie médiévale.

La haute qualité de l'industrie textile arménienne est attestée par les sources historiques, notamment arabes, surtout dans le domaine du tissage des tapis et des produits tinctoriaux. Une ramification de la route de la soie reliait le territoire arménien à la voie principale; très vite, la sériciculture s'y implanta avec succès dans les vallées du nord, et le pays put rapidement fournir de la soie en abondance.

En Arménie, outre la production de tissus de luxe pour les besoins des souverains, des hautes couches de la société et de l'Église, il y a la nécessité de produire ou d'importer[1] de grandes pièces pour la confection des rideaux d'autel; ceux-ci semblent avoir été utilisés depuis une époque reculée puisqu'on en a mention dès le milieu du IVe siècle[2].

Jusqu'à présent, très peu de tissus médiévaux ont été signalés et répertoriés en Arménie. Nous avons pu examiner l'un d'entre eux, une soierie de qualité conservée au Matenadaran.

---

[1] L'Arménie recevait des États voisins des textiles qu'elle ne pouvait produire ; on peut citer à ce propos Procope de Césarée, qui mentionne la chlamide en soie marine (filaments de *pinna nobilis*) offerte par l'empereur Zénon, *De Aedificiis*, III, i , 24-29, éd. Loeb Classical Library, Procopius, *Buildings* (Cambridge, Mass. et Londres, 1947), p. 183.

[2] On trouve mention du rideau d'autel dès 340, dans un canon adressé par Macarius, évêque de Jérusalem, au catholicos d'Arménie Vrtanes, voir P. Jacques Issaverdenz, *Rites et cérémonies de l'Église arménienne* (Venise, 1876), pp. 9-10.

Les produits tinctoriaux d'Arménie

La garance[3] et la cochenille d'Arménie, colorants rouges, s'exportaient dans tout le Proche-Orient.

La pourpre était connue des Arméniens, car elle est même mentionnée dans le texte fondateur du mythe de Vahagn[4]. Sa couleur est définie par celle de l'abricot (*tsirani*), fruit symbole de l'Arménie[5]. Cependant, par sa définition même de couleur abricot, un ton lumineux proche de l'orange, et non pas violet, et par l'absence de mer et d'océan, on doit penser à un autre type de produit tinctorial, beaucoup plus caractéristique du pays. La cochenille d'Arménie (*vordan garmir*), improprement appelée *kirmiz* par les Arabes et les Perses qui ne la distinguaient pas du point de vue linguistique du kermès, est de plus grande taille que les autres insectes tinctoriaux de ce type; elle se développe sur une catégorie de graminée (*sez*) ou sur un roseau commun[6]. Apparemment, on l'exportait sous une forme sèche, conditionnée en sac[7].

Les chroniqueurs arabes des IXe et Xe siècles demeurent nos principaux informateurs pour les sources non arméniennes. En Arménie, on possède très tôt des renseignements sur cette question chez Lazare de Pharbe au Ve siècle et chez Moïse de Khoren au VIIIe siècle[8].

---

[3] L'Arménie est grosse exportatrice de garance. Elle la cultivait intensément, Ibn Hawqal, *Kitab surat al-ard, Configuration de la terre*, trad. J. H. Kramers et G. Wiet (Paris, 2001), pp. 340-341.

[4] Moïse de Khoren, *Histoire de l'Arménie*, livre I, XXXI, Traduction d'Annie et Jean-Pierre Mahé (Paris, 1993).

[5] Bogos Levon Zekiyan, « La porpora in Armenia, tra mito, folklore, arte e religiosità », *La porpora realtà e immaginario di un colore simbolico*, Istituto veneto di scienze, lettere ed arte (Venise, 1996), pp. 277-297.

[6] Voir Dominique Cardon et Gaëtan du Chatenet, *Guide des teintures naturelles*, Neuchâtel (Paris, 1990), pp. 374-377.

[7] Dominique Cardon, « Les vers du rouge : insectes tinctoriaux (homoptera coccoidea) utilisés dans l'ancien monde au Moyen Age », *Cahiers d'histoire et de philosophie des sciences*, 28 (Paris, 1990).

[8] Maurice Lombard, *Les textiles dans le monde musulman : VIIe-XIIe siècles* (Paris, 1978), pp. 119-122.

Artashat est surnommé par Ibn Hawqal la ville de la teinture rouge[9] : il indique que le *kirmiz* arménien est employé pour teindre les étoffes en poil de chèvre et la laine[10]. De ces renseignements, on peut supposer que cette teinture était employée pour les tapis et les manteaux. Il précise encore que les tapis de Dabil (Duin en arménien) avaient un fond rouge à base de *kirmiz*.

Idrisi nous apprend que l'Arménie exportait des voiles de lin peut-être teints en noir avec de la noix de galle (*sabani*, du grec *savbanon*)[11]. Le lin était particulièrement difficile à teindre, et obtenir une couleur très saturée comme le noir par les moyens traditionnels devait être une gageure.

En raison de sa richesse géologique, le pays produisait aussi des mordants réputés comme la chrysocolle (silicate de cuivre), qui servait également pour la soudure de l'or.

Les tapis

Les sources arabes accordent une place importante aux tapis arméniens, *busut*, surtout ceux du lac de Van[12], les tapis de Garin K'aghak' (Erzeroum) ou Qaliqala en arabe, nommés *qali*[13], terme qui désigne en arabe le tapis noué. Particulièrement remarquable est la mention, chez Ibn Hawqal, du tapis nommé *armani mahfur*, ou tapis creusé, qui a été interprétée comme un tapis à deux hauteurs de poils[14], mais qu'il me semble plus approprié de rapprocher du kilim dont les relais non cousus formeraient ces fameux creux[15].

---

[9] J. Laurent, *L'Arménie entre Byzance et l'Islam depuis la conquête arabe jusqu'en 886* (Paris, 1919), pp. 41-42.

[10] Ibn Hawqal, *Kitab surat al-ard*, p. 135.

[11] Idrisi, *Géographie*, trad., P. A. Jaubert (Paris, 1836-1840), tome II, p. 326.

[12] Yakut al-Hamawi, *Mu`djam al buldan, Geographisches Wörterbuch* (Leipzig, 1866-1873), IV, 895.

[13] Ibid., p. 20.

[14] C'est l'interprétation de R. B. Sergeant, *Material for a History of Islamic Textiles up to the Mongol Conquest* (Ann Arbor, 1942) ou de Lombard, *Les textiles dans le monde musulman*, p. 41, *busut mahfura*, tapis creusé, « ce qui signifie qu'ils portaient des dessins en relief obtenus en coupant le poil de laine à des niveaux différents ».

[15] Ibn Hawqal, *Kitab surat al-ard*, p. 246. Un terme moderne de même racine exprime une carie dentaire, donc plutôt un sillon.

Dès la seconde moitié du VIIIe siècle, Ibn Khaldun témoigne de la considération que l'on avait pour les tapis arméniens, car ils sont cités dans la liste des contributions dues par les Arméniens au calife de Bagdad.

De même, en 917, le calife al-Muqtadir, recevant l'ambassadeur byzantin ordonna un important déploiement de luxe, parmi lequel figuraient des tentures arméniennes[16]. Ce calife disposait de textiles arméniens; en effet, le gouverneur de ce pays lui envoya en 912, en plus des tapis dus en paiement de l'impôt, deux longs tapis *armaniyya* de très grandes dimensions (surface estimée à 900 m^2)[17].

Autres textiles réputés

Dans les autres spécialités textiles de l'Arménie, sont cités les coussins, les vêtements de poils de chèvre ou de laine, les habits de laine rouges et verts pour les femmes, de précieux liens (*tikkah*) utilisés pour les pantalons[18]. Selon Maqrizi, un grand d'Égypte laissa à sa mort, parmi ses autres richesses, mille *tikkah* en soie d'Arménie[19]. Aucune mention dans les témoignages arabes ne nous permet d'identifier ce qu'étaient précisément ces *tikkah*, mais on peut imaginer que ces liens aient été tissés aux cartons, technique connue en Iran dès l'époque sassanide et qui fut largement pratiquée jusqu'à une date récente dans tout le Proche-Orient et en Arménie.

Les représentations des textiles dans l'iconographie aulique arménienne

Malgré les lacunes inhérentes à la technique de la sculpture, (manque de couleur, difficulté de transcrire les détails des textures), les décors architecturaux fournissent des informations remarquables sur la variété des tissus utilisés en Arménie durant le haut Moyen Âge. Quelques-uns de ces témoignages sont capitaux pour notre

---

[16] Lombard, *Les textiles dans le monde musulman,* pp. 191-192.

[17] Ibid., p. 184.

[18] Voir les différents textes comparés de Ibn Hawqal, Idrisi, Jahiz, Istahri, Muqaddasi dans Sergeant, *Material for a History of Islamic Textiles up to the Mongol Conquest*, pp. 95-96.

[19] Maqrizi, éd. de Sacy, *Chrestomathie arabe*, tome 1, p. 99 et Reinhart Dozy, *Dictionnaire détaillé des noms des vêtements chez les Arabes* (Amsterdam, 1845), pp. 95-99.

connaissance de la diffusion de certaines techniques. On peut citer à cet égard le tympan de la porte ouest de la cathédrale de Mren. David Saharouni y porte un long caftan dont les longues manches pendent librement. Le tissu dans lequel il est confectionné peut être identifié avec quasi certitude comme une toile de laine ou de cachemire grattée[20]. (Fig. 1)

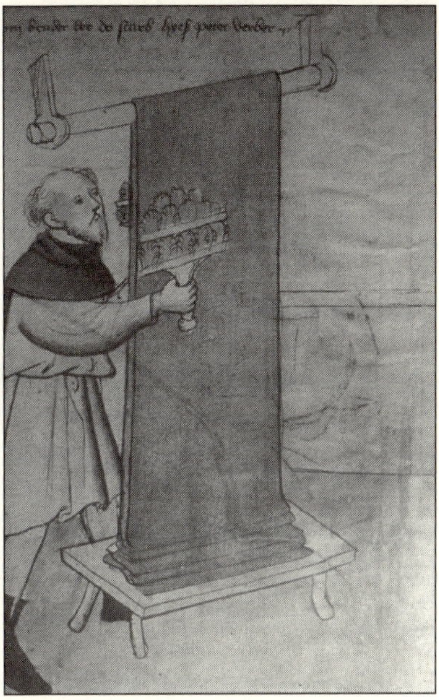

Fig. 1- Manuscrit, XIVe siècle, Stadtbibliothek, Nuremberg, la planche montre comment un artisan gratte une étoffe de laine à l'aide d'une brosse composée de chardons. *Autour du fil, L'encyclopédie des arts textiles*, tome 12 (Paris, 1990), p. 86.

---

[20] Voir l'illustration dans Sirarpie Der Nersessian, *L'art arménien* (Paris, 1977), n° 36, p. 57. Pour les toiles de laine grattées, technique très diffusée en Écosse ou dans le sud de la France pour la fabrication de couvertures. Les anciens témoignages de cette technique sont les tissus des manteaux sassanides ainsi que les jambières et bas de chausses, découverts en Égypte, en toile de cachemire rouge ou bleu, voir Marielle Martiniani-Reber, *Textiles et mode sassanides, Département des antiquités égyptiennes, Musée du Louvre* (Paris, 1997), pp. 41-74. Un petit fragment de sergé de laine grattée a également été découvert sur le site de Mistra en Grèce. Voir Marielle Martiniani-Reber, éd., *Parure d'une princesse byzantine*, *To evnduma miva « buzantinhv prigkivpissa »* (Genève, 2000), p. 120.

On en connaît de nombreux exemples produits en Perse sassanide et conservés en Égypte ainsi qu'un modeste fragment de sergé découvert à Mistra, datant probablement de l'époque paléologue. Cette opération rend le lainage plus chaud[21]. L'identification du tissu du caftan de Saharouni avec ce type de lainage gratté est confortée par le parallélisme des mèches qui montre une volonté délibérée de représenter un textile et non une fourrure.

Les tissus façonnés sont montrés de manière abondante dans les arts figurés; toute représentation d'étoffes portant une ornementation strictement répétitive peut être interprétée comme image de tissage façonné, c'est-à-dire, stricto sensu, à dessins plus ou moins complexes, obtenus par le croisement des fils de chaîne et de trame et dont l'exécution nécessite des procédés mécaniques, donc, à l'époque, un métier commandé par une tire[22].

Les reliefs des façades de l'église de la Sainte-Croix d'Aghtamar (915-922) constituent une mine de renseignements sur le costume aulique et les tissus de luxe. Dans l'une des scènes, le roi Saul assistant au combat de David et Goliath, symbole de la victoire du faible sur le fort, arbore un caftan en tissu façonné à petits motifs qui dessinent un décor très original, inspiré par une pseudo-calligraphie à caractères coufiques[23]. (Fig. 2)

---

[21] Une miniature d'un manuscrit du XIVe siècle, conservée à la Stadtbibliothek de Nuremberg, dépeint le procédé de façon extrêmement précise ; la laize de lainage est soumise à un grattage méthodique à l'aide d'une planche sur laquelle sont fixées des têtes de chardon. Voir *Encyclopédie, Autour du fil* (Paris, 1990), volume 12, p. 86.

[22] Définition dérivée de l'entrée « façonné » du *Vocabulaire technique du CIETA* (Lyon, 1959 et 1997), p. 17.

[23] Herman Vahramian et Sirarpie Der Nersessian, *Aght'amar, documenti di architettura armena*, 8 (Milan, 1974), pls. 39-40.

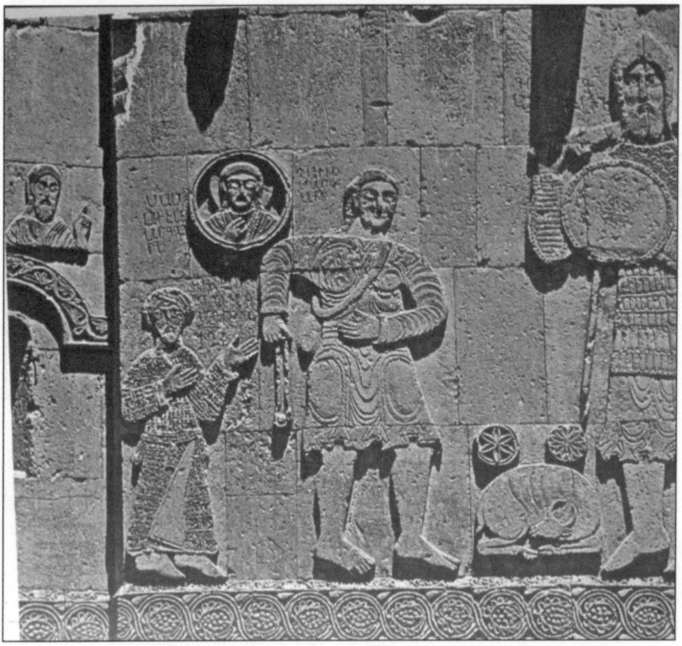

Fig. 2- Sainte-Croix d'Aghtamar (915-922), Saul assiste au combat de David et Goliath. Herman Vahramian et Sirarpie Der Nersessian, *Aght'amar, documenti di architettura armena*, 8 (Milan, 1974), p. 39.

Près de l'entrée, le roi Gagik tient la maquette de l'église[24]. Il porte un pallium orné de médaillons noués, à l'intérieur desquels s'inscrivent des oiseaux, bien connus dans les décors textiles sassanides[25]. Toutefois la disposition des médaillons, ainsi que l'échelle des motifs correspondent à cette époque plus tardive. L'encolure des oiseaux est soulignée d'un collier perlé. On remarque que la direction des oiseaux s'inverse selon les registres, disposition déjà observée sur les tissus sassanides[26]. (Fig. 3)

---

[24] Ibid., pls. 12 et 13-14.

[25] Voir par exemple in Marielle Martiniani-Reber 1997, *Textiles et mode sassanides*, n° 31, p. 19 et p. 82, mais, dans cet exemple, les oiseaux sont en registres.

[26] Voir *Musée des tissus de Lyon, guide des collections* (Lyon, 1998), p. 44, pour une soierie sassanide ornée de registres de bouquetins.

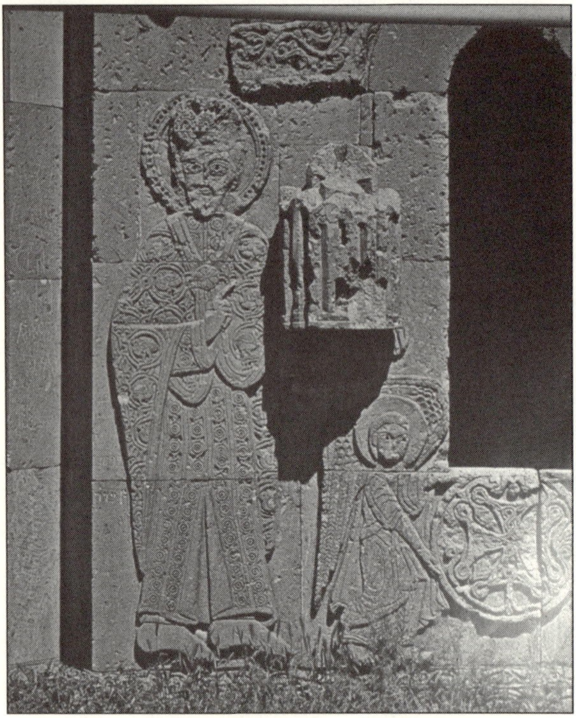

Fig. 3-Idem, Roi Gagik. Idem, pl. 12.

Enfin, sur la façade sud, deux princes martyrisés en 786 par les Arabes sont représentés habillés de précieux caftans, ornés de petits motifs répétitifs, de forme simple[27] ; le décor du vêtement d'Isaac est constitué de petits cercles pointés, celui du manteau de Hamazasp d'un réseau de quatre-feuilles.

L'évangile de Gagik de Kars (1029-1064), qui montre le portrait de la famille royale, soit le souverain, la reine et leur fille, est un témoignage essentiel pour notre connaissance des tissus de luxe portés par la cour arménienne[28]. (Fig. 4)

---

[27] Vahramian et Der Nersessian, *Aght'amar, documenti di architettura armena*, pl. 38.

[28] Voir une bonne photo de cette page de manuscrit conservée au patriarcat arménien de Jérusalem dans Sirarpie Der Nersessian, *L'art arménien*, p. 101.

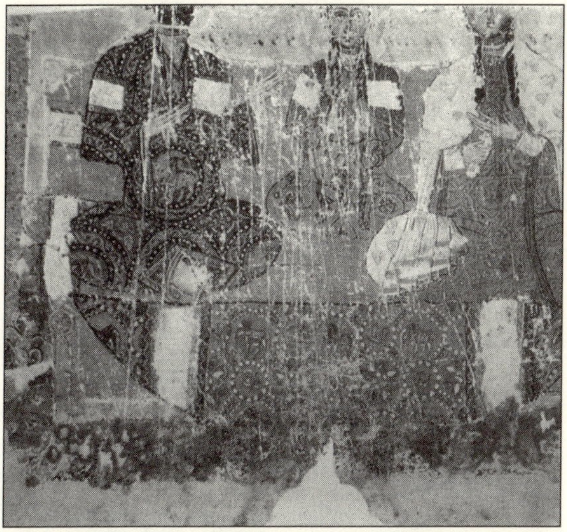

Fig. 4- Evangile de Kars (1029-1064), portrait de la famille royale. Sirarpie Der Nersessian, *L'art arménien* (Paris, 1989), p. ill. 75.

Le souverain porte un manteau à médaillons noués, à couronne perlée, dans lesquels s'inscrivent des bouquetins qui sont à rapprocher des exemples sassanides. On remarque le motif losangé des écoinçons dont le centre est composé d'une rosace. Le manteau possède des bandes de tiraz à caractères coufiques. La jeune fille porte aussi un manteau rehaussé de bandes de tiraz aux manches. L'ornement se compose de grosses palmettes en forme de pique, bleues sur fond rouge. Le vêtement de la reine Gorantoukht, offre à voir des médaillons noués enfermant des fleurons ou plus probablement des simurghs, verts sur fond rouge. Mais surtout, sur l'estrade où est installée la famille royale, est disposé un tapis, qui peut être interprété comme une pièce de tissu façonné. Il présente un intérêt exceptionnel en raison de sa ressemblance, tant au niveau du décor que des coloris employés, avec une soierie découverte en Catalogne et dont plusieurs fragments ont été dispersés dans diverses collections[29]. (Fig. 5)

---

[29] La soierie du monastère de Santa Maria de l'Estany a été découpée en six fragments connus. D'après la reconstitution faite par Milton Sonday, l'ensemble des fragments connus ferait originellement partie d'une

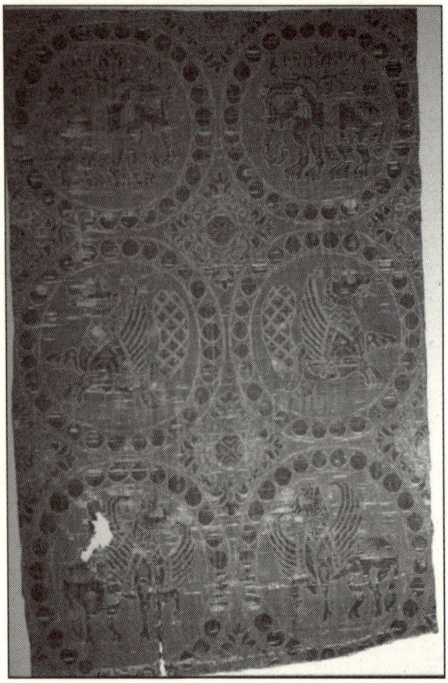

Fig. 5- Soierie de Santa Maria de l'Estany, Catalogne, XIe siècle (?) *The Glory of Byzantium* (New, York, 1997), p. 414.

---

chasuble. Celui du Bargello se présente comme une bande avec des découpures en arc de cercle. Il provient de l'ancienne collection Franchetti (inv. F 634). Le plus grand morceau appartient au Cooper Hewitt, National Design de New York (ancienne collection Miguel Pasco y Badia). Le tissu a été bien étudié dans le catalogue *The Glory of Byzantium* (New York, 1997), pp. 414-416, et le rapprochement avec la miniature de l'évangile de Gagik de Kars y est établi. Des chevaux ailés, des simurghs, et des éléphants sont disposés à l'intérieur de médaillons à couronne perlée (largeur 2 cm), de 28 perles chacun. La hauteur totale du médaillon est de 17 cm.
Qualification technique : samit façonné 3 lats suivis, sergé 2 lie 1, S.
Chaînes : 2 fils pièce pour 1 fil de liage, soie beige jaune tordue en Z pour les fils pièce et fils de liage, découpure de 2 fils pièce, réduction de 30 fils pièce au cm.
Trames : 1 coup de chaque passée, soie rouge, noire, bleue sans torsion appréciable, découpure de 2 passées, réduction de 46 l passées au cm.
Tous les termes techniques employés proviennent du *Vocabulaire technique du Centre international d'étude des textiles anciens* (Lyon, 1959 et 1997).

L'hypothèse d'une importation de soieries arméniennes en Occident, voire même d'une imitation espagnole de la production arménienne n'est pas établie par la présence de témoignage physique parvenue jusqu'à nous. Maurice Lombard mentionne que le souverain almohade Abu Yusuf Yaqub appréciait particulièrement la soie d'Arménie et qu'il laissa à sa mort, en 1199, deux cents paires de pantalons confectionnés avec des variétés différentes de cette étoffe[30]. À ce jour nous n'avons pu avoir confirmation de ce renseignement, car la note est erronée. Cependant, d'autres sources écrites témoignent de la connaissance qu'avaient les Espagnols des spécialités textiles arméniennes (Ibn Hawqal, décrivant les tapis d'Andalousie, les compare aux meilleurs tapis *mahfur* arméniens).

L'évangile du monastère de Horomos, près d'Ani, réalisé en1236 par le peintre Ignatios, représente un prince et son épouse, et atteste la continuité de l'usage du caftan à longues manches pendantes en tant que vêtement d'apparat ; il constitue sans doute aussi l'un des premiers témoignages d'un type de médaillon qui deviendra caractéristique du décor textile persan, et surtout ottoman. Cet ornement à contour perlé est visible sur le manteau de l'épouse du prince[31].

Sur une miniature de T'oros Ṙoslin (1262)[32], les souverains ciliciens revêtent des costumes issus de l'iconographie impériale byzantine, ornés de grands médaillons à figures animales. On remarquera la couleur beige du pallium du roi, qui n'est pas sans rappeler celle de la soierie du manuscrit 6263 du Matenadaran[33]. (Fig. 6)

---

[30] La mention dans la note de l'ouvrage de Maurice Lombard, *Les textiles dans le monde musulman*, p. 179, note 2, est erronée, Tanuhi, *Niswar al-muhadara wa-ahbar al-mu`dakara [The table-talk of a Mesopotamian judge]* (Londres, 1922), trad. D. Margoliouth, p. 137.

[31] Raymond Kévorkian et Berdj Achdjian, *Tapis et textiles arméniens* (Marseille, 1991), p. 109, ill. 21.

[32] Ibid. p. 33, ill. 21; manuscrit de Jérusalem 2260, fol. 288 r. Cette couleur pourrait peut-être se définir par le terme de *tsirani* (ton de l'abricot) ; elle n'est en tout cas pas sans rappeler une teinte que l'on trouve assez fréquemment sur des soieries persanes d'époque post-sassanide (VIIIe siècle).

[33] Les éléphants semblent représentés de manière plus maladroite que les autres animaux, en particulier parce que la tête et l'extrémité des pattes sont

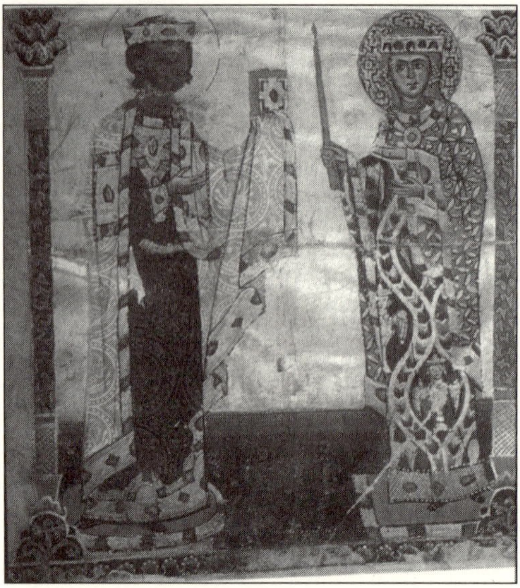

Fig. 6- Portrait des souverains de Cilicie, T'oros Ṙoslin, 1262. Raymond Kevorkian et Berdj Achdjian, *Tapis et textiles arméniens* (Marseille, 1991), ill. 21.

Examen d'une soierie médiévale conservée au Matenadaran

La soierie double la reliure du manuscrit mat. 6263, qui contient les actes des apôtres et les épîtres[34]. (Fig. 7)

---

importantes par rapport au corps. La queue est en revanche trop courte. Ils rappellent ceux d'un fragment de samit conservé au musée de l'Ermitage, provenant de l'église de Photrer en Géorgie, voir Anna Jerusalimskaja, « Soieries byzantines des Xe-XIe siècles provenant de Svanétie (Géorgie) », *Bulletin du CIETA*, 77, 2000, pp. 57-69.

[34] Il date du XIIe siècle (peut-être 1169). Son origine n'est pas connue (école d'Ani ?). Le copiste est Grigor, tandis que le commanditaire pourrait être Mekhitar Gosh, savant du XIIe siècle. Les deux fragments qui doublent les deux intérieurs de la reliure sont en bon état, malgré quelques traces d'usure. Ils sont collés dans la reliure et leur bord est partiellement recouvert par les rabats de cuir.

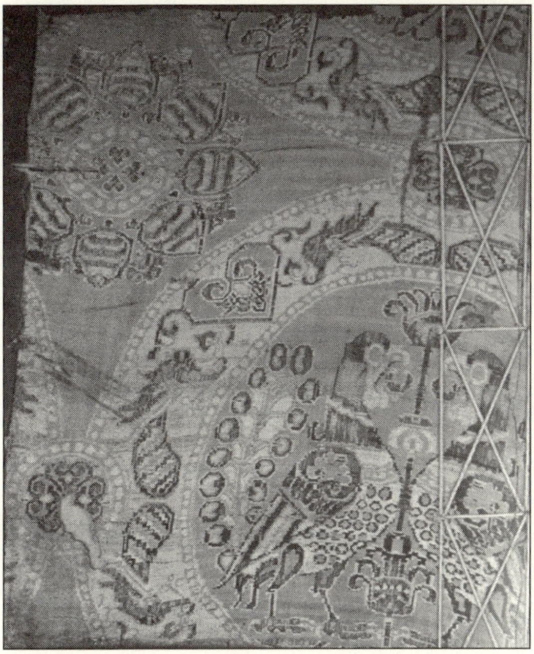

Fig. 7- Soierie doublant le manuscrit 6263, Matenadaran, Arménie (?), VIIIe-IXe siècle. Sirarpie Der Nersessian, *L'art arménien* (Paris, 1989), ill. 74.

Du point de vue technique, il s'agit d'un samit 4 lats suivis, dont la principale particularité est la faible torsion des deux chaînes (pièce et de liage)[35].

---

[35]*Dimensions* : hauteur 28 cm, largeur 20 cm (visible)
hauteur 28,5 cm, largeur 21 cm (visible)
Qualification technique : samit façonné 4 lats suivis, sergé 2 lie 1, S.
Chaînes : proportion 1 fil pièce pour 1 fil de liage, chaîne pièce en soie brun foncé 2 poils, très faiblement tordue en Z, chaîne de liage en soie brun moyen, 1 poil faiblement tordu en Z, découpure de 1 fil pièce, réduction de 16 fils pièce au cm.
Trames : proportion de 4 passées par 1 passée de chaque lat, matière : soie sans torsion appréciable rose, jaune, blanche et brun foncé, découpure de 1 passée, réduction de 25 passées au cm.

Des médaillons circulaires contiennent deux oiseaux affrontés, sans doute des aigles, mais pourvus d'une roue comme les paons. Ils tiennent un anneau dans leur bec. Leur corps est perlé et le haut de leurs ailes marqué d'une palmette. Les oiseaux ne sont pas posés sur un socle comme c'est habituellement le cas. Une palmette dérivée de l'arbre de vie marque l'axe médian vertical du médaillon.

La couronne des médaillons, bordée de perles, est ornée de paons affrontés et disposés de profil entre des motifs cordiformes. Le plumage des oiseaux est marqué de lignes obliques en zigzags.

Les médaillons ne sont pas complètement tangents[36]. Le point de tangence est marqué d'un médaillon perlé contenant une rosace composée de quatre motifs cordiformes.

L'espace des écoinçons s'orne d'une rosace composée de huit pétales ovoïdes. Le cœur correspond à un motif composite au centre marqué d'un médaillon perlé et de quatre cœurs.

D'une façon générale, l'importance et la qualité des étoffes arméniennes et des tapis ont été fréquemment évoquées par les auteurs arabes où elles sont souvent considérées comme le nec plus ultra de certains secteurs de la production textile de leur époque. Elles sont confirmées par les documents figurés, reliefs, peintures, qui montrent aussi la variété des décors reflétant des influences persanes et byzantines, voire même chinoises, ainsi que de probables importations.

La qualité des étoffes présentes en Arménie au Moyen Âge est également confortée par l'examen de la soierie du Matenadaran, étude qui devrait être complétée par celle d'autres exemples.

Sur le second fragment, apparaît une erreur de tissage rendant visible la chaîne pièce sur une longueur de 8 mm.

La couleur rose est très claire.

[36] Ils sont espacés d'environ 8 mm.

13

Le manteau arménien de Jean-Jacques Rousseau[1]

Yolande Crowe

Au siècle des Lumières, maints esprits curieux continuèrent à scruter l'Orient lointain et de nombreuses publications de voyage s'ajoutèrent aux écrits souvent fantaisistes des siècles précédents. En un sens la pratique du *Grand Tour*, voyage de formation à travers l'Europe, faisait partie de l'éducation des jeunes nobles en quête d'œuvres d'art et de culture. Mais au 17ème siècle déjà les compagnies des Indes Orientales s'empressaient de fournir une grande variété de produits exotiques, épices, soieries en tout genre, cotonnades peintes, tapis turcs, persans et indiens ainsi qu'une vaste quantité de céramique chinoise. Les voyageurs, tels Tavernier, se faisaient peindre dans leur costume persan.

Lorsque le Genevois Jean-Etienne Liotard séjourne à Constantinople de 1738 à 1742, il y peint marchands européens et autres personnages officiels, parmi lesquels le révérend Richard Pococke, lui-même en costume arménien. Dans son portrait, il se tient debout appuyé sur un autel antique; le fond de la toile représente la pointe du Sérail et au loin les îles des Princes. Par la suite Liotard exposera le dessin préparatoire pour ce tableau à Paris en 1771 lors de la vente de son propre *cabinet de tableaux,* Rue Montmartre. Il portait le numéro 10 avec l'inscription : *L'évêque Pococ, Anglois, avec l'habit Arménien qu'il portoit lorsqu'il voyageoit dans le Levant*[2]. (Fig. 1) La simplicité du sombre kaftan brun aux seuls parements de fourrure encore plus sombre le long de son ouverture et aux poignets, correspondait certes à l'habillement de voyage des marchands arméniens qui, au long des routes

---

[1] Je remercie vivement Renée Loche, Danielle Buyssens et Sabina Engel pour leur aide précieuse dans mes recherches.

[2] L'orthographe d'origine a été respectée, sauf mention contraire.

caravanières, évitaient de se faire remarquer par des vêtements ostentatoires. En outre, de se faire passer pour Arménien signifiait aussi que l'on appartenait à une minorité chrétienne, acceptée par les autorités musulmanes qui reconnaissaient leur honnête habilité à négocier et, le cas échéant, à prêter de fortes sommes d'argent.

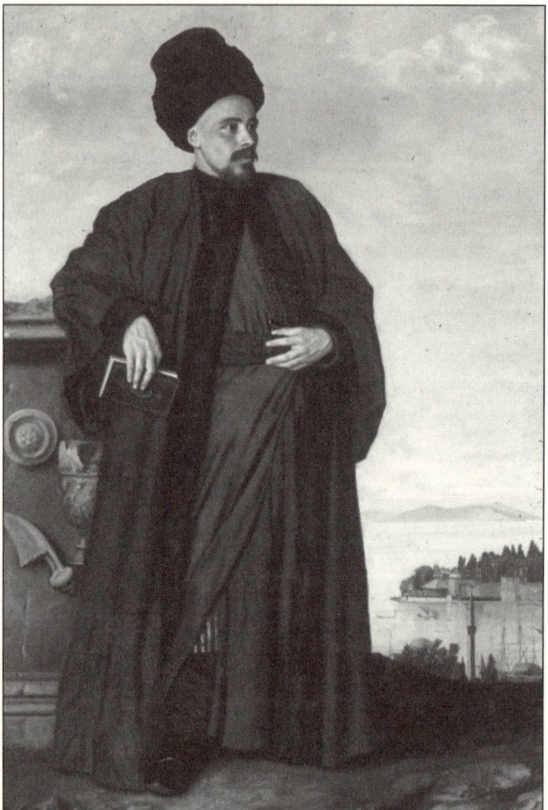

Fig. 1-Portrait du Révérend Richard Pococke 1738 ou 1739. J.E. Liotard, inv. 1948-0022. Centre d'iconographie genevoise. Musée d'art et d'histoire, Genève.

L'importance du réseau arménien aux 17e et 18e siècles, dont le centre se trouvait à la Nouvelle Julfa au sud d'Isfahan, la capitale de l'empire séfévide jusqu'à la débâcle persane de 1722, n'est plus à démontrer; en fait, ce réseau s'étendait de Lisbonne à Canton en passant par l'Inde et un des cheminements vers l'Europe passait par

Moscou. Dans le monde ottoman la communauté arménienne, au même titre que les minorités orthodoxe et juive, jouait aussi depuis longtemps un rôle important, en particulier dans le domaine du commerce de la soie et d'autres textiles importés des Indes et de la Perse. En outre, ces commerçants, n'ambitionnant ni rôle politique ni fonction militaire, ne menaçaient en aucune façon les autorités en place. Il semble que le port du vêtement arménien n'était pas inconnu dans le Paris du café Procope. Le café lui-même fut introduit d'abord à Marseille en 1671, puis à Paris, successivement par deux maîtres de café arméniens, Pascal puis Grégoire. D'ailleurs d'autres maîtres et leurs garçons n'hésitaient pas aussi à s'habiller en Arméniens même s'ils ne l'étaient pas[3]. En 1669 l'ambassadeur ottoman à la cour de Versailles, Aga Mustapha Rac, avait fait servir à ses invités du café dans des tasses de porcelaine japonaise.

De petits albums, consacrés à une variété de costumes exotiques, furent alors créés pour un public de diplomates et de commerçants européens fascinés par l'Orient et avides de dépaysement ; les accoutrements exotiques des personnages de la cour et de la ville illustraient la grande variété d'habits rencontrés dans l'empire ottoman, et visibles à Istanbul. On pouvait distinguer vers la fin de chaque volume un ou plusieurs personnages en habit d'Arménien (Fig. 2), côtoyant des représentations les costumes portés par les minorités orthodoxe et juive. Ainsi le manteau arménien, en d'autres termes le kaftan du monde musulman, devint le vêtement idéal du commerçant européen et de tout voyageur aventureux déjà aguerri par la traversée de la Méditerranée, ainsi que de la noblesse polonaise[4].

---

[3] J. Moura et P. Louvet , *Le café Procope* (Paris, 1929), p. 63, n. 3.

[4] A. Dziubinski, Introduction, *War and Peace. Ottoman-Polish relations in the 15th-19th centuries,* exposition (Istanboul 22 juin-20 septembre 1999).

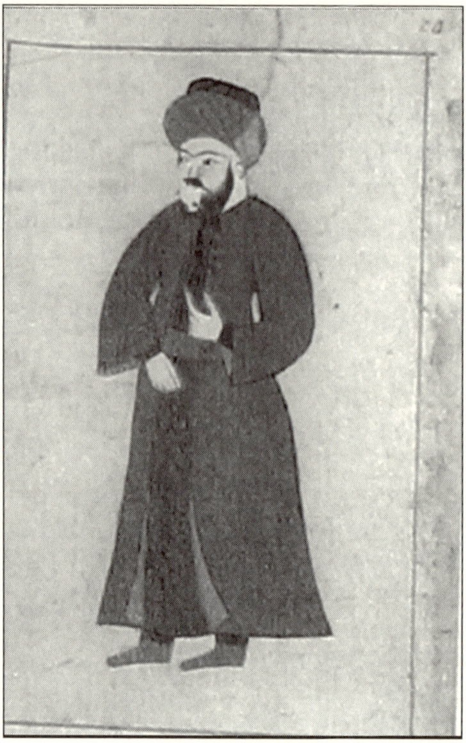

Fig. 2- Costume d'Arménien. Bibliotheca Narodowa. Cod. Boz 165 17yy, no. 20.

Dans sa retraite de Môtiers (Fig. 3), Jean-Jacques Rousseau le connaît bien et ne veut pas porter d'autre vêtement au quotidien. Avec un tel habit long, et de son propre aveu, malade, il peut se sonder plus facilement. D'ailleurs, dès la mi-avril 1762, alors qu'il est encore à Montmorency chez le Maréchal de Luxembourg, un dénommé La Roche, s'étant enquis auprès du fils d'un tailleur arménien, lui fait parvenir la liste des fournitures nécessaires pour la fabrication d'un habit arménien: échantillons de draps, aunages pour la robe et la veste, leur doublure et les ceintures d'usage ainsi que les fourrures pour le bonnet[5]. « Je me fis donc une petite garderobe Armenienne. Mais l'orage excité contre moi m'en fit remettre

[5] *Correspondance complète de J.J. Rousseau.* R. A. Leigh, ed. vol. 10 (Madison, 1969), lettre no. 1740, pp. 194-196, La Roche à Rousseau, 14 avril 1762.

l'usage à des tems plus tranquilles »[6]. En effet, il doit quitter la France car il est sous mandat d'arrêt du Parlement après la parution de l'*Émile*. Il s'arrête quelques jours à Yverdon où il fait la connaissance de Madame Julie-Anne-Marie Boy de la Tour dont il avait autrefois connu le père à Lyon. Mais il se voit à nouveau contraint de partir sous la menace d'un ordre d'expulsion des autorités de Berne. Malgré sa célébrité, il se sent traqué. Finalement grâce à ses nouvelles amitiés lyonnaises, un toit lui est offert à Môtiers dans la maison du frère de Madame Boy de la Tour, elle-même veuve depuis quatre ans de Pierre Boy de la Tour, de Neuchâtel et négociant à Lyon. « Je voudrois, Madame, que vous vissiez l'empressement avec lequel je m'établis dans votre maison.[7]» La bourgade se trouve dans le Val de Travers au sud-ouest de Neuchâtel. C'est un peu le bout du monde pour Rousseau, cependant au début de son séjour il apprécie la nature qui l'entoure ainsi que le bon voisinage de George Lord Keith, maréchal héréditaire d'Écosse, mieux connu sous le nom de Mylord Mareschal qui prit fait et cause pour les Stuart. Après une carrière mouvementée, il s'était mis au service de la Prusse dont il est alors le gouverneur pour la principauté de Neuchâtel depuis 1754. Il accueille Rousseau cordialement et l'invite régulièrement pendant son séjour de plus de trois ans, dans son château de Colombier à six lieux de Môtiers[8].

---

[6] J. J. Rousseau, Oeuvres complètes, vol. 1, *Les confessions* (Paris, 1959), p. 600.

[7] Vol. 12, (Madison 1970), lettre no. 2007, p. 51. À Mme Julie-Anne-Marie Boy de la Tour, Môtiers 18 juillet 1762.

[8] Rousseau, *Les confessions*, pp. 595-601.

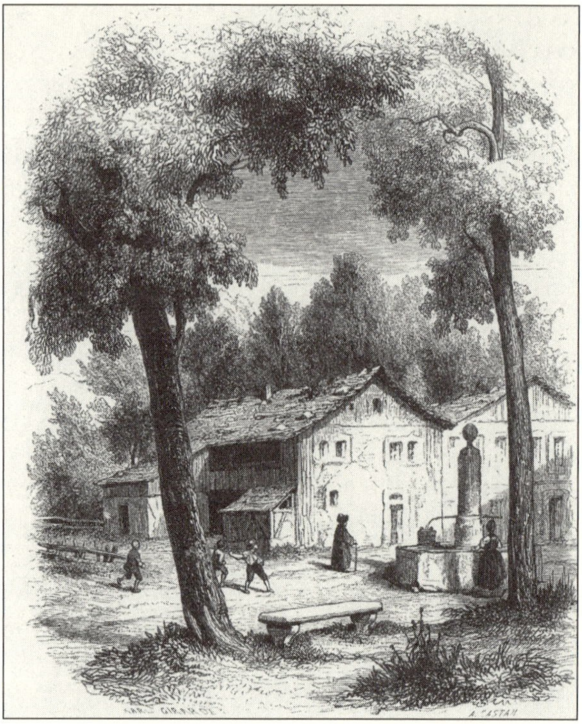

Fig. 3- Môtiers. K. Girardet, *Rousseau*, Genève 1848. GIR 2058/28. Bibliothèque de Genève, d'iconographie genevoise.

De toute évidence à l'approche de l'hiver, il lui manque les doublures de fourrure pour sa robe d'Arménien et pour ses bonnets. Rousseau demande fin août à Madame Boy de la Tour de lui en procurer les éléments nécessaires :

> Je vous envoie ci-joint une robbe et deux bonnets que je vous supplie de vouloir s'il est possible envoyer à Lyon pour être fourrés avant l'hyver. Je voudrais pour la robbe quelque fourrure fort commune, Souhaittant seulement qu'on mette à la bordure aux fentes et aux poches quelques fillets un peu honnêtes, comme fausse martre ou petit gris. Le bonnet de Bouracan[9] sera fourré comme la

[9] Bouracan: gros camelot de laine non croisée, en vogue au 18ème siècle. Voir note 11.

> bordure de la robe, et l'autre de quelque autre manière à volonté[10].

De telles commandes vont lui fournir de nombreuses occasions d'écrire également à une autre de ses admiratrices qui fera aussi de son mieux pour le satisfaire. Voici comment se déroulent la commande et la fabrication de plusieurs manteaux arméniens de Jean-Jacques Rousseau. Et dès la mi-septembre c'est madame Marie-Françoise de Luze née Warney (1728-1796) et parente de Madame Boy de la Tour, qui reçoit la requête suivante pour de nouvelles robes d'Arménien:

> Il s'agiroit de me rendre un service semblable à ce lui que vous avez rendu à Mme-Boi-de-la-Tour lorsqu'elle fut vous voir, en me choisissant dans vos magasins quelque coupon d'indienne dont je pusse me faire une robbe d'Arménien, même deux si le cas y écheoit. Je souhaiterois que le fond ne fût pas blanc et salissant, un petit dessin qui ne fut pas montant, une toile fine et non pas claire, car je l'aimerois encore mieux serrée et grosse, et je préfère aussi la qualité au bon goût. Au reste je soumets le mien au vôtre, et pourvû que l'indienne soit de vôtre choix, quand ces conditions ne s'y trouveroient pas, j'en serois toujours content.
>
> Quant à l'aunage, le moins que doit avoir le Coupon est trois aunes, mais quand il auroit le double, le triple et d'avantage, il n'importe, j'en trouverai toujours l'emploi ; et de deux.
>
> Ce n'est pas tout ; il faudroit aussi que vous voulussiez bien me faire l'emplette de quelque doublure chaude pour la dite robe, comme flanelle ou molleton ; il en faudrait la quantité qui répond à trois aulnes et demie d'Indienne, plutôt plus que moins[11].

Il est spécialement fait mention d'indiennes car le grand-père du mari de Madame de Luze avait créé une fabrique de toiles peintes au Bied dans le canton de Neuchâtel en 1734. En outre, les choix de la fourrure et des ceintures ainsi que celui d'un tailleur, préoccupent

---

[10] Vol. 12, lettre no. 2118, p. 260. À Mme Boy de la Tour, Môtiers 30 août 1762.

[11] Vol. 13, (Madison 1971), lettre no. 2158, p. 57. À Mme de Luze, Môtiers 13 septembre 1762.

assurément Rousseau de sorte qu'il envoie un mémoire, semble-t-il, le même jour que celui d'un courrier à Madame Boy de la Tour :

Mémoire:

> Ayant pris quelques instructions sur les fourures, on m'a dit que les plus belles étaient aussi les plus durables, et qu'on les pouvoient transporter successivement à grand nombre d'habits sans que le poil se détachât. Ainsi j'aime mieux mettre quelque argent de plus et avoir une fourure après laquelle je n'en aye plus dans la suite à acheter. Je souhaite surtout qu'il n'y ait aucun défaut ni au bout de manches, qui se retroussent, ni sur les bonnets.
>
> Indépendamment de la robbe de bouracan, je voudrois savoir ce que me coûteroit la garniture d'une autre robbe, non fourrée en plein, mais bordée seulement de filets noirs, soit de martre, soit de lapin, soit de quelque autre fourrure noire et si l'on ne pourroit pas m'envoyer ces filets, mesurés sur le tour de la robbe de bouracan, pour en faire ici border une autre, sans avoir besoin de l'envoyer là-bas.
>
> Ne pourrait-on pas trouver un tailleur entendu qui sur la coupe de la robbe de bouracan put en tailler une autre de camelot[12], ou de quelque autre étoffe de soye ou autre, légère pour les chaleurs, et qui sut entretailler les pièces, de maniére à ne point dépenser d'étoffe plus que n'en a dépensé le tailleur Arménien. En ce cas le dit tailleur pouroit garder avec soin le patron pour me faire au besoin tous mes dolimans ou robbes de dessus. Quant à la couleur, le gris seroit à préférer; mais je n'en excluds aucune que les couleurs vives que le soleil mange. [...].
>
> J'ai deux ceintures, il m'en faut encore autant. Ne pouroit-on pas trouver quelque ceinture de soye tissue à rézeau comme les filets de pêcheur. Ce sont les plus belles et d'un meilleur usage. Au deffaut de celles-là, on achèteroit quelque étoffe de soye qui soit le moins sujette à se couper et qui ait un peu de consistance, comme par éxemple, pou de soye ou autre semblable, au défaut de quoi on pourroit prendre un croisé ou serge de soye,

---

[12] Camelot: grosse et solide étoffe à poil ondulé qui se fabriquait dans le Levant puis en France, en laine ou en poil de chèvre ou de chameau, quelquefois avec une chaîne en laine et une trame en lin.

quoiqu'un peu trop mince pour ceinture. Chaque ceinture doit avoir deux aulnes et demie de long et comme on les plisse en écharpe, il faut leur laisser toute la largeur de l'étoffe ; au de bouts de chaque ceinture on attache une frange large de 4 doigts, et il manque aussi à chaque bonnet une houpe de la même couleur. (Fig. 4)[13]

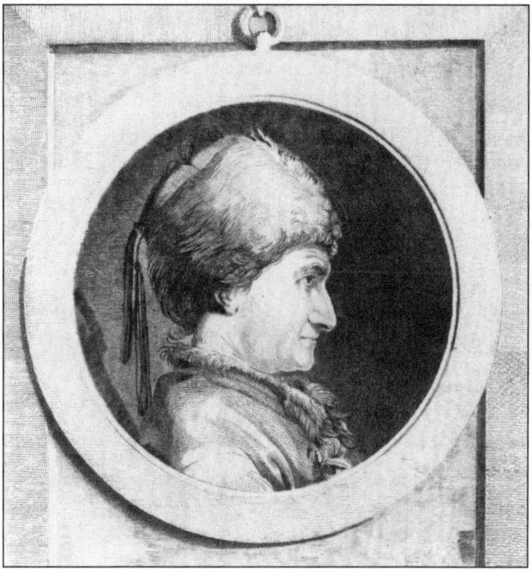

Fig. 4- Portrait de J.J. Rousseau. Gravure de J.B. Michel 1765. GIR 344. Bibliothèque de Genève, d'iconographie genevoise.

Fort rapidement cinq jours plus tard, Rousseau renvoie la série des échantillons dûment expédiés par Madame de Luze avec le message suivant:

> Voilà, Madame, les échantillons que vous avez eu la bonté de m'envoyer; j'ai marqué celui que je préfère quoiqu'à dire vrai j'eusse mieux aimé un dessin plus petit, mais tenons-nous, s'il vous plaît, à celui-là, plustôt que de prolonger l'embarras que vous donne cette négociation.
>
> J'ai laissé l'aunage indéterminé, comptant sur un coupon, mais puisqu'il faut prendre la pièce, je m'en

---

[13] Vol. 13, lettre no. 2160, pp. 59-60. À Mme Boy de la Tour, Môtiers 13 septembre 1762. Dans ce cas la houppe est une touffe de brins de frange.

> tiendrai d'abord, selon votre avis, à trois aulnes et demie, dont il vous plaira de marquer le prix en les envoyant, de même que la flanelle pareille à l'échantillon[14].

Une semaine après, ne voulant pas laisser passer l'occasion d'une seconde commande de cette indienne attrayante tant par son dessin que par son prix, le reclus de Môtiers s'adresse à nouveau à Madame de Luze:

> Il s'agit de cinq aulnes encore de la même Indienne, tant elle a paru jolie et à bon marché. J'ai déjà remis à M. d'Ivernois l'argent du précédent envoi et il voudra bien se charger encore de celui de ces cinq aulnes, lequel vous sera remis avec cette lettre, de même que la toile cirée qui couvroit le précédent pacquet, afin qu'elle serve encore à couvrir celui-ci.
>
> Il me semble au reste que l'échantillon que j'avois marqué était brun, au lieu que ce fond ci est lilac : mais n'importe; dans un beau caffetan couleur de lilac j'aurai l'air d'un petit agréable de Téflis ou d'Erivan, et je crois que cela m'ira fort bien. C'est domage que je ne sois pas à portée de vous éblouïr de ma magnificence arménienne, et de vous faire homage de ma parure. C'est domage aussi qu'avec un si bel étalage je ne sois pas de ceux qui peuvent offrir ni vous de celles qui daignent aggréer le Salamalec Lyonnois[15].

À nouveau, le 4 octobre Madame Boy de la Tour lui envoie un courrier détaillé, daté de Lyon:

> Voici une note qui contient la pelleterie qui sera de durée; si vous aimez le léger, il faut prendre le plus beau, rien de plus facile que de vous faire une semblable Robe dont j'ai le modèle. J'ai fait couper un patron devant moi vous trouverez ci-joint des échantillons de camelot et leur prix. Vous choisirez celui qui vous conviendra le mieux.
>
> J'ai commandé une ceinture ; il ne s'en est trouvé de faites qu'en rose, vert ou bleu. Je l'ai demandé de la couleur de votre habit et si elle est telle que vous la

---

[14] Vol. 13, lettre no. 2171, p. 75. À Mme de Luze, Môtiers 18 septembre 1762.

[15] Vol. 13, lettre no. 2189, p. 111. À Mme de Luze à Neuchâtel, Môtiers 25 septembre 1762.

désirez je serai toujours à temps d'en faire une seconde. Il se fait aussi de ces ceintures d'une étoffe Rayée comme les mouchoirs de col de femme dans des couleurs vives et claires, je ne déciderai rien qu'à votre réponse que j'attendrai avec impatience.

(après la signature) Il faut de camelot pour votre robe 4 aunes et demie. Je ne saurais vous choisir en soie que du grau de Naples ou taffetas, parce que vous voudriez de l'uni[16].

Le 9 octobre l'hiver approche, et la commande de l'exilé se précise. On le sent méticuleux à outrance. Il lui faut un ensemble aussi élégant que celui de l'Arménien rencontré chez Mylord Mareschal:

> Pour la fourrure de la robbe de Bouracan, je préféreroi la façon de martre no.1 à 75 livres. Mais j'ai peur que cette fausse martre ne dure pas ; c'est pourquoi je ne sais s'il ne vaudroit pas mieux sacrifier une vingtaine de Livres de plus, et choisir le petit gris no. 2 à 96 livres qui je crois, seroit plus léger et dureroit beaucoup plus. Je vous supplie de juger de cela, et de faire pour le mieux.
>
> Outre la ceinture que vous avez la bonté de me faire faire, je seroi bien aise d'en avoir une autre, de ces ceintures rayées dont vous me parlez. J'ai vu chez Mylord Mareschal un Arménien qui en a de pareilles, et je trouve qu'elles font fort bien.
>
> Je laisse la garnitures des bonnets à vôtre choix ou à celui du fourreur, pourvu que les deux fourrures soient jolies, légéres et différentes.
>
> La réflexion que vous me faites qu'on ne saura pas coudre ici la bordure à ma robe de dessous me fait prendre le parti de me passer de cette bordure ; Une autre année je pourrois vous envoyer une de ces robes, et si vous aviez la bonté d'en faire faire une semblable, vous pourriez en même tems la faire border par le fourreur.
>
> De tous les échantillons de Camelots que vous m'avez envoyés; je préférerois celui que je vous renvoye, laissant pourtant toujours le tout à vôtre choix. Les

---

[16] Vol.13, lettre no. 2210, p. 162. Mme Boy de la Tour, Lyon 4 octobre 1762 (orthographe corrigée).

> devants doivent être doublés de taffetas ou de fine toile grise. Voilà tout, à ce que je crois[17].

Dès le 26 octobre, Madame Boy de la Tour annonce l'expédition du manteau ainsi que celles des deux différents bonnets de fourrure:

> Votre pelisse, mon bon et cher ami, est partie hier, [...]. J'espère que vous trouverez votre pelisse belle et bonne et chaude, légère et qu'elle durera éternellement moyennant qu'elle soit préservée des arté. Un des bonnets est assorti et l'autre est en agneau de Tartarie, tout ce qu'il y a de plus beau et de plus de dure soyez assuré que j'ai plus ménagé votre bourse que je n'aurai fait la mienne, peut-être ai-je été trop à l'économie à l'égard de la ceinture, il [y] en a de la même espèce, double plus large qui coûte 24 ... et celle que je vous envoie n'en coûte que 9 [...].
>
> Je vous enverrai [le compte] dès que tout sera complet, dites-moi aussi, très naturellement si vous êtes content de mon envoi ; le taffetas n'aurait rien duré en doublure, je n'ai pu trouver une plus belle toile, vous l'allez trouver bien grossière. Adieu, mon bon ami, toujours tout à vous[18].

Presque un mois plus tard le désir de Rousseau de ne pas paraître négligé, le pousse à expliquer qu'il lui faut apparaître habillé avec un certain raffinement de façon à ne pas être pris au premier abord pour une personne en robe de chambre. D'ailleurs un libelle anonyme de Voltaire le décrit plus tard comme déguisé en saltimbanque[19].

> J'ai reçu, Madame, presque en même tems vôtre second envoi [...]. Je suis frapé du bon marché de vos empletes, et je me plaindrois presque du trop à cet égard, comme vous l'avez prévu. J'avois une ceinture à filoche semblable à celle que vous m'avez envoyée ; mais ce que j'aurois Souhaité étoit d'en avoir une autre de trés belle soye avec de belles franges, qui fut plus parante que

---

[17] Vol. 13, lettre no. 2220, pp. 184-5. À Mme Boy de la Tour, Môtiers 9 octobre 1762.

[18] Vol. 13, lettre no. 2256, pp. 254-5. Mme Boy de la Tour, 26 octobre 1762 (orthographe corrigée).

[19] J. Starobinski, *La transparence et l'obstacle, suivi de sept essais sur Rousseau* (Paris, 1971), p. 439.

> celles-là. J'espère que vous concevez bien que cette parure n'est pas pour satisfaire mon gout ; mais ne voulant plus quiter l'habit que j'ai pris, ni chez Mylord Mareschal, ni même à l'Eglise, il faut accoutumer les yeux à ne pas le prendre pour un habit négligé; et pour qu'on ne m'accuse pas d'aller au temple en robbe de chambre, il faut chercher à donner à mon vétement de la decence et même de la noblesse, surtout dans les prémiers tems; après quoi je pourrai reprendre sans inconvenient une façon plus simple[20].

De toute évidence les commandes ont satisfait Rousseau car jusqu'au printemps suivant il n'est plus question de nouvelles pelisses ou chapeaux. Cependant à la fin de mars 1763 malgré la transformation de certaines commandes en cadeaux de la part de ses bienfaitrices, il a besoin d'un bonnet et n'hésite pas à en faire la demande auprès de Madame Boy de la Tour : « Je vous envoye [...]dans le fil ci-joint la mesure de ma tête ; je l'ai prise entre les deux nœuds.[21] » Et à l'automne Rousseau songe déjà à un kaftan d'été pour remplacer celui en camelot qu'il dit trop rugueux. Il désire en outre pour l'immédiat deux bonnets fourrés et deux ceintures de soie.

> Je voudrois quelque petite étoffe légére pour un Caffetan d'été. Celui de Camelot que vous avez eu la bonté de me faire faire est un peu gros et rude, il lime trop le Doliman[22] de dessous, la doublure des devants est extrémement grosse, et il a été estropié par le tailleur. Si c'est du Camelot je voudrois qu'il fut doux et fin, et en le prenant gris, on prendroit aussi de la toile grise, mais très fine pour doubler les devants. Si c'est quelque autre etoffe légére de soye ou autre qui ne ronge pas la doublure, on pourra prendre un petit taffetas pour doubler les devants. La quantité d'étoffe doit répondre à peu près à une aune et deux tiers de drap.

---

[20] Vol. 14, lettre no. 2325, p.79. À Mme Boy de la Tour, Môtiers 23 novembre 1762.

[21] Vol. 15, Thorpe Mandeville House 1972, lettre no. 2569, p. 333. À Mme Boy de la Tour, Môtiers 27 mars 1763.

[22] Doliman, du turc *dolama*, robe longue et étroite ouverte par devant et qui se portait par-dessus les autres vêtements.

> Je voudrais faire fourrer encore deux bonnets l'un bien léger l'autre moins : mais je voudrais de belles fourrures et différentes. Les bonnets ne doivent point être fourrés en dedans. Si l'on a gardé ma mesure les bonnets peuvent être faits sur les lieux ; le choix de l'etoffe n'y fait pas grand chose. Sinon j'enverrai les bonnets tout faits [...].
>
> Il me faudrait deux ceintures de soye. L'une légére et pareille à celle que vous m'avez envoyée, l'autre double, de celles dont vous m'avez parlé. La couleur à vôtre choix[23].

On remarquera que la description des bonnets est fort précise et demande toute l'attention et la patience de Madame Boy de la Tour. Ceux de l'été ne seront pas doublés et restent de couleur modeste. Il ne faut à aucun prix une couleur criarde, mais semble-t-il, les lacets pour les bottines peuvent être en soie jaune.

> Hier, Madame, j'ai fait remettre [...] un bonnet de bouracan sur la mesure duquel je vous prie de vouloir bien faire faire deux autres. De ces trois bonnets j'en voudrais deux pour l'été savoir celui de boucaran « Sans fourrure », garni d'un petit galon et d'une houpe d'or comme l'année derniére, un autre bordé dans la même largeur de petit gris ou Martre ou autre jolie fourure légére ; quant au troisiéme, je le voudrois de quelque drap leger comme silesie ou carcassonne doublé de quelque étoffe un peu chaude, et fourré aussi, mais non pas en dedans. Le tout gris ou couleur modeste, et surtout point d'écarlatte. Je vous prie aussi de vouloir bien faire ajoûter aux autres articles deux piéces de padou[24], l'une bleue et l'autre grise, quelques lacets de soye jaune pour des botines de maroquin[25].

Ainsi s'achève les tribulations d'un trousseau en somme raffiné et aux accents orientaux. Jean-Jacques Rousseau continuera à porter

---

[23] Vol. 18, 1973, lettre no. 2962, p. 26. À Mme Boy de la Tour, Môtiers 9 octobre 1763.

[24] Padou, ruban de coton de 8 à 10 cm qui sert à border un vêtement pour éviter qu'il ne se déforme.

[25] Vol. 18, lettre 3029, p.143. À Mme Boy de la Tour à Lyon, Môtiers 19 novembre 1763.

son manteau arménien à la répétition générale du *Devin du village*, selon la remarque dans le Journal de Strasbourg du 9 novembre 1765: « Il est habillé en Arménien, excepté un bonnet de drap petit-gris, avec une bordure de poil de quatre à cinq doigts de hauteur. Je ne sais si le bonnet est doublé, car il ne l'ôte jamais à personne. » Le même accoutrement le revêt durant son séjour en Angleterre (1766-1767), comme le révèle le portrait peint par Ramsay de la National Portrait Gallery d'Écosse à Édimbourg (Fig. 5). La gravure en buste de Rousseau avec manteau arménien et toque de Taraval d'après un dessin de Watelet (Fig. 6) a été reproduite en bronze sous la Révolution, et sous la Restauration, en biscuit de Wedgwood. Quand le peintre François Gérard (1770-1837) envisagea de faire un portrait posthume de Rousseau, c'est revêtu de son costume arménien qu'il le peindra. (Fig. 7)[26]

---

[26] Galerie du Rhône, Martigny, Suisse, vente du 5 juin 2004.

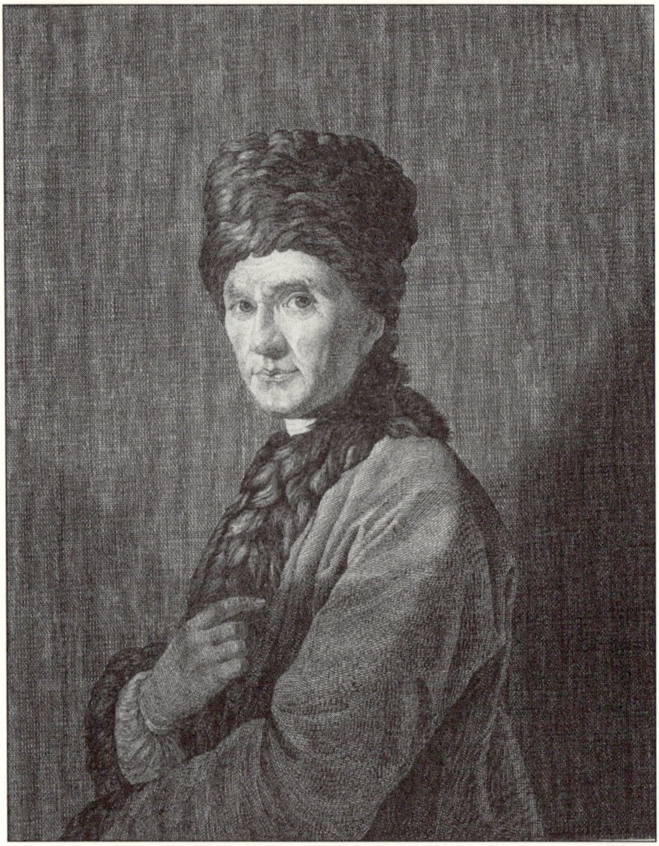

Fig. 5- Portrait de J.J. Rousseau. Gravure de I.E. Nocher 1769, d'après le tableau de Ramsay peint en 1766. GIR 349. Bibliothèque de Genève, d'iconographie genevoise.

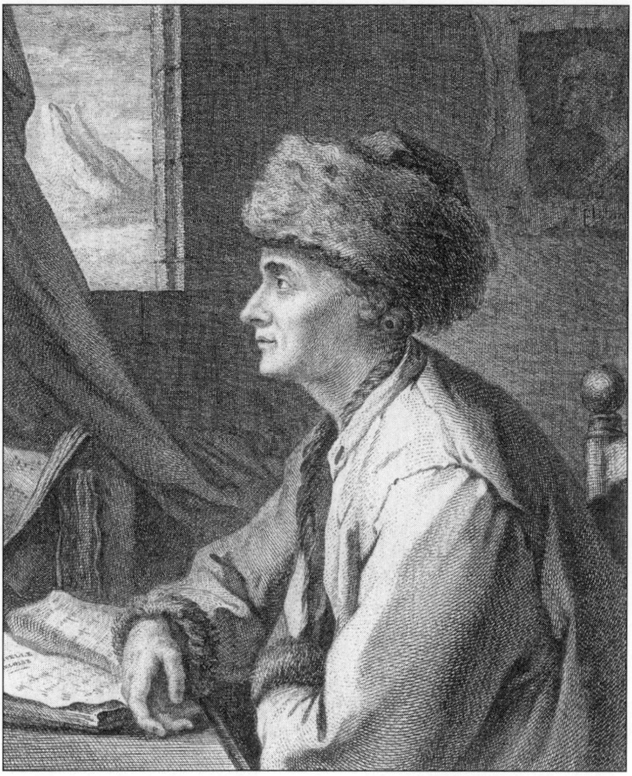

Fig. 6- Portrait de J.J. Rousseau. Gravure de C.H. Watelet d'après un dessin de Taraval 1766. GIR 386. Bibliothèque de Genève, d'iconographie genevoise.

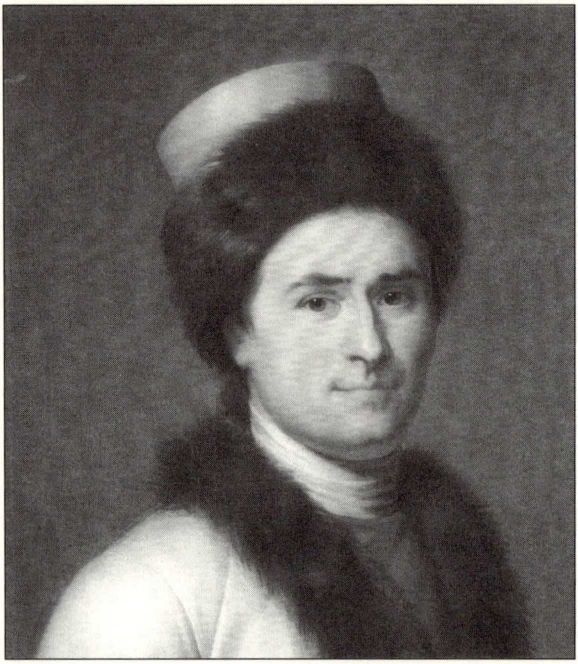

Fig. 7- Portrait de J.J. Rousseau. Huile de F.P.S. Gérard 1822. Galerie du Rhône, Martigny. Vente du 5 juin 2004 no. 524. Détail.

Il y a deux siècles et demi le mieux connu des personnages orientaux, et visible dans toutes les bourses de commerce et les foires internationales, aurait été assurément le marchand arménien. Riche de plusieurs cultures, il avait su s'imposer en particulier sur le marché des textiles aux soies multiples et aux cotonnades en tout genre, ainsi que dans le négoce des pierres précieuses. Toutes les routes caravanières depuis le sous-continent asiatique lui étaient connues, et son savoir-faire, basé sur un réseau religieux et familial, sous-tendu par de précis codes commerciaux, en faisait un négociant à la fois dur au négoce mais sur lequel on pouvait compter. Aussi n'est-il pas surprenant que son costume ait été aussi adopté par d'entreprenants voyageurs européens et par ceux qui, comme Rousseau, recherchant le confort d'un vêtement ample et exotique, s'attachèrent au kaftan, l'habit de l'Arménien persan, ottoman ou même indien au 18e siècle[27].

[27] Au 17e siècle, sur la place d'Amsterdam, c'est le turban persan qui caractérise le marchand arménien. Voir Gulbenkian R., « L'habit arménien, laissez-passer oriental pour les missionnaires, marchands et voyageurs européens aux XVIème et XVIIème siècles », in *Revue des études arméniennes* 25 (1994-1995), pp. 369-388.

Philology and Linguistics

14

Developments in Armenian Spirituality[1]

Boghos Levon Zekiyan

I would like to start with a preliminary observation on the title I have given this present contribution. Christian spirituality in general, and Armenian spirituality in particular, present a great variety of trends and facets not only in their diachronic evolution but also in their synchronic reality. It is difficult indeed to assign any spirituality a linear and homogeneous path of evolution. Therefore, I prefer to speak of "developments" in Armenian spirituality in plural, rather than of "development" in singular. Because we have to deal not only with a rich and long living heritage that does not escape the rules of historical evolution, but at the same time with an innerly dynamic entity exhibiting many different dimensions, movements, and tensions. These peculiarities of Armenian spirituality, in its capillary penetration and concrete manifestations, are seen in the life of a variety of persons, groups, communities, and institutions. Thus, the present study has no claim that the trends we shall be pointing to and taking into consideration are to be considered as those being the most dominant and specific ones in the whole or in a given period.

Yet some other delimitation of the topic I will deal with is still necessary. A first delimitation regards the diachronic dimension. First for reasons of space, since it is not possible to allude in the

---

[1] This article is a thorough re-elaboration of a paper originally presented to the International Symposium, held in Bossey, Switzerland, at the Institut Oecoménique de Bossey, 25 June-1 July, 2001, on "Armenian Spirituality: A Contextual Study for Our Time," in which Prof. Dickran Kouymjian also took part. This symposium was organized by the Great House of the Armenian Catholicosate of Cilicia, at Antelias, Lebanon, to celebrate the seventeenth centenary of the conversion to Christianity of the Kingdom of Armenia. The proceedings of the symposium have not yet been published.

limits of an article to a spiritual heritage of seventeen centuries, this article considers developments prior to the end of the Cilician period for which I take normally as a reference date, not the fall of the Kingdom, but the transfer of the Patriarchal See of the Catholicos from Sis to Etchmiadzin, its aboriginal place. Secondly, because developments successive to the Cilician era, that take their roots already in that same period, it places the intricate question of Latin influences on the main branch of the Apostolic community, thus, challenging a theoretical approach to decide to which extent given developments must be considered as harmoniously integrated with prior Armenian tradition, and hence as integral components of the overall Armenian tradition. This is the case, for instance, with Armenian scholasticism as it has been cultivated by the celebrated school of Tat'ew. One can suppose that this trend had a strong impact on Armenian spirituality.

A further delimitation of this article within the Cilician era itself is of a synchronic nature. This article covers the heritage of the Cilician era, in Cilicia proper. So developments taking place in Greater Armenia in that same period will rest for the moment outside of the horizon of this present paper. I hope to make it the subject of research from the standpoint of spirituality in a future study. Finally, I have to especially mention two of the great figures, who had a deep influence on their contemporaries and onwards, but who will remain outside of the range of this study: Yovhannēs Sarkawag (Hovhannes the Deacon, ca. 1050-1129) and Mkhit'ar Gosh (Gosh, ca. 1130-1213). Sarkawag's poem dedicated to the blackbird (without a title in the original) is to be considered as a religious manifesto to see in nature man's main interlocutor to find out the revelation of divine Grace. It certainly traces a deep wake in Armenian spirituality, to be put in parallel also with some basic trends of Armenian art, especially of Armenian architecture of which there already existed an extremely rich tradition when Sarkawag wrote his poem. On the other hand, although conceived and written in an erudite context and an accurately learned style, Sarkawag's *Poem on the Blackbird* discloses a keen spiritual syntony with the analogous attitude of St. Francis of Assisi (1182-1226), more than one century later in his *Cantico delle creature*.

Spirituality is a reflection, among many other factors-as cultural environment, education, socio-political influences, liturgy, and catechetical training, which contribute, each in its own measure and way-to shape it also and especially of theology. Thus a reference to the theological thought in the Armenian Church will help us. Some years ago, in 1998, at the International Symposium "Armenia and Christian Orient," organized by the National Academy of Sciences of the Republic of Armenia and the Armenian National Commission for UNESCO, held in Yerevan, I presented a paper under the title "Peculiar trends and exceptional figures in the development of the Armenian theological thought" (Ինքնուրոյն գիծեր ու եզակի մեծութիւններ հայ աստուածաբանական մտքի զարգացման մէջ) [*Ink'nuroyn gitser u ezaki metsut'iwnner hay astuatsbanakan mtk'i zargats'man mēj*], in *Armenia and Christian Orient* [Yerevan, 2000], pp. 101-108). This paper was only a first, and certainly elementary attempt to look into the rich heritage of the Armenian theological thought, for what may be the most specific and original contribution of the Armenian Church to universal Christian theology. Dealing now with spirituality, I shall refer to some ideas expressed in that paper as characterizing the theological horizon of some of the most eminent representatives of the Armenian theological tradition.

Another important component, especially in the Armenian case, related to the shaping of spirituality, is the Armenian Christian *Weltanschauung*, that I also like to call the Armenian Christian "ideology," giving this term its largest and deepest meaning in the wake of the French school of the history of ideas, represented by François Châtelet and his collaborators.[2] In several articles I dealt with the nature, the formation, the contents, and the main

---

[2] The term "ideology" may have different uses according to different levels and registers of thought: political, sociological etc. In this paper we use it in a meaning that we can define as "anthropologico-philosophical": as a whole of ideas, concepts, images, myths, in a word a whole of whatever kind of mental and imagery representation that may determine and orientate concrete options concerning the general statement of life of a community or of a person. This is, obviously, a very wide definition that embraces the whole range of mental and psychical factors capable to play some real role and impress their own seal in the manifold manifestations of human society and man's individuality. Thus intended "ideology" is very close to German *Weltanschauung*. This is the basic meaning in which the term has been used by the authors of *Histoire des idéologies*, sous la dir. de Fr. Châtelet, vols. 1-3 (Paris: Hachette, 1978): cf. vol. 1, "Introduction générale," pp. 9-13.

characteristics of this ideology as well as with the methodological premises and requirements for its study. Just for reasons of time and space I shall not repeat here the basic views and conclusions reached and formulated in those studies, limiting myself, when necessary, to textual references. This is also valid as far as some peculiar trends of Armenian spirituality are concerned in their relationship with the artistic expressions.[3]

---

[3] As main titles, the following may be considered: "L'«idéologie» nationale de Movsēs Khorenats'i et sa conception de l'histoire," *Handes Amsorya*, CI (1987), Kol. 471-485; "Ellenismo, ebraismo e cristianesimo in Mosè di Corene (Movsēs Khorenats'i). Elementi per una teologia dell'etnia," *Augustinianum*, XXVIII (1988): *XVI. Incontro di Studiosi dell'Antichità Cristiana. Cristianesimo e giudaismo: eredità e confronti, 7-9 maggio 1987* (Roma, 1988), pp. 381-390*; "Hrand Nazariantz, gli Armeni e l'Italia. Da una vicenda interculturale verso una nuova tipologia di confronto etnoculturale," *Annali di Ca' Foscari*, XXIX, 3 (Serie Orientale 21) (1990), pp. 135-150*; "Les identités polyvalentes et Sergueï Paradžanov. La situation emblématique de l'artiste et le problème de la polyvalence ethnique et culturelle," *Filosofia Oggi*, XVI (1993), pp. 217-231; "Riflessioni preliminari sulla spiritualità armena. Una cristianità di 'frontiera': *martyria* ed apertura all'*oikumene,*" *Orientalia Christiana Periodica*, 61 (1995), pp. 333-365 (pp. 343-346, under the title "*Segni di un mondo spirituale*" a paragraph is dedicated to spiritual trends present in artistic expressions); "Das Verhältnis zwischen Sprache und Identität in der Entwicklung der armenischen Nationalbewußttseins. Versuch einer begrifflichen Formulierung aus geschichtlicher Erfahrung," in *Über Muttersprachen und Vaterländer. Zur Entwicklung von Standardsprachen und Nationen in Europa*, G. Hentschel (Hrsg.), Frankfurf am M.-Berlin-Bern-New York-Paris-Wien (Peter Lang) (1997), pp. 277-297; "Lo studio delle interazioni politiche e culturali tra le popolazioni della Subcaucasia: alcuni problemi di metodologia e di fondo in prospettiva sincronica e diacronica," in *Il Caucaso: cerniera fra culture dal Mediterraneo alla Persia (secoli IV-XI). Atti della Quarantatreesima Settimana di studio del Centro Italiano di Studi sull'Alto Medioevo (aprile 1995)*, I (Spoleto, 1996), pp. 427-482; "In margine alla storia. Dal fenomeno dell'emigrazione verso un nuovo concetto dell'identità e dell'integrazione etnoculturale", in *Ad limina Italiae,* A? druns Italioy. *In viaggio per l'Italia con mercanti e monaci armeni*, a cura di B.L. Zekiyan, Editoriale Programma, Padova, 1996, S. 267-286*; *The Armenian Way to Modernity. Armenian Identity between Tradition and Innovation, Specificity and Universality* (Eurasiatica 49, Quaderni del Dipartimento di Studi Eurasiatici, Università degli Studi

The Formative Period (Fifth-Seventh centuries)

There may be no doubt, I think, that the first great period of the culture of Christian Armenia is that period of an extraordinary blossoming both in art and letters, and in heroism, as well as in religious and national consciousness, which we can call the formative period of the Armenian Christian identity. Formative, not in the sense that a full expansion of that identity is not yet realized in this period, but in the sense that the foundations of that identity were laid in this period. It starts with the conversion and the Baptism of the Kingdom, and it continues until the beginning of Arab domination in Armenia. If we look for a symbolic date, we can indicate 661, the year of the death of Catholicos Nersēs III and of the reaffirmation by Khalif Moawiya of the Arab power in Armenia.

There may also be no doubt that the height of this formative period is in the fifth century: the hallmarks of this period include the great era of the invention of the Armenian alphabet that brings to its full conclusion the process of rooting of the Christian religion in Armenia, that becomes the basis of the incarnation of the new religion in the Armenian culture, that gives birth to that extraordinary cultural blossoming that we all know; the great era also of the battle of Avarayr which is the first Baptism of blood that involves the Armenian Church and the Armenian nation as a whole, sealing definitively the historical marriage between Christian faith and

---

Ca' Foscari di Venezia) (Venezia: Supernova 1997), part. pp. 15-26, 83-96; "L'Armenia tra Bisanzio e l'Iran dei Sasanidi e momenti della fondazione dell'ideologia dell'Armenia cristiana (secc. V-VII). Preliminari per una sintesi", in *Crossroad of Cultures. Studies in Liturgy and Patristics in Honor of Gabriele Winkler*, Hans-Jürgen Feulner, Elena Velkovska, and Robert F. Taft, S.J., eds., *Orientalia Christiana Analecta*, 260 (Roma: Pontif. Ist. Orientale, 2000), pp. 717-744; *Ընդկովկասեան տարածաշրջանին մէջ քրիստոնէական ներմշակութային հայկական բնորդը. Նախադարեր ազգային ինքնութեան աստուածաբանութեան* [in transliteration HMB: Ĕndkovkasean taratsashrjanin mēj k'ristonēakan nermshakut'aynats'man haykakan bnordě. Nakhadarer azgayin ink'nut'ean astuatsabanut'ean] [The Armenian Model of Christian Inculturation in the Subcaucasion area. Preliminaries for a Theology of Ethnos], *Hask Hayagitakan Taregirk*, N.S., IX (1997-2001), pp. 53-69. (The titles bearing the sign of an asterisk are now gathered in *L'Armenia e gli armeni. Polis lacerata e patria spirituale: la sfida di una sopravvivenza*, [Milano, Guerini e Ass., 2000]).

Armenian identity; the era, in one word, of the *Surb T'argmanich'k'*, the Holy Translators, and of *Surb Vardanank'*, Vardan and His Companions, the "Holy Warriors,"[4] who will inspire the Armenian people throughout the various vicissitudes of its tormented history, and to whom Armenians will turn their eyes as models and supports to overwhelm their difficulties.

If the fifth century is the starting point of the liturgical, hierarchic, canonical, and monastic organization of the Armenian Church, and if the fifth century is the apex of this formative period, the sixth and seventh centuries also played their important role in giving the Armenian Christian identity some of its most specific traits. I would like to sum up in the following two points those respective roles. The sixth century marks the definitive orientation of the Armenian Church, in her main branch and majority, against Chalcedon. It places the Armenian Christianity within the orbit of that Christian world that we call today Ancient Oriental or pre-Chalcedonian Churches. The seventh century, on the contrary, brings a counter-balance in this orientation in that Armenians will not close, in a univocal, definitive, and almost sectarian way, all path of dialogue with Byzantine Christianity and its multifarious world.[5]

---

[4] It is in any case no "war of religion" in the habitual and current sense of the word. See "Riflessioni preliminari sulla spiritualità armena," pp. 337-341; ID., "A Historical Outline of the Armenian People," in Adriano Alpago-Novello, ed., *The Armenians* (New York, NY: Rizzoli International, 1986), p. 52.

[5] It is however an almost unanimous opinion nowadays that this opposition, as far as Christology is concerned, was not in the substance of the doctrine but in its theological and dogmatic formulation. On the Armenian Church and Chalcedon, Karekin Sarkissian's and Nina Garsoian's volumes that also furnish a wide bibliography, can be considered as the basic works of reference, in recent decades, notwithstanding differences of approaches and positions: Karekin Sarkissian, *The Council of Chalcedon and the Armenian Church* (London, 1965, New York, 1975); Nina G. Garsöian, *L'Église arménienne et le grand schisme d'Orient*, (Corpus Scriptorum Christianorum Orientalium, 574: Subsidia 100), 1998. Jean-Pierre Mahé's extensive insight into Armenian Christianity from 611 through 1066, although of a more general historical tenor, is also mainly concerned with the Chalcedonian and anti-Chalcedonian issue: "L'Église arménienne de 611 à 1066", *Histoire du Christianisme des origines à nos jours*, sous la dir. de Jean-Marie Mayeur ..., t. IV, Évêques, moines et empereurs (610-1054),

Let us now put a first and general question as to Armenian spirituality: what kind of spirituality do we meet in Armenia within this overall frame of the formative period? This is obviously a huge question that might be the subject of an entire monograph, or even of many monographs. On the other side, to attempt to give it a univocal reply would contradict what we said at the very beginning of our inquiry. I think however that we can and must try to find out some basic and, more or less, common trends that accompany the

---

sous la responsabilité de Gilbert Dagron ..., Desclée (1993), ch. II, 457-533. For some peculiar questions see: Poghos Ananian, "*Քննութիւն Հայ եկեղեցւոյ Պատմութեան (Ե. եւ Զ դար) [K'nnut'iwn Hay Ekeghets'woy patmut'ean (E. ew Z. dar*)], [Recherches sur l'histoire de l'Eglise Arménienne du Ve au VIe siècle] (St. Lazare – Venise 1991), a collection of articles published earlier in Pazmaveb/Bazmavep; Զաքարիա Հայոց Կաթողիկոսի եւ Աշոտ Իշխանաց Իշխանի թղթակցութիւնը Փոտ Պատրիարքի եւ Նիկողայոս Ա. Պապի հետ [Zak'aria Hayots' Kat'oghikosi ew Ashot Ishkhanats' Ishkhani tgh't'akts'ut'iwnĕ P'ot Patriark'i ew Nikoghayos A. Papi het] [La correspondence du Catholicos des Arméniens Zak'aria et du Prince des Princes Ashot avec le Patriarche Photius et le Pape Nicolas Ier], (Bibliothèque d'Arménologie « Bazmavep », 35) (St. Lazare-Venise 1992), (French Résumé: pp. 94-98); B. L. Zekiyan, "La rupture entre les Églises Géorgienne et Arménienne au début du VIIe siècle. Essai d'une vue d'ensemble de l'arrière-plan historique, *Revue des Études Arméniennes*, N.S., XVI (1982), pp. 155-174; ID., "Les relations arméno-byzantines après la mort de St Nersēs Shnorhali, in *XVI. Internationaler Byzantinistenkongress. Akten*, II/4: *Jahrbuch der österreichischen Byzantinistik*, 32/4, pp. 331-337; ID., "The Armenian Community of Philippopolis and the Bishop Ioannes Atmanos Imperial Legate to Cilicia," in *Between the Danube and the Caucasus: Oriental Sources on the History of the Peoples of Central and South-Eastern Europe*, G. Kara, ed., (Budapest, 1987), p. 363-373; Krikor Maksoudian, "The Chalcedonian Issue and the Early Bagratids: The Council of Shirakawan," in *Revue des Études Arméniennes*, N.S., XXI (1988-89), pp. 333-344; Viada A. Arutjunova-Fidanjan, "The Ethno-confessional Self-Awareness of Armenian Chalcedonians," ibid., pp. 345-363; Andrea Schmidt, "Die *Refutatio* des Timotheus Aelurus gegen das Konzil von Chalcedon. Ihre Bedeutung für die Bekenntnisentwicklung der armenischen Kirche Persiens im 6. Jahrhundert," *Oriens Christianus*, 73 (1989), pp. 149-165; Aleksej Lidov, "L'art des Arméniens chalcédoniens," in *Atti del V Simposio Internazionale di Arte Armena (Venezia 30 maggio-3 giugno)* (San Lazzaro, Venezia 1992), pp. 479-495.

expressions of Armenian spirituality at this early stage of its formation.

It is quite evident that Armenian spirituality also shares those basic and common trends which are a distinctive feature of almost all Christian spirituality at the Patristic era in its ecclesial, and more precisely ecclesial-communitarian expressions. I say "almost," and stress the word "communitarian," since such phenomena as early anachoretism, hermitism, with all their multiple and, sometimes, extravagant manifestations of different ways of solitary life, even if belonging to the overall reality of the Church, bear however the witness of a very peculiar aspect of Christian life, which cannot offer a pattern for basic and common trends of Christian behavior. Of course, they existed also in Armenia, although we must add that we do not find here, at least with the same frequency and relevance, the most extravagant manifestations of early Christian hermitism such as stylitism, and similar, affiliated practices, frequent, and typical indeed, specially in the Syriac area. Leaving apart hermitism, both in its more common and most extravagant features, we can consider early Christian life as centered on two prototypes: on one hand the community of faithful living in the world, and on the other hand the coenobitic or monastic communities. They both belong to the public, official, and communitarian expressions of life of the early Church. They share some of the following basic trends:

a) the centrality of liturgy, that means the public, communitarian organization of prayer;

b) a keen sensitivity for the local community, hence for the local Church;

c) a rigorous asceticism; and

d) a strong perception of Christianity as a witness, and a deep insight into the substantial correlation between the witness of word and the witness of blood.

These basic elements underwent, in Armenia, re-elaborations and new developments, following a basic and almost structural trend of the Armenian rite, which we can even observe in the Armenian language, that successive evolutions do not obscure what is earlier and archaic.[6] We can add that Armenia bears sometimes a unique

---

[6] Let me quote here what I was writing in note in my study on Eghishē ("Quelques observations critiques sur le "Corpus Elisaeanum," in *The*

witness to the famous law of *area serior*, which formulated originally in comparative linguistics, proves its validity in many fields of human life and behavior.[7] Thus the palaeo-Syriac theologoumenon of *bnay kyama* survives in Armenia in the marvelous synthesis of Eghishē's vision of the Church as *ukht* [alliance].[8] Similarly, the archaic and fecund Syriac conception of the

---

Armenian Christian Tradition. Scholarly Symposium in Honor of the Visit to the Pontifical Oriental Institute, Rome, of His Holiness Karekin I Supreme Patriarch and Catholicos of All Armenians, December 12, 1996, ed. by R. F. Taft, S.J. (Orientalia Christiana Analecta, 254), (Roma: Pontif. Ist. Orientale, 1997), n. 67, pp. 121-122): "Au fond, il s'agit peut-être, encore une fois, d'une caractéristique arménienne assez particulière. En général, on peut rencontrer dans le caractère et dans la culture arméniens ce trait assez paradoxal: ils font, souvent, preuve d'un fort conservatisme autant que de tendances poussée vers l'innovation, et même d'un certain esprit révolutionnaire ou 'anarchique.' Aussi la langue arménienne a été considérée comme une des langues qui ont maintenu quelques traits des plus archaïques du proto-indo-européen en même temps qu'elle a revolutionné certains aspects du système indo-européen. Dans la liturgie, l'étude de G. Winkler sur le Sacrement du Baptême, *Das armenische Initiationsrituale*, (OChA, 217) (Roma, 1982), a démontré, de façon incontestable, comment le rite arménien ait conservé, malgré les maintes évolutions postérieures, les moments les plus archaïques du rite, de provenance syriaques, qui ne sont pas restés avec la même pureté de traits dans la liturgie syriaque elle-même. Un procédé semblable vient d'être mis en lumière par deux thèses doctorales, défendues respectivement en 1996 et 1997 à l'Institut Pontifical Oriental. La première, par C. Gugerotti sur le rite arménien de l'ordination montre que ce rite, tout en s'enrischissant, à l'époque cilicienne, des apports de la liturgie latine, réussit à maintenir, dans son caractère original, le noyau le plus archaïque du rite; la deuxième, par M. Findikyan sur la Liturgie des Heures, met en évidence que la structure originelle de cette Liturgie reste intacte malgré les évolutions successives".

[7] Cf. Giancarlo Bolgnesi, "Tradition and Innovation in the Armenian Language," in *Studi glottologici, filologici, orientali* (Brescia: Paideia Ed. ce, 1990), p. 381.

[8] See our "Ełišē as Witness of the Ecclesiology of the Early Armenian Church," in Nina G. Garsoïan, Thomas F. Mathews and Robert W. Thomson, eds., *East of Byzantium: Syria and Armenia in the Formative Period*, Dumbarton Oaks Symposium 1980 (Washington, D.C.: Dumbarton Oaks Center for Byzantine Studies, 1982), pp. 187-197.

Holy Ghost as "Female" finds in Armenia a magnificent development in the *Vardapetut'iwn Grigori*, one of the most outstanding catechetical monuments of the Patristic age, while the echo of that very archaic theological vision is still perceivable in the late 10th and early 11th centuries by St. Gregory of Narek.[9]

Let us, however, go back to the above-mentioned four basic trends to see briefly what kind of new developments they underwent in Armenia.

a. The centrality of liturgy in the Armenians is shown by a very strong sense of the function of the church edifice as the place of the concrete incarnation of the spiritual Church. Eghishē leaves from this conviction to build, on the background of the *Vardanants' War*, his peculiar theology of the common priesthood of all the faithful, which has as its corresponding pole the fact that the bodies of all of them are the temples and the altars for the exercise of this priesthood. The extraordinary abundance of churches in historic Armenia,[10] often in smaller dimensions, especially in centuries subsequent to the formative period, is very significant, I think, with regard to this matter. In inverted proportions, the abundance and small sizes of those churches underline their function as indispensable reference points, milestones in the everyday life of the small local community

---

[9] Cf. G. Winkler, "Die Tauf-Hymnen der Armenier," in *Liturgie und Dichtung*, EOS Verl., Erzabtei St. Ottilien, 1983, pp. 381-419; EAD., "Überlegungen zum Gottesgeist als mütterlichem Prinzip und zur Bedeutung der Androgynie in einigen frühchristlichen Quellen," in *Frauenforschung aus liturgiewissenschaflicher Sicht*, ibid. (1990), pp. 7-29. Some passages of St. Gregory's teaching, *Vardapetut'iwn Grigori*, in Agathangeghos (for ex. par. 412), are among the major texts of the earliest Armenian literature on the female/maternal function of Holy Spirit. These traits remain somehow hidden in the English version of the *Teaching* by R. Thomson (*The Teaching of St. Gregory*, first published by Harvard University Press in 1970, has recently had a new revised edition in the series "AVANT: Treasures of the Armenian Christian Tradition – Number 1", St. Nersess Armenian Seminary [New Rochelle, NY, 2001]) which in any case follows in general a high level philological standard. Furthermore no allusion to that function is to be found in the Translator's "Introduction."

[10] There is a superabundant literature on Armenian architecture. Let us mention here one of the most comprehensive and rigorous recent works on the subject: Paolo Cuneo, *Architettura armena dal quarto al diciannovesimo secolo* (Roma: De Luca Editore, 1988).

in perfect harmony with the very peculiar sensitivity developed in Armenia for the local Church.

b. Indeed this sensitivity for the local Church lead the Armenians to build their theology of the *ethnos*, certainly one of the most original and specific Armenian contributions to the general theological thought. It needs to be seriously studied and re-evaluated at the light of all those instruments which are offered to us by the developments of contemporary theology, such as the reflection on the "local Church" and on the "peculiar Church," the value of earthly realities in order for the Salvation, and the concept of inculturation, etc. The theology of *ethnos*, implied in the creative activity and the whole behavior of St. Mesrob Mashtots', will be developed according to two different, but complementary, trends by Eghishē and Movsēs Khorenats'i. This is not the right place to go deeper into this subject, its various problems and implications. I dealt with them in some recent papers and articles,[11] even if I must add that the analytical research and the theoretical reflection on them are just at their first steps and much work in this sense is still to be done.

c. Ascetic rigor found in Armenia its highest expression in martyrdom. We would not be wrong, if we say that martyrdom impressed its own mark very soon on Armenian spirituality. Announced by P'awstos, formulated in its highest expression by Eghishē, put in its eschatological dimension by Sebēos, the spirituality of martyrdom goes through the entire Armenian historiography as a red thread. Let us remember that Armenian

---

[11] "Ellenismo, ebraismo e cristianesimo in Mosè di Corene," n. 3; "Das Verhältnis zwischen Sprache und Identität," n. 2; "Die Christianisierung und die Alphabetisierung Armeniens als Vorbilder kultureller Incarnation, besonders im subkaukasischen Gebiet", in print in the Proceedings of the International Symposium "Die Christianisierung des Kaukasus/The Christianisation of Caucasus (Armenia, Georgia, Albania) (Wien, 1999)"; "Das Ethnos und die christliche Heilsordnung. Überlegungen aufgrund der armenischen Erfahrung für eine Theologie des Ethnos", in print in the Proceedings of "Weltkonferenz Armenien 2000. Halle (Salle)"; "I processi di cristianizzazione e di alfabetizzazione dell'Armenia in funzione di 'modelli'. Verso una teologia dell'etnia e della 'Chiesa etnica'", in print in the Proceedings of the Symposium in Honor of H.H. Garegin II at the Pontifical Oriental Institute, Rome, 2000; "Ĕndkovkasean taratsashrjanin mēj k'ristonēakan nermshakut'aynats'man haykakan bnordě."

historiography, one of the richest historiographical productions among the Middle Eastern cultures in the Middle Ages, is at the same time a deep theological reflection on history, on human life, on the chosen People, on the Church, and on Christian mysteries. History offers the platform for this reflection, which for this very reason is also a theology deeply rooted in life. It offers the double feature of a *theology through history*, and of a *theology of history*, as we would say in modern terms. A leading idea in this theology is the typological vision of the history and of the function of the chosen People in the overall history of Salvation. A concrete typological relationship links the history of the Jewish people to that of the Christian Church, considered not only in its universal extension, but also and especially in its local dimension and above all its ethnical rooting. All that the Armenian people endure and dream of this world as *a people of the last days*, of the New Alliance, has its *antitypus* in the life and history of the People of the First Testament. The Maccabees especially play a prominent role in this respect in Armenian historiography.[12]

d. Finally, the Armenian insight into the relationship between the witness of word and the witness of blood became deeper in parallel with the Armenian perception of the imperative of the incarnation of the word in the culture of a people.

We see, thus, that the various aspects of early Armenian theology and spirituality are strictly linked, and correlated in multiple ways, one with the other.

To conclude this very essential survey of the formative period, I would like to add that the animated Christological debates of the sixth and seventh centuries have contributed to give Armenian spirituality its strongly emphasized christocentric character. This basic trend will mark Armenian spirituality, we can say, in almost all its future developments.

The pathos for the language – trends in the seventh through the eleventh centuries

---

[12] See in part, R.W. Thomson, "The Maccabees in Early Armenian Historiography," in *The Journal of Theological Studies*, n.s., vol. XXVI, part 2 (1975), pp. 329-341.

The second great period in Armenian theology and spirituality covers, in my opinion, the period going inclusively from the seventh to the eleventh centuries. This is the period dominated by two exceptional personalities: Yovhannēs of Otsun (Otsnets'i, ca. 650-728, Catholicos since 717) and Grigor of Narek (Narekats'i, ca. 945-1003), the latter being without any doubt one of the greatest poets and deepest mystics in the history of world cultures and religions. This is also the period in which the question of the language, namely in the sense of French *langage* or Italian *linguaggio*, to express correctly Christ's ontological constitution, becomes almost an obsession for the Armenians. Differently from the Byzantines, who are satisfied with their Chalcedonian definition and consider it as the last possible and absolutely perfect word in human language to say about Christ, the Armenians are, on the contrary, in a passionate search for a theological formulation that may be more and more perfect. Otsnets'i's balanced adhesion and explanation of the formula *yerkuts' bnut'eants'* (εκ δυαις φυσεσι) is not enough to stop that search.[13] The Armenian theory of *"anapakanut'iwn"* [incorruption], in the wake of Julian of Halicarnassus, whom the Armenians condemn, by some misunderstanding however, is one of the many examples that can be considered as an argument for that search.[14] One of the best specialists of this peculiar and highly delicate question in the history of Christian dogma, R. Draguet, regards these doctrines or, rather, these theologoumena as perfectly orthodox, if placed in their context. He writes: "Remises dans leur contexte, ces

---

[13] We lack unfortunately monographs both on Otsnets'i in general as well as on peculiar aspects of his rich personality and doctrine. On his Christology one can see: Arshak Tēr-Mikelian, *Die armenische Kirche in ihren Beziehungen zur byzantinischen (vom IV. bis zum XIII. Jahrhundert)* (Leipzig: Gustav Fock., 1892), pp. 73-74; Eruand Tēr-Minaseant', *Hayots' Ekeghets'u yaraberut'iwnnerě Asorwots' Ekeghets'ineri het. Haykakan ew asorakan aghbiwrneri hamadzayn*, [the Armenian edition of the author's *Die armenische Kirche in ihren Beziehungen zu den syrischen*, Leipzig, 1904] (S. Etchmiacin, 1908), *passim*, in part. pp. 172-175, 181-183, 207-209, 229-231; Maghak'ia Ōrmanean, *Azgapatum* [History of the Nation], I (Constantinople, 1912), par.s 573-575, col.s 838-842.

[14] As for the Armenians see Ōrmanean, *Azgapatum*, and especially Tēr-Minaseants', *Hayots'*.

formules n'expriment rien de contraire à la foi."[15] Also Step'anos of Siwnik' (Siwnets'i, ca. 688-735), one of the foremost figures in this period, and especially with regard to the Christological debates, shares the same trend.[16] The heartfelt cry, in the Benedictions of the Night Office traditionally attributed to him, "Christ is my God, and I will exalt him, the God of my father, and I will glorify him," paraphrasing once again the cry of the chosen People in *Exodus*, is a deeply touching expression of this radically Christological and Christocentric tension.

The question of language and of *linguaggio* reaches in the work of Grigor Narekats'i an abyssal dimension, to such an extent in which it probably has never been felt before or after, we may say, in human writing and conversation. I use expressly the term "abyssal," since, as I tried to demonstrate in a recent study,[17] it is the image of *bathos*, abyss, that expresses better the inner and deeper trait of Narekats'i's mysticism. Narekats'i has been in these last decades the most fortunate Armenian author to be studied according to the various aspects of his oceanic work. Krikor Beledian, James Russell, Jean-Pierre Mahé, Claudio Gugerotti, Hovhannes Davthyan and Emma Lalayan, Tamar Dasnabédian, and Poghos Khachatryan, to mention only some of the authors of many a remarkable study in the last two decades, have put in evidence with different, but complementary approaches, the depth, variety, richness, and complexity of Narekian poetry and mysticism letting us understand once again that Narekian research is still taking its first steps.

In relation with our present topic, I would like to call attention particularly upon the following themes that emerge from some of the

---

[15] René Draguet, *Julien d'Halicarnasse*, in *Dictionnaire de Théologie Catholique*, VIII, col. 1938.

[16] See Daniel Findikyan, *The Commentary of the Armenian Daily Office by Bishop Step'anos Siwnets'i († 735). Edition and Translation of the Long and Short Versions with Textual and Liturgical Study*, Dissertatio ad Doctoratum, yet unpublished, (Romae: Pontificium Institutum tudiorum Orientalium, 1997), p. 21. For general and bibliographical information on Siwnets'i, see ibid. pp. 13-25.

[17] *La spiritualità armena. Il Il libro della lamentazione di Gregorio di Narek*, traduzione e note di B. L. Zekiyan, Introduzione di B. L. Zekiyan e Cl. Gugerotti, Presentazione di D. Barsotti (Roma: Ed.ni Studium, 1999), p. 91.

above mentioned studies: a) the "wreck" [*erkp'eghkum*] of the language as Beledian calls it, implying the whole problem of God's absolute ineffability in intimate and unavoidable connection with the absolute necessity to confess and praise Him; hence, the problem of language as the *place* where God's Grace, Salvation, and Mercy appear to man in his total poverty and nullity;[18] b) the perception of *penthos* with its uniquely Narekian accents, rooted however in the long Armenian tradition of a cult of the word, put in light especially by Gugerotti;[19] c) the exceptional involvement, leading to a real implosion, of the personal *ego* in Narekats'i's spiritual adventure, for which some preceding parallel can be found perhaps but in St. Augustine's *Confessions*, and it will be equally difficult indeed to find something similar to that in subsequent centuries. As I have tried to point out, if we want to search at any cost for some parallel, the most fitting one we shall find, I think, in a very different expression however, on Monte Verna with Francis prostrated to earth, and "loam in the mouth" to use Narekats'i's words, asking and crying: "Deus meus, quis es Tu, et quis sum ego?", the highest peak or deepest bottom ever reached, I would say, in Christian mysticism.[20]

Evangelical radicality and opening to the *oikumene* – the Cilician component of the Cilician era (ca. 1045-ca. 1441)

The Cilician period, although very different indeed from the preceding ages in Armenian history for a number of reasons, is however, in strict links with the prior heritage. We all know the great, extraordinary opening of Cilician Armenia to the Christian *oikumene*, especially incarnated in two unique figures, sharing the same name Nersēs Shnorhali (1102-1173, Catholicos since 1165, from now on Shnorhali) and Lambronats'i (1152/53-1198, Bishop of

---

[18] With regard to this topic of Krikor Beledian's Narekian research, let us mention here especially: *Grigor Narekats'i lezui sahmannerun mēj* [*Grigor Narekats'i dans les limites du langage*], (Bibliothèque d'Arménologie "Bazmavep") (Venise–St. Lazare, 1985), in part. ch. II, B, pp. 69-80, French Résumé: pp. 155-157.

[19] See ch. III of the Introduction to *La spiritualità armena*, by Claudio Gugetotti, *La parola-lamento e Gregorio di Narek*, pp. 102-135.

[20] See B. L. Zekiyan, ch. II of the Introduction to *La spiritualità armena: San Gregorio di Narek, Surb Grigor Narekatsi*, pp. 76-91.

Tarsus/Tarson since 1180/1181), whose conceptions on the theological language, interecclesial relations, interconfessional debates, can find other terms of parallel but in the modern ecumenical movement that Pope Paul VI defined "something new with regard to the long and painful history which preceded us,"[21] and I would dare to add that modern ecumenism, even in its most advanced instances, has not yet achieved the whole corpus of principles and instructions formulated by those blessed souls. Since the basis of all this building is a very peculiar insight into the nature of human language in general, and of the theological language in particular, I think that we can understand it much better in its historical roots and cultural-ecclesial context if we consider it in the light of Narekats'i's mysticism of the "wreck" of language. And we know how deep a devotion and admiration nourished both Shnorhali and Lambronats'i for Gregory of Narek, whom they venerated as an "angel in body."

Even if this continuity in tradition from Narek to Hṙomkla (Shnorhali's patriarchal residence) and Tarson is clearly evident, we must, I think, consider yet some other important factor. At this point we touch upon a very deep, I would say, the ultimate link that, like an underground stream, unites these three figures: Narekats'i, Shnorhali, and Lambronats'i, apparently one so different from the other. It is a link that also unites the main expressions and orientations and the highlights of Armenian spirituality in its manifold and multifarious ramifications and developments.

The consciousness of the extreme fragility of human language, hence of human concepts and human thought, is a basic theme, a *leitmotiv* that both Shnorhali and Lambronats'i also develop and deepen, although in another contextual frame than Narekats'i: in relation to the Christological dogma, and to what we would call today the "ecumenical dialogue."[22] Such consciousness that goes far

---

[21] "L'ecumenismo è una cosa nuova rispetto alla lunga e dolorosa storia che ci ha preceduto… è cosa arcana, che affonda le sue radici nei misteriosi disegni di Dio" quoted by Germano Pattaro, *Corso di teologia dell'ecumenismo* (Queriniana, Brescia, 1985), p. 4.

[22] For a detailed analysis see: B. L. Zekiyan, "Un dialogue oecuménique au XIIe siècle: les pourparlers entre le catholicos St Nersēs Šnorhali et le légat impérial Théorianos en vue de l'union des Eglises arménienne et byzantine," *Actes du XVe Congrès International d'Études byzantines -*

beyond the perception of human fragility on simply a metaphysical and ethical ground is certainly a very important factor, even the most important, to explain Shnorhali's and Lambronats'i's outstanding opening in interecclesial dialogue, and to explain also the relative open-mindedness of the Armenian Church in comparison with other Christian realities. Such excesses, for instance, as reiterated Baptism never prospered among Armenians. Also their conception of *communicatio in sacris* has normally been wider than that of other Churches, including the Roman Catholic Church, whose practice in this matter up to recent times – practically up to Vatican II in the sixties of the last century – has been among the most rigorous ones. It will be interesting to quote here the following words of a Turkish author who certainly cannot be suspected of favoritism for Armenians: "They have a great capacity of adaptation to the ambiance. They are not fanatic in religion and in the use of the language. They are, however, faithful and tied to their faith and

---

Athènes, Sept. 1976, IV, *Histoire, Communications* (Athènes 1980), p. 420-441. See also: ID., Les relations arméno-byzantines après la mort de St Nersēs Shnorhali; ID., "The Armenian Community of Philippopolis; ID., "Nersēs de Lambron" e "Nersēs Shnorhali," *Dictionnaire de Spiritualité*, XI (Paris, 1981), col. 122-134, 134-150; ID., "Les disputes religieuses du XIVe siècle, prélude des divisions et du statut ecclésiologiques postérieurs de l'Église Arménienne," *Actes du Colloque «Les Lusignan et l'Outre Mer». Poitiers-Lusignan, 20-24 Octobre 1993,* Programme com'science, Conseil Régional Poitu-Charentes, [w.d.], pp. p. 314-315, n. 21; the same in English with light variants: "The Religious Quarrels of the 14th Century Preluding to the Subsequent Divisions and Ecclesiological Status of the Armenian Church," dans *Studi sull'Oriente Cristiano*, I (1997), pp. 175-76, n. 22; ID., "Un singolare itinerario di spiritualità dalla frontiera all'oikumene. Riflessioni sulla cristianità armena", in *Religioni e sette nel mondo*, 1 (1995), p. 37-53; P. Ananian, "Narsete IV Klayetzi", dans *Biblioteca Sanctorum*, IX, Rome, 1967, col. 750-753; E. Suttner, "Eine «Ökumenische Bewegung» im 12. Jahrhundert und ihr bedeutendster Theologe, der armenische Katholikos Nerses Schnorhali", dans *Kleronomia*, t. 7, fasc. 1, 1975, p. 87-97; H. Khatchadourian, "The Christology of St. Nerses Shnorhali in Dialogue with Byzantium," dans *Miscellanea Francescana*, 78 (1978), p. 413-434; Archbishop Mesrob Ashjian, *St. Nerses of Lambron, Champion of the Church Universal. His Synodal Discourse with English Translation and Annotations* (New York: The Armenian Prelacy, 1993), pp. 12-35.

beliefs as they are in friendship too. For this reason, notwithstanding pressures during the centuries, the great majority of them have not changed their religion and confession, even at the price of great privations and suffering."[23]

Shnorhali and Lambronats'i are not only at the highest rank, among a lot of exceptional masters in theology and spirituality in Cilician Armenia or the most representative figures of the Cilician era, but simply, they are at the peak of the greatest and most representative spirits of the Armenian Church and, for more than one reason, also of the Universal Church. They are certainly among the greatest and most original ecumenical minds of all of Christianity.

As far as their Armenian collocation is especially concerned, if the statement now made is absolutely evident for Shnorhali, it may not seem perhaps clear enough in so far as Lambronats'i comes into question. But such a suspicion has little ground. The debate on Lambronats'i's personality and value was rather a superstructural phenomenon that originated very late, although in passionate terms, in the nineteenth century within groups of definitely integralist attitudes. First it was a faction of Catholic Armenians who tried to denigrate him in the eyes of the Roman Holy See, taking as pretext for their venomous campaign the publication, in Venice by the Mekhhitarist Fathers of San Lazzaro in 1847, of his Commentary to the Holy Sacrifice. Somehow later an analogous campaign of denigration exploded among some influential groups of Apostolic Armenians. It reached the climax by some Caucasian Armenians, such as Karapet Ezeants'. This latter was totally deprived of that *esprit de finesse* which distinguishes, for instance, Patriarch Ormanian's evaluations and style, even when he has serious reservations to express as he does also for Lambronats'i'. There are, however, more than one positive and consistent signals that this sad chapter in the Armenian public and especially ecclesiastical opinion as far as Lambronats'i's evaluation and veneration is at issue is definitively overwhelmed.[24] We have to add that the opposition to his ideas and to his Church policy, led during his lifetime by some

---

[23] Sadi Koçaş, *Tarih boyunca Ermeniler ve Türk-Ermeni ilişkileri* [The Armenians and the Turkish-Armenian Relations through the centuries], 2nd ed. (Ankara: Altınok Matbaası, 1967), p. 45.
[24] Mesrop Ashjian, *St. Nerses of Lambron.*

leading groups of North-Eastern Armenia, did not dim either his glory nor his influence. The most influential mind within the Armenian Church since the fifteenth century, St. Gregory of Tat'ew (1346-1409), considered generally as the main pillar of Armenian orthodoxy, speaks of Lambronats'i as եռամեծ եւ սուրբ հայրն մեր, that is, "our threefold great and holy Father."

As to the extent of the influence exercised by Lambronats'i, let it be enough to mention here the following two facts: a) he succeeded in eradicating the largely diffused medieval usage of celebrating Eucharist in a totally private form, even if his model of daily solemn celebration did not take root leaving the place only to the solemn celebration of Sunday and of the great feast days; b) we owe to him the current canonical form of the Armenian rite of ordinations in which he made a great and wise synthesis between the Armenian up to his days and many Western elements borrowed from the Roman rite, which are not only assimilated and transformed, but also perfectly integrated into the main trunk of the Armenian rite without dimming in any way its aboriginal and archaic features.[25]

Besides their exceptional ecumenical *envergure*, Shnorhali and Lambronats'i left deep traces in Armenian spirituality also for other reasons. Among these latter we can consider at first the strongly personal accent they introduced into liturgy. To explain this evolution, I would like to stress once again the link of both Saints with Gregory of Narek. I already alluded to the vehemence of the irruption of the personal *ego* in Narekats'i's mysticism. Yet no *ban* of *Narek*, that is no "word" of Gregory's masterpiece *Matean Oghbergut'ean* [Book of Lamentations] as he called the single chapters of his work, was written for liturgical use. Some of them entered into liturgy later. In the best of hypotheses, we can consider some Narekian *ban*s, in the author's intention, as paraliturgical. Shnorhali, the inspired reformer and last great forger of the Armenian liturgy, and Lambronats'i, in his wake, introduced in it strong personal accents. Such hymns and *sharakan*s of Shnorhali, as *Aṙawōt Lusoy* [Morning of light], *Ashkharh amenayn* [The whole world], *Hawatov khostovanim* [I confess with faith], or the whole sequence of the hymns of the Vigil of Christ's Passion in the Night Office, etc., are like the icebergs of this new liturgical trend, of this

[25] See note 6.

typically Armenian "*devotio moderna*" which not only precedes its Western equivalent, but is at the same time very deeply rooted in the traditional humus of Liturgy and excellently integrated with its traditional structures and dynamics.

Lambronats'i went one step further, and introduced into the Liturgy of the Mass Narekats'i's wonderful invocation to the Holy Ghost. This is indeed peculiar to the Pontifical liturgy, celebrated by a Bishop. But if we consider that Lambronats'i celebrated Holy Eucharist everyday with solemnity and with the participation of his whole clergy, we realize then that he considered that invocation as an integral part of every day's eucharistic celebration.

Let us now go back, however, to both Shnorhali's and Lambronats'i's ecumenical attitude. No doubt, Shnorhali is the forger, inspirer, prototype, and the most balanced, humanly most perfect incarnation of that doctrine and spirit. I alluded to a basic factor to explain that opening: the consciousness of the substantial fragility of human language. Now I would like to touch here upon another factor: Shnorhali's evangelical radicality, in a sense very near to that of Assisi's *Poverello*.

When Lambronats'i explains in his *Synodal Discourse* that there is no substantial difference in the faith of the Greeks and of the Armenians, he asks then: "But why … has no one until this day shown us this clearly, but rather the contrary?". Lambronats'i's answer to the question is: "I find that they, although saints and sages, did not live in accordance with the Law of Compassion."[26] With great respect for those pastors, doctors, and theologians of past centuries and with deep wisdom, Lambronats'i introduces a distinction between canonical holiness and radically evangelical holiness. He thinks that a lot of canonized saints had the former, but only a few ones the latter. To this second group belonged, doubtless, St. Nersēs Shnorhali.

That Shnorhali had effectively a very adherent and radical perception of Christ's message in its deepest implications, we can also deduce from another fact. He openly invites priests working among the *Arewordi*s not to challenge secular strength for forced conversions, since "to choose and to gather the good in the good vessels, according to the allegoric words of the Gospel, and to throw

[26] Ashjian, *St. Nerses of Lambron*, pp. 79-80.

away the bad is the concern of the righteous Judge when He will sit on the throne of his glory and will repay every one according to his faith and deed."[27] If we consider that St. Bernard, the *Doctor mellifluus* of the Western Church, expressly theorized the convenience of imposing Christian faith with arms, we immediately realize the distance and difference between the two saintly Doctors. Once again it is Francis of Assisi to incarnate in the West a radically evangelical approach to such problems similar to that of Shnorhali, although both will remain for centuries *vox clamantis in deserto*.

Yet there is a difference between Shnorhali and Francis that I believe of topical interest to point out. Francis does not cultivate theology, even he willingly refuses to do it, to put more clearly in light the radicality of his evangelic attitude. But doing so, he gives up at the same time, the possibility of correcting, improving, reforming theology from inside, from its roots, in its basic elements, principles, methods, approaches and views. Shnorhali, on the contrary, does not give up this task. Of course, he is no theologian in the medieval scholastic sense. He really is, however, a theologian in the best, patristic sense of the word: a great, original, and intuitive theologian whose discovery of the conventionality and relativity of human language, including the theological language too, together with his tireless stress upon the necessity of permeating theology of the spirit of love and charity, must be considered as a milestone in the history of theology and of dogma. Shnorhali stays at the origin of a new theology which – it is true – remains unknown and inaccessible outside of his Church, and even in his own Church it will not be universally understood and followed, although some particularly illuminated spirits will every so often revive its basic message. Just to mention one of such wise figures, let us quote here a passage of the letter of Movses IV of Tat'ew to Urbanus VIII: "We are not heretic or schismatic, as you think of us, but we are orthodox, following the confession of our spiritual Fathers. We anathematize by name all heretics: Arius, Macedonius, Nestorius, Eutyches and all those who think like them. In fact, even though if we say one nature of Christ, which seems to you as sounding Eutychian, we add however: unconfused. If we did not say unconfused, that would be an abominable heresy. In the same way, when you say "two natures,"

---

[27] Edition of St. Petersburg (1788), p. 198.

which is [like] to [what] Nestorius [said], you add: indivisible. If you had not added "indivisible" while saying two natures, that would be an abominable heresy. But, while we affirm one the unconfused nature, you affirm two the indivisible natures. Thus the meaning of both the expressions is but one and [equally] correct."[28]

These last considerations belong – it is true – rather to the domain of speculative theology than of spirituality. But this is a very important point to make here: a peculiar feature of Armenian spirituality is its very close, deep, inner link with theology. In the Armenian tradition we often have a thrilling testimony that spirituality is but lived, innerly experienced theology, theology penetrating into every day's life. Lambronats'i gives a trenchant definition of this conviction of which he has also been one of the most fascinating incarnations in the Armenian Church. He says: "It is well known to those who have experienced it: love of study is by itself love of God."[29] The specifically Armenian institution of the *vardapet*s is, I think, a most fitting expression on the ground of Church institution of this privileged link between theology and spirituality. This opens, however, a new chapter in our topic that cannot be discussed here, in the limits of this paper.

[28] Letter, on the 17th of August 1626, by Catholicos Movses IV with the Bishop Khach'atur of Cesarea [Kesarats'i] and the *vardapet* Aristakes to Pope Urbanus VIII (Archives of Propaganda Fide, Scritture Originali Congregazioni Generali, edited by G. Amadouni, *Oskan Vardapet Erewants'i ew ir zhamanakě* [O. V. of Yerevan and his time] (Venezia - S. Lazzaro, 1975), p. 268.

[29] Colophon of the Saint to his translation from the Greek of the *Dialogues* of Pope Gregory the Great: Garegin I Kat'oghikos [Yovsep'eants'], *Yishatakarank' dzeragrats'* [Colophons of Manuscripts], fifth century-1250 (Antilias, Lebanon, 1951), coloph. N° 218, col. 479; the same in A. S. T'evosyan, *Hayerēn dzeragreri yishatakaranner* [Colophons of Armenian manuscripts], fifth-twelfth century (Yerevan, 1988), coloph. N° 244, p. 227 (unfortunately this more recent and enriched edition of the oldest colophons does not indicate references to Yovsep'iants'' edition). For other testimonies related to the importance of the book and learning in the Armenian world as seen from a general cultural standpoint, see Zekiyan, "Riflessioni preliminari sulla spiritualità armena," pp. 350-351.

15

Saint Nersēs of Lambron and the Book of Revelation

Robert W. Thomson

In this volume, dedicated to Dickran Kouymjian, I wish to address the adaptation of a Greek commentary on the Book of Revelation by Saint Nersēs of Lambron. This enigmatic Book of Revelation, purportedly written on the island of Patmos by Saint John as a record of angelic interpretation of his visions, is now found at the end of the Bible. It did not always have that position; indeed it was not always accepted in early times as part of the biblical canon. In Armenian tradition, there are some scattered references to the Book of Revelation, or "Apocalypse," but not until Nersēs of Lambron in the later twelfth century did it become a serious object of study. Nersēs not only translated, or rather retranslated it, thereby making it more popular, in the same year 1179 he also adapted the widely read *Commentary* by Andrew of Caesarea [who lived 565-614].

The Book of Revelation is never mentioned in any of the lists of canonical books found in the proceedings of church councils – either in those of Armenian councils, or those of other councils translated into Armenian and found in the *Kanonagirk' Hayots'*. Nor was Revelation used in the readings of the liturgical year. Armenian authors from Grigor Tat'ewats'i onwards do refer to it in connection with the canon – but that brings us to the fourteenth century, long after Nersēs of Lambron.[1]

[1] Michael E. Stone, "Armenian Canon Lists IV: the List of Gregory of Tat'ew [14th century]," *Harvard Theological Review* 72 (1980), pp. 237-244.

As for Armenian Bibles, the Book of Revelation does not appear until the twelfth century.[2] The earliest surviving copy of Revelation is in Matenadaran 5607, dated to the twelfth century. This manuscript is not a bible as such, but rather a collection of theological works with an emphasis on biblical commentaries that includes a text of Revelation. The earliest dated bible with Revelation is Mat 4243 of AD 1263-6, written at Bardzraberd near Sis by the scribe Step'anos from Vahka. This is not a complete bible; the manuscript begins with Revelation, then come Acts and the Epistles, followed by the Prophets and Wisdom books. The only other copy of Revelation datable to the thirteenth century is in the famous *Charĕntir* written at Geghard by Mkhit'ar Ayrivanets'i in 1283.[3] The manuscript begins with the New Testament, with Revelation at the end, then comes the Old Testament, and after that a series of important patristic and philosophical texts. In Armenian bibles Revelation could be placed as the first book of the New Testament, could appear after the Gospel of John, after Acts, after the Catholic Epistles, or elsewhere.[4]

The date of the first translation of Revelation into Armenian is unclear. There are very few direct quotations from it in early Armenian literature, despite the profound impact of biblical imagery and vocabulary on nearly all Armenian writers. The *History* of Agat'angeghos, for example, has no direct quotation from it. Conybeare saw the influence of Revelation in that work, however, in an allusion to the vision of the 24 elders in Revelation 5.9: they sang a new song to the Lamb, saying "Thou hast redeemed us by thy

---

[2] For the contents of early manuscripts of the Armenian Bible see Shahē Achēmian, *Grand catalogue des manuscrits arméniens de la Bible* (Lisbon: Calouste Gulbenkian Foundation, 1992).

[3] Matenadaran 1500, dated by a colophon to 1283. See the description in Michael E. Stone, Dickran Kouymjian, Henning Lehman, *Album of Armenian Palaeography* (Aarhus: Aarhus University Press, 2002), pp. 296-297, with further bibliography. [The vitriolic review of this important volume in *Journal of the Society for Armenian Studies* 13 (2003-4), pp. 147-156, by Vrej Nersessian, neither gives an accurate description of the book nor does justice to its originality and significance.]

[4] See the study of Augustin Sek'ulay, *Nor ktakarani grk'eru kargĕ Hayots' k'ov* (Vienna: Mkhitarean Press, 1949).

blood."[5] But redemption through the blood of Christ is a theme that appears in the Pauline letters. Since the Book of Revelation itself has innumerable quotations from, and allusions to, passages elsewhere in scripture, many of the verses cited in modern indices of Armenian authors as being from Revelation cannot be affirmed as *bona fide* quotations from that book. Similarly, Eznik refers to Satan as a "rebellious dragon," an expression found also in Sebēos.[6] But did these authors directly have in mind an Armenian version of Rev. 12.9: "The great dragon was cast out, that old serpent called the Devil, and Satan?". The image is so pervasive in early Christian thought, with other biblical images of a dragon [*vishap*], that I doubt these references can prove the use of an Armenian version of Revelation in general use at that early date.

Ghazar P'arpets'i seems to have closer affinity to Revelation. In the vision of Saint Sahak, he describes a four-sided throne described as "crystalline" and the people who gained wings and sang "Holy God."[7] But the Trisagion of Rev. 4.8 is not quoted directly; and besides, it was too common a feature of liturgical worship to mean that Ghazar had Revelation in mind, while "crystalline" is not used for a throne in Revelation, but of the "glassy sea." Furthermore, this vision in Ghazar's *History* also exists in Greek, and may well not form part of the original Armenian text.[8] In a different dream, that of Azhdahak in Movsēs Khorenats'i, Book I 26,[9] there are numerous

---

[5] Frederick C. Conybeare, *The Armenian Version of Revelation and Cyril of Alexandria's Scholia on the Epistle of Easter* (Oxford: University Press, 1907), pp. 78-86.

[6] Eznik de Koghb, *De Deo*, ed. Louis Mariès and Charles Mercier [*Patrologia Orientalis* 28, fasc. 3] (Paris: Firmin-Didot, 1959), § 51; Sebēos, *Patmut'iwn*, Georg V. Abgaryan, ed. (Yerevan: Matenadaran, 1979), p. 147.

[7] Ghazar P'arpets'i, *Patmut'iwn Hayots'*, Galust Tēr-Mkrtch'ean and Step'an Malkhasean, eds. (Tiflis: Martirosean Press, 1904; reprinted with a new Introduction and critical Bibliography by Dickran Kouymjian, [Delmar, NY: Caravan Books]), pp. 29-37.

[8] Gérard Garitte, "La vision de S. Sahak en grec," *Le Muséon* 71 (1958), pp. 255-278.

[9] Movsēs Khorenats'i, *Patmut'iwn Hayots'*, Manuk Abeghian and Set' Yarut'iwnian, eds. (Tiflis: Martirosian Press, 1913; reprinted with an Introduction by Robert W. Thomson, Delmar, NY: Caravan Books, 1981), pp. 74-77.

verbal parallels with the Book of Revelation. The king of the Medes saw a woman in purple at the summit of a mountain, wrapped in a veil the colour of the sky. She gave birth to three heroes, the first of whom was mounted on a lion, the second on a leopard, and the third was a dragon. But Calvert Watkins has put this passage in the context of other allusions in Movsēs to ancient themes expressed in fragments of Armenian song. The juxtaposition of a mountain, a sacred figure, fertility and wild animals goes back to a mythological Indo-European theme of fertility, with parallels in Hittite and other ancient literatures.[10]

My impression is that the first indubitable quotation from Revelation occurs in the *History* of T'ovma Artsruni, where he speaks of the gate of divine wrath being opened on Armenia by Bugha's invasion. T'ovma notes that human power cannot prevent the opening of the gate of destruction. Only for God is it easy: "As it is written: he will shut and there will be no one to open; he will open and there will be no one to close."[11] This is Rev. 3.7, where the author is adapting the theme of the key of David. Job refers briefly to it at 12.14, and it is also found in Isaiah 22.22, but not in the standard Septuagint text. The Hebrew reads: "The key of the house of David will I lay upon his shoulder; so he shall open and none shall shut, and he shall shut and none shall open." Here, however, the standard Armenian text, as usual, follows the Septuagint. Therefore, T'ovma was quoting Revelation not Isaiah, for it is most improbable that he had any knowledge of either the Hebrew text of Isaiah or its direct translation in Syriac.

One author who undoubtedly was familiar with Revelation is the poet Gregory of Narek. In his *Matean Oghbergut'ean* he specifically refers to John, the evangelist and author of Revelation, by describing his love for God as neither hot nor cold.[12] This is from Rev. 3.15. In their remarkable study of that most famous of all

---

[10] Calvert Watkins, "La famille indo-européenne de grec *orchis*," *Bulletin de la Société de Linguistique de Paris* 70 (1975), pp. 11-23.

[11] T'ovma Artsruni, *Patmut'iwn Tann Artsruneats'*, ed. K'erovbe Patkanian (St. Petersburg: Skorokhodov Press, 1887; reprinted with Introduction by Robert W. Thomson, Delmar NY: Caravan Books, 1991), p. 124.

[12] Grigor Narekats'i, *Matean Oghbergut'ian*, ed. Poghos M. Khach'atryan and Arshaloys A. Ghazinyan (Yerevan: Armenian Academy of Sciences, 1985), p. 344, being Prayer 26.1, line 13.

Armenian literary works, the Mahés identified over fifty allusions to the Book of Revelation.[13] But since Revelation is itself a quilt of biblical quotations and allusions, as noted above, many of these parallels may well reflect the Old Testament or Pauline expressions on which Revelation draws. Nonetheless, several passages are most likely to have been taken from Revelation – though whether this proves that Gregory used an Armenian version is not obvious, since he was familiar with Greek.[14]

From the citations in T'ovma and Grigor Narekats'i, it seems that Revelation was well known in Armenia by the tenth century, even if no manuscript with the full text survives from before the twelfth century.[15] On the other hand, when and by whom Revelation had been translated is unknown, and the surviving witnesses indicate that more than one Armenian version existed.[16] Our present concern,

---

[13] Annie and Jean-Pierre Mahé, *Grégoire de Narek: Tragédie. Le Livre de Lamentation* [*Corpus Scriptorum Christianorum Orientalium* 584, Subsidia 106] (Leuven: Peeters, 2000), p. 833 for the list of quotations from, and allusions to, Revelation.

[14] Here are a few examples from many:

Prayer 2.5.8. Gregory refers to the glory of the hair of the one on High – an allusion to Rev. 1.14 that describes the one like the Son of man.

16.1.9. God is alpha and omega – as Rev. 1.8 and elsewhere.

38.2.33. Gregory refers to the tree of life bearing its fruits – as Rev. 22.2.

92.2.20. Gregory frequently uses the image of a spouse in the context of the New Jerusalem. Here one might think of patristic exegesis of the Song of Solomon, but Gregory's expression "adorned and prepared" comes directly from Revelation.

92.3.11. The binding of Satan is from Rev. 20.1-3.

There are also themes in Narekats'i that might come from Revelation, but are featured elsewhere in the Bible. For example:

The moon turning the colour of blood – either from Rev. 6.12 or Joel 2.31.

[15] See above at note 2.

[16] For the various versions see the classic study by Frederick C. Conybeare, note 5 above. He notes, p. 87, that the text in Jerusalem dated to 1199 (published by Frederik Murat, *Yaytnut'ean Yovhannu hin hay t'argmanut'iwnĕ*, 3 vols. (Jerusalem 1905-11), is so different from other witnesses that he presumes that two different renderings were made from a common Greek text. But Conybeare's view that the pre-Nersēs Armenian version of Revelation shows the influence of a Latin text was challenged by Joseph Molitor, "Zum Textcharacter der armenischen Apokalypse," *Oriens Christianus* 55 (1971), pp. 90-148. Molitor concludes that the Armenian is

however, is with the commentary on Revelation translated, or more correctly, adapted by Nersēs of Lambron. Since that undertaking immediately followed his own new translation of the Book of Revelation in 1179, it will be useful to quote the colophon where Nersēs describes that biblical book.[17]

"This revelation of the theologian-evangelist John, honoured for the usefulness of its testimonies by the teaching of our holy fathers, was freed from the stumbling block of suspicion of many who had ridiculous thoughts about it. For the great Dionysius wove its testimony into his theological homilies,[18] and Irenaeus bishop of Megalu,[19] Gregory the theologian in his abdication homily,[20] and the great Cyril, Methodius, and Hippolytus, also the untested Origen,[21] whom the church has honoured for their trustworthiness, placed

---

a direct translation from Greek, though it includes errors from copying *viva voce*, scribal mistakes and differences in orthography based on dialectical variation.

[17] The Armenian text is published in the edition of the Armenian commentary, *Meknut'iwn Yaytnut'ean S. Awetaranch'in Yovhannu* [no editor named] (Jerusalem: St. James Press, 1855), pp. 319-321, in Artashes S. Mat'evosyan, *Hayeren Dzeṙagreri Hishatakaranner E-ZhB dd* (Yerevan: Armenian Academy of Sciences, 1988), pp. 301-302, and in Garegin Yovsep'ian, *Yishatakarank' Dzeragrats'* (Antelias: Press of the Catholicosate, 1951), cols. 623-626.

[18] But there are few direct quotations from Revelation in the Pseudo-Dionysian corpus.

[19] Megalu: sic! Irenaeus, originally from Asia Minor, was bishop of Lyons from circa 178 to circa 200. The Armenian versions of his Greek writings have attracted much attention for their style and language in the "philhellene" tradition. See details of the published texts in Robert W. Thomson, *A Bibliography of Classical Armenian Literature to 1500 AD* (Turnhout: Brepols, 1995), pp. 59-61. Unfortunately, his undoubted influence on Armenian thought remains little explored.

[20] I.e. Gregory of Nazianzus, whose homilies were extremely popular in Armenia. See especially Oration 42, the "Farewell Speech," given on his departure from Constantinople. The Armenian texts are being edited by Bernard Coulie and associates in the *Corpus Christianorum* series published by Brepols.

[21] The sense here of *anp'ordz* is unclear. Origen was not widely known in Armenia, and the published texts attributed to him are not authentic.

[Revelation] as allegorical[22] in the series of the divinely-inspired new testaments. We, following their course, have transmitted it to the children of the holy church for inclusion in the apostolic books, as truly the apostolic revelation. And it was accurately rendered, re-arranged from the Greek in translation by me the humble Nersēs, with which I have also introduced a critical explanation of the same into the church of Armenia.[23]

To those who after us are readers of the same and enjoy the splendour of this inspired book, may the grace of the holy Spirit grant you sweetly to receive in the palate of the mind of your soul's mind this word of God, which is more pleasing than honey to the mouth.[24] For when you truly gain understanding from it, you turn your backs in hatred from all evil ways, according to the psalmist.[25] But if you also demonstrate mercy for us, praying for expiation from the Lord, you too will have forgiveness, according to the command of the righteous-speaker,[26] as we have experienced the world in this time, in which its splendour has passed."

[The following passage was added at a later date, but its intrinsic interest merits its inclusion here.]

"For visibly to our eyes the holy city of Jerusalem where God has trodden has been ravished from the service of Christians by the sword of the Ismaelites in 636 of the Armenian era.[27] Over it many torrents of blood were shed of the many nations of the Latins, who had set sail in many companies in ships, and with firm faith and courageous valour arrived in Palestine. There they were struck down as corpses around the city according to the psalm: 'And there was no one who buried [them],'[28] and we remained 'an offence to our neighbours'[29] until the completion of the year 647.[30] In that year was

---

[22] As allegorical: *tarats'uts'*, not in the version of the colophon printed by Mat'evosyan.
[23] I.e. the commentary translated in the same year.
[24] Ps. 118.103.
[25] Ps. 118.128.
[26] Cf. Mt. 5.7. Righteous-speaker: *irawakhaws*, only attested in works by Nersēs of Lambron in the *Nor Bar̉girk' Haykazean Lezui.*
[27] I.e. 3 Feb. 1187 to 2 Feb. 1188.
[28] Ps. 78.3. The text in the colophon could also mean "... who was buried."
[29] Ps. 43.14, 79.7.
[30] I.e., 31 Jan. 1198-30 Jan. 1199.

raised to greater honour the king of the Armenians Leon, from the Rubenids, pious and victorious through God. The fame of his valour moved the great emperor of Old Rome, Henry, and of New Rome, Alexios; who crowned him with precious gems in the church of Tarsus, which is tended by my unworthiness. May Christ our God bless him for us with length of days and invincible victory; and at his departure hence may He grant him to share the crown of the holy kings and a dwelling in the realms of light. And to Him be glory forever. Amen."

The commentary on Revelation to which Nersēs refers was that by Andreas of Caesarea. Not until the sixth century was an extensive commentary on Revelation composed in Greek; in the west Revelation enjoyed a different and wider reception.[31] The first full Greek commentary was that by Oikoumenios, written around 550.[32] Not much is known about him, save that he was a lay figure, called "rhetor" and philosopher in the manuscripts. At the end of that century, Andreas, or Andrew, bishop of Caesarea, composed what became the most popular such commentary. An expanded version was edited around 895 by Aretas, also a bishop of Caesarea; but that is not the text used by Nersēs, even though Aretas's name appears alongside that of Andrew in some of the references to Nersēs' work.[33] Presumably, that expanded version was better known in later times and the double authorship cited by mistake. This Commentary on Revelation by Andrew was translated not only into Armenian, but also into Georgian and Slavonic.[34]

---

[31] For the history of the interpretation of the Book of Revelation see the recent commentary by Judith Kovacs and Christopher Rowland, *Revelation* (Oxford: Blackwell, 2004).

[32] Greek text in Herman C. Hoskins, *The Complete Commentary of Oecumenius to the Apocalypse for the first time from Manuscripts at Messina, Rome, Salonika and Athos edited* (Ann Arbor, MI, 1928).

[33] Even Nersēs himself refers to the dual authorship in the colophon quoted below. But there he is referring to a copy of the commentary in a western tongue, not the Greek text which he was to translate later.

[34] The Slavonic version is abbreviated, and may be as early as the tenth century. The Georgian also dates from the tenth century. It was translated by the famous Euthymius Mt'ac'mideli [of the Holy Mountain] between 975 and 977 along with the Book of Revelation. For these two translations see Schmid (next note), vol. 1, part 1, pp. 113-117.

Of Andrew's original Greek text more than 140 manuscripts survive, though none are earlier than the tenth century.[35] Hoskier, editor of the previous commentary by Oikumenios, did not think much of Andrew. He states: "Anyone who is at all familiar with Andrew, whose commentary is terribly commonplace, will soon accord to Oecumenius a superior position in these studies."[36] But Hoskier was more interested in the textual history of Revelation than in the exegesis of the book. I do not know of any references in Armenian to Oikumenios or his commentary, but that by Andrew in its Armenian rendering by Nersēs became remarkably popular. Well over 100 manuscripts survive, ranging from the thirteenth to the nineteenth centuries; most were written in Greater Armenia, but there are also examples from as far apart as the Crimea and Smyrna.[37]

It would be more accurate to describe Nersēs's translation of this commentary as an "adaptation," for it is not a straight rendering from Greek into Armenian, as we shall see. Luckily, the long colophon attached to the translation indicates not only the occasion but also the way in which it was done. The following text is taken from Matenadaran 1418, a Miscellany of 1280 that was written in Khorin Anapat near Vahka in Cilicia:[38]

---

[35] See the full study of the manuscript tradition and the critical edition of the text by Josef Schmid, *Studien zur Geschichte des griechieschen Apokalypse-Textes. I. Die Apokalypse-Kommentar des Andreas von Kaisareia* [Münchener Theologische Studien], two parts in three volumes (München: Karl Zink, 1955-6).

[36] Hoskier, p. 4.

[37] The list is too long to be cited here. The largest number of copies is to be found in the Matenadaran, but see also the catalogues to the collections in Antelias, Bzommar, Jerusalem, New Julfa, Nikosia, Paris, Rome, Sebaste, Tiflis, Venice, and Vienna. Details of the catalogues in Bernard Coulie, *Répertoire des Bibliothèques et des Catalogues de manuscrits arméniens* (Turnhout: Brepols, 1992), with supplements in *Le Muséon* 108 (1995), pp. 115-130, and 113 (2000), pp. 149-176.

[38] For the Armenian text see the 1855 Armenian edition of the commentary, pp. 321-324, Mat'evosyan, *Hayeren Dzeṙagreri Hishatakaranner,* pp. 228-229, and Yovsep'ian, *Yishatakarank' Dzeragrats'*, col. 473-476. As yet there is no full study of Nersēs as exegete. An excellent survey of his life, writings, and theology, with good bibliography may be found in Boghos L. Zekiyan, "Nersēs de Lambron," *Dictionnaire de Spiritualité* (Paris:

I, Nersēs, poor in Christ and slothful among lovers of study, offspring of the last and miserable time, on reading the Revelation of John was distressed at not knowing the solution to its amazing words. Hunting here and there for a commentary on the same in our own language, I did not find any. Afterwards I had occasion to visit the great Antioch; and as I was going around the monasteries of the Romans and Franks which were there, this desire burned in my mind. After investigation I found among the books of the famous monastery of Saint Paul in that city the commentary on Revelation in the Lombard language, in the same script which the Franks use, composed by two authors.[39] Desiring to translate it, I found no one who could turn it from that language into Armenian. Then, going out of the city to the holy mountain on the north side, in one of the monasteries of the Romans which is called Bet'ias, I found locked up[40] with one of the reclusive monks called Basil what I desired in the Greek language and script, well written and elegant, which had belonged to Athanasios, patriarch of that city. I requested it with entreaties from that well-disposed man, and on receiving it hastened with the book to the patriarchal throne, to my lord Catholicos, the saintly Grigorios. When he was informed of this he greatly rejoiced, and ordered it to be translated by the metropolitan of Hierapolis, Konstandeay, who was staying there under the auspices of the patriarch. With the help of God and of the holy Lord[41] we began – he to translate and I to write; and we dedicated

---

Beauchesne, 1982), vol. 11, col. 122-134. For details of the manuscripts containing Nersēs' various works, see Nersēs Akinian, *Nersēs Lambronats'i* (Vienna: Mkhitarean Press, 1956). Since the commentary on Revelation was not originally an Armenian composition, it is not described in the useful recent guide to manuscripts of Armenian biblical commentaries: Eznik Petrosyan and Armen Ter-Step'anyan, *S. Grk'i Hayerēn Meknut'yunneri Matenagitut'iwn* (Yerevan: Hayastani Astuatsashnch'ayin Ĕnkerut'iwn, 2002).

[39] This was therefore a copy of the revised version of Andrew by Aretas, already translated into Italian.

[40] Locked up: *knk'eal*, lit. "sealed," perhaps "hidden away."

[41] Lord: the manuscripts cited in the 1855 edition read either *tnn* "of the house [i.e. patriarchate]" or *tr̄nn* "of the Lord" [i.e. the Lord Catholicos Grigor]. Mat'evosyan prints the latter.

> this wonderful and divine commentary on Revelation to the studious children of the Armenian church.[42]
>
> I beg you readers and lovers of wisdom, that when you understand the depths of God's wisdom through examining this, you will pray Christ to preserve in peace the holy patriarch, my lord Grigor, the kindly disposed cause and instigator of this translation, during this life and to receive him as heir to his saints in the future kingdom of heaven. May Christ also make worthy of his mercy through your prayers the metropolitan Konstandeay who translated it, and Basil the monk who provided the exemplar.

This commentary to the divine Revelation was translated in 628 of the Armenian era[43] at the holy and patriarchal see called Hṙomklay, which is surrounded by the elysian waters of the Euphrates, that provides for all bodily needs of the inhabitants through God's providence, under the protection of the Cross that bore God of Vanik,[44] and of other wonderful saints who were put to rest there to the glory of God. But it was corrected from the copy in literary[45] style in the sheltered hermitage of saint George in the middle of the Taurus mountains, which is on the Bluff[46] of Cilicia at the beginning of Pamphylia,[47] by the hand of the humble bishop of that metropolis Tarsus, the miserable Nersēs, through the grace and mercy of Christ, who is blessed for ever. Amen."

As is clear, the translation was the result of a collaboration, in which Constantine read out his Armenian rendering and Nersēs took

---

[42] The expression *mankunk' ekeghetswoy* has a wide range of meanings in Armenian. See Manea Erna Shirinian, "Reflections on the 'Sons and Daughters of the Covenant' in the Armenian Sources," *Revue des études arméniennes* 28 (2001-2002), pp. 261-285.

[43] 5 Feb. 1179-4 Feb. 1180.

[44] Michel Thierry, *Répertoire des Monastères arméniens* (Turnhout: Brepols, 1993), does not note a monastery of Vanik in this region. For Hṙomklay I have not been able to consult the recent monograph by Hans-Peter Hanisch, *Hromklay, die armenische Klosterfestung am Euphrat* (Bregenz: VLM Press, 2002).

[45] Literary: *k'ert'oghakan.*

[46] Bluff: *gah*, "precipice," perhaps "defile."

[47] See Thierry, *Répertoire des Monastères arméniens,* nos. 286, 288, for two hermitages dedicated to St. George in this region.

notes. At a later stage Nersēs wrote up his rough draft – but he does not say whether or not he then had the Greek with him. In any event, it will come as no surprise that sometimes the Armenian is close to the original, sometimes it is but a paraphrase, often it is abbreviated, and quite frequently Nersēs introduces new material. Furthermore, the fact that two persons were involved gives greater scope for misunderstanding or misinterpretation, regardless of intentional changes.[48]

The format of the commentary is the common one of quotation of a verse followed by explanation. I am not here concerned with the particular text of Revelation used by Andrew; but it is worth noting that Nersēs generally, but not always, translates the lemmata – the verses quoted as headings – as they appear in Andrew's commentary. It appears that in this commentary Nersēs does not consistently attempt to introduce his newly translated version of Revelation, but sticks to the text before him.

What then of the commentary as opposed to the biblical text? First of all, Nersēs wrote a new Introduction, disregarding Andrew's tripartite explanation of the meaning of inspired scripture; Andrew compares scripture to the division of man into body, soul and spirit. Instead, Nersēs gives a summary of the contents of the Book of Revelation and explains how it is to be interpreted: "We understand it not as a vision visible to the eyes or as an appearance of dreamlike fancies, but as an imprint of the revelation formed by spiritual appearance before the sight of the inner man; so that through its agency the hidden and wonderful mystery of the deity and the ranking of the worship of the heavenly beings might be revealed to the faithful. … So if the narration of this book includes corporeal

---

[48] The edition of the Armenian text printed in Jerusalem in 1855 was based on three manuscripts. According to the editor, who is not named, his base MS was a copy made expressly for him of a MS written in 1306 by the famous scholar Yovhannēs Erznkats'i; this manuscript is now Matenadaran 2520. Yovhannēs is Tsortsorets'i, 1260-1335, who is noted for a commentary on grammar and for completing the commentary on the Gospel of Matthew begun in the twelfth century by Nersēs Shnorhali. Yovhannēs Erznkats'i Tsortsorets'i was writing not much more than a century after the translation had been made. But the printed edition has so many grammatical oddities that one worries about the accuracy of the copy made in the nineteenth century and the editor's competence.

apparitions, forms of beasts, varieties of colours of precious stones, let it not astonish the hearers. For we find this done also by the prophets in many places. ... We are to understand incorporeal qualities, and not that there are tangible substances in heaven. ... As for the various fearsome appearances of the Devil and the false Christ to the blessed ones, let no one reckon them pointless, because they must all be fulfilled in their own times." So although Nersēs does not offer explicit prognostications of the future, the warnings of judgement to come serve to help the righteous and to silence the impious.

In the body of the commentary, Nersēs gives a few other indications how scripture is to be interpreted. Things are not always to be taken literally. With regard to the 24 thrones and 24 elders, or priests, of Rev. 4.4 for example, he says: "Who among mankind these were, I am totally unable to confirm. However, first I say that one should not posit the number 24 as a limit. For it is a custom of scripture everywhere to indicate the many by means of a very small number, like forgiving 70 times seven. Likewise this number was posited mystically and not as a limit; either in accordance with the number of hours in the days in which they laboured, or according to the number of the 24 letters through which they became wise in knowledge of the truth." But Nersēs does not generally engage in numerology, often omitting Andrew's speculations on the significance of specific numbers. In that regard Nersēs differs from many Armenian commentators, who are often interested in finding meaning in, or at least parallels to, numbers mentioned in the Bible. As for Revelation, Nersēs several times adds that it must not be taken in a physical sense: for example at Rev. 14.8: "It is necessary to know that the appearance of this angel at that time [i.e. the angel who announced the fall of Babylon] did not happen sensibly, but is only an impulse to the mind's knowledge of things that occurred in those days, as I think."

The Armenian version is generally shorter than the original, and is often discursive in its rendering of the Greek. Nonetheless, Nersēs introduces a good deal of new material. First of all we may note the various sources, which he quotes by name; I list them in rough order of composition:

Irenaeus:

Rev. 12.7-9: Andrew refers to Justin saying that before the coming of our Lord, Satan never dared to blaspheme God, but after the coming of Christ he was emboldened to do so. Andrew does not cite his source, but Nersēs adds that this is from Irenaeus. There are several patristic citations of this opinion of Justin's, but Nersēs could be familiar with it from Irenaeus's *Contra Haereses*, Book V.[49]

Eusebius of Caesarea:

Rev. 6.5b, the black horse: Here Andrew refers to those who fell away from the faith, but Nersēs says: "By black horse one must understand the whirlwind of trouble of the persecutions under the Emperor Decius. For he was the third persecutor of Christians, as Eusebius narrates." This is from Book VI of the *Ecclesiastical History*, which is also the source of other additions in the next verse concerning the persecution in Alexandria and Novatian's activity in Rome. We shall see another expansion from the same Book VI later on.

The Life of Antony:

Twice Nersēs refers to Antony in connection with the saints in heaven, quoting from the *Life* by Athanasius.[50]

The Martyrdom of Cyprian of Antioch [Kiprianos]

Rev. 9.7 introduces the locusts like horses whose tails have scorpion stings. Their king, says Andrew, is the Devil, though he does not explicitly call them demons. Nersēs expands: "Among the demons there is a ranking of greatness and smallness, as we have learned in the confession of Kiprianos." Kiprianos, or Cyprian, was the magician in Antioch who employed the various ranks of demons

---

[49] See also Rev. 10.2-3: When the angel cried out, seven thunders spoke. This refers, says Nersēs, to the good order of the heavenly ones, who are in seven circles according to the holy Irenaeus and Epiphanius. Since Andrew had already mentioned these two authors in the same connection much earlier in the commentary, the additions here are not meaningful.

[50] Rev. 7.9-10: Antony joined the crowd of all races standing before the throne, "when the Devil fought in the air with the saint." And Rev. 12.5 refers to the martyrs raised up to glory, whom "the death-breathing dragon tried to swallow in the air, but was unable, as the great Antony saw."

in increasing order of importance to help him seduce the virgin Justina, before she converted him and he became bishop of the city. They were both martyred in the persecutions of Diocletian. Nersēs was no doubt familiar with the lengthy Armenian martyrology.[51] I do not know the date of that text, but already in the late fourth century Gregory Nazianzenus was aware of the story.[52]

Gregory Nazianzenus:

Nersēs sometimes adds references to a specific text of Gregory's where Andrew has mentioned his name. Gregory's homilies were extremely popular in Armenia and Nersēs was certainly familiar with them, as noted above.

Dionysius, i.e. the Pseudo-Areopagite:

Dionysius is also cited by Nersēs after Irenaeus and Epiphanius for the seven ranks of angels, but this does not tally with the Areopagite's system of three sets of three ranks. Rev. 22.1-2 refers to the squares of the heavenly city. Here Andrew refers to the angelic beings called "thrones" filling these public squares. Nersēs adds: "As the great Dionysius writes." But there is no direct reference to this verse of Revelation in Dionysius.

One noticeable feature of all of Nersēs' commentaries is his emphasis on the spiritual life. This translation is no exception. In it Nersēs emphasizes the role of one's conscience. Rev. 3.20 reads: "Behold, I stand at the door and knock." Nersēs interprets this as the daily examination of conscience, whereby one removes from oneself the burden of passions and through prayer and thanksgiving offers to God a sacrifice of blessing. Several times repentance is stressed, as is the danger of punishment, which God inflicts on those who transgress without being healed by repenting. When Andrew discusses the blessings of the future age for those victorious against demons, at Rev. 2.7, Nersēs adds that life eternal is for those who taste Christ's life-giving body. Elsewhere too he adds explicit references to the liturgy, *patarak*, literally "sacrifice," and at Rev.

---

[51] See the text in *Liakatar Vark' ew Vkayabanut'iwnk' Srbots'*, Mkrtich' Awgerian, ed. (Venice: Surb Ghazar, 1813), vol. 4, pp. 68-105.

[52] Further details in *The Oxford Dictionary of the Christian Church*, ed. Frank L. Cross and Elizabeth A. Livingstone, 3rd ed. (Oxford: University Press, 1997), pp. 441-442, s.v. "Cyprian of Antioch."

1.12 he refers to Christ as high-priest continually offering himself as a sacrifice in the churches before the Father. Likewise at Rev. 8.4 "the smoke of the incense rising up, the prayers of the saints," is interpreted as Christ "fanning the sacrifice of our thanksgiving and making it of sweet odour to the Father, as sharer in tribulation and tested high-priest and intercessor."

Other additions serve to enhance the rhetorical effect of the text. The son of man in Rev. 1.14, for example, had hair white as snow, which prompts Nersēs to remind us that "just as hair grows from the head, likewise too thoughts from the mind." The four living beings in Rev. 4.8 did not rest by day or night. Nersēs explains that not resting means not ceasing from praising, just as "rest for a servant is speaking with a kind Lord." Torments like stings of a scorpion are introduced in Chapter 9. Nersēs adds: "For as the poison of a scorpion makes the body itch, likewise too the poison of Satan ceaselessly tortures the soul through the compunction of the mind." Again he emphasizes the role of conscience. The heavenly city of Rev. 21.23 had no need of a sun, being illuminated by God's glory. Nersēs interprets: "Just as for the senses the ray of the sun is light, so is knowledge for the contemplative one."[53]

In this commentary, as in his others, Nersēs is primarily concerned with spiritual issues, and rarely introduces any topical references to contemporary matters. There is in fact one explicit reference to the Armenians, even though here Nersēs is elaborating on a passage in Andrew, not introducing them himself. The four horsemen of Chapter 6 have figured prominently in many explanations of the Apocalypse. They ride respectively on a white, a red, a black, and a pale horse; and on this last sat Death followed by Hell.[54] Andrew interprets this passage as the turbulence brought upon the Christians in the persecution of Maximin, for which he refers the reader to Eusebius's *Ecclesiastical History*.[55] Nersēs picks up Andrew's reference to Maximin and adds details from Eusebius's account, indicating his personal knowledge of that book. But his

---

[53] As for the metaphor of the sun, the only mistake I have detected in Nersēs' allusions to scripture is to ascribe the phrase "sun of righteousness" to Zachariah instead of Malachi.

[54] In the west Dürer's dramatic engraving is particularly famous.

[55] In Book IX Eusebius describes Maximin's war against the Armenians around the year 312 and the ensuing plague and famine.

interest is not in the Armenians as such. Rather he stresses the horrors of pestilence and the charity of Christians. It is very curious that early Armenian historians describing the conversion of Armenia do not quote this passage from Eusebius, even though the Armenian translation was an early one.[56] Agat'angeghos mentions Maximin, but only as one of the "impious kings" destroyed by Constantine.[57] It is Constantine and his relationship with Armenia that is stressed in early authors,[58] not the persecution of Maximin and the description of Armenians as Christians. In Rev. Chapter 6, where John describes the opening of the sixth seal and its accompanying violence, Andrew notes that this has been interpreted as the attack of Vespasian on Jerusalem, though he himself sees the prophecy as the troubles which precede the coming of Anti-Christ. Nersēs follows this, but adds: "For after Constantine the Great reigned and the church was confirmed, no other disturbance occurred to it at all, save the one to come in those times. This is a sign of the oppression which precedes the coming of Anti-Christ."[59]

Nersēs introduces no clear allusions to events of his own time. In Rev. Chapter 12, John refers to the woman clothed with the sun who brought forth a male child; he was to rule the gentiles with an iron rod. Andrew interprets this in terms of the church and the apostles. Nersēs adds: "He [Christ] now rules through the power of the Romans, who are sons of the font." In Chapter 17 an angel shows John the destruction of the fornicating city, the great harlot sitting on a beast which had seven heads. Andrew refers here to Old

---

[56] It was translated from the Syriac version, not the original Greek. The early translation is printed with a new translation from the Greek in Abraham Charian, *Ewsebiosi Kesarats'woy Patmut'iwn Ekeghets'woy* (Venice: Surb Ghazar, 1877).

[57] Agat'angeghos, *Patmut'iwn Hayots'*, Galust Tēr-Mkrtch'ian and Step'an Kanayeants', eds. (Tiflis: Martirosian Press, 1909; reprinted with Introduction by Robert W. Thomson, Delmar NY: Caravan Books, 1980), p. 456, § 868.

[58] The importance of Constantine in Armenian tradition is a subject which needs further research. For an initial survey see Robert W. Thomson, "Constantine and Trdat in Armenian Tradition," *Acta Orientalia* 50 (1997), pp. 277-289.

[59] Rev. 6. 12-13. At 7.4 Nersēs brings in Vespasian "as an image of the afflictions of Anti-Christ." See also 6.14-17, 7.2-3, 7.8.

Rome, which lies on seven hills, and interprets the seven heads as the seven impious kings from Domitian to Diocletian. Old Rome no longer exists, adds Nersēs, and the empire is ruled from Constantinople. As for barbarian attacks, which Andrew says currently afflicted the empire [Andrew died in 614], Nersēs has no comment.

Of particular interest are those passages where Nersēs has introduced changes or additions of a strictly theological nature, for these provide a clue as to his motivation in adapting this commentary. The majority hinge on interpretations of references to Christ's body. The first such discussion is at Rev. 1.5, where Andrew expands on Christ as "first born from the dead and king of kings." Christ is equal with the Father and consubstantial, and first born because he is not like those who died previously and rose again. Nersēs renders this accurately, then adds: "He is eternally immortal in the body which died." Verse 15 of that chapter refers to a son of man "whose feet were like smoking bronze in the midst of an incandescent furnace." In the Greek "bronze" is the compound noun *chalkolibanos*. Andrew interprets *chalkos* as Christ's human nature, *libanos* as the divine. But Nersēs ignores this and adds that "in the midst of an incandescent furnace" indicates the earthly body flaming in the divine fiery nature.

In Rev. Chapter 2 the angel tells John to write to the church of Smyrna: "Thus says the One without beginning, who was dead and came alive."[60] The phrase refers to Christ as God, says Andrew. Nersēs adds: "Co-eternal with the body, which he took from us." The expression "feet of smoking bronze" is repeated in the message to the church of Thyateira. Here Andrew speaks of the "indissoluble and unconfused union [*henôsis*] of Christ's divinity and humanity." This becomes in Nersēs: "the indissoluble and unconfused God-man, *astuatsamard*, in whom the earthly body flamed through the divine mingling, *kharnumn*." So Nersēs avoids "union" in favour of an ancient Armenian concept emphasized in early texts like the *Teaching of Saint Gregory*, where the relationship between divine

---

[60] Here the lemma diverges from the Greek of Andrew, which refers to "the first and the last." The Armenian versions of Revelation differ here. The Jerusalem text follows the version in Andrew, but the Oxford text in Conybeare and the standard Armenian of Zohrap read as the Armenian of Nersēs.

and human in Christ is defined in terms of "mingling."[61] Furthermore "God-man" is not a traditional Armenian expression, though variants of *Theandros* are very common in Greek. *The Nor Bargirk'* gives only two citations for *Astuatsamard*: this example in Nersēs and one in a letter from the Emperor Manuel to Nersēs Shnorhali.[62]

The longest discussion of Christ's body comes in Chapter 19, where John refers to the "robe dyed with blood, cast around the Word of God." Andrew offers three explanations, one being that this refers to the union of the physical hypostasis, *huikê hupostasis*, with the impassible birth from the Father. Nersēs picks this up in different terms. "The robe dyed with blood is the body of the Word of God which he received from the dough [*zanguats*] of Adam, in which he will come to judge the earth." This also fits into the ancient tradition of describing the Incarnation as Christ "putting on" or "robing" himself with a body.

To sum up: Nersēs follows Andrew in his use of technical terms such as "hypostasis," when this refers to one of the Persons of the Trinity, or "consubstantial," when this refers to Christ as consubstantial with the Father or his body consubstantial with our human nature. Likewise, when the term "nature, *phusis*," refers to human nature, or the nature of angels, or even Christ's divine nature, Nersēs translates Andrew directly. But he studiously avoids speaking of a union in Christ. Nersēs repeatedly emphasizes the true humanity of the body taken by Christ, in which he lived on earth, ascended to heaven, and will come again to judge. Why was this so important to him?

The answer, I think, lies in the discussions on matters of faith with the Greeks. This is not the occasion to enter into the substance of those discussions, but one text provides a valuable clue. In April 1179, the same year that he translated the Book of Revelation and Andrew's Commentary on it, Nersēs addressed an assembled Armenian council at Hṙomklay. This had been summoned by Gregory IV to discuss the Byzantine emperor Manuel's desire to

---

[61] See the discussion of such terminology in Robert W. Thomson, *The Teaching of Saint Gregory*, revised edition, Treasures of the Armenian Christian Tradition, 1 (New Rochelle NY: St. Nersēss Armenian Seminary, 2001), pp. 26-32.

[62] The Greek connection is significant in view of the conclusion below.

reopen discussions on matters of the faith. Nersēs' *Synodical Oration*, *Atenabanut'iwn*, is a lengthy eirenic document, in which he emphasizes that all the different churches of the world are members of the same body whose head is Christ. In the middle, he examines the Chalcedonian position that Christ has two natures, human and divine. Although he is prepared to accept that one can call Christ "ineffably united from two natures," he attacks those who distinguish the properties of the two natures, making two persons. This had always been the Armenian position: Christ is not two persons, which would make the Trinity a Quaternity. In the *Oration*, Nersēs defines the traditional Armenian expression *anchar kharnumn* [ineffable mingling], in terms of the Cyrilline definition: "one nature of God the Word incarnate."[63] What is particularly significant in our present context is that Nersēs rebukes those who attack the Armenians by alleging that they say that the human nature was changed [*p'okheal*] into the divine.

The commentary on the Book of Revelation was rendered into Armenian only a few months after the council at Hr̈omklay. Although Andrew had not been concerned with Christological controversy, Nersēs remained anxious to stress Armenian tradition and to rebut those who defamed it. Therefore, he repeatedly introduced new material emphasizing the human body of Christ, while at the same time avoiding controversial terminology.

[63] Pasquale Aucher, *Orazione sinodale di S. Nierses Lampronese* (Venice: San Lazzaro, 1812, Armenian text with facing Italian translation), p. 88. The more recent French translation by Charles Mercier, *Discours synodal de St. Nersès de Lampron* (Venice: Mekhitarist Press, 1948), was not available to me.

16

Scribal Errors Corrected by the First Hand

Claude Cox

For me, interest in how Armenian manuscripts were made was sparked by the presentations of Dickran Kouymjian at conferences and symposiums. We all remember the wonderful illustration by slides of manuscripts that are not readily available for personal examination. For more than twenty years, from time to time, I have listened to such papers, and learned much from this gentle, erudite man with the understated sense of humor and easygoing manner. It is a pleasure to contribute to this volume honoring him.

Recently, with Michael Stone, Dickran published a watershed volume on Armenian paleography.[1] For this *Festschrift*, my contribution focuses on errors that medieval Armenian copyists made and then corrected while copying the Book of Job. Some of these mistakes are rooted in paleography, namely orthography; others are the result of phonetic similarities among letters of the alphabet; the largest single category of mistakes finds a letter or letters left out by parablepsis. Another major group reveals that mistakes arose through attraction to a word or words found in the immediate context.

Some of these types of scribal error occur in manuscripts written in other languages, but, in some cases, "the way they happen" is unique to Armenian because the script of the Armenian alphabet is unique.

---

[1] Michael E. Stone, Dickran Kouymjian, and Henning Lehmann, *Album of Armenian Paleography* (Åarhus: Åarhus University Press, 2002).

Resources

The evidence presented here was collected in the course of collating eight manuscripts for a critical edition of the Armenian text of Job.

The manuscripts, their date, provenance, and scribe(s) are as follows.[2]

Jerusalem 1925	1269	Erznka	Mkhit'ar the monk, Hakob the monk, Movsēs
Matenadaran 1500	before 1282	Geghard	Mkhit'ar of Ayrivank'
Venice 841	13th cent.	Drazark?	T'oros, Barsegh, and Georg, mainly
Venice 280	1418-22	Khlat'	Karapet
Jerusalem 1934	1643-46	Isfahan	Step'anos, son of Martiros, pupil of Khach'atur the *vardapet*
Matenadaran 2587	1648	Isfahan	Ghazar
British and Foreign Bible Society	1667?	Cilicia?	Astuatsatur
British Library, Oriental 8833	17th cent.	unknown	P'illippos

I might mention that Zohrapian's printed text was also used for the new edition, but the underlying manuscript, namely Venice 1508, dated 1319, was not separately collated and therefore does not appear in the evidence presented here. For the sake of interest, the

[2] These data are derived from *The Armenian Translation of Deuteronomy*, University of Pennsylvania Armenian Texts and Studies 2 (Chico, CA: Scholars Press, 1981), pp. 16–31. The information there is derived, in turn, from catalogues whose bibliographical details are provided in the footnotes. For the folio numbers for Job in these witnesses see the catalogue of Shahē Ajamian, *Ts'uts'ak Astuatsashunch' Mateani Hayerēn Dzeragirnerun* [Catalogue of Armenian Biblical Manuscripts] (Lisbon: C. Gulbenkian Foundation, 1992).

qualifying mistakes in the eighth century Sinai fragment, collated for the critical edition, are also listed.[3] It is given the siglum "Sf."

The eight manuscripts are all written in types of *bolorgir* minuscule scripts, though some errors may derive from copying from manuscripts that were in the majuscule script, such as we see in the Sinai fragments.[4] The manuscripts vary in their scribal character; for example, Jerusalem 1925 and the British and Foreign Bible Society manuscripts are easy to read, while Matenadaran 1500 is famous for its difficulty in that respect.

The list of scribal errors

The list that follows was compiled from the manuscripts listed above. For ease of reference later I have numbered them. In all cases, the mistakes appear to have been corrected by the scribe; they are therefore corrections by the first hand and that fact is not noted after the first item. Some standard text-critical abbreviations are employed; they are:

*	original reading
>	omit
+	add
∩	indicates a minus due to parablepsis, i.e., the scribe skipped from one letter or letters to the same letter or letters later in the word or immediate context
(I)	indicates change of line
c	correction
pr m	*prima manus*, i.e., first hand
1° 2°	first occurrence; second occurrence
ditt	dittography, i.e., written twice
ex	from
om	omit
prae	before

---

[3] The fragment comprises Job 37:12–17; 37: 22–38:2; 38:7–13; 38:18–23. See S. Peter Cowe, "An Armenian Job Fragment from Sinai and its Implications," *Oriens Christianus* 76 (1992), pp. 123–157. Cowe provides plates of the fragments on pp. 126, 129.

[4] For plates of several manuscripts, see Michael E. Stone, *The Testament of Levi* (Jerusalem: St. James Press, 1969). Plates 1 and 2 are photos of two pages from Jerusalem 1925; plate 5 offers a page from Jerusalem 1934.

sed hab	*sed habetur*, i.e., "but it has"
tr	transposes
vid	*videtur*, i.e., "it appears"

The reading to the left of the square bracket is the reading in the critical text, which, since the mistakes that interest us here are likely unique, is also the majority text. The list does not include items where the copyist's error is shared with any other manuscript. The list is then a list of unique mistakes, unique at least among the manuscripts collated for the edition.

1. 1:3f մեծամեծք] ditt V280* (c pr m)
2. 1:4b առնեին] առէին J1925*
3. 1:6c ընդ նոսա] BF*
4. 1:20a պատառեաց] պատառեալ J1925*
5. 1:21d եւ 2° > J1934*
6. 1:22c ոչ > V280*
7. 2:3f յանմեղութեան] յանմեղութիւն V841*vid
8. 2:8b նստէր] նտէր M1500*
9. 2:9aa համբերից] համերից V841*
10. 2:9da հարկահար] հարկահարե[ա]լ BF*
11. 2:13a զեւթն 1°] զեւթ J1925*
12. 3:17a զսրտմութիւն բարկութեան] զբարկութեան սրտմտութիւն J1934*
13. 3:17b հանգեան] հանգեալք BF*
14. 3:25b պատահեաց] պատահաց J1925*
15. 4:8b նոցանէ] նցանէ V841*
16. 4:14b զոսկերս] զոսկեր V841*
17. 5:7b ձագք] ձագ M2587*
18. 5:12a խորամանկաց] խորամանկանց BF*
19. 5:14b ի 2°] զ(գիշերի) BF*
20. 5:18a միւսանգամ] միսանգամ J1925*
21. 6:10a քաղաքն] քաղաք V841*
22. 6:10a խնայեցից] խնայեցի V280*
23. 6:19a Թեմնացւոց] թեմնացւոյ V280*
24. 6:26b անսացից] սսացից J1925*
25. 6:29a Նստարուք] + դուք V841*
26. 7:18b դատիցիս] դատիցես BF*
27. 8:3a դատիցի] դատի J1934*
28. 8:6b դարձուսցէ] դարձուցէ J1925*vid

29. 8:12a արմատոց] արմաւոց V841*vid
30. 8:16b նորա > V841*
31. 9:12a դարձուսցէ] դարձուցէ J1925*
32. 9:16a կարդացից] կարդայց J1925*vid
33. 9:27b հեծեծեցից] հեծեծիցից V841* (|)
34. 10:3c ի > M1500*
35. 10:7b ի > V280*
36. 10:7b հանիցէ] հայիցէ J1925*vid
37. 10:11a ինձ] զիս V280*
38. 10:18a անդէն > V280*
39. 10:21a մինչչեւ] մինչեւ J1934*
40. 10:21a դառնայցեմ] դառնացեմ J1925*
41. 11:2a լսիցէ] լսիցի J1925*
42. 11:2b արդարանալ] արդանալ V841*
43. 11:11a զգործս] կգործս BF*
44. 11:11b զանարժանս] զարժանս J1934*
45. 11:16a մոռասցիս] մոռասցի V841*
46. 11:18b տատամսութենէ] տատամութենէ J1934*
47. 11:19a հանդարտեսցես] հանդարտեսցէ M2587*
48. 12:5a սահմանեալ պատրաստեցաւ] պատրաստեալ սահմանեցաւ J1934*
49. 12:8a զքեզ] քեզ BF*
50. 12:19b զզաւրաւորս] զօրաւորս V280*
51. 12:21a անարգութիւն] աարգութիւն J1934*vid
52. 13:4a մեղանչականք] մաղանչական J1934*
53. 13:7b նենգութիւն] նենգութեամբ BF*
54. 13:11a արհաւիրք] ահաւիրք V841*
55. 13:25b հողմավար] հողավար M2587*
56. 13:27c ոտից] ոտ M2587* (vid)
57. 14:1b սակաւակեաց] սակաւեաց J1925* (|)
58. 14:3b առաջի] առաջ V841*
59. 14:6b զվարձկան] զվարձկանի J1925*
60. 14:10a վախճանեալ] վխճանեալ J1925*
61. 14:15a զիս > J1934*
62. 14:17a ի > J1925*
63. 14:17b նշանակեցեր] նշանեցեր V841*
64. 14:17b նշանակեցեր] նշակեցեր J1934*
65. 14:18a փլանելոց] փանելոց M2587*
66. 14:21b եթե] թե J1925*
67. 15:7b յառաջ] առաջ V841*

68. 15:8a զհրաման] հրամ J1925*
69. 15:8b եհաս] հաս V841*
70. 15:21c կործանումն] կործանում V841*
71. 15:29a մի 2° > M2587*
72. 16:4c ես > J1925*
73. 16:4d իբրեւ > J1934*
74. 16:7 ընդարմացեալ] ընդարմացալ J1934*
75. 16:9b կրճտեաց] կրտեաց BF*
76. 16:13a զիս — (13b) զերիկամունս > J1934*
77. 17:9a հաւատարիմն] հաւատարիմ V841*
78. 17:10b ճշմարտութիւն] ճմարտութիւն J1925*
79. 18:4c ի հիմանէ] հիմանի J1925*
80. 18:9b ի վերա նորա] զնա J1934*
81. 19:5b էք] եմք J1934*vid
82. 19:21b տեառն > V841*
83. 19:22a դուք / զիս tr J1925* (c pr m[?])
84. 19:24b քանդակեալ] քանդեալ M2587*
85. 19:25 լուծանելոցն] լուծանելոց J1934*
86. 19:25 յերկրի] pr ի V841*vid
87. 20:3a իմոյ] > J1934*
88. 20:11a ոսկերք] ոսկեր M2587*: cf. 4:14b
89. 20:17b զկոգւոյ] pr մի V280*
90. 20:26c եկամուտ] կամուտ J1925*
91. 21:4a իցեն] իցեմ J1934*
92. 21:6a տագնապեցայց] տագապեցայց J1925*
93. 21:16b հայի > V280*
94. 22:12b զգածեալսն] զգածեալս V841*
95. 22:12b ամբարտաւանութեամբ] ամբարտաւութեանբ V841*
96. 22:13b դատիցի] դատիցէ J1934*
97. 22:17a տէր —(17b) մեր > J1934*vid
98. 22:23a դարձցիս] դարձցես J1934*
99. 22:28a զյարկն] յարկն J1934*
100. 22:30a փրկեսցէ] փրկեցէ J1934* (|)
101. 23:12a ոչ] + եւս թիւրեցայց J1934*: ex 11b
102. 24:5c լկտիս] լտիս J1925*
103. 24:6a տհաս] pr ի J1925*
104. 24:13b արդարութեան] արդութեան V841*
105. 24:15c զերեսաւք] երեսաւք V841*
106. 25:16b կնքեցին] կքեցին V841*
107. 25:20c հատուսցի] հատոցի V841*

108. 25:20c հատուսցի] հատուցի J1934*
109. 25:2a առ > J1934*
110. 26:4a ում] ոյր BF*
111. 26:5a ծնանիցին] ծանիցին V841*
112. 26:8a յամպս] pr ի V841*
113. 27:7a եին] in V280*
114. 27:11b ոչ] pr եւ BF*
115. 27:15a վախճանեսցին] վճարեսցին V841*
116. 28:1b կղկղի] կղղի M2587*
117. 28:2b հանգոյն] հանոյն V841*
118. 28:4a փոշոյ] փշոյ J1925*
119. 28:4b մոռանամ] մոռան J1925*
120. 28:7b ակն] ան M2587*
121. 28:10a գետոց] գետոյ M2587*
122. 28:17b ի > J1934*
123. 29:3a ճրագ] ջրագ V841*
124. 29:6b ոռոգանեին] ոռոգանային V841*
125. 29:13b այրւոյն] արոյն V841*
126. 29:20b նորա] իմում J1934*
127. 29:25c մխիթարեին > V841*
128. 30:1b խրատեն] խրատեսցեն V841*
129. 30:1c փախարակեի] պահարակէի V841*
130. 30:18b զժապաւէն] + քանդակ V280*
    So, "embossed hem?"
131. 30:24b զայլ] զայր BF*
132. 31:8b երկրի J1934*
133. 31:14b Եւ > J1934*
134. 31:19 անտես > M1500*
135. 31:22a յանրակէ] յանդրակ M1500*
136. 31:27a Եթե 1° ∩ (27b) 2° J1934*
137. 31:34b գոգով] զովով BF*vid
138. 31:35c մուրհակ] մուհակ V841*
139. 31:36 ընթեռնուի] ընթերնոյր BM*
140. 31:38a հեծեաց] հեծեաց V841*
141. 32:2a բուզացի] բոզացի V841*
142. 32:2d տեառն] նորա BF* (c pr m vid)
143. 32:3c լինել > M2587*
144. 32:10b եւ > M1500*
145. 32:11c քննիցէք] քննիցիք J1925* vid
146. 32:15b յինքեանց] ինքեանց M2587*

147. 32:15b զբանս] բանս V280*
148. 33:1a բայց] բաց V841*
149. 33:1 զբանս] զբան J1934*
150. 33:8b լուայ] լուա J1934*
151. 33:13 ամենայն] յամենայն V841*
152. 33:14a խաւսեսցի] խաւսի V841*
153. 33:17b կործանմանէ] կործմանէ J1934*
154. 33:23c դառնալ] դառն V841*
155. 33:24a չանկանելոյ] չանկանալոյ V280*
156. 33:4b մերում] pr ի V841*
157. 34:12b ամենակալն] ամենակն J1925*vid
158. 34:15a մարմին] մարմինք V841*
159. 34:16b բարբառոյ / բանից tr V280*
160. 34:17b զչարս] զչարէ J1925*vid
161. 34:24a հասանէ] ասանէ J1934*
162. 34:30a թագաւորեցուցանէ] թագաւորեցուցանել BF*
163. 34:33a որք] որ BF* vid
164. 35:13a տեսանել] տեսեալ J1925*
165. 36:6a կանդանացուսցէ] կանանացուսցէ V841*
166. 36:6b տացէ > V841*
167. 36:8b վարակեսցին] վարեսցին V841*
168. 36:12b անհնազանդք] անհնազանք M2587*
169. 36:16a զերծոյց] զերծոց V841*
170. 36:19a կամակորութեան] կամակորութեաքք BF*vid
171. 36:19c զաւրաւորս զաւրութեամբ] զաւրութիւնս J1934* (c pr m vid)
172. 36:21a Այլ > J1934*
173. 36:23b ասիցէ] ասաց BF*
174. 37:4c Եւ > J1925*
175. 37:5b գիտեաք] գիտաք BF*
176. 37:10a զսառամանիս] զսառնամանիս J1925*
177. 37:12c հրամայեսցէ] հրամեսցէ J1925*
178. 37:14a դիր > M2587*
179. 37:15a զգործս] զգորս Sf*
180. 37:22a ոսկեճաճանչ] ոսկէճաճ J1934*
181. 37:22b այսոցիկ] այսոցի Sf*
182. 37:22b ամենակալին] ամենակին V280*
183. 37:23b զարդարն] զար Sf*
184. 37:24a մարդիկ] pr ամենայն V280*
185. 38:2a զխորհուրդս] զխորհուրդ V841*

186. 38:3b եւ > V841*
187. 38:5b արկ > M2587*
188. 38:11a ցայդ վայր] ցվայր V280*
189. 38:14a զհողն կաւ] զկաւն J1934*
190. 38:18b ինձ > V841*
191. 38:19a ագանիցի] ագանիցէ J1934*
192. 39:21b իցէ] է J1934*
193. 39:22b իցես] իցիս J1934*
194. 38:25a անձրեւաց] անձրաց J1934*
195. 38:28a է հայր] եհար J1934*
196. 38:29a սառն] առն M2587*
197. 38:31b զպատրուակ] զպատուակ M2587*
198. 38:32a զմազուրովթն] զմազորվվթն BF*
199. 38:38a զհող փոշի] զփոշի J1925*
200. 38:41a ագռաւուց] ագառուց V841*
201. 39:2a թուիցես] թուիցիս V841*
202. 39:7b զքամբասանս] զամբասանս M2587*
203. 39:10a կապիցես] կապիցի J1925*
204. 39:10a կապիցես] կապիցիս V280*
205. 39:17b նմա > J1934*
206. 39:18a բարձրասցի] բարձրացի BF*
207. 39:25a փող > V841*
208. 39:25b հեռաստանէ] հեռատանէ V841*
209. 39:28 քարանձաւս] քարանձաւ J1934*
210. 40:2a զդատաստան որ] զդատաստանքն J1925*vid
211. 40:5 յերկրորդումն] յերկրդումն J1934*
212. 40:7b եւ դու > J1934
213. 40:9b որոտայցես] որտայցես J1934*
214. 40:21a ազգի 1°] ազի V280*
215. 40:22a հովանոցանանց] հովանացանան J1934*
216. 40:27b բարբառով] բառով J1934*
217. 40:28a դնիցէ] դնիցի J1934*
218. 40:28b Նուաճիցես] նուաճիցեց J1934*vid
219. 41:3a Կամ — Եւ > M2587*
220. 41:5a զպատրուակ / (յ- J1934) երեսաց նորա (> J1934*) tr J1934*
221. 41:7b գայլախազ] գայլահազ BM*
222. 41:9b մեկնեսցին] մեկնեսցեն J1934*
223. 41:12a նորա > M2587*
224. 41:16a Զի սիրտ] զսիրտ M2587*

225. 41:20a խոցոտէ] խոցէ J1925*
226. 42:3d զմածամեծս prae (3c) զոր tr M1500*
227. 42:5a զքէն] pr ի J1925*
228. 42:7c ճշմարիտ] ճշմարիտք J1925*
229. 42:7d զծառայ իմ] զծառայի J1934*
230. 42:8a եւ ∩ (8b) եւ BF*
231. 42:8b երթայք] երայք V280*
232. 42:8d om 8d M2587*
233. 42:8f ոչ > M2587*
234. 42:8f կասն > J1934*
235. 42:9a Սովփար] սովար J1925*
236. 42:11b անցին] անցն J1925*
237. 42:11f որոջ] որջ J1934*
238. 42:11f չորեքդրամեամ] չորեքդրամամ M2587*
239. 42:11f անգիր] ընդիր M1500*
240. 42:12b բիւր / բեւր] բեւրք J1925*
241. 42:15a դստերացն] դստերն M2587*

The major types of scribal error corrected by the first hand

1. *Loss of a letter, letters, words*

A scribal error corrected by the scribe himself—the scribes seem all to have been "hims"—usually has the character of "a slip." It is usually not a question of a major error, unless it involves a sizeable omission. Mistakes thus made almost always involve the loss of a letter, or two, which has been caused by parablepsis. For example, the scribe's eye skipped from one letter to the same letter repeated within a single word. Let's begin with this most frequent mistake, the loss of a letter by parablepis, where the scribe's eye slipped from a letter to the same, or sometimes similarly shaped letter that followed.

ա ∩ ա	42, 44, 51, 64, 143, 154
դ ∩ ո	104
ե ∩ ե	5, 47, 133: see also է ∩ ե[5]
զ ∩ զ	50, 76, 99, 171
զ ∩ գ	214
է ∩ ե	30, 90: see also ե ∩ ե
ի ∩ ի	27, 56
ի ∩ խ	34

[5] The letter է is often indistinguishable from ե in minuscule script.

ի ∩ հ	79
կ ∩ ն	120
մ ∩ մ	71 ∩
մ ∩ ն	68, 77
յ ∩ յ	3
յ ∩ ց	40, 148, 169: see also ց ∩ յ
ն ∩ ն	70, 82, 127
ն ∩ ո	15
ն ∩ ս	8, 24, 149
ո ∩ տ	213
չ ∩ չ	39
ս ∩ ս	61, 152[6]
ս ∩ ա	196
ս ∩ վ	209
ս ∩ տ	208
վ ∩ կ	187
վ ∩ փ	235
ր ∩ ր	211
ր ∩ ի	35, 138
ր ∩ ո	197
ր ∩ ռ	216
ր ∩ ք	231
տ ∩ ա	166, 205
ց ∩ յ	132: see also յ ∩ ց
ւ ∩ զ	141
ւ ∩ ս	20
փ ∩ ւ	65

We can add the following handful of instances of parablepsis to those just given.

ան ∩ ամ	119
էր ∩ եր	97
րդ ∩ րո	104
եթե ∩ եթե	136

[6] This corruption also involves the loss of -ս- before -ց-. One could argue that the corruption is more complicated than simple parablepsis since it results in the present tense instead of the subjunctive; the corruption makes sense to read.

ցէ ∩ ցէ	219
եւ ∩ եւ	230
ձեր ∩ ձեր	232

In the majority of these sixty-four instances of loss by parablepsis, we are only dealing with the loss of one or two letters, or rarely three (nos. 152, 216). The exceptions involve the loss of a word (nos. 5, 30, 61, 82, 127, 143, 166, 171, 187), or two (no. 3) or several words of text (nos. 76, 97, 136, 219, 230, 232).

In another twenty-six instances we also reckon with the loss of a single letter, but not as the result of parablepsis. In some cases we may be dealing with phonetic issues, where a letter is lost following a particular sound, that is, the problem may be one of sound rather than appearance. In the list that follows, the "lost" letter is in the middle, after the letter that precedes and before the letter that follows. For example, in the first instance, the lost letter ն is preceded by ռ and is followed by է.

No. 2	ռ	ն	է
9	մ	բ	ե
11	թ	ն	տ
14	հ	ե	ա
46	մ	ս	ո
54	ա	ր	հ
55	ղ	մ	ա
60	վ	ա	խ
74	ց	ե	ա
75	ր	ճ	տ
78	ճ	շ	մ
92	գ	ն	ա
102	լ	կ	տ
106	կ	ն	ք
111	ծ	ն	ա
116	ղ	կ	ղ
117	ն	գ	ո
146	ն	գ	ի
147	ց	զ	ա
161	ր	հ	ա
165	ն	դ	ա
168	ն	դ	ք
175	տ	ե	ա

202	զ	բ	ա
210	ն	ո	ք
238	մ	ե	մ

It is possible that here too, in a few cases, we must reckon with loss because letters look somewhat alike, e.g., մ and ա have an open structure.

Several other cases of the loss of a single letter involve loss of the demonstrative/definite marker -ն (nos. 21, 85, 94). In a couple of cases, the loss of a letter may be due to a loss of stress in a word (nos. 118, 140). In seven instances, the letter -ս- has been lost before -ց- (nos. 28, 31, 100, 107 [also loss of -ւ-, i.e., -ւս-], 108, 206) or -զ- (no. 45). Once the preposition ի was lost (no. 62); once թե was written for եթե (no. 66) — these are commonly confused, but differ by only one letter.

In yet another fourteen cases, two letters are lost within words. In the short list that follows, the "missing" letters are given after the number. One notes that in all but two instances the loss is -ա- followed by a consonant.

Nos. 57,[7] 63, 84, 167	ակ
95, 153, 164[8]	ան: cf. also no. 64
115	ախ
157, 182	ալ
177	այ
194	եւ
225	ոտ
241	աց

Five times the conjunction եւ has been lost (nos. 5, 133, 144, 174, 186) — two letters! (Only once has եւ been added: no. 114). Text critics will already know that the conjunction "and" is easily added or lost in biblical texts. Once we find the loss of the subject ես, again two letters (no. 72), or the loss of the negative particle ոչ (no. 6).

Still other cases of the loss of a single letter are: nos. 58, 67, 69, 105, 113, 122, 125, 150, 237.

---

[7] Change of line could also have contributed to this error.

[8] The loss of -ան- led to the participle տեսեալ.

So we can say that out of the total of 241 cases of mistakes corrected by the first hand, some 134, more than half, involve the loss of one or two letters, about half of these by parablepsis. These are the most common mistakes scribes make, and then correct, while copying.

A few other types of loss need to be mentioned. In four cases, the scribe lost a word following the direct object marker զ- or the preposition ց-, attaching these not to the correct word but to the one following (nos. 188, 189, 199, 224). In two cases, a change of line may have contributed to loss (nos. 33, 57; cf. also no. 100). In one instance, each a possessive pronoun (no. 223), indirect object (no. 190), or a negating particle (no. 233) has been lost. Once one, of two prepositions used together, was lost (no. 109).

2. *Assimilation to other items in the context*

The immediate context sometimes entices scribes to make mistakes. For example, the tense of a verb may be made to agree with another just before it in the sentence, or the number of a pronoun may inadvertently be made to agree with one just copied. This occurs in all types of copying, not just Armenian, and critical editions of the Hebrew Bible or the Greek New Testament will attest to this same phenomenon. In the list of 241 items, this occurs seventeen times. These are of interest and we can look at each briefly.

No. 4. 1:20a պատառեաց] պատառեալ J1925*

The finite verb has been attracted to յարուցեալ, which precedes.

No. 10. 2:9da հարկահար] հարկահարե[ա]լ BF*

The word հարկահար "servant" has been attracted to the participle մոլորեալ, which precedes.

No. 13. 3:17b հանգեան] հանգեալք BF*

The verb հանգեան "found rest" has been assimilated to the participle աշխատեալք, which immediately follows.

No. 16. 4:14b զոսկերս] զոսկեր V841*

It appears that the plural "bones" has been assimilated to the following singular possessive pronoun, իմ.

No. 17. 5:7b ձագք] ձագ M2587*
The plural "the young" has been assimilated to the singular in v.7a.

No. 22. 6:10a խնայեցից] խնայեցի V280*
The future, employing the subjunctive mood, has been assimilated to the past tense of the verb it follows. Alternatively it could be argued that the final -ց was lost before the following զ- because of the conjunction of similar sounding letters.

No. 49. 12:8a զքեզ] քեզ BF*
There is a dative earlier in the verse; the accusative has been assimilated to it.

No. 73. 16:4d իբրեւ > J1934*
The word իբրեւ follows the words եւ ես; the same words, i.e., եւ ես, appear in v.4c. It appears that the scribe assimilated v.4d to v.4c.

No. 89. 20:17b զկոգւոյ] pr մի V280*
The word մի occurs earlier in the line: the scribe of V280 inadvertently repeated it.

No. 101. 23:12a ոչ] + եւս թիւրեցայց J1934*: ex 11b
The scribe added these words from v.11b.

No. 110. 26:4a ում] ոյր BF*
Compare vv.3b (զոյր), 4b: the scribe has assimilated v.4a to v.3b where զոյր begins the line.

No. 114. 27:11b ոչ] pr եւ BF*
The conjunction եւ occurs earlier in the line.

No. 124. 29:6b ոռոգանեին] ոռոգանային V841*

The scribe inadvertently assimilated the imperfect ոռոգանեին "flowed" to the verb թանային "soaked" in v.6a.

No. 126. 29:20b նորա] իմում J1934*

The word իմ "my" occurs earlier in the line, so "and my bow goes in its hand" becomes in J1934* "my bow goes in my hand." The third person possessive pronoun has been assimilated to the first person, which precedes.

No. 160. 34:17b զչարս] զչարէ J1925*vid

The verb կորուսանէ "destroys" immediately precedes the direct object զչարս "the wicked." The scribe seems to have copied the ending of the verb onto its object.

No. 203. 39:10a կապիցես] կապիցի J1925*

The second person of the verb has been assimilated to the first person, which occurs in v.9a. There the verb is կամիցի, which is also visually similar.

No. 215. 40:22a ճովանոցանան] ճովանացանան J1934*

In this instance the "o" vowel in the middle of the word has been assimilated to the "a" vowel which precedes.

In all these cases the immediate context has led the scribe to make errors, "slips," which were then corrected.

3. *Confusion of letters*

In twelve cases, mistakes occur because individual letters of the alphabet look or sound similar. In the following list, the letter to the left is correct; that to the right is what the scribe first wrote and then corrected. The cases are:

Nos. 23, 32, 121	ց	յ
29	տ	ւ
43	զ	կ
91	ն	մ
131	ւ	ր
123	ճ	չ

129, 221	խ	ճ
137	գ	զ
218	ս	ց

4. *Dittography*

"Dittography" refers to the copying of something twice. There are five cases of this: nos. 1; 25 (-րուք becomes դուք); 156 (the scribe repeats ի on the end of միջի); 198; 227 (ի on the end of լսէի is repeated).

5. *Confusion of active and middle-passive moods*

In five cases, the scribe first wrote the middle-passive form where the active is correct (nos. 41, 145, 201, 204, 217); in five instances the reverse occurs, that is, the scribe first wrote the active where the middle-passive mood is correct (nos. 26, 96, 98, 191, 222). The occasion of error is about the same in either direction.

6. *Confusion of singular and plural*

In six cases, there is a confusion of the singular and plural: in the cases of nos. 52, 88, and 185 the plural is original; in the cases of nos. 158, 228, and 240 the singular is original. That is, the direction of corruption is about equal. Compare also no. 17, which is dealt with under cases of assimilation.

7. *Abbreviation of nouns ending in -թիւն*

This type of noun, so common in Armenian, is often abbreviated by scribes: -թիւն is abbreviated to -թի with a line above; the genitive –թեան is abbreviated to –թե with the line above to indicate it is abbreviated; the instrumental -թեամբ may be shortened to -թեբ, again with the line above. Such abbreviations can be confused. That possibility may lie at the root of the scribal errors, nos. 7 and 170. In the former, the scribe has corrected -թի to -թե; in the latter the scribe seems to have first written -թբք, then corrected it to -թե. At no. 170 the scribe may have been misled by the word անիրաւութբք, which appears immediately above; in that case, the corruption is rooted in assimilation to another word in the context. I might add that errors rooted in abbreviations also affect the presence or absence of the demonstrative/definite marker -ն: -թիւնն becomes

-թին, with the abbreviating line above, which is not much different than -թիւն. If the abbreviating line above is lost, a scribe can easily add the letter lacking, i.e., -ւ, and we have -թիւն instead of -թիւնն.

8. *Transpositions*

Six times in the list (nos. 12, 48, 83, 159, 220, 226) the scribe makes a slip by putting the words in the wrong order. Numbers 12 and 48, both in J1934*, are especially interesting and represent the same type of transposition. One suspects that sometimes, if a scribe transposed two words but it did not affect the sense, the scribe may have left the new order intact rather than make a correction. Such changes of word order then appear in the critical apparatus since they were left "uncorrected."

9. *Confusion of the active mood and the subjunctive*

Twice in the list we find this confusion: at no. 128 the subjunctive is first written where the active should appear; at no. 192 the reverse occurs—which happens with the loss of two letters.

The number of scribal errors corrected by the first hand as an indicator of the care with which a manuscript has been copied

Can the care with which individual scribes worked be assessed in a relative way by comparing the numbers of errors they made and then corrected? Here is the list of manuscripts and the numbers of such errors for the Book of Job.

J1925	44
M1500	7
BF	23
V841	56
BL	2
M2587	26
J1934	59
V280	21

This is a revealing set of numbers. What strikes the eye first is the amazingly low number of errors in the British Library manuscript—only two. On the other hand, V841 and J1934 have a very high number of errors corrected by the first hand. Matenadaran Ms. 1500 also has a low number of such corrections in comparison to the haste with which the manuscript seems to have been copied. Jerusalem Ms. 1925 also has a rather high number of first hand corrections, 44, almost twice as many as the British and Foreign Bible Society manuscript.

It should be said that these figures only tell part of the story about the care with which individual scribes worked because, in some instances, the scribe may have left an error uncorrected if it did not affect the sense, or even made changes to the text that he was copying. Uncorrected mistakes are not represented here, so that a rather high number of first hand corrections may only indicate that the scribe was careful! That said, I think we must give very high marks to P‘illippos, the scribe of the seventeenth Ms. of unknown provenance at the British Library.

First hand corrections: a clue to patterns of scribal errors?

It might be possible, by comparing the lists of errors corrected by the first hand, to find patterns of mistakes in a scribe's work. We have already noted in the analysis above that certain types of errors are frequently made, for example, letters or words are left out by parablepsis. To test this possibility, we can list the mistakes in Jerusalem 1925 that are corrected by the first hand.

2. 1:4b առնեին] առէին J1925*
4. 1:20a պատառեաց] պատառեալ J1925*
11. 2:13a զեւթն] զեւթ J1925*
14. 3:25b պատահեաց] պատահաց J1925*
20. 5:18a միւսանգամ] միսանգամ J1925*
24. 6:26b անսացից] ասացից J1925*
28. 8:6b դարձուսցէ] դարձուցէ J1925*vid
31. 9:12a դարձուսցէ] դարձուցէ J1925*
32. 9:16a կարդացից] կարդայց J1925*vid
36. 10:7b հանիցէ] հայիցէ J1925*vid
40. 10:21a դառնացեմ] դառնացեմ J1925*
41. 11:2a լսիցէ] լսիցի J1925*
57. 14:1b սակաւակեաց] սակաւեաց J1925* (|)
59. 14:6b զվարձկան] զվարձկանի J1925*
60. 14:10a վախճանեալ] վխճանեալ J1925*
62. 14:17a ի > J1925*

66. 14:21b եթե] թե J1925*
68. 15:8a զհրաման] հրամ J1925*
72. 16:4c ես > J1925*
78. 17:10b ճշմարտութիւն] ճմարտութիւն J1925*
79. 18:4c ի հիմանէ] հիմանի J1925*
83. 19:22a դուք / զիս tr J1925* (c pr m[?])
90. 20:26c եկամուտ] կամուտ J1925*
92. 21:6a տագնապեցայց] տագապեցայց J1925*
102. 24:5c լկտիս] լտիս J1925*
103. 24:6a տհաս] pr ի J1925*
118. 28:4a փոշոյ] փշոյ J1925*
119. 28:4b մոռանամ] մոռան J1925*
145. 32:11c քննիցէք] քննիցիք J1925* vid
157. 34:12b ամենակալն] ամենակն J1925*vid
160. 34:17b զչարս] զչարէ J1925*vid
164. 35:13a տեսանել] տեսեալ J1925*
174. 37:4c Եւ > J1925*
176. 37:10a զսառամանիս] զսառնամանիս J1925*
177. 37:12c հրամայեսցէ] հրամեսցէ J1925*
199. 38:38a զհող փոշի] զփոշի J1925*
203. 39:10a կապիցես] կապիցի J1925*
210. 40:2a զդատաստան ոք] զդատաստանքն J1925*vid
225. 41:20a խոցոտէ] խոցէ J1925*
227. 42:5a զքէն] pr ի J1925*
228. 42:7c ճշմարիտ] ճշմարիտք J1925*
235. 42:9a Սովփար] սովար J1925*
236. 42:11b անցին] անցն J1925*
240. 42:12b բիւր / բեւր] բեւրք J1925*

An examination of the list reveals the scribe's tendency with respect to errors in the course of copying. This list contains forty-four items and, in twenty-eight cases, the scribe has corrected the loss of one (nos. 2, 11, 14, 20, 24, 28, 31, 32, 40, 60, 62, 66, 78, 79, 90, 92, 102, 118, 236) or two letters (nos. 57, 68, 72 — the subject ես; 119, 157, 164, 174 — the conjunction եւ; 177, 225). There are three cases of assimilation (nos. 4, 160, 203); two cases each of singular-plural confusion (nos. 228, 240) and active / middle-passive confusion (nos. 41, 145). These types of mistakes together account for 35 of the 44 errors corrected by Mkhit‘ar.

Further analysis might compare such scribal tendencies among various manuscripts. That lies outside the limitations of this particular study.

The most fascinating error corrected by the scribe

Doubtless the reader paused at no. 130 in the list. Job 30:18b reads: Եւ իբրեւ զծապաւէն պատմուճանի իմոյ շուրջ կալաւ զիս "and he encircled me like the hem of my tunic." The scribe of V280* added the word քանդակ after զծապաւէն, so that we now have "embossed hem" instead of just the plain "hem." Text critics love to find such readings as this one! What was the scribe thinking? What does the addition tell us, if anything, about the world of the scribe?

Conclusion

This contribution to Dickran's *Festschrift* focuses upon one aspect of scribal work, namely, the mistake, or "slip," that is corrected by the scribe himself. It offers some insight into the kinds of mistakes that Armenian scribes tend to make, and then correct. At the same time, this contribution is of interest to text critics who wrestle with sorting out mistakes from original readings. The kinds of mistakes that a scribe is prone to make *may* be of use in determining the superiority of one reading over another where manuscripts differ.

The exposition here also raises questions about the way scribes worked, their posture — did they, for example, copy with one finger of one hand following the text being copied and with the stylus in the other hand? Such questions as these belong to Dickran's areas of expertise and so I leave my subject unfinished or, better, open-ended![9]

---

[9] Readers who are text critics may wish to look at the items in the list which are not dealt with in the discussion. They are nos. 18, 19, 36, 37, 38, 53, 59, 80, 81, 86, 87, 93, 103, 112, 134, 135, 139, 142, 151, 155, 162, 163, 170, 172, 173, 178, 180, 184, 195, 200, 207, 212, 229, 234, 239, all of them minor mistakes of various kinds.

17

An Armenian/Judaeo-Arabic Word-List in Cambridge

James Clackson

The publication of a word-list with Armenian written in Hebrew characters is, in a sense, a "return gift" to Dickran Kouymjian, since it was he who brought to light a word-list with Greek written in Armenian letters, that I later published with his help and advice.[1] The new word-list, recently found in the Cambridge University Library, dates from around the tenth century and contains Armenian in Hebrew script with Judaeo-Arabic glosses given above each word. The piece is to be published by Avihai Shivtiel, who identified the piece in the manuscript collections of the Cairo Genizali, and who was kind enough to alert me of his discovery before publication and provide me with his transcription and translation of the text.[2]

The Cairo Genizah is one of the richest collections of documents from anywhere around the Mediterranean. The Genizah, originally housed in the Ben Ezra Synagogue in Old Cairo, was the depository for all written documents for the Jewish community in Cairo from the middle ages to the nineteenth century. The Jews of Cairo tried not to destroy any written text during that period, for fear that it might contain the name of God, and so every scrap of paper was deposited in the Genizah through a hole in the wall which ran beside the street. As a consequence of this, the Genizah contained material

---

[1] Dickran Kouymjian, "Unique Armenian Papyrus" in Dora Sakayan, ed., *Proceedings of the Fifth International Conference on Armenian Linguistics* (New York: Delmar, 1996), pp. 381-386 and James Clackson, "A Greek Papyrus in Armenian Script" *Zeitschrift für Papyrologie and Epigraphik* 129 (2000), pp. 223-258.

[2] Avihai Shivtiel, "A Judaeo-Armenian and a Judaeo-Arabic word-list from the Cairo Genizah," in *Journal of Semitic Studies*, Supplement 16 (2005), pp. 140-142.

over a vast range, not just literary and biblical texts, but also legal, financial and commercial documents, informal letters, lists and accounts. Taken together, these texts have greatly increased our knowledge of Egypt and the Near East in the middle ages and have been used to reconstruct the social history of medieval Cairo.[3] The greatest part of the Genizah, around 140,000 documents in total, was donated to Cambridge University Library in 1898, by Dr. Solomon Schechter and Dr. Charles Taylor, after Dr. Schechter had negotiated with the authorities of the Ben Ezra Synagogue to remove it from Cairo for study. Since that date, the collection has been worked upon by a number of experts from around the world, but there are still thousands of pieces that remain unpublished or that still defy interpretation.

It is not surprising that amongst a collection of this kind an Armenian word-list has been uncovered. The Armenians are first identified in Egypt in antiquity and there is good evidence for a continuous Armenian presence since then.[4] Armenians visited and worked in Egypt as merchants, pilgrims, and craftsmen and it is most likely that a visiting Armenian dictated this word-list to a Jewish business associate or companion.

In the medieval world, there is a growing number of examples of informal word-lists, constructed mainly for the use of travelers and merchants, and also perhaps for the linguistically curious. The earliest example known to me of a word-list that was clearly dictated is the seventh century "Folium Parisinum," which contains Greek words written in Latin script with a Latin gloss provided.[5] Most of the other glossaries from antiquity belong to the more formal realm of structured education or scholastic commentary, and no other text so clearly belongs to an informal, travelers' phrase book category

---

[3] S. D. Goitein, *A Mediterranean Society; The Jewish Communities of the Arab World as Portrayed in the Cairo Genizah*, 6 vols. (Berkeley, California: University of California Press, 1967-1994).

[4] Angèle Kapöian-Kouymjian, *L'Égypte vue par des Arméniens* (Paris, 1988) and for evidence of Armenians from papyrus texts from the Greco-Roman period see Clackson, "A Greek Papyrus in Armenian Script."

[5] Published with a commentary by Johannes Kramer, *Glossaria Bilinguia in papyris et membranis reperta* (Bonn, 1983) as Text 14.

before the tenth century.[6] In the medieval period; however, the number of surviving informal glossaries appears to increase—if this does not just reflect the accident of survival, it may be linked to the fact that a smaller part of the population of the Mediterranean would have been able to communicate directly, as Latin and Greek ceased to be the *lingue franche* that they had been under Roman rule.[7] Armenian specialists will of course be aware of one of the most celebrated of these medieval word-lists, the Armenian-Latin glossary of Autun, which dates to the tenth century.[8]

The Armenian/Judaeo-Arabic glossary from the Cairo Genizah is shorter than the Autun glossary. It contains only 21 items written on eight lines of text. The Judaeo-Arabic (that is, Arabic written in Hebrew letters) is written above the Armenian word. The glossary contains words for foodstuffs on the first two lines, designations for persons on the next two lines, and then words for "white" and "black" followed by a word, which is obscure in Judaeo-Arabic and Armenian. The next line unusually has an easily identifiable Armenian word for "man" (Classical Armenian *mard)* and the text then ends with what may be three imperative verb-forms followed by a short phrase. In the reproduction of the text below, I have not given the Judaeo-Arabic forms themselves, but in translation, with the Judaeo-Armenian forms transliterated:

bread	*meat*	*water*	*wine*
hds	*mys*	*šwr*	*kyny*

rose	*apples*	*pears*

---

6 Johannes Kramer *Glossaria Bilinguia in papyris et membranis reperta (*Bonn, 1983), and *Glossaria bilinguia altera (C. Gloss. Biling. II).* Archiv für Papyrusforschung und verwandte Gebiete, Beiheft 8 (München/Leipzig, 2001).

7 See Bernhard Bischoff, "The Study of Foreign Languages in the Middle Ages," *Mittelalterliche Studien. Ausgewählte Aufsätze zur Schriftkunde und Literaturgeschichte* Band II (Stuttgart, 1967), pp. 227-245, for reference to and discussion of the evidence for glossaries and language learning in the medieval period.

8 Jos Weitenberg, "Armenian Dialects and the Latin-Armenian Glossary of Autun" in T. Samuelian and M. Stone, eds., *Medieval Armenian Culture* (Chico, California: Scholar's Press: 1983), pp. 13-28.

b'rt	*knzwr*	*d'nz*
woman	*virgin*	*your mother*
kwgnig	*kyys*	*myr*

father	*beautiful*	*face*	*singer*
d'd	*'gyh*	*'kš'kyn*	*kws'n*

white	*black*	*??*
'spyd'g	*syb*	*'stp'n*

m'rt

up!	*Go away!*	*Sit down!*
'ryg	*'knh*	*nyst*

How are you?
'yn škurn's

It must be remembered when trying to interpret these forms that the Hebrew alphabet does not contain separate letters for vowels, although *y* may be used to represent the vowel /*i*/ and *w* used for /*u*/ and *h* may represent the vowel /*a*/ when used finally. The letter for the glottal stop, *aleph* (represented in the above transliteration by ') is clearly used here to represent an initial schwa or medial /*a*/ as well. Difficulties are also caused by the use of the same Hebrew letter to represent lenited and unlenited sounds; thus, the word *b'rt* clearly represents the word that would be in Classical Armenian *vard,* and *syb* represents *sew;* in both cases, the letter *b* is used for the lenited form of the consonant, and here represents the voiced labio-dental fricative [v]. In the same way, the letters transliterated *k* and g may also stand for the Armenian fricatives [kh] and [gh] (i.e. խ and ղ).

Despite the difficulties of decoding the Hebrew transcriptions, the interpretation of most of the Armenian words is straightforward. It is easy to work out the following equivalences:

hds=hats'; mys=mis; šwr=jur; kyny=gini; b'rt=vard; knzwr= khndzor; d'nz=tandz; kyys=koys; myr=mayr; kws'n=gusan; 'spyd'g=spitak; syb=sew; m'rt=mard; nyst=nist.

The following words, however, need more comment: *kwgnig,* the word glossed as "wife" appears to contain *knik,* the post-Classical form of *kin* "woman" in many dialects. The first syllable may be an attempt to render the possessive pronoun *k'o* "your," which may have already taken the Middle Armenian form *k'u.* Note that the Judaeo-Arabic word for "mother" later in the same line is given as "your mother," although there is no pronoun or article given in the Armenian translation. The word glossed by "father" *d'd* is clearly the modem dialectal word for father *tat*, previously unattested in the Classical language. The phrase *'gyh 'kškyn* probably contains the word for "sweet, beautiful" (modem dialects have forms /aghi/ and /aghig/) and perhaps the word for "eyes' *ach'k',* although the exact analysis escapes me. The command *'ryg* must be Classical Armenian *ari ek* i.e. "up! come!" (from *yaṙnem* and *eki)* a collocation which survives into the modem language; *'knh* probably contains *gna* the imperative of *gnam* although it is unclear to me why it is written an initial vowel. The reading of the phrase *'yn škurn's* is problematic, and its interpretation is uncertain, although it is likely to have *inch'* as first word and could represent a Middle Armenian verb form *ku aṙnes,* giving a phrase "what are you doing?"

It is clear that if this text is as early as the tenth century—and the palaeography suggests that it is not much later, then it shows some interesting dialect features for a text of this date, including post-Classical words for "woman," "father" and "beautiful." Unfortunately, uncertainties over the representation of the sounds in the Hebrew script, and the absence of clear representation of the vowel sounds, means that it is difficult to associate the Armenian with a particular dialect or group of dialects. However, it is worth noting that in this text Classical Armenian voiced stops are usually devoiced, even in the vicinity of *r (vard* and *mard),* but voicing seems to be retained after *n* in *khndzor* and *tandz.* Unvoiced stops usually appear as voiced, except following *s* when *p* and *t* remain (in *spitak* and *nist).* The word final aspirate of *hats'* is written with a curious combination of *ds* (the writer does not use the Hebrew letter *tsade,* conventionally thought to have had an affricate value).

The exact circumstances of the creation of the word-list, and its intended use or purpose can only be speculated upon. The existence of the personal pronoun "your" in the Arabic phrase "your mother," and the possible existence of the same Armenian pronoun in the collocation *kwgnig,* if I am correct to see this as Armenian *k'u knik,* may suggest that the word-list was created through pointing at objects and eliciting a response.[9] On the other hand, the inclusion of Armenian *vard* may argue for a bilingual Armenian speaker participating in the creation of the list, since the Armenian word is very similar to the Arabic word given for "rose," *ward* (which has the same origin as the Armenian term—both are borrowed from Persian), and the speaker may have selected this lexical item as an example of a word that sounded similar in the two languages. However the word-list came about, it has survived as a unique record of contact between an Armenian and a Jew in medieval Cairo, and as such will, I hope, be thought a fitting offering to a man who has done much to integrate the story of the Armenians with their neighbouring cultures.

---

9 This seems to have been how the Autun glossary was constructed, see Weitenberg, "Armenian Dialects and the Latin-Armenian Glossary of Autun," p. 14.

18

The *Pentaglot Apostolos* in the Biblioteca Ambrosiana: Ms. B 20 inf. a-b

Gabriella Uluhogian

Introduction

The Biblioteca Ambrosiana of Milan was created in line with the original idea and desire of Cardinal Federico Borromeo (1564-1631) and was solemnly inaugurated on December 8, 1609.[1] In order to promote his project, Cardinal Borromeo wanted, even before the library was opened, to collect a large number of Greek and Oriental manuscripts, so that the Library could offer concrete material to scholarly studies and editions of texts. Among the numerous treasures that are preserved in this Library is a precious codex known as the *Pentaglot Apostolos*. This is a polyglot New Testament manuscript in two volumes (for the description see below), which comprises the *Letters* of St. Paul, the *Catholic Letters* and the *Acts of the Apostles*. Notwithstanding the singular nature of the artifact, one cannot say that it has been subjected to a complete study – which would require the collaboration of various experts – but not even to an accurate description.

In this paper, I propose to make the manuscript better known to scholars. Although I will concentrate my attention only on the Armenian text, I am convinced that the non-textual (codicological) details of the description could also be of use to other specialists. In addition, this multi-lingual manuscript poses an interesting historical question concerning a subject that has not been fully explored: the shared lives, in certain religious environments, specifically monastic,

---

[1] On the Biblioteca Ambrosiana cf. *Storia dell'Ambrosiana*, *Il Seicento* (1992), *Il Settecento* (2000), *l'Ottocento* (2001), *Il Novecento* (2002), Milan.

of people linked by a single underlying religious faith, but coming from different ethnic groups and speaking different languages.

Description of the manuscript

Ms. B 20 inf. is a paper codex made of thick Oriental paper,[2] 360x260mm (written surface 295x215mm), bound in two volumes, the second of which lacks the Armenian text. The first volume comprises ff. I, 275, I', numbered in pencil at the centre of the lower margin of each *recto*; in the upper external corner there is a previous numbering in pen with letters of the Coptic alphabet and, alongside, the corresponding Arabic number in pencil; the second volume comprises ff. I, 186, I' and is evidently organized like the first, except for the fact that the column intended for the Armenian remained blank.

The Armenian text occupies the ff. 1-175 of the first volume (the ff. 20-21 have a clear tear in the lower external part, with a loss of six to eight lines of text) and the text breaks off at f. 176; the leaves have been glued and sewn during restoration in such a way that it is not possible to analyse the original structure of the quires, even if from the integral part of the volume one can deduce that it was composed of quinions. Each leaf of the codex contains five columns of text, in the following sequence: on the *recto*, from left to right, Ethiopic, Syriac, Coptic, Arabic, Armenian; and as a mirror reflection on the *verso*: Armenian, Arabic, Coptic, Syriac, Ethiopic.

As concerns the Armenian, the text is set out in a column of 30/34 lines, 50/55mm width. The writing is *bolorgir*, by a single hand, in dense black ink. Towards the end of the column the Armenian scribe sometimes thins out the writing (ff. 40v, 49v, 120v) or he makes it more dense (ff. 39r, 96r, 101r, 121r), in order, it would seem, to make his text correspond with that of the other languages, even though some clues mentioned below raise some doubts about this.

For the Armenian, the decoration is limited to ff. 46v, 99v which have modest headbands, whereas titles and initials are written in

---

[2] Here one notes, among others, the phenomenon of the démariage, described by J. Irigoin, "Le papiers non filigranés: état présent des recherches et perspectives d'avenir" in M. Maniaci and P. F. Munafò, eds., *Ancient and Medieval Book Materials and Techniques* (Erice, 18-25 sett. 1992), Studi e Testi 357 (Città del Vaticano, 1993), p. 293.

large *erkat'agir*, traced in red ink; in the Coptic column the decorated initials and headings are more frequent; in the Syriac and Arabic sections, red ink is sometimes used for titles also. The binding is from the nineteenth century, in leather on card plates; the plates are framed with a blind-stamped double-line border along the external margins. On the spine (currently held together with strips of sticky tape) four raised bands delimit five areas: the second area bears in gold the words: *Epistolarum S. Pauli Pentaglotton*; in the final area at the bottom an oval label in green leather bearing *"20"* in gold has been glued in.

The margins of the codex are worn and the paper has yellowed. The first leaves, as was said, have been subjected to radical and crude restoration with inversions in the order, and frequent alteration of the quire structure through repair of the central part of the bifolia; furthermore, there are many holes from bookworms (especially at ff. 115-127).

The quire numbering, in letters from the Armenian alphabet in alphabetic sequence, rather than numerical, shed light on the composition of the whole manuscript. A hand other than that of the scribe has marked the original quires with Armenian letters, positioned at the centre of the lower margin of the *recto* of the first sheet and the *verso* of the last sheet of each quire. A curious detail is the fact that, unlike what usually happens, in the last leaf of each quire there is not the same reference letter as the first sheet, rather the letters follow on in alphabetic order with this sequence: ff. 9v դ, 10r ե, 19v զ, 23r գ, 26r է, 35v ը, 36r թ, 45v ժ, 46r ի, 55v լ, 56r խ, 65v ծ, 66r կ, 75v հ, 76r ձ, 85v ղ, 86r ճ, 95v մ, 96r յ, 105v ն, 106r շ, 115v ո, 125v պ, 126r ջ, 135v ռ, 136r ս, 145v վ, 146r տ, 155v ր, 156r ց, 165v ւ, 166r փ, 175v ք; at f. 176r, in which the Armenian text no longer appears, the start of a new quire is however marked, restarting from ա, the first letter of the alphabet.

The examination of the text makes it possible to establish with certainty the original order of the pages, in addition to establishing the quantity of text lost.

In fact, in the scant and meagre descriptions of the codex[3] it is indicated that the codex is mutilated at the beginning and, more

3 F. Macler, "Notices de manuscrits arméniens vus dans quelques bibliothèques de l'Europe centrale," *Journal Asiatique* (Sept.-Oct. 1913), p.

precisely, that it starts from Rom 3, 29.[4] Anyway, carefully examining the text, one notes that the missing part is smaller, since at the time of the final rebinding there was an inversion in the order of the sheets.

The leaves, in their current order, present these portions of the text, indicated in brackets: ff. 1-19 (Rom 3,29b-10,3a), 20-21 (Rom 1,20b-2,2), 22 (Rom 3,1b-3,9a), 23 (Rom 3,22-29a), 24-25 (Rom 2,3-2,21), 26-45 (Rom 10,3b-16,27). And inversely, the text is distributed as follows: Rom 1,20b-2,2 (ff. 20-21), 2,3-2,21 (ff. 24-25), 2,22-3,1a (missing), Rom 3,1b-3,9a (f. 22), 3,9b-21 (missing), 3,22-29a (f. 23), 3,29b-10,3a (ff. 1-19), 10,3b-16,27 (ff. 26-45).

Summarizing, the following parts are missing: Rom 1,1-1,20a (2 sheets), Rom 2,22-3,1a (1 sheet), Rom 3,9b-21 (1 sheet); calculating that each leaf contains between nine and eleven verses, on the basis of the evidence offered by the Armenian text we can conclude that the manuscript is missing four leaves only.

235; E. Galbiati, "L'orientalistica nei primi decenni di attività, in Storia dell'Ambrosiana," vol. 1, *Il Seicento* (Milan, 1992), p. 108; Idem, "I fondi orientali minori (siriaco, etiopico, armeno) dell'Ambrosiana," Atti del Convegno *La Lombardia e l'Oriente* (11-15 giugno 1962), Ist. Lombardo-Accademia di Scienze e Lettere (Milan, 1963), pp. 190-199.

[4] The same is said for the Ethiopic text, and that in Coptic and that in Arabic (cf. respectively S. Grébaut, "Catalogue des manuscrits éthiopiens de la Bibliothèque Ambrosienne," *Revue de l'Orient Chrétien*, 3 s., 9 (29), (1933-34), pp. 25-29; J. B. Chabot, "Note sur la polyglotte de la Bibliothèque Ambrosienne de Milan," *Orientalia Christiana Periodica*, 13 (1947), pp. 451-453, fig. 1-2; O. Löfgren – R. Traini, "Catalogue of the Arabic manuscripts in the Biblioteca Ambrosiana," I: Antico fondo and medio fondo, Vicenza [1975] (Fontes ambrosiani, 51), pp. 3-4 (n. I-II). It is curious to observe that none of these specialists has checked to see if we must really consider lost almost three initial chapters of the *Letters to the Romans*, despite the existence in the anterior counterguard of a manuscript note by the orientalist Antonio Maria Ceriani (1828-1907), which is very difficult to read, which indicated: *Initio folia transposita, desunt tamen prima folia…* . Very different is the value given to the description of the codex in the introduction to the Coptic text in [G.W. Horner], *The Coptic Version of the New Testament in the Northern Dialect*, vol. III, (Oxford, 1905), pp. XVII-XX.

The Armenian text

The Armenian text therefore comprises the following *Letters* of St. Paul: Rom (1,20-16,27, with gaps in the passages 2,22-3,1a and 3,9b-21) (ff. 1r-45v), 1 Cor (ff. 46v-99r), 2 Cor (ff. 99v-141v), Gal (ff. 142r-160r), Eph (1,1-6,22) (ff.160v 175v). This final *Letter* is interrupted abruptly at chapter 6, 22a, when at this point there are little more than two verses to the conclusion.

One will observe that between the end of Rom and the start of 1 Cor there is a leaf (f. 46r) where the Armenian column remains blank. This detail, together with the fact that there is another blank column at f. 155v, without interruption of the Armenian version of Gal between the f. 155r and the f. 156r, whereas the columns of the other four languages occupy in a regular manner the spaces reserved for them, raises the doubt that in reality the Armenian text does not always keep up with the others. It is only with the contribution of experts in the other languages that one can establish if the columns of text always correspond or if sometimes in one or other of the versions some additional pericopes have been inserted. The solution to this question does not answer a mere curiosity. Through this confrontation it would also be possible to have evidence about the level of knowledge of the reciprocal languages that the scribes had and about their procedure in the preparation of the manuscript.

The order in which the *Letters* are presented is for the Armenian that was found in the *Vulgata*.[5] The Euthalian prefaces are missing, but the final annotations are present (one sees for example at f. 99r, at the end of 1 Cor: *Առ Կորընթացիս թուղթ առաջին գրեցաւ ի Փիլիպպեայ ի ձեռն Ստեփանեայ եւ Փորտունատեայ եւ Աքակիոսի: Տունք Դ. Հ.* Even if the text is basically the same as that of the *Vulgata*, there are some interesting variants, on which more thorough investigations could be made. In fact, in addition to the absence or presence of the enclitic article, a phenomenon known to anyone who has experience of the transmission of Armenian texts, there is a different use of the cases which should be indicated: one

[5] Since there is no critical edition of the Armenian Bible, the comparison was made using the two principal editions of the Holy Text: *Աստուածաշունչ մատեան Հին եւ Նոր Կտակարանաց*, Y. Zohrapian, ed. (Venice, 1805), 4 vols., and *Գիրք Աստուածաշունչք Հին եւ Նոր Կտակարանաց*, A. Bagratuni, ed. (Venice, 1860).

can see, for example, Rom 6, 9: մահ նորա ոչ եւս տիրէ rather than մահ նմա ոչ եւս տիրէ or Rom 8, 31 մեզ հակառակ rather than մեր հակառակ. There are also variations in the mood and tenses of the verbs, important also from the point of view of meaning, such as at Rom 5, 19 եղեն ... եղեն rather than եղեն ... եղիցին or Gal 5, 1 մտանիցէք rather than մտանէք.Overall, however, the text is set out accurately and correctly, which indicates the work of an expert scribe.

The origins and source of the codex

Since the Armenian text does not give any indication about the place and date when it was transcribed,[6] it is necessary to search elsewhere for elements that are useful for the clarification of the history of the manuscript.

Useful information is provided by G.W. Horner who, in the introduction to his edition of the Coptic version of the New Testament text,[7] also undertook an accurate analysis of our codex and, on the basis of palaeographic evidence, affirms that the Coptic text was transcribed by two different scribes, and that its oldest part dates from the twelfth century and the most recent part from the fourteenth century. There are also some notes in Arabic which open a window on the environment where the texts comes from: at f. 150v there is the invocation of the mercy of God "for him who provided (for the work) and for the copyist the feeble Yuhanna the Syrian from the city Amida"[8]; at f. 160r "provided for it the presbyter Salīb the provider at Dayr al Siryan, known as our Lady the Virgin"; at f. 176r "O Lord, open the soul of thy little servant the transcriber of these letters and his brother Ḣadīd ....". From these memorial notes it seems that it is possible to find out that the promoter was the priest

[6] In volume II of the same tetraglot codex (ms. B 20 inf. b), containing the *Catholic Letters* and the *Acts of the Apostles*, in which the Armenian text is missing, despite there being a column reserved for it, a hand other than the scribe of volume I has written on f. 186v in *bolorgir* characters Ես մեղաւոր ծառայս [I, (this) servant sinner]. From this note one learns only that an unknown Armenian had contact with the codex at some time after its writing.

[7] Cf. note 4.

[8] This and the following two notes are taken word for word from Horner's *Introduction*.

Salib; one of the scribes (that is the transcriber of which text? Arabic or Syriac? This note, in Arabic, is under the column occupied by the Syriac text) is Yuhanna of Amida, and the unnominated "transcriber" of the f. 176r is either Yuhanna or another unknown person, whose the brother Ḣadīd is also remembered.

Löfgren and Traini, on the other hand, in their catalogue of the Arabic Christian manuscripts in the Biblioteca Ambrosiana[9] give a different interpretation of the note at f. 160r, in which the transcriber would have been the priest Ṣalīb "in the monastery of the Syrians known as the monastery of Our Lady the Virgin."

Aside from the different interpretation of the notes, the important fact is that the codex is placed in relationship with the Monastery of the Syrians (Dayr al-Suryān),[10] one of the most famous among the many places occupied by ascetics that animated the Egyptian desert of Wadi'n Natrum.

The information takes on greater value if we consider the existence of another manuscript parallel to ours: this is the pentaglot *Psalter* in the Vatican Library (Ms. Barb. Or. 2),[11] from the Monastery of St. Macarius, perhaps the most famous centre of Coptic asceticism in Egypt, it too is in the region of Wadi'n Natrum. The two manuscripts have many characteristics in common and they probably reflect a single original idea, which merits investigation. The Vatican *Psalter* has more or less the same dimensions (356x263mm), the same type of paper, the same organization of the

---

[9] O. Löfgren – R. Traini, "Catalogue of the Arabic manuscripts…, p. 3.

[10] Cf. A. Cody – P. Grossman, *Dayr al-Suryān*, in *The Coptic Encyclopedia*, vol. III, (New York-Toronto, 1991), pp. 876-881 and the bibliography shown; cf. also the most recent contributions by K. Innemée - L. van Rompay, "La présence des Syriens dans le Wadi al-Natrum (Egypte)," *Parole de l'Orient*, 23 (1998), pp. 167-202 and L. van Rompay – A.B. Schmidt, "Takritans in the Egyptian Desert: the Monastery of the Syrians in the Ninth Century," *Journal of the Canadian Society for Syriac Studies*, 1 (2001), pp. 41-60.

[11] *Codices Armeni Bybliothecae Vaticanae Borgiani, Vaticani, Barberiniani, Chisiani*, schedis Frederici Cornwallis Conybeare adhibitis recensuit Eugenius Tisserant (Rome, 1927), p. 343; *Codices Aethiopici Vaticani et Borgiani Barberinianus Orientalis 2, Rossianus 865,* recensuerunt S. Grébaut... et E. Tisserant..., in *Bybliotheca Vaticana* 1935-36, I, pp. 859-861; II, tav. III (f. 82v).

five texts in columns and in the same order in which they appear in the *Apostolos* of the Biblioteca Ambrosiana. There are also some other singular coincidences: in the Vatican manuscript the Armenian text which, unlike that of the Ambrosian codex, is the work of different scribes, breaks off before the others (at the end of f. 194r, with the *incipit* of Ps. 148 Աւրհնեցէք զտէր յերկնից), again here an Armenian colophon is missing, also here there is a later memorial note.[12] It is clear that there is a close relationship between these manuscripts; codicological evidence suggests that the Vatican *Psalter* dates from the fourteenth century, the same period as the most recent part of the *Apostolos*. The two codices are clear evidence that when they were copied there must have been some kind of cooperation between members of the Coptic, Arabic, Syriac, Ethiopic and Armenian churches.

This is no great surprise, because it is known that from the fourth century, with varying degrees of intensity, groups of Armenians not only made pilgrimages to Jerusalem, but that they also pushed on to the Egyptian deserts in search of solitude and the ascetic life. But it was above all during a later period that the contacts with Egypt became more intense and more frequent. This happened when a large part of the Armenian population moved West, because of the invasion of the Seljuks in the eleventh century, into Cappadocia and then in the mountains of Cilicia, where at a later date the Armenian Kingdom was to be set up. In particular in 1065, in the agitated period of transition that followed the fall of the city of Ani under the attack of Alp-Arslan, Grigor-Vahram from the illustrious family of the Pahlavuni was elected Catholicos. Because of his temperament he was inclined towards a life of prayer and study[13] rather than the government of the church, and he delegated to others for long periods the pastoral tasks, distancing himself from his see. During his periods of absence he undertook numerous journeys, the purpose and chronology of which are problematic, but it is known that

[12] At f. 193v one reads in *bolorgir* characters, in a different hand from all those used in the text, and different also from the scribe of the Ambrosian codex: զՄանուէլ անարժան երեց յիշեցէք ի Տէր [Remember to the Lord the unworthy priest Manuēl].

[13] He was called *Vkayasēr* [Martyrophile], because of his love for the life of the saints, studies to which he was dedicated personally and which also involved his disciples.

between 1074 and 1088, after having been at Constantinople, where he collected material for the lives of the saints, he went once or perhaps twice to Egypt.[14] Here, during the domination of the Fatimids (969-1171), there was a large Armenian colony: various sources[15] speak of 30,000 Armenians, some of whom reached positions of great prestige, such as the famous Badr al-Jamali (1074-1094), Vizier of the Caliph Al-Mutanṣir and again, in the twelfth century, the very powerful Vizier Bahrām.[16]

There could be a number of reasons behind the visit of Grigor-Vahram to Egypt: the desire to visit the monasteries in the desert; his wish to regulate the religious life of the numerous fellow nationals resident there; or chance – there is also talk of a storm which could have pushed his ship onto the Egyptian coast, while he was on his way to Jerusalem. It is also interesting to note that another Grigor,[17] son of the sister of the former, who had come to Egypt, it seems, before his uncle, was consecrated by him to the position of patriarch, in reality bishop, of the Armenians resident here.

For us here, the interest is not so much on the unravelling of the complex chronology of these visits of important Armenians, but rather the affirmation that the Armenian presence in Egypt between the eleventh and thirteenth centuries was well-established among the numerous other ethnic groups living there.

In the Scetis desert, in the great territory of the Wadi 'n Natrum, next to the mainly Coptic monasteries there were other monasteries which, taking on the name of the nation which populated them, were called the Monastery of the Armenians or of the Abyssinians or of the Syrians, the latter having already been brought to mind. Hugo G.

---

[14] For the personality of Grigor and his journeys see the article by Angèle Kapoian-Kouymjian, "Le Catholicos Grégoire II le Martyrophile [Vkayaser] et ses peregrinations," *Bazmavep*, 132 (1974), No. 1-2, pp. 306-325 and the numerous sources indicated there.

[15] Ibid.

[16] M. Canard, "Un vizir chrétien à l'époque fāṭimide: l'Arménien Bahrām," *Annales de l'Institut d'Etudes Orientales*, 12 (1954), pp. 84-113; Idem, *Notes sur les Arméniens en Egypte à l'époque fāṭimide*, ibidem, 13 (1955), pp. 143-157.

[17] Also concerning the possible homonymic confusion with his young nephew, son of his sister, cf. A. Kapoian-Kouymjian, *Le Catholicos Grégoire II le Martyrophile*.

Evelyn White, who made long studies of the monastic sites of this desert, attests the presence of Armenian inscriptions and graffiti[18] in the Monastery of St. Macarius, which are proof of the existence of people who wrote and spoke Armenian.

And also the singularity of the manuscripts in the five languages of the most important Oriental Christianities is explained if we consider that we are dealing with the prechalcedonian churches, among which, even though there were differences in language and rites, there was a common faith. Here we should remember that more than once Coptic, Armenian, Syriac, Abyssinian, and Nubian are mentioned together as representatives of the orthodox faith in opposition to the Nestorian doctrine and the Council of Chalcedon.[19] If we then consider the relative proximity of the various monasteries or perhaps even the shared lives of individuals of different nationalities[20] in the same monastery, it is not difficult to conclude that a type of (as they would say today) *team-work* could be organized, calling on scribes of various languages to collaborate. In fact, despite the renown that some of them had,[21] it remains difficult

---

[18] H. G. Evelyn White, *The Monasteries of the Wadi 'n Natrum* (New York, 1932), part III, at pp. 76, 70, 115 cites graffiti and inscriptions, interpreted for him by the learned Mekhitarist of Vienna, Father S. Kogian, among which it is worth reporting the most complete (p. 115), from the typical formulary of the memorial inscriptions or the Armenian colophons: "....in (this) place, whosoever shall read and remember us .../ may he be remembered in the presence of Christ on the terrible day (of Judgement) .... after this vain life./ ... to the Forerunner [*karapeti*], God shall remember you./ Remember the sinner, the servant of Jesus Christ, Tirat ...".

[19] Cf. Sawīrus Ibn Al-Mukaffa', *History of the Patriarchs of the Egyptian Church*, vol. II, part III, by A.S. Atiya et al, (Cairo, 1959), p. 346, and by the same author *Histoire des Conciles*, in the French translation by L. Leroy, *Patrologia Orientalis*, t. VI, pp. 517 and 521.

[20] Multilingual and multiethnic monasteries of Jerusalem, cf. Avedis K. Sanjian, "The Armenians and the Holy Places in Jerusalem," *Bazmavep*, p. 139 (1981), No. 1-2, pp. 424-445. Cf. also G. Hintlian, *History of the Armenians in the Holy Land* (Jerusalem, 1989).

[21] One thinks of John, son of Ezekiel, the man "skilled in Coptic, Syriac, Arabic and Egyptian (Ethiopic?)", for whom cf. S.E. Assemani-J.S. Assemani, *Bibliothecae Apostolicae Vaticanae Codicum Manuscriptorum Catalogus*, I/2: complectens codices Chaldaicos sive Syriacos (Romae, 1758), description of ms. Vat. syr. 26.

to believe that a single scribe was expert enough to be able to write in languages that were so profoundly different; the same also regarding writing technique. On the other hand one can easily believe that the Coptic text placed at the centre indicates the obvious priority of the national Church.

The content of these two manuscripts, the *Letters* of St. Paul, the *Catholic Letters* and the *Acts* in the Ambrosian volume, and the *Psalter* in the volume preserved in the Vatican Library and in addition the existence of two surviving leafs of the pentaglot *Gospels*, one the Bodl. Ms. Copt. C 2, and the other Ms. Or. 1240a of the British Museum (now British Library), lead one to reflect. It is no mere chance that one is dealing with the best-known and most widespread texts in Christianity: the *New Testament* and the *Psalter*. In conclusion to that which has been said, we can take on board the opinion only hinted at by Chabot,[22] that, as a consequence of an agreement between the five dissident Eastern churches, a prestigious *edition* of a polyglot Bible *ante litteram* was undertaken with a choice of the texts that had always been the most widely read by Christians.

The reason for the interruption of the Armenian text in both codices remains unresolved. If some other traumatic event was not responsible for the interruption of the planned transcription of the two manuscripts, this could also be a clue to a disagreement between the communities. Rivalry and contrast were sure to exist between the monks in the desert, as a curious particular in the codex itself would seem to indicate: at f. 99v, at the start of the 2 Cor, there is an Armenian heading in the space reserved for it, the Coptic, on the other hand, also occupies the Arabic column, and then the Arabic transcriber, almost as if he wishes an act of revenge, also writes to the right of the Coptic heading, above the Syriac column! The interlacing of the writings in this case could also express the order in which the columns were written, thus bearing witness to the priority of the Coptic text.

If the origin of the *Pentaglot Apostolos* of the Ambrosiana therefore appears to be ascertained, we do not know when or how it reached the library where it is now preserved, from its place of

---

[22] As observed by Chabot, "Note sur la polyglotte de la Bibliothèque Ambrosienne de Milan," p. 452.

production. On the other hand, we have knowledge concerning its parallel, the Vatican *Psalter*, and its adventurous journey that brought it from Egypt, where it was purchased in 1635, to Rome two years later.[23]

With regards to the arrival of our codex at the Biblioteca Ambrosiana, although there are no certain documents, such as regular entrance registers, it is known that, as earlier said, one of the primary concerns of Cardinal Federico Borromeo was to acquire manuscripts in the various oriental languages. For this purpose, he had no hesitation in sending his trusted expert collaborators on a special mission to the Orient where they were able to acquire precious codices. Among these envoys the name of Michele Maronita[24] sticks out in particular. In a period of only two years (1611-1613), he brought to Milan some of the jewels of the Library: the codex containing the second volume of the *Syro-Hexaplaris* version of the Bible (Ms. C 313 inf.),[25] and that containing the Peshitta version of the Old Testament (Ms. B 21 inf.). It has been ascertained that both codices come from Egypt. And the learned Mons. Enrico Galbiati, who was the Prefect of the Biblioteca Ambrosiana until a few years ago, suggests that also the *Pentaglot Apostolos* reached Milan thanks to Michele Maronita.[26]

Although we have no certain knowledge of its arrival, we have evidence of an early presence in the Biblioteca Ambrosiana, documented by two antique manuscript[27] indices of the books in the Library. In the Ms. I 133 sup., at f. 73r under *Pauli Epistolae cum*

---

[23] Cf. the annotation of Tisserant, *Codices armeni*, p. 343: *anno 1635 in monasterio s. Macarii ad desertum Scetense a P. Agathangelo Vindocino emptus* [est]. On the series of misadventures suffered by the codex, see F. Nau, *Patrologia Orientalis*, t. X, fasc. 2 (1913), pp. 53-57.

[24] Galbiati, *L'orientalistica*, pp. 101-108.

[25] I give sincere thanks to Mons. Cesare Pasini, vice-prefect of the Ambrosiana, who allowed me to read, before printing, the important contribution "Per la storia della siro-esaplare Ambrosiana (alla luce delle annotazioni siriache e copta recentemente rinvenute sul codice). Con un saggio di Emidio Vergani e un'appendice di Philippe Luisier," in *Orientalia Christiana Periodica*, 71 (2005), pp. 21-58.

[26] Galbiati, *L'orientalistica*, p. 108.

[27] C. Pasini, "Antichi cataloghi manoscritti dei codici della Biblioteca Ambrosiana," in *Aevum* 69 (1995), pp. 665-695.

commentariis (shelfmark: *Gr. F. B 6*), we read *Eiusdem Epistolae Arm.^e, Arab.^e, Gr. Syr.^e F. B 21*: it is true that the Ethiopic language is not nominated and that "Greek" is said rather than "Coptic", but it is difficult not to identify our *Pentaglot* in this annotation, also because the Library has no other similar polyglot manuscript of Paul's Epistles. This index was prepared, as Mons. Pasini informs us, in the years 1684-1685.[28] But it is possible to identify even the presence of the code in the Library even earlier on the basis of information found in Ms. Z 57 inf., where at f. 19r we read *Epistolae catholicae omnes triplicis characteris* (shelfmark: *MS. fol. P 365*) and at f. 59r: *D Pauli Apostoli Epist. ad Rom. triplicis characteris* (shelfmark: *MS. fol P 365*). Unfortunately, the nineteenth century binding eliminated all trace of previous shelfmarks which would have allowed certain identification. In any case, since this index originates from the first half of the seventeenth century, again in this case, by exclusion, even with the incorrect indication that we are dealing with a *triplicis characteris* codex, we cannot avoid identifying it as the *Pentaglot*, which therefore makes it one of the oldest and most precious relics preserved at the Biblioteca Ambrosiana from its very beginning.

[28] C. Pasini, "Antichi," p. 691.

A Fifteenth Century Bible from Khlat‘: Textual Character and Significance for the Text of Acts

Joseph Alexanian

The text of the Acts of the Apostles has received considerable attention from textual critics of the New Testament. Nevertheless, it has defied all efforts to account satisfactorily for its unusual features and to determine the earliest text of Acts. In an earlier paper, I dealt with the problems posed by the quest for the earliest text of Acts. The Greek and versional sources fall into two groups, referred to by New Testament textual critics as the Alexandrian text-type and the Western text-type. Both of these text-types include witnesses from the second century that are among the earliest sources of the New Testament text. Thus, both text-types have an arguable claim to being closest to the original text of Acts. Both texts cannot, however, be the original text of Acts, because they differ at many points, and the Western text is almost nine percent longer than the Alexandrian text of Acts.[1]

In the earlier paper, I listed the most important witnesses to the two text-types, described the textual character of the two texts, and

---

[1] Joseph M. Alexanian, "Remarks on the Armenian Text of the Acts of the Apostles," in *Text and Context: Studies in the Armenian New Testament*, S. Ajamian and M. E. Stone, eds., University of Pennsylvanian Armenian Texts and Studies, 13 (Atlanta, GA: Scholars Press, 1994), pp. 15-22. Note that the technical term used by New Testament textual critics for the two major textual groups is not "textual type" as printed in that volume, but "text-type" as used here. See, e.g., "Method in Establishing the Nature of Text-Types of New Testament Manuscripts," in Ernest C. Colwell, *Studies in Methodology in Textual Criticism of the New Testament* (New Testament Tools and Studies, IX; Grand Rapids, MI: Wm B. Eerdmans, 1969), pp. 45-55.

briefly discussed the scholarly debate during the past one hundred years attempting to explain the existence of these two texts of Acts. Most textual critics today believe that the Alexandrian text-type is the most accurate text and the closest to the original text of Acts.[2]

In order to advance the quest for the earliest text of Acts, the Institute for New Testament Textual Criticism in Muenster, Germany, is preparing a complete and accurate critical apparatus of the text of Acts listing all variants in the Greek manuscripts, early versions, and church fathers. This critical edition, edited by Dr. Carroll Osburn, Executive Director of the Caris Foundation, will be published as part of the Muenster Institute's *Novum Testamentum Graecum Edition Ciritica Maior*. The present writer is responsible for the Armenian version. Among the early versions, the ancient Armenian text of Acts has been little studied, and none of the more than 180 manuscripts has been fully collated. Supported by the Caris Foundation and the Muenster Institute, the collation of manuscripts, analysis of text, and preparation of a critical text and apparatus of Armenian acts is nearing completion.

In the earlier paper, I reported on a preliminary study of eleven manuscripts of the Armenian text of Acts. That study revealed that the texts of ten manuscripts, dating from the twelfth through the fifteenth centuries, are quite homogeneous and that the Armenian text is most closely aligned with the Alexandrian text-type. Agreement with the Western text is very weak, even though the text in the Armenian version of Ephrem's Commentary on Acts is, according to F. C. Conybeare, almost identical to the text of Codex Bezae.[3] Stanislas Lyonnet came to the same conclusion in his analysis of eleven Armenian manuscripts, published in Lagrange's *Introduction* in 1935. According to Lyonnet, the Armenian text of

---

[2] See "The Acts of the Apostles" in Bruce M. Metzger, *A Textual Commentary on the Greek New Testament* (London, New York: United Bible Societies, 1971), pp. 259-272, and the many sources cited there.

[3] F. C. Conybeare, "The Commentary of Ephrem on Acts," in *The Text of Acts*, ed. J. H. Ropes (vol. 3 of *The Beginnings of Christianity, Part I: the Acts of the Apostles*, ed. F. J. Foakes Jackson and K. Lake; London: Macmillan, 1926), pp. 373-453.

Acts agrees almost exactly with Codex Vaticanus, the primary witness to the Alexandrian text-type.[4]

There are, however, occasional readings that may indicate contact with the Western text. Whether these readings are remnants of the original translation of the New Testament from Syriac into Armenian (Arm 1) or are the result of Western influence, either Greek or Syriac, on the revised translation (Arm 2), we cannot yet say. The fact that Ephrem's Commentary on Acts, preserved only in Armenian translation, is strongly Western adds an intriguing piece to the puzzle.

Since 1992, the number of manuscripts collated has grown from eleven to eighty-seven. These manuscripts date from the twelfth through the seventeenth centuries and include some of the earliest extant manuscripts of Armenian Acts. The texts of the additional manuscripts appear to be essentially the same as the texts of the earlier group, with the usual differences in spelling and grammatical form, the substitution of one demonstrative for another, the minor additions and omissions, and the occasional errors.

One of the original eleven manuscripts, however, Jerusalem Ms. 297, shows more variations from the Zohrabian base text than any of the other manuscripts. In this paper, we will analyze the text of J297 in order to evaluate its relationship to Zohrab, shed further light on the Armenian textual tradition in Acts, and determine with greater precision the value of the Armenian text for the textual criticism of the text of Acts.

Manuscript 297 of the Armenian Patriarchate in Jerusalem is a fifteenth century Bible copied in Khlat‘ on the northwestern coast of Lake Van. The principal colophon indicates that the scribe was a priest Karapet and the sponsor was Hovhannes Vardapet. The Lake Van area was an important center of manuscript production during the fifteenth century, along with Khizan to the south, following the collapse of the Armenian Kingdom of Cilicia in 1375 and during the invasions of eastern Armenia by the Mongol and Turkoman tribes. J297 contains the books of the Old and New Testaments according to the Armenian canon, including 3 Corinthians in the New Testament.

---

[4] S. Lyonnet, "La version arménienne," in *Introduction à l'étude du Nouveau Testament, Deuxième partie, Critique textuelle, II: La critique rationelle,* ed. M.-J. Lagrange (Paris: Librairie Lecoffre, 1935), pp. 454-460.

The manuscript is written on paper, 664 folios, 26x19x10 cm. in size. The binding is tooled leather on boards. It is in good condition, though there is some damage to the margins from moisture and worms. The script is well-formed medium *bolorgir*, written in two columns of forty-two lines each. The manuscript is illuminated with headpieces, marginal ornaments, illuminated initial letters, enlarged *erkat'agir* initial lines, and enlarged initial letters. The colors are muted and earthy, and the style is in the monastic tradition.

Textual critics have learned that the text of a manuscript may differ in textual type from one section of the biblical canon to another. Though our concern in this study is with the text of Acts, I decided to check the text of J297 in the Gospels by means of seven test passages in the four Gospels, a practice begun by Ernest C. Colwell at the University of Chicago for the study of Armenian Gospel manuscripts. These passages involve the inclusion or exclusion of Matthew 16:2-3, of "the Son of God" in Mark 1:1, the choice between "in the prophets" or "in Isaiah the prophet" in Mark 1:2, and the inclusion or exclusion of Mark 16:9-20, Luke 22:43-44, John 5:4, and John 7:53-8:11. Most scholars today consider the "Isaiah" reading in Mark 1:2 and the shorter readings in the other six passages to be closer to the original text. We will refer to this older text as the "critical" text.

I have examined over 110 manuscripts containing the four Gospels, twenty-eight of which date from the ninth through the twelfth centuries. Virtually all of these twenty-eight manuscripts read the critical text in each of the seven passages, or, in the case of lacunose manuscripts, in all the passages that are extant. The picture changes in the thirteenth century. Manuscripts from Greater Armenia continue to read the critical text, while manuscripts from Cilicia, exposed to ecclesiastical influence – if not pressure – from Europe begin to conform to the current text found in both the Latin Vulgate and the Byzantine text-type of the medieval Greek manuscripts. Cilician manuscripts from the thirteenth century have an average of only four of the seven critical readings; by the fourteenth century the average has dropped to three.

As the influence of the Cilician manuscripts begins to spread throughout Armenia and the Diaspora, the number of manuscripts containing the critical text in all seven passages drops precipitously. Of fifty-seven manuscripts dating from the fourteenth through the seventeenth centuries, only five have the full critical text. The four whose provenances are known are from Erzinjan, Shirak, the Lake Sevan area, and possibly Jerusalem, all areas where conservative tendencies might prevail. The remaining fifty-two manuscripts have an average of 3.3 readings, and eleven of them have two, one, or none of the seven readings. Our fifteenth century Bible from Khlat' has only two of the seven readings, omitting Matthew 16:2-3 and Mark 16:9-20. Based on this limited data, J297 would appear to have a text of the Gospels similar to the mass of later manuscripts influenced by the fourteenth century Cilician text.

When we turn to the text of J297 in Acts, however, the picture changes. Our attention had been drawn to this manuscript because it appeared to have the greatest number of significant variations from Zohrab. More detailed study has confirmed this impression. In Acts, chapters 1, 2, 8, and 24, J297 differs from Zohrab 318 times, approximately once in every six words. By way of comparison, the well-known manuscript J1925, the Erznka Gospels, dated AD 1269, differs from Zohrab approximately once in every thirteen words, less than half the rate of J297.

An analysis of J297's differences from Zohrab will help to define the character of J297's text in Acts and will determine whether J297 represents a version of Acts different from the standard Arm 2 text. Has J297 preserved the ancient Arm 1 text? Whereas the standard text, including Zohrab, is a strong witness to the Alexandrian text-type, is it possible that J297 represents a different branch of the Armenian textual tradition with strong links to the Western text-type? These questions have serious implications for our understanding of the history of the Armenian text and the value of Armenian in helping the textual critic to determine the earliest text of Acts.

The 318 variations from Zohrab consist of 62 omissions of one to six words in the Zohrab text, 43 differences in the use of the demonstrative suffixes, 40 differences in the grammatical form of nouns, pronouns, and verbs, 37 variations in the spelling of proper nouns, 34 spelling variations in other words, 28 additions of one to three words to the Zohrab text, 19 substitutions of one to three different words for the words in Zohrab's text, 14 changes of singular to plural and plural to singular, 13 instances of transposition, that is, changes in word order involving two to six words, and 25 errors of various sorts. The term "error" refers to readings that produce nonsense due to either unintelligible spelling, grammar, or relationship to context. In addition, the scribe of J297 erred more than four times in his placement of punctuation marks.

Aside from errors, we have listed nine different types of variation above. Some of these, by their nature, are intra-versional variations, variations among Armenian manuscripts that arose during the course of the centuries of text transmission, with no influence from non-Armenian sources. These intra-versional types of variation include the use of the demonstrative suffixes, grammatical variations, and most spelling variations.

The three types of intra-versional variation, normally, cannot be used to determine the relationship of the Armenian text to the Greek text or to other versions. There can be exceptions, of course, in the case of individual readings. And certainly, since the Armenian biblical text is ultimately a translated text, all of the original readings of Arm 1 and Arm 2 are inter-versional. But the original texts of Arm 1 and Arm 2 are not available to us in the New Testament. Therefore, all the readings of our extant manuscripts must be viewed as part of the process of the transmission of the text through time. As part of the transmission process, some types of variation, by their nature, cannot clearly indicate contact with a non-Armenian source.

These intra-versional variations are essential, however, in evaluating the trustworthiness of a manuscript, in investigating the relationships between manuscripts, and in determining the manuscript groupings that help us understand the history of the text and reconstruct the fifth century Arm 1 and Arm 2 texts. The more than 100 intra-versional variations and the 25 errors suggest that J297 was not copied by a trained scribe in a scriptorium and that it may not be closely related to any of the other manuscripts in our study. But before arriving at such conclusions, we must analyze the intra- and inter-versional variations to determine more precisely J297's relationship to the other Armenian manuscripts and to the Greek and versional witnesses.

Fourteen manuscripts will be used as a control group to evaluate J297's relationship to the Armenian manuscript tradition. These manuscripts and J297 represent a wide diversity of location and time. One dates from the twelfth century, eight from the thirteenth, four from the fourteenth, J297 from the fifteenth, and one from the seventeenth century. The known provenances include many areas of Greater Armenia, Cilicia, Jerusalem, Cyprus, and Rome.[5]

The remaining six types of variation are – or can be – inter-versional, that is, readings that entered the Armenian text through contact with non-Armenian sources. In this paper, the non-Armenian sources will be limited to the witnesses cited in the Nestle-Aland *Novum Testamentum Graece*, 26th edition.[6] Though the citation of Greek witnesses in the Nestle-Aland apparatus is adequate, the citation of versional readings is quite inadequate. Since the Armenian version is closely related to the Syriac and Georgian versions, this study will need to be supplemented with a careful comparison of J297's readings with the texts of those two versions.

The most common type of inter-versional variation in J297 is omission. Sixty-two times J297 omits one to six words found in Zohrab. Twenty of these omissions involve the conjunction եւ. Thirteen are omissions of եւ alone and seven more are phrases containing եւ. The remaining forty-two omissions involve words of every sort. Most of these omissions are intra-versional, the product

---

5 The manuscripts with present location, library number, date, and provenance, if known, are as follows:

Location	Ms. No.	Date	Provenance
Yerevan	6263	12th cent.	unknown
Jerusalem	1925	1269	Erznka
Yerevan	142	1269	Rome
Vienna	245	1279-1280	Zhani anapat
Chicago	229	1284-1312	Cyprus
Jerusalem	540	1291-1298	Glats‘or (?)
Yerevan	196	13th cent.	Grner (?)
Manchester	2	13th cent.	unknown
Vienna	247	13th cent.	Cilicia
Vienna	261	13th cent.	Kamrik anapat
Vienna	71	13th-14th cent.	unknown
Yerevan	149	1331	Jerusalem
Yerevan	62	1371	Awag anapat
British Museum	8833	17th cent.	exemplar Cilician (?)

6 Eberhard Nestle, Erwin Nestle, Kurt Aland, et al, eds.; *Novum Testamentum Graece* 26. (Aufluge; Stuttgart: Deutsche Bibelstiftung, 1981).

of intentional or unintentional scribal activity during the centuries of text transmission.

The fact that the Alexandrian text-type is the shortest text of Acts suggests that we look for Alexandrian support for any of the omissions. Nine of J297's one-word omissions have some external support. None of the longer omissions have support from the witnesses cited in the Nestle-Aland apparatus. Five of the one-word omissions have Alexandrian and, in some cases, Western support. These include the omission of եւ (3) in Acts 1:13, իսկ in 2:33, եւ (1) in 2:33, եւ (2) in 8:26, and Յիսուս in 24:24. Two of the omissions are supported by virtually all Greek witnesses, the omission of Յիսուս in 8:5 and եւ(3) in 24:1. Two of the omissions, քով and Ներքինին, occur in 8:37, a verse which is found only in Western witnesses and the later Byzantine manuscripts.

Some of these omissions with Greek support may represent intentional corrections of the text by J297 or one of its parents, since western Armenia was in constant, if not always cordial, contact with the Byzantine Church through the centuries. The omission of Յիսուս in 8:5, supported by the majority of the manuscripts in our control group and by most Greek witnesses, may well be an original reading of Arm 2 which failed to displace the Arm 1 reading during the period when both versions were in existence, vying for acceptance by the church. The remaining omissions with non-Armenian support are probably examples of coincidental agreement, a judgment based on the type of omissions involved and the random nature of the support. Occasional coincidental agreement is inevitable, especially when one or more of the manuscripts involved has an uncontrolled text.[7]

The spelling of proper nouns is always a source of much variation among manuscripts, especially the transliterated names of people and places that are relatively unknown. Most of J297's thirty-seven variations from Zohrab are intra-versional, but some of them may represent transliteration from Syriac rather than Greek, one of the characteristics of Arm 1. In Acts 1:13, the fourteen manuscripts in our study and Zohrab have Յակովբոս for the three Jameses in the apostolic list. The diphthong -ով- is the usual transliteration of the Greek omega. J297 agrees twice, but the third

[7] Colwell, *Studies in Methodology*, pp. 57, 169.

time reads Յակոբեան in place of Յակովբեան, possibly reflecting a Syriac base. In 1:13 and 1:22, our fourteen manuscripts and Zohrab render John as Յովհաննէս, with the Syriac. In 1:13, J297 agrees, but in 1:22 it has Յովաննու, which is closer to Greek. In 8:9 and 8:13, eight manuscripts and Zohrab render Simon the magician as Սիմովն, reflecting a Greek source. J297 and six manuscripts have Սիմոն, suggesting a Syriac base. In 8:1 and throughout the chapter our fourteen manuscripts and Zohrab render Samaria as Սամարիա or Սամարիայ, with minor variations. J297 alone, in 8:1, has Շամրին, which clearly indicates a Semitic rather than a Greek base. It is interesting that Zohrab's apparatus knows of one manuscript with this reading. These transliterations of proper nouns, some of which indicate a Syriac base and others a Greek base, are typical of all Armenian manuscripts. They probably go back to the origins of Arm 1 and Arm 2, and the period when both texts were in circulation, rather than being adopted later through contact with Syriac or Greek manuscripts.

A third type of inter-versional variation is addition. J297 makes twenty-eight additions to Zohrab involving one to three words. Three of these additions are short phrases of two to three words including եւ; ten are additions of եւ alone. Only five of the twenty-eight additions find support from non-Armenian sources. The addition of եւ at the beginning of 8:6 and 8:14, քեզ following գոյ in 8:21, and the verb է following Քրիստոս in 8:37 have broad support from Greek witnesses. The addition of Քրիստոս after Յիսուս in 8:16 has meager support, which is no doubt coincidental, since the addition of titles to Jesus is a common scribal change.

The additions in 8:6 and 8:14 may be intentional corrections of the text, since Greek manuscripts were available to scribes in western Armenia. The additions in 8:21 and 8:37 are unique in that they are found in the majority of our fifteen manuscripts and also have broad support from Greek witnesses. As was suggested earlier, such readings may be original readings of Arm 2, which failed to displace Arm 1 during the period when both versions were in use.

The nineteen substitutions and thirteen transpositions in J297's text may be dealt with quickly. Though substitution and, to a lesser degree, transposition can be significant indicators of inter-versional contact, this appears not to be the case with J297. None of these readings finds support from any Greek witness or from the versions that are cited by Nestle-Aland. Some of the words substituted are synonyms. Most of the substitutions and transpositions simplify the syntax of the sentence or clarify the meaning. Scribal changes of this sort are common. It is inevitable that, during the centuries of text transmission, the Armenian biblical text – as the Greek text – would evolve toward a smoother, clearer text.

The fourteen differences in number, eight plurals for Zohrab's singulars and six singulars for Zohrab's plurals, are the sixth type of possible inter-versional variation. Five of the plurals occur in J297's text of the quotation from Psalm 69 (68):25 in Acts 1:20. Zohrab's text is as follows: եղիցի բնակութիւն նորա աւերակ· եւ մի ոք իցէ որ բնակիցէ 'ի նմա. J297's text reads: եղիցին բնակութիւնք նոցա աւերակք· եւ մի ոք իցէ որ բնակիցէ 'ի նոսա. There is some support for the pluralization of նորա in several Western witnesses, including the marginal notes of the Harclean Syriac. It is likely in this case, however, that the agreement is coincidental, and that J297, the only manuscript I have found thus far with this reading, has harmonized the quote to the text of Psalm 69 (68), where more than one word is pluralized and, thus, the sentence is closer to J297's text.

None of the other three plurals or six singulars finds support from the witnesses cited in the Nestle-Aland apparatus. However, a check of the Syriac and Georgian texts and Ephrem's Commentary on Acts will very likely produce evidence that some of these readings go back to Arm 1 and its Syriac *vorlage*. Based on the assumption that Arm 1 was translated from Syriac and Georgian from Arm 1, the frequent confusion between singular and plural in Syriac, Armenian, and Georgian has been explained by the fact that the *seyamé*, the sign of the plural, was often omitted in Syriac manuscripts.[8]

In their studies of the earliest sources of the Armenian biblical text, Lyonnet and Vööbus have listed fourteen characteristics of Arm 1 found in our extant manuscripts and Zohrab. Three of these occur

---

[8] Louis Leloir, "La version arménienne du Nouveau Testament," in *Die alten Übersetzungen des Neuen Testaments, die Kirchenväterzitate und Lektionare*, ed. K. Aland (Arbeiten zur Neutestamentlichen Textforschung, Band 5; Berlin: Walter de Gruyter, 1972), pp. 303-304; Joseph Molitor, "Das neue Testament in georgische Sprache," in *Die alten Übersetzungen*, pp. 319-320.

in J297's text. Proper nouns transliterated from Syriac and the confusion of singular and plural have already been discussed. A third characteristic is the addition of personal pronouns after verbs. An example of this is found in 24:21, where J297 alone adds the pronoun եւ following the verb կային.

We have examined the six types of inter-versional variation and have found that some of these readings may have arisen from contact with Alexandrian or Western manuscripts, but that most of them are better understood as the result of scribal editing or error by Armenian copyists. A few of them may preserve readings of Arm 1 and Arm 2 from the fifth century. In any case, it should be noted that these six types of variation are as important as the intra-versional variations in evaluating the quality of J297's text and in determining its relationship to other manuscripts and its place in the history of the Armenian text.

Before formulating our conclusions, we must analyze J297's readings from a different perspective, namely, the extent of J297's agreement with other manuscripts in differing from Zohrab. In Acts, chapter 8, J297 has 105 differences from Zohrab. Fifty-four of these are singular readings, that is, readings found in J297 alone. Every type of variation is represented, the most common being omission (17), addition (14), grammatical change (7), and substitution (6). Thirty-seven of the 105 variations have the support of two to six of the manuscripts in our control group. These constitute the minority readings in chapter 8. Fourteen of the variations are supported by seven to fourteen manuscripts. These, plus seven readings where eight of the fourteen manuscripts read against J297 and Zohrab, are the majority readings. Every type of variation is found among the minority and majority readings. Where J297 departs from the majority text, seven times it agrees with Zohrab and twice it has singular readings.

We have examined many of these 105 variations earlier in this paper. It is probable that most of the singular and minority readings are scribal changes, intentional or unintentional, which arose in the course of the transmission of the Arm 2 text. These include the intra-versional readings and the inter-versional readings with little or no non-Armenian support. Since our fifteen manuscripts cover such a broad geographical area, we can say that most of the majority readings preserve an ancient form of the text common in Greater

Armenia prior to the editorial and theological changes of the Cilician period. Some of these readings preserve Arm 1 readings and original Arm 2 readings that were replaced by Arm 1 readings in other branches of the textual tradition.

With the data from chapter 8, we can compute the percentages of agreement of our fourteen manuscripts and J297 in its variations from Zohrab. Excluding the fifty-four singular readings, J297 differs from Zohrab fifty-one times in chapter 8. In these fifty-one places of variation, the closest manuscript to J297 is E142, written in Rome in 1269, with 60.8% agreement. J540, written perhaps in Glatsor in 1291-1298, shows only 50.9% agreement. The remaining twelve manuscripts fall from 47.1% to 9.8%. Percentages below 70% are not considered by New Testament textual critics to be indicative of significant relationships between manuscripts. Thus, our earlier suspicion is confirmed, that J297 is not closely related to any of the other manuscripts in our study or to the Cilician-type manuscripts represented by Zohrab.

Our analysis of J297's text in Acts and its relationship to Zohrab and to a diverse group of fourteen manuscripts leads us to the following conclusions. First, J297 derives from the same fifth century version, the Arm 2 revision of Arm 1, as all other manuscripts of Acts examined thus far. As such, its primary witness is to the Alexandrian text-type. A few of its readings, shared with other manuscripts and Zohrab, indicate contact with the Western text-type, whether through Syriac influence over Arm 1 and early Arm 2 or through contact with Western manuscripts in later centuries.

Second, many of the 318 variations from Zohrab, including twenty-five errors, are due not to a different text of Acts but to the absence of quality control. The copying of J297 or its ancestors was a private enterprise rather than one under the supervision of a monastery or scriptorium. J297 seems to have the same characteristics as the Group W manuscripts of the Gospels, whose texts suffered from scribal carelessness, provincialism, and absence of control.[9]

---

[9] Joseph M. Alexanian, "The Armenian Gospel Text from the Fifth Through the Fourteenth Centuries," in *Medieval Armenian Culture*, Thomas J. Samuelian and Michael E. Stone, eds., University of Pennsylvania

Third, J297 shares with other manuscripts singular and minority readings that arose in several ways. Some readings reflect the Arm 1 and early Arm 2 texts; some entered the textual tradition through contact with later manuscripts; and, of course, many are due to scribal editing and sensible scribal error. Most of the majority readings preserve the standard text of Greater Armenia prior to the Cilician period.

Fourth, though J297 is descended from Arm 2, as are all known manuscripts, it is not closely related to any of the other manuscripts in our study or to Zohrab. It did not entirely escape Cilician influence, however, as evidenced by its having only two of the seven readings of the critical text in the Gospels.

Fifth, apart from its errors, the text of J297 is an excellent example of what happens to the biblical text over the centuries as it becomes more widely available in both production and distribution. As with the Greek Byzantine text of the late Middle Ages – and the modern English versions of today – J297 presents a text that has been expanded, smoothed, and simplified even more than the text of fourteenth century Cilicia.

Finally, the Armenian text of Greater Armenia, not Cilicia, remains a significant witness to the Alexandrian text of Acts and will be useful to textual critics as they seek to establish the earliest Greek text of the Acts of the Apostles.

Armenian Texts and Studies, 6 (Chico, CA: Scholars Press, 1984), pp. 384-386.

20

Syntactic Criteria for Classical Armenian Text Chronology: The Use of the Second Person Possessive Pronouns

Jos J. S. Weitenberg

This paper, to honor the multifaceted and lasting contributions of Dickran Kouymjian to Armenian Studies, concerns Classical Armenian text chronology: is it possible to follow the development of individual linguistic features from Classical Armenian (fifth century) up to the Middle Armenian period (thirteenth century) through individual texts? Conversely, would it be possible to roughly date a Classical Armenian text with respect to such a feature? This question will be approached here by charting the use of the attributive forms of the second person possessive pronoun (the paradigm of Arm. *k'o* [your]) in this period.

The underlying assumption in this type of research is the following: when writing Classical Armenian, all authors try to conform to the same language standards as these are conceived by them. But over the centuries the spoken language deviates more and more from the literary norm. Inevitably elements of the currently spoken language find their way into each author's text. Thus, there is a marked difference in the language of Eznik and Yovhannēs Kat'oghikos (Draskhanakertts'i, ninth-tenth centuries), though both aspire to conform to the norm of literary Classical Armenian. This has been demonstrated in great detail by Aṙak'elyan.[1] The authors themselves are not explicitly aware of this, except in the most evident cases. The area that is most susceptible to such unconscious intrusions of the spoken language into literary expression concerns

---

[1] Varag Aṙakelyan, *Grigor Narekats'u lezun ew ochě* (Yerevan: Academy of Sciences, 1975), pp. 5-39.

the field of the syntax of pragmatic elements (use of the article, use of *z*-, word-order) and the gradual loss, the natural decay as it were, of specific forms.

As an example of this approach one may mention the study of Düm-Tragut[2] on the development of word-order of the attributive possessives (our father, etc.) in Armenian. One notes that Classical Armenian prefers the word-order possessed-possessor *hayr mer* [father our] (postposed order), whereas Modern Armenian, like Modern English, prefers the inverse order *mer hayr* [our father] (preposed order). There is complete reversal of a syntactic feature over a period of more than a thousand years. Düm-Tragut followed this development in a corpus of Classical and Middle Armenian texts. Expressed in tabular form her results are:[3]

	postposed (Noun-Poss) (*hayr mer*)	preposed (Poss-Noun) (*mer hayr*)
5thc. Classical Armenian	72.13%	27.87%
13thc. Middle Armenian	32.89%	67.11%
20thc. Modern Armenian		(100%)

That is, in Classical Armenian an expression like *hayr mer, ordi im* occurs in 72.13% of all cases. About 600 year later, in Middle Armenian, we find that only 32.89% uses this order of constituents. In Modern Armenian this order is not usual any more. The linguistic change shows a gradual chronological development.[4]

This method yields good results within the larger chronological context. Is it also possible to trace such syntactic developments on a smaller scale, within the period of the fifth to around the eleventh centuries? By way of experiment I present a short study on the use of the second person possessive pronoun *k'o* [your] in Classical authors

[2] Jasmine Düm-Tragut, *Word Order Correlations and Word Order Change: An "Applied-Typological" Study on Literary Armenian Variation* (München: LINCOM Europe, 2002).

[3] Ibid., pp. 248-252.

[4] Düm-Tragut based the assessment of the Classical Armenian situation on the authors Eznik, Koriwn, Ps.-Faustus and Eghishē. Her Middle Armenian corpus *a.o.* comprises Mkhit'ar Heṙats'i and Smbat Sparapet. See Düm-Tragut, pp. 12-16.

from the fifth to the tenth century. The authors selected for this study are the following: Agat'angeghos (fifth century), Eghishē (sixth century), Ghewond (eighth century), Pseudo-Smbat Bagratuni (tenth century), Ps. Yovhannēs Mamikonian (eleventh century), Movsēs Khorenats'i. As a middle Armenian control text the corpus of the poet Frik (thirteenth century) has been used. The following question will be treated: on the basis of this material, is it possible to observe a change over time in the use of the various forms of the paradigm? The answer that seems to emerge is: there indeed is a measurable increase in the use of the form *k'o* from the seventh century onwards at the expense of other inflected forms.

With respect to the inventory of forms, one observes that, as opposed to a very rich Classical inventory, the Middle Armenian period basically only preserved the forms *k'o* and *k'u*.[5] Therefore one expects to find a gradual increase in the use of the forms *k'o* and *k'oy* in the Classical texts at hand. The data are as follows:

The total of all attributive forms of the pronoun *k'o* is:

Agat'angeghos	348
Eghishē	95
Movsēs Khorenats'i	82
Ghewond	126
Ps.-Yovh. Mamikonian	76
Ps.-Shapuh Bagratuni	132
Frik	51

The distribution of the individual forms is given in the following table. This table reads as follows: a given attributive possessive form (*k'o* etc. Col. I) occurs with a given author (e.g. Agat'angeghos) X (148) times in postposed order (Col. II), and Y (10) times in preposed order (Col. III). The form therefore occurs Col. II + Col. III (148 + 10) times (Col. IV) with this author. This is Z% (45.40% Col. V) of the total of all attributive second person possessive forms in this author as given in Col. VI (358); thus, 45.50% of all attributive possessive forms of the second person in Agat'angeghos has the form *k'o*.

[5] Joseph Karst, *Historische Grammatik des Mittel-Armenischen* (Strassburg: Trübner, 1901), 229f.

I Forms		II Noun-Poss	III Poss-Noun	IV Total II+III	V	VI (All 2nd person possessives)
K'o	Aga	148	10	158	=45.40%	(348)
	Egh	38	10	48	=50.52%	(95)
	MKho	33	7	40	=48.78%	(82)
	Lew	74	6	80	=63.49%	(126)
	Mam	47	7	54	=71.05%	(76)
	Bag	94	8	102	=77.27%	(132)
	Fri	9	35	44	=86.27%	(51)
Zk'o	Aga		2	2	=0.57%	(348)
	Egh		1	1	=0.95%	(95)
	MKho		6	6	=7.31%	(82)
	Lew		3	3	=2.38%	(126)
	Mam		5	5	=6.57%	(76)
	Bag					(132)
	Fri		5	5	=9.80%	(51)
K'oy	Aga	65		65	=18.67%	(348)
	Egh	2		2	=2.10%	(95)
	MKho	8	3	11	=13.41%	(82)
	Lew	9	1	10	=7.93%	(126)
	Mam					(76)
	Bag	6		6	=4.54%	(132)
(*K'ow*)	Fri	1		1	=1.96%	(51)
Zk'oy	Aga					(348)
	Egh					(95)
	MKho					(82)
	Lew		2	2	=1.58%	(126)
	Mam					(76)
	Bag					(132)
	Fri					(51)
K'oyoy	Aga		7	7	=2.01%	(348)
	Egh		6	6	=6.31%	(95)
	MKho		5	5	=6.09%	(82)
	Lew		1	1	=0.79%	(126)
	Mam					(76)
	Bag					(132)
	Fri					(51)
K'owm	Aga	24	2	26	=7.47%	(348)
	Egh	4	2	6	=6.31%	(95)
	MXo	2	2	4	=4.87%	(82)

	Lew	4		4	=3.17%	(126)
	Mam	3	2	5	=6.57%	(76)
	Bag	1		1	=0.75%	(132)
	Fri					(51)
K'owmē	Aga	10		10	=2.57%	(348)
	Egh					(95)
	MKho	1	5	6	=7.31%	(82)
	Lew	2	1	3	=2.38%	(126)
	Mam					(76)
	Bag	4		4	=3.03%	(132)
	Fri					(51)
K'ov	Aga	10		10	=2.57%	(348)
	Egh	4		4	=4.21%	(95)
	MKho					(82)
	Lew					(126)
	Mam	6		6	=7.89%	(76)
	Bag					(132)
	Fri					(51)
K'oyov	Aga		6	6	=1.72%	(348)
	Egh		3	3	=3.15%	(95)
	MKho		1	1	=1.21%	(82)
	Lew					(126)
	Mam					(76)
	Bag					(132)
	Fri					(51)
K'ots'	Aga	53	4	57	=16.27%	(348)
	Egh	22	1	22	=23.15%	(95)
	MKho	5	3	8	=9.75%	(82)
	Lew	21	2	23	=18.25%	(126)
	Mam	5		5	=6.57%	(76)
	Bag	18	1	19	=14.39%	(132)
	Fri	1		1	=1.96%	(51)
K'oyots'	Aga		3	3	=0.86%	(348)
	Egh					(95)
	MKho		1	1	=1.21%	(82)
	Lew					(126)
	Bag					(76)
	Mam		1	1	=1.31%	(132)
	Fri					(51)
K'ovk'	Aga	2		2	=0.57%	(348)
	Egh	2		2	=2.10%	(95)
	MKho					(82)

	Lew Bag Mam Fri					(126) (76) (132) (51)
K'oyovk'	Aga Egh MKho Lew Bag Mam Fri		2	2	=0.57%	(348) (95) (82) (126) (76) (132) (51)

A number of observations can be made on the basis of this table; these of course have a limited value at this point of our research:

Not all forms show free word-order. As stated by Minassian,[6] preposed order is generally found in the long forms *k'oyoy, k'oyov, k'oyots', k'oyovk'*. To a certain extent these are in complementary distribution with the short forms *k'oy, k'ov, k'ots', k'ovk'*. The consistently preposed order of *zk'o* is surprising. The long forms tend to disappear after the eighth century, but their overall very low frequency makes it difficult to establish any chronological criterion upon this.

With respect to word-order, the occurrences of the attributive forms of the second person possessive, considered together as a group, confirm the results of Düm-Tragut: there is a clear break between the Classical (regularly postposed possessive) and the Middle Armenian period (regularly preposed possessive). This is shown in the next table.

Frequency of all forms of 2nd. person Poss. with various authors:

[6] Martiros Minassian, *Grammaire descriptive de l'Arménien Classique* (Genève, 1996), p. 391, §932.

		Total	Postposed (Noun Poss.)	% of Total	preposed (Poss.-Noun)
5c	Aga	348	312	=89.65%	36
6c	Egh	95	72	=75.78%	23
	MKho	82	49	=59.75%	33
8c	Lew	126	110	=87.30%	16
10c	Mam	76	61	=80.26%	15
10c	Bag	132	123	=93.18%	9
13c	Fri	51	11	=21.56%	40

But though one sees the clear break between the Middle Armenian poet Frik and the previous Classical authors, within the Classical authors no further stratification emerges: postposed attributive second person possessives are the most frequently occurring order in all texts before Frik. Therefore, one must conclude that this material, studied in this particular way does not allow an additional chronological precision of the word-order change in the period from the fifth century to the Middle Armenian period.

On the other hand, with respect of the use of the single form *k'o* one notices an increasing frequency of usage. That is, the table shows that the form *k'o* tends to expand over time at the expense of other forms. This is what one expects on the basis of the actual linguistic development: in Middle Armenian the forms *k'o* and *k'u* are predominant. The breaking-point (the moment where one prefers to use *k'o* over the other forms of the paradigm) seems to lie in the eighth century (Ghewond): over 60% of the second person possessives consists of the form *k'o*. This result becomes clearer still when we add the percentages of the occurrences of *k'o* and *zk'o* (that are the same morphological forms) together.

	Noun-Poss I	Poss-Noun II	Total I+II	Percentage	(Number of all 2nd pers. poss. Forms)
Aga	148	12	160	=45.97%	(348)
Egh	38	11	49	=51.57%	(95)
MXo	33	13	46	=56.09%	(82)
Lew	74	9	83	=65.87%	(126)
Mam	47	12	59	=77.63%	(76)
Bag	94	8	102	=72.27%	(132)
Fri	9	40	49	=96.07%	(51)

The results may be of some relevance for the dating of the text of Movsēs Khorenats'i: the frequency of use of *k'o* in this text is not quite reconcilable with the fifth century (Agat'angeghos) text. Beyond this indication, no conclusion on the date of Khorenatsi can be drawn from this material, however.

The result may be distorted because the form *k'oy* has not been taken into account in the table above. There are two considerations here: on the one hand, the form *k'oy* is not simply an orthographic variant of *k'o*. They are of different etymological origin (*k^{w}*osyo* --> *k'oy* but *k^{w}*os* --> *k'o*) and they result in two different Middle Armenian forms: *k'o* and *k'u*. So, in principle it is necessary to keep the occurrences of Class. *k'o* and *k'u* strictly separated (as has been done here). On the other hand, it is uncertain to what extent the forms *k'o* and *k'oy* have been confused in manuscript and text-editions because of the instability of final *-y*. One has the impression, that the 1909 Tiflis Agat'angeghos edition prefers to write *k'oy* as a genitive singular form, whereas the nominative (-accusative) form is given as *(z)k'o*. To be sure on this one must go back to the manuscript basis of the text.

The results given above for the gradual expansion of the attributive possessive form *k'o* also need reinforcement through a study of grammatical agreement. There is loss of forms in the possessive but there is no parallel loss of grammatical categories in the noun. Therefore, spread of *k'o* should go hand in hand with loss of grammatical agreement, also from a chronological point of view.

Nevertheless, the data given above show a very smooth development. They may support the view that the breaking point between Classical and Middle Armenian lays somewhere around the eighth century. This would agree with the periodization of Chahukyan,[7] who places the start of his Pre-Middle Armenian period around the same time.

---

[7] G. B. Chahukyan, *Hayots' lezui zargats'umě ew kaṙuts'vatsk'ě* (Yerevan: Mitk', 1969).

21

Zok: The Armenian Dialect of Agulis

Bert Vaux[1]

As someone who was drawn to academia primarily by the prospect of discovering and reconstructing our linguistic past, I am honored to contribute this essay in recognition of Dickran Kouymjian, who among his many accomplishments counts the (re)discovery of the long-lost sixth-seventh century Greco-Armenian papyrus.[2] What I would like to discuss here is my attempts to recapture yet another unique component of the lost Armenian past, namely Zok, the armenoid language formerly spoken by the indigenous Armenian inhabitants of the city of Agulis and neighboring villages.

The data presented here rely heavily on the kind assistance of Yervand Melik-Moussian, who passed away on Thanksgiving Day, November 23, 1995, two months shy of his 97th birthday. Mr. Melik-Moussian was born in January of 1899, in the city of Agulis, located in southeastern Nakhichevan. Following the massacre of the Armenian population of Agulis by the Turkish army in 1919, Mr. Melik-Moussian made his way to Tiflis and thence to Teheran. He subsequently emigrated to New Jersey following the Revolution; I had the pleasure of meeting with Mr. Melik-Moussian and his family in Freehold on February 25 and May 20, 1995. In addition to being an accomplished painter, photographer, and author, Mr. Melik-

---

[1] Thanks to Hrach Mardirosyan for many helpful comments on an earlier draft of this work.

[2] Dickran Kouymjian, "A Unique Armenian Papyrus," *Acts of the Vth International Conference on Armenian Linguistics*, D. Sakayan, ed. (Delmar, N. Y.: Caravan Books, 1996), pp. 381-386 and James Clackson, "A Greek Papyrus in Armenian Script," *Zeitschrift für Papyrologie und Epigraphik* 129, pp. 223-258.

Moussian was a gifted native speaker of Zok. Before his death he composed a manuscript dealing with the history, culture, and language of Agulis,[3] which is still awaiting publication. In this chapter, I present some of the linguistic materials that I collected from Mr. Melik-Moussian, together with supporting materials from other sources on the dialect.

1. The Zok Language

Though closely related to it linguistically, Zok is completely unintelligible to speakers of Standard Eastern Armenian, and is therefore properly considered a separate language. Speakers of the language refer to it as zokerēn "Zok language." Because Zok is so different from other varieties of Armenian, many myths about its nature and origins have arisen in the Armenian community. The most commonly held opinion is that the Zoks are half-Armenian, half-Jewish merchants who intentionally formed a secret language so that outsiders would be unable to understand their business dealings. According to another opinion, expressed to me by a prominent Armenologist who will remain unnamed, the Zoks are the descendants of Irish settlers from India!

The reality is that the Zoks are simply one of the indigenous Armenian communities of Nakhichevan, and have probably lived there since the Classical Armenian period. Their language is closely related to the nearby dialects of Karabagh and Julfa, and its unintelligibility to other Armenians is due primarily to a major realignment that occurred in its vowel system at an unknown point in the past.

In his 1935 grammar of Zok,[4] Hrach'ya Achaṙian states that the language was at that time spoken by approximately 10,000 Armenians in Upper and Lower Agulis (Azeri Yuxarı Äylis and Aşağı Äylis respectively, the latter also sometimes called Dasht) and the neighboring towns of Allahi (Älähi), Ts'ghna (Çänänäb), Disar, Handamēch' (Andamiç), K'aghak'ik (Käläki[k]), Nasrvaz (Nasırvaz), P'aṙaka (Parağa), Ṙamis, Tanakert (Danaqırt), and

---

[3] Yervand Melik-Moussian, Agulis/Igülis, Manuscript (Tehran and Freehold, New Jersey, 1981).

[4] Hrach'ya Achaṙian, *K'nnut'iwn Agulisi Barbaṙi* [Study of the Agulis Dialect] (Yerevan: State University Press, 1935.)

Khurs. I have depicted the location of these villages in the map (Fig. 1), using the modern Azeri names and geographical coordinates provided at http://www.fallingrain.com/world. (The three largest cities in Nakhichevan, namely Nakhich'evan (Naxçıvan), Julfa, and Ordubad, have been added for reference.) Řamis does not appear on this website; I have done my best to interpolate its location from Yervand Lalayian's map.[5]

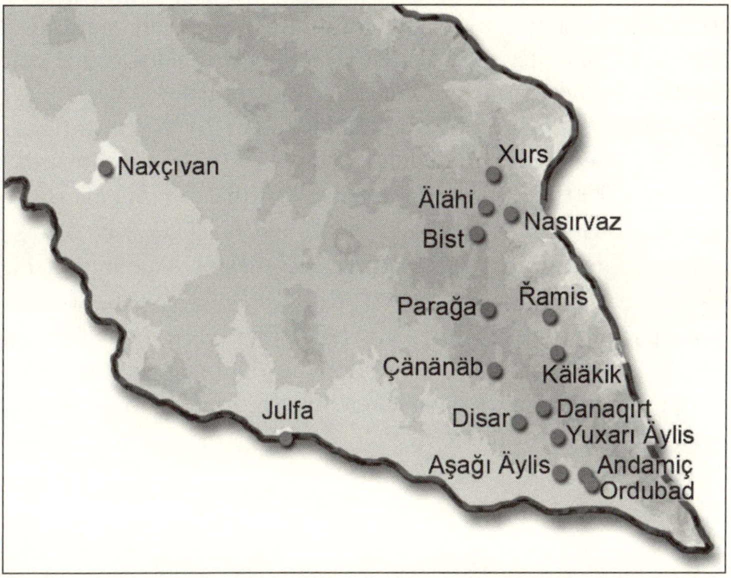

Fig. 1-Villages in Nakhichevan that spoke Zok, according to Achaŕian.[6]

A number of Zoks were forced to leave Nakhichevan by Shah Abbas at the beginning of the seventeenth century; many of these migrated to Nazilli in western Turkey.[7] At the present day, it is not clear how many native speakers of Zok remain; when I last visited

---

[5] Yervand Lalayian, ed., *Varanda*, *Azgagrakan Handēs* (1897) 2, pp. 5-244; 3, pp. 338-349.

[6] Ibid.

[7] Nerses Mkrtch'yan, *Burduri barbaŕĕ* [The Dialect of Burdur] (Yerevan: SSH GA Hratarakch'ut'iwn, 1971).

Yerevan in 2001, my friends in the Nakhichevan Compatriotic Union knew of only two, both living in Yerevan. Nona Shahnazaryan and I spent an evening recording our conversation with one of these, Nazik Avakyan, who was born in Ts‘ghna (Çänänäb) in 1922 and actually lived there for some time before moving to Yerevan. In the summer of 2007, I learned of a speaker of the Tanakert subdialect, Mrs. Jenyan, living in the Meghri region close to Agulis.

The Armenian community in Agulis played an important role in international trade in the seventeenth to the nineteenth centuries, and elements of Zok enter into Armenian trade documents of the period, particularly in the writings of Zak‘aria Agulets‘i.[8]

The first written record of Zok was made by Joachim Schröder in his 1711 *Thesaurus*, where he transcribes a few isolated words and a brief text.[9] He first observes, on page 303, that *Goghthanenses vero inter duas consonantes in o mutent, ut:* հոց *pro* հաց *panis,* խոչ *pro* խաչ *crux* “the residents of Goght‘n [the ancient Armenian name of the province containing Agulis] truly change [a] between two consonants into o, as in hots‘ for hats‘ [bread], khoch‘ for khach‘ [cross].” He then provides the following dialogue on page 356, of which at least the first line of Gh’s speech appears to be in Zok or something closely related to it:

(2) Schröder’s Zok dialogue

a. text

Գ. Ճաղավաթ կոնես, մա Պարոն Տիրատուր ինչ որ կոսես սիրով լինի։
Տ Այ ջոն փեսա քո տաղդ ասա՛, Կոնես կոսսես մըռա նիլմա՛։
Ղ Խայի լիզուն մոյն լիզու ա։
Ծոկռ մոռ խուսուղ Զուղեցին ա։

---

[8] V. Kazhyan, *Bayĕ ew nra khonarhman hamakargĕ Zak‘aria Agulets‘u Ōragrut‘iwnum* [The verb and its conjugational system in Zakaria Agulets‘i’s Journal] *Patmabanasirakan Handēs*, No. 2, (1977) pp. 137-150 and Grigor Khalat‘ian, “*Shṙöderi t‘ght‘erits‘. Nmoysh Agulets‘ots‘ barbaṙov*” [From the pages of Schröder: a text in Agulis dialect] *Yushardzan* (Vienna: Mekhitarist Press, 1911), pp. 181-185.

[9] Johann Joachim Schröder, *Thesaurus Linguae Armenicae, antiquae et hodiemae, cum varia praxios material, cujus elenchum sequens pagella exhibet* (Amsterdam: [s.n], 1711). Schröder also collected another Zok text that did not appear in his book but was published by Khalatian in 1911.

Որ նասիլըն գուլն գոլման ա
Լիզվի քա′նդուղ Ղափանցի ա·
Միր Վիլեաթի լիզուն պորզ ա·
Աման լիզու պորզ խուսիլա·

b. transcription

G Shaghavat‘ kones, ma Paron Tiratur inch‘ or koses sirov lini.
T Ay jon p‘esa k‘o taghd asá, Kones koses měřa nilmá.[10]
Gh Khayi lizún moyn lizu a.
Tsovṙ moṙ khusugh Jughets‘in a.
Or nasilěn guln golman a
Lizvi k‘ándugh Ghap‘ants‘i a.
Mir vileat‘i lizun porz a.
Aman lizu porz khusila.

c. Schröder's Latin translation

G Gratum erit, sed Domine Tiratur, quidquid dixeris, amice dictum sit.
T Ast, dilecte Gener, ipse tuum carmen cantes; kuenies, kuesies ne obliviscaris.
L Armena Lingua est unica Lingua,
Sed mendose loquitur Sjulfajensis,
Dicens: Guln gulmana [sic] (lupus venit.)
Linguae Corruptor Siunensis.
Nostrae provinciae lingua clara est.
Omnem linguam clare loquitur.

d. My English translation of the Armenian[11]

G Excuse me, but Mr. Tiratur, may whatever you say be amicable.

---

[10] The original text places the boundary incorrectly; it should read měřanil má 'don't' forget.'

[11] Thanks to Dan Lassiter, who renders the Latin version as "It will be pleasing, but Sir Tiratur, whatever you say, please say it in a friendly way. / But, my dear Gener, sing your song yourself; do not forget 'kuenies, kuesies' / The Armenian language is a single language, / But the man from Julfa speaks it incorrectly, / Saying: 'Guln gulmana' (The wolf comes.) / The man from Siuna is a corruptor of the language. / The tongue/language of our province is clear/pure. / It speaks every tongue/language clearly.

T Oh, dear bridegroom, say your verse: don't forget kones and koses.

L The Armenian language is one language
The Julfatsi is a deceptive speaker
Who says 'the wolf comes'
The Ghapantsi[12] destroys the language
Our vilayet's language is simple
Every language is spoken simply.

The first extensive treatment of the Zok language is by Kerovpe Patkanov,[13] who presents a number of texts as well as a brief description of the morphology and historical phonology of the dialect. I reproduce and translate four of his texts at the end of this chapter.

Ṙstam Sargsiants' presents the first book-length treatment of Zok,[14] including an impressive number of texts in addition to a treatment of the grammar. Ms. Lena Petrosyan, herself a descendant of Zok stock, kindly provided me with a recording of some of these texts by a native speaker of Zok. The recording differs significantly from Sargsiants''s original in pronunciation, most likely because the woman Ms. Petrosyan recorded speaks a subdialect other than that of Ts'ghna, the one that Sargsiants' described.

Zok subsequently enjoyed a brief literary history thanks to the efforts of Ṙstam Zargariants', who wrote twelve plays, poems, and stories in the Zok language, including the play *Adat'ch'i* (1912) and the journal *Zoki Chroygĕ* (1919, 1932).[15] Achaṙian 1935 is the most linguistically sophisticated analysis of the dialect to date, and

---

[12] The Latin has 'the Syunetsi,' referring to the name of the region in which the city of Ghapan is located.

[13] Kerovpe Patkanov, *Izsledovanie o dialektax' armjanskago jazyka* [Study of the dialects of the Armenian language] (Sanktpeterburg': Tipografija Imperatorskoj Akademij Nauk', 1869), pp. 27-55.

[14] Sargis Sargsiants', *Agulets'ots' barbarĕ (Zōkeri lezun)* [The dialect of the Agulets'is (The language of the Zoks)] (Moscow, 1883).

[15] Ṙstam Zargariants', *Adat' ch'i. Komedia erku gortsoghut'iamb* [Isn't It Normal. A comedy in two acts] (Tiflis: Elektratp, Or. N. Aghaniani, 1912). I am profoundly indebted to Kevork Bardakjian for obtaining copies of *Adat' ch'i* for me in Yerevan, and to Lena Petrosyan for sending me legible copies of the two issues of *Zoki Chroygĕ*.

presents a number of new texts from various Zok subdialects. Achaṙian adds a long discussion of many Zok words.[16] Most recently, Russell offers translation of and commentary on a Zok benediction that we collected in a 1995 session with Mr. Melik-Moussian.[17]

2. Linguistic features

Linguistically, Zok is interesting among other reasons for possessing a system of vowel harmony, showing penultimate stress,[18] participating in Achaṙian's Law (cf. fnn. 21 and 31), undergoing an intricate set of vowel shifts, and employing the particles *nel* and *mätil* to form the past tense and obligatory mood respectively. The past particle *nel*, which appears to derive from the verb *linel* 'be', can be seen for example in the phrase օր տուեծ ա նել իրան [*or tvets ä nel irän*] 'which had been given to him' in the excerpt from T'umanyan's *The Little Fisherman* presented in section 3 of this chapter. *Mätil* most likely derives from Old Armenian *piti* 'it is necessary', plus an unknown suffix. A variant *matam/mätäm* appears in text (6) below.

Zok vowel harmony requires that word roots share a single value for [back], for which the vowels are specified as in (3):

(3)	[+back]	a	o	u		
	[-back]	ä	ö	ü	{e	i}

The back vowels {*a o u*} occur in [+back] domains, but become {*ä ö ü*} respectively after a [-back] segment (i.e., a front vowel or palatal velar consonant). The brackets surrounding *i* and *e* indicate that both are neutral; in other words, they do not show harmonic alternations, and can occur after [+back] or [-back] vowels (4a), but spread [-back] to following vowels (4b).

---

[16] Hrach'ya Achaṙian, *Hayots' lezvi patmut'iwnĕ* [History of the Armenian Language] Vol. 2, (Yerevan: State University Press, 1951), p. 364ff.

[17] James Russell, "Scythians and Avesta in an Armenian Vernacular Paternoster, and a Zok Paternoster," Le Muséon 110 (1997), pp. 1-2.

[18] Compare Zok *g^y^ákhti* 'belt', with penultimate stress, vs. SEA *gotí*, with final stress.

(4)	underlying form	surface form	gloss
a.	g^yákhti	g^yákhti	belt
	kah-e-l	káhil[19]	trample
	aghandz-nér	aghandznér	roast-plural
b.	Avetís-a	Avetísä	Avetis-genitive
	aghandz-nér-av	aghandznéräv	roast plural-instrumental

The diphthongs *ey*, *oy*, *ay* and *uy* select [-back] suffixes. The epenthetic vowel ĕ arises after the application of harmony, and therefore does not play a role in harmony processes. However, in the variety of Zok spoken by Mr. Melik-Moussian, *ĕ* undergoes a separate harmonic process, becoming *u* when it follows a round vowel, as in *dürk'-u* 'door-definite', *ánun-u* 'name-definite'. (See text [11] for examples. This type of harmony is found in several other dialects as well, including Marash and Karchevan.)

The innovations just described conspire to make Zok one of the most divergent varieties of Armenian. Nevertheless, in certain other respects it is one of the most archaic dialects. Some notable archaisms include the preservation of the proto-Armenian consonant series (group 6); the survival of the reflex of proto-Armenian *l* in *kakhts'* 'milk' < IE **glkt-* (cf. Greek *galaktos*; all other forms of Armenian show variants of *kat'*, with no trace of the original **l*); the maintenance of original plain voiced stops after *r* (most forms of Armenian develop voiceless aspirates in this position); and the preservation of the original diphthong *ay*, which in most other dialects becomes *e* or *a*. Achaṙian argues that the so-called penultimate stress systems found in Agulis, Karabagh, and neighboring dialects cannot be a preservation of the penultimate stress system postulated for proto-Armenian, but rather must be innovations.[20]

The Agulis dialect is closely related to the Karabagh and New Julfa dialects; for further details of this relationship, see the

[19] *E* regularly raises to *i* in final syllables of polysyllabic words.

[20] Hrach'ya Achaṙian, *Hayots' lezvi patmut'iwnĕ*, pp. 371-372. See Jos Weitenberg, "Thoughts on Early Armenian Accentuation," *Annual of Armenian Linguistics* 21 (2001), pp. 673, for further discussion.

introductory section of Achařian's grammar of the new Julfa Dialect.[21]

3. Texts

In order to provide a flavor of the Zok language I present a number of translated texts here, arranged in chronological order.

(5) The old man and Death, from Patkanov[22]

a. text

Հըլավուրը եւ մոհը

Մոյն հըլավուր մորդ մեշումը փայտա նել կըտարած եւ հորզնը կապած, դըրեծ յոնսին, տանամ տոն: Իբոր վըստակածա նել բեռնի ծընդրութիւնիցը եւ ճընըփահիցը, փայտը վերա դըրել եւ ինքը իւրան սըրտամը տըրտընջալիս ա նել ուրան աղկատութեան վարա, պարկ սասավ կանչալա մոհին, որ գիւ իւրան պըրծըցանի դարտիցը: Բրդան մոհը նըրվահալա սըրո եւ ահալաթա՝ ու՞նչըս նիզամ անձանից: Հըլավուրին ջունը ոհ ու դուղ ա ընկել եւ ահալ ա թա՝ քիզանդուր ուջայըմ կանչալ, որ գիւս հոկ հորզնը փայտը բըցըրցանիս, դըրիս յոնսիս վարան:

b. transcription

Hĕlavurĕ ew mohĕ

Moyn hĕlavur mord meshumĕ[23] p‘ayt a nel kĕtarats ew horznĕ kapats, dĕrets yonsin,[24] tanam ton: Ibor vĕstakatsa nel beřni tsĕndrut‘iwnits‘ĕ ew chĕnĕp‘ahits‘ĕ, p‘aytĕ ver a dĕrel ew ink‘ĕ üran sĕrtamĕ tĕrtĕnjalis a nel üran aghkatut‘ean vara, park[25] sasav[26]

---

[21] Hrach‘ya Achařian, "K‘nnut‘iwn Nor Jughayi Barbaři," [Study of the New Julfa Dialect] (Yerevan: State University Press, 1940).

[22] Patkanov, *Izsledovanie o dialektax‘ armjanskago jazyka.*

[23] *meš-um-ĕ* = forest-locative-definite, from the common Armenian dialectal form for 'forest', *meša* (cf. Azeri *mešä*, Turkmen *meše*).

[24] *yons-i-n* = SEA *us-i-n* 'shoulder-genitive-definite'. The *n* in the Zok form may be a preservation of the nasal in the Indo-European ancestor of this word, **omso-*, or it may be the same sort of pre-strident nasal insertion that we see in non-standard dialect forms like *mendz* 'big' (< *mets*). Cf. also Zok *unch‘* 'no(t)' < *och‘* in footnote 36.

[25] *park* (Achařian, *K‘nnut‘iwn Agulisi Barbaři*, has park‘) = SEA *pirk* 'strong, loud'.

[26] *sas-av* = *sas* 'voice' (also used in Karabagh dialects, from Turkic *säs* 'mouth') + instrumental *-av*.

kanch‘ala mohin, or gü üran pěrtsěts‘ani dartits‘ě: Běrdan[27] mohě něrvahala[28] sěro ew ahalat‘a` u̇nch‘ěs nizam andzanits‘: Hělavurin juně oh u dugh a ěnkel ew ahal a t‘a` k‘izandur[29] ujayěm[30] kanch‘al, or güs hok[31] horzně p‘aytě běts‘ěrts‘anis,[32] děris yonsis varan:

c. translation

The Old Man and Death

An old man had cut wood in the forest and bound it as firewood. He put it on his shoulder and took it home. When he had become tired from the weight and the journey, he put the wood down and grieved in his heart at his poverty. He began to call loudly to Death, that it come and free him of his pain. Suddenly, Death appeared to him and said: “What do you want from me?” The old man’s soul fell into fear and trembling, and he said: “I called you so that you would come and take this load of wood and put it back on my shoulder.”

(6) The dog and the thief, from Patkanov[33]

a. text

Շոնը եւ գուղը

Քըշարան գուղը հոց ա գիցել շուն առաչք, որ փերզի, յարաբ կահիլ ա դըրոնավ խաբիլ նըրո. ամա շոնը ահալաթա՝ այ՛ մորդ, դու մայտկըս նարամ որ ամ լուզըս կապիս, որ իս հաչիմունչ ամտայրիս խայրին ուջա, ամա շոտ խաբվամըս, անդուր որ քու ստի բեղափիլ արած ըղկոթիւնիցդ նըրվալիս ա, որ մատամա որթուն մընոմ որ դու կէարիս ունչ վընաս տոս:

b. transcription

Shuně ew gughě

K‘ěsharan gughě hots‘ a gits‘el shun aṙach‘k‘, or p‘erzi,[34] yarab kähil[35] a děronav khabil něro. ama shoně ahal a t‘a` áy mórd, dü

---

[27] *běrdan* (from Turkish *birden* ‘suddenly’) = Std. Arm. *mekēn*.

[28] *něrvahal a* = SEA *erewel ē* ‘appeared’.

[29] *k‘izandur* = Std. Arm. *k‘ez andur* ‘you-for.that’.

[30] *ucha-y-ěm* = *ucha* ‘for’ + *ěm* ‘I am’, with epenthetic *-y-* inserted to break the vowel hiatus.

[31] *hok* ‘this’.

[32] *Běts‘ěrts‘anis* = Class. Arm. *bardzrats‘anes* ‘you (sg.) raise’.

[33] Patkanov, *Izsledovanie o dialektax‘ armjanskago jazyka.*

[34] *p‘erzi* = SEA *p‘ordzē* ‘try. subjunctive. 3rd. singular’.

[35] *kähil* = Class. Arm. *karenal* ‘be able to’.

maytkēs naram[36] or am lüzēs kapis, or is hach‘im unch‘[37] am tayris khayrin uja,[38] ama shot khabvamēs, andur or[39] k‘u sti beghap‘il arats ĕghkotyunits‘ĕd[40] nĕrvalis a, or matam a[41] ort‘un[42] mĕnom or du käris unch‘ vĕnas tos:

c. translation

The dog and the thief

At night the thief threw bread in front of a dog so that [the dog] might try it and [the thief] be able thereby to deceive him. But the dog said, O man, you think you can bind my tongue that I not bark for my master's benefit, but you are quite deceived, since from your sudden false kindness it appears that I have to stay awake so that you are unable to do harm.

(7) The frog and the ox, from Patkanov[43]

a. text

Գյառնուկը եւ իզնը

Գյառնուկը ըզահալ ա որ իզնի չունք դառնայ, սկըսել ա ըռոհնիլ, գյառնուկին ձէօգը հըրոտ ա տըվել իւրան մորը, որ ատ բանիցը հըռանա. ամա նո ալ նիւրի սկըսելա ըռոհնիլ, ձէօգը սաս արալ թա՛ դիւ ճըղվիս ալ իզնին հըսանալ չիս: Իրինքինճին ալ նուրի գյառնուկը ըռոհալ ա եւ ճըղվել:

b. transcription

G^{y}ařnukĕ[44] ew iznĕ

G^{y}ařnukĕ ĕzahal a[45] or izni ch‘unk‘ dařna, skĕsel a ĕřohnil.[46] g^{y}ařnukin dzögĕ[47] hĕrot[48] a tĕvel üran morĕ, or at banits‘ĕ hĕřana.

---

[36] *dü maytk əs naram* = ‘you think’. Note the application of Achařian's Law in *du* ‘you (sg.)’ > *dü. maytk* = Std. Arm. *mitk‘* ‘mind’, *naram* = SEA *anum* ‘do’.

[37] *hach‘im unch‘* = Std. Arm. *hach‘em och‘* ‘I don't bark (subjunctive)’.

[38] *am tayris khayrin uja* – literally ‘for the good of my master’. *am* = Std. *im* ‘my’, *tayr* = Std. *tēr* ‘lord’, *khayr* = dialectal *kher* ‘good’, *uja* = ‘for’.

[39] *andur or* ‘since’.

[40] *ĕghkot‘yun* = Std. Arm. *aghekut‘yun* ‘kindness’.

[41] *matam a* ‘it is necessary’. Ačařyan 1935 has *mätäm ä*.

[42] *ort‘un* = Std. Arm. *art‘un* ‘awake’.

[43] Patkanov, *Izsledovanie o dialektax‘ armjanskago jazyka*.

[44] *G^{y}ářnuk* = Std. Arm. *gortnuk* ‘frog’.

[45] *ĕzahal a* ‘wanted’ = (as it were) Std. Arm. *uzatsats ē*.

ama no al nüri[49] skěsel a ěřohnil. dzögě sas aral t‘á dü chěghvis[50] al iznin hěsanal ch‘is: Irik‘inchin[51] al nüri g^yařnukě ěřohal a ev chěghvel:

c. translation

The frog and the ox

The frog wanted to be like an ox, so it began to swell up. The frog's child advised its mother to stay away from such a thing, but the frog began to swell up again. The child called out: you'll burst and still not attain the ox's [size]. On the third try the frog swelled up again and burst.

(8) Two friends, from Patkanov[52]

a. text

Արկու բարիկամ ճընափահըն նել նելիս. սըրուց ըռաստակալ մույնը որջ. սըրուց մույնը շոտ վիրա ելալ ծառի վարան, որ ունչա իւրան խաթո չը գիւ, ան մույն ընալ մայտն ա բարալ որ, որջը մառած ուխմանին դիպիլ չի, գյատնին վարան ձըգահալ ա, յանի թա՛ մառած ա: Որջը մըտըկահալ ա նըրո դըրուր տըվել, բարանը դըրել ա նըրո բըրանին եւ ընկըճնարին վարան. իբոր տահալ ա որ ըսկի նափաս չը տուս գելիս. թուղ ա արալ, հըռահալ: Յատնան ան մույն հընգիրը որ ծառիցը վերա ակալ, սըրհոանից հըրցահալ ա թա՝ որջը ան ունչա ահալ սըրո ընկճին. սոյալ ջըղոբ ա տըվել թա՝ որջը անձ հըրոտ տըվել թա՝ ան ուխմանին անձ դոստ չի յիմանամ, իբոր փերզած չիմ ամ քյամբախտըթիւնիս մաչը:

b. transcription

Arku barikam chěnap‘ahěn nel nelis. sěruts‘ ěřastakal[53] muyně orj. Sěruts‘ muyně shot vira elal tsaři varan, or unch‘a üran khat‘o[54] ch‘ě

46 *ěřohnil* = Std. Arm. *uřch‘il* ‘swell up’.

47 *dzög* = SEA *dzag* ‘offspring’, with the regular Zok sound changes of rounding of *a* to *o* in stressed syllable and fronting of the vowel after a voiced obstruent (Achařian’s Law).

48 *hěrot* = Std. *khrat* ‘advice’.

49 *nüri* = SWA *norēn* ‘again’?

50 *chěghvis* ‘you (sg.) burst/split (subjunctive)’ = Std. *chegh(k)es*.

51 *irik‘inch‘in* ‘third’ = *irik‘* ‘3’ + the Turkish ordinal suffix *-inci* ‘-rd’ + the Armenian definite article *-n*.

52 Patkanov, *Izsledovanie o dialektax‘ armjanskago jazyka.*

gü. an muyn ĕnal maytn a baral or, orjĕ mar̊ats[55] ukhmanin[56] dipil ch'i, gʸatnin varan dzĕgahal a, yani t'á mar̊ats a: Orjĕ mĕtĕkahal a[57] nĕro dĕrur tĕvel,[58] baranĕ dĕrel a nĕro bĕranin ew ĕnkĕchnarin[59] varan. ibor tahal a or ĕski nap'as[60] ch'ĕ dus gelis, t'ugh a aral, hĕr̊ahal: Yatnan[61] an muyn hĕngirĕ or tsar̊its'ĕ vera akal, sĕrohanits' hĕrts'ahal a t'a` orjĕ an unch' a ahal sĕro ĕnkchin. soyal[62] jĕghob a tĕvel ta` orjĕ andz hĕrot tĕvel t'a` an ukhmanin andz dost ch'i yimanam, ibor p'erzats ch'im am kʸambakhtĕt'yunis mach'ĕ:

c. translation

Two friends

Two friends were walking on the road. A bear encountered them. One of them quickly went up a tree, so that it might not reach him. The other one had the thought that a bear would not touch a corpse. He cast himself upon the ground as if he were dead. The bear approached and came up close to him, put its mouth to his mouth and ears. When he saw that no breath at all was coming out, he left him and went away. Afterwards his friend who was up the tree asked him what the bear said in his ear. He replied: The bear advised me, 'a person cannot be known to me as a friend until I have tried him in my misfortune.'

---

53 *ĕr̊ast akal* < *r̊ast* 'encounter, meeting' + *akal* = SEA *ekel* 'come.ppl.'.

54 *khat'o* = Arabic *ḥattā* 'until, up to'.

55 *mar̊ats*, literally 'dead', here = 'corpse'.

56 *ukhman* = Std. Arm. *ok'min*, *omn* 'one, a certain one'.

57 *mĕtĕkahal a* = SEA *motkats'el ē* 'approached'.

58 *dĕrur tĕvel* 'moved', from Classical Arm. *ĕnd irear tal* (cf. New Julfa *dirur tal*, Karabagh *tü'rür tal*).

59 *ĕnkĕj-nar-i-n* 'ear-pl.-genitive-definite'.

60 *nap'as* < Arabic/Persian *nafas* 'breath'.

61 *yatnan* = SEA *yetnits'* 'afterwards'. (Note that Zok uses the "Western"/Classical ablative *-ē* (> *-a*).

62 *so-y-al* = SWA *sa al* 'he too'.

(9) In praise of Agulis, nineteenth century[63]

a. text

Ի Գովեստ Ագուլեաց

Ըկիւլիսը արկու ձիւրի մաջի ա,
Վունքն ու տանիրն նրո մաջտիղ տըրվիծ ա
Էկինարիքն էլ նրոնց կորքքան ընկիծ ա
Գիւտն էլ գէաղի մաջտաղիցը նելիս ա:

Ըգըլիցիք յարգ ահողու սայրող նել,
Արտի օր գուրքիրը նրուց շոտ լեվ գյավամ նել,
Արտուր ոջայ օր՝ Հոր ա Բինարո ամրամ նել,
Արդի օր էօրտոկս սարին խողարն նահամ նել:

Թ՛ա օր Ծոհաբաաը քյանտի ունչ նել Ըգիւլիս,
ուվ ա գիտամ ունչ ա նելիլ Ըգիւլիս,
սող աշխարքամ մոյն [հ]ոտ ա նելիլ Ըգիւլիս
Անտուր հզոր տոն ա ըլած Ըգիւլիս:

b. transcription

I Govest Aguleats‘

ĕgülisĕ arku dzüri maji a,
vunk‘n u tanirn nro majtigh tĕrvits a,
ek‘inarik‘n[64] el nronts‘ kork‘k‘an ĕnkits a,
gütn el gäghi majtaghits‘ĕ nelis a:[65]

ĕgĕlits‘ik‘ yarg ahoghu[66] sayrogh[67] nel,
arti or gurk‘irĕ nruts‘ shot lev g^{y}avam nel,[68]
artur ojay or` Hora Binaro amram nel,[69]

---

[63] Recorded by the teacher Khach‘atur Khojamireants‘ in Tiflis; held in the HSSH state central archive, font 429, work 17, page 91. Reproduced with glosses of thirty of the words in Argam Ayvazyan, *Agulis: patmamshakut‘ayin hushardzanner* [Agulis: historico-cultural monuments] (Yerevan, Hayastan Hratarakch‘ut‘iwn, 1984), pp. 18-19.

[64] *ek‘inarik‘n* = Std. Arm. *aygineřĕ* ‘the vineyards’.

[65] *nelis a* = SEA *gnum ē* ‘he/she/it goes’.

[66] *ahogh* = SEA *asogh* ‘saying’.

[67] *sayrogh* = SEA *sirogh*‘loving’.

[68] *gyavam nel* = SEA *govum ēin* ‘they praised’.

ardi or örtoks[70] sarin[71] khogharn[72] naham nel:[73]
t'a or Shohabasĕ k^{y}anti unch' nel[74] ĕgülis,
uv a gitam unch' a nelil[75] ĕgülis,
sogh[76] ashkhark'am muyn khot[77] a nelil ĕgülis,
antur hzor[78] ton a ĕlats ĕgülis:

c. translation
In praise of Agulis

Agulis is in two valleys
The monastery and houses are placed in its middle
The vineyards fall on their sides
And the river flows through the middle of the village.

Aguletsis love to recite songs
That's why the books praised them highly
And Hora Binaro [...???]
That's why even now they talk about its beautiful games.

If Shah 'Abbas hadn't destroyed Agulis
Who knows what Agulis might have been
In the entire world there was only one Agulis
That Agulis of a thousand homes.

---

69 The meaning of this line is unclear to me. Ayvazian 1984 glosses *hora* as *hayi/hayots^h* 'Armenian-gen.', *Binaro* as *banirn* 'things', and *amram nel* as *asum en* 'they say', but all three of these are probably incorrect.
70 *örtoks* = Std. Arm. *ayzhm isk* 'even now, still'.
71 *sarin* = Std. Arm. *sirun* 'lovely'.
72 *kho[gh]arn* = Std. Arm. *khaghern* 'games'.
73 *naham nel* = SEA *asum ēin* 'they said'.
74 *k'ranti unch' nel* = Std. Arm. *ch'k'ander*, *ch'averer* 'hadn't destroyed'.
75 *unch' a nelil* = SEA *inch kliner* 'what would have been'.
76 *sogh* = Std. Arm. *hamayn* 'all'; from Turkish *sağ*.
77 *khot* = Std. Arm. *hat* 'unit, piece'.
78 *hzor* = Std. Arm. *hazar* '1000'.

(10) Our endangered homeland, by Harut‘yun T‘umanyan (from Achaṙian[79])

a. text

Միր հըգյադառն վաթանը

Օհի մաջին, մոհի մաջին
Միր վաթանը լելիս ա.
Ովման չիկո, քոմագ արի
Սեվ խըբերը գյելիս ա:

Ծոռ ա տըվեծ
Միր ըշխարքի ուլուրը,
Հարամիք ակած լըցվեց
Միր ազգի չուրք բուլուրը:

Ըկընլուսի, մըշտըլըղի,
թոզա կյանքի գյարունքին՝
սեվ մըռոջ ա, թոխպ ա ակած
կետված հայոց յերկընքին:

Դուշմունն ակած, չափմիշ նարամ,
Միր ոջաղը քձանդամ ա,
Հայի ճըրոգը հընգըցանամ,
Աշխարք ըրնով նարկամ ա:

Միզ կյանք տըվող, միզ շունչ տըվուղ
Ջոկըստունը մառնամ ա,
Նոր ըք, նոր ըք, քյամբախտ զոկար,
Ծուտ հըսահիք-մառնամ ա:

Թումանանաց Հարըթյուն

b. translation

In fear, in death
Our homeland weeps
No one is there, I made a mound
Black tidings come

It is turned away and twisted
The turbulence of our land

79 Achaṙian, *K‘nnut‘iwn Agulisi Barbaṙi.*

Brigands have come and filled
All four corners of our nation

In the spring of good news, good fortune, and fresh life
A black fog and a cloud have come
and clumped over the Armenian sky

The enemy has come and is pillaging
He is destroying our home
The candle of the Armenian wanes
The land is dyed with blood

Giver of life to us, giver of breath
Zokastan is dying
Come back, o ill-starred Zoks
Arrive quickly--it is dying.

The following translation of the Lord's Prayer was collected from Mr. Melik-Moussian in 1995. This is the lone sample for which I have been able to indicate the position of word stress, as I have a recording of Mr. Melik-Moussian reading it.

(11) The Lord's Prayer

a. text

անուն հոր եւ օրթօ եւ օքոյն սըրփօ ամմեն: միր ափի օր երկընքումըս, սուրփ նէան քու անունու. քու թաքավորությունը միր վէարին մընօ միշտ, համման ըցէահէածըթ կատարվի, ուրտի երկընքումն, անտի էալ երկրի վէարին: Միր որվա հոցը հըսանի միզ, եւ թուղ միշտ միզ պարտական, որ միք էալ պորտք չըմընոնք միրուց, եւ միշտ միզ հէառի պէահիս չարից, մէանէակ փըրկիս չարությունից. քանի որ ըշխարքամըս թաքավորությունու, ուժու, նան պատիվը, քունն ա միշտ: ամմեն:

b. transcription

ánun hor yev ort'ó yev ok'úyn sĕrp'ó amen. mir ap'í or yerkĕnk'úmnĕs, surp' nän k'u ánunu. k'u t'ak'avorut'yúnĕ mir värín mĕno misht, hamman ĕzähätsĕt' katarvi, úrti yerkĕnk'úmn, ánti äl yerkrí värín: mir orva hots'ĕ hĕsáni miz, yev t'ugh misht miz partakan, or mik' äl portk' ch'ĕmĕnonk' miruts', yev misht miz hä́ři pähis ch‘arits‘, mänäk p‘ĕrkis ch‘arut‘yúnits‘, k‘ani or ĕshkhárk‘amĕs t‘ak‘avorut‘yúnu, úzhu, nän pátivĕ, k‘unn a misht: ammen:

c. translation

[In the] name of [the] father and of [the] son and of the holy spirit, amen. Our Father, who art in heaven, Hallowed be thy Name. Thy kingdom come. Thy will be done, On earth as it is in heaven. Give us this day our daily bread. And forgive us our trespasses, As we forgive those who trespass against us. And lead us not into temptation, But deliver us from evil. For thine is the kingdom, and the power, and the glory, for ever and ever. Amen.

(12) Excerpt translated from Hovhannēs T‘umanyan's *The Little Fisherman* (Melik-Moussian[80])

a. text

Խեղճ Ուրաշիմա, յիմահալ չի որ ջոհիլութեան գաղտնիքը ջադու արուած սանդուղի մանջին էա էլէած բնդուեծ, որ տուեծ էա նել իրէան ծօվի տակին ապրուղ նախշուտ Սէն-Նինին: Թիթիվ խելքէավ վռազ-վռազ բեց էա արալ սանդուրը եւ ամման բիւն կրցահալ: Զրկուել ա ջօհիլ եւ երկար կեանքից եւ բախտաւոր ապրելու վայելքից: Համա նո սայրուղ, ազնիւ սարտ օնի նել եւ նէահէալ էա իրէա սրտին եատքից: Ատ ա պատճառը, որ մինչեւ հրդիօ էալ Եապոնական երկրու մըռահած չին Ուրիշիմային, եւ նրօ գաղտնի պատմութիւնը: Եւ շոտ տեղերէամ նրօ պաշտամըն անդուր հէատի օր, մինչեւ անգամ աստուածների անհոգ աշխարամ, Սէն-Նինիի նմուն շախշուտին սըյրելու վախտամ ալ, մոռահալ չի իրէա հարազատներին եւ իրէա ախքատ վէաթէանը:

b. transliteration

Kheghch Urashima, yimahal ch‘i or johilut‘yan gaghtnik‘ĕ jadu arvats sandughi manjin ä eläts bĕndvets, or tĕvets ä nel irän tsovi takin aprugh nakhshut Sen-Ninin: t‘it‘iv khelk‘äv vĕřaz-vĕřaz bets‘ ä aral sandughĕ ew amman bün kĕrts‘ahal: Zĕrkvel ä johil yev yerkar kyank‘its‘ yev bakhtavor aprelu vayelk‘its‘: Hama no sayrugh, azniv sart oni nel yev nähäl ä irä sĕrtin yatk‘its‘: At a patchaře, or minch‘ev hĕrdö äl Yaponakan yerkru mĕřahats ch‘in Urashimayin, yev nĕró gaghtni patmut‘yunĕ: Yev shot tegheräm nĕro pashtamĕn

---

[80] Melik-Moussian, *Agulis/Igülis.*

andur häti or, minch'ev angam astvatsneri anhog ashkharam, Sen-Ninii nĕmun nakhshutin sĕyrelu vakhtam al, mořahal ch'i irä harazatnerin yev irä akhk'at vät'änĕ:

c. translation

Poor Urashima didn't know that the secret of youth was bound up in the magic box, which had been given to him by the beautiful Sen-Nini, who lived under the sea. With a light mind he impatiently opened the box and lost everything. He was deprived of youth, long life, and the enjoyment of living happily. But he had a kind and loving heart, and he went after his heart. This is the reason why even up to the present day in Japan they have not forgotten Urashima and his secret history. And in many places they worship him for this reason, that even in the carefree realm of the gods, loving a beauty like Sen-Nini, he did not forget his family and his poor homeland.

22

Ակն/Ական (*AKN/AKAN*) ‘*Eye’

Eric P. Hamp

The noun ակն/ական (*akn/akan*), best glossed ‘*eye,’ but also ‘spring, opening, gem, and (-) Sun,’ has been well observed and studied descriptively, and long, attentively, learnèdly, and admirably known and studied philologically and historically.[1]

This excellent literature and scholarship will here be mentioned and alluded to only briefly, but I hope sufficiently, and on salient or essential pertinent points to our argument. It is proposed that one aspect to this discussion has been scanted, nearly omitted, leaving in limbo a solution to a crucial set of conclusions: phonological, morpho-syntactic, and subtly semantic, which also carry implications for related nominal paradigms (*otn*, *dzukn*, *unkn*) and for important relics of Indo-European and Indo-Hittite dates ($*ʕ^w$ or H_3, and *-*n*-).

Olsen, in her valuable and frank preface to her mammoth, masterly, and milestone work,[2] has identified Armenian as a Cinderella among more opulent Indo-European kin, but then goes on to exemplify appropriately features that in fact enrich in significant ways our picture of PIE by considering the Armenian evidence. Indeed, her list could easily be lengthened, and some scholars may consider Olsen’s taste for morphological, inflexional, and derivational detail too fine-grained for typological or cultural adventure. Be that as it may, and with gratitude for the stimulating

---

[1] Antoine Meillet, *Altarmenisches Elementarbuch* (Heidelberg: Carl Winter, 1913), p. 59b; Hans Jenson, *Altarmenische Grammatik, Chrestomathie* (Heidelberg: Carl Winter, 1959, 1964), p. 149; and Birgit Annette Olsen, *The Noun in Biblical Armenian: Origin and word-formation, with special emphasis on the Indo-European heritage* (Berlin; New York: Mouton de Gruyter, 1999), Index 1005 and references 969ff.

[2] Olsen, *The Noun in Biblical Armenian*, pp. v-x.

presentation of lively points open to past and present debate, we owe an enormous debt to Olsen for this centennial gift.

I propose here, in tribute to our valiant friend and colleague Dickran Kouymjian, who has contributed so much to Armenian Studies, an addition to Olsen's list where Armenian (no Cinderella) presents us with a priceless IE dimension to one of our most basic IE lexemes and bases, and not an indirect or displaced survival.

It is clear that the history of Armenian _n_-stems is manifold and complex.[3] There are for _akn_ a number of separate lexemes, as mentioned at the outset above. Therefore, we may reasonably expect a derivational suffix to have carried a semantic distinction for this versatile base, and perhaps variously.

For example, in analyzing and discussing Welsh _llydan_ 'broad' recently;[4] with Old Breton _litan_, Old Irish _lethan_, Gaulish toponym _Litana_, Hittite _paltana-_, _palhí_, Lith. _pló-na-s_, Latv. plâ-ns, Greek πλάτη, πλάθανον, πλατ-ύ, πλάτ-αια; Welsh _Llyd-aw_, German _Fuld-a)_, I have had occasion to remark that "we may have here the leveled residue of the IE nominal paradigm outlined and described in Hamp."[5] We are looking here at a pre-IE paradigm *_pl(e)t(eH_$_a$_/-n-/-l)_ _–ú-_, contextually determined by syntax and desinence. In that discussion I introduced the following footnote: Armenian _layn_ 'wide' must be *_laθin-_ < *_lə_$_{(a)}$_ten-_ (_o-_) < *_lḤ_$_a$ _t-(e)n-(o-)ə_ < metathesis and/or conformation to *(_p_)_let-~_ *(_p_)_ltH_$_a$_-n-_(_o-_). Thus Helleno-Armenian shows both the *_-n(o)_ and *ú- synonyms.[6]

On the other hand, we must not lose sight of the lexeme first and foremost for the 'eye.' This bids us to pay fundamental attention to the noun ակն/ական, _akn/akan_, pl. աչք _ach'k'_;[7] on _ach'k'_ and cognate forms I have already remarked upon.[8] While Olsen carefully notes the detail of stem formation, it seems to me that she neglects a

[3] Ibid., pp. 115-143, 117ff, esp. pp. 119, and 132-143.

[4] _Studia Celtica_ 36 (2002), pp. 149-150.

[5] Eric P. Hamp (1994 and 1995), listed in 2002, "Llydan," footnote 4 above; _Donum Balticum_ (_Stang Festschrift_), Velta Rūķe-Dravina, ed. (Stockholm: 1970), pp. 173-177.

[6] _Studia Celtica_, pp. 149-150.

[7] Meillet, _Altarmenisches Elementarbuch_, p.59b and Jensen, _Altarmenisches Grammatik_, p. 149.

[8] See Hamp (1970), note 4 (1997) in the _Gedenkschrift_ for Zbigniew Gołab (2007).

real possibility. She notes correctly that *ach'k'* is a genuinely ancient form; it appears then as if the *yod* of this old dual was incorporated in the final of the root stem form or else was considered part of this dual ending, as in '20.' Then 'eye' would have started as a root noun, and unlike ὄσσε, ὄμμα < *$H_3k^w m̥nt$-*[9] would be a fact of later Greek history, replacing an apocopated Greek *ὄ=; likewise *ach'ats'* would reflect, I propose, a later neuter plural *–a-*.[10] We shall see that syllabic **-n-* > *an* would syllabify by Siever's Law.

The regularity of initial *a-* for the vocalization of *$ʕ^w$-(*C*), which Olsen states[11] was pointed out by me in connection with **H_3bhel-* in Hamp[12] 'increase' and 'be of use', giving three homophonous possible roots, yet separate by virtue of their distinct morphologies (and syntaxes, though unified by Clackson[13] through ambiguous arithmetic-increase or gain = deficit or debt : sweep = heap up). The Armenian comparanda are mentioned by Olsen (*awel*, *aweli*),[14] but are not fully analyzed, doubtless because they are classed basically as adjectives (from verbs) and not as nouns. They also happen not to involve a consonant susceptible of voicing. In 1982 I credited, hypothetically, *the voicing* in *akn* to position in final of a root noun; that is wrong, I will now claim, and not necessary. Otherwise I remain convinced, except on the voicing mechanism, of my 1982 analysis, which does not appear in Olsen,[15] and appears in Clackson,[16] only to be branded as uncertain, "a crux," or a doubt among most 'prothetic' vowels, where reasoned and informed argument has already gone beyond powerless doubt, which declares merely an obvious absence of exactly comparable cognates.

We turn now to profit from the remaining separate items of reference listed in Olsen's index.[17] The reference to p. 5 has to do

---

[9] Olsen, *The Noun in Biblical Armenian,* pp. 170-171, 763.

[10] Ibid., p. 171 on neuter *–an* vs. animate *ot-in.*

[11] Ibid, p. 763.

[12] Eric P. Hamp, "Two Roots *$H_o$bhel-* ," *Glotta* 60: (1982), pp. 227-230.

[13] James Clackson, *The Linguistic Relationship Between Armenian and Greek* (Oxford, UK; Cambridge, USA: Blackwell, 1994) (Publications of the Philological Society, No. 30), p. 157.

[14] Olsen, *The Noun in Biblical Armenian*, pp. 211, 436.

[15] Ibid., p. 976.

[16] Clackson, *The Linguistic Relationship*, pp. 33-36.

[17] Ibid., p. 1005.

with Godel's rejection of the accusative singular, (but see p. 817), as the source of the *–n* in old root nouns; Godel is perfectly right that *akn* in particular would be a very bad example for that argument, assuming that it was an old meuter, as the plural (i.e., old dual) suggests. Toch B *ek* 'eye,' dual *eś* and *yneś* appears to indicate an old neuter.[18] I do not follow Olsen's suggestion that *akn* might have been influenced by feminine gender of *unkn* 'ear,' but of course gender shift in the Caucasus region is an argument that would call for additional motivation. However, because I attach weight to arguments that link features of Greek to comparanda in Armenian, but without insisting every time on the accusative source for **n* (e.g. *akn* could be the source semantically for *unkn*), I call attention to the feminine ὤψ[19] seen in εἰς ὦπα ἰδέσθαί "look directly in the face" or the Ionism θεῇς εἰς ὦπα ἔοκεν "in the face she resemble the goddesses." The eye or the face is the 'see-er' or 'sight.' It is quite natural to find this verbal root-noun (to the suppletive future ὄψομαι 'I shall see') as a feminine. I discuss elsewhere the merger in form of the nominative and accusative singular of Armenian nouns.

We see then that the original gender correlation, reflected through the inherited singular and dual in the attested phonology is appropriate for the functional derivation classes.

Olsen discusses interestingly,[20] but inconclusively, *mowkn*, mouse and *dzukn* fish, while velar *–k* reminds one of the –α gravity postfix of Indic *ásṛ-k* (with the voicing in ἀστϱά-γ-αλος 'neck-vertebra' suggesting $*ʕ^w = H_3$). The alternation in length of Greek υ in the cognates could have arisen in different syllabic contexts by absorption of the rounded laryngeal next to the rounded υ. Therefore, $*muʕ^w$-, $(id)\acute{g}^h uʕ^w$-. Thus, we know that H_3 had a feature of rounding, like a labio-velar.

ap'n –in[21] looks to me like H_2aH_2p-*(e)n- (r/n-)* (Germanic) or $H_2(a)pH_2/(e)n$- (Armenian).

---

[18] Douglas Q. Adams, *Dictionary of Tocharian B* (Amsterdam; Atlanta, GA: Rodopi, 1999), p. 75.

[19] Eric P. Hamp, "Slavic *oko* 'eye'," *Balkanistica* 10 (1997), Donald L. Dyer, et. al, eds., pp. 220, 221-226 and Hamp, "Addenda to Slavic *oko*," *Balkanistica* 10 (2007), p. 57.

[20] Olsen, *The Noun in Biblical Armenian*, p. 130-131.

[21] Ibid., pp. 136-137.

P. 141-Here we have (with the above) the Indo Hittite oblique *n-[22] as confused in *ospn* 'lentil,' with the $H_3(V)n$- suffix.

Pp. 170-171 is Olsen's basic reference for our noun: see also pp. 839, 763 (for *H_3) and for compounds pp. 662, 675-676. For the dual see p. 773 for *-H_1 and 811 for *-$k^w iy$. See also Olsen's remarks, p. 175, which, with Lindeman's suggestion, are non-committal, and I think, ultimately not essential (although Meillet may be right for *otn*.)[23]

We have now attended to every aspect of *akn*, *akan* except the voicing. There can be no doubt that a reconstruction of *ak-(a)n* permits *$ʕ^w k^w$-*n*- ; and *$ʕ^w k^w$ may be treated as phon-et/olog-ically and uni-segmental. In this instance, the prevailing presence of *w* lip-rounding may have aided. We would then have a merger with the situation referred to by Olsen[24] and which I have discussed more recently, e.g., in *Festschrift Schmalsteig* (2004) and Darden.[25]

In such cases we do not find irregularities. They are monadnocks of ancient Lantgesetze not overtaken by analogy. We must be grateful to Armenian for the bequest of such riches to science.

---

22 Hamp (2002).

23 Ibid., p. 175.

24 Ibid., p. 591, footnote 786.

25 Eric P. Hamp, "Unexpected Laryngeals in Initial Clusters in Baltic (-Slavic)," *The Bill Question: Contributions to the Study of Linguistics and Languages in Honor of Bill J. Darden on the Occasion of his 66th Birthday*, H. I. Aronson, V. A. Friedman, D. S. Hristova, and J. M. Sadock, eds. (Bloomington, Indiana: Slavica, 2006), pp. 117-119.

History

23

Plutarque et le théâtre grec dans l'Arménie ancienne[1]

Giusto Traina

1. La *Vie de Lucullus* conserve l'une des versions du récit sur la troisième guerre contre Mithridate Eupator, qui vit la participation du roi d'Arménie, Tigrane dit le Grand. Il y est question de la capitale, que le roi avait fait construire près de la frontière sud-ouest du royaume de la Grande Arménie, et qu'il avait nommé Tigranocerte/*Tigranakert* (l'emplacement de cette ville est encore sujet à discussion). Pour sa politique d'urbanisation, Tigrane avait adopté une pratique suivie depuis des siècles par les souverains orientaux, qui prévoyait des transferts massifs de population[2]. A Tigranocerte, il avait fait venir des Cappadociens et des Ciliciens, mais aussi des nomades arabes, utiles au trafic caravanier. Lors de sa prise par Lucullus, en 69, Tigranocerte contenait déjà une population assez importante qui a été évaluée, à tort ou à raison, à plusieurs centaines de milliers de personnes. Tigrane avait obligé ses sujets les plus en vue à venir s'y établir avec tous leurs biens, fait qui semblerait indiquer que, dans la pensée de son fondateur, Tigranocerte était destinée à tenir lieu de capitale de l'Empire : selon Appien (*Mithr.* 67), c'est dans cette résidence que Tigrane avait revêtu le diadème de roi d'Arménie. Quand Lucullus, en 69 av. J.-C., entra dans la ville conquise, il y trouva grand nombre de comédiens

---

[1] Je remercie Brigitte Le Guen et Michel-Yves Perrin pour leurs précieuses observations.

[2] Sur le site de Tigranocerta, voir T. Sinclair, « The site of Tigranocerta » I-II, *Revue des études arméniennes*, n.s. 25, (1994-1995), pp. 183-254; 26, (1996-1997), pp. 51-111. Voir aussi R. Hovannisian, ed., *Armenian Tigranakert/Diarbekir and Edessa/Urfa* (Costa Mesa: Mazda Press, 2006).

« que Tigrane avait rassemblés de toutes parts », et s 'en servit pour les spectacles qu'il donna pour célébrer sa victoire[3].

Comme Brigitte Le Guen l'a remarqué, le passage de la *Vie de Lucullus* « atteste conjointement de l'importance de la circulation des artistes et de la diffusion de l'art dramatique »[4]. D'ailleurs, Tigrane ne constituait pas un cas isolé dans cette région : une soixantaine d'années plus tôt, la confrérie des *technitai* dionysiaques d'Athènes avait envoyé une ambassade à la cour d'Ariarathe V de Cappadoce[5]. La mobilité des acteurs semble être confirmée par l'adverbe *pantachothen* « de toutes parts » utilisé par Plutarque, ce qui conviendrait très bien à l'esprit « théâtral et démesuré » de Tigrane, évoqué par Plutarque dans le chapitre 21.4 de la *Vie de Lucullus*, d'ailleurs comme un élément qui aurait rendu « la domination arménienne ...intolérable pour les Grecs, et même pénible ». Bien entendu, ce genre de théâtralité est propre à plusieurs souverains hellénistiques[6]. Et Tigrane ne faisait que suivre le modèle d'Alexandre le Grand, qui aurait fait venir trois mille acteurs à Ecbatane (Plutarque, *Vie d'Alexandre* 72.1).

La question de Tigranocerte est encore ouverte car il n'y a pas de documentation archéologique à l'appui, et le site de la ville n'a pas été identifié avec assez de certitude. Si Strabon mentionne la présence de colons grecs à Tigranocerte, Plutarque nous parle du caractère hellénique que Tigrane avait voulu lui conférer. D'autres sources nous présentent une connotation différente. C'est ainsi qu'Appien met en valeur les éléments les plus typiques de cette

---

[3] « ...apprenant qu'il était resté dans la ville beaucoup d'artistes dionysiaques que Tigrane y avait rassemblés de toutes parts pour l'inauguration du théâtre qu'il y avait construit, il s'en servit pour les concours et les spectacles pour célébrer sa victoire ».

[4] B. Le Guen, *Les associations de technites dionysiaques à l'époque hellénistique,* Nancy, I, p. 343.

[5] Deux décrets rédigés peu avant 130 av. J.-C., respectivement en l'honneur du roi et de sa femme Nysa, témoignent de l'importance accordée au théâtre grec dans ce royaume : Le Guen, *Les associations*, II p. 32.

[6] A. Chaniotis, « Theatricality Beyond the Theater. Staging Public Life in the Hellenistic World », dans B. Le Guen, éd., *De la scène aux gradins. Théâtre et représentations dramatiques après Alexandre le Grand* [Pallas, 47], (1997), pp. 219-259.

fondation : « une enceinte haute de cinquante coudées, dont la base était truffée d'écuries, et il avait créé un palais et de grands parcs d'agrément dans les faubourgs, ainsi que de nombreux terrains de chasse et des étangs » (*Mithr.* 380). De surcroît, ses habitants avaient été déportés de Cilicie et de Cappadoce (*ibid.* 285) : selon Appien, Tigrane avait fondé la ville « pour se faire honneur à lui-même » (*ibid.* 379). Certes, le récit d'Appien relève de la propagande de Lucullus qui avait tout intérêt à faire passer le roi pour un tyran oriental. Mais le titre de « philhellène » dont il est affublé sur des émissions monétaires sans doute destinées à ses mercenaires, n'était pas que de la propagande[7]. Non content d'être un monarque dans la plus pure tradition iranienne, Tigrane, à l'exemple de son beau-père et allié, Mithridate Eupator, s'appliquait à diffuser et à promouvoir la culture hellénique dans son Empire[8].

Certes, la situation de Tigranocerte est particulière car il s'agissait d'une capitale de frontière. Malgré la présence attestée de la plupart des peuples sujets de Tigrane, une partie des sources nous donnent l'impression que c'étaient les Grecs ramenés des villes ciliciennes et cappadociennes qui formaient le gros de la population. Mais en réalité, Tigrane avait rassemblé non seulement des Grecs, des Anatoliens plus ou moins hellénisés, (plus les Juifs mentionnés seulement par les sources arméniennes)[9], mais aussi des « barbares » (Plut. *Lucull.* 29.5). Et d'ailleurs, Tigranocerte n'était pas qu'une fondation de type hellénistique. Dans sa description de la ville, Appien met clairement en évidence ses éléments les plus typiquement iraniens – le complexe du palais royal, avec jardin, terrain de chasse et les étangs qui se trouvaient en périphérie. Et dans l'unique évocation précise relative à la cité, Appien s'arrête sur la présence de nombreuses écuries attenantes aux enceintes. A la différence de Plutarque, Appien se tait sur la présence de colons grecs, et définit tous les habitants de la ville comme Cappadociens.

---

[7] L. Breglia Pulci Doria «Plutarco e Tigran II *filhellên*», *Annali Facoltà Lettere Napoli*, 16 (1973-1974), pp. 37-67.

[8] Voir M.-L. Chaumont, G. Traina, « Les Arméniens entre l'Iran et le monde gréco-romain » dans G. Dédéyan, éd., *Histoire du peuple arménien* (Toulouse, 2007), pp. 101-162.

[9] Voir A. Topchyan, « Jews in ancient Armenia (1st century BCE-5th century CE) », *Le Muséon*, sous presse.

Appien utilisait des sources romaines hostiles à Tigran, qui mettaient en évidence l'élément barbare de Tigranocerte afin de souligner le caractère oriental, donc négatif, du roi. L'analyse des sources nous permet d'en conclure que la fondation de Tigrane était une cité hétérogène, au caractère mixte qui reflétait le projet ambitieux de constituer un royaume multiethnique, gouverné par un roi qui se voulait en même temps hellénique et iranien. Dans ce dessein, qui prévoyait une réorganisation radicale des espaces et des populations, comme dans le cas des nomades arabes « bousculés dans leurs habitudes », on peut peut-être déceler un modèle utopiste.

Quoi qu'il en soit, Tigrane suivait un modèle assez répandu dans le monde hellénistique. Il considérait comme fondamentale la construction de cités « grecques » pour consolider son royaume, créant ainsi de nouveaux marchés commerciaux et en même temps d'imposantes places fortes, capables de résister pas seulement aux ennemis internes, c'est-à-dire aux nobles et aux dynastes, susceptibles de créer des désordres et des scissions. En créant un nouveau centre aux marges de la Grande Arménie, qui donnait sur le Tigre et non plus sur l'Araxe, le roi voulait consolider ses nouvelles conquêtes, mais aussi établir des relations commerciales avec le monde des cités d'Anatolie, ce qui évidemment l'amenait à entrer en opposition avec la politique romaine et permet de considérer autrement l'allusion de Plutarque à la grogne des Grecs à l'égard du despotisme « théâtral » de Tigrane.

2. Le passage de la *Vie de Crassus* est le témoignage le plus célèbre sur l'hellénisme en Arménie. Nous sommes en 53 av. J.-C., après la conclusion de la bataille de Carrhes et la mort de Crassus. Tandis qu'à Séleucie sur le Tigre on célébrait une macabre parodie du triomphe romain ; le dignitaire Surenas avait prélevé la tête et la main droite du cadavre de Crassus pour les amener au roi Orode, qui se trouvait à la cour d'Artawazd II, roi d'Arménie[10] : on célébrait les noces de la sœur de ce dernier avec Pacoros, fils du roi parthe. Le banquet se tenait au palais royal, sans doute à Artaxata, capitale de la Grande Arménie. Le repas fini, on assistait à des « *akousmata* venus

---

[10] Marc Antoine infligera le même traitement à Cicéron : voir G. Traina, *Marco Antonio* (Rome-Bari, 2003), p. 58.

de Grèce ». Imaginant la réaction étonnée de ses lecteurs, Plutarque précise que le roi parthe connaissait très bien le grec, tandis que l'Arménien était même féru de culture hellénique et composait des ouvrages dans cette langue, dont des tragédies. Un acteur d'Asie mineure, Jason de Tralles, était en train de réciter le rôle d'Agavè dans les *Bacchantes* d'Euripide, accompagné par le chœur. C'est alors que Silacès, satrape de Mésopotamie à qui Surenas avait confié la tête de Crassus, entra dans la salle avec celle-ci. Par une macabre présence d'esprit, l'acteur s'empara de la tête, confia à l'un des choreutes les habits de scène de Penthée[11], et reprit son chant dans l'enthousiasme général des Arméniens et des Parthes[12]. Étant donné

---

[11] Plutarque parle de *skeuopoiêmata*, un terme qui peut indiquer le costume, le masque ou bien les deux. Le *Greek-English Dictionary* of Liddell-Scott-Jones (=*LSJ*), qui se réfère au passage de la *Vie de Crassus*, propose de traduire « *mask and dress* of a tragic actor ». Le *Vocabolario greco-italiano* (=*GI*) de F. Montanari précise que ce terme peut indiquer le masque *ou* le costume.

[12] « A ce moment Orodès s'était déjà réconcilié avec l'Arménien Artabazes (=Artavasdès), et avait obtenu la promesse de marier à la sœur de ce dernier son propre fils Pacoros. Dans les banquets et les beuveries qu'ils donnaient à tour de rôle, on représentait plusieurs auditions venues de Grèce. Car Orodès n'ignorait ni la langue ni les lettres grecques ; quant à Artabazès, il composait même des tragédies, et écrivait des discours et des récits historiques, dont quelques-uns sont conservés. Lorsqu'on apporta la tête de Crassus à l'entrée du palais, les tables venaient d'être enlevées. Un acteur tragique nommé Jason, originaire de Tralles, chantait le rôle d'Agavé dans les *Bacchantes* d'Euripide et y remportait un grand succès, lorsque Silacès entra dans la salle, se prosterna et jeta au milieu la tête de Crassus. Les Parthes se levèrent en battant les mains et en criant de joie, tandis que sur l'ordre du roi, les serviteurs donnèrent une place à Silacès. Alors Jason, remettant le masque de Penthée à l'un des choreutes, prit dans ses mains la tête de Crassus et, en jouant à nouveau le délire dionysiaque, il chanta ces vers avec transport :

(Agavè) « Nous apportons de la montagne au palais
un lierre fraîchement coupé.
Heureux trophée de chasse ! »

Tout l'auditoire était sous le charme, mais, au moment où fut chanté ce dialogue avec le chœur,

(Chœur) « Qui l'a tué ? »
(Agavè) « A moi revient cet honneur »,

le déclin des associations de Technites dionysiaques au Ier siècle av. J.-C., peut-être elles n'ont pas joué un rôle particulier pour entretenir le banquet nuptial tenu au palais d'Artawazd, sans doute dans sa résidence d'Artaxata comme le veut la *Vie de Crassus*. En effet, Plutarque parle de « plusieurs *akousmata* venus de Grèce »[13], mais il mentionne le nom d'un seul artiste, l'acteur Jason de Tralles.

D'après la *Vie de Crassus*, Artawazd ne se serait pas limité à connaître le grec, ce qui était assez compréhensible pour le fils de Tigrane, un roi qui se présentait comme « philhellène », mais il aurait même écrit des tragédies. La tradition arménienne a gardé une mémoire bien différente de ce souverain : D'après Moïse de Khorène (II 22), « adonné à la bonne chair et à la boisson, il errait dans les marais, dans les roselières et dans les rocailles ; paissant les onagres et les sangliers. Peu soucieux de sagesse, de valeur et de bonne renommée, véritablement esclave et serviteur de son ventre, il ne faisait que remplir ses latrines ! ». Dans son commentaire de ce passage, Jean-Pierre Mahé a observé que l'accusation de manque de sagesse est une appréciation paradoxale, étant donnée la renommée d'Artawazd comme auteur littéraire et historien[14]. En réalité, les deux textes ne se contredisent pas. D'après le point de vue oriental, l'hellénisme d'Artawazd était fort critiquable car éloigné des valeurs originaires d'*imastut'iwn*, « sagesse », et *k'ajut'iwn*, un terme qu'on peut traduire par « bravoure » mais qui, en réalité, reflète une gamme sémantique assez complexe qui correspond en grec aux catégories d'*andreia* et d'*arêtê*. A part les anachronismes flagrants présents

---

Exathrès, qui se trouvait au banquet, s'élança et s'empara de la tête, en disant que c'était plutôt à lui, plutôt qu'à l'autre, de prononcer ces vers. Le roi, ravi, lui donna la récompense conforme à l'usage du pays, et remit à Jason un talent. Telle fut, dit-on, le final tragique de l'expédition de Crassus ». Cette anecdote est reprise, en forme abrégée, par Polyen, *Strat.* VII 41.

13 Selon le *LSJ* et le *Diccionario Griego-Español*, ce terme désigne des auditions musicales. Le *GI* propose une signification plus large qui comprend « tout ce qu'on peut écouter », donc aussi des déclamations et, évidemment, des extraits de théâtre.

14 A. et J.-P. Mahé, *Histoire de l'Arménie par Moïse de Khorène. Nouvelle traduction de l'arménien classique (d'après Victor Langlois)* (Paris, 1993), ad l.

dans l'*Histoire des Arméniens* de Moïse, on remarquera que ce dernier caractérise Artawazd comme un souverain doublement négatif car il ne se limite pas à pratiquer les chasses chères à l'aristocratie iranienne – et d'ailleurs à l'aristocratie macédonienne aussi – mais il s'adonne à la *tryphè* des banquets, dans son interprétation personnelle du « dionysisme royal ». Selon les légendes arméniennes relatées par Moïse (II 61), Artawazd aurait disparu durant une partie de chasse : englouti dans la terre, il aurait été enfermé dans un antre et attaché par des chaînes de fer[15]. C'était une manière symbolique pour exorciser et rattacher à l'ancien mythe caucasien une réalité bien plus prosaïque : en 34, Marc Antoine avait emprisonné le roi à Alexandrie, avant de le faire exécuter, après la bataille d'Actium.

3. On a évoqué la présence du théâtre grec en Orient soit comme la preuve de l'existence d'une communauté grecque, soit comme l'indicateur privilégié de l'hellénisation d'une région[16]. Aux témoignages écrits qu'on vient de discuter, on ajoutera les vestiges de théâtres grecs retrouvés par les archéologues à Séleucie sur le Tigre, à Babylone et à Aï Khanoum.[17] D'autre part, ces bâtiments ne

---

[15] Sur les divers aspects de ce passage de Moïse de Khorène voir au moins J.R. Russell, « Some Iranian Images of Kingship in the Armenian Artaxiad Epic » (1986-1987) = *Armenian and Iranian Studies* (Cambridge, Mass., 2004), pp. 157-174 ; G. Charachidzé, *Prométhée et le Caucase. Essai de mythologie contrastive* (Paris, 1992) ; L. Abrahamyan, « Hero chained in a mountain : on the semantic and landscape transformations of a proto-Caucasian myth », *Aramazd. Armenian Journal of Near Eastern Studies*, 1, (2006), pp. 208-221 ; voir aussi Id. « The Chained Hero : The Cave and the Labyrinth », *Iran & the Caucasus*, 11 (2007), pp. 89-99.

[16] Voir G. Traina, « Hellenism in the East : some historiographical remarks », *Electrum*, 6 (Cracovie, 2002), pp. 15-24 ; « Notes on Hellenism in the Iranian East (Classico-Oriental Notes, 6-8) », *Iran & the Caucasus*, 9 (2005), pp. 1-14.

[17] Pour une carte de distribution des théâtres grecs en Orient voir B. Le Guen, « Théâtre, cités et royaumes en Anatolie et au Proche-Orient de la mort d'Alexandre le Grand aux conquêtes de Pompée », dans F. Prost dir., *L'Orient méditerranéen de la mort d'Alexandre aux campagnes de Pompée* [Pallas 62] (Rennes – Toulouse, 2003), pp. 329-355. Voir aussi R. J. Van der Spek: « Ethnic segregation in Hellenistic Babylon », dans W. H. van

sont pas que des modèles grecs transplantés en Orient : il montre les traces d'un processus d'orientalisation qui reste encore à comprendre dans ses détails[18]. D'ailleurs on est loin des temps où l'hellénisme en Orient était considéré comme un phénomène homogène : la recherche actuelle est de plus en plus sensible aux variantes régionales, en un mot à l'*interpretatio* des modèles grecs dans d'autres sociétés. Et je suis tout à fait d'accord avec R. Boucharlat quand il observe, à propos du site de Suse en Iran, que « Dans la mesure du possible, il faudrait distinguer la *présence* grecque sous la forme d'une administration et d'une colonie, et l'*influence* grecque, perceptible, pour nous, dans l'évolution et le style des constructions et des objets »[19]. D'ailleurs, de même que nous avons une *interpretatio Graeca* de motifs orientaux, il ne faut pas exclure des formes d'*interpretatio Orientalis* des divers langages de l'hellénisme : à propos de certains mythes géorgiens, G. Charachidzé a parlé de "processus de transposition"[20]. La présence d'un véritable théâtre grec à Tigranocerte en 69 av. J.-C., ainsi que les «*akousmata* venus de Grèce », représentés sans doute à Artaxata en 53 av. J.-C., ne doivent pas être considérés comme les éléments d'un vernis d'hellénisme introduit dans un contexte oriental, mais d'un hellénisme réélaboré pour chanter la grandeur de Tigrane et la victoire des Parthes, alliés des Arméniens. Probablement, un texte comme les *Bacchantes* était approprié pour une célébration de la victoire contre Crassus[21]. D'ailleurs, la célébration sur scène n'était

---

Soldt, R. Kalvelagen, D. Katz éds., *Ethnicity in Ancient Mesopotamia. Papers Read at the 48th Rencontre Assyriologique Internationale, Leiden 1-4 July 2002* (Leiden, 2005).

18 A. Invernizzi, « Appunti sulla cultura ellenistica nell'impero seleucide », *Topoi*, 4.2 (1994), pp. 521-530.

19 R. Boucharlat, « Suse, marché agricole ou relais du grand commerce. Suse et la Susiane à l'époque des grands empires », *Paléorient* 11/2 (1985), pp. 71-81.

20 G. Charachidzé, « Ecriture de l'histoire géorgienne ou la mythologie travestie », dans M. Detienne, éd., *Transcrire les mythologies: tradition, écriture, historicité* (Paris, 1994), pp. 213-224 ; 262 s.

21 Voir G. Gojan, *2000 let armjanskago teatra. 1. Teatr drevnej Armenii, po pamjatnikam material'noj kul'tury i drevnim tekstam* [2000 ans de théâtre arménien. 1. Le théâtre de l'Arménie ancienne, d'après les monuments de la culture matérielle et les textes anciens] (Moscou, 1952), p. 134 ss. ; J.

pas étrangère aux cours iraniennes ou iranisantes car on y déclamait des textes sacrés ou bien les compositions épiques, généralement orales, chantés par des bardes locaux appelés *gusan*. Si la tragédie grecque est certainement unique, d'autres littératures pouvaient contenir des éléments dramatiques à qui le langage du théâtre grec ne devait pas sembler totalement étranger. Mais cela ne concernait pas Plutarque qui avait sa propre conception de l'hellénisme qui a influencé la tradition classique : comme le remarquait Claire Préaux, Droysen n'a fait que fondre Plutarque dans un moule hégelien[22]. En même temps, le contexte historique justifiait l'intérêt de Plutarque pour ces aspects 'dégénérés' de l'hellénisme en Arménie, car il ne faut pas oublier que les biographies de Lucullus et de Crassus furent écrites à l'époque où Trajan préparait sa campagne orientale.

Nadolny, « Die "Bacchantinnen" des Euripides auf armenischen Bühne im 1. Jahrhundert v. u. Z. », *Das Altertum*, 21 (1975), pp. 99-102.

[22] C. Préaux, «Réflexions sur l'entité hellénistique», *Chronique d'Egypte*, 40 (1965), pp. 129-139.

Le maître des milices d'Orient, Vahan, de la bataille de Yarmouk (636) au complot d'Athalaric (637)

Mikaël Nichanian

Alors qu'Héraclius avait réussi en 628, pour la première fois dans l'histoire de l'Empire, l'exploit digne d'Alexandre d'envahir et de soumettre la Perse, cette victoire sans précédent fut suivie d'une défaite, elle-même inouïe, contre les Arabes à Yarmouk[1] en 636. Considéré classiquement comme un basculement du monde antique à l'époque médiévale, c'est bien là un des tournants de l'histoire du Proche-Orient ancien, qui entraîna, en quelques années, la perte des trois quarts des territoires, des ressources et des populations de l'Empire et une fragmentation de l'espace méditerranéen unifié par l'Empire romain. En l'espace de quelques années, l'Empire romain d'Orient passait ainsi d'une situation hégémonique de grande puissance internationale à celle de puissance régionale écrasée par la supériorité militaire du Califat.

Le général qui dirigea les troupes byzantines à Yarmouk était le maître des milices d'Orient Vahan (Vaanes). Son origine familiale, inconnue jusqu'ici, peut être déduite d'un passage du chroniqueur arménien Sebēos qui permet d'avancer l'appartenance lignagère de

---

[1] Sur la bataille de Yarmouk, voir Goeje M.J. de, *Mémoire sur la conquête de la Syrie* (Leyde, 1900) [= Goeje, *Syrie*], pp. 84-85, 103-106 ; F.M. Donner, *The Early Islamic Conquests* (Princeton, 1981) [= Donner, *Islamic Conquests*], pp. 133-146 ; W.E. Kaegi, *Byzantium and the Early Islamic Conquests* (Cambridge, 1992) [= Kaegi, *Islamic Conquests*], pp. 112-145 ; A. Stratos, *Byzantium in the Seventh Century*, H.T. Hionides trad., vol. II (Amsterdam, 1968) [= Stratos II], pp. 64-72 ; *L'Encyclopédie de l'Islam*, vol. XI, (Leyde-Londres 1960) [= *EI XI*], « Yarmuk », pp. 315-317.

ce Vahan au clan des Khorkhoruni. L'identification de ce dignitaire contribue ainsi à la compréhension des luttes politiques de la fin du règne d'Héraclius. Une source byzantine accuse, en effet, Vahan de trahison et de révolte à Yarmouk à la tête des contingents arméniens, mais en fait cet officier n'était pas à la tête des troupes arméniennes, mais de l'ensemble de l'armée impériale. En outre, ni les sources arabes, syriaques, ni même l'autre chronique byzantine, celle de Nicéphore, n'évoquent de révolte militaire dans l'armée romaine à Yarmouk. Comme après la défaite de Manzikert en 1071, l'accusation officielle de trahison des contingents arméniens[2] était destinée à masquer les graves défaillances du haut commandement de l'armée impériale qui menaçait l'existence même de l'Empire. En fait, le complot auquel participa Vahan était celui de 637, organisé dans la capitale par un fils naturel d'Héraclius exclu de la succession impériale. Athalaric tenta alors de profiter de la grande défaite de Yarmouk pour rallier à sa cause les officiers et dignitaires, inquiets de l'affaiblissement physique et politique d'Héraclius et de la menace militaire arabe.

Ainsi, la fin du règne d'Héraclius est marquée par deux tentatives majeures d'insubordination militaire. La première, celle de Baanes en 636, est sujette à caution, car mentionnée par le seul Théophane. Elle constituerait selon lui une des causes de la grave défaite subie par les troupes impériales face aux Arabes à Yarmouk. La seconde est celle d'Athalaric, aidé dans sa tentative de putsch, sans doute en 637, par plusieurs membres de la noblesse arménienne, notamment Varaz-Tirots' Bagratuni, Vahan Khorkhoruni et David Saharuni.

Les textes anciens présentent quatre versions incompatibles de ces complots, ainsi que des séquences événementielles contradictoires. Une réinterprétation globale des sources permettrait d'harmoniser, dans une certaine mesure, leurs divergences et de proposer l'identification de Vahan Khorkhoruni, attestée par Sebēos, au général Baanes de 636 mentionnée par Théophane.

---

[2] Cette prétendue révolte des Arméniens à Yarmouk figure même dans l'historiographie la plus récente. Voir Kaegi, *Islamic Conquests*, p. 4, en contradiction avec les pp. 120, 133 et 186 du même ouvrage.

1. Les sources
1.1. Théophane le Confesseur

Une première version des faits est présentée par le chroniqueur Théophane. Selon cet auteur qui est le seul à connaître les antécédents de ce dignitaire, Baanes exerçait, au cours de l'expédition d'Héraclius en Perse, la charge de stratélate[3], qui équivaut sans doute à la fonction de maître des milices d'Arménie ou d'Orient. En décembre 627, il s'illustra par une victoire décisive sur les troupes perses juste avant la prise de Ctésiphon[4]. Plus tard, après deux défaites face aux Arabes essuyées d'abord par Serge[5] en janvier 634, puis par le frère d'Héraclius, Théodore[6], en juillet, Baanes fut nommé pour superviser les opérations militaires comme maître des milices d'Orient[7]. L'identification des deux occurrences de Baanes ne semble pas poser de problème[8], dans la mesure où il s'agit d'un officier attesté au sommet de la hiérarchie militaire byzantine et qui a déjà manifesté ses compétences en Perse. De concert avec le sacellaire Théodore[9], il remporta une victoire – ignorée des autres sources – sur les Arabes à Emèse et les poursuivit jusqu'à Damas. L'année suivante, en 636, les Arabes organisèrent une grande expédition dans la région de Damas. Baanes opéra, une nouvelle fois,

---

[3] Un sceau pourrait être attribué à ce dignitaire : G. Zacos et A. Veglery, *Byzantine Lead Seals* I, 3 vols. (Bâle, 1972) [= ZV], n° 2831 (*The Prosopography of the Later Roman Empire*, vol. III, A.D. 527-641, J.R. Martindale éd. (Cambridge, 1992) [= *PLRE* IIIB], p. 1349) : Baanou stratèlatou. Voir aussi Kaegi, *Islamic Conquests*, p. 34, n. 23.

[4] C. de Boor éd., *Theophanis Chronographia* (Leipzig, 1883) [= Théophane], p. 318, 4-7.

[5] Théophane, p. 336, 16-19. En 631/32 selon la chronologie de Théophane. La tradition que reprend Théophane, selon laquelle Serge trouve la mort dans cette bataille, est conforme à la version de Michel le Syrien. Sur la date de 633, voir Donner, *Islamic Conquests*, pp. 115-116 et n. 132-133.

[6] *PLRE* IIIB, pp. 1277-1279, « Theodorus 163 » ; Kaegi, *Islamic Conquests*, pp. 98-100.

[7] Théophane, p. 337, 1-5. En 632/633 selon la chronologie erronée de Théophane.

[8] *PLRE* IIIA, p. 161, « Baanes ».

[9] *PLRE* IIIB, pp. 1279-1280, « Theodorus 164 ».

la jonction avec les troupes de Théodore. Selon Théophane, le mardi 23 juillet 636, les troupes du sacellaire subirent une première défaite. C'est alors que se produisit la révolte des troupes d'Orient qui proclamèrent Baanes empereur, ce qui entraîna le retrait de l'armée centrale du sacellaire. Les Arabes profitèrent de cette confusion des armées byzantines pour lancer l'assaut et les anéantir[10]. Cette séquence événementielle n'est attestée par aucune autre source. Quant au complot de Jean-Athalaric, Théophane ne le mentionne pas.

1.2. Nicéphore

Le patriarche Nicéphore présente une version différente des débuts de l'expansion arabe. Selon lui, les premiers raids arabes eurent lieu peu de temps après la célébration du triomphe consécutif à la victoire sur la Perse[11]. Héraclius se déplaça alors en Orient où il démit son frère Théodore de ses fonctions[12], conformément à la version de Théophane, mais pour d'autres motifs. Selon Théophane, Théodore fut écarté à la suite des défaites infligées par les Arabes, alors que, pour Nicéphore, ce sont les critiques lancées contre Héraclius et son mariage impie avec Martine qui étaient en cause et qui équivalaient en fait à un crime de lèse-majesté. C'est d'ailleurs bien comme un rebelle que Théodore fut puni et non pas comme un général vaincu, puisqu'il subit un déshonneur public et une peine d'emprisonnement.

Chez Nicéphore, c'est à ce moment qu'intervient l'épisode de la mort de Serge[13] « ὁ κατὰ Νικήταν » que les Arabes jugeaient responsable de la rupture d'un accord commercial. Nicéphore fournit ainsi une version intéressante et originale de la cause du conflit[14] : à la demande de Serge qui avait l'oreille de l'empereur, les marchands

---

[10] Théophane, pp. 337, 27-338-6. En 633/634 selon Théophane.

[11] C. Mango éd. et trad., *Nikephoros Patriarch of Constantinople*, *Short history*, CFHB 13 (Washington DC, 1990) [= Nicéphore], §19, p. 66,1-6.

[12] Nicéphore, §20, p. 68,1-9.

[13] *PLRE* IIIB, pp. 1134-1135, « Sergius 43 ».

[14] L'historiographie retient plus souvent la tradition rapportée par Théophane, pp. 335, 25-336, 3, selon laquelle les *foederati* arabes, gardant la frontière du désert, ne furent pas payés par le trésor impérial et qu'ils dirigèrent alors les pillages des tribus arabes du désert.

arabes n'eurent plus le droit de venir commercer dans l'Empire et furent donc privés des trente livres d'or annuelles qu'ils retiraient de leur activité[15]. Michel le Syrien mentionne également un Serge patrice dans le cadre de la première défaite byzantine face aux Arabes en janvier 634, qui est sans doute identique au Serge mentionné par Nicéphore. Cyril Mango[16] préfère écarter l'identification de ces deux mentions de Serge, parce qu'une tradition[17] rapporte la mise à mort du général Serge à l'issue de la première défaite byzantine face aux Arabes. Mais en fait, il apparaît clairement que Nicéphore a brouillé la séquence chronologique et placé par erreur la notice sur la mort de Serge au milieu des préparatifs de la troisième bataille arabo-byzantine. De fait, cet épisode est complètement autonome dans la narration et ne s'insère pas dans le fil du récit. Dans le *Breviarium* de Nicéphore, apparaît une confusion chronologique due à l'homonymie du frère de l'empereur et du sacellaire. Tout le passage qui s'étend du châtiment de Serge aux velléités séditieuses de l'armée d'Orient a été décalé par Nicéphore et se révèle donc antérieur à la nomination en Orient du sacellaire Théodore « Trithyrios » : il renvoie aux deux défaites byzantines antérieures à la défaite de Yarmouk. Du coup, l'identification des diverses occurrences de Serge est sûre et l'attribution des troubles de l'armée d'Orient, difficilement

---

[15] Nicéphore, §20, p. 68, 11-20.

[16] Mango, *Nikephoros*, p. 187.

[17] Théophane, pp. 336,16-18 ; J.-B. Chabot éd. et trad., *Chronique de Michel le Syrien, Patriarche jacobite d'Antioche (1126-1199)*, vol. II (Paris 1899-1910) [= Michel le Syrien II], p. 413 ; E.A.W. Budge éd. et trad., *The Chronography of Abu'l Faraj, the son of Aaron, the Hebrew physician commonly known as Bar Hebraeus* (Oxford, 1932) [= Bar Hebraeus], p. 93 ; V. Déroche éd. et trad., « Doctrina Jacobi nuper baptizati », *Travaux et Mémoires* 11, 1991 [= *Doctrina Iacobi*], p. 209, l. 4. Cette dernière source fournirait, selon Mango, un *terminus ante quem* pour la mort de Serge en juillet 634, date prétendue de la rédaction du document. Mais il semblerait que la *Doctrina* ait en fait été composée au début des années 640, ce qui invalide l'argument de Mango. En outre, cette bataille et donc la mort de Serge aurait eu lieu en 633 selon Donner, *Islamic Conquests*, pp. 115-116 et n. 132-133, mais en janvier 634 selon A.D. Beihammer, *Nachrichten zum Byzantinischen Urkundenwesen in Arabischen Quellen (565-811)* (Bonn, 2000) [= Beihammer, *Arabischen Quellen*], §53, p. 73-74.

imputables à l'eunuque Théodore, renvoie certainement au frère de l'empereur, comme le soulignent les variantes de Théophane et de Michel le Syrien.

Dans tous les cas, l'identification entre les deux mentions de Serge prime sur les contradictions apparentes concernant sa mort en janvier 634[18] et semble d'autant plus probable qu'il s'agit, dans toutes les sources, du gouverneur de la région[19], officiellement *dux Palaestinae*, responsable à la fois des affaires civiles et militaires et du déclenchement du conflit. Son rang élevé est attesté par sa capacité d'influence sur les décisions impériales et par le surnom « ὁ κατὰ Νικήταν[20] » qui le rattache à un membre de la famille impériale, le cousin germain de l'empereur, Nicétas. Cette tournure[21], en effet, désigne un lien de dépendance, lié à la parenté ou au service. Elle place le dignitaire Serge dans un contexte aristocratique caractéristique qui permet d'écarter l'hypothèse d'un officier militaire de rang subalterne. Cette position importante est encore confirmée par le titre de patrice que lui accorde Michel le Syrien qui désigne dans les chroniques orientales un gouverneur ou un général. Sa dignité réelle est en fait celle de candidat qui est encore, en cette première moitié du 7e siècle, une dignité importante[22].

En revanche, il faut écarter une autre identification proposée par une partie de la tradition historiographique[23]. La *Chronique de 640*[24] désigne, en effet, un général byzantin mort en février 634 comme « BRYRDN », qui pourrait être interprété soit comme Vardan, soit comme fils de « YRDN ». Par conséquent, De Goeje avait suggéré

---

[18] Beihammer, *Arabischen Quellen*, §53, pp. 73-74.

[19] A.A. Vasiliev éd. et trad., *Kitab al-'Unvan, Histoire universelle écrite par Agapius, Mahboub, de Membibdj, PO* 8-3, (Paris, 1912) [= Agapius], p. 454 : « Un patrice grec dont le nom était Serge résidait à Césarée [Palestine] et en était gouverneur pour les Grecs. »

[20] Nicéphore, §20, p. 68,11.

[21] A. Cameron, *Glotta* 56, 1978, pp. 87-94.

[22] *Doctrina Iacobi*, p. 209, trad. V. Déroche, p. 208 : « Lorsque le candidat fut tué par les Saracènes, j'étais à Césarée–me dit Abraamès … On disait : Le candidat a été tué ! Et nous les juifs, nous étions dans une grande joie. »

[23] Beihammer, *Arabischen Quellen*, §65, p. 86.

[24] A. Palmer trad., *The Seventh Century in the West-Syrian Chronicles* (Liverpool, 1993) [= Palmer, *Chronicles*], pp. 18-19, AG 945, indiction VII, le 4 février (= 4 février 634).

une identification avec le patrice Serge, alors que Hoyland préférait distinguer les deux personnages[25]. En s'appuyant sur les parallèles de la tradition arabe, notamment Al-Azdi qui précise que ce dignitaire était gouverneur d'Emèse (Hims), Kaegi[26] choisit la solution « Vardan », puisque Serge était basé à Césarée. On peut distinguer sans hésitation les deux dignitaires Serge et Vardan[27].

Ensuite, alors que Théophane voit Baanes comme le successeur du frère d'Héraclius, Théodore, dans la charge de maître des milices d'Orient, Nicéphore voit au contraire le sacellaire Théodore « Trithyrios » à cette fonction[28]. Ici, les différences entre les deux chroniqueurs s'accroissent encore, puisque Nicéphore ne mentionne pas Baanes, mais attribue au sacellaire des velléités de complot[29]. Ainsi, selon cette version, les consignes impériales d'attentisme ne furent pas respectées, car les prétendus rebelles voulaient se parer du prestige de la victoire pour renforcer leur entreprise séditieuse. La grande défaite de l'armée byzantine eut lieu, selon Nicéphore, à Gabitha, alors que Théophane disjoint la bataille de Gabitha de celle de Yarmouk et que les sources syriaques associent Gabitha à la bataille de Yarmouk[30]. Tout ce qui, chez Théophane, faisait

---

[25] De Goeje, *Syrie*, pp. 30-34, vs. R. Hoyland dans Palmer, *Chronicles*, p. 19, n. 119.

[26] Kaegi, *Islamic Conquests*, pp. 98-100.

[27] Kaegi, *Islamic Conquests*, p. 99, avance une autre identification entre les anthroponymes Vardan et Artaban attestée par les sources arabes. Or, cette identification est difficile à accepter dans la mesure où Vardan est tombé à la bataille de Datin le 4 février 634, alors qu'Artaban a participé avec Théodore, le frère d'Héraclius, à la bataille d'Ajnadayn en juillet 634.

[28] Nicéphore, §20, pp. 68, 9-10.

[29] Nicéphore, §20, pp. 68, 21-27.

[30] Voir Michel le Syrien, II, p. 420 et l'*Historia subiectionis Syriae*, trad. J.B. Chabot, *CSCO*, Scr. Syri, 3e sér. 4, 1904, p. 60, 20-21 (= trad. Palmer, p. 3,20-21). Ce que Théophane désigne comme la bataille de Gabitha renvoie en fait à celle d'Ajnadayn en juillet 634, voir Beihammer, *Arabischen Quellen*, §65, p. 86. Kaegi, *Islamic Conquests*, p. 120-121, dissocie la bataille de Gabitha (= Jabiya, Gabiya) le 23 juillet 636 perdue par Théodore « Trithyrios » de la bataille de Yarmouk le 20 août 636 ; mais selon P. Speck, *Das geteilte Dossier. Beobachtungen zu den Nachrichten über die Regierung des Kaisers Herakleios und die seiner Söhne bei Theophanes und Nikephoros* (Bonn, 1988) [= Speck, *Dossier*], pp. 172-173,

partie des caractéristiques du frère d'Héraclius, Théodore, ou de Baanes, le commandement de l'armée d'Orient et l'organisation d'un complot, est attribué au sacellaire Théodore dans la version de Nicéphore. En fait, les chroniqueurs arabes voient Baanes en activité dès l'été 635 et le considèrent comme le successeur du frère d'Héraclius[31].

Dans le *Breviarium*, la séquence des événements se poursuit avec la supervision des opérations militaires par Héraclius toujours présent en Orient et la défaite de Jean de Barkaina en Égypte. Mais, après la défaite de Marianos et la perte de l'Égypte, Héraclius revint non loin de la capitale, dans son palais de Hiereia. C'est alors qu'eut lieu, selon Nicéphore, le complot[32] de Jean-Athalaric[33] contre son père Héraclius, passé sous silence par Théophane. Nicéphore mentionne comme acolyte uniquement le magistre Théodore[34], fils du frère de l'empereur Théodore, alors que Sebēos cite un plus grand nombre de dignitaires.

---

et Beihammer, *Arabischen Quellen*, p. 86, l'*Historia subiectionis Syriae* atteste avec certitude que les deux toponymes renvoient à la même bataille.

[31] Beihammer, *Arabischen Quellen*, §89 (21 août -19 septembre 635), p. 108.

[32] Nicéphore, §24, pp. 72, 8-18. Sur le complot, voir Stratos III, p. 231, n. 24.

[33] *PLRE* IIIA, p. 706 (Ioannes 260 = Athalaricus). Ce n'est sans doute pas un hasard, si ce nom germanique, jamais attesté à Byzance, renvoie au roi des Ostrogoths entre 526 et 534 (*PLRE* II, pp. 175-176). Il est significatif pour la continuité des lignages qu'un fils d'Héraclius soit lié à cette famille royale, nécessairement par sa mère. Sur le nom, voir M. Schönfeld, *Wörterbuch der altgermanischen Personen-und Völkernamen* (Heidelberg, 1911), pp. 33-34. On peut sûrement mettre ce lien avec la famille royale ostrogothique en rapport avec Germanus 3 (*PLRE* IIIA, p. 528), né en 551 d'une lignée royale ostrogothique, sans doute le même dignitaire que Germanus 5. Il serait tentant de faire d'Athalaric un descendant de Germanus 3, sans doute son petit-fils, ce qui en ferait également un parent de l'empereur Justinien I. Etant donné la tendance pour les empereurs, relevée pour Tibère et Maurice, à s'allier aux parents de Justinien I, une union entre Héraclius et une parente de Justinien, même illégitime, est probable. Les prétentions d'Athalaric au trône impérial s'expliquent mieux encore dans ce contexte.

[34] *PLRE* IIIB, pp. 1284-1285, « Theodorus 171 ».

1.3. Michel le Syrien

Michel le Syrien présente une troisième version des premières victoires arabes : Après une défaite subie par le patrice Serge, l'empereur envoya son frère « Theodoricus » dans la région d'Antioche[35]. Outre la défaite sur laquelle toutes les sources s'accordent, Michel le Syrien rejoint Nicéphore sur les prétentions impériales de Théodore, mais dans l'intention de stigmatiser l'orgueil des chalcédoniens châtiés pour leur égarement hérétique. Théophane ne reprend pas à son compte cette version, qu'il a dû pourtant trouver dans les chroniques syriaques, alors que Nicéphore y a vu une occasion de remplacer cet épisode anti-chalcédonien par une interprétation traditionnelle, rattachant la défaite militaire aux péchés commis par l'empereur.

Chez Michel le Syrien, la troisième étape de l'affrontement arabo-byzantin en Syrie est bien Yarmouk[36]. Mais ce chroniqueur se distingue des auteurs précédents par sa mention de trois généraux byzantins : Baanes et le fils de Sahr-Varaz (Sarbarios), rejoints en 636 par le sacellaire. Dans cette version, Baanes semble être à la tête de l'armée d'Orient. Il est désigné à la fois comme général et comme patrice, ce qui peut effectivement, dans la terminologie des chroniques orientales, correspondre au titre de maître des milices d'Orient. Chez Michel le Syrien, nulle trace de complot ou de rébellion dans les troupes romaines. Il est, par ailleurs, le seul à rapporter la mort des généraux Théodore et Baanes[37].

---

[35] Michel le Syrien II, p. 418. Sur les sources arabes, auquel Michel le Syrien a eu accès, voir Kaegi, *Islamic Conquests*, p. 34, n. 23.

[36] Michel le Syrien II, pp. 420-421 : en l'an 5 d'Omar, ce qui équivaut à 638.

[37] Sur les différentes versions, plus ou moins légendaires, concernant le sort de Baanes après la bataille, voir Kaegi, *Islamic Conquests*, p. 139 et n. 74, et p. 278 et n. 93. Les sources byzantines, les seules fiables sur ce point, ne mentionnent pas le sort du général. Les sources arabes qui n'auraient pas manqué de rapporter la mort du général byzantin, sont également muettes sur ce point. Selon Eutychius, *Annales*, §279, trad. Breydy, p. 116, Vahan s'était retiré dans un monastère du Sinaï. W.E. Kaegi, *Heraclius. Emperor of Byzantium* (Cambridge, 2002) [= Kaegi, *Heraclius*], p. 244, assure, sans justification, que de toutes façons Vahan n'était pas revenu à Constantinople.

1.4. Sebēos

Enfin, une quatrième version est connue par le pseudo-Sebēos. Comme le patriarche Nicéphore, il désigne le fils d'Héraclius, Athalaric, et le magistre Théodore comme les meneurs du complot ; mais il connaît aussi les noms de certains nobles arméniens qui acceptèrent, à des degrés divers, de participer au renversement d'Héraclius, notamment Vahan Khorkhoruni, David Saharuni et Varaz-Tirots' Bagratuni, fils de Smbat. Cet épisode n'est relaté que par Nicéphore et Sebēos, mais selon une chronologie différente, puisque Sebēos place le complot d'Athalaric avant la bataille de Yarmouk.

Le pseudo-Sebēos s'accorde avec les autres sources pour mentionner deux batailles entre les armées arabes et byzantines avant celle de Yarmouk. L'une dirigée par un patrice qui y trouva la mort, le patrice Serge de Michel le Syrien, l'autre par le frère de l'empereur.

Le chiffre de 70 000 hommes dans l'armée byzantine à Yarmouk rejoint celui donné par Michel le Syrien, mais pour l'essentiel, la version de Sebēos est proche de celle de Nicéphore. Il ignore, en effet, l'existence de Baanes et ne connaît qu'un général, un eunuque d'Héraclius, donc le sacellaire Théodore. Il rejoint encore Nicéphore sur la consigne impériale de ne pas attaquer, mais d'attendre les renforts. Toutefois, l'attaque byzantine, contraire à l'ordre impérial, n'est pas attribuée chez Sebēos au désir d'usurpation du sacellaire.

Enfin, selon le pseudo-Sebēos, Varaz-Tirots‘ Bagratuni et Vahan Khorkhoruni furent réhabilités sous le règne de Constant II, après la mise à l'écart de Valentinos et la nomination de Théodore « l'Arménien » à la succession de Valentinos, sans doute comme maître des milices en 643[38].

2. Synthèse sur les troubles de 636-637

2.1. Les complots de 636 et 637

Pour résumer, Sebēos et Nicéphore mentionnent le complot d'Athalaric, alors que Théophane et Michel le Syrien n'y font pas référence. Nicéphore et Michel le Syrien évoquent une volonté d'usurpation chez le frère d'Héraclius, Théodore, alors maître des

---

[38] Robert W. Thomson trad., *The Armenian History attributed to Sebēos*, vol. I (Liverpool, 1999) [= Sebēos I], §143, p. 107.

milices d'Orient. Nicéphore est le seul à évoquer aussi des menées séditieuses de la part du sacellaire Théodore, alors que Théophane, de son côté, est le seul à rapporter la proclamation de Baanes comme empereur par l'armée d'Orient.

Nicéphore rapporte donc trois menées séditieuses, alors que Théophane, Sebēos et Michel le Syrien n'en mentionnent qu'une seule, mais différente pour chacun des chroniqueurs : Théophane, celle de Baanes ; Michel le Syrien, celle du frère d'Héraclius ; et pour Sebēos, celle d'Athalaric. Quant à Nicéphore, la seule tentative de rébellion qu'il ne rapporte pas est celle de Baanes, mais, il rapporte bien celle d'Athalaric et du frère d'Héraclius et en ajoute même une autre, inconnue par ailleurs, celle de l'eunuque Théodore, pourtant bien incapable d'avoir la moindre prétention impériale.

En fait, il semble bien qu'il y ait eu confusion à plusieurs niveaux. Une première source de confusion tient à l'homonymie des deux Théodores[39], le frère d'Héraclius et l'eunuque sacellaire, qui a contaminé les sources sur lesquelles s'appuie Nicéphore, en transférant le désir d'usurpation du frère d'Héraclius vers le sacellaire et qui, du coup, a décalé également la notice concernant la mort de Serge.

Une seconde source de confusion tient à la figure de Baanes[40], qui pouvait difficilement être impliqué à la fois dans les deux complots rapportés par la tradition historiographique, celui d'Athalaric et celui de l'armée d'Orient à Yarmouk. Nicéphore a choisi de conserver l'épisode du complot d'Athalaric, par conséquent, il ne pouvait attribuer à Baanes les troubles de l'armée d'Orient et supprime donc le dignitaire de son récit, transférant à Théodore les attributs de Baanes, notamment le titre de maître des

---

[39] Sur cette confusion qui a touché les deux batailles qu'ont dirigées les deux Théodores, celle d'Ajnadayn de juillet 634 et celle de Yarmouk en août 636, voir Beihammer, *Arabischen Quellen*, §65, pp. 85-86. Cette homonymie a semé la confusion dans les sources anciennes, mais aussi dans la littérature moderne. Voir Kaegi, *Islamic Conquests*, p. 67 : en août 636, les opérations militaires sont conduites par Vahan et Théodore, frère d'Héraclius, selon Kaegi, au lieu du sacellaire. Kaegi lui-même identifie correctement les deux Théodores à la p. 100.

[40] Sur ce dignitaire, voir W.E. Kaegi, *Byzantine Military Unrest. 471-843. An Interpretation* (Amsterdam, 1981) [= Kaegi, *Military Unrest*], p. 150-151 ; *PLRE* IIIA, p. 161, « Baanes ».

milices d'Orient. Théophane a choisi la solution inverse qui consistait à attribuer les désordres de l'armée d'Orient à Baanes, mais à passer sous silence le complot d'Athalaric. En fait, Baanes exerça certainement la charge de maître des milices d'Orient[41] plutôt que d'Arménie, puisque Mzez Gnuni semble occuper les fonctions de prince d'Arménie et Georges, celles de maître des milices d'Arménie à la même époque. Un argument supplémentaire tient à l'accusation calomnieuse de rébellion lancée contre Baanes, sans doute après sa participation au complot d'Athalaric. Baanes ne pouvait être accusé d'avoir été proclamé empereur par son armée que s'il était un officier byzantin dirigeant des troupes byzantines, et non arméniennes. Enfin, les sources arabes sont unanimes pour dire qu'Héraclius a confié le commandement-en-chef des troupes byzantines à Baanes qui exerçait donc sûrement la charge de maître des milices d'Orient[42].

L'identification entre Vahan Khorkhoruni, impliqué dans le complot d'Athalaric, et Baanes, maître des milices d'Orient en 636, n'a encore jamais été tentée. Cette identification est très probable du fait de la présence de ce dignitaire dans l'état-major impérial depuis la guerre perse des années 620 où Baanes est attesté en décembre 627 comme maître des milices[43], puis à nouveau parmi les généraux byzantins[44] confiés à Sahr-Varaz pour sa rébellion contre Artasir III en 629/630. Par ailleurs, aucun autre Baanes n'est attesté sous le règne d'Héraclius. Enfin, à ce niveau élevé de responsabilités, la probabilité d'une homonymie est très faible.

---

[41] Kaegi, *Islamic Conquests*, p. 119, voit en Théodore le maître des milices d'Orient et en Vahan le commandant-en-chef. Cette interprération est contradictoire, car si Vahan est commandant-en-chef, il exerce bien la charge de maître des milices d'Orient. Quant à Théodore, envoyé spécialement de la capitale, il supervise certainement des contingents de l'*Obsequium*, venus en soutien. Il a d'ailleurs modifié son analyse dans Kaegi, *Heraclius*, p. 242 : Vahan y est désormais considéré comme maître des milices d'Orient.

[42] Beihammer, *Arabischen Quellen*, §97 (début 636, Antioche), pp. 122-126, et §103, p. 133.

[43] Théophane, p. 318,4.

[44] J.-P. Mahé, « Critical Remarks on the newly edited Excerpts from Sebēos », dans *Medieval Armenian Culture*, T. Samuelian et M. Stone, éds., (Chico, Cal. 1983), pp. 218-239, pp. 225-226 et 231.

Cette identification permet de résoudre un certain nombre de problèmes chronologiques. Elle permet d'abord de donner raison à Nicéphore contre Sebēos sur la question de la chronologie, en plaçant le complot après la bataille de Yarmouk d'août 636[45]. De fait, il aurait été impossible de nommer Baanes au poste de maître des milices d'Orient après sa participation à un complot contre l'empereur. La séquence chronologique inverse permet au contraire de donner un sens à la participation de Baanes au complot d'Athalaric, puisqu'il tentait d'échapper ainsi à une disgrâce certaine, consécutive à sa grave défaite militaire. La date de 636/637 est confirmée également par un autre biais [46] ; Théodore Rshtuni fut nommé prince d'Arménie au cours de l'hiver 640/641; or, David Saharuni, qui participa au complot d'Athalaric, avait occupé pendant trois ans cette fonction avant Théodore. Ces données chronologiques permettent de placer la nomination de David vers la fin de l'année 637 et le complot entre la fin de l'année 636 et le début de 637.

L'identification de Vahan Khorkhoruni avec le général de 636[47] permet, enfin, de clarifier le tableau confus que présentent les chroniqueurs sur les complots de ces années. Elle contribue à écarter du maître des milices Baanes les accusations[48] de révolte au cours de la campagne de Syrie, puisque, dans ce cas, le même dignitaire n'aurait pu participer tranquillement au complot d'Athalaric dans la capitale entre la fin de 636 et le début de 637. Comme cette accusation ne peut pas concerner davantage l'eunuque Théodore,

---

[45] Sur la chronologie, voir Kaegi, *Islamic Conquests*, p. 67 ; Howard-Johnston, *Sebēos*, pp. 240-242 ; Palmer, *Chronicles*, p. xlix : la première défaite byzantine eut lieu le 4 février 634, près de Gaza (*Chronique de 724*, pp. 18-19) ; la seconde à la fin de 634, à l'est de la Mer Morte (Sebēos, trad. Thomson, §136-137, pp. 96-99) ; la troisième qui conduisit à l'occupation de la Palestine en 635 (Sebēos) et de la Syrie en 636 (*Chronique de 724*).

[46] Howard-Johnston, dans Sebēos, vol. II, p. 229.

[47] Stratos II, p. 209, rassemble toutes les traditions concernant le nom du général byzantin de 636. La *PLRE* mentionne le Baanes de Yarmouk (*PLRE* IIIA, p. 161, « Baanes »), mais pas le Vahan Khorkhoruni de Sebēos.

[48] Sur ces accusations de même nature que celles lancées contre les contingents arméniens lors de la bataille de Mantzikert, voir Kaegi, *Islamic Conquests*, pp. 120, 133 et 186 qui ne croit plus à la révolte de Vahan à Yarmouk, alors que dans Id, *Military Unrest*, pp. 149-151, il analyse les causes de la révolte de Vahan en 636.

elle renvoie nécessairement au frère d'Héraclius, Théodore. Toutes les références aux troubles de l'armée d'Orient, imputées chez Nicéphore au sacellaire Théodore et chez Théophane au maître des milices Baanes, s'appliquent en fait au frère d'Héraclius, qui fut d'ailleurs sanctionné pour crime de lèse-majesté[49].

L'emprisonnement de Théodore explique d'ailleurs bien son absence du complot d'Athalaric où son fils, le magistre Théodore, fut pourtant impliqué et renforce encore la probabilité de la séquence chronologique plaçant la bataille de Yarmouk avant le complot d'Athalaric, puisque la punition du père précède certainement le complot du fils.

La probabilité d'une identification des diverses mentions de Baanes est encore renforcée par la place qu'il occupe dans la liste des complices, cités par Sebēos, du projet séditieux d'Athalaric. Sont cités, en effet, dans l'ordre le magistre Théodore, un groupe de hauts dignitaires de la capitale puis Vahan Khorkhoruni. Les autres nobles arméniens, comme Varaz-Tirots' Bagratuni ou David Saharuni, sont mentionnés à part. Ainsi, deux groupes se dessinent nettement, un groupe de hauts dignitaires impériaux impliqués dans les affaires de l'État et, par ailleurs, quelques nobles arméniens qui servaient dans l'armée impériale et qui, à ce titre, étaient présents dans la capitale et participèrent au complot. Cette image des complices du complot d'Athalaric correspond bien à l'influence réelle exercée par Baanes au sein de l'appareil dirigeant de l'Empire. Occupant, en effet, la charge de maître des milices d'Orient, il se rangeait bien au niveau des plus grands personnages de l'État.

Les informations prosopographiques livrées par Sebēos permettent de cerner un peu mieux le contexte politique du complot de 636/637. Elles permettent de distinguer un groupe d'officiers écartés du premier cercle du pouvoir impérial ou menacés de disgrâce à des degrés divers. Ainsi, le fils naturel d'Héraclius, Jean-

---

[49] Cette rébellion de l'armée doit en effet être surtout liée au contexte financier désastreux qui entraîne un règlement irrégulier de la solde militaire dont témoignent plusieurs sources (notamment Théophane, pp. 335, 25-336, 3), mais aussi à la crise de légitimité que rencontre Héraclius à cause de son mariage impopulaire qui a pu être interprété par les clercs comme la cause principale des défaites de l'Empire (Nicéphore, §20, p. 68, 4-7).

Athalaric, pourtant de lignée royale, fut éloigné de la succession impériale qui devait revenir à Constantin III, puis à Heraklônas, le fils de Martine. La mise à l'écart d'Athalaric est encore soulignée par son envoi comme otage chez les Avars en 622[50]. L'implication du magistre Théodore peut s'expliquer, quant à elle, par le déshonneur public qui avait frappé son père, accusé de vouloir usurper le trône, quelques années plus tôt, à la suite de sa défaite face aux Arabes. Directement ou indirectement, on relève à des places de choix, parmi les comploteurs de 636/637, les deux grands généraux vaincus des années précédentes, Baanes et le frère d'Héraclius, Théodore, par l'intermédiaire de son fils Théodore magistre, qui exercèrent successivement la responsabilité décisive de maître des milices d'Orient face à l'expansion arabe en Syrie. Ce complot était donc lié aux récents événements militaires et à la crise de légitimité que rencontrait l'empereur, non seulement dans la population, mais aussi et surtout dans le groupe dirigeant. Les soubresauts politiques des années suivantes ne peuvent que confirmer ce diagnostic.

2.2. Présence de la famille des Khorkhoruni à Byzance

La carrière de Vahan ne prit pas fin à cette époque, puisque Sebēos mentionne son retour en grâce, en même temps que Varaz-Tirots' Bagratuni exilé en Afrique, après la mise à l'écart de Valentinos au profit de Théodore « l'Arménien », comme maître des milices, au début du règne de Constant II. Au moment où ce dernier devait se séparer des officiers qui l'avaient soutenu face à Martine lors son ascension politique en 641, il chercha de nouveaux soutiens du côté des rebelles de 637.

L'identification permet enfin de cerner plus précisément l'origine sociale du maître des milices d'Orient de 636. Les Khorkhoruni sont, en effet, un des anciens lignages de la noblesse arménienne[51]. Ils jouissaient certainement d'un prestige égal aux plus

---

[50] Nicéphore, §13, 4-6, p. 58.

[51] Sur cette famille, voir C. Toumanoff, *Studies in Christian Caucasian History* (Washington, DC, 1963) [= Toumanoff, *Caucasian History*], pp. 208-209 ; Garsoïan N., *The Epic Histories Attributed to P'awstos Buzand* (*Buzandaran Patmutiwnk'*) (Cambridge, Mass., 1989), p. 429 ; H. Acharean, *Hayots' Andznannuneri Bararan*, 5 vol., (Erevan 1942-1962), n° 31 ; Garitte G., *Documents pour l'histoire du livre d'Agathange*, Studi e

grandes familles, comme les Mamikonean ou les Bagratides. De fait, leur rang, attestée par le *Gahnamak*[52], les place au quatrième rang des grandes familles, entre les Arcruni et les Mamikonean. Si l'on met de côté les marches[53] du royaume d'Arménie qui s'en détachent et manifestent leur autonomie, on peut mettre au rang des grandes principautés centrales, celles des Mamikonean, des Bagratuni, des Mardpets, des Artsruni, des Kamsarakan et des Khorkhoruni[54]. Ceux-ci comptent donc au nombre des plus grands princes régionaux dont le contingent militaire n'était pas négligeable : la *Liste Militaire*[55] leur attribue ainsi l'obligation de fournir mille cavaliers pour la défense de la frontière occidentale du royaume. En termes de puissance militaire, on compte vingt-quatre familles qui fournissent un contingent égal ou supérieur à celui des Khorkhoruni. Les domaines de la famille étaient situés dans la région du Turuberan, dans la vallée de l'Arsanias, au Nord-Ouest du lac de Van[56], dans un secteur où les bonnes relations avec Byzance étaient nécessaires à la survie du clan. Comme les Saharuni, leur bonne relation avec Byzance valut d'ailleurs aux Khorkhoruni leur disparition de l'Arménie arabe en tant que lignage.

Leur présence à Byzance à la fin du règne d'Héraclius témoigne sans doute d'une implication importante en faveur des intérêts impériaux, par rapport aux autres membres de la noblesse arménienne. C'est peut-être cet engagement qui entraîna la confiscation de leurs domaines et leur disparition en Arménie arabe, ainsi que l'entrée complète de ce clan dans les rangs de l'administration impériale. De fait, deux membres de cette famille

---

testi n° 127 (Vatican, 1946), pp. 223, 239 ; Hübschmann H., *Die altarmenische Ortsnamen* (Strasbourg, 1904), pp. 330, 435.

[52] Adontz N., *Armenia in the Period of Justinian*, Lisbonne 1970 [= Adontz, *Justinian*], pp. 191 et 67*. Les Khorkhoruni portent le titre de Malxaz qui les désigne souvent dans les sources arméniennes. Sur l'étymologie de ce mot qui signifie « roi » en assyrien et qui atteste l'ancienneté de cette famille, voir Justi F., *Iranisches Namenbuch* (Marburg, 1895), pp. 188-189 ; Adontz, *Justinian*, pp. 311 et 321.

[53] On peut placer dans cette catégorie notamment les principautés du Siwnik', de Mokk', de Tayk' et de Tsopk' (Sophène).

[54] Adontz, *Justinian*, p. 344.

[55] Ibid., pp. 193 et 68*.

[56] Toumanoff, *Caucasian History*, p. 209.

avaient servi l'Empire une génération avant Baanes, Atat[57] en Thrace sous le règne de Maurice et Théodose[58] en Arménie sous le règne de Phocas. Quelle que soit la nature exacte de leur parenté, Baanes est issu d'un lignage qui connaissait une tradition de service dans l'Empire et qui avait déjà été honoré de charges et de dignités par l'empereur.

Dans ce contexte, la haute charge de maître des milices d'Orient exercée par Baanes prend un sens particulier. Elle révèle que ce dignitaire n'avait pas été propulsé à la tête du corps d'armée le plus prestigieux de l'Empire par ses seuls mérites, mais qu'il devait cette faveur à la familiarité de son clan avec les cercles dirigeants. Cette familiarité cultivée par le clan Khorkhoruni avec l'aristocratie byzantine, depuis deux ou trois générations au moins, et redoublée peut-être par des liens de mariage qui nous échappent, valut finalement à Baanes la faveur insigne d'occuper la charge de maître des milices d'Orient. La direction des opérations militaires à Yarmouk, conjointement avec le sacellaire Théodore, mais aussi la participation au complot d'Athalaric constituent à cet égard autant d'indices d'une entrée réelle dans le premier cercle du pouvoir.

---

[57] Sur ce dignitaire, voir Sebēos I, pp. 31-33, 53-56 ; *PLRE* IIIA, p. 140, « Atat Khorkhoruni ». Sous le règne de Maurice se produit une tentative d'unité des princes arméniens : ils s'emparèrent de la caisse d'un officier fiscal perse (Sebēos I [87], p. 32). Mais après des manœuvres d'intimidation conjointes des troupes byzantines et perses, Mamak Mamikonean, Kotit Amatunik' et Step'anos Siwni, dont les domaines se trouvaient en Persarménie, se soumirent au souverain perse. Inversement, Atat Khorkhoruni et Samuel Vahewuni, dont les domaines se situent à l'ouest du lac de Van, se soumettent à l'empereur (Sebēos I [88], p. 33). Atat Khorkhoruni fut même spécialement comblé d'honneurs et reçut une mission en Thrace (Sebēos I [88], p. 34). Un an avant la mort de Maurice, Atat, honoré d'une haute charge ou dignité impériale, fut à nouveau envoyé en Thrace, mais il décida de passer du côté perse (Sebēos I [104], p. 55). Après l'arrivée au pouvoir de Phocas, il chercha à regagner les territoires byzantins et fut mis à mort par Khosrov (Sebēos I [105], p. 56).

[58] Sur ce dignitaire, voir *PLRE* IIIB, pp. 1297-1298, « Theodos 38 Khorkhoruni ». Sous le règne de Phocas, un autre membre du clan Khorkhoruni, Théodose, dirigea une armée byzantine et subit une défaite face à l'armée perse près de la rivière de l'Aratsani. Il fut fait prisonnier et fut exécuté en Perse (Sebēos [109], trad. Thomson, pp. 60-62).

La hiérarchie ecclésiastique arménienne au Proche-Orient et dans les Balkans : la mention des évêchés arméniens de l'Empire byzantin dans la *Racine de la foi* d'Anania de Narek

Gérard Dédéyan

Nous voulons ici mettre en évidence les informations de première importance qu'Anania, abbé du couvent de Narek, oncle maternel de Grigor et auteur d'une *Réfutation des Thondrakiens* commandée par le catholicos Anania de Mokk'[1], nous fournit à propos de l'extension de la hiérarchie arménienne à l'intérieur des frontières de l'Empire byzantin, dans son ouvrage la *Racine de la foi*, réfutation du chalcédonisme dédiée au catholicos Khach'ik Ier Arsharuni (971-992), qu'il vint personnellement lui remettre à la résidence patriarcale d'Argina, durant l'été 980 (ou 987 ?)[2]. Nous ne sommes plus, comme le souligne Jean-Pierre Mahé, à l'âge de la tolérance dans les relations interecclésiales arméno-byzantines, inauguré par le catholicos Zak'aria de Jagk' et le patriarche Photios, à l'issue du concile de Shirakawan (862)[3]. La lutte contre les *cayt'*, les « déficients », c'est-à-dire les Arméniens chalcédoniens, bat son plein : Anania remet la *Racine de la foi* à Khach'ik Ier le jour même

---

[1] Annie et Jean-Pierre Mahé dans *Grégoire de Narek*, *Tragédie. Matean oghbergut'ean. Le Livre de Lamentation*, Introduction, traduction et notes par Annie et Jean-Pierre Mahé, *CSCO*, vol. 584, t. 106 (Louvain : Peeters, 2000) (dorénavant *Narek*), pp. 54-56.

[2] Id., Ibid., pp. 57-58.

[3] Id., Ibid., p. 56. Sur ce concile Igor Dorfmann-Lazarev, *Arméniens et Byzantins à l'époque de Photius* : *deux débats théologiques après le triomphe de l'orthodoxie*, *CORPUSCO*, vol. 609, *Subsidia*, T. 117 (Louvain : Peeters, 2004), n. 26.

où Uxt'anēs décide d'écrire un ouvrage relatif à la rupture religieuse entre Arméniens et Géorgiens[4].

Mais nous ne pensons pas que l'installation de hiérarchies non chalcédoniennes à l'intérieur des frontières de l'Empire byzantin, fait sans précédent[5], ait pu être réalisée sans l'aval des autorités de Constantinople, Khach'ik Ier n'étant assurément pas en mesure d'imposer de telles dispositions.

En effet, si, du côté arménien, on observe un raidissement au plan doctrinal et disciplinaire (la hiérarchie estime indispensable de baptiser une deuxième fois les *cayt'* qui rallieront l'Église arménienne)[6], les empereurs macédoniens, bon gré, malgré, inaugurent alors une période de tolérance religieuse due à la présence croissante d'Arméniens à Byzance, d'une part à la suite de l'annexion de territoires arméniens (la principauté de Tarōn en 968, le royaume de Vaspurakan en 1022, d'autre part et surtout en raison de la politique de colonisation conduite dans les territoires (Crète, Chypre, Cilicie, Syrie et Mésopotamie du Nord) soustraits aux Arabes lors de la Reconquête byzantine (de 950, date de la première intervention des Phokas, à 1031, date de la prise d'Édesse par Georges Maniakès): dans ces territoires, vidés de leur population musulmane à la suite de déplacements forcés ou de massacres, la colonisation a un caractère militaire, avec l'installation, assez généralisée, de garnisons arméniennes, et un caractère civil, avec l'organisation d'une immigration – à des fins de réactivation économique, et principalement en Euphratèse, autour de Mélitène -, de Syriaques jacobites. Le rôle des Arméniens est assez décisif pour que la zone-frontière ainsi délimitée soit organisée, suivant la terminologie administrative byzantine (le terme de thème s'appliquant d'abord à un contingent de soldats, puis au territoire du recrutement de contingent), en « petits thèmes arméniens »[7], par

---

4 Mahé, *Narek*, p. 58.

5 L'empereur Maurice (582-602), après la rétrocession d'une partie importante de l'Arménie par le souverain perse Chosroès, en 591, y installe une hiérarchie arménienne chalcédonienne placée sous l'autorité d'un anticatholicos chalcédonien.

6 Mahé, *Narek*, pp. 56-57.

7 Sur les *mikra armènika thèmata*, cf. Nicolas Oikonomides, « L'organisation de la frontière orientale de Byzance aux X°-XI° siècles et le Taktikon de l'Escorial », dans *idem, Documents et Études sur les*

opposition aux « grands thèmes romains » d'Asie Mineure ou des Balkans.

Pour fixer ces immigrants hétérodoxes, garants de la sécurité et du développement des marches orientales de Byzance, les autorités de Constantinople sont amenées à autoriser l'installation des hiérarchies arménienne et syriaque jacobite à l'intérieur même des frontières de l'Empire[8]. De fait, dans la période d'expansion de Byzance, depuis Nicéphore Phokas (963-969) jusqu'à Constantin VIII (1025-1028), principalement aux dépens du *Dār al-Islām*, c'est plutôt la tolérance qui a dominé, de la part des autorités centrales et, à défaut, de la part des autorités locales, les minorités dans l'Empire étant devenues « majorités régionales », comme l'a montré Gilbert Dagron[9].

Rappelons, avec Jean-Pierre Mahé, que le texte de la *Racine de la foi*, longtemps considéré comme perdu, a été presque entièrement conservé, avec diverses additions, dans la compilation d'Anania de Sanahin, composée sur l'ordre du catholicos Petros Ier Getadarts' (1019-1058)[10]. Anania de Narek passe en revue toutes les régions et provinces comptant, selon lui, des diocèses arméniens et pour lesquels l'Église arménienne a consacré des évêques : « Il est absolument évident que ceux de notre peuple qui ne se trouvent pas sous leur autorité [celle des Grecs] n'ont pas accepté la foi de Chalcédoine, ce que prouve le nombre de provinces dépendant de

---

institutions de Byzance, VII°-XV° siècles, Variorum Reprint, (Londres, 1976), ch. 24.

8 Sur la politique byzantine d'immigration arménienne au Proche-Orient, nous nous permettons de renvoyer, entre autres, à notre article « Le rôle des Arméniens en Syrie du Nord pendant la Reconquête byzantine (vers 945-1031)» dans Astérios Argyriou, Catherine Otten, Pierre Racine (dir.), *Byzance et l'Asie*, 7° Symposium Byzantinon, Strasbourg (8 déc. 1997), *Byzantinische Forschungen* (Amsterdam : Hakkert, 1999), pp. 249-284.

9 Nous renvoyons à son article « Minorités ethniques et religieuses dans l'Orient byzantin à la fin du X° siècle et au XI° siècle : l'immigration syrienne », dans *Travaux et Mémoires du Centre d'Histoire et de Civilisation de Byzance*, t. 6 (Paris, 1976) (dorénavant Dagron, « Minorités »), pp. 177-216 ; voir, du même, dans Jean-Marie Mayeur (dir.), *Histoire du christianisme*, t. IV, Gilbert Dagron (dir.), *Evêques, moines et empereurs (650-1054)*, ch. V, « Le temps des changements, fin X°-milieu XI° siècle », pp. 333-337.

10 Mahé, *Narek*, p. 57, n. 223.

nous qui n'acceptent pas, jusqu'à aujourd'hui, la foi de ceux-ci. Quant à ceux qui sont sous leur autorité [celle des Grecs], ne sont-ils pas nombreux à recevoir, non pas la foi de ceux-ci, mais la nôtre ? Et vois, combien il y a d'évêques, sous notre autorité, à l'intérieur des terres, à savoir en Asie et dans le *Gamirk'* [Cappadoce au sens large], en Bithynie, en Galatie, en Asie Propre, en Isaurie, en *Liwstria*, en Cilicie et à Tarsus, en Mésopotamie, en Phrygie, et dans toute la Syrie, ainsi que dans le *Gamirk'* et à Gangra, et près du Pont, et de l'autre côté » [de la mer] à T'arsis et en Macédoine ; et quant à ceux qui sont sous votre autorité n'y a-t-il pas là parmi eux de nombreux évêques consacrés par les Arméniens, qui restent fermes dans la foi en la vérité, puisque ne s'étant pas détournés des trois saints conciles de Nicée, Constantinople et Éphèse, ancrés dans la foi définie par saint Grégoire ? »[11].

Quelques remarques préalables doivent être faites à propos de certains noms ici mentionnés : *mējerkreays* doit être substitué à *i mēj erkrē aysd*, le mot *erkreay* équivalant au grec *mesogaios,* « qui est à l'intérieur des terres »[12]. Des erreurs ou des maladresses du compilateur ou du scribe sont à signaler. *Gamirk'*–le pays de Gomer, fils de Japhet, nom arménien de la Cappadoce - est cité deux fois ;[13] certains noms sont mal lus : après la locution *yayn koys*, « de l'autre côté [du bras de mer] et associé à *Makedonia*, le mot *T'arsis* (repris du Psaume 71, annonçant la venue du Messie, « les rois de Tarsis et des îles/ apporteront des présents » ?) n'a rien à voir avec la Tarse cilicienne – déjà mentionnée plus haut sous le nom de *Tarsus*, mais est une mauvaise lecture pour *T'rakia*, la Thrace ; nous traduisons

---

[11] Cité par Hratch T'amrazyan, *Anania de Narek, sa vie et son oeuvre* (en arm.), (Erevan : Editions de l'Académie des Sciences d'Arménie, 1986), pp. 144-145, en partie traduit dans Mahé*, Narek*, p. 58.

[12] Lecture rectifiée par J.-P. Mahé. Cf. aussi *Nor bargirk' haykazean lezui*, t. 2 (Venise, 1837), p. 259. *Mesogaios* équivaut à *mediterraneus.* Il semble que J.-P. Mahé traduise *mējerkreay* par « Anatolie ».

[13] Postérieurement, l'appelation de *Kapadovkia* désigne la Cappadoce proprement dite (i.-e. Première Arménie), avec Césarée pour capitale ; celle de *Gamirk'* désigne, plus largement, « toute la contrée renfermée entre l'Euphrate, à l'est, le Pont, au nord, la Phrygie et la Galatie, à l'ouest, et le Taurus cilicien, au sud » ; cf. Édouard Dulaurier, *Recueil des Historiens des Croisades, publié par l'Académie des Inscriptions et Belles-Lettres*, *Documents arméniens*, t. 1 (Paris, 1869) (dorénavant *DA* I), p. 59, n.1, et p. 576, n.1.

Mijagedk' par son équivalent exact, « Mésopotamie », *Asorik'*, par « Syrie », *Sōnay* par « Isaurie».

Il semble que l'auteur suive–au moins de loin– l'*Ashkharhats'oyts'* dans sa version longue, sans pour autant chercher consciemment à faire coïncider les provinces énumérées avec celles de cette « Description du monde », composée au V° siècle et attribuée à l'historien Movsēs de Khoren, ou au tournant du VII° siècle et attribuée soit au même Movsēs, soit au mathématicien Anania de Chirak [14] : il cite d'abord l'Asie dans l'acception large du terme, l'appelant, comme *Ashkharhats'oyts'mējerkrayk* « Milieu des terres » [15] ; puis il énumère certaines provinces, en excluant d'autres, comme celles qui constituent l'Arménie elle-même, puisqu'il a déjà pris celle-ci en considération, ou celles (par exemple l'Arabie, la Sarmatie) d'où le christianisme – en tout cas sous sa forme arménienne – est absent, cette énumération étant effectuée plus ou moins dans l'ordre de l' *Ashkharhats'oyts'* (à l'exception de *Gamirk'*, cité ici en premier) : la Bithynie, la Galatie, l'Asie Propre, (ou l' *Ashkharhats'oyts'* situe Éphèse, Smyrne, Pergame, Tralles) ; puis, après l'Isaurie (*Sawṙeay*), est mentionnée *Liwstria*, peut-être Lystra, en Lycaonie (entre la Phrygie et la Cappadoce) ; on passe ensuite (après la Cilicie et Tarse, et la Mésopotamie) à la Phrygie, et (après la Syrie), au *Gamirk'* – à nouveau – et à Gangra (ville mentionnée par l' *Ashkharhats'oyts'* avec la Paphlagonie). C'est dans ce passage que l'auteur de l' *Ashkharhats'oyts'*, parlant de la Paphlagonie, la situe *aù eri covun Pontosi*, « près de la mer du Pont »[16], phrase qu'Anania de Narek (ou son compilateur) emploie lui aussi, après avoir mentionné Gangra.

L'impressionnante liste d'évêchés arméniens livrée par la *Racine de la foi* pourrait donc pâtir d'une amplification littéraire due à une connaissance un peu anarchique, mais réelle, de l' *Ashkharhats'oyts'*,

---

[14] Sur cette oeuvre, on consultera Babken Harut'yunyan, *L'Ashkharhats'oyts' et le problème des quatre Arménies* (en arm.), (Erevan, 1997), et Robert H. Hewsen, *The Geography of Anania of Shirak (Ashkharhats'oyts')* (Wiesbaden, 1992). Nous nous référerons à la publication bilingue du P. Arsène Soukry, *Géographie de Moïse de Khorène* d'après Ptolémée (Venise, 1887).

[15] Nous renvoyons globalement à la publication du Père Soukry, texte, pp. 21-38, trad., pp. 29-51.

[16] Texte, p. 23, trad., p. 31.

voire, mais cela est moins sensible, à des réminiscences néotestamentaires (à Jérusalem, le jour de la Pentecôte, chacun entend les Apôtres parler dans son propre idiome, par exemple les Juifs et les prosélytes originaires de Mésopotamie, de Cappadoce, du Pont et de l'Asie, de Phrygie et de Pamphylie).[17]

Il est vrai que, au tournant de l'an Mil, le moine Step'annos Asoghik de Tarōn, dans son *Histoire d'Arménie*, évoque la situation délicate où se trouva le catholicos Khach'ik Ier Arsharuni, confronté à la dispersion de ses ouailles vers « l'Occident » (*Arewmutk'*) – c'est-à-dire vers l'Empire byzantin –, à l'occasion de la Reconquête effectuée par les empereurs macédoniens : « Aussi il consacra des évêques pour Antioche de Syrie, Tarse de Cilicie, Séleucie, et pour tous ces cantons »[18]. Il est peu probable qu'Asoghik, qui mentionne aussi la présence de deux évêchés arméniens en Cappadoce – Sébaste et Larissa (à relier à la colonisation militaire arménienne de la première moitié du X° siècle, dans le cadre de la création des « thèmes » de Sébaste et de Lykandos)[19], ait entendu, par l'expression *ew yamenayn gawaṙs yaynosik*, « et pour tous ces cantons », l'ensemble de l'Asie Mineure, comme le fait pratiquement Anania de Narek.

Certes, dans tous les lieux cités par Anania – et en dehors des diocèses arméniens cités par Asoghik – l'on trouve, aux X°-XI° siècles, des communautés arméniennes (au sens ethnoculturel) ; en allant d'est en ouest : en Isaurie, nous avons vu que Séleucie est un siège épiscopal à la fin du X° siècle ; on trouve des Arméniens à Platanion, dans le thème des Anatoliques – qui coïncide plus ou

[17] Actes 2, 8-12, suggestion de J.-P. Mahé.

[18] Cité par Gérard Dédéyan, « Reconquête territoriale et immigration arménienne dans l'aire cilicienne sous les empereurs macédoniens (de 867 à 1028) », dans Michel Balard et Alain Ducellier (dir.), *Migrations et diasporas méditerranéennes (X°-XVI° siècle)*, Publications de la Sorbonne, (Paris, 2002), p. 30 et n° 194, où nous préférons la lecture *Selewkay* à *Sulnday* - Sélinonte en Cilicie, traduction donnée par Frédéric Macler - et identifions *Selewkay* à Séleucie d'Isaurie plutôt qu'à Séleucie de Piérie, près d'Antioche (identification retenue par J.-P. Mahé, *Narek*, p. 57), car une présence militaire arménienne, outre celle attestée à Platanion, au nord-ouest de Séleucie, est encore mentionnée à proximité de Séleucie, à la fin du XI° siècle (Dédéyan, ibid., p. 30).

[19] Cf. Gérard Dédéyan, « Mleh le Grand, stratège de Lykandos », dans *Revue des Études Arméniennes*, NS, t. XV (Paris, 1981), pp. 73-102.

moins avec la Lycaonie, vers le milieu du IX° siècle [20] : ils participèrent à l'expédition de Crète sous Léon VI (886-912) ; il y aurait eu, vers 1097, des Arméniens à l'ouest d'Iconium [21] ; à Priène, dans le thème des Thracésiens, qui recouvre en gros l'Asie Propre, stationnaient des stratiotes arméniens qui participèrent à l'expédition de Crète, en 949[22]. Les exemples sont moins probants pour la Bithynie, qui coïncide en partie avec les thèmes des Bucellaires et de l'Opsikion : sous l'empereur Léon IV le Khazar (775-780), lors d'une expédition contre les Arabes, l'armée byzantine est commandée par quatre généraux (sur cinq) de souche arménienne, Tatzatès/Tachat, stratège du thème des Bucellaires, Grigor, fils de Musulak, stratège du thème de l'Opsikion, Artawazd, stratège du thème des Anatoliques, Baristèrotzès/Varaztirots', stratège du thème des Arméniaques [23] ; mais peut-être cet exemple n'est-il pas plus probant que la mention, par les sources franques de la IV° Croisade (1202-1204), de contingents militaires arméniens (dont une vingtaine de milliers suivirent le futur empereur Henri de Hainaut en Europe) répartis sur la côte ouest de l'Asie Mineure (à Smyrne, Abydos et dans la vallée du Scamandre) et qui se joignent aux Latins pour combattre les Grecs, après la prise de Constantinople par les premiers, en avril 1204 [24] ; enfin, le transfert forcé des Arméniens en Thrace et en Macédoine (d'où est originaire la dynastie macédonienne), pour éradiquer certains mouvements sectaires de l'est de l'Asie Mineure et surtout pour combattre les Avars, puis les Bulgares, est une constante dans la politique byzantine, du VI° au X° siècle ; en Thrace, les Arméniens étaient particulièrement nombreux

---

[20] Gérard Dédéyan, *Les Arméniens entre Grecs, Musulmans et Croisés. Étude sur les pouvoirs arméniens dans le Proche-Orient méditerranéen (1068-1150)*, Bibliothèque de la Fondation Calouste Gulbenkian, 2 vols. (Lisbonne, 2003), t. 1, p. 95. L'empereur Léon V l'Arménien (813-820) avait été auparavant stratège des Anatoliques (Georges Ostrogosrsky, *Histoire de l'État byzantin*, 2° édition, Payot (Paris, 1976), p. 230.

[21] Dédéyan, *Les Arméniens*, t. 1, p. 649.

[22] Peter Charanis, *The Armenians in the Byzantine Empire*, Bibliothèque de la Fondation Calouste Gulbenkian (Lisbonne, 1968), p. 16.

[23] Nicolas Adontz, « L'âge et l'origine de l'empereur Basile I », dans *Études arméno-byzantines*, (Lisbonne : Bibliothèque arménienne de la Fondation Calouste Gulbenkian, 1965), p. 91.

[24] Charanis, *The Armenians*, p. 54.

à Constantinople, depuis l'avènement de Basile Ier (867-886)[25], mais aussi à Philippoupolis (actuelle Plovdiv) et à Andrinople [26] : mais on ne mentionne pas d'évêque arménien de Philippoupolis avant la fin du XII° siècle[27]. Pour la Macédoine (qui, selon *l'Ashkharhats'oyts'*, comprend « la Thessalie, d'où sont sortis les Arméniens »)[28], les témoignages les plus probants (celui d'Eustathe, archevêque grec de Thessalonique lors du siège de la ville par les Normands, en 1185, et celui du clerc autrichien, Ansbert, qui accompagne l'expédition de l'empereur germanique, Frédéric Barberousse, en 1190) sur l'existence d'une communauté arménienne (active économiquement et sans doute très nombreuse, comme la communauté juive de la ville) sont postérieurs de deux siècles[29].

La liste fournie par Anania de Narek nous paraît donc un peu « enflée », au sens littéraire du terme, et peut-être influencée par la lecture de *l'Ashkharhats'oyts'*. Il n'y a probablement pas d'évêchés arméniens à l'ouest de la Cappadoce, en Asie Mineure occidentale, mais certainement des contingents militaires (quoique ceux-ci soient surtout concentrés dans les régions reconquises sur les Arabes et organisées en thèmes « arméniens », ou vers la frontière du Danube) et souvent des communautés.

En revanche, peut-être faut-il, dans de nombreux cas, susbstituer – s'agissant de l'Asie Mineure occidentale ou des Balkans – le mot *vanoray*, au sens de « monastère », à celui d'*ēpiskopos*, « évêque ». C'est ce que nous suggère un passage des *Réflexions sur les institutions de l'Église*, opuscule de Nersēs de Lambron, archevêque

[25] Adontz, « L'âge et l'origine de l'empereur Basile I », *passim*.

[26] Dédéyan, *Les Arméniens*, t. 2, pp. 735-740. Cf. aussi Adontz, « La famille de Théodorokan », dans *Études arméno-byzantines*, qui signale la présence du duc T'ot'orakan à Philippoupolis et celle de son lieutenant Yovhannôs à Andrinople aux alentours de l'an Mil, pp. 153-156.

[27] Dédéyan, « De la prise de Thessalonique par les Normands (1185) à la Croisade de Frédéric Barberousse (1189-1190) : le revirement politico-religieux des pouvoirs arméniens », dans *Chemins d'outre-mer. Études d'histoire sur la Méditerranée médiévale, offertes à Michel Balard*, (Paris : Publications de la Sorbonne, 2004), p. 191. Certaines sources comptent en tout, dans les Balkans, à la fin du XII° siècle, trois évêchés, dont un seul – Philippoupolis – est connu (ibid., p. 187).

[28] Texte, p. 17, trad., p. 21.

[29] Dédéyan, « Le revirement politico-religieux », *passim*.

de Tarse (1175-1198), composé vers 1177[30], qui fait curieusement écho au passage susmentionné de la *Racine de la foi*. Nersēs (dont l'oncle maternel était le catholicos Nersēs Chnorhali), très sensible à l'influence d'une Église latine, présente au Proche-Orient, qu'avaient dynamisée la Réforme grégorienne et le ressourcement du monachisme bénédictin sous sa forme cistercienne (dont Bernard de Clairvaux avait donné l'illustration la plus marquante), oppose le zèle religieux des Francs – dotant d'églises et de sièges épiscopaux les régions du Proche-Orient où ils s'étaient établis, au lendemain de la Croisade – à la tiédeur manifestée selon lui par les princes arméniens – à l'exception des Arcruni du Vaspurakan et des Bagratuni de Kars lors de leur établissement à Sébaste[31] – dans la zone méditerranéenne où ils avaient émigré : « Lorsque ceux-ci [les Francs] arrivèrent, toute la Mésopotamie et la Syrie, l'Isaurie[32] et la Cilicie, la Pamphylie, la Cappadoce et tout le *Gamirk'* étaient peuplés d'Arméniens qui avaient des princes et des monastères autant qu'ils pouvaient en posséder, et les pouvoirs princiers n'ont pas diminué jusqu'à maintenant »[33]. Embrassant la même aire territoriale qu'Anania de Narek (moins l'Asie Mineure occidentale – sauf la Pamphylie – et les Balkans), Nersēs parle, à l'arrivée des Francs – « Il n'y a pas soixante-dix ans » –, de l'existence d'innombrables *krōnastank'* (synonyme de *menastank'*, « monastères »), mais déplore que, par la suite, les Arméniens n'aient ni construit d'églises ni érigé de sièges épiscopaux (mentionnant, dans plusieurs cas le repli de prélats arméniens vers les *vanorayk'*, c'est-à-dire les « monastères »)[34].

---

[30] Mgr Norayr Bogharian, *Les écrivains arméniens* (en arm.), (Jérusalem, 1971), pp. 253-255.

[31] En réalité, ces derniers – les rois de Vanand – avaient eux-aussi reçu des Byzantins, en échange de leur royaume, des terres en Cappadoce, mais pas la ville de Sébaste, jamais mentionnée par les sources (cf. Gérard Dédéyan, « L'immigration arménienne en Cappadoce au XI° siècle », dans *Byzantion*, t. XLV, fasc. 1 (Bruxelles, 1975), pp. 82-85).

[32] Nous pensons que le mot *Siwria* ne doit pas être traduit par « Coelè-Syrie » (*Kiwlisiwria*, dans *l'Ashkharhats'oyts'*, p. 36), mais, étant une mauvaise lecture pour *Sawr̄eay* (« Isaurie » dans *l'Ashkharhats'oyts'*, p. 24), désigne l'Isaurie même (où résidaient les Hét'umiens), que *l'Ashkharhats'oyts'* associe volontiers à la Cilicie.

[33] *DA* I, p. 577.

[34] Ibid.

On ne conserve pas de liste des participants (deux mille cinq cents ecclésiastiques, nous apprennent les sources) au synode de la Montagne Noire, réuni en 1113 par le catholicos Grigor III (1113-1166), frère de Nersēs Chnorhali, peu après l'érection du siège d'Aght'amar en siège catholicossal[35]. Une lettre du catholicos Grigor IV Tghay (1173-1193), adressée en 1178 au patriarche de Constantinople, mentionne, comme prélats arméniens venus de régions autres que l'Arménie, l'Aghuanie ou la Géorgie et présents au concile de Hr̊omkla (résidence patriarcale, en Euphratèse, depuis 1150), la même année 1178 : pour la Cappadoce (au sens large du terme), l'archevêque de Césarée, les évêques de Néocésarée, Sébaste, Kokison ; pour la Cilicie, l'archevêque de Tarse, les évêques d'Anazarbe et de Mamistra ; pour l'Isaurie, l'évêque de Séleucie ; pour Chypre, un évêque dont le siège n'est pas précisé ; pour la Syrie, l'archevêque d'Antioche, les évêques de Laodicée et d'Apamée ; pour la Mésopotamie, l'archevêque d'Édesse, l'évêque de Samosate (les évêques de Mélitène et d'Ashmushat/Arsamosate ayant leur résidence respectivement en Quatrième Arménie et dans le Tsop'k'/Sophène)[36]. L'évêché de K'esun, en Commagène, dont la durée n'a peut-être excédé le règne du prince Gogh Vasil (1080-1112), maître de la région – sa piété est louée par Nersēs de Lambron, mais le siège épiscopal, dont la résidence était Karmir Vank'/le Couvent Rouge, à K'esun), semble ignoré de lui –, n'apparaît plus sur la liste établie par Grigor IV ; c'est le cas également pour Marash, dont le chroniqueur Matt'ēos d'Ur̊hay/Édesse cite l'évêque, au tout début du XII° siècle[37], tandis que Nersēs de Lambron, mal informé, nie l'existence d'un siège épiscopal à la même époque[38].

On remarque, d'une part, que contrairement à l'assertion de

---

[35] Mgr Maghak'ia Ormanean, *Azgapatum*, t. 1, réimpression anastatique (Beyrouth, 1969), col. 1354.

[36] Lettre encyclique de saint Nersēs Chnorhali (en arm.), Les Saints-Jacques, Jérusalem, 1871, p. 198-199. Sur cette lettre, voir Isabelle Auge, *Grecs, Arméniens et Latins d'Orient au temps de la Croisade. Politique religieuse et reconquête en Orient sous les Comnènes (1081-1185*) (sous presse, Geuthner, Paris, 2006), document d'avril 1178 et carte « La participation au synode de Hor̊omkla ».

[37] *DA* I, p. 52.

[38] Ibid., p. 577.

Nersēs de Lambron, et à peu près à l'époque où il compose son opuscule, il existe de nombreux évêchés arméniens dans le Proche-Orient méditerranéen ; d'autre part que l'archevêque de Tarse, oubliant le penchant des évêques arméniens – ou syriaques – à résider dans les monastères (penchant confirmé par la liste des prélats arméniens contemporains du couronnement royal de Lewon le Magnifique, en 1198)[39] et séduit par l'usage latin de la résidence dans la *civitas*, en vient à ignorer l'existence de nombreux sièges épiscopaux, quand ils ne correspondent pas à une résidence urbaine. Cependant la répartition géographique qu'il présente pour la Diaspora arménienne, à la fin du XI° siècle, nous paraît correspondre – avec une extension consécutive à l'invasion turque de la deuxième moitié du XI° siècle – à l'ancienne zone-frontière, au sud-est de l'Empire byzantin, celle-là même où la nécessité de fixer les soldats des thèmes « arméniens » et leurs familles en leur ménageant une desserte spirituelle, avait amené les *basileis*, au tournant de l'an Mil, à autoriser la coexistence d'une double hiérarchie ecclésiastique.

Pour conclure, les évêchés arméniens de l'Empire byzantin mentionnés dans la *Racine de la foi* ne peuvent être situés que dans les régions de colonisation militaire arménienne et donc, principalement, dans l'ancien thème « romain » de Sébaste et dans les nouveaux thèmes « arméniens » du Proche-Orient. Ailleurs – sauf, peut-être en Thrace, et dans la mesure où l'on n'a pas affaire à une amplification due à la lecture de *l'Ashkharhats'oyts',* voire du Nouveau Testament, il ne peut s'agir que de couvents, sans résidence épiscopale. Anania ne confirme les données d'Asoghik que sur la création de sièges épiscopaux au Proche-Orient ; peut-être l'abbé de Narek confirme-t-il, en revanche, en dépit d'exagérations dues à sa culture personnelle celles de diverses sources sur l'existence de communautés arméniennes dans presque tout le territoire de l'Empire, à l'ouest de la Cappadoce.

---

[39] *La Chronique attribuée au Connétable Smbat,* (Introduction, traduction et notes par Gérard Dédéyan, *Documents relatifs à l'histoire des Croisades* publiés par l'Académie des Inscriptions et Belles-Lettres, XIII (Paris, 1980), p. 74-75. Presque tous les archevêques arméniens sont mentionnés à la fois comme titulaires d'un siège, généralement urbain, et comme supérieurs d'un monastère, peu éloigné de la ville mentionnée, plus de la moitié des évêques le sont au titre d'un monastère.

26

Les documents ecclésiastiques arméno-byzantins après la quatrième croisade

Azat Bozoyan

Les relations ecclésiastiques arméno-byzantines remontent à une époque très ancienne, alors que la notion d'Arménie cilicienne n'existait pas encore.

Après le concile de Chalcédoine, les initiatives d'union entre les deux Églises vinrent tantôt de l'Arménie, tantôt de Byzance[1]. Dans *Les regestes des actes du Patriarcat de Constantinople*, on trouve un assez grand nombre de documents qui ont trait aux relations arméno-byzantines. Par ailleurs, ces dernières années, J. Darrouzès, R. Bartikian, A. Heisenberg, H. Hunger et d'autres spécialistes, ont édité un grand nombre de lettres échangées entre les dignitaires des deux Églises sous le gouvernement des empereurs macédoniens, comnènes, anges, lascaris et paléologues.

La situation géopolitique de la Cilicie arménienne était relativement complexe. Le dangereux voisinage de l'empire byzantin, du sultanat d'Iconium, des émirats, sultanats et atabégats seldjoukides, mongols et turcomans, puis mamelouks et ottomans, contraignit le royaume arménien de Cilicie à de délicats compromis diplomatiques.

À partir des années 70 du XIe siècle, les relations ecclésiastiques arméno-byzantines s'interrompirent. Elles ne reprirent que dans les années 30 du XIIe siècle quand Grégoire III Pahlavouni écrivit une

---

[1] Sur les relations ecclésiastiques arméno-byzantines après le grand schisme de Chalcédoine voir N. Garsoïan, *L'Église arménienne et le grand schisme d'Orient* (Louvain, 1999), [CSCO, v. 574, subs., t. 100].

lettre à Jeanne II Comnène[2]. Il fallut attendre cependant le catholicossat de Nersēs IV le Gracieux (1166-1173) pour voir apparaître un véritable renouveau. En 1165, alors qu'il n'était encore qu'un simple évêque, Nersēs se rendit à Mopsueste chez le protostrator Alexis afin d'y mener de longues négociations dogmatiques et de lui présenter la lettre dogmatique de la confession arménienne. En 1167, celle-ci servit de référence à l'empereur Manuel Ier Comnène, quand il proposa à Nersès, désormais catholicos, de venir débattre de l'union des deux Églises à Constantinople même. Nersēs refusa par crainte d'être isolé parmi les docteurs byzantins. Les relations entre les deux Églises se poursuivirent jusqu'en 1178, date de la réunion du concile de Hṙomkla. Sur ces relations, nous possédons à peu près 25 documents écrits en grec et en arménien[3].

Pour la période postérieure, nous disposons d'une lettre d'Isaac II Ange (1185-1195, 1203-1204) au catholicos Grégoire IV Tgha, écrite en grec[4], d'une lettre de Grégoire VI Apirate à l'empereur Alexis III Ange en arménien[5], et d'un compte rendu des débats intervenus à Constantinople en 1197 entre Nersēs Lambronats'i et le patriarche Grégoire II Xiphilinos, également en arménien. Il est intéressant de constater que si Nersēs de Lambronats'i avait au départ une grande sympathie pour Byzance, son attitude s'inversa à son retour en Cilicie[6].

Après la chute de Constantinople en 1204, les relations arméno-byzantines entrèrent dans une nouvelle phase. Nous possédons le contrat des fiançailles scellé entre Théodore Lascaris et Philippa, nièce de Léon Ier, en 1213, ainsi que les dispenses patriarcales et synodales rédigées pour l'occasion.

---

[2] J. Darrouzès, *Trois documents de la controverse gréco-arménienne*, Revue des étude Byzantines (1990), pp. 89-153 et 147-153.

[3] A. Bozoyan, *Documents on the Armenian-Byzantine Ecclesiastical Negotiations (1165-1178)* (Erevan, 1995), pp. 29-90 (en arménien, avec un résumé en anglais, pp. 226-231).

[4] H. Bartikian, *Studia Armeno-Byzantina,* Vol. II*: Articles in foreign languages* (Erevan, 2002), pp. 21-25 (en russe).

[5] « Kavkaz i Vizantija », t. 4 (Erevan, 1984), pp. 224-231. J'ai découvert le texte de la lettre dans deux manuscrits arméniens.

[6] Bozoyan, *Documents*, pp. 138-141.

Nous avons connaissance, en outre, d'une lettre du patriarche Germain II (1223-1240) adressée au catholicos Constantin Ier de Bardzraberd (1222-1267), d'une lettre du patriarche Manuel II (1243-1254) au roi Het'oum Ier (1226-1270) et au catholicos Constantin Ier et d'une lettre du patriarche Isaïe (1323-1332) au catholicos Constantin IV (1323-1326) et au roi Léon IV (1320-1341). Dans ces documents rédigés en grec, il est question des lettres envoyées par les catholicos et les rois arméniens au sujet de l'union des deux Églises, mais aucun original ou aucune copie de ces lettres écrites en arménien n'est parvenu jusqu'à nous. On possède uniquement, et ce dans plusieurs manuscrits arméniens, la copie de la lettre que Constantin Ier adressa au patriarche Manuel II. Pour ce qui est de la correspondance écrite en grec par les Arméniens, nos connaissances sont là encore bien maigres. Nous devons nous contenter des lettres de Nersēs IV le Gracieux et de Grégoire IV dans lesquelles, bien que l'union soit qualifiée de souhaitable, il n'est à aucun moment question d'une soumission de l'Église arménienne à l'Église byzantine; preuve que les démarches des dignitaires arméno-byzantins étaient à but plus politique que dogmatique.

L'empire byzantin connut une période tourmentée après que Constantinople fut tombée aux mains des Latins en 1204. Durant toute la première moitié du XIIIe siècle, le Proche-Orient fut le théâtre de bouleversements géopolitiques spectaculaires et lourds de conséquences. Il est à cet égard significatif que, dans l'historiographie byzantine du XIIIe siècle, les Arméniens soient appelés des alliés de l'empire latin de Constantinople du fait de l'aide apportée par des détachements arméniens dans les premières années de la création de cet état[7]. Ainsi, de nouveaux états étaient apparus sur la scène internationale, parmi lesquels: le royaume arménien de Cilicie et l'empire de Nicée, principal porteur de l'héritage culturel byzantin.

Menacé par l'empire latin de Constantinople, au nord, et le sultanat de Roûm, au sud, l'empire de Nicée s'efforça rapidement de

---

[7] La collaboration arméno-latine dans les Balkans s'est manifestée pour la première fois à l'occasion de la troisième croisade. L'historien byzantin Niketas Choniates, qui était le maire de la ville de Philipople (aujourd'hui Plovdiv) fut le contemporain de ces événements. Il évoque ces relations sur un ton hostile (voir Bozoyan, *Documents*, pp. 218-219).

nouer des alliances de revers. Le royaume arménien de Cilicie, devenu un puissant état sous le règne de Léon Ier (1199-1219), était le partenaire idéal. D'où ce mariage arrangé en 1213 entre Philippa, fille de Ruben, frère de Léon Ier, et Théodore Ier Lascaris (1208-1222). Traditionellement les princesses arméniennes appelées à épouser des empereurs byzantins changeaient et de confession et de nom, mais vraisemblement cela ne fut pas le cas pour la nièce de Léon Ier. Pour ce mariage nous possédons une « lettre patriarcale et synodale [adressée] au roi Léon Ier d'Arménie pour le rassurer sur les dispositions de l'empereur concernant son mariage avec sa fille[8] ». Léon mena une brillante diplomatie religieuse face au pape Innocent III, tout au long de son règne. Dans le domaine politique, le rapprochement avec le Saint Empire qu'il initia, fut lui aussi un succès. Sa diplomatie matrimoniale fut, en revanche, moins heureuse. Certes, en l'an 663 du calendrier arménien (1214), Léon Ier accorda la main de sa fille Rita au souverain de Jérusalem, le roi Jean de Brienne[9] ; mais l'accord qu'il conclut en 1216 avec le roi André de Hongrie[10], alors en route pour l'Égypte, théâtre de la cinquième croisade, prévoyant le mariage de sa fille Zabel avec ce dernier, n'aboutit pas. De même, le mariage entre Philippa et Théodore Lascaris fut rapidement suivi d'un divorce en 1218[11].

---

[8] V. Laurent, *Les regestes des actes du Patriarcat de Constantinople. Vol. I: Les actes des Patriarches*. Fasc. IV: Les regestes de 1208 - 1309 / (Paris, 1971), N.1214; A. Pavlov, *Lettre synodale de l'an 1213 au sujet du mariage entre l'empereur byzantin et la fille du roi d'Arménie* (en russe), dans Viz. Vremenn., IV (1897), pp. 160-166. Philippa était en réalité la nièce et non la fille de Léon Ier comme nous l'avons déjà constaté.

[9] G. Dédéyan, *La chronique attribuée au connétable Smbat* (Paris, 1980), p. 89.

[10] *Sembat le Connétable, Chronique*, éd. Akelian (Venise, 1956), p. 221; *La chronique attribuée au connétable Smbat*, p. 90-92; Pontificia Commissio ad redigendum Codicem iuris canonici orientalis, *Fontes*, Series III, vol. III, éd Tautu et al (Vatican, 1950), 56, p.81.

[11] *Sembat le Connétable*, *Chronique*, p. 221; *Georges Acropolite, Chronique*, 15 & 18; éd. Bekker (Bonn, 1836), pp. 29 & 34 (trad. Allemande Blum, Stuttgart, 1989, p. 83 & 86); Théodore Skutariotes, «Chronique », in Constantin Sathas, Bibliotheca Graeca Medii Aevi, 7 vol., t. VII (Paris, 1894), p. 462; Nicolas Mésarite, 52, in August Heisenberg, «Neue Quellen zur Geshichte des Lateinischen Kaisertums und der

Il est à plusieurs reprises question des Arméniens dans une lettre synodale rendant compte de la prise d'Antioche par Levon Ier en 1216. On y apprend que le patriarche grec d'Antioche, Syméon II,avait trouvé refuge en Cilicie en 1214, et qu'il y resta jusqu'en 1217[12]. Des 1212, Wilbrand d'Oldenburg avait pu faire le constat des bonnes relations entre le patriarcat antiochain et le royaume arménien. Le pèlerin allemand assista en effet à Sis, la capitale cilicienne, à une procession celebrant la fête de l'Épiphanie dirigée par le patriarche d'Antioche en personne[13]. Après ce séjour en Cilicie, Syméon II gagna Nicée au début du patriarcat de Manuel Ier qui, sans doute, se saisit de son cas et de celui des évêques qui l'accompagnaient. Ce voyage intervint, à mon avis, après l'annulation du mariage entre Philippa et Théodore Lascaris (1218). Il est clair que le royaume arménien de Cilicie désirait voir en fait le patriarcat antiochain s'installer sur ses terres. On trouve cette idée formulée pour la première fois, dans un document présenté lors du concile de Hṙomkla de 1178[14].

La phase suivante des relations arméno-byzantines est liée à un nouveau bouleversement de la géopolitique levantine: les invasions turco-mongoles.

Jean III Vatatzès (1222-1254), successeur de Théodore Ier Lascaris, continua à entretenir des relations amicales avec la Cilicie, dans un but analogue à celui de son prédécesseur: avoir un allié de revers contre le sultanat d'Iconium. En proposant aux Arméniens un plan d'union avec l'Église byzantine il tenta également de rompre l' entente entre l'Église arménienne et la Papauté.

Kirchenunion », *Sitzungsberichte der Bayerischemn Akademie der Wissenschaften, Philosophisch-Philologische und historische Klasse*, Munich, Jhg. 1923, 3. Abhd., p. 47; voir A. Heisenberg, « Zu den armenisch-byzantinischen Beziehungen am Anfang des 13. Jahrhunderts », *Sitzungsberichte der Bayerischen Akademie der Wissenschaften, Philosophisch-Pilologische und historische Klasse* (Munich, Jhg. 1929), 6, Abhandlung, pp. 3-20.

[12] *Les regestes,* N. 1220.

[13] P. Halfter, « Die beschreibung des Armenischen Königreiches Kilikien durch den Hildesheimer Domherren Wilbrand von Oldenburg, » *Armenia and Christian Orient* (Erevan, 2000), pp. 406-407.

[14] Bozoyan, *Documents,* pp. 231-233.

À cette étape importante des relations ecclésiastiques arméno-byzantines reste attaché le nom de Germanos II, patriarche de Nicée de 1223 à 1240. Nous possédons une lettre qu'il adressa au catholicos Constantin Ier Bardjraberdzi (1221-1267) en 1239/40. Elle a été publiée pour la première fois par le byzantiniste S. Lagopetès en 1913[15]. On dispose, en outré, de la copie d'une lettre que le patriarche Manuel II, successeur de Germanos II, écrivit à Het'oum Ier et à Constantin Ier durant l'hiver 1247-1248. Elle est du plus grand intérêt car le patriarche s'y livre à un bref historique des tractations passées entre l'Église arménienne et l'Église byzantine au cours des années 1239-1247. Jusqu'à récemment encore cette lettre était restée inédite, mais, en 2002, R. Bartikian en a assuré l'édition et la traduction en arménien pour la revue *Gandzasar*[16]. Il y a ajouté le texte grec et la traduction en arménien de la lettre de Germanos II. Grâce à cette dernière on peut dire avec certitude que ce sont cette fois-ci les Arméniens qui prirent l'initiative des pourparlers. Le patriarche d'Antioche, Dorothéos (1219-1245) joua le rôle d'intermédiaire. Après que le roi d'Arménie cilicienne, Het'oum Ier, l'eut informé de ses bonnes dispositions à l'égard de l'Église byzantine, celui-ci dépêcha auprès de Germanos II un certain moine Basilios (Blasios dans la lettre du patriarche Manuel II)[17] et Théodoret, higoumène du monastère de Saint-Théodose à Skopèle. Aussitôt, le patriarche de Nicée manda à Sis le métropolite Jean de Mélitène, en prenant soin de lui remettre une lettre adressée à Constantin Ier de Bardzraberd. C'est le même document qui a été publié par S. Lagopatès.

Comme il le lui avait été ordonné, Jean de Mélitène remit la lettre de Germanos II aux dignitaires du royaume et repartit avec leur réponse et la profession de foi de l'Église arménienne (ἀντιγράμμα πάλιν ἔλαβε καὶ τῆς τῶν Ἀρμενίων λίβελλον πίστεως)[18]. Nous reviendrons un peu plus tard sur ce dernier document. La lettre de

---

[15] Sp. Lagopatès, *Γερμανὸς ὁ Β πατριάρχης Κωνσταντινουπόλεως-Νικαίας* (Tripoli, 1913), pp. 354-357.
[16] *Gandzasar*, t. VII (Erevan, 2002), pp. 62-71 (en arm).
[17] *Gandzasar*, t. VII, pp. 68-71, 78-79.
[18] *Gandzasar*, t. VII, p. 81.

Manuel[19] nous apprend qu'il reçut, en outre, des Arméniens l'assurance qu'une ambassade serait prochainement envoyée au patriarche[20]. Ce qui eut effectivement lieu, peu de temps après le retour de Jean de Mélitène à Nicée. Les informations apportées par *l'Histoire* de Kirakos de Gandzak, laissent supposer que le chef de la délégation arménienne fut le vardapet Jacques (qui deviendra plus tard catholicos sous le nom de Jacques Ier Klayetsi; 1268-1296)[21]. Celui-ci arriva à Nicée alors que le patriarche Germanos était déjà mort. Selon la lettre de Manuel II, l'empereur Jean III Ducas Vatatzès (1222-1254) réunit les évêques de l'Église byzantine, qui, après avoir examiné attentivement la profession de foi de l'Église arménienne, décidèrent d'envoyer une nouvelle fois à Sis (capitale de la Cilicie) le métropolite Jean de Mélitène, accompagné d'un archonte patriarcal, dans le but de réaliser l'union des deux Églises. À cet effet, ils reçurent des documents émanant et de l'empereur et du synode. Il est à remarquer que le trône patriarcal était alors vacant. Contre toute attente, les négociations n'eurent pas lieu. La lettre de Manuel II nous en révèle la cause: le catholicos Constantin Ier ne se trouvait pas à Sis. Probablement était-il resté à Hṙomkla dans le but de faire échouer la tentative d'union entre les deux Églises. Ces événements durent se produire en 1240, ou entre 1241 et 1244, durant la vacance du trône patriarcal. Puis les négociations entre les Églises arménienne et byzantine s'interrompirent jusqu'en 1247.

Dans l'intervalle eurent lieu d'intéressants pourparlers entre l'Église arménienne et l'Église catholique romaine. En 1246, le légat du pape Innocent IV, Dominique d'Aragon (appelé Dimanje dans les documents arméniens) rendit visite au roi Het'oum Ier et au catholicos. Nous sommes renseignés sur son séjour en Cilicie non seulement par les récits des chroniqueurs arméniens, mais également par une lettre écrite à l'occasion par l'historien Vardan Arevelts'i,

---

[19] D'après les *Regestes* de Grumel-Darrouzès, les lettres de Germanos II et Manuel II sont conservées en trois copies (Monac. 207, f. 14v-16; Vatic. gr.1455, f. 25-27; Otteb. gr. 77, ff. 25v-28v).

[20] *Gandzasar*, t. VII, pp. 80-81: φάσκοντα μετ ὀλὶγον καὶ πρέσβεις σταλῆναι παρὰ τῆς σῆς ἐξουσίας τὸν ἴσον λίβελλον ἀποκομισαμένους, écrit le Patriarche Manuel II.

[21] Deux historiens arméniens, *Kirakos de Gandzak*, XIIIe s., *Histoire d'Arménie*; Oukhtanès d'Ourha, Xe s., *Histoire en trois parties*; traduit par M. Brosset (St-Pétersbourg, 1870), p. 177.

dans laquelle il s'oppose fermement aux propositions du légat concernant l'union des deux Églises[22].

En 1247, le roi Het'oum Ier prit, une fois de plus, l'initiative de relancer les négociations avec l'Église byzantine. Il fit remettre par ses ambassadeurs une lettre au patriarche Manuel II. Comme il a été mentionné plus haut, nous possédons la réponse qu'écrivit Manuel au roi et au catholicos. Il y note qu'il s'agit de la troisième fois que l'affaire de l'union est débattue entre Grecs et Arméniens.

Durant l'hiver 1247-1248 commença donc la seconde étape des négociations ecclésiastiques arméno-byzantines au XIIIe siècle. Manuel II convoqua un synode qui examina une nouvelle fois la profession de foi (λίβελλον) de l'Église arménienne. Cette fois, on exigea d'elle quelques concessions dogmatiques. L'inévitable Jean de Mélitène fut derechef envoyé à Sis en compagnie du métropolite Jean de Philadelphie. On n'a conservé aucun document sur ces négociations qui se déroulèrent dans la capitale arménienne en 1248. Il faut d'ailleurs noter que, jusqu'à la reprise de Constantinople en 1268, nous ne possédons aucun document sur les relations ecclésiastiques arméno-byzantines. Il est probable néanmoins que ni les Arméniens, ni les Byzantins ne firent des concessions dogmatiques.

Il ne nous reste à present qu'à examiner un dernier document dont la rédaction la plus ancienne est conservée au Vatican, dans les Archives Secrètes de la bibliothèque apostolique (AA Arm. I–XVIII 1804). Il a été mis en circulation au cours des controverses dogmatiques qui ont opposé Arméniens, Byzantins et Latins. Il s'agit de la « profession de foi de l'Église arménienne » qui a été envoyée à Innocent IV (1243-1254) à l'occasion de la venue en Cilicie du légat pontifical Dominique et que le catholicos Constantin Ier de Bardzraberd a signé de sa main. À ce document originel, conservé maintenant à Rome, a été ajoutée aux XVII-XVIIIe siècles une traduction en italien sur le titre de laquelle la « profession » est datée de l'année 1225, ce qui est probablement faux.[23] Ce texte est en fait la profession dogmatique arménienne de Nersēs IV Chnorhali, envoyée à Constantinople entre 1165 et 1166. Constantin Ier de Bardzerberd a donné une nouvelle vie à l'oeuvre de son devancier en

[22] Voir *Le Livre des Épitres* (Jérusalem, 1994), pp. 657-665 (en arm.).

[23] Bozoyan, *Documents*, pp. 34-38.

la considérant comme un énoncé impartial de dogmatique arménienne. Si l'on en croit la lettre de Manuel II, cette «profession» a été envoyée pour la première fois au patriarche Gérmanos II, par l'intermédiaire de son ambassadeur, le métropolite Jean de Mélitène. C'est ce même document qu'aurait apporté à Nicée, entre 1240 et 1243, l'ambassadeur du roi Het'oum Ier et du catholicos Constantin Ier: le vardapet Jacques. Dans les deux cas, le document est appelé λίβελον πίστεως [La profession de foi]. Le patriarche Manuel II précise qu'on lui a envoyé une confession semblable et qu'elle fut soumise au jugement des évêques byzantins. Rappelons que ceux-ci exigèrent par écrit plusieurs concessions dogmatiques de la part des Arméniens. « La profession de foi » envoyée au patriarche Manuel est conservée dans le manuscrit arménien N 2174 du Maténadaran Mesrop Macht'ots' de Erevan.

Pour finir, il nous faut préciser que cet écrit dogmatique, qui a été envoyé à Constantinople, Rome et Nicée par Nersēs IV et Constantin Ier, existe également dans une version adressée au roi de Pologne Henri III en 1574. Il s'agit de la profession de foi de l'Église arménienne de la colonie de Lemberg-Lvov. Cette version figure à la suite d'une lettre destinée au roi de Pologne. Elle est aujourd'hui conservée à la bibliothèque Saltikov Schedrin de St-Pétersbourg, dans le fonds des documents en langue étrangère. L'original de cette profession de foi est écrit sur parchemin, parallèlement en arménien, en grec moderne et en latin. Les traductions grecques et latines datent du XVIe siècle. Sur les titres des versions arménienne, latine et grecque, qui sont écrits en rouge, il est dit que la profession est adressée au patriarche de Constantinople. Ce texte correspond donc à celui envoyé par Constantin Ier au patriarche Manuel II, qui lui, n'est conservé qu'en arménien. La version latine en a été publiée par P. Anton Sterck en 1907.

Trente-six erreurs concernant l'Arménie cilicienne (XIIe-XIVe siècle)

Claude Mutafian

L'État arménien fondé en Cilicie au début du XIIe siècle fut érigé en royaume à la fin du même siècle, et sa chute en 1375 marqua la fin de toute royauté arménienne. Ce dernier royaume d'Arménie est un peu le « mal-aimé » de l'arménologie. Comme son cadre géographique, la Cilicie, se trouvait hors du territoire historique, on le considère souvent, plus ou moins consciemment, comme marginal, presque comme une diaspora périphérique. Les appellations fréquentes du genre *Petite Arménie* ou *Nouvelle Arménie* sont à cet égard significatives, car elles traduisent une réticence à y voir une « Arménie » tout court.

Dans toute recherche historique, moins il y a de sources, plus il y a d'erreurs, car on en est réduit à se baser sur des récits tardifs. Ainsi, si le XIIIe siècle arménien est remarquablement bien documenté, le XIIe l'est moins et le XIVe est encore plus déficient. Il n'en reste pas moins vrai que parmi tous les États arméniens qui ont existé depuis l'antiquité, celui de Cilicie est de très loin le plus riche en documentation, avec des sources d'une extraordinaire diversité. Or, paradoxalement, les trois siècles de son existence correspondent probablement à la période de l'histoire arménienne la plus fertile en erreurs et en affirmations gratuites qui se transmettent d'un auteur à l'autre. Parfois, on énonce comme une vérité quelque chose qui ne se trouve que dans des sources très tardives, sans signaler qu'il y a place au doute. Ailleurs, on donne des interprétations sans aucune preuve, souvent erronées. Plus grave, on rencontre fréquemment de flagrantes fautes factuelles, qui se recopient d'un auteur à l'autre. Dans la plupart des cas, une simple recherche ou vérification de sources aurait permis de rectifier, mais en général elle n'est pas faite et les erreurs se perpétuent.

Lorsque, par chance, les auteurs mentionnent le ou les ouvrages d'où ils ont tiré telle ou telle affirmation qui se révèle a posteriori erronée, on peut essayer de remonter la filière. En cas de succès, on arrive presque inéluctablement soit à l'un des deux plus prestigieux pères mékhitaristes de Venise, Tchamtchian[1] (XVIIIe s.) et Alichan[2] (XIXe s.), soit au généalogiste Rüdt-Collenberg[3] (XXe s.). Les deux pères mékhitaristes ont été de fabuleux pionniers de l'arménologie, mais à leur époque on n'avait pas la discipline scientifique actuellement exigée – malheureusement pas toujours satisfaite, loin de là – consistant à mentionner ses sources, si bien qu'on en est réduit soit à les croire sur parole, soit à essayer de retrouver chaque fois leurs sources, quitte à affirmer, au cas où la recherche n'aboutit à rien, qu'ils devaient avoir sous la main des sources disparues depuis ! C'est là un pur acte de foi, battu en brèche depuis qu'on a explicitement réfuté certaines de leurs affirmations. Leur immense valeur n'est pas en cause, mais elle ne nous dispense pas d'un examen critique. Quant à Rüdt-Collenberg, si son remarquable travail sur les généalogies de l'Arménie cilicienne et des États voisins reste une référence inégalée, il doit être manié avec précaution pour plusieurs raisons. Tout d'abord, l'auteur était handicapé par son ignorance de la langue arménienne. En second lieu, s'il mentionne en général ses sources, c'est de manière sibylline et incomplète, sinon erronée. Enfin son ouvrage date de 1963, si bien que Rüdt-Collenberg n'avait pas à sa disposition la masse de catalogues de manuscrits et de recueils de colophons publiés depuis. En résumé, aucun de ces trois grands historiens n'est à prendre pour « argent comptant ».

La liste qui suit est plus ou moins classée par ordre chronologique.

Dans toutes les notes, l'astérisque * désigne un ouvrage en arménien.

[1] Mikaël Tchamtchian, *Histoire de l'Arménie**, 3 vols., t. III (Venise, 1786).
[2] Ghévont Alichan, *Sissouan** (Venise, 1885), traduction française en deux parties, *Sissouan ou l'Arméno-Cilicie* (Venise, 1899) et *Léon le Magnifique* (Venise, 1888).
[3] Weyprecht Rüdt-Collenberg, *The Rupenides, Hethumides and Lusignans, The structure of the Armeno-Cilician dynasties* (Paris, 1963).

1) Commençons par l'une des erreurs de base, le nom même de l'État. Comme on l'a signalé, bien des auteurs parlent de *Nouvelle Arménie*[4] ou de *Petite Arménie*[5]. Or le premier terme n'a jamais existé, et le second n'a été que très exceptionnellement utilisé, seulement durant les dernières décennies du royaume et dans de rares sources, presque exclusivement latines, sous la forme *Armenia Minor*, et ceci uniquement dans les cas où il était également question de l'Arménie historique, ou *Armenia Major*. Or, dès les années 1160, Benjamin de Tudèle écrivait qu'à Korykos commençait l'*Arménie*[6], et pratiquement toutes les sources, arméniennes ou voisines, ont appelé ainsi le pays jusqu'en 1375. Les rois portaient en arménien, sur tous leurs documents, sceaux et monnaies, les titres de *T'agavor Hayots*' ou de *T'agavor amenayn Hayots'*, respectivement traduits dans les sources occidentales par *Roi d'Arménie* et *Roi de toute l'Arménie*. N'oublions pas en effet qu'en arménien classique *Hayots* est le génitif de *Hayk'*, qui signifiait « Arménie ». Il y eut ainsi, durant cette période, coexistence entre un « royaume d'Arménie » en Cilicie et une « Grande Arménie » sans État sur le territoire historique. Le terme de *Petite Aménie* pour désigner le royaume est à rejeter non seulement au vu des sources, mais également parce qu'il s'appliquait depuis des siècles à un autre territoire, la région de Sébaste et Mélitène, à l'ouest de l'Euphrate, donc bien loin de la Cilicie.

2) Il ne faut pas croire que la chute des royaumes de Grande Arménie et l'invasion turque ont provoqué une émigration massive des Arméniens vers la Cilicie, sous la bannière de tel ou tel chef. La politique byzantine, qui consistait à protéger ses marches frontalières face aux Arabes en y déplaçant des Arméniens, avait déjà eu pour conséquence l'installation d'un noyau arménien en Cilice, en Cappadoce et en Euphratèse. Il s'enrichit avec l'arrivée de certaines

---

[4] Jacques De Morgan, *Histoire du peuple arménien* (Paris, 1919), pp. 161, 193; Hrand Pasdermadjian, *Histoire de l'Arménie* (Paris, 1949), 3e édition, 1971, p. 196.

[5] René Grousset, *L'Empire du Levant* (Paris, 1946), p. 385.

[6] Benjamin de Tudèle, « Itinéraire », trad. in Haïm Harboun, *Les voyageurs juifs du Moyen Age, XIIe siècle* (Aix-en-Provence, 1986), p. 89.

familles fuyant le joug turc, mais la majeure partie de la population arménienne demeura en Grande Arménie.

3) La fondation de l'État arménien a été facilitée par l'arrivée de la croisade à la fin du XIe siècle, c'est un fait indiscutable. Il ne faudrait pas en déduire que les seigneurs arméniens se sont comportés en auxiliaires des croisés, comme on le lit trop souvent depuis la célèbre déclaration en ce sens du pape Grégoire XIII en 1584[7]. Pour les croisés venus s'emparer de Jérusalem et fonder des États en Orient, les Arméniens étaient utiles comme élément chrétien autochtone, mais ils restaient des « hérétiques » et se trouvaient souvent en position de rivalité. Inversement, pour les Arméniens, l'arrivée de ce nouvel élément antigrec et antimusulman dans la mosaïque du Levant ouvrait des perspectives diplomatiques et stratégiques prometteuses quant à leur but ultime, la reconstitution du royaume détruit en Grande Arménie au milieu du XIe siècle. Chacune des deux parties essayait donc d'utiliser l'autre pour parvenir à ses propres fins. Les constants conflits arméno-francs en Euphratèse, puis avec Antioche, ainsi que la description que fit Matt'ieu d'Édesse du comportement des Francs vis-à-vis des Arméniens[8], devraient suffire à détruire cette image idyllique d'un partenariat soi-disant naturel.

4) A la suite de la destruction par les croisés des pouvoirs arméniens en Euphratèse, le flambeau fut repris en Cilicie par les Roubénides. Il était utile, pour leurs ambitions étatiques, de se forger un passé royal, d'où les affirmations de plusieurs sources postérieures au couronnement qui présentent les Roubénides comme des parents des Bagratides[9], créant ainsi une continuité entre Ani et Sis. Cette généalogie n'a aucun fondement.

---

[7] François Tournebize, *Histoire politique et religieuse de l'Arménie depuis les origines des Arméniens jusqu'à la mort de leur dernier roi (l'an 1393)* (Paris, s.d. [1910]), p. 170; De Morgan, p. 239; Pasdermadjian, p. 196.

[8] Matt'ieu d'Édesse, *Chronique* avec continuation par Grégoire le Prêtre*, éd. Mambrē Mēlik' Adamian & Nersēs Tēr Mikayēlian (Vagharchapat, 1898), pp. 337-339 (trad. française Édouard Dulaurier, *Chronique de Matt'ieu d'Édesse (962-1136) avec la continuation de Grégoire le Prêtre jusqu'en 1162* (Paris, 1868), pp. 293-295).

[9] Vahram Raboun, *Histoire rimée des Roubénides**, vers 161-162, éd. et trad. Édouard Dulaurier, « Chronique rimée des rois de la Petite Arménie »,

5) Le fondateur du comté d'Édesse et premier roi de Jérusalem, Baudouin de Boulogne, épousa une princesse arménienne. Les sources contemporaines n'en donnent pas le nom, et il faut attendre le XVIIIe siècle pour en trouver un, en l'occurrence sous la plume de Pauli, qui l'appelle *Arda* sans donner de justification[10]. Il convient donc de l'adopter sous réserves. En revanche, plusieurs chroniqueurs donnent le nom de son père, *Taphnouz* ou *Taftoc*[11]. Quel est ce personnage, inconnu par ailleurs sous ce nom ? Certains croient y reconnaître le prince T'at'oul de Marache, alors que d'autres lisent « T'oros », auquel cas ils ont le choix entre les princes T'oros d'Édesse et T'oros Ier le Roubénide[12]. Inutile de dire qu'aucune de ces identifications n'a le moindre fondement. Il y a beaucoup plus

---

in *Recueil des historiens des croisades, Documents arméniens* (= *DA*), t. I, (Paris, 1869), p. 497; *Colophons de manuscrits arméniens, XIIIe siècle* (= *CM XIII*)*, Artachēs Mat'ēvossian, éd. (Erevan, 1984), n° 474, p. 583; Hét'oum de Korykos, « Lignages », in *Petites chroniques* (= *PC*)*, Vazguēne Hakobian, éd., t. II, (Erevan, 1956), p. 100; Nersēs Palients, « Chronique et chronologies »*, in *Id.*, p. 179. Voir Gérard Dédéyan, *Les Arméniens entre Grecs, Musulmans et Croisés, Étude sur les pouvoirs arméniens dans le Proche-Orient méditerranéen (1068-1150)*, 2 vols. (Lisbonne, 2003), t. I, pp. 365-374.

10 Sebastiano Pauli, *Codice diplomatico del sacro militare ordine Gerosolimitano oggi di Malta*, 2 vols., (Lucques, t. I, 1733), pp. 346, 355. Voir Claude Mutafian, « Prélats et souverains arméniens à Jérusalem à l'époque des croisades : légendes et certitudes (XIIe-XIVe siècle) », *Studia Orientalia Christiana, Collectanea* 37 (2004) (Le Caire-Jérusalem), pp. 114-119.

11 Albert d'Aix, « Historia Hierosolymitana », III 31, in *Recueil des historiens des croisades, Historiens occidentaux* (= *HOcc*), 5 vols., t. IV, (Paris, 1879), p. 361; Guillaume de Tyr, X 1, *Chronique*, Robert Huygens, éd., 2 vols. (Turnhout, 1986), p. 453; Pauli, t. I, pp. 346, 355.

12 Pauli, t. I, p. 517; Alichan, p. 47 (trad. fr., p. 43); Hrach'ia Adjaṙian, *Hayots' andznanunneri baṙaran* [Dictionnaire prosopographique arménien]*, 5 vols. (Erevan, t. I, 1942), p. 303; Rüdt-Collenberg, n°s 3 & 7, tableau I (Rup.) et pp. 49-50; Cyrille Toumanoff, *Les dynasties de la Caucasie chrétienne de l'Antiquité jusqu'au XIXe siècle, Tables généalogiques et chronologiques* (Rome, 1990), p. 427; Ernst Honigmann, « Mar'ash », in *Encyclopédie de l'Islam, Nouvelle édition* (= *EI*), (Leiden, t. III, 1971), réimpr. 1990, p. 492; Monique Amouroux-Mourad, *Le comté d'Édesse, 1098-1150* (Paris, 1988), p. 60.

d'indices en faveur du prince Tavt'ouk, frère de Constantin seigneur de Karkar[13].

6) Selon Guillaume de Tyr, le troisième comte d'Édesse, Jocelin Ier, avait pour épouse une sœur des princes roubénides T'oros et Léon[14]. On ne sait pas comment elle s'appelait, et le nom de *Béatrice*[15] qu'il est admis de lui attribuer résulte d'une confusion avec l'épouse de son fils Jocelin II, la princesse franque Béatrice de Saône[16]. Il aurait d'ailleurs été surprenant que leur père, le prince roubénide Constantin mort au tout début du XIIe siècle, ait donné un tel prénom à sa fille née à une époque où l'onomastique franque n'avait pas encore pénétré le monde arménien.

7) Le plus controversé de tous les princes roubénides est incontestablement Mleh (1170-1175), qui, plutôt que de continuer à jouer Grecs et Latins alternativement les uns contre les autres, prit le pari risqué – et réussi – de se débarrasser des deux en s'alliant au puissant émir d'Alep, Noûr al-Dîn. De nombreux historiens, encore à l'heure actuelle, transforment abusivement cette pure alliance militaire en une communion religieuse, présentant Mleh comme converti à l'islam[17]. Non seulement cette affirmation n'a rigoureusement aucun fondement, mais elle est catégoriquement contredite par le rôle que certaines sources chrétiennes lui font jouer dans la résolution du conflit de succession qui éclata en 1173 à la mort du catholicos Nersēs Chnorhali, frère de son beau-père.

8) La troisième croisade, réponse à la prise de Jérusalem par Saladin en 1187, donne à bien des auteurs une nouvelle occasion de s'étendre sur la soi-disant alliance naturelle entre Arméniens et

---

[13] Dédéyan, t. II, pp. 1036-1038.

[14] Guillaume de Tyr, XIV 3, p. 635.

[15] Rüdt-Collenberg, n° 5, tabl. I (Rup.) et p. 49; Amouroux-Mourad, tableau généalogique; Dédéyan, t. I, pp. 413, 495, 513.

[16] *Lignages d'Outremer* (= *LOM*), éd. Marie-Adélaïde Nielen (Paris, 2003), p. 111.

[17] De Morgan, p. 180; Pasdermadjian, p. 205; Claude Cahen, in « Arminiya », in EI^2, t. I, 1960, réimpr. 1991, p. 660; Ani Atamian Bournoutian, « Cilician Armenia », in *The Armenian People*, Richard Hovannisian, ed., 2 vols. (New York, 1997), t. I, p. 280.

croisés. Leur argument est l'attitude bienveillante du prince roubénide Léon II, futur roi Léon Ier, envers l'empereur germanique Frédéric Barberousse arrivé aux frontières occidentales de la Cilicie. Ils oublient que l'attitude du prince avait deux motivations essentielles : la crainte devant l'approche de cette puissante armée et l'espoir de la remise par l'empereur d'une couronne royale. Pis, ils ne tiennent pas compte du savant partage des tâches entre le prince et le catholicos Grégoire IV Tgha, qui à deux reprises envoya à Saladin des messages l'informant de la marche de l'armée allemande[18]. Certes, cette dernière information ne se trouve que dans les sources arabes, mais il n'y a aucune raison de douter de son authenticité comme le fait par exemple Alichan[19]. L'attitude des autorités arméniennes est fidèle à la diplomatie « tous azimuts » menée depuis le début du siècle par les Roubénides et les Pahlavouni. Elle allait bientôt porter ses fruits avec le couronnement de Léon.

9) Le couronnement eut lieu le 6 janvier d'une année arménienne qui est 646 (31 janvier 1197-30 janvier 1198) selon certaines sources[20], 647 (31 janvier 1198-30 janvier 1199) selon d'autres[21], bien plus nombreuses. Il s'agit donc soit du 6 janvier 1198, soit du 6 janvier 1199. Or, dans d'autres sources qui donnent la date suivant l'ère chrétienne, on lit toujours 1198[22]. On possède en outre un

---

[18] 'Imâd al-Dîn al-Isfahânî, *Conquête de la Syrie et de la Palestine par Saladin*, trad. Henri Massé (Paris, 1972), pp. 193, 229; Bahâ' al-Dîn Ibn Šaddâd, « Vie de Saladin », in *Recueil des historiens des croisades, Historiens orientaux*, 6 vols., t. III, (Paris, 1884), pp. 161-164.

[19] Alichan, p. 447 (trad. fr., *Léon*, pp. 103-104).

[20] Samuel Anets'i, *Havak'munk' i grots' Patmagrats**, Arshak Tēr-Mik'elian, éd., (Vagharshapat, 1893), p. 144; Kirakos Gandzakets'i, *Patmut'iwn Hayot's**, Karapet Melik'-Ohanchanian, éd., (Erevan, 1961), p. 162; Vardan Arevelts'i, *Havak'mun Patmut'ian Hayots'**, Ghévont Alichan, éd., (Venise, 1862), p. 139; Hét'oum II, « Chronique »*, in *PC*, t. I, 1951, p. 77.

[21] Sembat Sparapet, *Chronique**, Sérovbé Aguelian, éd. (Venise, 1956), p. 208 (trad. fr. Gérard Dédéyan, *La chronique attribuée au Connétable Smbat* [Paris, 1980], p. 73); Connétable Sempad, « Chronique du royaume de la Petite Arménie », in *DA*, t. I, p. 634; Nersēs Palients, p. 180.

[22] « Chronique historique traduite du français par l'humble serviteur du Christ Hét'oum seigneur de Korykos »*, in *PC*, t. II, p. 61; *Les Gestes des*

manuscrit copié en 647 de l'ère arménienne dont le colophon est explicitement écrit après le couronnement et l'année de la mort de Nersēs de Lambron[23], qui décéda en juillet 1198[24]. Il n'y a donc aucun doute sur la date de 1198[25], mais 1199 continue à avoir ses partisans.[26]

10) La fondation du royaume s'accompagna d'un spectaculaire développement du commerce, essentiellement avec les grands ports italiens. Le symbole de ce commerce est le port d'Ayas, que Marco Polo décrivit en 1271 avec émerveillement. Or, contrairement à ce qu'on lit parfois[27], l'essor d'Ayas ne date pas des débuts du royaume, les sources ne le mentionnent pas avant les années 1260.

11) Il est courant de parler de *l'union de 1198* entre les Églises arménienne et romaine. Or, s'il est vrai que le pape a posé ces conditions d'union comme préalable à la reconnaissance pontificale de la royauté naissante, Kirakos de Gandzak est bien clair sur le fait que l'acceptation était purement tactique : Léon convoqua les prélats arméniens, ceux-ci opposèrent un refus catégorique et unanime à

Chiprois, Gaston Raynaud, éd. (Genève, 1887), § 56, p. 16; « Annales de Terre Sainte », Reinhold Röhricht & Gaston Raynaud, éds., in *Archives de l'Orient Latin*, 2 vols., t. II B, (Paris, 1884), p. 435.

[23] Ms. n° 989 du Matenadaran d'Erevan, in *Colophons de manuscrits arméniens, Ve-XIIe siècle**, Artashēs Mat'evossian, éd., (Erevan, 1988), n° 306, pp. 305-306.

[24] Sahag Djemdjēmian, *Grand catalogue des manuscrits arméniens de la bibliothèque des Mékhitaristes de Venise** (Venise, t. V, 1995), coll. 19, 27, 96, 176; Maghakia Ormanian, *Azgapatum* [Histoire nationale]* (Constantinople, 1912-1913), § 1059, col. 1539.

[25] Sirarpie Der Nersessian, « The Kingdom of Cilician Armenia », in Kenneth Setton et al., eds., *A History of the Crusades*, t. II, (Madison, Wisc., 1969), p. 648, n. 2.

[26] Alichan, pp. 469-470 (trad. fr., *Léon*, pp. 168-173); Ormanian, § 1063, col. 1545; Claudio Gugerotti, *La liturgia armena delle ordinazioni e l'epoca ciliciana, Esiti rituali di una teologia di comunione tra Chiese*, (Rome, 2001), p. 20; Abraham Terian, « Church-State Relations at the Dawn of Kingship in Cilician Armenia », *Journal of the Society for Armenian Studies* 13 (2003, 2004), p. 5.

[27] De Morgan, p. 200; Atamian Bournoutian, p. 284.

toute concession, mais le prince les convainquit de simuler tant que c'était nécessaire[28]. Les protestations ultérieures de nombreux dignitaires latins accusant les Arméniens de ne pas respecter leurs engagements corroborent ce récit, bien loin de toute « union »[29].

12) Une fois couronné, le prince roubénide Léon II est devenu le roi d'Arménie Léon Ier. C'est un fait parfaitement logique, confirmé par toutes les sources, sans exception. Quatre autres rois homonymes se trouvent dans la liste des titulaires du royaume. Les sources indiquent rarement les rois d'Arménie avec un numéro d'ordre, mais lorsqu'elles le font pour les rois du nom de « Léon » c'est toujours en commençant à Léon Ier, appelant ensuite Léon II son petit-fils, Léon III et Léon IV les petits-fils de ce dernier qui sont à leur tour montés sur le trône, et Léon V le dernier roi[30], un Lusignan dont le mausolée se trouve à Saint-Denis, avec la mention *quint*. Il est donc totalement absurde de faire commencer la liste au prince Léon Ier, grand-oncle du premier roi, ce qui a pour effet de numéroter les cinq rois « Léon » de II à VI. Cette ancienne habitude avait disparu au début du XXe siècle, mais elle retrouva un second souffle à la suite de son adoption par l'historiographie soviétique, qui l'imposa à la plupart des historiens. Elle compte encore de nombreux adeptes[31].

13) Une chronique abusivement attribuée au connétable Sembat contient une précieuse liste de prélats et seigneurs. On n'a longtemps connu qu'un manuscrit de cette œuvre, en partie publié, avec traduction française, dans les « Documents arméniens » du « Recueil

---

[28] Kirakos Gandzakets'i, pp. 156-157.

[29] Jacques de Vitry, « Historia Iherosolimitana », in Jacques Bongars, *Gesta Dei per Francos*, 2 vols. (Hanau, 1611), t. I, p. 1095; [Pseudo-]Brocardus, « Directorium ad Passagium faciendum », éd. Louis de Mas Latrie, in *Documents arméniens*, t. II, 1906, p. 488.

[30] Voir Claude Mutafian, « La titulature et la numérotation des rois d'Arménie en Cilicie », in Robert Dermerguerian, dir., *Armeniaca*, (Aix-en-Provence, 2004), pp. 74-78.

[31] Tchamtchian, index, pp. 152-153; Victor Langlois in *Le Trésor des chartes d'Arménie ou Cartulaire de la chancellerie royale des Roupéniens*, Venise, 1863; Dulaurier, in *DA*, t. I, p. 795; *DA*, t. II, pp. 927-929; Grousset, pp. 394-403; Pasdermadjian, p. 207; Der Nersessian, p. 658; Thomas Boase, *The Cilician Kingdom of Armenia* (Edinbourg, 1978), p. 186.

des historiens des croisades ». Il y est écrit que cette liste est celle des présents au couronnement de Léon Ier en 1198[32]. Or, Alichan mentionne souvent sous le nom de *notre Historien Royal* un second manuscrit, manifestement plus « authentique », sur lequel cette précision n'existe pas[33]. La liste n'est donc que celle des dignitaires civils et religieux arméniens de Cilicie à l'époque du couronnement, mais pas nécessairement des présents.

14) A Léon Ier, mort en 1219, succéda sa fille Zabel, encore mineure. On oublie trop souvent que cette succession n'était pas évidente, le défunt roi ayant eu une fille de son premier mariage[34], certes non porphyrogénète mais aînée, ce qui primait et en faisait l'héritière naturelle.

15) Le premier régent de Zabel s'appelait *Sire Adam*, on en fait traditionnellement un seigneur franc en se basant sur la simple consonnance de son nom[35]. Pourquoi aurait-on délibérément choisi un Franc pour diriger provisoirement le jeune royaume d'Arménie ? La découverte récente d'un colophon prouve définitivement que Sire Adam était arménien[36].

16) Après la mort de Sire Adam la régence passa au père du futur roi Hét'oum Ier, Constantin, seigneur de Papéron, d'une branche cadette des Hét'oumides. Il avait un cousin issu de germains homonyme, seigneur de Lambron, de la branche aînée de la dynastie, qui allait plus tard être exécuté pour haute trahison par Hét'oum Ier.

---

[32] Connétable Sempad, p. 634.

[33] Sembat Sparapet, p. 208 (trad. fr., p. 73).

[34] Continuations de Guillaume de Tyr, in *HOcc*, t. II, 1859, p. 320; *Chronique d'Ernoul et de Bernard le Trésorier*, éd. Louis de Mas Latrie, (Paris, 1871), p. 411; Sembat Sparapet, p. 218 (trad. fr., p. 89).

[35] Voir René Grousset, *Histoire des croisades et du royaume franc de Jérusalem*, 3 vols., (Paris, t. III, 1936), p. 267; Rüdt-Collenberg, n° 68, p. 60.

[36] Anna Sirinian, « Da Drazark a Roma : una pagina di storia ciliciana nel colofone del manoscritto *Arch. Cap. S. Pietro* B 77 », in Valentina Calzolari, Anna Sirinian & Boghos Levon Zekiyan (a cura di), *Dall'Italia e dall'Armenia, Studi in onore di Gabriella Uluhogian* (Bologna, 2004), p. 74.

Ce *prince des princes* Constantin de Lambron avait une épouse nommée Stéphanie. Il est admis d'en faire une fille de Constantin de Papéron[37], mais c'est impossible vu les listes, qui nous sont parvenues, des enfants de ce dernier[38]. En réalité, on n'en sait pas plus sur cette Stéphanie.

17) Le roi Hét'oum II a laissé par intermittence le pouvoir à l'un ou l'autre de trois de ses frères. Le second, Sembat, a été effectivement couronné. Le troisième, Constantin, ne semble pas l'avoir été, mais il a porté le titre de roi, comme le montrent, entre autres, ses monnaies. En revanche, le premier, T'oros, n'a jamais été roi,[39] il convient donc de ne pas l'inclure dans les listes royales.

18) On montre au patriarcat arménien de Jérusalem une longue canne en ambre, avec embouts en argent ciselé, connue sous le nom de *Sceptre du roi Hét'oum.* Selon la légende, ce roi Hét'oum serait entré en vainqueur à Jérusalem, et aurait fait don de son sceptre au patriarcat. Les deux rois de ce nom ont effectivement participé aux campagnes syriennes des Mongols, Hét'oum Ier en 1260 et Hét'oum II en 1299. Parmi les nombreuses sources relatant ces événements, certaines mentionnent bien un séjour royal dans la Ville sainte, mais ce ne sont pas les plus fiables, et aucun colophon n'en parle. Un tel épisode est en réalité pratiquement exclu pour le premier, et fort improbable pour le second[40].

19) A un certain moment au début du XIVe siècle, Hét'oum II a transmis formellement la royauté à son jeune neveu, Léon, fils de T'oros. On admet en général la date de 1301 pour cette passation de

---

[37] Rüdt-Collenberg, n° 100, tableau III (H2), et n° 58 bis, p. 58; Toumanoff, pp. 281, 284.

[38] Alichan, p. 75 (trad. fr., p. 77); *CM XIII*, n°s 282, 477, 519, pp. 343, 593, 639, 641.

[39] *CM XIII*, n° 597, p. 742; Paul Bedoukian, *Coinage of Cilician Armenia*, 2e éd., (Danbury, 1979), p. 90; Connétable Sempad, p. 679; Nersēs Palients, pp. 182, 205; *LOM*, p. 92.

[40] Voir Mutafian, « Prélats ... », pp. 139-140, 141-144.

couronne[41], mais selon la grande majorité des sources elle eut lieu plus tard, probablement en 1305/6[42].

20) En se basant sur le dominicain Etienne de Lusignan[43], source peu sûre du XVIe siècle, on donne souvent pour épouse à ce roi Léon III une de ses cousines germaines du nom d'*Agnès*, fille de sa tante Zabel[44]. En réalité, si cette fille a bel et bien existé, aucune source contemporaine ne la donne pour épouse de Léon III[45] qui ne semble d'ailleurs pas avoir été jamais marié.

21) Cette princesse Zabel donnée par erreur comme belle-mère de Léon III était l'épouse du prince Amaury de Tyr, frère du roi de Chypre Henri II. En 1306, Amaury renversa son frère, qui fut plus tard envoyé en Cilicie pour être confié à la garde du roi d'Arménie Ochine, frère de Zabel. L'usurpation tourna court avec l'assassinat d'Amaury en 1310. Les sources relatives à cette « mise sous tutelle » de Henri II sont essentiellement chypriotes et « légitimistes », donc hostiles aux Arméniens, qui ont effectivement trempé dans le complot. Zabel y est présentée comme une intrigante assoiffée de pouvoir. Cette image de la princesse lui est restée attachée, sans aucune preuve. On pourrait pourtant suggérer, sans d'ailleurs plus de preuves, d'autres explications à son attitude. A cette époque le royaume d'Arménie avait perdu la protection mongole, Chypre restait sa seule alliée au Levant, et il pouvait sembler naturel de songer qu'une union entre les deux royaumes était la seule planche de salut. Zabel a pu avoir cette motivation, anticipant l'offre de la couronne d'Arménie qui allait être faite six décennies plus tard au roi Pierre Ier peu avant son assassinat en 1369.

---

41 Adjarian, t. II, 1944, p. 423; Rüdt-Collenberg, n° 177, tableau III (H2); Toumanoff, p. 290.

42 Norayr Bogharian, *Grand catalogue des manuscrits des Saints-Jacques**, 11 vol. (Jérusalem, t. IV, 1969), pp. 47, 536, t. XI, 1991, p. 388; *Colophons de manuscrits arméniens, XIVe siècle* (= *CM XIV*)*, Levon Khach'ikian, éd., (Erevan, 1950), nos 66, 73, pp. 52, 56; Tchamtchian, p. 301.

43 Estienne de Lusignan, *Description de toute l'isle de Cypre*, (Paris), 1580, fº 143r.

44 Rüdt-Collenberg, n° 178, tableau III (H2) et p. 74; Toumanoff, p. 290.

45 *LOM*, pp. 91, 169.

22) Le patriarcat arménien de Jérusalem est l'une des quatre plus hautes instances actuelles de l'Église arménienne. Quand et comment a-t-il été fondé ? La version presque universellement admise donne un rôle essentiel à un Sarguis, alors évêque de Jérusalem, qui faisait partie des nombreux opposants aux concessions faites par l'Église arménienne à l'Église latine au concile de Sis (1307). Ce Sarguis aurait alors fait sécession, obtenant en 1311 la confirmation de son indépendance par un décret de son suzerain temporel, le sultan mamelouk du Caire. Ce récit se trouve, pour la première fois semble-t-il, chez Tchamtchian[46]. Aucune source antérieure n'en parle, même si on connaît par ailleurs ce Sarguis comme un opposant au courant latinophile alors de rigueur au catholicossat. De plus, avant 1311 certains archevêques de Jérusalem avaient déjà porté le titre de patriarche, et après 1311 il y en eut d'autres qui ne portèrent pas ce titre. On peut donc difficilement garantir l'authenticité de la version de Tchamtchian en attendant la découverte éventuelle de nouvelles sources[47].

23) Au XIVe siècle, comme dans tout royaume en état de décadence, les assassinats devenaient monnaie courante à la cour d'Arménie. Ce n'est pas une raison pour en rajouter. Certains auteurs suggèrent ainsi que le roi Ochine en 1320 et/ou son fils Léon IV en 1341 ont péri assassinés[48], alors qu'aucune source ne permet de justifier de telles affirmations. On ne peut pas non plus invoquer Tchamtchian, qui n'écrit rien d'analogue[49].

24) Le successeur de Léon IV, Guy de Lusignan, a, lui, été bel et bien assassiné en 1344. Quelques sources tardives et imprécises l'appellent *Constantin*[50], d'où une tradition aussi tenace qu'erronée

---

[46] Tchamtchian, p. 313; Ormanian, § 1262, col. 1830; Adjaṙian, t. IV, 1948, p. 431.

[47] Mutafian, « Prélats ... », pp. 144-147.

[48] Alichan, p. 559 (trad. *Léon*, p. 376); Ormanian, § 1289, coll. 1865-1867; Rüdt-Collenberg, p. 25; Boase, p. 30; Atamian Bournoutian, p. 288; Gugerotti, p. 209; Terian, p. 14.

[49] Tchamtchian, pp. 318, 341.

[50] Jacobus Dachian, *Catalogue des manuscrits arméniens de la bibliothèque des Mékhitaristes de Vienne** (Vienne, 1895), p. 111; *CM XIV*, n° 529, p. 441; Samuel Anets'i, p. 168.

qui veut qu'il ait pris ce nom au moment de son couronnement[51]. D'autres auteurs ont adopté une variante encore plus fausse, attribuant ce nom royal à son frère Jean, qui en réalité n'a jamais régné[52].

25) Au milieu du XIVe siècle, à Avignon, le pape Benoît XII demanda à un dominicain arménien, Nersēs Palients, de dénoncer toutes les « erreurs » de l'Église arménienne. Inspiré par son zèle fanatique de récent converti, celui-ci dressa son impressionnant catalogue des *cent dix-sept erreurs* ! La version latine qui nous est parvenue n'est certainement pas celle qu'il a rédigée, car elle comporte des erreurs grossières qu'un esprit cultivé comme lui n'aurait jamais faites. La plus caricaturale concerne le catholicos d'Aghvanie, appelé dans le texte *catholicos Columbarum*[53], c'est-à-dire « des Colombes », par confusion entre les mots arméniens *aghvanits*, qui signifie « d'Aghvanie », et *aghavniats*, pour « des Colombes » ! On peut supposer que Nersēs a rédigé sa liste non en latin mais en arménien, et que le texte latin a été préparé à la curie par un traducteur dont la connaissance de l'arménien laissait à désirer.

26) Afin de préparer une par une les réponses aux 117 accusations, un concile s'est réuni à Sis, et rédigea le texte sous le règne de *Constantin*. A cause de l'une des erreurs ci-dessus signalées, on a vu en lui Guy de Lusignan, ce qui conduisait à dater la fin du concile d'avant 1344[54]. En réalité, c'est le successeur du roi

---

[51] Grigor Mik'ayelian, *Histoire de l'Etat arménien de Cilicie* (en russe) (Erevan, 1952), p. 51; Rüdt-Collenberg, n° 179, tableau (H2) et p.74; Toumanoff, p. 322; Boase, p. 186, n. 2; Henriette Kühl, *Leo V. von Kleinarmenien*, (Frankfort/Main, 2000), p. 28; Terian, p. 15.

[52] Tchamtchian, p. 347; Dulaurier, in *DA*, t. I, pp. 423 (n. 1), 680 (n. 2), 703, 714; Ormanian, § 1309, col. 1905; Adjaṙian, t. II, pp. 670-671, n° 137; Bogharian, t. III, 1968, p. 597.

[53] Aloysius Tautu, *Acta Benedicti XII (1334-1342)* (Vatican, 1958), p. 132.

[54] Tchamtchian, p. 341; Dulaurier, in *Documents arméniens*, t. I, p. LXXI; Alichan, pp. 221, 559 (trad. fr., p. 253 et *Léon*, p. 376); Ormanian, § 1291, col. 1869; Adjarian, t. III, 1946, p. 382, n° 134; Louis de Mas Latrie, in *Documents arméniens*, t. II, p. 560, note; Jean Richard, *La papauté et les*

assassiné qui s'appelait Constantin, et la date du concile est postérieure, très certainement 1345.

27) On lit parfois qu'à partir de Guy la couronne passa à la dynastie des Lusignan. En réalité, Guy fut assassiné en 1344 au bout de deux ans de règne, après quoi la royauté revint à la dynastie hét'oumide. Deux rois « Constantin », de la branche hét'oumide cadette de Néghir, se succédèrent, et ce n'est qu'à la suite de l'assassinat du second qu'on revint aux Lusignan, avec le dernier roi d'Arménie, Léon V, neveu de Guy. Couronné en 1374, capturé en 1375, il régna moins d'un an. En tout et pour tout, il n'y eut donc que deux rois d'Arménie de la dynastie Lusignan, et ils ne totalisèrent pas plus de trois ans de règne.

28) Les autorités arméniennes ont mené depuis le début du XIVe siècle une politique religieuse très latinophile, qui n'a manifestement donné aucun résultat concret quant aux espoirs d'aide européenne. On admet que, devant l'inefficacité de cette politique, un concile réuni à Sis en 1361 changea de cap et revint à une politique religieuse plus « nationale »[55]. On n'a apparemment aucune source contemporaine sur ce revirement, dont la première mention semble due à Siméon Erevants'i, qui écrivait au XVIIIe siècle[56]. Il est fort probable qu'il ait raison, mais on ne peut pas l'affirmer catégoriquement.

29) Fils d'un cousin germain de Guy, le roi de Chypre Pierre Ier se vit proposer la couronne d'Arménie en 1368. Il l'accepta, mais fut assassiné l'année suivante, il ne fut donc jamais roi d'Arménie, et ne doit pas être compté dans la liste des souverains.

30) L'une des raisons de vouloir considérer comme rois des personnages qui ne l'ont jamais été réside dans l'erreur, ci-dessus

---

missions d'Orient au Moyen Age (XIIIe-XVe siècles), 2e éd., (Rome, 1998), p. 213; Gugerotti, pp. 218 & 281-283.

[55] Abel Mekhit'ariants', « Histoire des conciles de l'Église d'Arménie avec leurs statuts », *Ararat** (1874), pp. 168-169; Ormanian, § 1322, coll. 1922-1923; Gevorg Tēr-Vardanian, « Les synodes religieux de Sis », in *Arménie chrétienne, Encyclopédie** (Erevan, 2002), p. 921.

[56] Siméon Erevants'i, *Djambr**, Vagharchapat, 1873, p. 17.

signalée, sur la numérotation des rois « Léon », selon laquelle le dernier roi, Léon V, devenait Léon VI. Or, sur son mausolée est écrit, sans ponctuation, *lyon de lizignê quît roy latî du royaume darmenie*[57]. Au lieu de la lecture correcte « Léon de Lusignan quint, roi latin du royaume d'Arménie », incompatible avec la fausse appellation « Léon VI », on a alors lu « Léon de Lusignan, quint roi latin du royaume d'Arménie ». Le problème, c'est qu'il fallait alors trouver avant lui quatre autres rois latins, alors qu'en réalité il n'y en eut que deux, Philippe d'Antioche et Guy de Lusignan. C'est pourquoi on a appelé à la rescousse Jean et Pierre Ier de Lusignan, en en faisant par erreur des rois d'Arménie[58].

31) La capitale du royaume, Sis, se rendit aux assiégeants mamelouks en avril 1375, et le roi Léon V fut emmené en captivité en Égypte. Est-ce pour en finir de manière plus romanesque que Tchamtchian, encore suivi par plusieurs auteurs, a préféré montrer le roi résistant neuf mois dans la forteresse de Kapan avant de se rendre[59] ? Là encore, aucune source ne justifie un tel récit[60], qu'on doit définitivement considérer comme faux depuis la découverte de la chronique du confesseur de Léon V, Jean Dardel. L'auteur, qui a toujours tendance à exagérer l'histoire en faveur du roi, n'aurait pas manqué de s'étendre sur un tel exploit[61].

32) Dardel, confesseur catholique du roi catholique Léon V, en arrive souvent à de forts partis pris antiarméniens lorsqu'ils sont utiles au panégyrique du roi. Il rend ainsi responsable de la chute de Sis la trahison de dignitaires arméniens, qui auraient préféré l'islam à la foi catholique. Il lance en particulier de graves accusations de connivence avec l'ennemi sur la personne du catholicos de l'époque,

---

[57] Karapet Basmadjian, *Léon V Lusignan, dernier roi d'Arménie** (Paris, 1908), pp. 136-137; Kühl, pp. 314-315.

[58] Mutafian, « La titulature ... », pp. 76-77.

[59] Tchamtchian, pp. 359-364 (trad. anglaise Avdall, Michaël Chamich, *History of Armenia*, 2 vols. (Calcutta, 1827), t. II, pp. 305-308); Dulaurier, in *DA*, t. I, pp. 720, 723; Basmadjian, p. 64.

[60] Alichan, p. 192 (trad. fr., p. 211) ; Mutafian, « Prélats ... », pp. 149-151.

[61] « Chronique d'Arménie par Jean Dardel », Ulysse Robert, éd., in *Documents arméniens*, t. II, pp. 68-85.

en 1375. Elles sont souvent reprises, mais très douteuses vu la partialité de la seule source qui en parle[62].

33) Dardel ne donne pas le nom de ce dernier catholicos du royaume, c'est en général Paul Ier qui est mentionné en cette année 1375[63], mais les colophons sont formels, il s'agit de son prédécesseur, Constantin V, mentionné dès 1373 et mort le 15 août 1380[64].

34) Léon V fut finalement racheté de captivité et finit ses jours en France, d'où l'opinion bien répandue suivant laquelle la rançon aurait été payée par le roi de France. C'est faux, le dernier roi d'Arménie dut sa libération à la générosité du roi Jean Ier de Castille[65].

35) Le mausolée de Léon V se trouve dans la basilique de Saint-Denis, d'où l'opinion bien répandue suivant laquelle il y fut enterré en 1393. En réalité, c'est au couvent des Célestins que se trouvait son tombeau jusqu'à la Révolution. A la suite du saccage du couvent et de la dispersion des cendres, seule la pierre tombale fut sauvée, et à la Restauration elle fut placée sur un nouveau mausolée, vide, au milieu de ceux des rois de France[66].

36) On parle souvent, pour ce dernier royaume d'Arménie, d'un *royaume roubénide*. En réalité, il y eut un seul roi roubénide, le fondateur. Après lui, les souverains furent presque tous de la dynastie hét'oumide, les seules exceptions étant les trois rois latins, Philippe d'Antioche qui régna deux ans et les deux Lusignan, qui totalisèrent trois ans. Sur les 177 ans de royaume, il y eut ainsi 21

---

[62] Dardel, pp. 79-80; Tournebize, p. 724.

[63] Tchamtchian, pp. 358, 362; Tournebize, pp. 712, 718; Basmadjian, p. 52; Ormanian, §§ 1336-1342, coll. 1937-1946; Adjaṙian, t. IV, p. 280, n° 69; Carrière, in *DA*, t. II, p. 58, n. 4; Kühl, p. 139; « Paul Ier de Sis », in *Arménie chrétienne*, p. 866.

[64] *CM XIV*, n°s 628, 630, 639, 663, pp. 511, 514, 518, 534; Bogharian, t. IV, p. 424.

[65] Dardel, p. 102.

[66] Basmadjian, pp. 136-142; Kühl, pp. 314-319.

ans de règne roubénide, 5 ans de règne latin, tout le reste étant hét'oumide : il convient donc de parler d'un royaume hét'oumide fondé par les Roubénides.

28

Some Notes on a Letter Sent from an Armenian Priest in Bengal to the All Savior's Monastery at New Julfa in 1727

Sebouh Aslanian[1]

In 1727, an Armenian priest in Bengal wrote a letter to the primate of All Savior's Monastery in New Julfa, the rich Armenian commercial suburb of the Safavid capital of Isfahan. The priest was one of two clerics in charge of the Armenian Church of Saint John the Baptist in the town of Chinsura (also known as *Chichra*[2]) on the banks of the Hugli River in Bengal, not far from the English settlement of Calcutta. In his letter, he informed the Primate in New Julfa, to whom he was subordinate, of the latest news concerning his parish community in Bengal and, in particular, notified him about the various promises Armenian merchants in his parish had made regarding alms donations both to the Church in Chinsura as well as to the mother convent back home in New Julfa.

This letter is an important primary source for the history of Armenian relations with India and is especially significant in shedding light on the relationship between New Julfa, as the "nodal center" of a global network of Armenian commercial settlements and its offshoot colonies in India.[3] (Fig. 1)

---

1 I thank Houri Berberian, Rudi Mathee, Francesca Trivellato, Willem Floor, Bedross Der Mattosian, and Levon Boghos Zekiyan for their comments on an earlier draft of this essay. A slightly different Armenian version of this essay, translated by Vartan Matiossian, appeared in *Patma-banasirakan Handes*, no. 1 (2006), pp. 254-271.

2 Chichra is a Julfan corruption of "Chuchura," the old Bengali name for the town of Chinsura. Julfan sources use this toponym until the late nineteenth century.

3 For background on New Julfa, its trade networks and the role of new Julfa as a "nodal center," see Aslanian, "From the Indian Ocean to the

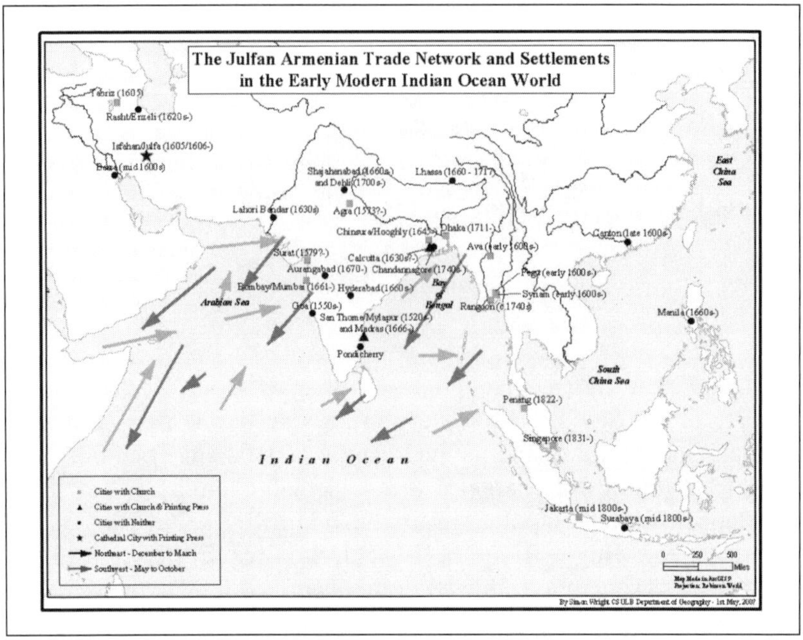

Fig. 1-The Julfan Armenian Trade Network

To help the reader understand the historical context of the letter, of which I provide a full annotated transcription and partial translation below, it is necessary first to say a few words about 1) the history of Armenian relations with India and the establishment of Armenian settlements there beginning in the sixteenth century and, 2) the commercial mail or courier system used by Julfa merchants and clergy alike to share information between India and Julfa.

Armenian Relations with India and Settlements

The earliest extant source on Armenian relations with India is an interesting twelfth-century Armenian itinerary of India and the

---

Mediterranean: Circulation and the Global Trade Networks of Armenian Merchants from New Julfa, Isfahan, 1606-1747," (Ph.D. dissertation, Columbia University, 2007). See also Edmund Herzig, "The Armenian Merchants of New Julfa: A Study of Premodern Trade," (Ph.D. dissertation, St. Antony's College, Oxford, 1991).

neighboring islands of the Malay Archipelago, entitled "Names of Cities in the Indies and on the frontier of Persia," published and scrupulously analyzed most recently by Kéram Kevonian.[4] This work, whose provenance can be traced to the first quarter of the twelfth century, indicates that Armenians were already familiar with the distant lands of India and the Indian Ocean at such an early date. As Kevonian remarks, "[i]f their [i.e., the Armenians'] presence in Asian trade is known for the sixteenth-eighteenth centuries, this text demonstrates that the latter was probably only a continuation of an ancient tradition that had its ups and downs."[5] Nonetheless, it is necessary to remark here that, though evidence suggests that individual Armenians such as the anonymous author of this geographical tract had visited India as early as the twelfth century, if not earlier, there is little evidence to indicate the presence of Armenian settlements in the Indian subcontinent prior to the early modern era.[6]

The first reliable references to Armenian communities in India date from the first quarter of the sixteenth century. When the Portuguese first appeared on the western coast of India in 1498 and shortly afterwards began to settle in the southern region of the country, they found many Armenians already living in those parts. The small town of Mylapur (later renamed San Thomé) on the

---

[4] Kéram Kevonian, "Un Intineraire Arménienne de la Mer de Chine," *Histoire de Barus: Sumatra Le Site de Lobu Tua: Etudes et Documents*, Claude Guillote, ed. (Paris: Cahiers d'archipel 30, 1998), pp. 35-118.

[5] Ibid., p. 116.

[6] In addition to the author of the itinerary mentioned above, there is the even earlier tradition of the visit to Southern India of an Armenian merchant known to the locals as Thomas Cana, who seems to have traveled to Southern India in the early ninth century and played an active role in the revival of the Jacobite church of Christianity there. Mesrovb Seth, *Armenians in India* (Calcutta, 1937), p. 618; Gulbenkian, "Jacobo Abuna: An Armenian Bishop in Malabar (1503-1550)" in *Estudos Históricos: Relacoes entre Portugal Armenia e Medio Oriente* (Lisboa: Academia Portuguesa da Historia, 1995), vol. 1, pp. 111-112 and Thomas Khojamalian *Patmut'iwn Hndustani* folio 85 (mansuscript no. 535 All Saviors' Monastery, New Julfa). As far as early communities or settlements are concerned, Mesrovb Seth's claim that there was an "Armenian colony" at Benares during the first millennium of the Common Era is unsubstantiated.

outskirts of Madras had Armenian inhabitants in the first quarter of the sixteenth century. According to Portuguese sources, it was Armenian merchants residing in Pulikat (in the kingdom of Vijayanagar) who first led them to the tomb of the apostle Saint Thomas in Meliapur where a small church had been built.[7] Later in the seventeenth century, when Francois Martin, the founder of the French colony of Pondicherry retired in San Thomé to write his famous memoirs, he noted the following about Armenian relations with the town:

> It is held that the commencement of the building of San Thomé was the work of many Armenians who were frequenting there on account both of trade and also of their pious devotion to the Saint whose name the town bears. When the Portuguese secured themselves in India, the members of that nation settled in all parts of the country, and a number of them in San Thomé, where they united with the Armenians who were already in residence there. They then built a town and residences by the help of their trade with other parts of India. It is assured that in former times there were families in this place whose opulence reached millions, and the trade in this place in the early days was a gold mine.[8]

---

[7] See the accounts of Gaspar Correa and Jao De Barros quoted in Gulbenkian, "Jacomo Abuna: An Armenian bishop in Malabar (1503-1550)," pp. 103-131. The Armenian version of this article was published in Roberto Kulbenkian, *Hay Portukalakan Haraberut'iwnner* [Armenian-Portuguese Relations] (Yerevan, 1968) pp. 286-310. The passage quoted from De Barros appears on p. 295.

[8] *Memoire de Francois Martin Fondateur de Pondichery (1665-1696)*, publies par A. Martineau, vol. 1, (Paris: Societe d'editions geographique, maritime et coloniales, 1931), pp. 335-336. "On tient que les premiers commencement de la ville de San Thomé ont été l'ouvrage de plusiers Arméniens qui s'y étaient habitués pour y faire leur commerce et encore par une dévotion qui'l y avait au saint dont la ville porte le nom. Aprés que les Portugais eurent affermi leur domination dans les Indes, il y eut des gens de cette nation qui s'établirent dans les Indes, il y eut des gens de cette nation qui s'établirent partout, plusiers s'arrêtèrent à San Thomé; ils s'y allièrent avec les Arméniens qui y étaient déjà, ils y firent bâtir des maisons et en firent ainsi une ville qui devint très coniderables dans la suite par le commerce qu'on faisait de là dans l'une et l'autre Inde; on assure qu'il y a

In the middle of the same century, Armenian merchants were invited to settle in the Mughal capital of Agra by Emperor Akbar the Great (1552-1605).[9] According to Mesrovb Seth, an Armenian church was built there in 1562.[10] Many decades later, when Father Manrique passed through Agra (1640), he paid a visit to the Armenian caravanserai of the city.[11] The important commercial port of Surat to the north, the first port of call in India for most visitors traveling to the East from the Persian Gulf ports of Basra and Ormuz, had also attracted Armenian merchants starting in the sixteenth century. Mesrovb Seth notes that the earliest tombstone in the city's old Armenian cemetery dates from 1579 and belongs to the wife of an Armenian priest.[12] Based on this evidence, Seth concludes that that there must have been a sizeable community of Armenians in the city to warrant having a priest and most likely a Church to meet their religious needs. According to an Armenian treatise on historical geography published in Venice in 1805, one of Surat's Muslim governors is said to have destroyed the Armenian Church (most probably in the early part of the seventeenth century under Shah Jahan's rule) upon complaints by Muslim merchants returning from the pilgrimage in Mecca.[13] No remains of this early church (either

---

eu autrefois des familles riches de plusieurs millions, et il est certain aussi que le commerce dans les premiers temps était une mine d'or."

[9] On the Armenians in Agra, see Seth, *Armenians in India*, p. 2; Terenig Polatian, *Akrayi Hayerě* [Armenians of Agra] (Beirut, 1963); and Rev. H. Hosten, SJ., "Mirza Zul Qarnain, A Christian Grandee of three Great Moghuls, with notes on Akbar's Christian Wife and the Indian Bourbons" in *Memoirs of the Asiatic Society of Bengal,* (Calcutta, 1916), pp. 115-194. Hosten does not find any proof for the existence of an Armenian Church in Agra at such an early date, though he does provide much evidence for the presence of Armenians in Agra during that time.

[10] Seth, *Armenians in India*, p. 2. Seth provides no evidence for this assertion. His source was most likely the appendix to Thomas Khojamalian's *Patmut'iwn Hndustani* (see footnote 6 above) where the author briefly mentions the existence of an Armenian Church in Agra in the second half of the sixteenth century.

[11] *Travels of Fray Sebastian Manrique (1629-1643),* issued by the Hakluyt Society (1927), vol. 2, p. 159.

[12] Seth, *Armenians in India*, p. 225.

[13] Stepanos Giuver Akonts, *Ashkharagrut'iwn chorits' masants' hator 4 hndiks* [Geography of the Four Parts (of the World) vol. 4 The Indies],

physical or documentary) seem to have survived, though another church was built later in the seventeenth century to serve to needs of the city's growing Julfan community. Several dozen tombstones from this church and other Armenian cemeteries in Surat have been preserved, the oldest of which dates from the 1690s.[14] Lahori Bandar in the Punjab also seems to have had a small Armenian community in the first decade of the seventeenth century. At least two important manuscripts copied by Armenian priests in Lahor in 1635 have survived.[15]

Two events helped accelerate Armenian migration and settlement in India during the seventeenth century. The first and most important was the founding of New Julfa in 1605 through Shah Abbas' forced deportations of Armenians from Old Julfa. In less than fifty years, merchants from New Julfa were already visiting the markets of Hyderabad, Golconda, and Masulipatam in southern India and Hugli, Patna, and Calcutta in the north. Like other merchants traveling to India from the West, Julfan Armenians must have traveled there on ships leaving for India from the Persian Gulf. Since it was difficult to make a return trip to India from the Persian Gulf during the same year due to the monsoon regime regulating maritime travel across the Indian Ocean, merchants traveling to India usually allowed themselves up to two years to dispose of their goods and return home. This long layover encouraged the forming of new settlements in places not settled by Armenians before the almost sudden arrival of New Julfans in India. By the end of that century, Julfans had crossed the Himalayas from Patna to establish a small

---

(Venice: San Lazzarro, 1805), pp. 84-85. The author provides no dates or motives for the destruction of this little-known church. If such a church was destroyed it is unlikely that the destruction would have taken place during Akbar's religiously tolerant rein, nor that of his successor Emperor Jahangir. It is more probable that the event took place during Shah Jahan's reign, which saw the first major reversal of Akbar's religious policies. See Richards, *The Mughal Empire*, pp. 121-122, for background discussion.

[14] I thank Elizabeth Lambourn for sending me images of some of these tombstones.

[15] Vazgen Hakobyan and Ashot Hovhannisyan, eds., *Hayerēn dzeragreri Zh E dari hishatakaranner hator b, 1621-1640* [Colophons of Armenian Manuscripts from the seventeenth century, vol. 2, 1621-1640], (Yerevan: Haykakan SSH Gitut'iwnneri Hratarakch'ut'yun, 1978), pp. 587 and 633.

community in Lhassa, the capital of Tibet[16] (1680s- 1717); around the same time, they had settled in Spanish-ruled Manila[17] on the outer limits of the Indian Ocean. They had also settled in the Dutch colony of Batavia by the middle of the eighteenth century. [18]

The second event that spurred Armenian settlement in India was a trade agreement, signed in London on June 22, 1688, between the "English East India Company and the Armenian Nation." For the Company, the main objective of the Agreement was to encourage the

---

16 For the colony in Tibet, see Levon Khach'ikian, "The Account Ledger of Merchant Hovhaness of Julfa," *Journal of the Asiatic Society*, vol. VIII, no. 3 (1966), and the Introduction to *Hovhaness Tēr Davtian Jughayetsu Hashvetumarĕ* [The Accounting Ledger of Hovhaness Tēr Davtian of Julfa] (Yerevan, 1984). See also *I Missionari Italiani nel Tibet e nel Nepal*, a cura di Luciano Petech, 7 volumes, (Rome: Libreria delo Stato 1952-56); L. Petech "Un itinirario della Persia alla Cina" *Bolletino della Società Geografica Italiana*, 1950, especially pp. 169-170; Krosi Csoma "A Tibetan Passport dated 1688 A.D," *Journal of the Asiatic Society of Bengal*; as well as *Storia do Mogor; or, Mogul India, 1653-1708, by Niccolao Manucci*. Translated with introduction and notes by William Irvine, vol. 2, (Calcutta: Editions Indian, 1966) p. 413.

17 Serafin D. Quiason, *English country trade with the Philippines, 1644-1765* (Quezon City: University of the Philippines Press, 1966). Quiason's work is the only reliable source that discusses the settlement of Armenian merchants in Manila. *The Archivo de Indias* in Sevilla (Spain) has hundreds of pages of documentation on Armenian merchants in Manila, which have not yet been examined. I am currently in the process of preparing some of this material for publication. See also chapter three of Aslanian, "From the Indian Ocean to the Mediterranean" for a detailed treatment of Julfan connections with Manila and beyond to Mexico in the New World.

18 Hordanan Hordananian, *Netrlandakan Arewelean Hndkastanay hay gaghuti patmut'iwnĕ skzbēn minch'ev mer orerĕ* [The History of the Armenian colony of the Dutch East Indies from the beginning down to our days] (Jerusalem, 1937); Margaret Sarkissian, "Armenians in South-East Asia" in *Crossroads: An Interdisciplinary Journal of Southeast Asian Studies,* vol. 3 no. 2-3 (1987), pp. 1-33; and B. C. Colless, "Traders of the Pearl: The Mercantile Activities of Nestorian Christians and Armenians," *Abr Nahrain*, periodically from 1969-1976. For the presence of Armenian merchants in Mallaca in the early sixteenth century, see Tome Pires, *The Suma Oriental of Tome Pires: An Account of the East, from the Red Sea to Japan, Written in Malacca and India in 1512-1515*, trans. and edit. by Armando Cortesao (London: Hakluyt Society, 1944), vol. 2, p. 269.

Armenians "to alter and invert the ancient course of their Trade to and from Europe,"[19] that is, to have the Armenians transport their silk to Europe on English Company ships around the Cape of Good Hope, as opposed to the overland routes across Ottoman Territory. To this end, the Company accorded the Armenians special privileges, such as "liberty at all time hereafter to pass and expedite to and from India on any one of the Company's ships on as advantageous terms as any Freeman whatsoever," as well as low customs fares.[20] The most important clause in the Agreement, at least as far as Armenian migration and settlement in India is concerned, was the following:

> that they shall have liberty to live in any of the Company's Cities, Garrisons, or Towns in India, and to buy, sell, and purchase Land or Houses, and be capable of all Civil Offices and preferments in the same manner as if they were Englishmen born, and shall always have the free and undisturbed liberty of the exercise of their Religion.[21]

In an addendum to the Agreement, the Company further agreed that:

> whenever forty or more of the Armenian Nation shall become Inhabitants in any of the Garrisons, Cities or Towns belonging to the Company in the East Indies, the said Armenians shall not only have and enjoy the free use and exercise of their Religion, but there shall be also allotted to them a parcel of Ground to erect a Church thereon for the worship and service of God in their own way and that we will also at our own Charge, cause a convenient Church to be built with stone or other Solid Materials to their own good liking and the said Governor and Company will also allow fifty Pounds per annum during the space of Seven Years for the maintenance of such Priest or Minister as they shall choose to officiate therein.[22]

---

[19] See Ronald Ferrier. "The Agreement of the East India Company with the Armenian nation 22nd June 1688," *Révue des études arméniennes,* new series, vol. VII, p. 438.

[20] Ibid., p. 438.

[21] Ibid., p. 439.

[22] Ibid., p. 442.

Low tax breaks, promises of integration within the English settlements of India, and especially religious tolerance wooed greater numbers of Julfan merchants to the shores of India in the seventeenth and eighteenth centuries and stimulated the establishment of new settlements alongside older ones.

Armenian merchants had settled in Bengal (the richest province of Mughal India) during the first half of the seventeenth century. They seem to have already established themselves in Calcutta at least half a century before the English East India Company leased, through the mediation of the Armenian merchant named Khwaja Sarhat di Israel, the villages of Sutanati, Govindapur, and Kalikata in 1698, and established in Kalikata their factory of Fort William. This factory and the villages surrounding it became the nucleus of modern-day Calcutta. It is interesting to note that the Armenian Church of Holy Nazareth in Calcutta (built in 1724 on the grounds that served as an old Armenian cemetery) has a tombstone dating from 1630. Until the discovery of this tombstone in 1885, it was assumed that the English were the first foreign settlers and founders of Calcutta.[23]

In 1665, Armenians were invited to settle in Saidabad, a suburb of the provincial capital of Bengal at Murshidabad. In a manner

---

[23] The authenticity of this tombstone as evidence of Armenian settlement in Calcutta before the arrival of the English in the 1690s was disputed first by C. R. Wilson who argued that the stone was an isolated incident and that it was probably brought to Calcutta from somewhere else at a later date. See his *Early Annals of the English in Bengal: Being the Bengal Public Consultations for the first half of the 18th Century* (London: W. Thacker, 1895-1919), vol. 1, p. 137. More recently, Bhaswati Battacharya, in her otherwise informative account of Armenian trade in India (Bhaswati Bhattacharya, "Armenian European Relationship in India 1500-1800: No Armenian Foundation for European Empire?" *Journal of the Social and Economic History of the Orient,* Vol. 48, no. 2 (2005), pp. 277-322 (see p. 292, fn. 62), seems to agree with Wilson. Both Wilson and Battarcharya, however, disregard the fact that Armenians in India had the habit of building their churches on sites previously used by members of their community to bury their dead. This was the case with the Armenian Church of the Holy Virgin in Madras, which, like the Church of Holy Nazareth in Calcutta, has tombstones predating its construction in the mid-eighteenth century.

reminiscent of their settlement in New Julfa, they were granted land on the outskirts of the city (through a royal Farmān from Emperor Aurangzeb) to build a predominantly Armenian commercial suburb.[24] The Armenian church of the Virgin Mary was built in Saidabad in 1758.

Another notable place in Bengal where Armenians had also settled was Chinsura or Chichra, a small town about 28 miles north of Calcutta near the thriving port town of Hugli. According to Seth, their presence there dates from 1645. Armenian merchants were attracted to Chinsura because the nearby settlement of Hugli was the leading port in Bengal at the time, and because the area acted as the commercial headquarters in Bengal of first the Portuguese followed by the Dutch East India Companies.[25] Despite the importance of this community, our sources concerning its early history are very meager until the last decade of the seventeenth century. In November of 1692, the Armenian merchant, Hovhaness of Julfa, visited Chinsura after his return from Tibet, and noted in his commercial diary that he donated funds to an Armenian priest there for the celebration of church services.[26] Since the town's Armenian Church was not built until three years after Hovhaness's visit there, we may conclude that the Chinsura Armenians were probably using a private house to

---

[24] There is here an interesting parallel with the founding of New Julfa as an Armenian suburb of Isfahan sixty years earlier through a farmān from Shah Abbas I. See Ina Baghdiantz-McCabe, *The Shah's Silk for Europe's Silver* (Atlanta, Georgia: Scholar's Press, 1998), p. 291.

[25] The Portuguese had a base in Bandel, a few miles from Chinsura where they built a church in 1595. For Hugli's importance as a port town, see Sushil Chaudhuri, "The Rise and Decline of Hugli: A Port in Medieval Bengal," *Bengal Past and Present: A Journal of Modern Indian and Asian History*, (January-June 1967) pp. 33-68.

[26] Levon Khach'ikian and H. D. Papazian, *Hovhaness Tēr Davtian Jughayetsu Hashvetumarě* [The Accounting Ledger of Hovhaness Tēr Davtian of Julfa] (Yerevan, 1984), p. 281 for Hovhaness's journal entry. Khach'ikian notes in his Introduction (p. 33) that Hovhaness donated money to the "Armenian Church" of Hugli (i.e., Chinsura) but fails to notice that, since such a "Church" did not exist at the time of Hovhaness's visit there (i.e., 1692), religious ceremonies must have been held in a private house.

perform their religious services.[27] In 1695, a wealthy Armenian merchant originally from New Julfa named Khwaja Hovsep Margarian, whose relatives were most likely among the first Armenian settlers of Chinsura in the middle of the seventeenth century,[28] provided 20,000 rupees for the construction of the Armenian Church of Saint John the Baptist, where he buried his brother Hovhaness Margarian.[29]

---

[27] This seems to have been a custom among Armenian merchants, where Armenian churches did not yet exist. For instance, the same Hovhaness mentions in his business diary that he came across an Armenian priest in Patna, where the Armenians did not have a church, but were most likely using a private house to perform their religious services. See Khach'ikian and Papazian, *Hovhaness Tēr Davtian Jughayetsu Hashvetumarĕ,* pp. 21-22.

[28] See the important "legal brief" printed in Paris by Hovhaness' father, Marcara Avacintz (known among the Armenians as Martiros (or)di Marcara Avakshints), one of the first directors of the French East India Company in India, for his court case against the Company in the 1670s. The document is entitled *Factum Contenant l'histoire tragique; pour le Sieur Martin Marcara Avachinz de la ville d'Hispahan, Capitale de Perse, conseiller au Conseil Souverain de l'sle Daufine, & directeur des comptoire de la Compagnie Francoise des Indes Orientales dans les Indes et dans la Perse, demandeur en requeste presentée au conseile de sa majesté du 6 Mars 1676. Et Michel Marcara, son fils.* Bibliothèque National de Paris (BNF) Manuscrits Fr. 15529. See also the similar "brief" contained in BNF Ms Fr. 8972. Marcara states that he had traveled to India at a young age (most likely in the 1640s) and conducted commerce there with his brothers for many years. Seth, *Armenians in India*, states that the Margarian family was associated with the establishment of the Armenian community of Chinsura in the 1640s. Unfortunately, Seth does not provide any sources for this statement. For an insightful discussion of the career of Marcara Avachinz, see chapter 7 of Baghdiantz-McCabe's *The Shah's Silk for Europe's Silver*, pp. 295-225.

[29] Hovsep Margarian's will is quoted at length in Tēr Hovhaneants', *Patmut'iwn Nor Jugha i Spahan* [History of New Julfa at Isfahan], Eastern Armenian translation (Julfa, 1980), vol. 1, pp. 198-201. The original document of this valuable will was stored in the archives of All Savior's Monastery, but seems to have disappeared since it was last used by Tēr Hovhaneants' in the 1850s. The Church in Chinsura was named after Hovhaness (John) Margarian whose ornate tombstone was still well preserved inside the Church when I visited the town in the summer of 2003.

At the beginning of the seventeenth century, the Armenian communities in India came under the religious jurisdiction of the All Savior's Monastery in Julfa. In order to maintain the identity of these communities, the religious hierarchy of the All Savior's Monastery led by the primate, periodically staffed the churches in India with Armenian priests sent from their mother colony in New Julfa.[30] These priests served many functions not all of which were purely religious. First, they were tasked with meeting the spiritual needs of Julfan Armenians residing far away from their home in New Julfa. In fulfilling this task, priests also helped to maintain the economic and cultural integrity of the Julfan network as a whole. Second, priests serving in the overseas Julfan settlements played an essential role in vouchsafing the financial survival of the Diocesan center of their church in New Julfa. As Vazken Ghougasian points out, the Church relied on three principal sources of income to meet its expenses: 1) individual donations and wills, 2) land income from *vakf* properties owned by the Church, and 3) various types of taxes collected from the community. In the last category were special taxes known as *khostmunk* and *nverk,* which were essentially pledges of money made by wealthy merchants to be used after their death in the form of *hogepazhin* (literally the soul's portion) or money set aside for priests to pray for the deceased person's soul. There does not seem to have been a set standard for how much merchants were expected to pay for their *hogepazhin*; however, an examination of wills containing data on *Khostmunk* or *nverk* reveals that this portion

---

[30] As the Diocesan center for the Armenian churches in the East, the All Savior's Monastery in New Julfa not only periodically sent out priests to India, but also to the Armenian communities in Pegu and Syriam (both in present-day Burma/Miyanmar), as the following passage from a letter from Madras dated 1711 indicates: եւ այլ կու խնդրեմ հրամանուցդ առատ նախախնամութ[են]էդ որ մօսումիս Գ[3] լէվ ընտիր քահանայ ողորկես Բ[2] քն մադրասիս համ[ա]ր մէկն փէկու ճումիաթն միշտ խնդրուման որ առանց քահանայի մնացելան պիտի որ ողորկես [And I also beg from your eminence's generous affection, that, during this monsoon season, you send us three fine priests, two for this place at Madras and one for Pegu, for the [Armenian] community of Pegu are always beseeching us [saying] that they have been left without a priest. It is necessary that you send them (i.e., the priests)] (Letter stored in "Letters from Madras, folder 104," All Savior's Monastery Archive.)

varied from individual merchant to merchant, but was generally in the range of 5 to 10 tomans.[31] Priests sent to serve the parish churches across the New Julfan network overseas were thus expected to secure sizeable sums of *nverk* and *khostmunk* from the wealthy merchants residing abroad. They did this by regularly reporting back to their Primate in New Julfa concerning the financial fortunes of the notable merchants belonging to their parish. If a merchant had passed away while traveling to a distant market such as Manila, for instance, the priests were expected to arrange for the execution of the deceased merchant's will and to secure his donation to the All Savior's Monastery and send that money to New Julfa by means of letters of credit or other commercial instruments used by the merchant class.[32]

---

[31] This is based on the money bequeathed to the Church by two Julfan merchants in Chinsura, one of whom, a wealthy merchant named Ulukhan, left 110 rupees or between 5.5 to 6.9 tomans (each toman being worth between 16 and 20 rupees) and a low level merchant who left 90 rupees. Another merchant, Poghos son of Zeni aghazar, who passed away in Surat in 1682, left a more substantial sum of 1,000 rupees for the All Savior's Monastery and 500 rupees each to the Saint Catherine's Nunnery and the Meydan Church both in Julfa, thus bringing his total donation to between 100 and 125 tomans. This same merchant also left 300 rupees each to three Armenian priests in Surat. (See "Ktakner-Surat," All Savior's Monastery Archives).

[32] For instance, writing a long letter to Primate Movses Vardapet on November 16, 1711, a Julfan priest in Madras named Avet, reports on the cases of several wealthy Julfan merchants who had recently passed away in India and in one case Manila and outlines the steps he had taken to secure a *hogepazhin* for the All Savior's Monastery. The writer also informs the Primate that two years prior to his letter a Julfan merchant in Madras named Almaz had traveled by ship to Pegu, but his ship had not been heard from again. The writer states that people there were of the opinion that the merchant was lost at sea with the ship and informs the Primate that this merchant had no heirs but his wife in Julfa. He therefore asks the Primate to tell the merchant's wife to appoint a power of attorney and send him to Madras to settle the deceased's accounts and receive her share of the inheritance. The writer doesn't forget to mention that, since this merchant had no heirs but his wife, the share bequeathed to the All Savior's Monastery as *hogepazhin* would be significant. In this connection, he asks the primate to write a document regarding the *hogepazhin* and send the appropriate papers to Madras so that he, the writer of this letter, could receive this *hogepazhin* and send it to the All Savior's Monastery.

In addition to collecting *nverk* or *khostmunks* from wealthy merchants, the letter reproduced below suggests that each priest serving overseas was expected to make his own donation of two tomans in *Khostmunk* to the All Savior's Monastery on an annual basis. We do not know where this money came from, but it would seem reasonable to assume that it was paid from the income priests made while serving their mostly merchant flock in places like Madras, Surat, or Hugli.

The genesis of New Julfa's diocesan expansion in the world of the Indian Ocean is largely unexplored.[33] Our knowledge of the Diocese's early history in India remains obscure and must be pieced together through a careful examination of surviving documents such as merchant wills, encyclicals, and church correspondence from the first half of the eighteenth century. What is known is that by 1793, the following hierarchical system of diocesan authority had emerged. The senior priest of the church in Surat had authority over Armenian priests in Bombay, Shahjehanabad, Aurangabad, and Hyderabad; that of Madras had authority over the priests in Muchlibandar, Nagapatan, Pegu, and Batavia; and, after its establishment in 1724, the Church of Holy Nazareth in Calcutta had jurisdiction over the churches of Chinsura, Saidabad and Dhaka.[34] The evidence suggests that throughout the eighteenth century, Armenian churches in India had two or three priests posted there at any given time. While it is not surprising that priests stationed in the Julfan communities in India and elsewhere in the Indian Ocean needed to be in regular communication with each other and especially with their primate in New Julfa, what is more interesting and unexpected is that these priests relied on the same commercial mail system devised and used

---

[33] Goughassian does a good job of describing how the Diocese of New Julfa expanded in the seventeenth century, but the bulk of his discussion focuses on the relationship between the Diocese and the Holy See of Etchmiadzin, on the one hand, and the European Catholic missionaries, on the other. Ghoughassian hardly touches on the diocesan expansion into the world of the Indian Ocean. See Ghougassian, *The Emergence of the Armenian Diocese of New Julfa in the Seventeenth Century*.

[34] Tēr Hovhaneants', *Patmut'iwn Nor Jugha i Spahan*, vol. 1, p. 419 and Shushanik Khachikian, *Nor Jughayi Hay Vacharakanut'iwnĕ ew nra tntesakan kaperĕ Rusastani het* [Armenian Trade of New Julfa and its commercial ties with Russia] (Yerevan, 1988), p. 53.

by Armenian merchants across New Julfa's vast commercial network.

The Commercial Mail between Julfa and India

Elsewhere, I have referred to New Julfa's commercial mail as constituting an "Intelligence network"[35] that consisted of what we might call an elaborate postal system, where correspondence was delivered from one Armenian settlement in India to another and eventually to the "node" or center of the network in New Julfa itself.[36] Sometimes, this was done by means of professional couriers (known by the Persian and Arabic terms as *chapars*,[37] *shatirs* or most commonly as *qasids*), but more frequently through traveling merchants. Most mail from India to Julfa traveled on European company vessels (usually those of the English, French, and Dutch East India Companies) as well as ships freighted or owned by Armenian merchants. Armenian merchants also used Mughal ships such as those in the formidable commercial flotilla belonging to the Surat-based famous maritime merchant family known as the Chalabies. When professional couriers were not used, mail would be handed over ("taslim") to an Armenian merchant traveling to Isfahan or the Persian Gulf. Mail traveling from Bengal to New Julfa would generally follow two routes. The first and most frequent route was the maritime one relying on ships embarking at the port of Hugli or the busier harbor of Calcutta where mail was likely to travel in stages

---

[35] I have borrowed this term from Rene Barendse's pathbreaking essay, "The Long Road to Livorno: The Overland Messenger Service of the Dutch East India Company in the Seventeenth Century" in *Itinerario*, vol. XII (1988), no. 2, pp. 25-45.

[36] Sebouh Aslanian, "Trade Diaspora versus Colonial State: Armenian Merchants, the East India Company and the High Court of Admiralty in London, 1748-1752" in *Diaspora: A Journal of Transnational Studies*, vol. 13:1 (2006), pp. 37-100, and especially ibidem., "The Salt in a Merchant's Letter: The Culture of Julfan Correspondence in the Indian Ocean and the Mediterranean," *Journal of the World History*, (forthcoming 2008).

[37] On the "chapar" system in Safavid and post Safavid Iran, see Willem Floor's article on "Chapar" in *Encyclopedia Iranica*, as well as his "The Chapar-khana System in Qajar Iran," *Iran*: (London). [Iran: (Lond.)] (2001), vol. 39, pp. 257–291. I thank Rudi Matthee for the reference to the latter article.

down the eastern coast of India making calls on Madras and thence to Surat from where it would be shipped to the Persian Gulf port of Basra. In Basra, it would be transferred to Armenian merchants traveling overland to Isfahan. Sometimes, there would be professional couriers working for Julfan family firms waiting at the port of Basra to deliver important mail to their masters in Julfa.[38] In some cases, mail would be unloaded at the port of Bandar Rig in the Persian Gulf where it would be handed over to couriers to be delivered from there overland north to Julfa. The second mail route from Bengal was the overland one through a messenger (*Pattamar*[39] or *dak*[40] to use terms in currency in Mughal India) across the Deccan

[38] For instances of this, see the fascinating correspondence seized from the Armenian-freighted ship, the *Santa Catharina*. Freighted by the Khwaja Minasian Family in Bengal, this ship was seized in 1748 by the English navy in India on the pretext that it was a French ship. After its capture, the British shipped all the paper cargo of the ship (consisting of approximately two thousand family and business letters from India and Julfa) to London in order to use them as "exhibits" for a protracted law suit at the High Court of Admiralty in London, during which the Ship's Armenian merchants unsuccessfully tried to contest the illegal seizure of their vessel. For the story of the *Santa Catharina's* capture and its trial, as well as my discovery of its documents in the spring of 2003, see my "Trade Diaspora versus Colonial State." For references to professional couriers waiting at Persian Gulf ports, see Letter No. 20, folios 90-91 in the HCA-44 series.

[39] On the role of *pattamars* and mail during the Mughal period, see Irfan Habib, "The Postal Communications in Mughal India," in *Proceedings of the Indian Historical Congress*, pp. 236-252; Christopher Bayly's short treatment in *Empire and information: intelligence gathering and social communication in India, 1780-1870* (Cambridge [England]); (New York: Cambridge University Press, 1996), pp. 10-14; and Usha Agarwal, "An Account of the Postal System in India from 1650 to 1750" in *Bengal Past and Present*, 1966, (January-June), pp. 40- 57.

[40] For a discussion on the term Dak or "dawk" see, *Hobson Jobson: A glossary of colloquial Anglo-Indian words and phrases, and of kindred terms, etymological, historical, geographical and discursive.* New ed. edited by William Crooke, B.A. (London: J. Murray, 1903). "DAWK, S. H. and Mahr. *dak*, 'Post,' *i.e.* properly transport by relays of men and horses, and thence 'the mail' or letter-post, as well as any arrangement for travelling, or for transmitting articles by such relays." It is interesting to note that Julfans also used this term in reference to the overland delivery of their mail in Mughal India. Thus in a letter sent by an Armenian priest from

plain to Surat and from there by ship to the Persian Gulf. This combination of overland and maritime route could shave off a few weeks in travel time.

The mail service between India and Julfa was predicated on many contingent factors, the most important of which was the monsoon regime (known in Julfa dialect as *Mowsum*, from the Arabic *mawsim*[41] (trading season) from which in turn the Indian and English "monsoon" derives) that dominated the lives of everyone living along the shores of the Great Ocean. There were two general monsoon seasons in the Indian Ocean.[42] The first or the northwest

---

Madras to Julfa in 1711, the writer states: եւ յայտ լիցի վեհափառութեանդ որ մեծ թիւն ՌՃՁԹ [1159=1710] յուլիսի մէկէն եւ ԻԲ [22] քէն գրած ս[ուր]բ որհնութե[ան] թուղթն սուրաթին վերայ հասաւ թիւն ՌՃԿ [1711] յամսեանն ապրիլի ԻԶ [26] եւ մայիսի Ի [20]. Մէկն ձեռամբն շահրմանենց պ[ա]ր[ո]ն սարհադին եւ մէկն փայեկի /դայեկի՞. (This letter is stored in All Savior's Archives, Folder 104, "Letters from Madras"). The word that interests us here is almost certainly day[e]k which would be a corruption of the Mughal term dak or dawk (see above). However, it could also be a misreading on my part (the writing is unclear here) of the Persian word "Paik," which according to, Francis Joseph Steingass's *A Comprehensive Persian-English dictionary, including the Arabic words and phrases to be met with in Persian literature* (London: Routledge & K. Paul, 1892), means, among other things, the following: "A running footman; a carrier, messenger; a guard; a watchman; a footman." See p. 268.

41 See Solomon Goitein, A *Mediterranean Society: The Jewish Communities of the Arab World as Portrayed in the Documents of the Cairo Geniza*, vol. 1, *Economic Foundations* (Berkeley, Los Angeles: University of California Press, 1967), pp. 276-277. As Goitein points out, "the word *mawsim* designated both the caravan and the fair or business season connected with its arrival." It was only later associated exclusively with the oceanic seasons dependent on the wind patterns of the Indian Ocean. The Julfa dialect word was most likely a direct borrowing from Arabic.

42 I have drawn and simplified my information on the monsoon seasons from K.N. Chaudhuri. *Trade and civilisation* in the *Indian Ocean*: *an economic history from the rise of Islam to 1750*, Cambridge [Cambridgeshire]; [New York: Cambridge University Press, 1985], p. 127, and Janet L. Abu-Lughod. *Before European hegemony*: the world system A.D. 1250-1350 (New York: Oxford University Press, 1989), pp. 251-260 and chapter 8. The locus classicus for a discussion of the monsoons remains

monsoon extended from October to March marking the beginning of the season for the departure of ships from India to the Persian Gulf. Ships wishing to travel to the Persian Gulf had to usually depart India in January in order to catch the winds blowing west. Failure to do so and thus "missing the monsoon" meant a delay of up to one year. The other monsoon season lasted from April to September, with easterly winds blowing from the African coast toward the western shores of India. This meant that ships heading from the Persian Gulf (or the Red Sea) to India had to depart early in the summer to make landfall in India by late fall (see the arrows in Fig. 1). The voyage in either direction usually lasted from three to six months. This peculiar eco-structure of the Indian Ocean set limits on what men could accomplish. It is virtually impossible to understand commercial and social life in the Indian Ocean without first taking into account the impositions of the Ocean's geography and ecology. This was particularly the case for communities of merchants like the Julfa Armenians, whose settlements in India and beyond needed to be constantly replenished with the regular circulation of merchants, credit, priests and above all information from their nodal center in New Julfa. The circulation of all these objects was dependent on the monsoon system. This was especially the case with the mail service.

There are no available published data on the speed with which mail traveled between India and Julfa. Fortunately for us, however, it is possible to calculate the time it took for letters to travel from Julfa to Bengal because merchants receiving important correspondence had the habit of writing the date when a letter reached their hands. Based on an examination of hundreds of such letters that have come down to us through the All Savior's Monastery archives as well as

---

Arab navigation in the Indian Ocean before the coming of the Portuguese, being a translation of Kitab al-fawaidfi usul al-bahr wa'l-qawa'id of Ahmad b. Majid al-Najdi, together with an introduction on the history of Arab navigation, notes on the navigational techniques and on the topography of the Indian Ocean, and a glossary of navigational terms by G. R. Tibbetts (London: Royal Asiatic Society of Great Britain and Ireland, 1971), pp. 360-382. George F. Hourani's classic, *Arab seafaring in the Indian Ocean in ancient and early medieval times revised and expanded by John Carswell,* (Princeton, N.J.: Princeton University Press, 1995), also has a useful discussion on the monsoon system, as does Michael Pearson's excellent *The Indian Ocean* (London: Routledge, 2003), pp. 19-23.

archives in Venice and London, the average time of postal delivery in the mid-eighteenth century between Isfahan and Calcutta ranged from three months (the fastest speed found in the documents in our collection) to seven months for urgent business letters and only two weeks between Chinsura and Calcutta. We have one recorded case of a letter sent from Surat to Calcutta that reached its destination in forty-seven days. This was likely sent not by ship but by an Indian runner or Pattamar across the great Deccan plain. Mail, from Basra to Isfahan in 1747, was delivered by overland courier in sixteen days, from Bushir to Isfahan in two months.[43] These are the times for business letters containing vital information for the conduct of trade. Since time was of the essence in sharing commercial information, we would expect to discover the fastest time of delivery for business letters. This was not the case with letters sent by the clergy. Thus, we discover in the letter reproduced below that a letter of blessing from the Primate in New Julfa for the Church of Chinsura was dated June 18, 1725, and arrived in Chinsura on September 23 of the following year by way of the senior Priest in Madras who must have received the letter first. This means that it took about one year and three months to reach its destination in Bengal.[44]

Needless to say, the mail system in the eighteenth-century Indian Ocean was very slow and inefficient by modern standards. Mail often got lost in delivery; ships fell prey to pirates, were lost at sea, or were captured as prizes during one of the many wars fought in the Indian Ocean between European powers. Long delays also resulted from messengers getting robbed en route.[45] This is why if a letter was

---

[43] I discuss the postal times both for the Indian Ocean and the Mediterranean zones of the Julfan trade network in a chapter devoted to this topic in my dissertation, where I have a table with figures derived from a representative sample of fifty letters from the New Julfa-India circuit and fifty from the New Julfa-Livorno/Venice one. See also "'The Salt in a Merchant's Letter': The Culture of Julfan Correspondence in the Indian Ocean and the Mediterranean," *Journal of World History* (Spring 2008). Forthcoming.

[44] See paragraph 3 of the letter below.

[45] In a letter mailed from Isfahan to India, the author apologizes to his correspondent for the delay in writing him and explains the reasons why: "After having delivered this letter for those eight days to the Post, the same

important enough, as was often the case, the writer made sure to send as many as four or five copies via different couriers. A common complaint in Julfan correspondence between Persia and India was the failure of one of the parties to send news to his family either in Julfa or India. Thus, in a letter written from Pegu (Burma) by a Julfan merchant to a family member in 1676, the writer bitterly complains: "Let it be known to your benevolence that you have been gone now for 15 years and what do you have to say? Is there no pity in your heart? Your father passed away last year from the pain of longing to see your face, your mother's eyes have gone blind from crying and your wife has withered away."[46] He ends his melancholic letter by chiding his brother for not responding to a single one of his letters. We come across a similar complaint in another letter posted from Tokhat (a town in the Eastern provinces of the Ottoman Empire) and addressed to an Armenian merchant residing in Canton (China): "My dear one, it has been five letters, including this one, that I have written and sent by way of sea and land, and I have not received a single response to any of my letters. I don't know whether they have arrived there and you have ignored them, or if they haven't arrived. Only you know that."[47] To be sure these are rare cases since most

---

was returned to us because the man was robbed on the road." See *HCA-44 series* (log book of Spanish and English translations) letter No. 16, folio 56.

[46] Letter from Pegu addressed to a certain Paron Hovhaness either in Julfa or in Livorno, stored in folder 2 in *Documenti Armeni* Busta 2, *Archivio di Stato di Venezia (ASV)*. Since the letter was originally part of the Shahriman/Sceriman family papers before it was deposited at the *ASV* in the nineteenth century, it is safe to assume that it was a family letter addressed to one of their members. The verso side of the letter has the following notation in Italian: "*Lettera familiare scritta dalle Indie nell'anno 1676.*" (Family letter written from the Indies in the year 1676). The letter does not contain the author's name. The opening lines, in Julfa dialect read: մալում լինի վալինամաթ դու ԺԵ [15] տարիա գնացել աս ինչ կասես ապա քո սիրտն ըռախմ չկայ խալա ւոր խերու զարուդարդու ձերտեսուն կարօտ մեռաւ մէր ուլալու քօռացել: տան խիզանն ցամաքել պռըրկձած.

[47] PRO (Public Record Office) HCA 30/682, letter No. 1172 «Ի սոյն գրովս սիրելի իմ հինգ գիր եղեւ, զոր գրեցի եւ յղեցի՝ ծովով եւ ցամաքով եւ ո՛չ մի ամենեւին զպատասխան գրեանցն իմոց ընկալայ, ո՛չ գիտեմ թէ էհաս զանց արարեր, եւ թէ ո՛չ էհաս, այլ զայն դու գիտես, եւ ոչ ես».

family members managed to keep in touch with each other at least once every two years and often more regularly even when they traveled fast and far. Nonetheless, frequent complaints about delays in receiving mail are found in most of the correspondence that has reached us, thus indicating the difficulties of communicating across the Indian Ocean in the seventeenth and eighteenth centuries.

Despite these drawbacks, the commercial mail system must have been relatively efficient given the standards of the time; otherwise people would not have relied on it to transmit information. Besides, it was indispensable for Julfan society. In fact, almost every aspect of Julfan life was dependent on the functioning of the courier network. Merchants needed it to circulate vital information from their headquarters in New Julfa to their agents and business associates in India. Often their ability to expedite information in a timely fashion meant the difference between making a favorable investment in a volatile market and being stuck with merchandize when the market was down. *Commenda* agents in far away India needed to receive orders (*ordnagir:* from the Italian *ordine* for order and the Armenian *gir* for letter[48] and advice on what to do with their consignment of goods from masters back in Julfa; when they needed to make money transfers, they had to do so by mailing their letters of credit. Families also needed to hear from their members residing overseas from time to time. Most importantly, merchants residing in India needed to be apprised of the latest developments and news (including political news) concerning the welfare of their mother community in Julfa; in this connection, it is interesting to note that almost every business letter sent to India in the mid eighteenth century begins with a rapid summary of the political and social news in New Julfa that transpired during the last monsoon season. Finally, the circulation of information was vital in generating high levels of "social capital" required for the maintenance of "trust" and collective cooperation in the Julfan coalition of merchants. I have argued elsewhere that circulating information through family and business correspondence was vital for Julfan merchants because it allowed them to be constantly apprised of other merchants' reputation. In the absence of

[48] For an etymology of this term, see Edmund Herzig, *The Armenian Merchants of New Julfa: A Study in Premodern Trade*, (Ph.D. dissertation, University of Oxford, St. Antony's College, 1991), p. 434.

an effective legal system for policing merchant behavior, most merchants in the seventeenth and eighteenth centuries relied on informal "reputation mechanisms" to ascertain whether or not to trust fellow merchants with large sums of credit. If a merchant had a solid reputation, he would be trusted in carrying out transactions. A bad reputation, by contrast, almost certainly led to collective ostracism and boycott by other merchants and meant financial ruin. Therefore, given the importance of one's reputation for commercial success, merchants were guided by self-interest to remain honest. The greatest fear of a merchant was thus to have his reputation and honor slandered through gossip or rumors that often filled merchants' business correspondence in the early modern period. Since correspondence contained information often in the form of what we today would call "gossip" or "rumor," on the activities of various merchants, its circulation through the courier system was pivotal for generating and maintaining high levels of monitored "trust" between Julfan merchants and was, therefore, an important factor in their commercial prosperity and success.[49] In this connection, it is important to note that priests' letters also played an important role in supplementing the circulation of information in official business correspondence. Most letters sent by Julfan priests from India (including the letter reproduced below) to the All Savior's Monastery in New Julfa contained information (in the form of social gossip) on merchants and their status in the communities belonging to the parish where the priest in question was stationed. Since many Julfan merchants had priests in their families, news of a particular merchant's reputation abroad would filter to merchants in New Julfa and then find its way, through the "multiplex" nature of the Julfan information network to other merchants in the Julfan trade coalition through business correspondence.

But, as we have already noted, merchants were not the only ones to depend on the intelligence network connecting the communities in India and the East with the nodal center in Julfa. The Church equally depended on this system to send information to its Diocesan sees in

---

[49] On trust and reputation in the Julfan network, see Aslanian, "Social Capital, 'Trust' and the Role of Networks in Julfan Trade: Informal and Semiformal Institutions at Work," *Journal of Global History* 1, 3 (2006): pp. 383-402.

India. General encyclicals, pontifical bulls from Etchmiadzin, letters of blessing, alms donations, payment of church taxes, correspondence between priests overseeing a parish in India and the Primate in New Julfa, and in rare cases letters of excommunication all circulated between the Diocesan center of the All Savior's Monastery in Julfa and its daughter churches in India and further east by means of the same courier system. The ability of this system to circulate information from one end of the New Julfan network to another was, thus, just as crucial for merchants as it was for the clergy, whose job it was to maintain the integrity of the commercial network by ensuring that its members stayed firm in their identity as Julfans and Armenians.

The letter of 1727

The document that is reproduced and translated here for the first time throws light on many aspects of Julfan life in India that we have briefly touched upon in our discussion above. (Fig. 2)

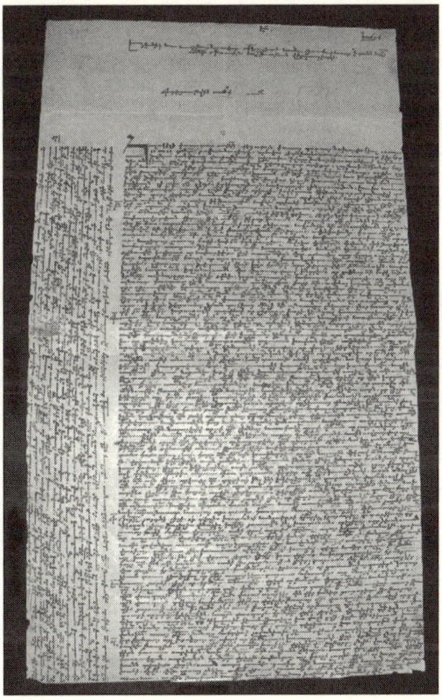

Fig. 2-First page of the letter of 1727.

It is stored in the Archives of All Savior's Monastery in New Julfa, Isfahan, in a folder entitled "Letters from Bengal No. 48."[50] Addressed to David Vardapet in Julfa, this interesting letter was written from the Armenian Church of Saint John the Baptist in Chinsura. Its author was a priest named Tēr Harut'iwn, who was most likely sent from the All Savior's Monastery in Julfa to serve the spiritual needs of the Armenian community of Chinsura/Chichra sometime in the first two decades of the eighteenth century, when the communities of India and the East came under the jurisdiction of the Diocese of Julfa.

Consisting of two large pages measuring approximately 40 centimeters by 30 centimeters with neat small handwriting, this letter reads like a "report" from the field; it contains useful information on local conditions in the Diocese of Bengal (including the Church and community of Calcutta to which the Church of Chinsura/Chichra was subordinate) as well as information on a number of wealthy merchants who had made promises of money and other donations to the All Savior's Monastery. Most importantly, the letter contains vital information on the role of Julfan merchants in Bengal in bankrolling the local Armenian churches there as well as donating funds to the All Savior's Monastery in New Julfa and indicates that this patronage activity, which was crucial for the maintenance of Armenian Churches in the communities dispersed along New Julfa's trade network, was carried out through the direct involvement and constant prodding of the religious hierarchy in Julfa. In light of what has been said above regarding the importance of the New Julfan intelligence network, the letter confirms that such a network played a vital role in keeping Julfan residents in Chichra informed of the most important developments in Julfa. For instance, we learn from reading the letter that its author, writing from Bengal in 1727, was already informed about the outcome of the 1725 Persian Embassy to the Ottoman Empire (in which a prominent New Julfan played an important role) (see paragraph 10); he was also informed about the passing away of Catholicos Astuatsatur in Etchmiadzin a little more than a year after the event (paragraph 11).

---

[50] See the catalogue entry in Levon Minasian, *Divan Surb Amenap'rkich' Vanki* [Archives of All Savior's Monastery] (1983), p. 31.

For those interested in the economic history of the Armenian communities in Bengal, the letter contains several important references to the commercial decline of the Armenian community of Chichra/Chinsura in the second decade of the eighteenth century as a direct result of the rise of the neighboring English settlement of Calcutta. This information challenges the conventional accounts on Bengal's Armenian merchant community as represented by Seth:

> [t]he once flourishing Armenian colony of Chinsurah...was deserted by the Armenians when [Chinsura] lost its commercial importance and they [i.e., the Armenians] transferred their trade to Calcutta about the middle of the last [i.e., the nineteenth] century.[51]

The letter, on the contrary, indicates that the leading members of Chinsura's Armenian merchant community had already abandoned their formerly prosperous base on the banks of the Hugli River for Calcutta as early as the 1720s. According to the letter, the principal motives for this were the commercial growth of the English factory at Fort William at Calcutta and the construction there of the Armenian Church of Holy Nazareth in 1724. The letter also provides important information, heretofore unavailable, concerning the identity of the merchant who provided the funds for the construction of Calcutta's Armenian Church. Moreover, it contains information on the legal dispute between this merchant and another Julfan merchant active in the Bengal trade.

Lastly, the letter is of great interest from the linguistic point of view since it is written mostly in Julfa dialect (the language used by merchants) interspersed with elements of Classical Armenian (*Grabar*) (the official language of the clergy). This makes it difficult to follow at times. In keeping with eighteenth-century customs, the letter has irregular punctuation and no paragraph breaks; it does, however, have numbers on the left margin (following the numeration scheme of the Armenian alphabet) to indicate thirteen paragraph sections.

The date of 1721 inserted at the top of the letter is certainly a mistake. There is one other almost identical copy of this letter in the same folder bearing the Armenian calendar date 1176 (i.e., 1727).

---

[51] Mesrovb Seth, *History of the Armenians in India*, p. 306.

The reference, in the letter, to the construction of the Armenian Church in Calcutta (built in 1724 according to most authorities[52]) also indicates that 1727 is the correct date for the letter.

Original orthography and awkward word breaks have been maintained in my transcription. I have also opened up words that appear in abbreviated form in the original by placing the missing vowels or letters in brackets. In deciphering and translating the Julfa dialect component of this document, I have benefitted from the pioneering works of Levon and Shushanik Khach'ikian,[53] as well as Edmund Herzig.[54] I have also relied on Bert Vaux's important manual on Julfa Dialect and especially on the useful glossary of Julfa dialect terms at the end of his manual.[55] For help in Julfa dialect vocabulary, I have benefited from the excellent glossaries in Herzig, Khach'ikian and Papazian, as well as dictionaries by Steingass,[56] Redhouse,[57] Yule,[58] Ghazarian and Avetisian,[59] Malkhaseants', and Bedrossian.[60]

---

[52] Seth, *History*, p. 429, and Anne Basil, *Armenian Settlements of India* (Calcutta, 1969), Chapter 21.

[53] Levon Khach'ikian and Hakob Papazian, *Hovhanness Tēr Davtyan Jughayetsu Hashvetumarĕ* [The Accounting Ledger of Hovhaness Tēr Davtyan of Julfa] (Yerevan: Haykakan SSH GA Hratarakch'ut'yun, 1984); and Shushanik Khach'ikian, *Nor Jughayi hay vacharakanut'iwnĕ ew nra arewtratntesakan kaperĕ Rusastani het XVII–XVIII darerum* [The Armenian Trade of New Julfa and its Commercial and Economic Ties with Russia in the Seventeenth and Eighteenth Centuries] (Yerevan: Haykakan SSH GA Hratarakch'ut'yun, 1988).

[54] Edmund Herzig, "The Armenian Merchants from New Julfa: A Study in Premodern Trade" (Ph.D. dissertation, Saint Antony's College, Oxford University, 1991).

[55] Bert Vaux, *The Armenian Dialect of New Julfa*, (unpublished manuscript, 2002, in press). I am grateful to Bert Vaux for sharing his valuable manuscript and his linguistic expertise with me.

[56] Francis Joseph Steingass, *A Comprehensive Persian-English dictionary, including the Arabic words and phrases to be met with in Persian literature,* (London: Routledge & K. Paul, 1892).

[57] Sir James Redhouse, *Ottoman/Turkish-English Dictionary*, (Istanbul, 1999).

[58] Henry Yule, and Arthur Coke Bunell, *Hobson-Jobson: A Glossary of Colloquial Anglo-Indian Words and Phrases, and of Kindred Terms,*

երջանիկ եւ սրբայնուէր ք[ա]հ[ա]ն[ա]յապէտի եւ հովիվ հոգեւոր ի տանն Ա[ստուծո]յ Տ[եարն]դ դավիթ Ա[ստուա]ծաբան վարդապետի

գրեցաւ թվին ՌՃՑ [1170-1721] ումն

Հոչակելի փառաւորութ[եա]մբ գերագոյն փառաց պատուոց նախայգահեալ Տ[եար]նդ դավիթ Ա[ստուա]ծաբան վարդապետի րաբունապետի որ եւ ես յետնեալնուաստս աստուստ իբր մօտու ծընրա հանգուց գագաթեամբ զգլուխս ի վայր խոնարհեցուցանելով եւ ի ծունկս անգեալ ըղձայ փափաք համբուրելով զգարշաբար ոտիցդ, զորթախանձանօք հայցեմ եւ աղաչեմ իբր զծառայ զտեարդ իմ, հարցանելով զգլուխդ հանուրց ազգիս զոր տ[եա]րն բոլորից պահեսցէ զգլուխն ամենեցուն ք[րիստո]ս ա[սդուա]ծ մեր. Նա եւս խնդրեցես ի յայ՞ ծերունի հայրդ իմ հգեւոր վասնբարիօք կելոյն ծառայիտ աստ եւ ի հանդերձեալն զի լսէ տեր զկամս երկիւղածացն եւ կատարէ զխնդրուածսն եւ ես [՞…՞] ցանգ եւ յաւեճ աղաչեմ զաստուածն բոլորից որեւ զիս խփիուռս հեթանոսաց անսաթաքելի պահեսցէ պառզ երեսօք եւ անամօթ մնայցեմ միւս անգամ արճանի լինիմ եւ լսեմ զերան աւ էտ ձայն սրբազանիմ որ ասես եկ ծառայիմ եւ լինեմ արճանի համբուրելոյ զգարշապար վեհին

Բ

զոր տ[է]ր յ[իսու]ս արացէ արժան. եւ ընդ ծառայական նուիրառս յայտնի լիցի ա[ր]ք[ա]զան վեհին որ

Etymological, Historical. Geographical and Discursive. 2nd. ed. (London: W. Crooke and J. Murray, 1903).

[59] R. S. Ghazarian and H. M. Avetisian, *Mijin Hayerēni Bar̄aran*, [Dictionary of Middle Armenian] 2 vols. (Yerevan: Yerevani Hamalsarani Hratarakch'ut'yun, 1987).

[60] S. Malkhaseants', *Hayerēn Badzatrakan Bararan* [Explanatory Dictionary of Armenian], 1st. edition (Yerevan, 1944) 4 Vols. and Rev. Matthias Bedrossian, *New Dictionary: Armenian-English.* Facsimile edition. (Beirut: Librairi du Liban, 1985). 1st edition published in San Lazarro, Venice: 1871.

հր[ա]մ[ա]ն[ու]ցդ[61] ահնութ[եա]ն նամակն ի թվին ՌՃՀԴ [1174=1725] յունիս ԺԸ [18] էն գրեալ յերկրիս հասարակ ք[ա]հ[ա]ն[ա]յից եւ ժողովրդեան վերայ թիւն ՌՃՑԵ [1175=1726] թիրայ է [7] ումն մադրասէն տ[ե]ր սիմօնին ձեռօքն մեզ է հաս ուրախութ[եամ]բ եւ համբիւրիւ ընկալաք եւ հր[ա]մ]ա[ն[ու]ցդ ս[ուր]բ ահնութե[ան]ն տիրացանք եւ ի մէջ ս[ուր]բ եկեղեցումն ի մէջ ժողովրդեան ընթերձաք ամենեքեանս փառս ա[ստուծո]յ մատուցաք եւ հր[ա]մ[ա]ն[ու]ցդ ս[ուր]բ աթոռնստիլդ շնորհաւորեանք եւ բազում ուրախութիւն արարաք եւ յետոյ լուսայհոգի եվ ի ք[րի]ս[տոս] հանգուցեալ մովսես վ[ա]րդ[ա]պ[ե]տին միմեանց մխիթարեցաք եւ հոգւոցն ասացաք· ի ձեռն պաշտմամբ եւ պադարագօք եւ նորին կենդանի աղօթքն մեզ օգնութի[ւն] կօչեցաք որ եւ բարեխօս լիցի առ ք[րիստո]ս ա[ստուա]ծըն մեր որեւ մեզ ողրմելոցս ողորմեսցի ճար եւ օգնութի[ւն] հասցի որ այս տառապանաց եւ պանդխդութե[ան] ազատիմք գամք համբուրենք զգարշայպար ծերունի վեհի. եւս հր[ա]մ[ա]ն[ու]ցդ այտ ծերութե[ան] ժամանակին եւ էս խրնթին եւ դառն եղանակումն մեք մեղաւոր գոլով խնդրեմք որ ամենայ ս[ու]րբ հոգի աստուածն հր[ա]մ[ա]ն[ու]ցդ ամենայզօրութենէ օգնէ կարողացուցէ եւ հաստատ հիմն արասցէ որ մայր ս[ուր]բ աթոռտ հաստատ շէն եւ աւատան պահեսցես հայր ս[ուր]բ ամենայ կարողն ա[ստուա]ծ ամենայզօր զօրութենէ հր[ա]մ[ա[ն[ու]ցդ պահեայ որ մինչի վիճակիտ եւ թէմիտ վերայ առաջնորդ հաստատեաց զրա հր[ա]մ[ա]ն[ու]ցդ թէմն եւ վիճակն ս[ուր]բ ամենայ փրկչի վանուցդ եւ ջուղայու վերայեր մեք ամենեքեանս փառս ա[ստուծո]յ մատուցինք եւ գոհացանք զաստուծոյ որ հր[ա]մ[ա]ն[ու]ցդ սիմէօն ծերունոյ նման պահեաց մինչի սուրբ աթոռդ ընկալար շնոռհաւոր լինի տ[է]ր յ[իսու]ս հր[ա]մ[ա]ն[ու]ցդ

[61] The genitive/dative singular in Julfa dialect in this case is formed with suffix "ուց" instead of the Classical Armenian ending "ոց."

կարողութիւն պարգեւի որ զհօտըդ բարեկենցաղ կառաւարեսցես ի փառըս ա[ստուծո]յ.

Գ.

եւ այլ յատնի լիցի որ վ[ա]ս[ն] ողորմութե[ան] սուրբ տանդ նուէրքի եւ օգնութե [ան] համարէիր շնորհարարեալ· հայր ս[ուր]բ տեղս այլ այնպիսի կենդանի մարդ ոչ գոյ որ մին արդիւնք եւ նուէրք ունենայ ամենեքեանն այլ ուրեանց խղջութե [ան] եւ ուրեանց կենցաղայվարութե[ան] հոքս ունեն թէ որպիս լիցի իւրեանց կենդանութիւնն այս դառնացեալ ժամանակիս որ ամենից կողմանց աշխատութե[ան] դուռն խափանվելէ. ամենեքանն այլ պաշարած մնացերէն· տեղս գ [3] կենդանի մարդգոյ որ փողկայ ձեռնեռանումն· թէ չէ այլքն ամենեքեան ձեռն ծոցի պաշառաց կան· մէկ պ[ա]ր[ո]ն աղայնազարնէ[62] որ հր[ա]մ[ա]ն[ու]ցդ ահնութ[եանմ]քն ունի անուն ունի յերես, եւ ա[ստուծո]յ տուած ունի դօլվաթ·[63] նա էս օր կալկատու եկեղեցին հաստատեաց· մօտ էռ.../ [7,000] ըռուփի[64] խարճէլ[65] դերեւս խարճումէ· եւ շինութիւն շինում նորանէ խօվ չի շինել եղանակումս ողորմութ[իւն] ուզել մէք ակնունէինք թէ տարումս պ[ա]ր[ո]ն նազարին մէկ մեծ ահնութ[եա]ն թուղթ կու գրէիր որ գիրն կարդայր ահնութիւնդ առնէր եւ ուռախանէր·[66] եւ կու խնդրեմ

---

[62] Paron Agha Nazar mentioned here as the patron of Calcutta's Holy Nazareth Church was Agha Nazar Jacob Jan, the wealthy Julfan merchant who passed away in Madras in the early 1740s, leaving a huge fortune to Khwaja David Sultan who was married to Agha Nazar's sister, Anna Khatoon. Agha Nazar was the maternal uncle of Shahamir Shahamirian of Madras.

[63] Dolvat<A/P *dalwa/dalva*: wealth.

[64] For the addition of the vowel "ĕ" before foreign words starting with the consonant "r," see section on "Linguistic notes on Julfa Dialect" in Appendix of Aslanian, "From the Indian Ocean to the Mediterranean."

[65] Kharjel (to spend) Julfa dialect verbal form<A/P *kharaj:* expense.

[66] Unusual third person present tense suffix.

ս[ր]բ[ա]գ[ա]ն վեհէն որ տարոջս մին ահնութե[ան] թուղթ գրես պ[ա]ր[ո]ն նազարին եւ բ [2] եկեղեցին[67] այլ յանձնես ուր[ե]ն որ չիչրուս եկեղեցին այլ հոքս քաշե. լուսայհոգի մովսէս վ[ա]րդ[ա]պ[ե]տին[68] ժամանակին այլեմ ազդումն արարեալ թէ չիչրուս եկեղեցուն հոքսն արարեք որ ձերաց գնացելէ եւ ժողովուրդէնէլ ինչ կայ գնացելէն կալկաթայ մին քանի աղքատ տնայ դ[ե]րայ մնացել տեղս. գլխաւորն ուլուխաններ[69] առա[ստու]ծ փոխեցաւ[70] եւ միսանին հաց եւ ջուր մեզանէ են ուզում. եւ չիչրուս սովդայգարերն գլխաւոռ մին նազարէթի որդի պ[ա]ր[օ]ն լիօննայ եւ սահակի որդի մինասն որ շարիմանէնց

---

[67] The reference to the two churches here is to the Saint John the Baptist Church of Chinsura and the Church of Holy Nazareth in Calcutta, which were constructed in 1695 and 1724, respectively.

[68] The Primate of New Julfa 1706-1724. See Vazken Ghougassian, *The Emergence of the of The Armenian Diocese of New Julfa in the Seventeenth Century* (Atlanta, Georgia: Scholar's Press, 1998), p. 293.

[69] Unknown word, perhaps a compound of Turkish (Ulu: high, sublime) and Persian/Turkish, *khan* (ruler, head, chief) The word may therefore signify an honorific as in head of senior merchants. It could also be a personal name.

[70] The reference here could be to a certain Paron Yedikar, who is described in other letters from Chinsura from a slightly earlier period as the "ulukhan" and "mutaveli" (<P. for custodian of pious institutions), as well as the Kadkhuda (<P. for district head or village elder) of Chinsura's Armenian community. In a letter written in Chinsura in 1713, we read the following: "մութավելին ժողովրդոց մասլահաթօվ [<P/A, Maslahat: interest] պարոն եդիկարնա որ է մեր թարվիզեցի մելքոնի որդի. ԻԵ[25] տարիայ որ տեղսայ տնաւորվելա, լէվիստակ քաթխութ մարդա. Բ[2] տարիայ որ մութավելիա…" [In the interests of the people, the caretaker (of the Armenian Church in Chinsura) is Paron Edikar who is the son of our Paron Melkon of Tabriz (most likely not the city in Persia but one of the districts of New Julfa bearing that name). He has been settled here for 25 years and is a judicious man. He has been the caretaker for the past two years.] This suggests that Paron Yedikar was already a resident merchant of Chinsura in the early 1690s, that is, before the Church of Saint John the Baptist was consecrated in 1695.

պ[ա]ր[ո]ն մանուէլին եւ պ[ա]ր[ո]ն յարութիւնին[71] յընկերան.[72] սոքայ հր[ա]մ[ա]ն[ու]ցդ յատնի եւ մին սովտայգար[73] այլ միրզայջանի որդի պ[ա]ր[ո]ն մարգարնէ որ խալտարէնց պ[ա]ր[ո]ն պետրոսին յընկեր նա էս տանս եւ մեզ քահանայիցս մին օգնութիւն անում թէ մոմի, ձիթի եւ եկեղեցոյ ըսպասավորութ[եան] էլ ոնչով էս տանս հոքս անող չկայ. հայր սուրբ վասն այն կուխնդրեմ որ պարոն նազարին մէկ լաւ ահնութեան թուղթ գրես եւ բ [2] եգեղեցինէլ ուր[է]ն յանձես[sic] կալկաթունն ինքնայ շինել

---

[71] Manuel and Harut'iwn Shahrimanian were members of Julfa's richest Armenian Catholic family. One branch of this family migrated and settled in Italy in 1698 and was granted titles of nobility in most Italian city-states as well as in the Austro-Hungarian Empire. Paron Manuel and Harut'iwn remained in Julfa in the first half of the eighteenth century. Manuel served as the secretary to the Persian Embassy to the Sublime Porte in 1725 (see fn 110 below) and later as the Persian Ambassador to Russia. Thus, in a family memoir written in Italian in the nineteenth century, we read: "*Emanuele di Marcarà: fu Ambasciatore di Persia alla Corte di Pietroburgo, ove lasciava la vita*" [Emanuel son of Marcara: was the Ambassador of Persia to the Court of Saint Petersburg where he passed away] (See the manuscript of Fortunato Sceriman, *Brevie Memorie sulla famiglia Sceriman,* Archives of the Biblioteca di Museo Correr in Venice. Mss. Cod Cigogna no. 3403, folio 9) and *Resultato del Processo per la verificazione de Requisiti alla N.V. nella famiglia de Co. Fr[at]elli Sceriman* also in the same folder. See also my upcoming commercial biography (with Houri Berberian) of the Sceriman family in Julfa and Venice provisionally entitled *The Cosmopolitans: The Sceriman/Shahrimanian Family Between Julfa and Venice*. Harut'iwn Shahrimanian was burned alive at the stake in Isfahan in January of 1747 upon the orders of Nadir Shah. Both brothers, it appears, were conducting trade in Bengal during this period as this reference to their factor suggests.

[72] *Ĕnker* in Julfa dialect is almost exclusively used to denote a *commenda* agent or factor. For a detailed discussion, see Aslanian, "The Circulation of Men and Credit: The Role of the *Commenda* and the Family Firm in Julfan Society," in *Journal of the Social and Economic History of the Orient* (JESHO), 50:2 (2007), pp. 124-171.

[73] Sovdaygar <P. *saudāgar*: Merchant.

էնտուր[74] հոքսն բարի սրտօվ կու հոքայ, չիչրուս եկեղեցինէլ ուր[է]ն յանձես որ էստուր այլ խնամք ածե. զրայ[75] փէտերն ողջ փթելայ. տարիս անցաւ միւս տարումն փէտեր ողջ վերկուրընկանի.[76] հոքսն անող չկ[ա]յ քոյ ս[ուր]բ աչն վկայ որ էս օրդ [4] տարիայ ինչ ինձ եգեղեցականն դառամաթէ[77] գոլման[78] ողջ էս ս[ուր]բ տանս վերայ խառջումեմ. այս տան հոքսն քաշում թէ ինչայ այլազգից միջում նախատինք չկռեմք թէ հայոց ազգեն յերկրումս եկեղեցի ունին կարեցանոչ պահել հայր ս[ուր]բ այսչափ աղաչանսէ. քո հր[ա][մա]ն[ու]ցդ յատնի լինի որ յերկրումս կենդանի մարդ չկայ, որ թէ ս[ու]րբ աթոռիտ եւ թէ էս ս[ու]րբ տանս հոքսն քաշէ. եւ ակն առհր[ա]մ[ա]նու]ցդ ս[ու]րբ աղօթքն ունիմք որ նախ ս[ու]րբ աթոռտ եւ ապայ այս տունս հաստատ մնասցէ, որ այլազգից միջում ամօթչկրեմք.

Դ.

Դարձ/եալ յայտնի լինի որ տեղիս խոստմունքի եւ նուէրքի հ[ա]մարիր հրամայել Դ[4] տարիէ որ տ[ե]ր նիկողոսն չիչայ[79] բողէլէ գնացել կալկաթայ յառաջն ինչ խոստմունք որելէլայ ուրձեռնումն լուսայ հոգի մովսես վ[ա]րդ[ա]պ[ե]տին քանի գրով ազդեմ ար[ա]րեալ ապայ

---

[74] *ēstowr/ēntowr*: Julfa dialect: for this for that. Compare with Western Armenian "Asor, anor."

[75] Zra< P, *zira*: Because, on account of, since.

[76] That is, "will fall down" or in Std Arm. *վայր կ'ընկնի:* I thank Vazken Ghougassian for this information.

[77] Daramad<P *daremad*: revenue, profit.

[78] *Golman.* Julfa dialect present continuous ending, which uses the "man" suffix after the stem of the infinitive. Forming the present continuous with the "man" ending distinguishes the Julfa dialect from all other Armenian dialects. See Achaṙian *K'nnut'iwn Jughayi Barbaṙi* (Yerevan, 1940), and the same author's, *Hay baṙbaṙagitut'iwn-uruagits ew dasaworut'iwn hay barbaṙneri barbaṙagitakan ēartersov, Ėminean Azgagṙakan zhoghovatsu*, vol. 8, (Moscow, Nor Nakhichevan, 1911), p. 89.

[79] Read "Chichra" Julfan term for Chinsura.

իմուս ժամանակին այս է որ ուլուխանն վասիէր[80] ար[ա]րէլ ս[ու]րբ ամենայ փրկչի վանքին գրէլէր ԱՃԺ/ ի [110] բանդայ յինք առի եւ մին յովանէս անուամբ տղայ կայր տեղս նա եւս վանքին Ղ/՟Ի [90] ասացէլ պ[ա]րոն մարգարն վաքիլայ զայն զայն եւս յինք կառում. սրբազանիս ԲՃ [200]ի կուլինի տեղս եւ մեր տարէն Բ [2] թ[օ]մ[ա]ն այլ կու շինենք ինչ լինի գրուս յետոյ վեհին կու գրեմք եւ կու ուղարկեմք հր[ա]մ[ա]ն[ու]ցդ հայր ս[ու]րբ էն ակն կալութիւնն ունի թէ ողորմութիւն լինէր տարումս մին Բ [2] ք[ա]հ[ա]ն[ա]յ ուղարկեր մեք գայինք հր[ա]մ[ա]ն[ու]ցդ գարշայպարն համբուրենք երեւումայ որ դառճանայպարէրն կապայ՞ ձեռն տու չէ ելէլ որ ք[ա]հ[ա]ն[ա]յ ուղարկես տարուս մովսումիցս այլ մնացինք տեղեքս:

Ե

եւ այլ յատնի լիցի որ հր[ա]մ[ա]ն[ու]ցդ ահնութե[ան] գրերն որ բանդիս վերայ գրէլեր եւ նախատինք առ տ[ե]ր նիկողոսն գրէրն ուր[ե]ն ցոյց տվի. վանուց փողին եւ ուր տարէն Բ [2] թ/օ/մ/ա/նն ուզեցի ասաց թէ պ[ա]ր[ո]ն գասպարին ձեռնովն Ի[20] թ[օ]մ[ա]ն փողամ աղարկէլ մին գիր հանէց ցուցարետ[81] թէ պասրայ պ[ա]ր[ո]ն գասպարն տվելայ եւ հր[ա]մ[ա]ն[ու]ցդ գիրն որ գրէլիր պասրայ պ[ա]ր[ո]ն գասպարին թէ մուքէլի որդի պ[ա]ր[ո]ն յարութիւնիցս Ի[20] թ[օ]մ[ա]ն յինք առի[82] բարաթ[83] գրեցի որ պասրայ պ[ա]ր[ո]ն գասպարդ տաս ծատուրի որդի պ[ա]ր[ո]ն չընթլ[ու]մին եւ պ[ա]ր[ո]ն գասպարն հրամանուցդ գրին յերեսն վեռէլեր տ[ե]ր

---

80 A "corruption" of the Julfa dialect term "Varis"<A/P. *wāris*: An heir; master, lord, owner. (Steingass, 1449)

81 The more common Julfa dialect term here նշանց արետ, or "he showed." "Aret" is Julfa dialect for third person past tense of the verb *tal* (to give).

82 Hinkarel< CA, *yinkn arnul.* verbal form meaning to take or to receive. This form is peculiar to Julfa dialect and not found in other dialects of Armenian. (Vaux, glossary).

83 Barat<A/P. *Berat.* A generic term for letter of exchange.

եղնայզարին մրէլ[84] տվէլ ուղարկէլ տ[ե]ր նիկողոսին ձեռն թէ տեղս էս երբ տ[ե]ր նիկողոսն էս գիրն նշանց արետ ասացի բարիայ էս օր Ժ [10] տարէ տեղէքսաս էտ քոյ տարէն փողն ապա վանքինն. ասաց ԺԵ [15] թօման այլ մահտեսի յովանիսին ձեռնովն ամ ուղարկէլ. էստուր գիր չումէր.

Ձ

բանդայ[85] այլ խօսեցայ ոչ ախտիար[86] հր[ա]մ[ա]ն[ու]ցդայ: եւ այլ յատնի լիցի հր[ա]մ[ա]ն[ու]ցդ շնորհալի ահնութե[ան] թուղթն որ արզ պ[ա]ր[ո]ն լիոնն եւ պ[ա]ր[ո]ն խաչիկին գրէլիր վ[ա]ս[ն] եղբօրդ ընչին վաքիլեք արարէլ[87] գիրն հասաւ ուրէնցն նախ հր[ա]մ[ա]ն[ու]ցդ ահնութիւն ընկալան եւ ապա գրոյ զօրութիւնն վերայհասուելան իւրեանքն հր[ա]մ[ա]ն[ու]ցդ գրեցին եւ բանդայ այլ փոքրի շատէն գրեմ որ էս օր պ[ա]ր[ո]ն թարխանն տեղէքս յերկնքումն աստղ չունե ումիտ պ[ա][ո]ն նազառնայ պ[ա]ր[ո]ն նազարի եւ պ[ա]ր[ո]ն թարխանի մէջն մեծ զրուց ընկէլ ամեն գրում լուսայ հոգի մօվսէս վ[ա]րտ[ա]պ[ետ]ին ազդեմ արարել՞ սա պ[ա]ր[ո]ն թարխանն եւ պ[ա]ր[ո]ն նազարն իւրեանց խսէպն իւրեանց միչումն

---

[84] Mrel<A/P, *Muhr*: Stamp, seal. As in many cases, this phrase demonstrates how Julfa dialect absorbs foreign words and conjugates them as though they were Armenian. In this case, *Mrel* is the infinitive of "to stamp" or "to seal." Note, however, that Classical Armenian also has verbal form of *m'rrel*, meaning to scribble or to write, probably from Persian root of *muhr* or "stamp/seal." Some Eastern Armenian dialects also have the form *mohrel*, "to stamp or to seal." See Malkhaseants, *Hayerēn Badzatrakan Baraṙan*. vol. 3, p. 379.

[85] Banday<A/P. *banda*. Servant, slave, bondman, domestic. Used here to denote your servant (i.e., the writer).

[86] Akhtiar<A/P. *akhtiar*. Reason, right. In this context, the term is used to denote that a decision is up to the discretion of someone.

[87] Vakil ararel<A/P. A/P. *Vakil*. representative, agent. The term means to appoint someone as one's representative through a power of attorney or to use the Julfan term, vakilagir.

Է

տեսէլեն եւ գիր շինեէլ մեզ կանչեցին գրէրն երկքնոց հուղարովն մօճրեցինք որ ԽԵՌ/Ի [45000] պ[ա]ր[ո]ն նազարն սանատ գրէց արետ պ[ա]ր[ո]ն թարխանին որ մինչի Ա[1] տարի վադայ[88] որ ընկերայգիրն[89] տայ ուր փողն յինք առու· էս կերպն կտրվացք ելավ երկուքն այլ ղապուլ[90] ար[ա]րին յետոյ պ[ա]ր[ո]ն թարխանն շուռ արեկ[91] թէ ես նորմէ խսեպ[92] կուզեմ· էս գոֆդու գուին[93] վերայ էս քանի տարին էսպէս մնաց· էս տարի պ[ա]ր[ո]ն նազարն փողն կապեց տարած եդիր ինկլիզի կունպանումն թէ ես էն մարդին սանատամ[94] տվել փողն տեղս մնայ· իմ ընկերայգիրն բերի ուր փողն տանե· ինկլիզին մեծն մեզ գանչեց թախեխ[95] ար[ա]ր որ խսէպն կտրէլան ֆարխաթիան[96] շինել թարխանին ջուղապարետ

---

[88] Vaday<A/P. *Vadah*. Period or payment period.

[89] Enkeragir. Julfa dialect for *commenda* contract.

[90] Ghabul ararel<A/P. Ghabul<A/P/T, *qabūl*. A favourable reception, concession; approbation. *qabūl kardan,* To agree, consent, accept, approve, submit to (Steingass, p. 953). Julfa dialect has two formulaic phrases or expressions to indicate that something written in a document is acceptable to the people who have sealed and signed it. One is to say that such and such is *ghabul* (acceptable) to the signatory, as in this case. The other is to use the word mafegh<A/P, *muwāfiq,* One who consents, agrees, approves; conformable, agreeable. (Steingass, p. 1339) JD usage seems to parallel Persian, *muwāfiq uftādan,* To be acceptable, to please. (Steingass, p. 79)

[91] *Shur arek*. Julfa dialect literally meaning, “he turned around” in this case used to denote “he changed his mind.” *Arek* is Julfa dialect third person past tense of the verb “to come.”

[92] Khsep<A/P, *Hesap*: Account.

[93] Gofd u gu<P. *guftgū kardan*: To converse, dispute, to quarrel.

[94] Sanad<A/P. *sanad*: document, order, promissory note. Julfa dialect uses this word as a generic term to indicate one of a variety of promissory notes used by Julfan merchants.

[95] Takhekh<A/P. *taqīq* (v.n. 2 of حقّ), Ascertaining the truth, verifying; verification.

[96] Farkhati<Farkhat? The act of acquittance. See Hermann Michael Kisch, Andrew Wallace Mackie, Herbert Hope Risley, William Wilson Hunter, *A*

ասաց դու քոյ ձեռն կտրելաս էլ պ[ա]ր[ո]ն նազարին խետ բանչունես քո փողն մեր կումպանումնայ քօթումս[97] կու պահեմք մինչի պարոն նազարին ընկերագիրն բերէք եւ Գ[3] ախբեր մին տեղ տեղս հազիրելէք[98] ձեր փողն յինք առէք. փողն մնաց քօթումն եւ ուրենքն պաշարած եւ պարտայտէրք հայ հընդու պ[ա]ր[ո]ն թարխանին նեղացանում մինչնի ուր[ե]ն այլ խառջի չունի՞ սրուրն խառջԻ առե ջումիաթով մասլահաթ ար[ա]րինք պ[ա]ր[ո]ն լիոնն պ[ա]ր[ո]ն խաչիկն բանդայ որ մին ֆիքր առենք պ[ա]ր[ո]ն նազարիցս շեն/կամ լեն/ըլթմազ[99] առենք էտ փողին քարսազին լինի բանդայ եւս քանի անգամ գնացելամ կալկատայ պ[ա]ր[ո]ն նազարին աղաչելամ որ հր[ա]մ[ա[ն]ու]ցդ խաթեր խմար մին ֆիքր առէ եւ հր[ա]մ[ա[ն]ու]ցդ ահնութեան թուղթն որ արզ պ[ա]ր[ո]ն նազարն գրէլիր ուրն հասաւ. լինի որ աստուծով շինեմք որ մին ճար լինի էտ փոշին հոքս առէ եւ էլինչ հր[ա]մ[ա][նու]ցդ ս[ու]րբ աղոթքն առաջնորդե բարիայ կու լինի: եւ այլ յայտնի լիցի որ քալանդար աւետի որդի յովանէսն տեղս թիվն ԱՃԺԱ/[111] համիրայ Է/[7] ումն առ ա[ստուա]ծ փոխեցաւ կարի յոյժ պարտական վալանդիզի[100] հայի եւ քուրդի[101] մինչի ԵՌ/[5000] յի պարտք ունէ եւ ԱՌ/[1000] յի թանխայ[102] ցաք ցրիւ տեղ որ ա[ստուծո]յ է գիտելի դուս գոյ թէ ոչ նայ եւս էս կերպն դառն ողորմելի աշխարէս գնաց շատ մարդի պարտական աստուած ուր հոգոյն ողորմի:

Statistical Account of Bengal vol. 6 (London, 1875), p. 270. The common Julfa dialect term for this is ghatilayagir<A/P. *qatīl*: To cut or sever, hence letter of severance of quittance.

[97] Kot<E. Court, as in the court of directors of the English East India Company in London where money was invested in interest bearing bonds.

[98] Hazir<A/P/T. *ḥāẓir*: Present, at hand, ready, prepared.

[99] Eltmaz<A/P. *iltimās kardan (guftan)*: To petition, to beg, to solicit.

[100] Valandiz. Dutchman.

[101] In this context, kurd probably is generic for Muslim.

[102] Tankha<A/P. *tan-k͟hwāh:* An assignment on lands, or order on the treasury for the payment of a stipend, salary, and the like; cash; fortune.

Ը

ե այլ յայտնի լիցի որ պ[ա]ր[ո]ն մանուկին որպիսութիւնն կամիս ըմանալ տեղսայ. հր[ա]մ[ա]ն[ու]ցդ ս[ուր]բ աղոթիւքն չաղժիր եւ հր[ա]մ[ա]ն[ու]ցդ սուրբ աչն կու համբուրե. ինքն իւր գլուխայ մարդի բայբաստայ չե. աստուած ուրն անփորձ պահե իւր մեհնաթին ուր աշխատանքի ֆքրումնայ որ ուր խիզանիցն շարնամդութիւն չքաշե աստուծոյ տուածն քանի Ճ/Ի [100] ուր ձեռնումն ունի տեղեքս արանկանի[103] խրիտ[104] կու գնայ ուրն խմար խրիտն կառե կու բերի ֆրանկսիսի կուծախե ինչ ուր նսիպ լինի աստուած ուր կարողութիւն տայ լէվ մէհնաթէ առում ա[ստուծ]ով լէվ կու լինի եւ ս[ր]բ[ա]զ[ա]ն վեհին գրէրն արեկ ինքն արանկում էր գրէրն խասացուցի ուրն կարդացէլեր արանկէ արեկ գրէրն բանդիս նշանցարետ ֆքրում կայ որ տարումս խիզանին խմար խառջուղ[105] ուղարկե աստուծով որ կաղարկե սրբազանին աղօթքն ուրն եւ մեզ օգնութիւն խասանե ճանայպարէրն բացվե գամք հր[ա]մ[ա]ն հր[ա]մ[ա]ն[ու]ցդ գարշայպարն համբուրեմք. քոյ ս[ու]ր[բ] աչն վկա որ գրեանքն կարդացելամք եւ դառն արտասուօք լացէլ. տառապանքն եւնեղութիւնն որ մեր սիրելիքն քաշումեն: եւ հր[ա]մ[ա]ն[ու]ցդ ծառայ ժամարարն եւսէր գրէլ թէ ոչ մեզ օգնող կայ եւ ոչ մին դի[ա]ն մեզ խառջի տըւող հայր ս[ու]րբ լինի օր մի որ փրկութիւն եւ ողորմութիւն խասանի մեր խեղջ ողորմելի

[103] Arank< H. from P. *aurang*, 'a place where goods are manufactured, a depôt for such goods.' During the Company's trading days this term was applied to their factories for the purchase, on advances, of native piecegoods, &c. Yule and Burnell, *Hobson Jobson: A glossary of colloquial Anglo-Indian words and phrases…*, entry under "Aurung." Note here the use of the Persian plural marker, "an." In some cases, especially involving Persian words, the plural in Julfa dialect is formed not by the classical Armenian marker "k" or "er/ner" but by the Persian marker "an," as in "arankani." Both Achaṙian (*K'nnut'iwn Nor Jughayi Barbaṙi* (Yerevan, 1940) and following him Vaux (*A Grammar of Julfa Dialect*) do not take into account the role of the Persian plural marker in Julfa dialect.

[104] Khrit<A/P. *k̲h̲arīdan, k̲h̲irīdan*: To buy, to purchase.

[105] Kharjukh<T. *Kharjlik*: Expenses, spending money.

խիզանինոր[106] մին դիւրութիւն գտանեն եւ պ[ա]ր[ո]ն մանուկին կողմանէ միամիտ լեր ա[ստուծո]վ չաղէ եւ առողջ հր[ա]մ[ա]ն[ու]ցդ սուրբ աչն կու համբուրէ ինքն այլ հր[ա]մ[ա]ն[ու]ցդ

Թ

գիրէ գրեալ ուր յանցանքն յատնի կու լինի. եւ այլ կու խնդրեմ հայրա գութ ողորմութենէտ որպես լուսահոգի մովսես վ[ա]րդ[ա]պ[ե]տն գութն եւ ողորմութիւնն մեզ վերայ ունէր հայրդ հոգեւոր այլ ողորմելոցս ողորմիս գութըդ եւ հայրայխնամ սերտ մեզ նուաստիցս վերայ պահես եւ մանավանդ ի պարապ ժամու ժամարարին խպարն[107] առնուս որ խիսդ եմք անտեր մեր տ[եա]րն եւ գլխաւոր թէ հոգեւոր եւ թէ մարմնաւոր հայրն հր[ա]մ[ա]նքդես չլինի ծառայքդ մոռանաս հայրայխնամ գութ շարժես ծառայիցդ վերայ:

Ժ

եւայլ յայտնի լիցի ս[ր]բ[այ]զանին որ էս մովսումիս բասրուց խապար էհաս թէ աղուանին էլչին[108] որ գնացերէ հոռմաստան անարգանօք դուսան արարէլ եւ էլչին յետդառցել եկէլ բաղտատ. փաշէն ուրայնօքն բռնել բանդխանայ տվել պարոն մանուէլն եւ քանի ջումիաթ որ խդուրանօցն ելէլ ողջոնցնայլ բռնէլ եւ ինչունեցէլան զափտէլ եւ բաղտատու փաշէն վերկացել իսպահանայ վերէն որ գոյ յերկիրդ[109] էս համբաւն[110] լսեցինք

[106] Khizan: Julfa dialect for family, children, wife.

[107] Khbar<A/P. *khabar* (v.n.), News, information, advices, intelligence; notification.

[108] Elchi<T. *ilchī*: An ambassador, plenipotentiary.

[109] On Manuel Shahrimanian's role in the Persian Embassy to the Sublime Porte in 1725, see among others, Gian Pierro Bellingeri, "Sugli Sceriman Rimasti a Giulfa: Devozione Agli Ultimi Safavidi?" in *Gli Armeni e Venezia: Dagli Sceriman A Mechitar, Il Momento Culminante di una Consuetudine Milenaria*, acura di Levon Zekiyan e Aldo Ferrari, (Venezia, 2004) pp. 93-124.; Laurence Lockhart, *The fall of the Safavi dynasty and the Afghan occupation of Persia,* (Cambridge [Eng.]: University Press, 1958), p. 282, and especially Krusinski, Judasz, and Tadeus. *The history of*

կրկնայպատիկ սուք դարայժամ եկն մեզ վերայ ամենից կողմանց դառնութեան լուր եւ համբաւ կու լսեմք.

ԺԱ

տեր յիսուս մեր խեղջ ազգին օգնութիւն խասանէ. եւ այլեւս լսեցինք թէ սրբազան վեհայպետ կ[ա]թ[ու]ղիկոսն առ ա[ստուա]ծ փոխուել եւ անկիւրիոյ կարապետ վ[ա]րդ[այ]պ[ե]տն յաջորդել կաթուղիկոս նստել զրուցս բերանօքէ եւ ոչ գրով. եւ ս[ր]բ[այ]զ[ա]ն վեհ ոչ ինչ չէիր գրեալ. սուտն եւ իրաւն չգիդեմք. խապարէսպէս լսեցինք. ապայ մէք մինչի թարիղս աստուածայտուր կաթուղիկոսն կու յիշատակեմք մինջեւոր ս[ուր]բ[այ]զան վեհն գրե որպես հուքմ[111] լինի. այնէ իրաւն

ԺԲ

եւ այլ յատնի լիցի ս[ու]րբ[այ]զան վեհին որ էս մովսումին հր[ա]մ[ա]նուցդ փողին խ[ա]մար շատ թլաշ[112] ար[ա]րի թէ աւաք վերառող լինէր աւաք տե խով [??]

---

the late revolutions of Persia: taken from the memoirs of Father Krusinski, Procurator of the Jesuits at Ispahan... done into English from the original...by Father Du Cerceau, (London: J. Pemberton, 1733), vol. 2, p. 185 ff. Concerning the Embassy, Krusinski writes: "The Person he [Shah Ashraf] made choice of for this Embassy, was an *Aghvan*, who from a mule driver, was advanc'd [sic] to be a Colonel. But because a Man of that Stamp was not very proper to manage a Negotiation, he gave him only the Title of Ambassador, and joyn'd [sic] with him *Manuel-Cheriman*, Head of the Family of that Name, the most noble and considerable of all the *Armenian* Families at *Zulfa*, to act and negotiate according to his Intentions, with the *Grand-Signior's* Ministers." (p. 185). On the failure of the Embassy in Constantinople see p. 190 ff.

[110] *Hambav*. Classical Armenian. News, rumor.

[111] Hukm<A/P. *ḥukm* (v.n.), Exercising authority; judgment, sentence, decree; verdict, doom, award; judicial authority, jurisdiction; rule, control, direction, management; a statute, law, enactment. (Steingass, p. 426) Julfa dialect usage normally refers to the authoritativeness of a document or decision.

[112] Tlash ararel<A/P. *talāsh kardan*. To take pains, to exert oneself; to inquire.

ելաւոչ· եւ բաւրայ ալ էս տարի ջումիաթէլ[113] չգնացին վ[ա]ս[ն] յերկիւղի որ էսպէս [??..] վրուցանիք լսելոց: անճառացայ ա [1] խակ ովրանգ շահի առի ինկլիզի նավում բառցի ուղարկեցի բաւրայ մեր յերեւանցի յոնոփրիոսի որդի պ[ա]ր[ո]ն ամիռ աղէ աղայվալէ որդի պ[ա]ր[ո]ն մարտիրոսին եւ ղեոնդի որդի պ[ա]ր[ո]ն մուրատ խանին ձեռն որ նոքայ տեղն ձախեն արասուն թ[օ]մ[ա]ն փող հընդուի առէն որ իսպահան շարիմանէնց մուքելի որդի պ[ա]ր[ո]ն յարութիւնն եւ կամ խալդարէնց ողորմած հոգի յովանէսի որդի պ[ա]ր[ո]ն պետրոս աղէն սօցայ երկքնոցն որոնցն որ խէրիաթ տեսնեն գիրն ուղարկեն հր[ա]մ[ա]ն[ու]ցդ ձեռն որ հր[ա]մ[ա]նքդ փողն յինքառուս քսան թ[օ]մ[ա]նն վեռուս եւ Ժ թ[օ]մ[ա]նն ողորմութիւն առես տաս ժամարարին եւ իմ պառաւմօրն որ իւրեանց խղջութիւնն հոգան եւ պարտք ունեն տան հայր ս[ուր]բ հր[ա]մ[ա]ն[ու]ցդ փողն Ժ թ[օ]մ[ա]նն իմ տարէն Բ [2] թ[օ]մ[ա]նի կողմանէնայխնդրեմ հր[ա]մ[ա]նուցդ հայրայգութողորմութենէն որներումն շնորհես եւ ահնութիւնդ միշտ ձառայիդ վերայ պահես· քո ս[ուր]բ աչն վկայ որ իմ կենդանութիւնն հր[ա]մ[ա]ն[ու]ցդ ս[ու]րբ ահնութեամբնայ եւ մեք ս[ու]րբ տանդ ձառայեմք ոչ թէ միայն մեղաւորս իմ պապն եվ իմ հայրն եւ մեք ահնութիւն ս[ուր]բ տանէդ ունեմք եւ միշտ պատռաստեմք ձառայութեան ապայ էս ժամանակիս կարողութիւնս էտ եհաս խնդրեմ շնորհես կենդանի մնամ գարշայպարդ համբուրեմ եւ սուրբ հօրս արծաթայգին ծառայոց նման ծառայեմ·

ԺԳ

եւ այլ յայտնի սուրբայզան վեհին որ տեր ըստեփաննոսին տարէն Բ [2] թ[օ]մ[ա]նին խ[ա]մար հր[ա]մ[ա]ն[ու]ցդ շնորհալի ահնութեան թղթովն ուզեցի ասաց մովսումին կտամ եւ ինքն գնաց մախսուտայպատ չուն որ տեղն ժողովուրդ շատ կային ամէնքն այլ էն արանկնին գնացէլ տեղս դարտակուելեր էսպէս խորհուրդ

113 Jumiat<A/P. *Jamiat*: Community, people. Julfa dialect uses this word almost exclusively to denote the community of Julfan merchants.

ար[ա]րինք որ մեղավորս տեղս մնամ եւ ինքն գնաց տեղն որ ժողովուրդք միշտ պատարաք տեսնեն եւ երբ արանկէ արեկ էր յունվարի Դ [4] նավէրն վերկալման որ լանկարեն[114] քաշէլ գետիցն դուս ելէլ որէլ օր չեր մնացել որ ֆիքրի արարէլըն առի եւ բանդայ էլ շատ բէջիթելայ.[115] փողն ուզեցի լիներ որ մին կերպէլ ար[ա]րէլ ուղարէլ, առեւտ ոչ. ջուղապէս արէտ թէ ես իմ տանի գրումն գրէլ ամ իմ խոր, որ տեղն տայ. ինչեւիցէ սա էլ առեւտոչ. հայր ս[ուր]բ, յանդքնութիւնս ներես, որ ով որք բանկալայ եկել ջումիաթէ հրամանքդ տեղդ հարցանես. էստուր էութիւնն հրամանուցդ կու պատմեն. էս թէ բանկալայ մուլք բի վառիս[116] տեղս ամեն մարդ ինքնայգլուխ այ, ինչ առէ էլ ոնջ ով հարցանող չկայ ոչ մեծ կայ ոչ փոքր. ամեն մարդ ուր կամքովն մին իշխանութեան տէրայ. էլ մէծաւորի հրամանի ականջ դնող չկայ: Յայտնին գրէմ հրամանուցդ որ ոնչով հրամանուցդ գրին ականջ չէ դնում. տեր նիկողոսն կալկաթայ էպիսկոպոնց նայխով.[117] էնպէս ջուղապարետ եւ տ[է]ր ըստեփաննոսն էսպէս. եւ գիտեմ իւրեանքն այլ հր[ա]մ[ա]ն[ու]ցդ յատուկ գիրեն գրեալյատնի կու լինի ախտիար[118] վեհիննէ. եւ այլ այնպէս յատուկ աֆալ[119] չունի որ վեհին ազդումնէր ար[ա]րեալ: եւ սրբազան վեհին ներումն եւ ողորմութիւն կու խնդրեմ որ գրուս երկարայբանութեանն եւ ախալանացս ներումն շնորհես եւ ծառայիտ մեղացն թողութիւն խնդրես եւ ս[ու]րբ ահնութիւնդ անարժանիցս անպակաս լիցի քանզի ծառայ բոյեմ տ[ե]ր յիսուս արժանի արասցէ զգարշայպար վեհին համբուրիցեմ եւ ընդ հովանեաւ ս[ուր]բ հօրս լինիցեմ ամէն. գրէս Բ [2] գրեցի մին ոճ[120] ա[1] գիրն ֆռանկսիսի

---

[114] Lankar<P *langar*: anchor.

[115] Bejit<P *bejad, bija*: to be disconcerted, to feel out of place.

[116] Literally, heirless rule?

[117] Phrase of uncertain meaning.

[118] Akhtiar<P *Akhtiar*: Authority.

[119] Afal<P/A *hafal:* condition, state.

[120] Julfa dialect commercial documents use the phrase "girs yerku grets'i min mazbun" [I wrote two copies of this document with the same contents].

նավումն ուղարկեցի եւ էս մէկն ինկլիզի նավումն ողարկեցի ղուլուղ

Ի նուաստից նուաստայգոյն եւ յետնեալ
Ծ[ա]ռ [ա]յ տ[ե]ր յարութիւնէ նուէրս աղաչանաց
Մատուցանեմ եւ գառշայպար վեհին ըստէպ ըստէպ
համբուրեմ
վերջ·

Partial Translation of Letter

To the blessed high priest and spiritual shepherd of the house of God, lord David the theologian Vardapet

Written in the year 1170 [1170+551=1721][121]

The first paragraph contains flowery language expressing the author's humility, self-deprecation, and rhetorical gestures of self effacement, such as kissing the soles of the feet of the letter's recipient, David Vardapet, who had been appointed as the Primate of New Julfa and by extension, the spiritual head of the Armenian

[121] Julfan documents use three calendars, sometimes simultaneously. The most popular of these was the small Calendar known as the Calendar of Azaria, which began in the year 1615/1616. Another calendar was the Greater Armenian Calendar that began in 552 and for the conversion of which one has to add 551 to arrive at the Gregorian equivalent. Lastly, Julfans also used the Roman Gregorian calendar, which they referred to as the year of our savior. This document only uses the Greater Armenian Calendar. In general, church documents use the Greater Armenian calendar in combination with the Azaria calendar. This document only has the greater Armenian calendar. Note, however, that the correct date should be 1727 and not 1721. On the calendars used by Armenians see Abrahamian, *Hayots' Gir yev Grch'ut'iwn* [Armenian Writing and Literature] (Yerevan, 1972).

churches in India and elsewhere in the East. The rest of the letter may be translated as follows:

Paragraph 2:

And let it be known to your holiness that your eminence's letter of blessing written on June 18, 1725 and addressed to the priests and people of these lands reached us from Madras on Tira 7 [September 23[122]], 1726, through the hands of Tēr Simon, and we accepted it with joy and kisses. We also received your eminence's holy letter of blessing and read it in the church and among the masses, and all of us gave glory to God and celebrated your eminence's assuming the seat of the primate and made much fanfare, and later we consoled each other on the passing away in Christ of the deceased Movses Vardapet and gave a mass for the blessing of his soul and called upon your own prayers to support us, that they may console us, send us assistance and a way out so we may be saved from being vagabonds and return to kiss the soles of your aged holiness' feet. [...]

Paragraph 3:

And concerning your pardoning[123] of alms and assistance to the holy house [All Savior's Monastery], holy father, let it be known to you that there are three well-to-do people here who have money in their hands. The others are all without any means. One [of these people] is Paron Agha Nazar who, with your eminence's blessing, has a [good] name and reputation, as well as the wealth that God has given him. It is he who established the Calcutta Armenian Church.[124]

---

[122] I have converted this date based on the conversion tables in Abrahamian, *Hayots' Gir yev Grch'ut'iwn*, pp. 118-120.

[123] The original text seems to be unclear here. The context suggests that the primate had *ordered* the collection of alms, *not* pardoned it. See paragraph 4 of letter below.

[124] Paron Agha Nazar mentioned here as the patron of Calcutta's Holy Nazareth Church was most certainly Agha Nazar Jacob Jan, the wealthy Julfan merchant who passed away in Madras in the early 1740s, leaving a huge fortune to Khwaja David Sultan who was married to Agha Nazar's sister, Anna Khatoon. Agha Nazar was the uncle of Shahamir Shahamirian of Madras. I discuss Agha Nazar's career in Bengal and Madras in "From

He spent about seven thousand rupees on this church and built the building with this money. Perhaps, he is still spending more money on it. Who hasn't built in this fashion and not asked for blessing?[125] We were expecting that you would write a grand letter of blessing to Paron Nazar this year, so that upon reading [it] he would receive your blessing and become glad. And I beg your holy eminence that you write a letter of blessing to Paron Nazar this year and also submit the two churches to him, so that he would look after this church of Chichra [Chinsura] as well. I had also notified [the All Savior's Monastery] during the time of the deceased Movses Vardapet that the Church of Chichra, which has been derelict, needs to be looked after. There are no well-to-do people [here] to look after it. It has been entirely abandoned, and whoever of the population had remained [here] has also gone to Calcutta. A few destitute houses have remained. The leading person here was Ulukkhan who passed away. All the others appeal to us for their bread and water. And the principal merchants of Chichra [at this time] are Paron Leon, son of Nazareth, and Paron Minas son of Sahak, who are *commenda* agents of Parons Manuel and Harut'iwn of the Shahrimanian family.[126] Another merchant is Paron Margar, son of Mirzajan, who is an agent of Paron Petros of the Khaldarian family. He assists this house and us priests both in the services of this Church as well as [in purchasing] candles and oil. There is no one else who cares after this house. Holy father, on account of this, I beg you to write a letter of blessing to Paron Nazar and hand over the two churches to him. He is the one who has built the Church of Calcutta, and he looks after its needs with a good heart. Hand over this church of Chichra to him so that he can look after it as well because the boards are rotting, and they have held up this past year, but next year they will entirely fall apart. Your holy hand is witness that it has been four years that whatever church revenue is coming, I am spending all of it on this house and taking care of it, in order for us not to bear the contempt

---

the Indian Ocean to the Mediterranean: Circulation and the Global Trade Networks of Armenian Merchants from New Julfa, Isfahan, 1606-1747."

[125] The meaning of this phrase is uncertain.

[126] Manuel and Harut'iwn Shahrimanian were members of Julfa's richest Armenian Catholic family. See footnotes 71 and 110 above.

of foreigners that the Armenian nation has a church in these lands and is unable to maintain it. Holy father, this much is my plea, that it becomes known to your eminence that there are no well-to-do people in these lands for them to look after both your Holy See as well as this sacred house. And we anticipate from your eminence's holy prayers first that the Holy See and then this house shall remain firm in order for us not to be humiliated among foreigners.

Paragraph 4:

Also concerning the *khostmunk* and *n'verk* contributions to the All Savior's Monastery that you had ordered, let it be known that it has been four years since Tēr Nikoghos has left Chinsura and moved to Calcutta. Whatever financial pledges were in his hands I have notified in several letters to the deceased Movses Vardapet. As to my own time, the [situation] is this that, Ulukhan had made the All Savior's Monastery the heir and had written [a pledge] of 110 [rupees] which I, your servant, took, and there was also a low level employee named Hovannes who had also promised 90 rupees to the Monastery; Paron Margar is his appointed representative. That portion as well I will receive. This will make the donations for the All Savior's Monastery pledged in this place 200 rupees, in addition to the 2 tomans that I will earn this year. Whatever the [total sum] will be, I will write your holiness later and will send it to your eminence. Holy father, I had the expectation that, [???], you would send one or two priests this year so I could come and kiss the soles of your eminence's feet. It appears that the roads are still closed and it has not been possible to send a priest during this year's monsoon season. So I shall stay in this place.

Paragraph 5:

And let it also be known that I showed Tēr Nikoghos your eminence's letters of blessing that you had written to me and the disdain you had shown towards him. I [also] asked him for the money [pledged to the Monastery] as well as his own share of yearly earnings of two tomans. He said that he has sent twenty tomans of money with Paron Gaspar. He took out a document and showed it to me [claiming] that he has given it to Paron Gaspar in Basra, as well as your eminence's letter that you had written to Paron Gaspar in Basra saying that you have received twenty tomans from Paron

Harut'iwn, the son of Mukel, and have written a receipt so that Paron Gaspar in Basra should give to Paron J'entloom, and Paron Gaspar had taken your eminence's document [i.e., the receipt] and had had Ter Yeghnazar seal and send it to Ter Nikoghos, so that when Ter Nikoghos showed me this document, I said good, now you have been in these places for ten years, that money you have sent to the All Savior's Monastery is from the portion of your yearly income. What happened to the money pledged to the Monastery? He said I have also sent fifteen tomans with the Pilgrim Hovhanes. But he didn't have the document to prove this.

Paragraph 6 and 7:

And I didn't say anything else; what you do regarding this matter is up to your discretion. And let it also be known that your eminence's letter of blessing that you had written to Paron Leon and Khach'ik concerning the power of attorney that you had arranged for [their?] brother has reached them. They first received your eminence's blessing and then became informed regarding the force of the document. They have written to you [about this matter] and I too shall say a few words about it here. [Suffice to say that] at the moment, Paron Tarkhan seems to have lost his star in heaven here. I hope that the person who has a star at the moment in Paron Nazar. There was a big discord between Paron Tarkhan and Paron Nazar, and I have notified the late Movses [vardapet] about this in all my letters. This same Paron Tarkhan and Paron Nazar had settled their accounts between them and drafted a contract. They called me and I sealed the document in their presence, testifying that Paron Nazar had written a *sanad* of forty-five thousand tomans and given it to Paron Tarkhan with a time period of one year in order for Paron Tarkhan to give him back his *commenda* contract and take his money. In this fashion, they both agreed to have a severance from each other, but later Paron Tarkhan changed his mind, saying that I have claims on this person [Nazar]. Because of this discord, matters stood like this. This year, Paron Nazar took his money and gave it to the English Company, saying that I have given that man a *sanad*, let this money stay here and let him bring my *commenda* contract and take his money. The head of the English company called me and made an investigation as to whether they had settled their accounts and drafted *farkhati* and he told Paron Tarkhan that you have settled this account and have no claims on Paron Nazar. Your money is at the court of our company, and we shall keep it at our court until you bring Paron Nazar's *commenda* contract and all you three brothers are present in this place and take your money. The money stayed at the court ... And let it also be known that Hovannes, the son of Kalantar Aved passed away here on Hamira 7 [??], in the year 111 (1726). It is possible that he owed up to 5,000 [rupees] in debt to the Dutch, Armenians, Muslims, and a 1,000 [rupees] in cash here and there about which only God knows. He left this wretched and miserable world indebted to many people. May God have compassion on his soul.

Paragraph 8:

And if you wish to know how Paron Manuk is doing, let it be known that he is here. He is robust and healthy as a result of your eminence's prayers, and he kisses your holy right hand. He is his own master and is not dependent on anyone. May God keep him away from temptation. His strength lies in the care he puts into his work, so that he may not be covered in shame before his family. He has a few hundred tomans of profit granted by God and purchases things in the manufacturing places in these parts, brings them, and sells them to the Europeans. May God give him strength. He is doing good work. With God's help he will be fine. When your holiness' letters arrived, he was away in the manufacturing centers/markets. I sent him the letters and he read them, came from manufacturing centers and showed the letters to me. This year, he might send spending money to his family, and with God's help he will do so. May your holiness' prayers bring succor to him and to me so that the possibility may present itself, and I shall come and kiss the soles of your eminence. Your holy right hand may stand witness that I have read your letters and cried with bitter tears. Our loved ones have been going through many difficulties and sufferings, and your eminence's servant priest [i.e., the letter writer?] had written that there is no one here who is helping us and no one who gives us a penny. Holy father, let there be a day that redemption and [God's] compassion shall reach our miserable family so that they shall find some rest. As far as Paron Manouk is concerned, do not worry. With God's help he is healthy and robust and will kiss your eminence's right hand.

Paragraph 9:

He too has written a letter to your eminence, and in it his fault shall become evident. And, moreover, I beg of your compassionate father that, as the deceased Movses Vardapet had pity and compassion on us, so too you shall have compassion on us humble ones and keep your pity and fatherly love on us, especially during your free hours, that you should receive the priest's [i.e., the letter writer's??] news, who feels very forlorn. Your eminence is our lord, leader, and father both spiritually and corporally. Let it not be that you shall forget your servants; rather take fatherly pity on your servants.

Paragraphs 10 and 11:

And let it also be known to your holy eminence, that news reached [us] from Basra that the Afghan Ambassador who had gone to the Ottoman Empire has been sent away with disrespect. And the ambassador had returned and arrived in Baghdad. The Pasha [of Baghdad] has seized him with his retinue [?] and belongings and sent him to prison. And they have seized Paron Manuel and all the people who were with him and confiscated all their belongings. And they have left Baghdad on their way to Isfahan to be in that place [i.e., Julfa?]. We heard this rumor, and we were doubly afflicted with ill-opportune sorrow and from all sides we are hearing news and rumors of misery. May the Lord Jesus come to the support of our poor nation. And we also heard that the venerable Catholicos has passed away and that Karapet Vardapet of Ancyra has sat as the next Catholicos. This information is by word of mouth only and not by letter. Since your venerable eminence had not written a thing [on this matter] we do not know what is true and what is false. This is how we heard the news. And to this date, we continue to remember Astuatsatur Catholicos [and will do so] until your venerable eminence writes [to us] so that it becomes authoritative as the truth. And let it also be known to your venerable eminence that I exerted much effort during this season for your eminence's money, if there had been someone to accept an *avak* [respondencia loan/letter of exchange]...but there was no such person and it did not happen. And there was no one from our community going to Basra this year.

Paragraph 12:

And let it be known to the holy father that I made much effort during this monsoon season on account of your eminence's money. If there had been people willing to take a promissory note. ... And none of the merchants of our community went to Basra this year on account of fear, and listening to such discussions I became hopeless. I bought one bale of Aurangshah's and loaded it on the English ship and sent it to Basra in the care of Paron Martiros, the son of Paron Amiragha Aghaval son of our Honoprios of the Yerevan quarter of Julfa, and Paron Muratkhan son of Ghevont, for them to sell it there [i.e., in Basra] and take out a *hundi* of thirty tomans so either Paron Harut'iwn son of Mukel of the Shahriman family or Paron Petros son of the deceased Hovhanes of the Khaldarents' family, whichever of the two finds it safe shall send the document [i.e., the *hundi*] to your eminence. Your eminence can then take the money, keep the twenty tomans [for the All Savior's Monastery] and give the ten tomans as alms to the priest [? Zhamarar] and to my elderly mother, so they can look after their own poverty and pay whatever debts they may have. Holy father, of the money you shall receive, ten tomans is from the pledge made by Ulukhan and Hovhanes and ten tomans from my own yearly two-toman contribution. I beg of your eminence's fatherly compassion that you shall be forgiving and always keep your blessing upon your servant. Your holy right hand is the witness that I am alive and well because of your holy blessing, and not only I the sinful one, but also my grandfather and father are servants of your holy house [the All Savior's Monastery] and we have had the blessing of your holy house and we are always ready to serve you.

Paragraph 13:

And let it also be known to the holy father that I requested the two-toman yearly donation from Tēr Stepanos, and he said that he would give it during this monsoon season and went to Makhsudabad because there were many people there all of whom had gone from here to the markets there, leaving this place empty. And we decided that I the sinful one would stay here and he [Tēr Stepanos] would go there, so the people would always have mass. When he returned from that textile-manufacturing place [i.e., Makhsudabad] it was January 4 and the ships had [already] lifted their anchors and were leaving the river. There was no time left and I tried to take care of this matter but was much confounded. I asked for the money [...] but he did not give it. He responded saying that he had written his father [in Julfa] for him to give the money in that place. Be that as it may, he did not even give me this [letter to his father?]. Holy father, forgive my audacity, but you should ask anyone from our community who has arrived there from Bengal and they will tell you the truth about this. In this place of Bengal where there is no real authority [literally no heirs for the *mulk* or authority/power] everyone acts on his own, no one asks them to be accountable, there is no ruler and no follower. Everyone is an authority according to his own will and there is no one who listens to the orders of a leader. I am only writing to you what is evident, that no one is paying heed to what you have written in your letter. Tēr Nikoghos in Calcutta ... responded in that fashion, and Tēr Stepanos in this fashion. I know that they have written their own letters to your eminence, so things shall become known to you. It is up to your discretion to do as you please. And I do not have any more news to inform the holy father [??]. I ask the forgiveness and the blessing of the holy father, so you may forgive my lengthy letter and its errors and may ask forgiveness for the sins of your servant. May I, the undeserving one, not be deprived of your holy blessing. And because I am your servant, may the lord Jesus find me worthy so that I may kiss the soles of your feet and be under the shield of my holy father. Amen. I wrote two identical copies of this letter, one of which I sent on a French ship, the other on an English ship.

From your most humble servant, Tēr Harut'iwn
I present my offering and continuously
kiss the soles of the holy father's feet.
The End.

29

The Armenian Church and Czarist Russia

George A. Bournoutian

Armenian contacts with Russia began in Kiev as early as the tenth century. By the end of the fourteenth century, Armenians, employed by the Mongols as traders, emissaries, and tax collectors, had reached Moscow and had established small trading posts along the Volga River. When Ivan IV defeated the last remnants of the Mongols and took Kazan (1552) and Astrakhan (1556), there were Armenian communities in both cities. The *Time of Trouble* following the death of Ivan IV and the Perso-Ottoman wars precluded further contacts until peace was restored by the election of a Romanov prince (Michael) as the Czar of Russia (1613) and the Peace of Zuhab between Safavid Persia and the Ottoman Empire (1639). The new, favorable conditions encouraged the wealthy Armenians merchants of New Julfa, Isfahan, to use the Caspian Sea-Volga River route for trading silk and other merchandise in Europe. After preliminary contacts and the presentation of a splendid diamond throne to the Russian ruler in 1660, an official trade agreement was signed on 31 May 1667, between the Persian Armenian Company and Czar Alexis (1645-1676), which gave special privileges to the Armenian merchants from Persia.[1] It was not long after that Armenians began building a tanning factory in Moscow and large trading depots in Astrakhan.

---

[1]The original contract (in Russian) is in the Central State Archives of Ancient Documents in Moscow [File: Russia's Relations with Armenia, 1667], group 1, ff. 14-22. All the documents cited here are available in English translation (slightly altered and with different spellings) in George A. Bournoutian, *Armenians and Russia, 1626-1796: A Documentary Record* (Costa Mesa, Ca: Mazda Publishers, 2001) and George A.

The rise of the number of Armenians in Russia, as well as the privileged position of the Persian Armenians there, prompted the leaders of the Armenian Church in Persia to officially contact the Russian Czar and to present their credentials. The earliest record is that of Catholicos of Aghuank' (Caucasian Albania), Petros III (1653-1675), who resided at the Holy See of Gandzasar, in the semi-autonomous Armenian region known as the *khamse*[2] (present-day Nagorno-Karabagh) in Karabagh. A letter, dated 2 December, 1672, states:

> [To] the Czar, crowned by Christ...[from] the slave of God, Petros, the Armenian Catholicos, with prayers of Gregory the Great of Greater Armenia. I am the Patriarch of the Holy See of Gandzasar, where the holy relics of St. John the Baptist, Gregory the Great, Joseph of Arimathea, and others are located and where we call upon the apostles of Jesus Christ and the Holy Ghost to guard your throne, the city of Moscow, and your entire kingdom...
>
> Your Majesty is aware that merchants are like sheep and need a safe place to multiply. Great Sovereign, you have given our Armenian people the right to trade in your lands. The Persian Shah has confirmed that right and the Armenian notables of Isfahan are overjoyed...We pray that your enemies will be vanquished and you, like King Solomon, will spread your justice to embrace our people and safeguard them from harm...[3]

A few months later, Hakob of Julfa, the Catholicos at the Holy See of Etchmiadzin (1655-1680), the mother Church of Armenia, wrote a letter to the Czar in which he complained about the enormity of taxes imposed by Persian officials and the forceful conversions of Armenians to Islam. He concluded:

> I hope that when Your Majesty sends envoys to the Persians, they can use their influence and say a few words on our behalf. The Russian State is important in the eyes

---

Bournoutian, *Russia and the Armenians of Transcaucasia, 1797-1889: A Documentary Record* (Costa Mesa, Ca: Mazda Publishers, 1998).

[2] From the Arabic five, which stood for the five autonomous districts of Karabagh: Khachen, Jraberd, Gulistan, Dizak, and Varanda.

[3] The original (in Armenian) is in the Central State Archives of Ancient Documents in Moscow (1672), folder 3, ff. 4-5.

> of the Persians and they may stop their harassment once they witness your concern. Thus the Armenian Church and I, by the Grace of God, its servant in Christ, bow our heads in supplication and in public prayer.[4]

At the close of the seventeenth century and the dawn of the eighteenth century Peter the Great (1689-1725) was petitioned by Armenian *melik*s of Karabagh, as well as by the Armenian emancipatory figure, Israel Ori, to help liberate Christian Armenia from Muslim rule.[5] Realizing the importance of the Armenians to his goals of expanding the borders of Russia, Peter permitted the construction of a wooden church in Astrakhan at the start of the eighteenth century, which in 1706 was replaced by a stone structure. Further letters from Armenian leaders in the Caucasus and Persia convinced Peter to examine the internal conditions in Persia more closely and to check the proposals of the Armenian *meliks* of Karabagh.

Meanwhile, as the Armenian population in Russia increased in size, the Catholicoi of Gandzasar and Etchmiadzin both began to vie for the jurisdiction over the lucrative donations and dues that could be collected from the Armenians in Russia. The mother Church, Etchmiadzin, which already collected dues from the many prelacies in Persia and the Ottoman Empire, assumed that it would be granted the same privilege in Russia. The internal struggles within Etchmiadzin and the election of a very militant and pro-Russian Yesayi Hasan-Jalalean as the Catholicos of Gandzasar (1702-1728) began a major rivalry between the two Holy Sees, which was to continue until 1768.

Yesayi fired the first salvo. Upon assuming his post, he immediately sent a letter to the Armenians of Astrakhan and Moscow informing them that he and not the Catholicos at Etchmiadzin was responsible for their welfare. It reads:

> From the servant of Christ, Yesayi, Catholicos of All Aghuank‘, the successor of Gregory the Illuminator and the Patriarch of the Holy See of Gandzasar, to the Armenians of

[4] The original (written in Latin sometime in 1673) is in the Central State Archives of Ancient Documents in Moscow (1724), folder 2, ff. 5-6.

[5] See documents no. 40, 43-49, 55, 59, and 67 in Bournoutian, *Armenians and Russia*.

> Moscow and Astrakhan...Catholicos Simēon[6] has died...As his successor, elected to the chair at Gandzasar, we are now responsible for your welfare and charge you to obey our directives...It is your duty to inform us of your needs and we shall respond...[7]

When Etchmiadzin, which was under the strict supervision of the Persian khans, feared to get involved with Ori's plan for the liberation of Armenia, Yesayi not only embraced Ori's idea, but also appointed a cleric, Vardapet Minas, as Ori's assistant and as his official envoy to Russia. Minas was dispatched to Moscow and began to work on behalf of Ori and Gandzasar.

Seven years later, the new Catholicos at Etchmiadzin, Alexander of Julfa (1706-1714), finally sent a letter to Peter the Great, but it was too late.[8] Minas had the ears of the Department of Foreign Affairs and had prejudiced the mind of the Russian officials against any Armenian not known to Ori or Yesayi.[9]

The rivalry intensified when Peter decided to grant formal recognition to the Armenian Church in Russia and a prelacy was established in 1716, with its center in Astrakhan. Catholicos Alexander dispatched Bishop Hovakim as the Prelate of the Armenians in Russia. When Hovakim left Russia to collect the Church dues in Europe, Catholicos Yesayi made Minas an archbishop and named him as Prelate of the Armenians in Russia. Minas, who had the ear of the Russians, accused Hovakim of being a Persian spy and had him arrested by the Russians upon his return from Europe in 1718. Two years later, Hovakim died in a Kazan jail and the rift between the two Sees widened. Yesayi and Minas acted as the sole representatives of the Armenians in Russia and completely ignored Etchmiadzin in their correspondence with Peter the Great. Yesayi and Minas went so far as to accuse Etchmiadzin of being friendly to Persia and an enemy of Russia.[10] The czar finally accepted Minas and Yesayi as the only religious leaders of

---

[6] Catholicos at Gandzasar from 1675-1701.

[7] Central State Archives of Ancient Documents in Moscow: Group 100 (1701-1703), folder 3, f. 237.

[8] In Armenian, Ibid., (1707-1711), folder 1, f. 32.

[9] Ibid., ff. 47-49.

[10] Bournoutian, *Armenians and Russia*, doc. 87.

the Armenians in Russia and Transcaucasia. It is not surprising that the Armenian archbishop of Tiflis began sending reports to Minas as well.

The fall of Isfahan to the Afghans, civil war in Persia, the occupation of Etchmiadzin by the Ottomans, as well as the armed resistance of the Armenians of Karabagh and Ghap'an, prompted Yesayi to extend his authority even further. Soon, Peter's successor, Czarina Catherine I (1725-1727) addressed Yesayi as the sole representative of the Armenians in Russia and Transcaucasia.[11]

The death of Yesayi encouraged Etchmiadzin to try and reassert its position. Catholicos Abraham II (1730-1734) dispatched a vardapet to distribute holy oil to the Armenians in Astrakhan and to collect dues for Etchmiadzin. The death of Minas (1740) and the anti-Armenian policies of Czarina Elizabeth (1741-1762)—discussed below—destroyed much of Gandzasar's power in Russia. On 17 October 1750, Catholicos Ghazar (1737-1751) of Etchmiadzin sent a letter to the Armenians of Astrakhan, which stated:

> The servant of Jesus Christ, Patriarch Ghazar, Catholicos of All Armenians...to the Armenians of Astrakhan—persons of property, notables, elders of the community, sacristans, wise merchants, able craftsmen, hardworking farmers, and all others, both males and females, young and old—Amen.
>
> You know that St. Gregory after bringing Christianity to Armenia sent a Catholicos to Georgia and another one to Caucasian Albania to convert the inhabitants of those regions. When the Persian kings came to our land they drove most of the Albanian Armenians to Khorasan, Kabul, and Qandahar. Armenians were also forced to live in [New] Julfa, Farahabad, Maznadaran, and Hamadan...
>
> The Catholicos of Aghuank' was to oversee the Albanian Armenians and no others. He, however, usurped his authority and now plans to extend it over our community. I write to you, once again, to remind you of your duty to the Holy See of Etchmiadzin...[12]

[11] Ibid., doc. 148.

[12] Matenadaran Archives, Archives of the Catholicosate of Etchmiadzin, folder 155, doc. 3.

During the reign of Peter the Great and his immediate successors, Archbishop Minas had tried to utilize his connections, overcome the opposition of the Russian Orthodox Church, and gain permission to construct an Armenian church in St. Petersburg.[13] Minas could not accomplish his goal and lost his power after the death of Catherine I (1727). The single church in Astrakhan remained the only Armenian church on Russian soil. Following two decades of petitions, the dream of new churches in Russia finally came true only during the reign of Czarina Anna (1730-1740). Anna, the daughter of Ivan V, had been married to the Duke of Courland. A childless widow, she brought a group of Germans, headed by her lover Biron, who disdained everything Russian. The construction of Catholic and Protestant churches was permitted. Armenians took advantage of this and, since the Armenian population of Astrakhan had grown considerably, they petitioned Anna for permission to construct a new church in that city. Permission was granted in 1737, a wooden foundation was begun and soon a number of services were conducted in the yet unfinished church.[14]

In 1739, a wealthy Armenian merchant, Luke Shirvanov, petitioned the czarina to permit the construction of a small Armenian church on the land he owned in St. Petersburg.[15] Anna granted the petition and a year later, the Senate and the Holy Synod affixed their seals to the petition. A few months later, Bogdan Khristoforov, a prominent Armenian merchant in Moscow asked the czarina to permit the construction of an Armenian church in the *Kitai-gorod* (Oriental) section of the city. Permission was granted for that as well.[16]

None of these churches were constructed, however. The reign of Czarina Elizabeth changed everything. She not only replaced the German party with Russians, but also stopped all non-Orthodox

---

[13] G. A. Ezov', ed., *Snosheniia Petra Velikogo s' armianskim' narodom* (St. Petersburg, 1898), doc. 202.

[14] Archives of the Foreign Policy of Russia in Moscow (1738), folder 1, f. 3.

[15] Central State Historical Archives in St. Petersburg, Collection 796, group 21, folder 60, ff. 2-4.

[16] Ibid. group 22, folder 651, f. 4

religious activities in Russia. One of her earliest decrees dated 1 February 1741, reads:

> We have ordered that upon completion of the Lutheran churches, whose construction was permitted by Count Münnich[17] in the Ukraine, they be consecrated according to the Greco-Russian rite. The first shall be named the Church of the Holy Resurrection and the second of the Holy Virgin. We also ask that the Synod inform us immediately where in Our Realm are they currently constructing Armenian churches and on whose order.[18]

A year later she sent the following note to the Holy Synod:

> After receiving your report of December 1741, We decree that all the construction permits for Armenian churches in Moscow, St, Petersburg, as well as the wooden church in Astrakhan, be cancelled and any existing construction be halted.[19]

Although the Armenian bishop of Astrakhan, Step'an, went to Moscow and begged the Holy Synod to reconsider the order, the governor of Astrakhan locked the church to prevent the conducting of services. A few months later an order arrived to demolish the unfinished church and raze its foundation.[20] The czarina, the daughter of Peter the Great, did not go against her father's wishes, however. The Armenians of Russia continued to have a prelate and a prelacy with its single church in Astrakhan. Ten years later, Armenian merchants from Moscow and St. Petersburg once again petitioned the government to permit the construction of churches in their respective cities. They stated that such structures would attract more Armenian merchants and bring more capital to Russia. They

---

[17] General Burkhard Kristof von Münnich (Khristofor Antonovich Minikh in Russian) was the president of the War Collegium. He was a friend of Biron and was exiled by Elizabeth.

[18] Ibid., f. 1.

[19] Archives of the Foreign Policy of Russia in Moscow (Relations with Armenia, 1752-1760), folder 1, f. 8.

[20] Central State Historical Archives in St. Petersburg, Collection 796, group 21, folder 60, ff. 63-64.

added that even the Muslims had more houses of worship, while the stone church in Astrakhan remained the sole Armenian church in Russia, despite the very large number of Armenians living in the Empire.[21] Although the Senate and the Collegium of Foreign Affairs accepted their petition, no official decree came from Elizabeth.[22]

The czarina even went further when she decided to encourage the conversion of Armenian soldiers who had joined Peter's army in special Armenian and Georgian squadrons. On 30 June 1742, the Holy Synod decreed that:

> The priest belonging to the Armenian faith, who is currently serving in the Georgian Regiment be expelled and not permitted to return to the regiment. The Armenians serving in this regiment should, according to the order of Her Imperial Majesty to the Holy Synod, dated 6 April 1742 and her order of 14 April to the War Collegium, be strongly and carefully coached to convert to the Orthodox faith. Those Armenian heretics who express a desire to convert should be taken by the regimental priest to an Orthodox church and be converted.[23]

Catherine the Great (1762-1796) completely reversed Elizabeth's policy of intolerance. Her enlightened policies brought greater economic prosperity and religious freedom for the Armenians living in Russia. A few months after taking the throne, the czarina issued a decree, which permitted all her non-Orthodox subjects, except the Jews, to build their own houses of worship in Russia. The previous petitions of the Armenians of Astrakhan, Moscow, and St. Petersburg now received positive responses.[24] A decade later, Armenians had a second church in Astrakhan, a church in Moscow, and a large church on Nevskii Prospect in St.

---

[21] Archives of the Foreign Policy of Russia (Relations with Armenia, 1752-1760), folder 1, ff. 1, 3-7.

[22] Ibid., f. 37.

[23] Central State Archives of Military History in Moscow, Collection 10, group 2/109, folder 2, f. 548.

[24] *Sobranie aktov' otnosiashchikhsia k' obozreniiu istorii armianskogo naroda*, I (Moscow, 1833), pp. 172-173.

Petersburg.[25] Ten years later, Catherine permitted the Armenian immigrants from the Crimea to construct a large church in New Nakhichevan (Rostov-on-the-Don).[26] By the end of the eighteenth century an Armenian church was also constructed in Grigoriopol‘ for the Armenian immigrants from Moldavia,[27] and smaller chapels had opened in Moscow, St. Petersburg, Astrakhan, and New Nakhichevan.[28]

Catherine's reign witnessed another major change vis-à-vis the Armenian Church. The czarina's wars with the Ottomans and her slow move in establishing ties with Georgia, re-established Etchmiadzin as the sole representative of the Armenians in Russia. The Catholicos who initiated and completed the process was Simēon of Yerevan (1763-1780). To by-pass the suspicion of the Persian khans, Simēon, in 1773, appointed Archbishop Hovsēp Arghutean (Iosif Argutinskii) as the new Prelate of the Armenians in Russia. Argutinskii was an ardent supporter of Russian expansion into Transcaucasia and a major exponent of the Russian orientation among his people. He soon complained that the Holy See was politically too cautious. To safeguard their position vis-à-vis the Persians, both Simēon and his successor Catholicos Ghukas (1780-1799) totally detached themselves from the actions of Argutinskii. The archbishop, for all intents and purposes, operated independently from Etchmiadzin. It was Argutinskii, and not the Catholicos, who, in 1780, insisted that Russia forbid Catholic missionaries from converting Armenians.[29]

Argutinskii's connections with the Russian State gave Etchmiadzin total control over the Armenians in Russia. In 1779, Catherine instructed the Armenian clerics from the Crimea that they had to be subordinate to Etchmiadzin.[30] Soon after, the czarina

---

[25] *Polnoe sobranie zakonov Rossiskoi Imperii*, XIX, no. 13464.

[26] Central State Historical Archives in St. Petersburg, Collection 880, group 1, folder 19, ff. 85-86.

[27] Central State Historical Archives in St. Petersburg, Collection 1374, Group 1, folder 55, f. 22.

[28] *Polnoe sobranie zankonov Rossiskoi Imperii*, XXIII (Moscow, 1830), no. 16945.

[29] Matenadaran Archives, Archives of the Catholicosate, folder 3, doc. 7.

[30] Central State Historical Archives in St. Petersburg, Collection 88, group 1, folder 19, ff. 85-86.

ordered that no Armenian priest from Persia, Georgia, or the Ottoman Empire could enter Russia without Etchmiadzin's written permission.[31] Argutinskii's personal friendship with the Potemkin brothers and General Suvorov prepared the way for what he hoped would be the liberation of historic Armenia by Russia. The Catholicoi of Gandzasar, the *meliks* of Karabagh, and the Armenian leaders of Yerevan and Tiflis were now subordinate to Argutinskii's directives. Argutinskii corresponded with the Lazareans of Moscow and St. Petersburg, King Erekle II of Georgia, Shahamir Shahamirian of India, and with every noted Russian military and state official.[32] The death of Catholicos Hovhannēs Hasan-Jalalean at the hands of Ebrahim Khan of Shushi, left Gandzasar without a leader for eight years and made Argutinskii, hence Etchmiadzin, the unofficial spiritual leaders of Armenians of Karabagh. Argutinskii even authored a draft for a future Armeno-Russian treaty in which the new Armenian State would be a kingdom blessed by the Armenian Church under Russian protection.[33] Argutinskii accompanied the Russian army during the invasion of Transcaucasia in 1796, and could almost taste the fruits of his labor, when Catherine's death halted the Russian advance at the Kur River. He did not give up hope and was instrumental in convincing Czar Paul (1796-1801) to reassess his policy regarding Russian diplomatic involvement in Transcaucasia.

The last year of the eighteenth century and the dawn of the nineteenth century witnessed a major change in the election of the Catholicos at Etchmiadzin. Throughout the seventeenth century, the powerful Persian Armenian community had exercised great influence in having their own candidates elected. The haughty behavior of the Persian Armenians angered the western Armenians, so much so that they even elected their own Catholicos.[34] The fall of the Safavids and the Ottoman occupation of the Holy See opened the way for the election of candidates from the Ottoman

[31] *Sobranie aktov'*, III, pp. 323-327.

[32] See Bournoutian, *Armenians and Russia*, documents nos. 323, 326, 327, 332, 348, 355, 369, 373-375, 378-379, 381-383, and 386.

[33] *Diwan Hayots' Patmut'yan*, IV (Tiflis, 1899), pp. 731-737.

[34] Krikor Maksoudian, *Chosen of God: The Election of the Catholicos of All Armenians* (New York: St. Vartan Press, 1995), p. 85.

Empire or those acceptable to the Armenians of Constantinople and Jerusalem. The Russian involvement in Transcaucasia now challenged both Persian and Ottoman influence. Russia adopted the Muslim stance of viewing the Catholicos, the Prelate of the Armenians in Russia, and the Patriarch of Constantinople as the leaders of the Armenian people. As long as Etchmiadzin was under Muslim rule, Russia tried to use its influence to elect a pro-Russian Catholicos and acted as the protector of the Holy See of Etchmiadzin. The death of Catholicos Ghukas and the upcoming election brought, for the first time, Russia into the fray. The Patriarch of Constantinople, Daniēl of Surmari and Archbishop Dawit‘ of Eneget‘ were supported by the Ottoman and Persian factions, respectively. Russia wished to see Argutinskii as the new Catholicos. A letter from Czar Paul to the Russian ambassador in Constantinople dated 16 March 1800, states:

> Make sure that in the upcoming election of the Catholicos of All Armenians, the Porte does not go against the wishes of the Armenian nation and elect someone who is not worthy of that position; someone who manages to receive the throne and robes of the leader of the Armenians through intrigues and bribery. I suggest that you explain, in a friendly manner, our position to the Turkish ministry.[35]

Russian pressure made Daniēl withdraw his candidacy and silenced Dawit‘'s ambitions. Argutinskii was elected the Catholicos of Etchmiadzin, but died in Tiflis in 1801, on his way to the Holy See. Although Daniēl was elected Catholicos in 1801, he was kidnapped by his rival, Dawit‘, in 1802 and imprisoned, first in Etchmiadzin, and then in Yerevan, and Maraghe for five years.[36] The new Russian czar, Alexander I (1801-1825) followed his grandmother's policy and sent troops to Georgia. Russians now reversed their position, supported Daniēl, and used his imprisonment as one of the excuses for the unsuccessful attack on

---

[35] Archives of the Foreign Policy of Russia (Relations with Armenians, 1780-1801), folder 184, f. 26.

[36] For more details see George Bournoutian, *The Khanate of Erevan under Qajar Rule, 1795-1828* (Costa Mesa, CA: Mazda Publishers, 1992), pp. 75-79.

Yerevan in 1804, during the first Russo-Persian War (1804-1813). Russian pressure finally removed Dawit‘ and re-installed Daniēl as Catholicos in 1807. Following his death Russia managed, once again, to install the new Prelate of the Armenians in Russia, Yep‘rem of Dzoragegh as the Catholicos (1809-1830).

Yep‘rem was not another Argutinskii, however. His weakness and indecision suited neither Russia nor Persia. He soon fled to the monastery of Haghpat and the See remained without a leader. Russia found another Argutinskii in the person of the Armenian Archbishop of Tiflis, Nersēs of Ashtarak. Nersēs was an active proponent of Russian rule in Transcaucasia and of Armenian autonomy under the direction of the Church and Russian protection. Following the first Russo-Persian War, Karabagh, together with eastern Transcaucasia became part of Russia. With Gandzasar under Russian control, Nersēs feared the machinations of Sargis Hasan-Jalalean, who had returned to Gandzasar from his exile and had assumed the title of Catholicos. He corresponded with the Russian military commanders in Transcaucasia and seems to have convinced them to end the Catholicosate of Aghuank‘ in 1815; Sargis was given the title of Metropolitan of Karabagh.[37] Realizing that the Armenians of the *khamse* region were a minority in Muslim-dominated eastern Transcaucasia under Russian rule, Nersēs sought to separate it and form an Armenian region under the control of the Armenian general Madatov. He thus asked Russia to conduct a population survey there. His actions forced the last khan of Karabagh, Mahdi-qoli to flee to Persia (1822).[38] The survey proved beyond any doubt that the *khamse* region was predominantly Armenian.[39] Nersēs now formed Armenian militia units and encouraged the Russian commanders to break the peace treaty of Gulistan (1813) and liberate western Transcaucasia, which included Yerevan, Etchmiadzin, and Nakhichevan. The Second Russo-Persian War gave Nersēs the opportunity to accompany his units and take part in the defense of Etchmiadzin against Persian attacks.

---

[37] *Akty*, V, document 522.

[38] *Akty*, VI/1, document 1299.

[39] Ibid., document 601.

Following the war, Nersēs was one of those responsible for the establishment of the Armenian Province from the khanates of Yerevan and Nakhichevan. He was also instrumental in the inclusion of article XV of the Treaty of Turkmenchay, by which Armenians in Persia had one year to immigrate into the newly established Armenian Province.[40] Russia also became the protector of the Armenians and their Church in Persia. The death of Alexander I and the ascension of the conservative Nicholas I, however, isolated Nersēs and his Russian supporters. The *khamse* region was not included in the Armenian Province and Nersēs was dispatched far away from Etchmiadzin as the new Prelate of the Armenians of Bessarabia.

With the Holy See in the hands of Russia, the czar wished to assure Russian control over the affairs of the Holy See. The new Catholicos, Hovhannēs of Karbi (1831-1842) was a pro-Russian candidate from Tiflis, who cooperated with Russia and enabled it to enact the *Polozhenie* (Regulation or Statutes) of 1836, without much resistance.[41]

Much has been written on the *Polozhenie*, or statutes that defined the relationship between the Russian government and the Armenian Church until the Russian Revolution of October 1917. Some historians view it as a set of restrictions imposed by Russia to limit the power of the Catholicos at Etchmiadzin and to place the Armenian Church under the virtual control of the central government. Other historians view it more benignly, as a document that not only officially recognized the autonomy of the Armenian Church and gave the Armenians full freedom of worship, but also permitted Church control over Armenian schools and other institutions. On one hand, it clearly shows that although Czar Nicholas and most of his advisors wished to restrain the

---

[40] The English text of the treaty is in J. C. Hurewitz, ed., *Diplomacy in the Near and Middle East: A Documentary Record*, I (Princeton, N.J.: Van Nostrand, 1956), pp. 96-102. The Russian text is in T. Iuzefovich, *Dogovory Rossii s Vostokom* (St. Petersburg, 1869), 223-227. The Persian text is in the *Asnad-e Vezarat-e Omur-e Khareje*, documents 61-62.

[41] The complete text of the *Polozhenie* is available in English, in Bournoutian, *Russia and the Armenians of Transcaucasia*, pp. 350-368. The original Russian text is in *Polnoe sobranie zakonov Rossiskoi Imperii*, XI, no. 8970.

independence of the Armenian Church, the Russians felt that the constant arguments and accusations among the Church hierarchy gave them sufficient justification to introduce the regulations. On the other hand, although the cooperation of some clerics enabled Russia to interfere in the affairs of the Armenian Church, other clerics did not always adhere to the statutes and, at times, defied it completely.

Furthermore, the *Polozhenie* was not a document dictated wholly by Russia. The Armenian religious hierarchy was consulted in its preparation. Moreover, Russia took into account the traditional and administrative formalities of the Armenian Church in preparing the document. Russia was convinced that the financial, administrative, and electoral difficulties experienced by Etchmiadzin between 1801-1807, and 1822-1829, mandated certain reforms. The *Polozhenie* also curbed the influence of Persian and Ottoman officials in the affairs of the Holy See. The *Polozhenie* did, unquestionably, place certain restrictions on the autonomy of the Church and officially gave Russia a major and unique voice in the election of the Catholicos. Moreover, the Synod at Etchmiadzin was now given power to balance the authority of the Catholicos. Furthermore, Russia maintained a strong role in the appointment of the Catholicos; for the czar chose him from among two candidates presented to him by the Governor-General of Transcaucasia (Articles 18-19). The Russian procurator at Etchmiadzin served as a day-to-day informer and submitted reports to the chief Russian administrator in Transcaucasia and to the central government in St. Petersburg (articles 45-46). The Russians thus both regulated and interfered in the affairs of the Armenian Church far more than the Muslims had ever done. Nonetheless, the power of the procurator over the Catholicos was limited and the provisions of the *Polozhenie* were, at times, totally ignored. Most important, however, was the fact that the Armenians were referred to as a separate ethnic and religious entity within the Russian Empire. The *Polozhenie* called them the People of Hayk and their Church was referred to as the Armenian Gregorian Church. The Armenian Church could appoint their own clergy, who were under the jurisdiction of their own superiors. Its members were exempt from taxes, duties, services, and from corporal punishment. The Armenian Church and its members were free to practice their faith throughout the Russian Empire. The Church could resolve all civil suits in its own religious courts. The Armenian Church had the right to possess immovable property (articles 1-9). Hence, the Armenian Church kept its autonomy and was not absorbed or dominated by the Russian Orthodox Church, a fate that befell the Georgian Church.

The Armenian Church thus enjoyed a privileged position and with the cultural awakening of the Armenians became involved in the education of the Armenians in Transcaucasia. Academies, schools and printing presses were established in Tiflis and Etchmiadzin. The Church was generally conservative and did not encourage modern changes. It was the Russian government that inadvertently forced it to alter its behavior and become more revolutionary. On 12 June 1903, Czar Nicholas II (1894-1917), wrongly convinced that the Church was instigating anti-Russian feelings among the Armenians, ordered the confiscation of Armenian Church properties. The violation of the *Polozhenie* was a shock to the clergy, as well as the mostly apolitical population.

Catholicos Mkrtich‘ of Van (1892-1908), known as Khrimian Hairik, refused to accept the new law and Armenian revolutionaries began a terrorist campaign against Russian officials. By 1905, the resistance had joined the revolutionary activities that followed Bloody Sunday (9 January 1905). The czar finally gave in and appointed Count Vorontsov-Dashkov as the new viceroy of the Caucasus. Considered a friend of the Armenians, he convinced Nicholas to repeal the act and restore the *Polozhenie* on 1 August 1905.

The Armenian Church remained loyal to the Russian State and when World War I broke out, Vorontsov-Dashkov met with the leading Armenians in Tiflis to recruit Armenian volunteers to join the Russian army. Catholicos Gevorg V (1911-1930) also called upon his flock to assist Russia in the upcoming war. The Armenian mayor of Tiflis, and other Russian Armenian religious and lay leaders in Baku, Yerevan, Moscow, St. Petersburg, and New Nakhichevan also encouraged their people and Armenian volunteer units were formed and blessed by the Catholicos to fight for

Russia.[42] The Armenian Church continued to enjoy the favor of the government even after the fall of the Romanov dynasty. The short-lived Provisional Government was even more cooperative with the Church.

Throughout the reign of the Romanov dynasty (1613-1917), the Armenian Church was subject to the changing policies of the individual czars and czarinas. Russia realized that the Armenian Church had more faith in a fellow Christian nation than that of Muslim Persia or the Ottoman Empire and used this to its advantage. The Church benefited as well. A printing press and a seminary produced some important historical and religious books and a more educated clergy. Both the *Polozhenie* and the Russian Orthodox Church made it possible to practically stop all Catholic and Protestant missionaries from converting Armenians, as they had done in the Ottoman Empire. The extortions and bribes collected by the Persian khans ceased after 1828. The landholdings of the Church remained intact and the power of the Russian government helped Etchmiadzin to assert its primary position vis-a-vis the Armenian clerics in Constantinople, Aght'amar, and Jerusalem. The demise of Gandzasar assured Etchmiadzin to become the sole Holy See and the Armenian religious center for the entire Russian Empire. The Catholicos could now truly be called The Catholicos of All Armenians.

---

[42] Ronald Suny, "Eastern Armenians under Russian Rule," in R. G. Hovannisian, ed., *The Armenian People*, II (New York: St. Martin's Press, 1997), p. 136.

30

Periodizing Armenia's Past (A Critique of the Armenian Academy of Sciences' *Hay zhoghovrdi patmut'yun*)

Rouben Paul Adalian

The Spanish philosopher José Ortega y Gasset, in one of his essays on "Historical Reason," argues: "Man has no nature; what he has is history; because *history* is the mode of being of the entity that is constitutionally, fundamentally, *mobility* and *change*."[1] Even if one disagrees with Gasset's premise, his astute observation about history itself being the nature of man has particular relevance given the reexamination of historiography that is transpiring in the states of the former Soviet Union.

This reconsideration of a range of restricted topics that began during the Gorbachev years of glasnost has moved to a stage where each independent state can now forge a new national history. While the defects of Soviet historiography were many, the chances that the effort to write history from a national viewpoint will be more objective are slim also if precautions are not taken. In the current context of the goal of defining new national identities freed of Soviet domination and rooted arguably in a more authentic past, the risks of invention are as many as the practices of omission for which Soviet historical writing was so well known. These risks are especially great when the citation of historical evidence becomes part of the discourse of claims and counterclaims over disputed issues, interests, and contested lands. In this respect, the uses of history quickly reach

---

[1] Jose Ortega y Gasset, *Historical Reason*, trans. Philip W. Silver (New York and London: W.W. Norton & Company, 1984), p. 118. Ortega adds: "The hour of the historical sciences is at hand. Pure reason... must be replaced by narrative reason.... therefore, to understand what he [man] is today we have only to relate what he was *yesterday*."

beyond the bounds of scholarly pursuit as the fruits of that work, genuine or spurious, immediately enter the political debate and the competition for verification and justification.

When traditional moorings become loosened in a discipline, sometimes the irreverent observations of non-specialists get to the heart of the matter more quickly than the more deliberate argumentation of those who remain responsible for the rules of scholarly discourse. An article on this very subject that appeared in the British trade journal *The Economist* stated the problem without any circumlocution when glasnost had just ushered in the new debate on history. "In Russia, history is far from being the 'academic' matter it often seems in the West. History is politics."[2] The same may be argued for the other states of the former Union of Soviet Socialist Republics.

This confusion between past and future worked its telling distortions in Soviet historiography. Marx's suggestive blueprint of history as employed by Soviet interpreters led to the practice of insisting on the infallibility of the blueprint. The test of evidence or the reconstruction of the past without the assumption that it was bound to a predictable evolutionary process was presumed a redundant practice. The drift observed in so many works of Soviet historical writing from the application of more or less rigorous methods of analyzing a topic only to run for shelter in the safety of the doctrinaire modeling of the past, when reaching for conclusions, made Soviet historiography disappointing reading. Given that an entire society observed its own dialectic through this single lens, understanding the nature of that history has been made all the more compelling now that alternative methods may be tried.

For a people such as the Armenians, who for seventy years lived in a very tense state of ambivalence toward the Soviet system, the comprehension of their history for themselves had become an acutely difficult exercise. On the one hand, the discipline required the positing of the thesis of a unique historical experience. On the other hand, this experience was expected to adhere consistently in its evolutionary course to a predetermined design. The challenge of creating a coherent historiography that at times was internally conflicted by the apparent contradictions of two opposed obligations

---

[2] "Luther Calvin Gorbachev," *The Economist* (June 25, 1988), p. 49.

did not result in a satisfactory body of thought on the course of Armenian history.

From the earliest, i.e., the fifth century, native authors coined the expression "*patmut'yun hayots'*" [history of the Armenians]. Conceived at a time when Armenian statehood was in question and unable to locate its narratives in objective structures, as an intellectual enterprise Armenian historiography sought its principles in the most tangible of subjective forms. Not the body politic, but the social collective, animated by its presumed sense of patriotic consciousness, was adopted as the driving force of Armenian history. The symbolic representation of institutional behavior through events and personages compensated for the amorphity of the collective. Since an encompassing state was absent as a framework through the course of much of recorded Armenian history, writers expecting to make sense either of chance, or of process and purpose, working their effect on Armenian society selected the social unit as their subject. Since the social collectivity could not articulate its ends through proactive policies and programs, the writer was convinced that only self-consciousness could explain sensibly the regularity of response and reaction from the people of Armenia.

In modern times the expression was inverted to read "*hayots' patmut'yun*" [Armenian history], which is consonant with modern Armenian word order, but which also placed the emphasis on the ethnicity of the subject. This new historiography strived to construct a comprehensive picture of the Armenian historical evolution. The older method of historical writing had been selective to the extent that it emphasized the historical event. The modern practice argued that the valid subject of the discipline was found in the ethnic collective. Though both practices shared in the belief of a self-conscious society, they diametrically differed in the manner they comprehended the symbolic significance of their pensive craft. The former understood history as the record of acts upholding the character of a distinct society. The latter interpreted the past as a series of events that outlined the cumulative experiential basis of a collectivity for whom recognition of identity was more important.

Lastly, Soviet Armenian historiography advanced this line or reasoning a step further by reworking the expression into "*hay zhoghovrdi patmut'yun*" [history of the Armenian people]. The key word has been "people." The principal contribution of Soviet historiography to the understanding of Armenian history is not found in any clarification of the fundamental causes of change in Armenian society. Defining the process of class formation and the relations of social forces among the Armenian people has been difficult on account of the colonization of Armenia and the dispersion or suppression of the dynamic elements of Armenian society. The substantive rereading of the texts of Armenian historiography during the Soviet era brought into the picture the bulk of the Armenian populace, which earlier historians had not been technically or ideologically equipped to develop as a subject.

This rectification, however, introduced its own problems, most of which stemmed from the near silence of a people in captivity. Retrieving this overlooked history of the "people" was a laborious undertaking, made all the more difficult by its negation of the concept of a self-consciousness working its shaping influence among the Armenians. The immobilized mass of the Armenian people has remained a complicated subject to analyze. Recourse was found in the theme of national liberation, which, unfortunately, when contrasted with the reality that a populist historiography must underline, has been shown to be all too transparent. Until the late nineteenth and early twentieth century experience, the so-called movements for national liberation were very marginal phenomenon. As this problem in turn had to be rectified by acclaiming the thesis of a vanguard laboring to create the conditions for the articulation of conscious self-interest, the role of the masses again was put into question. Even if done with contortion, it has remained a difficult exercise to map out the course of Armenian history in its evolution from all the definable antitheses to observable syntheses on which professional and intellectual consensus could be obtained. The non-Marxist school held that Armenian history moved from anti-thesis to anti-thesis, or, more precisely, was actually confined to an anti-thetical duration. This has left many questions unanswered, since the pace of change in modern times has been so rapid as to impose conditions requiring response. A suspension of the dialectic is a highly dubious proposition in modern circumstances. Therefore, some of the fundamental issues and questions of at least modern history, if not of the earlier eras, have received no treatment satisfactory by the standards of those concerned with the discipline.

When a work appears in print that makes an attempt at responding to all of the substantive problems and questions of Armenian history, it must be taken seriously and treated with the respect that a major enterprise in historiography deserves. It also offers an opportunity to reconsider once again what constitutes the valid study of a subject whose very definition is problematic. It is more than history or historiography as a discipline that is at stake. A deeper inquiry also must be made, whether the self-consciousness that must be invested, and which manifests itself in the act of authorship, is an authentic and valid, or an inauthentic, invalid, and false, consciousness.

There is little question that the eight-volume *Hay zhoghovrdi patmut'yun* [History of the Armenian People] produced by the Academy of Sciences in Soviet Armenia was a major scientific achievement for Armenian scholarship.[3] A comprehensive history of the Armenian people, from its beginnings to the year 1965, was created. The first tome, volume VII, was released in 1967. The last tome, volume II, was released seventeen years later, in 1984. The series was not issued in sequence. In all, the endeavor took over twenty years, and required the services of one hundred and seventeen contributors, and thirty-four editors. *Hay zhoghovrdi patmut'yun*, therefore, was the product of an entire generation of Soviet Armenian scholars who themselves required the span of an additional generation to complete their massive project. Virtually all the prominent specialists trained in the various disciplines that supported Armenian historical studies, such as archeology, art

---

[3] Volume I, *Armenia in the Period of Prehistoric-Communal and Slave-Owning Society* (Yerevan, 1971); Volume II, *Armenia in the Period of Early Feudalism* (Yerevan, 1984); Volume III, *Armenia during the Period of Advanced Feudalism (Middle of the Ninth Century to the Middle of the Fourteenth Century)* (Yerevan, 1976); Volume IV, *The Armenian People during the Period of the Decline of Feudalism between the Fourteenth and Eighteenth Centuries* (Yerevan 1972); Volume V, *Armenia between 1801 and 1870* (Yerevan, 1974); Volume VI, *Armenia between 1870 and 1917*, (Yerevan, 1981); Volume VII, *The Victory of Soviet Rule in Armenia: The Armenian Soviet Socialist Republic during the Period of the Building of Socialism 1917-1941* (Yerevan, 1967); Volume VIII, *The Armenian People during the Years of the Great Patriotic War and the Post – War Communist Development 1941-1965* (Yerevan, 1970).

history, literature, economics, geography, and ethnography, were involved in its authorship. As such, *Hay zhoghovrdi patmut'yun* registered the intellectual synthesis of a generation largely educated in the Stalin era and published in the Brezhnev years.

This is the generation that witnessed the "thaw" of the Khrushchev interlude and the subsequent reaction to liberalization and criticism. They were a hardened, or politically quiet, lot. They had to be conservatives practicing a profession that constantly skirted the dangers of overt nationalist expression. The 6,622 pages of the series contain no real surprises. Because it was bound to achieve the status of a standard reference on Armenian history for some time to come, its authors, one expects, were prone to be even more cautious. Nevertheless, the obligation to weave a continuous narrative required that attention be dedicated to subjects that tended not to receive monographic treatment in Soviet Armenia. Thus assembled, the many layers of civilization, i.e., society, culture, politics, economy, added a depth to the volumes of the series that is frequently lacking in other general works of historiography.

Even so, *Hay zhoghovrdi patmut'yun* would not re-interpret Armenian history. It would standardize, reconcile, synthesize, and relay Armenian civilization as a total, continuous, singular, and comprehensible unit of history. That it was completed upon the heel of one era and at the dawn of a new epoch in Soviet life makes *Hay zhoghovrdi patmut'yun* that much more a generationally-defined product. The Gorbachev era ushered in the promise of a new historiography. Formerly forbidden subjects were explored and certain difficult themes were re-examined in the light of additional evidence. Yet they were piecemeal revisions. The subsequent challenges of the post-independence era in Armenia delayed, if not undermined, any hope of a new synthesis. Therefore, *Hay zhoghovrdi patmut'yun* remains a significant landmark in the intellectual history of the Armenian people. For now, it is the only comprehensive synthesis of their millennial history.

Given the scope of *Hay zhoghovrdi patmut'yun*, its eight volumes cannot be approached with the common suppositions of a reviewer. It would take a hundred specialists, each with his or her own area of expertise, to analyze all 191 chapters. Therefore, the proposal here is not to review the work, but rather to use this great synthesis to observe and reflect upon the intellectual construct of

Soviet Armenian historiography; that is, to consider whether the frameworks devised to explain Armenian history were structurally sound and whether the elements that compose those frameworks were conceptually reasonable and objectively measurable. Could this whole concept, this total synthesis, justify the course of Armenian history? Did it respond persuasively to the fundamental search for causation? In this effort, the question must be asked as to who ultimately, and in its most concrete form, makes Armenian history?

It needs to be added, at this juncture, that dealing with this issue has required Western scholars to face constantly the challenge of grappling with certain practices of Soviet historiography as the artifice of those whose exterior habits appeared rational, but whose ulterior motives involved distortion, even destruction, inducing confusion, a will to power, or a desire to control destinies large and small.

Given these difficult challenges, a set of criteria for examining *Hay zhoghovrdi patmut'yun* must be found. Additionally, these principles must be located in the Western tradition of historical inquiry. Because a confrontation on the order of a struggle between past and future has been submitted, the criteria for assessing *Hay zhoghovrdi patmut'yun* must have relevance at that level of discourse also.

The German philosopher Friedrich Nietzsche put some of the instruments of Western historical analysis, relevant to our purpose here, in perspective in the mid-nineteenth century. In his essay on *The Use and Abuse of History*, he remarked: "History is necessary to the living man in three ways: in relation to his action and struggle, his conservatism and reverence, his suffering and his desire for deliverance. These three relations answer to the three kinds of history-the *monumental*, the *antiquarian*, and the *critical*."[4]

A quick overview of the historiographical literature indicates that Armenians responded to these necessities with considerable thoughtfulness. From the fifth century to the present, historical writing has remained one of the strengths of the Armenian

---

[4] Friedrich Nietzsche, *The Use and Abuse of History*, trans. Adrian Collins, The Library of Liberal Arts, 2nd ed. (Indianapolis: Bobbs-Merrill Educational Publishing, 1980), p. 12. Only "monumental" historiography is discussed in this paper.

intellectual endeavor. Those fifteen hundred years of self-registered national history makes for one of the oldest and continuous records of historical writing, exceeded only by that of the Greeks and the Jews in the western half of the world. Nor does one have to rely on the yardsticks of time to gain perspective on the value given to historical writing in Armenian life. National tradition hailed an early author as the father of Armenian history for his cognizance of the method of monumentality in historical writing. Many an Armenian historian has found justification for taking the pen in Movsēs Khorenats'i's emblematic rationalization for writing Armenian history: "For although we are a small country and very restricted in numbers, weak in power, and often subject to another's rule, yet many manly deeds have been performed in our land worthy of being recorded in writing."[5] And he added that he wanted "to write the history of our nation in a long and useful work, to deal accurately with the kings and the princely clans and families: who descended from whom, what each of them did, which of the various tribes are indigenous and native and which are of foreign origin but naturalized, to set down in writing each one's deeds and times from the time of confusion at the building of the tower to the present..."[6] Monumental historiography, as it related the "struggles and actions" of men, has dominated Armenian historical thinking. This is a normal response in literate societies challenged by the needs of constant defense.

With the Enlightenment, the concept of natural law shifted the focus of interest from deeds and actions to motives. Historical writing, in its monumental design, concerned itself with general principles articulating the broad social forces driving the engines of historical change. Institutions, rather than individuals, were regarded the comprehensible units of history. Lastly, with Marx, a consistent methodology was formulated wherein both change and the causes for change were made applicable to all historical experience by the social dialectic of materialism. Thereby, a model of history could be

---

[5] Movsēs Khorenats'i, *History of the Armenians*, trans. Robert W. Thompson (Cambridge, Mass. and London: Harvard University Press, 1978), p. 69.

[6] Ibid., pp. 69-70.

constructed that could uphold the notion of progress comprehensively through time.

As the culmination of fifty years of Soviet Armenian scholarship applying the methods of class analysis, *Hay zhoghovrdi patmut'yun* is now planted as one of the major signposts of the modern intellectual advance of the Armenian people. The desire to issue such a major statement underscored a way of thinking that hoped to bring a semblance of order to a very complicated and difficult history. The sponsorship of the Armenian SSR Academy of Sciences and the cooperative effort to write it make *Hay zhoghovrdi patmut'yun* a social product in excess of the intellectual enterprise that it represents. Since it does not purport to break new ground, its social contribution, from this standpoint, does indeed exceed its intellectual distinction. Yet, because it aimed for the socialization of the historical discipline, *Hay zhoghovrdi patmut'yun* goes beyond earlier attempts at a comprehensive synthesis of Armenian history. Hakob Manandian's multi-volume *Critical Study of the History of the Armenian People*,[7] one of the finest works of Armenian historical scholarship, is in the strictest sense an academic treatise for the use of specialists alone. *Hay zhoghovrdi patmut'yun*, on the hand, speaks of a new awareness of who the Armenians are and how deeply they are a historically defined people. Lacking the instruments of political persuasion and constituting a society void of the more easily observable frameworks that help distinguish peoples from one another, it appears to suggest that historical consciousness became the badge of Armenians. As John Lukacs has pointed out, "historical consciousness" embodies much more that just another modern Western concept. It represents a way of thinking that has grown tandem to rational reasoning. It involves a form of thinking that potentially can achieve "philosophical unity." It is no less a new form of humanism.[8]

---

[7] Hakob Manandian, *K'nnakan Tesut'yun Hay zhoghovrdi patmut'yun* [Critical Study of the History of the Armenian people], vols. 1-3 (Yerevan: Haypethrat, 1945-1952). Reprint, *Erker* [Works], vols. 1-3 (Yerevan: Academy of Sciences of Armenia SSR, Institute of History, 1977-78).

[8] John Lukacs, *Historical Consciousness or the Remembered Past* (New York: Schocken Books, 1985). See pp. 22-30, pp. 44-49.

Consequently, though socialism was imposed upon the Armenian people, it can be argued that historical materialism has, despite many delays, further promoted an ancient intellectual current in Armenian thought. Monumentalism in Armenian historical writing was restored because modern methodologies accelerated the integration of the older samples of that tradition into a unified theory of the Armenian national evolution. Through *Hay zhoghovrdi patmut'yun*, a clear and significant step was taken by the Soviet Armenian intellectual elite toward an increased Western outlook on the role of history, as a social science, in the making of a nation.

The intellectual awareness of the emergence of new socio-economic formations is demonstrated in the periodization of historical time. Because a people defines its identity and engages in behavior in accordance to certain cultural patterns, and as these patterns, be they linguistic, artistic, spiritual, legal, or political, are the accumulated result of the many epochs in the history of this same people, the proper understanding of these characteristics requires the accurate identification of the socio-economic formations that contributed to their emergence. These cultural determinants must also be seen in context. The succession of cultural responses, their sequence, and the distinctive accumulation of those responses modify the abstractions of an epochal description of history.

Given the historical consciousness of the modern age, the very ordeal of responding to new challenges requires a clear understanding of the historical process itself, for in comprehending the quality of choices made in earlier challenges modern society finds a rational agency for making new decisions. Therefore, the subversion of the discipline of history in modern times is a highly deliberate political act. For by distorting the past, the objective of the re-shaper of historiography is revealed as the further manipulation of the present. It follows, therefore, that the periodization of Armenian history is one of the most crucial areas of inquiry that ought to be explored in *Hay zhoghovrdi patmut'yun*. After all, in that structure lies the fundamental characteristics of a people. Distortions at that level of analysis become the source of profound alienation as it robs a people of the ability to define its image and cope with its many aspects.

The periodization of Armenian history is presented in the following manner in *Hay zhoghovrdi patmut'yun*: communal society in the prehistoric era is traced in Armenia from the Old Stone Age; the dissolution of tribal society and the beginning of class relations is dated from the Middle Bronze Age at about 2,000 B.C.; slave-owning society appears with the formation of the Urartuan state in the ninth century B.C. and attains full growth in the Hellenistic period (Vol. I); the early feudal era lasts from the third to the eighth century (Vol. II); advanced feudalism spans the ninth to the middle of the fourteenth century (Vol. III); the period of the decline of feudalism covers the fourteenth through the eighteenth century (Vol. IV); most of the nineteenth century, from 1801 to 1870, is characterized by economic changes and social and political trends, and receives no formal specification (Vol. V); in 1870 the era of capitalism is introduced, with its imperialistic phase marking the beginning of the twentieth century (Vol. VI); the period of building socialism starts in 1917 and runs through to 1941 (Vol. VII); after the interruption of World War II (1941-1945), the final victory of socialism is secured between 1946 and 1955 and the construction of communism can be seen since 1956.

At first glance it might be presumed that the ordinary Marxian model of historical evolution was applied. At its barest, Armenian society progresses from the communal, to the slave-owning, the feudal, the capitalist, the socialist, and, lastly, the communist stages of history. The availability of some evidence to justify the application of each of the modes of social production in succession facilitated the adoption of this model.

Upon closer examination, however, some serious problems begin to emerge. This periodization and the typologies applied are fraught with internal and external inconsistencies. These complications originate from the methodological compromises that Soviet Armenian historiography had to reach. The problems are twofold: first, those of history, and second, those of historical analysis. Dealing with the second is easier since the point can be logically argued. The first requires that sufficient evidence be presented.

In and of itself the Marxian model is total abstraction. It outlines the course of dialectical materialism for humanity overall. It is in large part derived from the Western European experience as synoptically sketched, for example, by Frederick Engels in *Socialism: Utopian and Scientific.* The positive derivation of the model, however, is a matter apart from "the materialist conception of history."[9] Class conflict could be studied in specific countries, such as France, England, and Germany, and differentiated on the basis of property, labor, and class relations peculiar to each. Equally, in *Hay zhoghovrdi patmut'yun* when Armenia is described in the period of communal, slave-owning and feudal society, the typologies are area-specific to Armenia, but it is explained that they adhere to the type of socio-economic formation characteristic of the time frame. Armenian society specifically is observed to evolve from the communal to the slave-owning and the feudal.

While the ascriptions of the more remote ancient and medieval eras may be less troubling, those of the modern era, in contrast, cause considerable difficulty. To begin with, the fourteenth through the eighteenth centuries are described as the period of the decline of feudalism. In Western parlance, if the modern era is post-feudal, in Armenia it would not begin until the nineteenth century. This proposition is usually not questioned and it is customarily demonstrated with the evidence on the cultural revival of the Armenian people that was concentrated in the nineteenth century.[10] A new pattern of culture as the indicator of a social transformation is commonly cited. Given that feudal relations, according to *Hay zhoghovrdi patmut'yun*, begin to take form in the third century, then Armenia went through a fifteen hundred-year feudal experience. If Western feudalism was implanted the earliest in France and is dated from the time of Charlemagne, say, formally from 800, and was abolished again formally in 1789, Armenian feudalism lasted longer by half a millennium. If, at the end of feudalism, French society yielded to new forms of social and economic relations characterized by private property, wage labor, commercial capital, commodity manufacture, the bourgeois ownership of the means of production, and the concentration of wealth in the cities, the four hundred-year decline of feudalism in Armenia resulted in, and from, none of these. The forms of advanced feudalism may have been decaying, but the

---

[9] Friedrich Engels, *Socialism: Utopian and Scientific*, trans. Edward Aveling (New York: International Publishers, 1975), p. 53.

[10] See Richard G. Hovannisian, ed., *The Armenian Image in History and Literature* (Malibu, Calif.: Undena Publications, 1981). See also Anne Paolucci, ed., *Review of National Literatures*, vol. 13, *Armenia*, Vahe Oshagan, ed. (New York: Griffon House Publishers, 1984).

argument that feudalism was dissolving because of the social and political conflicts that the many contradictions of late feudalism imposed on an increasingly dynamic form of economic association cannot be sustained. According to Marx, an "age of dissolution" must also be an age of transition.[11] It is not required that an age of transition result in a more advanced and rational network of relations. The only thing this transition does, however, is to put the Armenians in the nineteenth century. The designation of this era, as that of the decline of feudalism, verges upon being nothing more than that of a mystifying euphemism for the unproductive centuries of Turkish rule.

Nor is the inadequacy of a universalizing ascription the only difficulty in dealing with this period of Armenian history. The feudal organization of Armenia in the early modern period has no subjective correspondence with the feudalism of the medieval centuries. Whereas, in the rough, the objective means of appropriating surplus and exploiting labor seem to correspond, the social division of classes, however, was most notably featured by its ethnic differentiation. Hence, for a long time the aggravation of the condition of the laboring masses did not find expression in the dialectic of class conflict. Given that Turkish and Islamic law and practice at this time completely precluded any form of opposition or even resistance from the lower and oppressed classes, it might appear that the materialist dialectic was dysfunctional. Actually the dialectic was manifest in a course opposite to that which the typological designation would suggest. The methods of appropriating surplus by the propertied element contributed not just to the impoverishment of the laboring class and its alienation from the land, but by that method of confiscation the social and cultural foundations of one people were also destroyed by another, and its territories, in the form of alienated property, were usurped by a dominant class. Thereby, gradually, increased political control of the land led to the formation of a new ethno-social organism, which replaced the original owners of the land. The decline of feudalism, which led to the "emancipation" of the serf in Europe, therefore served a contrary purpose in Armenia.

---

[11] Karl Marx, *Pre-Capitalist Economic Formations*, trans. Jack Cohen (New York: International Publishers, 1965), p. 109.

This brings into question the very designation of a "feudalism" wherein the means of appropriating surplus destroyed those who produced it. There may be no objective difference between surrendering agricultural surplus to an Armenian nobleman or a Turkish overlord. However, there is a marked difference between surplus invested to defend the state and surplus utilized to destroy the demographic residue of the conquered state. In this relationship the questions are not on the order of superstructural adjustments, but of existential continuity. Marx, in *The German Ideology*, wrote that "the first premise of all human existence, and therefore, of all history, [is] the premise, namely, that men must be in a position to live in order to be able to 'make history.'"[12] The premise no less applies to a self-conscious collectivity. If its "production of material life" is in jeopardy, then it is in no position to be making history. It might be asked at this point, if the existence of a people was being unmade, was its history being unmade also? That is a difficult question to answer. It is easier to say that the Armenians were not making history, but that others with the power to determine their fate were doing it for them. The Armenians were the passive viewers of this drama. The active players were the dominant and alien element that was holding them in passivity.

Because of the way *Hay zhoghovrdi patmut'yun* is divided, the next span of time covered is the years 1800 to 1870. Neither year marks a significant moment in Armenian history. They are dates of convenience, with the beginning of the century marking the entry of the Russians to the Transcaucasus (1801), though not Armenia proper for another four years (1805), and 1870 marking the time the reforms of tsar Alexander II were extended to the area. Visible changes could be measured in Armenian life during the first half of the nineteenth century. The basic structure of socio-economic relations, however, was little altered, other than the replacement of the governing class of Persians and Muslims by Russian soldiers and Christian administrators. Armenia remained rural and feudal, with the Muslim overlords acquiring increased property rights over their landholdings. In West Armenia, which remained under Ottoman rule, the feudal modes of production were hardly altered by the Tanzimat

[12] Karl Marx, *The German Ideology*, in Robert C. Tucker, ed., *The Marx-Engels Reader* (New York: W.W. Norton & Company, 1972), p. 119.

reforms. Therefore, clearly, for the first fifty years of the century, change was incremental and old patterns were not brought under strain by new modes of production. George Bournoutian's study on East Armenia documents, in detail, an economy based on peasant agriculture and nomad pastoralism.[13] The wars of conquest caused economic disruption and social dislocation, but as Vartan Gregorian's study of Russian rule in Armenia shows, the fundamental changes in social and economic organization occurred in the second half of the nineteenth century with the introduction of railway transport, factory production, cash crop farming, and rapid urbanization.[14] Given the combined area of East and West Armenia, the country was still in the feudal era. At best, it was a transitional era, as *Hay zhoghovrdi patmut'yun* disingenuously characterizes the period.[15]

Determining when the fundamental transformations in Armenian life occurred is no mere game in chronological calibration. The Armenians entered the twentieth century with great expectations. By the end of the second decade of the same century, without exception, all of their edifices came crashing down. Though the Armenian catastrophe in the second decade of the twentieth century ought not to predetermine how the history of the nineteenth is to be studied, nevertheless, the years of unmitigated disaster between 1915 and 1920 stamped a finalizing conclusion to nearly everything that men in the nineteenth had strived to accomplish. Those years were not the

---

[13] George A. Bournoutian, *Eastern Armenia in the Last Decades of Persian Rule 1807-1828: a Political and Socioeconomic Study of the Khanate of Erevan on the Eve of the Russian Conquest* (Malibu, Calif.: Undena Publications, 1982). Revised and reprinted as *The Khanate of Erevan Under Qajar Rule 1795-1828* (Cosa Mesa, Calif.: Mazda Publishers, 1992).

[14] Vartan Gregorian, "The Impact of Russia on the Armenians and Armenia," in Wayne S. Vicinich, ed., *Russia and Asia: Essays on the Influence of Russia on the Asian Peoples* (Stanford, Calif.: Hoover Institution Press, 1972), pp. 167-218.

[15] An ordinary textbook, *Hay zhoghovrdi patmut'yun* [History of the Armenian People] by V. A. Parsamian and Sh. R. Harut'yunian (Yerevan, 1979), suggests with clarity that the disintegration of feudalism and the rise of capitalism occurred in the second half of the nineteenth century. This implies that feudalism remained the dominant mode of production in Armenia through the first half of the nineteenth century.

final moment of an epoch. They were the last days of West Armenia and a time when the physical survival of the remaining Armenians was in jeopardy. Since there is such a clear ending to the existence of the West Armenians, it becomes all the more imperative to understand how much time the Armenians had to adjust to the new world of capitalism, and to ask whether the changes registered in Armenian society introduced weakness in its organization that made it destructible. Or, was Armenian society adapting at such a promising pace that imperialist cliques deemed it thoroughly impermissible and thus targeted the Armenian population for annihilation?

The basic questions are these: when did the Armenians begin to enter the modern era, how long did they have to learn and react, and at what pace did they Westernize? Did modernization increase the stratification in Armenian society, and did this in turn alienate the classes from one another? Or, did it contribute toward greater solidarity and a better understanding of the plight of the underprivileged? Did different classes resort to contradictory strategies of adaptation and response to the increasing interference by Ottoman and Russian administrators in Armenian national life, or did the classes find channels through which to forge a sense of greater national solidarity? Given the insecurities that capitalization of an economy introduces, and the class warfare that industrial exploitation, at its worst, can incite, how did the emergence of bourgeois society among Armenians contribute to the making of their history? Did the new leadership on the scene command sufficient loyalty and marshal the necessary legitimacy to carry through its programs? Was authority fractionalized and what were the consequences of opposing currents of thought? What intellectual positions did Armenians adopt? What organizational efforts did they make? To what degree did the social and economic transformations contribute to the integration or disintegration of Armenian society?[16] In all, what was the challenge of modern society for Armenians?

---

[16] See Louise Nalbandian, *The Armenian Revolutionary Movement: the Development of Armenian Political Parties Through the Nineteenth Century* (Berkeley, Los Angeles, London: University of California Press, 1963). See also Christopher J. Walker, *Armenia: The Survival of a Nation* (New York: St. Martin's Press, 1980); and *Armenian Review* 36, 1 (Spring, 1983), special issue on "Modernization an Armenian Society."

From 1839, when the Tanzimat was introduced in the Ottoman Empire to 1915, the span of time is seventy-six years, or about three generations. However, if the era is measured from 1863, when the Armenian Constitution was adopted for the Armenian *millet* in the empire and the year most historians date the modern period for West Armenia, the span is only fifty-two years, a mere half century and less than the lifespan of an individual. In East Armenia, if the era is dated from 1828, when a large section of Armenia was incorporated by the Russian Empire, to 1918, the span is ninety years, almost a century. But if the era is measured, say from 1861 when serfdom was abolished in Russia, the time frame is reduced to fifty-seven years and a mere five years more than in the Ottoman Empire. Whether in Turkey or Russia, Armenians were allotted much less than a hundred years to lift themselves from their lethargic obedience to feudal authority and enter the era of a self-conscious nationality.

The subsequent era, dated between 1870 and 1917, is marked by the presence of a burgeoning capitalist system in Armenia, with the twentieth century segment of that era designated as the period of imperialism. Certainly this does not mean Armenian imperialism. Nor can it mean Russian or Turkish imperialism as both empire predate the twentieth century and had occupied Armenia, in the case of the Russians since the early part of the nineteenth century, and in the case of the Ottomans since the first part of the sixteenth century. Obviously, this periodization is an exercise in the Leninist concept of imperialism as the last phase of advanced capitalism faced with the crisis of overproduction and resorting to territorial conquest in order to capture new markets. The concept may apply to Russia and may apply to the Western European colonialist states, but what does it mean as far as Armenia is concerned, other than to put it in a certain global context? The objective of periodization is not universalization, but just the opposite, to find and define the successive phases of organization that characterized a given society and that helps explain its adaptation to changing circumstances. The containment in broad historical time-bands might give a society universal context, but it has to be asked how much light this sheds on the specific geographic and ethnic unit under consideration.

The complications inherent in this approach to historical contextualization are most evident with the smaller problem of the introduction of socialism in Armenia. Since socialism in Armenia did not evolve, but rather was legislated by decree and implemented by force, then a very precise dating of the start of socialism can be obtained. On November 29, 1920, the Red Army established Soviet rule in Yerevan, and the nationalization of commercial institutions began in December of the same year. Yet the era of socialism is dated from 1917. The October Revolution occupies a place in world history and is one of the prime reference points of the twentieth century. Within Marxist historiography, it is the main reference point of history. In this respect, the year 1917 is just as applicable in Armenian historiography as in that of any other people, but quite understandably all the more for Armenia, since it constituted a frontier region of the Russian Empire. Yet because of that revolution Transcaucasia did not recognize Bolshevik authority and drifted away from Russia. Between 1918 and 1920 Armenia led an independent course.[17] Armenia would be reincorporated into the new Russian state at the end of 1920.[18] Therefore, to be true to the methodological principle of socio-economic organization as the basis of historical analysis, one has no choice but to adhere to the year 1920.

When observed in sequence, first, the debate surrounding the notion of advanced feudalism in Armenia, second, the uncertain date of the entry of capitalism, and third, the question of the socialist context, the difficulty of reconciling the inconsistencies of the periodization of Armenia history with objective facts is exposed. Armenian historiography is not understood as the record of the Armenians, but of the Armenians within certain conventions independently variable of the Armenians. Armenians perhaps were making their own history, but they certainly were not the ones periodizing it, which means to say there were not the ones changing it. More precisely, in the absence of a state, the context of Armenian

---

[17] See Richard G. Hovannisian, *Armenia on the Road to Independence: 1918* (Berkeley, Los Angeles, London: University of California Press, 1967). See also by the same author, *The Republic of Armenia*, Vol. 1, *The First Year, 1918-1919*, and Vol. 2, *From Versailles to London, 1919-1920* (Berkeley, Los Angeles, London: University of California Press, 1971 and 1982, respectively).

[18] See Mary Kilbourne Matossian, *The Impact of Soviet Policies in Armenia* (Leiden: E.J. Brill, 1962) and Ronald Grigor Suny, *Armenia in the Twentieth Century* (Chico, Calif.: Scholars Press, 1983).

history grows complicated. The question becomes: whose evolution is to be given primacy in explaining history? Were, and are, the Armenians the focal point of their own historiography? Or, were they the shadow actors on a stage constructed by another production company, another state? What of the necessity of consistency in the field of historical writing?

To try to understand Armenian history only in terms of Armenians can be very confusing. It is a given of the historical discipline that the facts in themselves, and the facts in correct chronological sequence, are not sufficient evidence for positing an explanation. The context in which these facts occur suggests its own configuration of history. Whereas, one can study Englishmen in England and Frenchmen in France, by observing the Armenian in Armenia, more often that not, only a spatial context is achieved. A more proper scale of context is necessary. On the other hand, the scale at the macro-historical end of the spectrum may be disproportionately remote from the truer dimensions of applicable reality.

The typologies used in *Hay zhoghovrdi patmut'yun* are on a global order. Nevertheless, they are temporally coincident with another context, which in the modern period is that of Russian history. It has to be noted that if the theory on successive transformation lends a certain structure to history, altering the basis of that theory casts doubt on the strength of that structure. The powerful force of context cannot be minimized, and the contexts of time and space are entirely insufficient for the Armenian story. Armenian society, as a subordinate collectivity, itself was in whole, contextualized by dominant frameworks. Therefore, Armenian behavior has to be evaluated within social and political contexts, which are largely defined by Muslims, or Russians, or rulers, or imperialists. The legitimate principles of definition were not Armenian. In fact, Armenian definitions were outlawed. Thus, ironically, Armenian historiography had to adhere to frameworks that not only subordinated the Armenian people, but also delegitimized it as a political body.

Hay zhoghovrdi patmut'yun leaves many unresolved problems in Armenian historiography because of the restricted methodology of the Marxian model. As Khachik Momjan, a Soviet Armenian philosopher working in Moscow and erstwhile head of the department of Marxist-Leninist philosophy at the Academy of Social Sciences, put it so neatly and emphatically: "One can definitely say that there are five socio-economic formations which are the basic phases of mankind's development, the chief stages of social progress. These are: the primitive communal system, the slave-owning system, feudalism, capitalism, and communism, whose first phase—socialism—has already been built in many countries."[19] First, how is this model to be understood in view of the fact that Armenians lived under foreign rule for very long stretches of time? What provisions must be made to analyze the progress of Armenia as a conquered country? Second, how must this be done in a comparative fashion, given that Armenia was all too often a divided country also? How can the parts be balanced such as to permit an equalizing definition that can sustain the argument for progressive change? Lastly, with the dispersion of the Armenians taken into consideration, how can any model contain so much diffusion, so much fragmentation, and so much disintegration?[20] A model is, by its purpose, an integrative concept. Is the model in *Hay zhoghovrdi patmut'yun* actually, or artificially, integrating the Armenians into a historical unity? Does its integration hold at the conceptual level, or is it just held together because the pages of the books are bound within a cover and everything Armenian is thrown in it?

Further underlining the standard Soviet thesis, Momjan also states: "The succession of socio-economic formation best illustrates historical progress."[21] The extreme and numerous structural cleavages in Armenian history, such as the extinguishing of native political institutions in Armenia, the partitions transfiguring the people into social segments culturally alienated from one another, the decomposition of the collective unity and collective destiny of this people in their own homeland, and the dispersion of many parts to the four winds, altogether raise sufficient doubt about the

---

[19] Khach'ik Nishanovich Momjan, *Landmarks in History: The Marxist Doctrine of Socio-Economic Formations* (Moscow: Progress Publishers, 1980), p. 45.

[20] Gerard Libaridian, "Armenia and Armenians: A Divided Homeland and a Dispersed Nation," in William O. McCagg Jr. and Brian D. Silver, eds., *Soviet-Asian Ethnic Frontiers* (New York: Pergamon Press, 1979), pp. 27-60.

[21] Momjan, *Landmarks in History*, p. 71.

progressive course of history. Add to this the wreckage of the twentieth century, and the whole notion of progressive integration is challenged by the Armenian experience. The formal model of progress even mocks the Armenian tragedy, since the demise of the Armenian nation is obscured by the semblance of dialectical materialism operating by the laws of class conflict while the human material itself diminished at a rapid rate.

In the modern era, in *Hay zhoghovrdi patmut'yun,* the Armenian people are not only overtaken physically by Russian dominion, but their evolution is demonstrated to have aligned itself with the pace of progress and revolution in Russia. Yet that is only half the story as West Armenia remained under Turkish rule and was then entombed. The objectivity of materialism requires that upon death what was rationally measurable at one moment should cease being nothing other than a mental construct with no reference to physical reality an instant later. Materialism, in consonance with the laws of nature, abhors a vacuum also, and West Armenia is consigned to dwell in memory. Therein materialism also invalidates the function of memory as an idealism removed from the reality of concrete propositions. However, John Lukacs reminds us that history is the "remembered past." Remembrance is also at the core of an Armenian consciousness conflicting with a materialism that pretends an injustice is removed once the subject is erased. This pretense also made an accomplice of materialism in denial itself.

The sovereign state may not be obligated to behave in accordance to moral principles. The impulse of society seeking collective justice on the other hand cannot be overlooked as a powerful motivational force introducing its own rescripts for a comprehension of the world and of human behavior. Eghishe Charents, the Armenian Communist poet, wrote in 1934, three years before his own death: "I erect a monument to myself/ in a time difficult for monuments, / when everything called immortal/ is collapsing." But where to build such a memorial was the question? "I was born in Kars but the sun/ of Iran lights my soul/ with an old but inextinguishable homesickness."[22] A place of birth has much to

---

[22] Diana Der Hovanessian and Marzbed Margossian, trans. and eds., *Anthology of Armenian Poetry* (New York: Columbia University Press, 1978), pp. 214-215.

recommend itself as the sight of a memorial. For Charents, Kars was beyond reach; it was a place in his memory. His native town had been handed over to Turkey from Russia. Again John Lukacs: "The functions of remembering, therefore, transcend space and time and mechanical causality."[23]

Another difficulty with the periodization developed in *Hay zhoghovrdi patmut'yun* is the perfunctory application of the total model of historiography as summarized by Momjan. The very typological designation of certain periods of Armenian history can be questioned. For example, the evidence on the structure of the Urartuan state is considerable. Its material remains, in the form of major architectural complexes, such as fortresses and temples, suggest a stratified society exercising a vast degree of power over the workers. Its very rapid rise also suggests the use of labor in a highly organized fashion and concentrated in certain locations where labor-intensive projects, such as construction, had taken place. It is also evident from the material remains of Urartu that this was a military society, with armed forces in occupation of fortified citadels that oversaw the collection of the land's produce as deposited in vast storage facilities. A centralized monarchy, a considerable political hierarchy, a class of priests in charge of temples serving as treasuries, a military force implanted across the country, all depended upon a system of labor exploitation that clearly was appropriating the maximum. As the records indicate, slave labor was relied upon extensively. The very short time in which all this was accomplished (the Urartuan state lasted three centuries) also indicates that the creation of this state brought about major conflicts between the nucleus of Urartu, centered in the region of Van, and rest of the Armenian highlands which were entirely absorbed into Urartu. The conflicts were those between a military state at the center and tribal confederations at the periphery. Urartu prevailed swiftly with the attendant disruption of the political organization of the tribal societies and the enslavement of a sizable percentage of the population. From start to end, Urartu, outside of Van, was an alien presence, and inimical in its social values and organization to tribal

---

[23] Lukacs, *Historical Consciousness*, p. 247.

society and the communal ownership of land and labor prevailing throughout the rest of the country.[24]

The role of slavery as the dominant mode of production by which Urartu organized the labor force at its disposal diminished with it. Upon Urartu's demise no new state emerged with the kind of organization seeking a similar degree of control. The beginnings of the Armenian state which replaced Urartu may perhaps be discerned in the legend of the struggle between two eponymous leaders, Hayk, the patriarch of the Hay, (as the Armenians call themselves), and Bel, possibly the Armenian rendition of the Semitic term *bal*, or lord.[25] A close reading of the legend shows Hayk's entourage consisting of his sons and their families, whereas Bel advanced with an anonymous army. According to Movsēs Khorenatsi‘:

> Among the giants he [Hayk] was the bravest and most famous, the opponent of all who raised their hand to become absolute ruler over all the giants and heroes. He intrepidly raised his hand against the tyranny of Bel...Hayk refused to submit to him, and... he journey[ed] to the land of Ararad...with his sons and daughters and son's sons, martial men about three hundred in number...[26]

Bel, on the other hand, "mustered his army against him, and with a mass of infantry arrived in the north..."[27] The contrast between two radically different value systems and the concomitant forms of social organization are very evident.

By this interpretation, it may be argued that what may have been Armenian rebellions against Urartu resulted in the overthrow of a class of rulers forming a government based on the exploitation of

---

[24] See B. B. Piotrovsky, *Urartu: The Kingdom of Van and its Art*, trans. and ed. Peter S. Gelling (London, 1967); Nicolas Adontz, *Histoire d'Armenie: Les origins du Xe siecle au Vie (Av. J.C.)* (Paris: Union Generale Armenienne de Bienfaisance, 1946).

[25] See Grigor Artashesi Grigorian, *Hay Zhoghovrdakan Vipergerĕ ew Patmakan Ergayin Banahiusut‘yunĕ* [Armenian Popular Legends and Historical Epic Poetry] vol. 1 (Yerevan: Armenian SSR Academy of Sciences, 1972), pp. 97-144.

[26] Khorenats‘i, *History of the Armenians*, p. 85.

[27] Ibid., p. 86.

slave labor. In its place was restored the tribal domain and the communal ownership of the land. Writing more than a thousand years later, Movsēs Khorenats'i still conceived the history of the Armenians in terms of families, clans, and tribes. The memory of those forms of social organization was still strong because feudalism in Armenia evolved within the framework of the tribal system. The thesis of the great Russian-Armenian historian, Nicholas Adontz, marshals very powerful evidence on the tribal and feudal systems in Armenia. According to his demonstration, Armenian society grew from a tribal pattern, drawn on the map of Armenia by its mountainous terrain, into a unified feudal polity that continued to respect the individualism of local and regional identities and loyalties.[28] Slavery played a limited role in this evolution. In fact, the Adontz thesis contradicts the entire method of periodization in *Hay zhoghovrdi patmut'yun*.

Manandian also traced the evolution of Armenian society from the tribal to the feudal mode. Only he disagreed with Adontz's explanation of the breakdown of tribal society as the consequence of the wars of the first and second centuries B.C.[29] He argued that "economic inequality" and the "process of social differentiation" occurred at an earlier date:

> The clarification of the period of disintegration of clan society and of the development of estates is closely tried to the problem of the beginning of feudalism in Armenia. In all probability the development of specific ties of subordination took place simultaneously and side by side with the disintegration of the clan structure. Consequently, the creation of estates and the birth of feudalism in Ancient Armenia may be expected in an early period, probably before the appearance of the Armenian Arsacids, or even earlier.[30]

---

[28] Nicholas Adontz, *Armenia in the Period of Justinian: The Political Contradictions Based on the Naxarar System*, trans. Nina G. Garsoian (Lisbon: Calouste Gulbenkian Foundation, 1970). For a study on Adontz, see Rouben Paul Adalian, *Nicholas Adontz: The Quest for a Rational History* (Diss., University Microfilms International, 1987).

[29] H. A. Manandian, *The Trade and Cities of Armenia in Relation to Ancient World Trade*, trans. Nina G. Garsoian (Lisbon: Livraria Bertrand, 1965), pp. 42-43.

[30] Ibid., p. 43.

Manandian's proposition has a number of implications. First, it contradicts the pat correspondence of Antiquity with a socio-economic system based on the exploitation of slaves. Manandian, as a student of Armenian economic history, could not have overlooked the evidence of slavery if it existed. Both he and Adontz had full command of the historical sources. Second, he proposed a periodization that put the feudal mode of production in Antiquity with the suggestion that its origins lie as far back as the last centuries of the first millennium B.C. If *Hay zhoghovrdi patmut'yun* proposed a feudal era in Armenia lasting from the third to the eighteenth century, Manandian's timetable adds at least another five centuries. This would imply that in Armenia a pattern of socio-political relations prevailed for over two thousand years and that a fundamental mode of production endured despite all vicissitudes. Third, it also suggests an unusual continuity between this people and its land. Herein lies the great value of alternate methods of periodizing, for they emphasize the continuities, the persistent success of coping with ordeal upon ordeal and therein also the monumental struggle to persevere.

Nor are Nicholas Adontz's and Hakob Manandian's propositions inconsistent with Marx's postulations on societal evolution. As Eric Hobsbawn explains in his introduction to Marx's *Pre-Capitalist Economic Formations*: "Feudalism appears to be an alternative evolution out of primitive communalism..."[31] This course is suggested by the Germanic model with the settlement of the tribal community and the rise of a feudalism characterized in its later phase by a sharp division of labor between city and country.

As to the problem of slavery in ancient Armenia, *Hay zhoghovrdi patmut'yun* buttresses its hypothesis for the prevalence of slavery in Armenia by analogy. In large part, the contention is based on the comparison of the dynastic ideology of the Artashesian family that ruled in the last two centuries B.C. and which assimilated the Hellenistic concept of divine monarchy.[32] Whereas all the research in demonstrating the linkage of Armenia with the rest of the Hellenistic

---

[31] Marx, *Pre-Capitalist Economic Formations*, p. 28.

[32] G. Kh. Sargisian, *Hellenistakan Darashrjani Hayastanĕ ew Movsēs Khorenats'in* [Armenia in the Hellenistic Period and Moses of Khoren] (Yerevan, 1966).

societies of the Middle East is admirable, and art historians, archaeologists, numismatists, and urban historians have contributed in reconstructing this aspect of Armenian history, nevertheless it is also evident that the veneer of Hellenism hardly reached beyond the upper crust of Armenian society. As for city life and urban design, there is nothing in Armenia to compare with Ephesus, Antioch, or Palmyra in fact or fiction. Artashat, the ancient capital of Armenia, which was laid out as a Hellenistic city, unfortunately was leveled long ago. More than a few points of comparison are needed as evidence of the prevalence of slavery in Armenia during Antiquity.

Marx's theory on historical materialism rests on the foundation that the dominant mode of production defines the pattern of socio-economic relations and the context of the political superstructure. There is little question about the critically determining function of the dominant type of economic organization. Therefore, it is imperative to demonstrate as rigorously as the evidence permits, that a certain society at a specific time in history was defined by a division of labor characteristically coherent across a span of space. Hobsbawn asserts: "The general theory of historical materialism require only that there should be a succession of modes of production, though not necessarily any particular modes, and perhaps not in any particular predetermined order."[33]

Therefore, without even being inconsistent with Marx, the entire model of Armenian history as constructed by Soviet historiography can be challenged. On some vital issues the system of periodization can be brought to task. Instead of an analytical methodology, ideological formalisms and scholastic conventions were relied upon, and these homogenized Armenian history to a degree where the Nietzschian concept of struggle and the dialectic of historical materialism were often defeated by compromise, contrivance, and obedience. Nietzsche asked: "What is the use to the modern man of this 'monumental' contemplation of the past, this preoccupation with the rare and classic? It is the knowledge that the great thing existed and was therefore possible, and so may be possible again."[34] It was this hope of engaging the dialectic that Soviet historiography tried to preempt.

---

[33] Ibid., p. 18.

[34] Nietzsche, *The Use and Abuse of History*, p. 14.

That era is now ended. It remains to be seen whether Armenian historians will rise to the challenge of remaking the monumental aspect of their craft into a reasonable and useful science for those they hope to educate and inform. In their search they may find yet again that Khorenats'i's choices of the true subjects of their discipline may have been close to the mark after all.

Modern History and Genocide

Social Relations in the American Mission to Kharpert: The Story of Arabella L. Babcock, 1862-1864

Barbara J. Merguerian

The mission of the American Protestants among the Armenians in Ottoman Turkey during the nineteenth and early twentieth centuries was replete with complexities and inner contradictions concerning both motives and results. Most observers agree that a major impact of the American missionaries on the Armenian people resulted from the education provided through a wide network of schools and colleges. Yet the content of that education, the level of instruction, and the choice of students remained subjects of contention. Should missionary schools be available only to the children of the converted, or was education a means of conversion? Should schools seek to reach a high level of instruction comparable to that available in the United States, or was a lower (and less costly) system adequate? Amid general agreement that basic instruction be provided in the native languages, should the study of English (very much desired by local populations) be offered as well? [1]

The first and outstanding missionary schools were founded in the Ottoman capital of Istanbul (Constantinople), but the impact of Protestant education was perhaps more remarkable in the outlying Armenian-inhabited provinces, particularly in Cilicia (Aintab and Marash were important centers) as well as in the eastern areas (Kharpert was considered one of the most successful stations). A distinguishing feature of the American effort was an emphasis on instruction for women and girls. An examination of the American effort to build an educational network for women in Kharpert

---

[1] Several of these issues are discussed in William R. Hutchison, *Errand to the World: American Protestant Thought and Foreign Missions* (Chicago: University of Chicago Press, 1987), especially chapter 1.

illuminates the sometimes contradictory principles advocated by the Americans, the various responses of the Armenians, and the resulting social tensions.

A detailed, if superficial, impression of the American effort can be gleaned from the prolific reports and letters penned by the American missionaries, whose motivation was to glorify their efforts. Careful analysis is required, therefore, to discern underlying, sometimes unconscious, attitudes. The story of the heartbreak experienced in Kharpert by the first principal of the Girl's Boarding School, Arabella L. Babcock, offers useful insights into the character of the missionaries and inconsistencies in their approach. Coming from a nation founded on the principle of the equality of all citizens and preaching a religion that assumed the common parentage of humankind, the American evangelists clearly perceived themselves as distinct from the indigenous peoples among whom they lived and worked. This sense of distinction easily came to imply superiority, an attitude that did not escape the attention of the local populations, and thus adversely affected the outcomes of missionary efforts.

It is difficult to overestimate the role played by women in the American missionary movement, as donors to the cause, as wives of missionaries or missionaries in their own right, and as objects of evangelism.[2] Missionary policy in the United States from the beginning encouraged the recruitment of men who were married, and evangelistic lore of the early days is full of romantic tales of the

---

[2] The number of studies on the subject of women in missions has been rapidly increasing. They include: R. Pierce Beaver, *American Protestant Women in World Mission: History of the First Feminist Movement in North America* (Grand Rapids, MI: William B. Eerdman's, 1980); Fiona Bowie, Deborah Kirkwood, Shirley Ardener, eds., *Women and Missions, Past and Present: Anthropological and Historical Perceptions* (Providence/Oxford: Berg, 1993); Patricia R. Hill, *The World Their Household: The American Woman's Foreign Mission Movement and Cultural Transformation, 1870-1920* (Ann Arbor: University of Michigan Press, 1985); Mary Taylor Huber, Nancy C. Lutkehaus, *Gendered Missions: Women and Men in Missionary Discourse and Practice* (Ann Arbor: University of Michigan Press, 1999); Helen Barrett Montgomery, W*estern Women in Eastern Lands: An Outline Study of Fifty Years of Woman's Work in Foreign Missions* (New York: MacMillan, 1910); Dana L. Robert, *American Women in Mission: A Social History of Their Thought and Practice* (Macon, Georgia: Mercer University Press, 1997).

women who accompanied their husbands to far-off lands, where they participated in the work (and suffered the hardships) as assistant missionaries; the names of the pioneering wives, such as Ann Judson and Harriet Newell, who set off with their husbands to India in 1812, became legendary. Initially, assignment of single female missionaries was discouraged, though not barred; as early as 1820 Mary Reynolds had accompanied Josiah Brewer and his wife to Smyrna, where Reynolds established and directed a school for Greek girls. With the impetus given to women's higher education in the United States in this period, and the interest in missions demonstrated by such leaders in the field as Mary Lyon (founder and president of Mount Holyoke Seminary), many talented women were attracted by the prospect of serving abroad. The example of Mount Holyoke graduate Fidelia Fiske, who established a Female Seminary in Urmia, Persia, in 1843, provided a popular model.[3]

Indeed, it can be argued that both the missionary movement and the crusade to provide higher education for women took their impetus from the same great spiritual revival in the United States in the early nineteenth century. Both shared a strong belief in the powerful moral force exerted by educated women in the family and in the community. Religion was a central aspect of student life at Mount Holyoke Seminary, a pioneering and trend-setting institution established in 1837; the day began with prayer, there were frequent Bible-reading sessions, and periods of religious revival were encouraged – all of these were features duplicated in the American girl's schools in Turkey. Lyon's movement represented a repudiation of the kind of education often provided to American women, basically finishing schools that taught social graces, dancing, fancy needlework, and music. Lyon was a pioneer in advocating instruction in arithmetic, algebra, and geometry to women. Knowledge of the natural sciences was considered especially important as exemplifying God's order in the universe. Closing exercises at the end of the school year, when students recited and were quizzed in front of

---

[3] The story of these pioneering women can be found in the official history by William E. Strong, *The Story of the American Board* (Boston: Pilgrim Press, 1910), pp. 14-16. On the significance of Mount Holyoke Seminary in general, as well as on Fidelia Fiske in particular, see Amanda Porterfield, *Mary Lyon and the Mount Holyoke Missionaries* (New York: Oxford University Press, 1997).

parents and community members, were a highlight (and this custom was carried over into the schools in Turkey, where it created a sensation). A major principle at Mount Holyoke was that all of the maintenance, cooking, and cleaning was done by the students themselves, the only male on campus being the person who chopped the wood. This practice was adopted partly to keep costs down, but also as a means of preparing students for life. Lyon considered it a "sin of omission not to accomplish as much as possible every moment" and taught her students to plan the use of every half-hour of every day.[4]

The American missionaries did not consider the possibility that the educational needs of Armenian women in Turkey might differ from those of their counterparts in the United States. Just as they were convinced that Protestant Evangelical Christianity was suited for all peoples in all countries, so they believed that a basic Christian education should be the same everywhere. Of course, some adjustments were made. At first the secondary and higher schools in Turkey operated on a lower level than their American counterparts. The vernacular Armenian language (*ashkharhabar)* was substituted for English as the basic instrument for reading and writing (except in the Turkish-speaking areas of Cilicia, where Armeno-Turkish was the language of instruction and Armenian was taught as a second language). In the case of history and geography, the missionary teachers were inspired by the realization that they were teaching in or near the areas where the events of the Bible took place, and therefore they stressed biblical history and geography. Religion was a key element in education; and while the schools in general were not limited to Protestant students, the pressure on the young and impressionable minds to accept evangelism was strong. The tradition of requiring students to share in the cooking, cleaning, and other household chores provided useful training, as did instruction in sewing and needlework. Generally, although the curriculum was not tailored to meet the specific needs of Armenian women, the Americans were flexible in adapting their schools to meet local

---

[4] Louise Porter Thomas, *Seminary Militant: An Account of the Missionary Movement at Mount Holyoke Seminary and College* (South Hadley: Mt. Holyoke College, 1937); Frank A. Stone, "Mt. Holyoke's Impact on the Land of Mt. Ararat," *The Muslim World* 46:1 (January, 1976), pp. 44-57.

needs. The emphasis on reading, understanding, and writing the Armenian language fluently as the core of the curriculum for both males and females had a major impact on the Armenian awakening that took place in the nineteenth century.

The Kharpert Mission

The American mission in Kharpert (the name of both the city and the province, usually called Harpoot or Harput by the Americans) was established by the Reverend George Dunmore in 1855. "There cannot be found a vaster or more promising field in Turkey than Kharpoot for evangelical missionary effort," Dunmore reported at first. This initial enthusiasm was considerably dampened after incidents in which he and his Armenian associate were stoned by local Armenians, leading him to complain that "the Christians are so hostile that any day I may die like a dog in the streets." The illness of his wife compelled Dunmore to return to the United States, but not before he had welcomed to Kharpert a newly assigned American missionary, the Reverend Crosby H. Wheeler, in 1857.[5] Wheeler quickly came to share Dunmore's enthusiasm for the mission, though he did not minimize the problems faced. Wheeler was a man of strong opinions, but he also had a practical American bent of mind, often devising innovative approaches to unanticipated problems and willing to learn from experience. Accompanying Wheeler was his wife, Susan Anna Brookings Wheeler, as well as the Reverend and Mrs. Orson P. Allen (Mrs. Allen was Crosby Wheeler's sister). Wheeler and Allan had been classmates at Andover Theological Seminary (class of 1855), and both wives were graduates of Mount Holyoke Seminary. Joining the mission two years later were the Reverend Herman N. Barnum and his wife Mary (daughter of the

---

[5] Papers of the American Board of Commissioners for Foreign Missions, Houghton Library, Harvard University (also available on microfilm), ABC 16.7.1, Mission to the Armenians, 1846-1859, vol. 9, Documents, Station Reports, Letters: Dunmore (Kharpert), no. 92 (April, 1855) and no. 95 (April, 1857). Susan Anna (Brookings) Wheeler, *Missions in Eden: Glimpses of Life in the Valley of the Euphrates* (New York: Fleming H. Revell, 1899), p. 21. Upon his return to the United States, Dunmore volunteered as a chaplain in the Civil War and was killed by a stray bullet (Dunmore's obituary appears in *Missionary Herald* (October, 1862), pp. 321-322).

pioneering missionary in the Middle East, William Goodell, who was continuing his service in Istanbul). The three couples were to form a mission circle in Kharpert that was to continue unbroken for 37 years and that was unique in its longevity.[6]

The biblical associations that made the Near East so attractive to the romantics of the mission (and romanticism played an important role) were particularly prominent in Kharpert, with its proximity to Mount Ararat. The area was often described, probably for the benefit of patrons at home, as the site of Eden; or if not Eden itself, at least as the spot to which Adam and Eve had been driven when expelled. Not the least of its appeal to the American mission was the suggestion that its inhabitants had retained through the ages some remnants of early religious movements (such as the Paulicians) of the seventh to the ninth centuries that were believed to have contained the seeds of Protestantism. Although non-committal regarding the claim of the native Armenians to be the oldest nation on earth and to speak "the language of Noah," the missionaries were enthusiastic about the rich historical associations of the area and its medieval fortress.[7]

The Kharpert mission was established by the American Board of Commissioners for Foreign Missions (ABCFM), the first and by far the largest such organization in the nineteenth century in the United States, with headquarters in Boston. Founded in 1812 and made up largely of Congregationalists and Presbyterians, the American Board embarked on its mission in the Near East in 1819 in a burst of enthusiasm to revive Christianity in the lands of the Bible. With an initial focus on converting the Jews and with an eye on the large

---

[6] On the Kharpert mission, see Barbara J. Merguerian, "Saving Souls or Cultivating Minds? Missionary Crosby H. Wheeler in Kharpert, Turkey," *Journal of the Society for Armenian Studies*, Vol. 6 (1992-1993), pp. 33-60.

[7] Crosby H. Wheeler, *Ten Years on the Euphrates, or Primitive Missionary Policy Illustrated* (Boston: American Tract Society, 1868), pp. 54, 62. The identification of the Kharpert area as Eden is common in the missionary literature of the time, for example in the title of the memoir by Susan Wheeler, *Missions in Eden*. An example of the claim of inhabitants to be the descendents of the early Paulician dissenters can be found in an 1859 report by missionaries Dunmore and Trowbridge regarding the villagers of Khanos who claimed to be direct descendents of the Paulicians and until recently kept their ancient faith; in becoming Protestants they say that "they do but publicly profess the faith of their fathers." ABC 16.7.1, vol. 9, no. 180.

Muslim population in the area, the Americans for a number of reasons turned their attention instead to the ancient Christian churches. With the opening of the mission in present-day Turkey in 1830, the Americans found Armenians prominent among their early disciples. Initially welcomed warmly by the Armenian Patriarch in Istanbul, the Americans concentrated their efforts on translating, publishing, and distributing religious literature in the Armenian vernacular language, an effort facilitated by the employment of Armenian assistants. The Armenian Patriarchate, itself engaged in an effort to raise the educational level of the clergy, welcomed Protestant support at first, but became alarmed when the reform effort moved to issues of dogma and faith. Increasing belligerence led, on one side, to the excommunication by the patriarch of the Armenians who sympathized with the Americans and, on the other side, to a decision by the missionaries to promote the establishment of the First Armenian Evangelical Church in 1846 and an Armenian Protestant millet (community) in Ottoman Turkey in 1850. The struggle left a legacy of hostility that persisted for decades.[8] Encouraged by the potential for the work among the Armenians, the American Board embarked on a crusade to meet "The Urgent Needs of the Armenian Reformation," particularly after 1851. Americans found that they could work more effectively in the Turkish provinces, away from the political intrigues and direct reach of the Armenian Patriarchate in Istanbul, and Kharpert became one of the most promising of the new centers. Efforts to expand the work, however, were hampered by the growing abolitionist movement in the United States, which made it difficult to raise funds or to attract volunteers for service. These conditions explain the assignment of three missionary couples to Kharpert in the late 1850s, as well as the chronic shortage of funds and the inability to satisfy the need for additional workers requested repeatedly in the Kharpert station reports.

In Kharpert, the missionaries found themselves dealing with a largely agricultural and impoverished population. On the one hand

---

[8] On the conditions leading to the establishment of the Armenian Evangelical Church, see G. H. Chopourian, *The Armenian Evangelical Reformation: Causes and Effects* (New York: Armenian Missionary Association of America, 1972).

fascinated by the local way of life that had not changed significantly since biblical days, the missionaries at the same time became exasperated with the prevailing conservative frame of mind that distrusted innovation of any kind. The Turkish government's hostility to proselytizing among the Muslims left the missionaries to concentrate their attention largely on the Armenians. The local population was curious about the Western dress and lifestyle of the Americans, but skeptical, if not hostile, concerning their motives. The Armenians found it difficult to understand why these strangers had come such a great distance to find fault with their Armenian Apostolic Church, to which they had clung for so many centuries and which defined their identity under the prevailing millet system of the Ottoman Turkish Empire. References to the stoning of the missionaries by the local population in the early days are frequent in the literature. Slowly, with persistence, especially as they became fluent in the Armenian language, the missionaries learned to take advantage of the curiosity of the local population in order to gain a hearing for their teachings. Any weapon would be used by the missionaries to attract attention; his spy glass, Wheeler wrote, was very effective in attracting the attention of a crowd and arousing their interest in listening to a sermon. The Americans also took advantage of the Christian reverence demonstrated by the Armenians; on one occasion, when pandemonium broke out after Wheeler had found himself in the unusual position of being asked to deliver a sermon in an Armenian Apostolic Church, he managed to restore order by making the gesture of kissing the cross.[9]

The emphasis on education that became a hallmark of American missions in the Middle East was a direct result of the Congregational/Presbyterian denominational belief that the source of all religious truth is to be found in the Bible. The individual's road to salvation therefore was to be found in reading with understanding and following the truths set forth in the Bible. Such a religion requircs a literate public, but schools were few in number and low in quality in Kharpert. Amelioration of this situation became a first order of business for missionary Dunmore. A small Protestant school that opened in 1855 was taught by a 16-year-old local Armenian, M. A. Melcon, who was to go on to become a professor at Euphrates

[9] Wheeler, *Ten Years on the Euphrates*, p. 145.

College. As no evangelical school existed then for women, Melcon brought his sister and one other girl into his classroom, where they studied along with the boys. Later we are told that Melcon's class included eight boys and four girls.[10]

Female education had been especially neglected, though it was not unknown. Missionary Dunmore reported from Kharpert upon his arrival the existence of two or three Muslim schools for girls as well as an Armenian school taught by the daughter of a priest. Dunmore soon had his associate, the priest Kevork, organizing a Bible-study class for local women, while Kevork's wife was at work teaching a class of 15 Protestant women to read. Dunmore appealed urgently to Boston for the assignment of a female missionary who could "devote her time to teaching and laboring among her own sex," since the pastor's wife "can do little" and his missionary wife was overtaxed.[11] Herman N. Barnum later recalled:

> Education was in the most primitive state then. Female education was unknown, and it was unthinkable so far as the majority of the people were concerned, except that the ladies already here had, with great persistence, persuaded a few women and girls to read. It was a form of "women's rights" that brought no little reproach upon those who first began to read.[12]

In 1858, soon after her arrival in Kharpert, where the houses had flat roofs, Susan Wheeler took the first steps to establish a girl's school. She gathered together, on one of those house-tops, a band of little girls, to teach them the rudiments of education and of the Christian religion, hoping to fit them to be wives of native pastors and teachers of their countrywomen. The missionary could read the spoken language of the people, but could not speak it freely. The

---

[10] Frank Andrews Stone, *Academies for Anatolia: A Study of the Rationale, Program and Impact of the Educational Institutions Sponsored by the American Board in Turkey: 1830-1980* (Lanham: University Press of America, 1984), pp. 111-112; Dunmore (Kharpert), no. 92 (April, 1855), ABC 16.7.1. vol. 9.

[11] Dunmore, no. 35 (June 18, 1857), no. 26 (Feb. 12, 1856), and no. 27 (May 14, 1856), ABC 16.7.1, vol. 11, Letters [DU-DW].

[12] "Forty Years in Harpoot, Eastern Turkey," *Missionary Herald* 95(10) (October, 1899), p. 402, quoted in Stone, *Academies*, p. 111.

women, of course, could talk with ease, but they could not read; and so, the instruction became mutual – the one learning to talk, the others to read.[13]

The early missionaries no doubt exaggerated local indifference to education in order to emphasize the need for Protestant schools and to encourage financial support at home. Of the state of literacy locally, Wheeler wrote:

> Our first effort, then, was to rouse all whom we met to a sense of the importance of learning this art, and of possessing a Bible... We endeavored to attract the public attention by asking every man we met, "Do you know how to read?" It was sometimes amusing to witness the wonder and incredulity with which our assertion was received, that an adult man, and even a woman, can learn to do this. Then too the idea of doing it, even if possible, was to some ludicrous enough. "What! Am I to become a priest," exclaimed many a man, "that I should learn to read!"[14]

If it was difficult to gain popular acceptance for spreading literacy among the male population, it was even more so when the question arose of educating women. Yet saving the souls of women was regarded by the Americans as equally important as saving the souls of the men. Moreover the importance of women as mothers and as primary educators of the new generation called for special attention.

Thus the establishment of schools for girls and women was among the early projects in the city of Kharpert and also in the outlying stations (there took place a steady growth of these, so that by 1870 there were 70 outstations in the Kharpert mission). Formal schools were only one way for American women to reach their counterparts in an effort to carry out their "women's work for women." Bible-reading and similar sessions were designed to teach women how to read and to interpret the Bible. These women, often older and no longer overburdened with household responsibilities, were then encouraged to go out and read the Bible to women in their

---

[13] "Girls' Schools in Turkey (4): Harpoot Female Seminary," *Light and Light for Women* 8:10 (October, 1878), pp. 289-290.

[14] Wheeler, *Ten Years on the Euphrates*, pp. 114-115.

neighborhoods or villages, often in the process teaching these women how to read for themselves. In all of these activities, the importance of women missionaries was apparent; the social structure and customs of peoples in the Ottoman Empire made it impossible for male missionaries to have access to the indigenous women. Hence the need arose for female teachers to carry on this work. The early reports from the Kharpert mission are full of appeals for the assignment of a single woman missionary to the field.

The basic thrust of all the American Board missions among the Armenians after 1846 was to establish independent evangelical churches headed by native clergymen. The name of Crosby Wheeler is especially associated with the effort to prepare Armenian preachers and to oversee the establishment of independent churches by parishioners willing to support both building and pastor.[15] Establishment of the Kharpert Theological Seminary in 1859 to educate Armenian clergy was a strong priority of the mission. As a matter of policy, American clergy did not serve as pastors and did not conduct services for the local population, although they eagerly solicited invitations to deliver sermons. Wheeler and fellow missionary Allen went so far as to refuse to give communion to local Armenians, telling them to establish their own parishes with their own pastors instead. The education of potential Armenian pastors drew attention to the need for suitable Armenian wives able to serve as helpmates and companions for their husbands as well as models for the community. As the work expanded and as local opinion permitted, educated women were also needed as teachers. A major problem hindering the higher education of Armenian women was the fact that many of them were married at the early age of 11, 12, or 13, and moved in with their husband's family, where they were required to stay at home to perform chores. The Americans adapted to this situation by establishing, in 1862, a Girl's Boarding School in Kharpert specifically for married women, the wives of students in the

---

[15] Father Mardiros, a native of Diyarbekir, was ordained as the first Armenian pastor in Kharpert in 1860; in 1865 the Kharpert Evangelical Union was established, with 11 churches, six pastors, and 325 members. *Missionary Herald* (1891), pp. 23-24.

theological school. Single girls were also to attend the school both as boarders and day students.[16]

The plans for the female boarding school called for a three-year course of study. The minimum age for admission was 12, and students were required to pass an entrance examination in basic skills. The curriculum consisted of reading, writing, spelling, composition, arithmetic, grammar, geography, and history, along with singing, catechism, and daily Bible lessons. Practical instruction in needlework and plain sewing was also included. The living arrangements for the students were designed to "conform as far as practicable to the customs of the country." In other words, students were to wear native dress, sleep on mattresses rolled out every evening, and eat their meals seated on the floor and without utensils.[17]

Assignment of Arabella L. Babcock

Establishment of the American Board School for Girls required the appointment of a woman missionary as principal. The senior secretary and chief policy-maker of the American Board, Rufus Anderson, though a friend of Mary Lyon and a strong supporter of higher education for women in the United States, opposed the appointment of single women to the missions. But he could not disregard the compelling reasons dictating the need for such women. When the request was made for a principal to head the Boarding School for Girls in Istanbul, Anderson agreed to the appointment of Harriet Martha Lovell in 1844, and when Lovell retired following her marriage to missionary educator Cyrus Hamlin, of Maria West in 1853. After the decision was made to establish women's boarding schools in the interior, Myra Proctor was assigned to Aintab and Ann Eliza Fritcher to Marsovan.[18] It was under these circumstances that

---

[16] Maria A. West, *The Romance of Missions: or Inside Views of Life and Labor, in the Land of Ararat* (New York: Anson D. F. Randolph, 1875), pp. 407-408; M.B. Norton, "Harpoot Female Seminary," *Life and Light* 6:8 (August, 1876), pp. 226-227.

[17] "Minutes of the First Annual Meeting of the Mission to Eastern Turkey," ABC 16.9.7, Eastern Turkey Mission, 1860-1871, no. 28 (June, 1861).

[18] Barbara J. Merguerian, "The Beginnings of Secondary Education for Armenian Women: The Armenian Female Seminary in Constantinople," *Journal of the Society for Armenian Studies* 5 (1990-1991), pp. 103-124.

the first single female missionary was assigned to Kharpert in the person of Arabella S. Babcock, of Framingham, Massachusetts, a friend of Proctor's, who was appointed in 1862 to head the newly established Girls' Boarding School.

A native of Thetford, Vermont, and the daughter of a Protestant pastor, Babcock was 22 years old when she left New York City on May 31, 1862, on assignment to Kharpert. She traveled with missionary Fayette Jewett and his wife as far as Istanbul, where she was met by Maria West, former head of the Girl's Seminary there, who accompanied her on the ship across the Black Sea to Samsun. There the two women were met by missionary Julius Leonard and taken over land to the missionary station in Marsovan. Wheeler met Babcock in Marsovan and brought her to Kharpert, where a small room for her use had been added to the house shared by the Allen and Wheeler families. In the basement of the house, a school room and sleeping rooms for the pupils had been prepared; it was the former site of the Theological Seminary, which had been moved to the second floor of the nearby newly constructed chapel.

Babcock left a favorable first impression. "We are very much pleased with Miss Babcock," missionary Barnum reported soon after her arrival in Kharpert on September 28, 1862. "She appears to be admirably fitted for the post," Barnum continued, "and if life and health are spared, I do not doubt that she will do a great work both in the school and out of it." He added that she "is taking hold of the Armenian language finely." [19] Wheeler later recalled that he had found her at first "much under the influence of romance and enthusiasm and wanting in judgment and discretion." But he came to admire her strong streak of independence, especially in running the school, which relieved him of this responsibility. "As far as the school was concerned, she was a model of excellence," Wheeler later wrote, noting that her rules were few, but strictly enforced, and her religious influence a good one. Although she had spells of discouragement, "her spirits lifted as the students progressed," Wheeler observed.[20]

---

[19] Barnum, no. 202 (October 15, 1862), ABC 16.9.7, Eastern Turkey Mission (1860-1871), vol. 1, Documents, Reports, Letters.
[20] Wheeler, no. 445 (Nov. 20, 1863), ABC 16.9.7, vol. 2, Letters.

Babcock must have been instructed in the general philosophy of the Kharpert mission (and for all Armenian missions) in regard to policy toward native customs. As Susan Wheeler put it:

> We were not sent to change the customs of the people, or to make sport of them because they were unlike our own. Our customs were just as strange to them as theirs were to us. In fact we did not go to Americanize the people; we soon learned that many of their customs were better for them than ours would be.[21]

Babcock exhibited an uncommon interest in the local customs and in the Armenian community. She became a special friend of two young Armenian sisters: one was her assistant in the school and the other was the wife of the local Armenian clergyman, Pastor Mardiros. Both sisters had been educated in the mission's Female Seminary in Istanbul. It was probably as a result of this association that Babcock came to believe that the missionaries paid too little deference to the native population. In any event, the first school year went well, and closing exercises were held in late November 1863. (Because Kharpert was an agricultural area and most inhabitants were to be found working out in the fields during the summer, the school year had been organized to begin in the spring, run through the summer, and close in late fall, thus allowing the students to work in the villages during the winter months when people could be found at home.) Missionary Allen wrote a glowing report of the Girl's Boarding School's first closing exercises, which had attracted a number of missionaries from neighboring stations as well as parents and friends. Of the female students, 36 in number (15 boarders, 10 day students, and 11 wives of theological students), Allen wrote:

> The examinations in reading both Turkish and Armenian, in writing, composition, geography with map drawing, arithmetic and Bible lessons showed thorough instruction and excellent progress.

Allen went on to discuss the significance of the event:

> Judging from this first year of the school, we are led to hope that it will prove an important aid in our mission work. Some of the pupils are employed as teachers at

---

[21] Susan Wheeler, *Missions in Eden,* pp. 50-51.

> other stations and in our own field seven are teaching schools in various places. The wives of the helpers also accompany their husbands and will accomplish among the women a work which a man could not do. The simple example of a woman in these dark villages, able to take up a book and read, is a great wonder, and at the same a convincing argument to the women that they too can do the same thing.[22]

At the end of the exercises, Babcock invited the missionaries to a reception in her sitting room, where to their astonishment she announced her engagement to marry the brother of her Armenian friends, the popular pastor in the nearby city of Diyarbekir, the Reverend Tomas Boyajian. Though she must have anticipated a negative reaction from her associates, Babcock was completely taken aback by the strong opposition to such a union expressed by all of the missionaries present. "This announcement was received in such a manner," Babcock later wrote to her mother, "and after that the course pursued by the missionaries was such, that I have since considered it as beneath me as your daughter as well as compromising my Christian character to retain any longer the position of teacher of this school." Her resignation was submitted a few weeks later.[23]

Of the sterling qualities represented by Pastor Tomas, there was no disagreement. A native of Diyarbekir, he was a graduate of the mission's famed Bebek Seminary in Istanbul, after which he had returned to preach in his native city. His reputation quickly grew, so that his ordination in 1863 had attracted such a huge audience that it had to be held out of doors, with an estimated one thousand adults and several hundred children in attendance. A widower – his wife, a graduate of the Female Boarding School in Istanbul, having passed away the previous year – he was left with a 4-year-old son. From all evidence he represented a strong endorsement of the positive outcome of missionary endeavors. Yet the missionaries in their letters home could only express contradictory emotions regarding this startling turn of events. They all praised the outstanding qualities and strong character of the Reverend Boyajian, while at the same

---

[22] Allen, no. 131 (Dec. 12, 1863), ABC 16.9.7, vol. 1.
[23] Babcock, no. 182 (Jan. 5, 1864), ABC 16.9.7, vol. 1.

time condemning the possibility of a marriage between an American missionary woman and an Armenian Protestant man. Wheeler exhibited a fortress mentality as he expressed fears about the precedent that would thus be set:

> Hitherto our supposed elevation in social position above the people has kept those seeking wives from attempting to invade our family circles; but with such an example before them, we shall have constant anxiety, lest others try to delude our daughters into an equal or greater discretion.[24]

Wheeler also predicted that Pastor Tomas would be unable to support Babcock in the manner to which she had become accustomed, and therefore he would be forced to leave the ministry for a higher-paying profession, thus depleting Protestant preaching resources. Allen admitted in a letter to Babcock's mother that Pastor Tomas would make "a very worthy husband, who will make every effort to make her happy" and that Babcock was clearly "deeply in love." According to Barnum, the missionaries had objected that "we all regard this proposed union as impeding the happiness of both the parties concerned and as compromising our influence and our relations with the people about us and likely to injure our work in many ways" and he went on to label the affair as "the greatest trial of our missionary life."[25]

Babcock herself has offered a touching account of the courtship in a letter to her mother, announcing her engagement "to a young man whose excellencies I cannot essay to describe," someone "whose high reputation and character" had became known to her long before she had "any idea that we should ever be personally interested in each other." Given the social customs of the country, the two had no opportunity to be alone together, she explained; their personal contact came only in larger settings with others present; she had listened to him preach repcatedly, dined in his presence in missionary and Protestant Armenian homes, and had welcomed him to her school on the occasions when he had visited the pupils from Diyarbekir. In fact, the two had only one brief private interview, at

---

[24] Wheeler, no. 445 (Nov. 20, 1863) ABC 16.9.7, vol. 2.

[25] Allen, no. 132 (Dec. 15, 1963); Barnum, no. 208 (Dec. 18, 1963), ABC 16.9.7, vol. 1.

the school, when he had proposed to her and she had accepted. "I should, however, have desired that he should have further opportunity of becoming acquainted with me before an engagement, if we had been in America," she explained to her mother. "But here the customs of the country are different and I felt that I could not permit it." The fact that he was Armenian presented no barrier, she wrote:

> With regard to his being an Armenian I wish to say that if you knew him, and the Armenians, and knew all about the missionary work in this country, I think you would feel just as I did, that I could be happier and more useful in being united to him, than to one of my own nation. He is in manner, refinement of feeling and cultivation of mind and heart, as perfect a gentleman, as those whom I have met in America.

The engaged couple agreed that the marriage would be put off for two years, to give the missionary board time to appoint a successor at the school; meanwhile Babcock could continue her work as principal. As the situation unfolded, however, Babcock was left with no recourse but to resign her position and return home.[26]

From all of the available evidence in this matter, it appears that Babcock was completely bewildered by the adamant opposition of her fellow missionaries to her engagement. Nowhere is there any hint that they had anything but the highest regard for the character, intelligence, and personality of Tomas Boyajian. Their disapproval was based solely on the perceived impropriety of a union between an American and a native Armenian. Such a point of view, however, did not appear to follow in any logical way from the morals or the philosophy espoused by the missionaries. It was argued that Boyajian would be unable to provide Babcock with the standard of living to which she had become accustomed. But, aside from the absence of any indication that this was a matter of concern to her, the missionary philosophy was based on a rejection of the importance of worldly material and goods. It was true that Babcock would have to resign her position and that her services as a teacher would be lost to the mission, but on the other hand the couple's marriage plans were based on her potential role as a helpmate in her husband's ministry,

---

[26] Babcock, no. 182 (Jan. 5, 1864), ABC 16.9.7, vol. 1.

all of which was an accepted part of the Americans' mission in Kharpert. Babcock took seriously the Protestant teachings about the equality of all peoples, whereas the other Americans, consciously or unconsciously, assumed the superiority of the Americans.

The sequence of events that followed is unclear in the surviving sources. Babcock accused the missionaries of destroying her opportunity for a happy and fulfilled life, and became increasingly angry and upset; the missionaries could not understand why she did not appreciate their point of view. They described her conduct as erratic, and then implied that she was mentally unbalanced. For a time she came to stay with the Barnum's, and then "escaped" to live with Pastor Mardiros and his wife (Tomas Boyajian's sister). Then she returned to live with the Allen's, but refused to speak with them after they repeated their firm disapproval of the engagement. Though she initially renewed her engagement with a ring, it was soon reported that Boyajian had broken it off due to "her singular conduct, and without any influence from us" [i.e. the missionaries]. A local couple was engaged to make sure that Babcock did not run away, thus placing her under virtual house arrest. It was suggested that she was pretending to be insane, though for what reason is not clear.[27]

It was finally decided that Babcock must return home; but since travel was impossible during the winter, she had to wait until spring, when she was sent on her way in the care of the Reverend Augustus Walker of Diyarbekir, who was returning to the United States via the southern route, through Aintab, Aleppo, and Beirut. His account of the harrowing two-and-a-half month journey home has survived. He had been in Kharpert when Babcock first arrived, and had been impressed with her potential; he had been present also when she had announced her engagement. Now, in March 1864, he found her a different person, with strange notions and queer doings (i.e., on the way home, while waiting for the ferry to cross the Euphrates, she insisted that she was being sold to the Kurds). She was cheered by her friend, Myra Proctor in Aintab, and seemed her old self as they set off on the transatlantic trip. After passing Malta, however, her

[27] The incident is described in letters from the Kharpert missionaries, including Allen, no. 132 (Dec. 15, 1863); Barnum, no. 208 (Dec. 18, 1863), no. 210 (Jan. 7, 1864), and no. 211 (Mar. 1, 1864); ABC 16.9.7, vol. 1. Also Wheeler, no. 445 (Nov. 20, 1863) and no. 446 (Jan. 26, 1864), ABC 16.9.7, vol. 2.

strange behavior reoccurred. Walker kept his eye on her; and when she tried to jump off the ship, he was there to stop her. Subsequently she refused to speak with him, and the captain was obliged to assign crew members to watch her constantly. Once back in the United States, with great relief Walker placed her in the care of her mother and sister.[28]

The Kharpert missionaries continued to justify their actions in regard to Babcock and claimed to have no regrets. Yet a note of defensiveness pervades their confidential assurances, and they express concern over possible censure by their colleagues. "I think that some of our brethren are a little disposed to criticize us for not cheerfully acquiescing in the engagement when it was first made," Barnum admitted. One missionary defense was to find flaws (retroactively) in Babcock's character. Barnum reported suspicions that Babcock suffered from a "secret vice," a charge he claimed to be confirmed by the Protestant woman who had been assigned to sleep in her room, for "besides the practice of this vice, she several nights insisted on getting into the same bed with the woman."[29] Such reports are difficult to assess based on sketchy missionary correspondence. It does not seem unreasonable to conclude from this sad episode that Babcock's mind had become unsettled as a result of her treatment at the hands of her colleagues. This was apparently the interpretation adopted by Pastor Boyajian. Upon his return to Diyarbekir, missionary Walker found the pastor "unpleasantly affected" by the Babcock matter. "His disappointment was great, and he cannot divest himself of the idea that her derangement resulted from opposition to her marriage," Walker reported.[30]

The entire affair must have reinforced Secretary Anderson's reluctance to assign single women to missions; but with the end of the Civil War in the United States there was no way to stop the enthusiasm of women to become more significantly involved in missions, both as fundraisers (with the establishment of the Women's Boards of Missions) and as missionaries. One of the lessons learned from the Babcock incident was the undesirability of assigning one single woman missionary to a station; henceforth

---

[28] Walker, no. 347 (Aug. 8, 1864), ABC 16.9.7, vol. 2.
[29] Barnum, no. 211 (Mar. 1, 1864), ABC 16.9.7, vol. 1.
[30] Walker, no. 349 (Dec. 16, 1864), ABC 16.9.7, vol. 2.

every effort was made to assign single women in pairs. Babcock's place at the Female Boarding School was taken by Maria West and Ann Eliza Fritcher, who were temporarily available because of delays in the opening the Girl's Boarding School in Marsovan. With her years of experience in Istanbul, West was particularly successful in continuing to place the Kharpert Girl's Board School on a strong footing.[31]

There were repercussions in Kharpert. Boyajian's ministry in Diyarbekir (which was part of the Kharpert mission) became a great trial to Wheeler, and one cannot help but suspect that the Babcock affair affected attitudes. At one point it was suggested to Wheeler by his colleagues that in order to ameliorate relations he might apologize to Boyajian for his "harsh language" used at the time of the Babcock affair; but Wheeler countered by asserting that he did "not recollect using any harsh language to or about him either then or since."[32] Boyajian displeased the missionaries when he expressed an interest in suggestions by the American Episcopal cleric Horatio Southgate that Armenians should adopt the Episcopal form of Protestantism because it is much closer in theory and practice to the Armenian national religion than the Congregational or Presbyterian faith expounded by the missionaries; this loomed as a particular threat because the Anglo/Prussian Archbishop in Jerusalem, Samuel Gobat, was sending emissaries to the Diyarbekir region with similar proposals during this period. Also Wheeler became exceedingly irritated when Boyajian subsequently traveled to the United States and to England to raise money to build a new church in Diyarbekir. Wheeler always tried to keep the local Protestant churches modest so that they could be supported by the local population, and he expressed concern that generous financial and other resources would corrupt the local Protestants. Moreover, Wheeler had come to Kharpert as a critic of the Bebek Seminary, where Tomas had been trained, because (he argued) it provided a much higher level of education than was needed locally and therefore put too many ideas into the heads of its students. With the passage of years, however,

---

[31] West, *Romance of Missions,* describes her experiences in Kharpert in chapter 11; she does not mention Arabella Babcock.

[32] Wheeler, no. 492 (Nov. 20, 1867) to Rev. George Wood, ABC 16.9.1, Letters, vol. 2.

and with Wheeler's gradual embrace of the value of higher education for the Armenians (evident in the establishment of the American Euphrates College in Kharpert), Boyajian and Wheeler became reconciled, and Boyajian served as an instructor in the college as his time permitted.

Underlying Tensions

The Babcock affair was not the first instance in which the missionaries faced the issue of intermarriage, nor was it the last. In the early days of the American Board, a school had been established in Cornwall, Connecticut, in order to train and socialize potential native leaders from the various mission fields. When two of the students – one of whom was a Cherokee Indian leader – married white women, a controversy erupted, which partly explains the discontinuance of the school soon after. As one missionary scholar explained, the school's leadership "supported most plans to civilize, socialize, and protect Indians, but not if this meant treating them as equals."[33] The executive body of the American Board, on the other hand, took a more egalitarian approach.

> How does it appear to be the will of God," the corresponding secretary of the Board wondered, "that individuals of different tribes and nations should not intermarry?
>
> Is there anything in the Bible, that asserts or implies, that man and wife be precisely of the same complexion? . . . Does it not tend strongly to irritate the young men, who have been educated at Cornwall, not only in the Cherokee nation, but wherever else they live, will it not strike their minds as equivalent to a declaration that their people are doomed to perpetual inferiority, and that every attempt to rise to an equality with the whites is impudent and criminal?[34]

While the situation in the American mission among the Armenians did not raise the problem in the same way, underlying social tensions between the Americans and the Armenians undoubtedly existed. Relations were harmonious on the surface, and the missionaries often

---

[33] Hutchison, *Errand to the World,* p. 65.

[34] Quoted in Ibid., pp. 66-67.

visited the Armenian Protestant families, and vice versa. But while preaching the equality of all people in the eyes of God, the Americans nonetheless drew clear boundaries between themselves and the indigenous peoples among whom they lived and worked. At the missionary compound in Kharpert, for example, there were two cemeteries: one for the local Protestants and the other for the missionaries and their families (the refusal of the Apostolic church authorities to permit the burial in their cemeteries of those who espoused Protestant views had been a major impetus for the formation of the Evangelical community). The missionary children, when little, as a rule did not play with the Armenian children, and when older were sent to the United States for their education.

Serious philosophical disagreements that had arisen during the 1850s regarding the operation of the missions also served to create differences between the Americans and the Armenians. Specifically, this decade marked the ascendancy of the philosophy espoused by Rufus Anderson, the powerful foreign secretary of the American Board, who rejected the "civilizing" function for missions and insisted on limiting the work to direct evangelism. Anderson was particularly scornful of efforts to provide education to native populations beyond the basics needed to read the Bible with understanding. The role of the missionary, according to Anderson, was to preach, and all other activities were of secondary importance. Students were to be limited to the families of the converted. Higher education was barred, as was instruction in English, both of which were considered by Anderson as unnecessary, expensive, and likely to raise the students above their station in life, leaving them dissatisfied and unfit for service among their people. Anderson believed that Christianity would bring with it a generally "civilizing" tendency, but he emphatically did not see it as the missionary's duty to interfere with established patterns of life and customs, even less to introduce Western technology.[35]

The leading figure in the Kharpert mission, the Reverend Wheeler, was an outspoken disciple of Anderson's and on his way to the Turkish interior he had sided with Anderson in debates then

---

[35] The foreign secretary's views are best summarized in Rufus Anderson, *Foreign Missions: Their Relations and Claims* (New York: Scribner & Co., 1869).

taking place in Istanbul. Wheeler took direct issue with the veteran missionary Cyrus Hamlin over the question of higher education and the teaching of English. (Hamlin, founder of the famed Bebek Seminary that had trained the first generation of Armenian Protestant pastors, was to resign from the American Board in protest to the Anderson policies and is now best remembered as the founder of Robert College in Istanbul, the first American-sponsored college in the Middle East.) Hamlin believed in the development of a system in which the native Armenian pastors would have an education comparable to that of the missionaries, while Anderson (and Wheeler) argued that Bebek had provided too advanced a level of education, one that removed the students from their native society and unfitted them for service in the small and unsophisticated communities of the Turkish interior. Wheeler enthusiastically undertook the challenge of establishing the Kharpert Theological Seminary in 1859, but tried to keep it on a lower educational level at first. Wheeler was also a strong advocate of self-supporting congregations; and given the relative poverty of the people, this meant modest church structures and low pay for pastors. The Armenians were understandably disappointed to be told that a second-rate education was good enough for them and that pastors should not seek higher wages nor should congregations try to raise money outside of their communities to build imposing church edifices. The Armenians also resented the fact that they had no voice in decisions about the distribution of mission funds; they asserted that they understood as well as (if not better than) the missionaries what these local needs were. The Armenians interpreted these policies to indicate that they had been placed on a level lower than the Americans, an interpretation that ill-fitted the evangelical Christianity preached by the Americans. As a result of all of these developments, many Armenians felt betrayed by the missionaries and charged that earlier promises made by the Americans had not been fulfilled.

A time went on, conditions changed. The success of the mission educational programs possessed an inner dynamic that pushed the educational level ever upward and prompted the Kharpert missionaries to devise a much admired comprehensive educational system crowned by Armenia (later Euphrates) College. American Board philosophy now adopted the "social gospel" and stressed educational and medical programs. To what extent underlying attitudes changed, however, is open to question. Assuming intermarriage to be a significant indicator, it may be noted that three decades later, although the particular circumstances were different, the reaction of missionaries to intermarriage remained the same. When in 1900 a single American missionary woman in Kharpert, Theresa Huntington, received a marriage overture on behalf of a young local Armenian doctor, she not only immediately rejected it but went so far as to look upon it as an insult. Huntington at least understood the innate contradiction in her position. "I feel inclined to resent it," she wrote to her mother regarding the overture. "Well, there's no use in feeling insulted. You see it is our pride which is insulted really, because they should consider themselves our equals, and yet we always try to treat the Armenians as equals."[36]

---

[36] *Great Need Over the Water: The Letters of Theresa Huntington Ziegler*, Stina Katchadourian, ed. (Ann Arbor: Gomidas Institute, 1999), pp. 208-209.

32

The Quest for Henry Finnis Blosse Lynch

Christopher Young

In August 1893, Henry Finnis Blosse Lynch, usually known as Harry, with his cousin Major Henry Charles Blosse Lynch[1] set off from Constantinople by steamer along the coast of Asia Minor. Their destination was Batum where they arrived after spending a few days at Trebizond on the way. From Batum by rail, then carriage and then horseback, they struck inland together with the usual posse of bearers and a dragoman. Lynch kept a diary together with copious notes. He also brought his camera along with a Mr. Wessum, a photographic expert from the London Polytechnic; with the latter's help he took a remarkable series of photographs of the peoples, the buildings and landscapes of this remote part of the Caucasus, which were then developed on the spot, and which were intended to illustrate the written record Lynch was keeping.

The expedition's first objective was the ascent of Ararat before winter set in. This was duly achieved after which Major Blosse Lynch, who had been in charge of horses and camping arrangements, left to rejoin his regiment. Lynch and Wessum continued, recording and photographing as they went along, encountering all sorts of hardships on the way. Their route was as follows: Erivan – Etchmiadzin – Ani – Kars – Van – Aghtamar – Bitlis – Mush – Erzerum and Trebizond. But this was no ordinary expedition and Lynch was no ordinary traveller. With a potent combination of intelligence, perception, sympathy and scholarship he revealed the Armenians in their remote homeland to the world beyond. He understood the thwarted aspirations of a proud but suppressed

---

[1] Son of General Edward Blosse-Lynch. Born 1856, he died in 1936. He saw action in the South African War. Retired as colonel in 1906. High Sheriff of County Mayo 1911, he spent the rest of his days at Partry.

people. He was able to see that nothing had been done to follow up the representations of the Armenians at the Congress of Berlin 15 years earlier. And it was clear to him that, while Czarist Russia was seeking to assimilate Armenia by subverting its religious and educational institutions, combined with territorial expansion in the region, the Ottoman Turks, with a mixture of indifference and connivance, were ready to destroy it by violence.

Lynch was quickly proved right by the massacres in Ottoman Armenia not long after he returned home. But four years later he was back, this time with a geographer and geologist called Oswald. Together they concentrated on the physical characteristics of the country, taking with them a variety of scientific instruments with which to gather data. The camera went too, except that this time Lynch developed the negatives himself after the end of the four months' expeditions during which he also brought himself up to date with the present state of the country.

Back in Britain, Lynch, with acknowledged help from others, collected together his written material and photographic record and studied the available material on his subject. The result, four years later, was his great work *Armenia: Travel and Studies*, published in 1901.

This is a work which exists at several levels: for the student of Armenian, Ottoman, Russian and even Byzantine history, it remains an indispensable source of information; for the architectural historian, it contains a unique record of buildings, many now destroyed or in ruins. The mountaineer will delight in the epic accounts of the ascent of Ararat, Nimrud, Sipan and Bingöl. The modern traveller will continue to find a useful if somewhat weighty guide to an area which remains remote today. And for our political leaders, who, with no apparent sense of history, seek to control affairs in that region, it should be compulsory reading, with a stiff examination to follow to ensure it has been properly understood.

But above all, it is for Armenians, the best evocation on words and pictures of a lost homeland only years before the hammer blow of deportation and massacre in 1915. As R. H Kevorkian has written: "Henry F. B. Lynch, par son temoignage fondamental, s'avère être pour l'Armenie, le plus grand voyageur des temps modernes."[2]

---

[2] In R. H. Kévorkian, *Fragments d'un Discourse d'Armenie* (Paris, 1990).

And as Archbishop Mesrob Ashjian wrote in his introduction to the 1990 reprint: "This is no ordinary travel or history book but a marvellous amalgam of history, geography personal observation, philosophical reflection and literary expression." He concludes there is no other book on Armenia published in the twentieth century that matches it in the excellence of its total presentation.[3]

Lynch's quest for Armenia was, therefore, spectacularly successful; but what about the author himself? We can tell from his book that he was intrepid, physically strong and able to endure hardship. We can see from his analysis of the political situation that he was an able polemicist. He rated the value of education, particularly as a way of advancing the interests of the underprivileged and preserving their culture, very highly. He was a good enough classicist to be able at short notice to address a school assembly in Latin. He was moved by the grandeur of landscape; and had a penchant for pretty village girls, barefoot and clad in loose cotton dresses.

But in many ways the book is curiously impersonal. For example, we cannot tell what he looked like: of the many photographs in the book chosen from several casefulls, there is not one of the author himself. He parleys much with various clerics, but we never find out what his own religious views were although he was, in fact, an Anglican. In the preface, we are told that he had no interests, public or private, in Armenia yet, as we shall see, he was partly Armenian and was the chairman of his family firm which had important business connections not far to the south. Indeed, when the family name is mentioned in the text, he makes no attempt to establish a connection. Nor, when passing through Arghana, does he mention the death of his uncle, William Michael Lynch, there. His family connections, background and his private thoughts are not mentioned. Why should this be? The reason, I believe, for his reticence is simple. His book, which contained a clear political message, had to be objective and impartial to get that message across. Mention of background and business connections could have resulted in accusations of special pleading, depriving the book's message of some of its force; that had to be avoided at all costs. That

[3] Introduction to reprinted edition (New York, 1990).

the book is objective is beyond question, but it does mean that we shall have to look beyond in our quest for Harry Lynch.

We start with his family background. Until the recent sale of house and estate, the Blosse-Lynches had been landowners in County Mayo, in the extreme west of Ireland, since the middle ages. From the seventeenth century onwards the family owned the lands of Cloonlagheen, subsequently called Partry, and it was there that Lynch's grandfather, Major Henry Blosse-Lynch (1778-1823) returned after soldiering with distinction under Wellington in the Peninsular War, having been mentioned in Despatches for bravery at the siege of Ciudad Rodrigo. At Partry, he resumed family life with his wife Elizabeth (née Finnis). She bore him 11 sons, of whom the eldest was 19 and the youngest not yet born when their father died; all except one, who died early, distinguished themselves and seven were drawn to the East.

In 1834, the British Government, in order to confront the threat of Russian influence in the Middle East, and to explore the feasibility of a river and land route to India, launched an expedition up the Euphrates, consisting of two steam vessels. No fewer than five of the Lynch brothers were involved. The most important was Lieutenant Henry Blosse-Lynch (1807-1873) who commanded one of the ships – *The Tigris* – and was second-in-command of the expedition. On board was Captain Robert Blosse-Lynch, Indian Army, who was unfortunately drowned when *The Tigris* sank in a hurricane in 1836.

A second expedition involving three steam vessels, the property of The East India Company, followed. One of them was commanded by another brother, Lieutenant William Michael Lynch (1811-1841); he was joined by two more brothers, Dr. George Quested Lynch (1814-1848),[4] the medical officer, and Thomas Kerr Lynch (1818-1891), recently graduated from Trinity College, Dublin. In the event, the route to India was abandoned, but the vessels remained in use under Henry Blosse-Lynch's command, by now resident in Baghdad and also responsible for the postal service. Above all, he recognized the commercial viability of river navigation and with his brother, Thomas Kerr Lynch and Stephen Lynch (1820-1896) founded Lynch Brothers in 1841, an enterprise which brought imported goods by fast clipper from England to Basra from where they were sent up

[4] Died of typhus when treating victims of the Irish potato famine.

river on convoys of rafts. Finally, in 1861, under the protection of the British Government, the Euphrates and Tigris Steam Navigation Company was founded, in which the brothers acquired the four steamers owned by the now defunct East India Company, and with them created a highly lucrative business, which survived until after the end of the second World War.

At the time of the Euphrates expeditions, there lived at Baghdad Colonel Robert Taylor, the East India Company's representative who was closely linked with what was going on. The Colonel was plainly out of the ordinary. "He keeps a capital table and lives in fine style: he has some good horses, an ostrich, a lion and a leopard," noted one observer. Others commented on his fine collections of Arabic and Persian manuscripts and on his bizarre style of dress.[5] He had an Armenian wife, born of a merchant family in Shiraz, and two charming daughters. The eldest, Caroline Ann, married Henry Blosse Lynch, by this time a captain in the Indian navy. The youngest, Harriet, married Thomas Kerr Lynch; their only son, Henry Finnis Blosse Lynch, the subject of this piece, was born into this exotic background in London on 18th April 1862.

Young Harry was sent to Eton College, the first member of his family to go there. The College records contain no mention of any sporting or academic achievements. However, at Trinity College, Cambridge, he held high office in the Union, played polo for the University and obtained a first class honours degree in Classics. He joined the Inner Temple and was called to the Bar, but never practised in law. He spent two years at Heidelberg studying classical philosophy. But as the only son of a father who was a Persian and Arabic scholar, chairman of the family firm and Consul General for Persia in London from 1869-75, and of a mother who was half Armenian, it was always likely that he would be drawn to the East. And so it proved.

Having now become a partner in the family firm, he set out on horseback from Alexandretta via Aleppo to Diyarbakir and then floated down the Tigris by raft to Baghdad. He followed this by inaugurating, on behalf of the firm, a river service under the British flag along the Karun river to the Caspian Sea, and then set about the

---

[5] See John S. Guest, *The Euphrates Expedition* (London, New York: K. Paul International, 1992), p.123

survey of a new trade route from that river to Isfahan. On his return home, he contributed an account of these experiences to the records of the Royal Geographical Society. And then, on his father's death in 1891, he became vice-chairman of the family firm, plainly a thriving concern.

The next decade is dominated by the two expeditions to Armenia, which together provided the material for his book. But between these expeditions, he had begun to contribute to the political debate by a series of articles in the *Contemporary Review* in which he discussed the plight of the Armenian nation and expressed his concerns about Russian expansion in that area. He also arranged his father's memoirs to be published privately. On the death of his uncle Stephen in 1896 he became chairman of the family firm. And in February 1898, he was elected to membership of the Athenaeum Club. In his certificate of candidature, he described himself as a barrister and a contributor to proceedings of the Royal Geographical Society without mention of his chairmanship of the family business! But what is of particular interest are the names of his supporters, which indicates his association with those who were involved at a high level with the Eastern question. For the list includes Lord Curzon, about to depart as Viceroy of India, whose views as expressed in "Persia and the Persian Question," (London 1892), Lynch cites with approval in his book. There is also Douglas Freshfield, the mountaineer and authority on the Caucasus and James Bryce, the Liberal politician who was the first Briton to scale Ararat, the founder of the Anglo-Armenian association, and the advocate of Christian government in Armenia. Also of interest, as an indication of the circles in which Lynch moved, are the eminent composers, Sir Hubert Parry and Sir Charles Villiers Stanford.

In 1901, Lynch was approaching 40. He had started to take an interest in political affairs at home and was actively involved in Toynbee Hall, an institution that provided education for the London poor, echoing his interest in the education of Armenian children. He enjoyed the life of a man-about-town, keeping his London home at 44 Pont Street, South Kensington; but, he also became a country gentleman, resident at Wardington Manor in Oxfordshire and a vice-president of the Banbury Agricultural Society. In that year, his career was marked by two defining achievements. The first was the publication of his book; the second the opening of the 270-mile caravan route which he had helped to survey across the Bahktiari region, and which had been constructed, complete with steel suspension bridges, by his firm. But it was time to move on and he decided to launch himself on a political career.

Years earlier, Lynch had served, as a weekend soldier, in the West Yorkshire Yeomanry and had attended the school for auxiliary cavalry in Aldershot. This may explain his outstanding horsemanship in Armenia and his interest in local military activities. But it also led to friendships being made in Yorkshire; these friends suggested that he should offer himself as the Liberal candidate for the traditionally Conservative constituency of Ripon. The Liberal Party was the obvious choice for Lynch as it supported, through James Bryce, substantial autonomy for Armenia, and its other policies, such as Home Rule for another oppressed race, the Irish, free trade, educational and social reform and the relief of poverty all naturally appealed to Lynch. So, accordingly, he was nominated and, exchanging the crags and deserts of the East for the green hills and dales of Northern England, he set about vigorously to climb a political mountain.

The political mood of the country was swinging towards the Liberals in the years preceding the general election of January 1906. This undoubtedly helped Lynch. The south of the constituency was dominated by the large, urban middle-class town of Harrogate, but the remainder was more isolated, consisting of some 90 villages, the country town of Knaresborough and the small and ancient city of Ripon. In the three years before the election, he concentrated on the rural areas, visiting each village several times over and winning the trust of the farm labourers, small holders and artisans. According to *The Ripon Gazette*, which it must be admitted, was strongly pro-Liberal, he won over some of the opposition as well: 'his command of the great questions of the moment are masterly, and are received with enthusiasm. Conservatives changed party to vote for him.' His efforts bore fruit and in the general election of 1906 he was returned as the Liberal Member of Parliament for Ripon by 300 votes.

It is difficult to form a view about Lynch's performance as a Member of Parliament. He was subsequently described as an ornate and attractive speaker, listened to with respect when the House discussed Middle Eastern questions.[6] A trawl through Hansard reveals that, except on one occasion, his interventions were principally concerned with the problems in Macedonia, Russia and its designs on Persia, Turkish atrocities against Armenians in Van, and the opium trade in China. He always had the facts at his fingertips, causing the Foreign Secretary, Sir Edward Grey, to concede on one occasion that Lynch knew more about the subject than he did. The single exception came about when he complained about the police handling of a crowd problem during a Royal procession near Oxford Circus. The injured party was plainly Lynch himself and he was promptly put down by the Home Secretary who told him that no one else had complained and that the police were doing their best. But Lynch was plainly not doing his best as far as his constituents were concerned. On no occasion did he raise matters in Parliament concerning their interests and he was rarely seen in the constituency. It looks as if he were using Parliament largely as a platform to air his views on the Eastern question, where, of course, he had important trading interests to protect. He had a precariously small majority, and when the next general election came in January 1910, the voters forsook the election cry of "Never Flinch, Vote for Lynch" in large numbers and he was badly beaten by his Conservative opponent, the Hon. Edward Wood, who, some 28 years later as Lord Halifax, was the British Foreign Secretary during the Munich crisis. Lynch never returned to Ripon, but in the second general election of 1910, he stood as Liberal candidate for the City of Gloucester, and had the disappointment of losing again, this time by four votes.[7]

---

[6] In this and other aspects of his political life, see *The Times* obituary, 26th November 1913.

[7] The *Ripon Gazette* is the source for his activities as an Member of Parliament (MP) in the constituency.

Bibliography and Sources

Athenaeum Club archives and library
Blosse-Lynch family papers
Dictionary of National Biography (first and second editions)
Eton College Register
Hansard: Parliamentary Reports (1906 – 1910).

Lynch, by this time a bachelor of nearly 50, never returned to Parliamentary politics and for the last three years before his untimely death, together with his business activities he concentrated on articles, lectures and speeches. He remained a severe critic of Government policy in the East and was an active member of the Persian Committee. In challenging on the Government, he occasioned considerable friction; and as his obituary in *The Times* went: 'with all his suavity of manner, he could attain a high pitch of indignation in his public references to Middle Eastern policy and did not always weigh his words with care.' The events of 1915 would of course justify his indignation but, sadly, by then, he was no longer alive, dying of pneumonia in a Calais hotel on the November 24, 1913. He is buried in the town and is therefore one of the very few members of the Blosse Lynch family not to be buried in the family burial place at Partry.

What, then, was Henry Lynch like as a person? And what did he look like? *The Ripon Gazette* carries a photograph of him during his election campaign in 1910. He appears, clad in an immaculately tailored tweed suit, as a man of medium build with dark hair, a dark bushy moustache and dark in complexion with neat, regular features. He is in every way an Edwardian gentleman. But what was he like as a person? We know nothing of his private life, but he comes across as a clubbable and genial person, intrepid and brave both in facing physical challenge and in putting forward what he believed in. He was clearly able to establish a rapport with both Armenian peasant and Yorkshire farm labourer and had a keen sense of justice for the marginalised and oppressed. He was also an innovative and impressive businessman. We can surely forgive him for occasional

---

Lynch, HFB: *The Armenian Question: Contemporary Review* (London 1894 and 1896), *Armenian Travels & Studies* (London, 1901), *The Ascent of Mount Ararat in Mountain Climbing* (London, 1897).

Across Luristan to Isfahan in Vol. III, Royal Geographical Society of London (1890).

Oharian-Achdjian: Lynch, sa vie, son oeuvre in *Fragment d'un Discours D'Armenie* (Paris, 1990). (n.b. this has many factual inaccuracies).

The Ripon Gazette (1906–1910).

Who was Who (1897–1916).

bouts of pedantry and self-importance. His connection with two leading composers of the day and his skills as a photographer suggest an artistically creative side to his nature. But a nickname is often a very good guide. And Lynch had a nickname. In the first volume of *Armenia: Travel and Studies* that Lynch presented to the Athenaeum, there is a letter placed there by a friend of his, George Leveson Gower, some ten years after Lynch's death. It reads in part: 'The author (an intimate friend of mine) was much assisted in the later stages of the production of this work by one who was, and in my case still is, an intimate friend of us both, Mr. Leonard Shoobridge, who is also a member of this club, as was the late Mr. Lynch.

It will be observed that in the gilt decorative band representing various animals that ornaments the outside of the binding, a squirrel and a dormouse are depicted. These were affectionate nicknames given to each other by Mr. Lynch and Mr. Shoobridge, the former being known as the Squirrel and the latter as the Dormouse. Mr. Lynch wished to commemorate this affection by introducing these two figures into the design, which otherwise is a reproduction of a frieze outside one of the old ruined churches of Armenia.

A squirrel, of course, is bright-eyed and bushy-tailed, cheerful and busy, climbs high and stores nuts like knowledge. Such was Harry Lynch.

His greatest achievements were surely his book and his success as chairman of the family firm, which was handling a million pounds worth of trade a year by 1900. His least satisfactory venture was surely as a Member of Parliament. His speeches on the Eastern Question were heard with respect but not heeded: in those circumstances it is only too likely that the speaker might not always weigh his words with care. And, of course, he lost his seat. But Lynch was miscast as the representative of a rural constituency in the north of England. His true constituency lay between Erzerum and Yerevan, and had he lived, there can be no doubt that the massacres of 1915 and the upheavals which followed the dismemberment of the Ottoman Empire would have been brought fully to the attention of the West. The decline in the fortunes of the Liberal party meant that he would never have returned to Parliament, but, with his predictions vindicated, it is highly likely that one who was described in *The Times* obituary column as "the well-known authority on

Eastern questions" would have played an important role as a diplomat, or in an advisory capacity at the Foreign Office.

The remarkable family from which he sprang has continued to do what it always did best: business, adventure, public life and soldiering. In spite of the vicissitudes of two world wars, it was not until the end of the second that the family firm finally had to give way to a changing world and was wound up. Partry remained in the family until recently. And without the help of Major Henry Blosse-Lynch, formerly of the Irish Guards, the present head of the family, whose grandfather climbed Mt. Ararat with Harry Lynch a century and more ago, some of this could not have been written.

The Emotions of Genocide: Revisiting Morgenthau's Account of the Armenian Genocide

Ronald Grigor Suny

I have never been interested in discussing whether there was a genocide in Ottoman Anatolia during World War I. Once acquainted with the overwhelming evidence of deportations and mass murder of a designated ethno-religious group, planned, initiated, and carried out by the Young Turk authorities, I was convinced that no serious investigator can doubt that, by any conventional definition, genocide had occurred. I have also been less interested in the "what" or "how" of genocide, the methods by which the Ottomans in power dealt with their Armenian subjects, except in so far as those methods illuminated the "why" and "when" of genocide. My own research in the historiographical literature and the available evidence in languages that I read – English, French, Armenian, Russian, Georgian, Italian, and German (not Turkish, regrettably) – has been directed toward the causal explanations provided by historians, whether social environmental, political strategic, or, more recently in my own work, psychological. In three different papers at various times in my intellectual evolution, I have tried each of these modes of explanation.[1] Here I am presenting the third, based on a theory of

---

[1] For my version of a social environmental analysis, see Ronald Grigor Suny, "Rethinking the Unthinkable: Toward an Understanding of the Armenian Genocide," in Suny, *Looking Toward Ararat: Armenia in Modern History* (Bloomington and Indianapolis: Indiana University Press, 1983), pp. 94-115. For my version of a strategic political explanation, see "Religion, Ethnicity, and Nationalism: Armenians, Turks, and the End of the Ottoman Empire," in Omer Bartov and Phyllis Mack, eds., *In God's Name: Genocide and Religion in the Twentieth Century* (New York and Oxford: Berghahn Books, 2001), pp. 23-61.

how emotions operate in history, while linking that explanation to the earlier two.

Surprisingly, the existing literature has either avoided explanations of the causes of the Genocide or implied an explanation even while not systematically or explicitly elaborating one. For deniers of genocide there is simply no need to explain an event that did not occur as stipulated by those who claim it did. What did occur, in their view, was a reasonable and understandable response of a government to a rebellious and seditious population in a time of war and mortal danger to the state's survival. *Raison d'état* justified the suppression of rebellion, and mass killing is explained as the unfortunate residue ("collateral damage" in the now fashionable vocabulary) of legitimate efforts at establishing order behind the lines.

Equally disturbing is the avoidance (frequently by Armenian authors) of any explanation for why the Young Turks embarked on this destructive and vicious policy. Fearing that explanation of the causes for Turkish action may be seen as justification for their policies, many authors have relied on essentialized notions of how Turks customarily act. It is the essential nature of Turks that leads to the systematic killing of Armenians during World War I. No further explanation is required.

Neither denial of such extensively documented events nor avoidance of causal explanation is acceptable for historical scholarship. Arguments for the Genocide have generally circled around two poles: nationalism and religion, sometimes combining the two. Consider, for example, the recent popular work of Peter Balakian, which, among others, is exemplary (in the second and third meanings of that word given in the *Webster New World Dictionary* – not "serving as a model…worth imitating," but "serving as a warning or deterrent" and as "serving as a sample," "typical") – of a narrative without any sustained explanation of why genocide happened.[2]

---

[2] After praising Balakian's *The Burning Tigris: The Armenian Genocide and America's Response* (New York: Harper Collins, 2003), the reviewer, Belinda Cooper, expressed her disappointment that "Balakian fails to weave the various strands of his account – the genocide, the relief efforts and the wider issue of why the great powers failed to intervene – into a consistent historical or analytical framework. Instead, he presents a disorganized, largely descriptive narrative that ultimately raises more questions than it

Balakian's beautifully written account reproduces in evocative detail the horrors of what happened, but only hints at a causal argument. Following the lead of Vahakn Dadrian in his *Warrant for Genocide*, who made a similar argument some years ago, Balakian sees mass killing as a product of religion – the deep antagonism of Islam toward Christianity – and he refers to the proclamation of *jihad* by the Ottoman Sheik ul-Islam and its influence on officers and ordinary people who carried out the killings. Why religion should have led to genocidal violence at this time and not throughout Ottoman and Islamic history, when the two religious communities managed to coexist for centuries without mass killing is not explained.

There are two principal questions that need answering: why the Young Turk leaders embarked on a policy of destruction of a people within their empire; and why ordinary people participated in this program of mass murder. For the second question – why people carried out the crime – *jihad* would be an independent variable and part of the explanation for mass killing. For the first question – why did the Committee for Union and Progress decide to deport and kill the Armenians – the proclamation of *jihad* would be part of the policy that needs to be explained. It is here a dependent variable.

In this chapter I would like to take a fresh look at a major text – Ambassador Henry Morgenthau's memoir – that in many ways combines the best and the worst in trying to explain the nearly inexplicable. Morgenthau employs both religion and nationalism, as well as attendant emotions, in his explanation. At the base of the arguments from nationalism are both cold, calculating strategic choices by leaders, as well as emotional impulses on the part of the leaders and responses from the population. Religious explanations gravitate more to the affective side of motivations, emotions aroused by faith, solidarity with your own community, and alienation from infidels. The ambassador provides both strategic and emotion

---

answers. His main story, the genocide itself, is an unremitting depiction of irrational barbarism by sociopathic Turkish leaders and a fanatical population against a generally unresisting minority." And then she speaks to the fears of many that explanation can be seen as justification: "Attention to the complexities of causation and context in no way reduces the evil of the genocide or the culpability of the perpetrators." (*The New York Times Book Review*, October 19, 2003) motivations of the major initiators of the Genocide, as well as his own interpretation of the motives of the ordinary perpetrators of the killings.

In the absence of an abundance of archival documents on Young Turk decision-making in 1914-1915, the memoir of the American ambassador to Constantinople, Henry Morgenthau, has taken on exceptional importance. For Genocide scholar Roger W. Smith, "It is the classic, contemporary account of the first large-scale genocide of the twentieth century."[3] For Holocaust scholar Robert Jay Lifton, Morgenthau's account is a unique and remarkable source because of its view of genocide from the top." "I do not know of any other example of a critical outsider who had regular access to the highest-ranking planners and perpetrators of genocide, even as it was taking place."[4] The narrative presented by Morgenthau was considered devastating enough for one of the professional deniers of the Genocide, Dr. Heath Lowry, now the Mustafa Kemal Atatürk Professor of Ottoman and Modern Turkish Studies at Princeton University, to issue a small book that attempted to undermine the authenticity and veracity of the ambassador's witness.[5] We now have a published edition of the original diaries, which provides the record of Morgenthau's original observations.[6] While the diary offers more details, there are no significant divergences between the diary itself and the memoir.

---

[3] Roger W. Smith, "Introduction," in Henry Morgenthau, *Ambassador Morgenthau's Story* (Detroit: Wayne State University Press, 2003), p. xxv. The original publication (New York: Doubleday, Page & Co., 1918) has been followed by successive reissues, among them one published by the Gomidas Institute in Princeton, NJ (2000), with an introduction by Ara Sarafian. All references in this essay are to the 2003 Wayne State University Press edition.

[4] Ibid., p. xxi.

[5] Heath Lowry, *The Story Behind Ambassador Morgenthau's Story* (Istanbul: Isis Press, 1990). See also the website "Tall Armenian Tale" (http://www.tallarmeniantale.com/morgenthau.htm).

[6] Henry Morgenthau, *United States Diplomacy on the Bosphorus: The Diaries of Ambassador Morgenthau, 1913-1916*, compiled with an introduction by Ara Sarafian (Princeton and London: Gomidas Institute, 2004). See also, *United States Official Records on the Armenian Genocide1915-1917*, compiled with an introduction by Ara Sarafian (Princeton and London: Gomidas Institute, 2004).

First, the provenance of the book should be noted. Based on his diaries, now preserved at the Franklin Delano Roosevelt library at Hyde Park, New York, Morgenthau's memoir was written up in the last year of World War I, a time of intense passion about the enemies of the Allied powers. In answer to an inquiry by Morgenthau about his plans to publish a book, President Wilson wrote on November 27, 1917, to encourage him to write up his "full exposition of some of the principal lines of German intrigue."[7] In his preface to the work, dated a month before the armistice, Morgenthau goes as far as to begin: "By this time the American people have probably become convinced that the Germans deliberately planned the conquest of the world," which he labels "the greatest crime in modern history."[8] The book was a product of its time. While hardly the propaganda piece that his critics have claimed, the memoir reveals a mind and an experience of its own time, with unguarded expression of the kind of essentialist views of national character that determined the understanding of human motivation in those years. Rather than avoiding or being embarrassed by Morgenthau's attitudes, a sensitive reader should attempt to understand how prejudices and perceptions shaped his (and others') emotional and cognitive responses in the Ottoman drama of 1914-1916. The ambassador reveals himself as a keen observer privileged in his access to power, judicious in his evaluations of both the political context and the key players, and highly ethical and fearless in his defense of his government and his own values, but he also speaks as the representative of a Christian power that at the time of publication was at war with Germany, an ally of the Ottomans.

The book is today read largely for its account of the Armenian Genocide, but it is principally concerned with Germany's role in the war, the intrigues of the German ambassador in Constantinople, Baron Von Wangenheim, and German influence on the Young Turk leaders. There is an attempt, one that in my opinion ultimately fails, to link the Germans to the Armenian Genocide. Morgenthau frames his story with the larger global ambitions of German imperialism personified by the imposing figure of Wangenheim. Prussian in

---

[7] Henry Morgenthau III, "Epilogue: the Rest of the Story," in Morgenthau, *Ambassador Morgenthau's Story*, p. 296.

[8] Morgenthau, *Ambassador Morgenthau's Story*, p. xxxix.

character if not by birth, dedicated to his "aristocratic and autocratic" homeland, Wangenheim was key to the German-Ottoman alliance that balanced against the Franco-Russian entente. In Morgenthau's view, he was the perfect instrument to deal with the Young Turks, who "had disappeared as a positive regenerating force" and by 1913 existed only "as a political machine" akin to the big city bosses of the United States.[9]

Morgenthau believed that the driving motivation of Talaat, Enver, and Djemal was no longer reform but "an insatiable lust for personal power."[10] Real power in Turkey was not in the state, but in the Committee of Union and Progress, the forty-man executive dominated by Talaat Bey. The triumvirate had achieved full power in the bloody coup d'état of January 26, 1913. Morgenthau achieved an extraordinary intimacy with Enver and Talaat, not only dining with them, riding together in the Belgrade forest, but at the same time confronting them with naïve frankness about his objections to their policies. His subtle, rounded portraits of these men betray both fascination with them as persons and abhorrence at their deeds. He probed their psychology in a vain attempt to comprehend their actions.

The hulking figure of Talaat, broad backed, with iron grip, was particularly intriguing to Morgenthau. Rising from humble origins, beginning as a mailman and later a telegraph operator, Talaat was not an ethnic Turk and was uninspired by Islam or any religion. "I hate all priests, rabbis, and hodjas," he told Morgenthau.[11] By the time the ambassador befriended him, Talaat had become disillusioned about the possibility of reform in the Ottoman Empire. "I have been greatly disappointed at the failure of the Turks to appreciate democratic institutions. I hoped for it once, and I worked hard for it – but they were not prepared for it."[12] Talaat, like all the Turkish leaders – according to Morgenthau – was motivated primarily by fear, most particularly, fear of Russia, the most serious threat to the empire's territorial integrity. "This fear of Russia, I

---

[9] Ibid., p. 10.
[10] Ibid.
[11] Ibid., p. 14.
[12] Ibid., p. 16.

cannot too much insist, was the one factor which, above everything else, was forcing Turkey into the arms of Germany."[13]

Morgenthau carefully distinguishes Enver from Talaat. A more diminutive figure, he was suave, elegant, audacious, and fond of luxury, in contrast to the plain living Talaat. Enver was Germany's principal supporter in Istanbul, and once he became Minister of War in January 1914, he helped pave the way for the empire to ally itself with the Germans.

The third member of the triumvirate, Djemal Pasha, was a sincere Pan-Turkist. "He despises the subject peoples of the Ottoman country – Arabs, Greeks, Armenians, Circassians, Jews; it was his determination to Russify the whole empire."[14]

In characterizing both the Germans and the Turks, Morgenthau depends on the familiar catalogue of national stereotypes. If the Germans are the cool, calculating men driven by *realpolitik*, the Turks are driven by emotions, most particularly fear, "the only emotion which really actuates the Turk." "The descendants of Osman hardly resemble any people I have ever known. They do not hate, they do not love; they have no lasting animosities or affections. They only fear. And naturally they attribute to others the motives which regulate their own conduct."[15] That fear was understandable, given the precarious position of the empire in the deadly power struggle in Europe and the internal instability of the country. The Turks especially felt threatened by Russia, a sense of danger that could easily be transferred to the Armenians perceived as internal enemies allied with that rapacious foreign power. The Germans played on these Turkish fears, and for the Young Turk leaders, particularly Enver, the German alliance was the only salvation for the empire.

A theme throughout the memoir is the manipulation of the Turks by the Germans. Morgenthau credits the Turks with an instinctive sense of survival but the Germans with strategic vision. It was the Germans who suggested to the Turks that the Anatolian Greeks living on the Aegean littoral be "moved from the seashore" for

---

[13] Ibid., p. 18.
[14] Ibid., p. 121.
[15] Ibid., p. 69.

military reasons.[16] In anticipation of the war to come, the government ordered the removal of more than one hundred thousand Greeks from the Mediterranean littoral to the Greek islands or the interior of Anatolia. These actions, Morgenthau reports, "were bona-fide deportations; that is, the Greek inhabitants were actually removed to new places and were not subjected to wholesale massacre."[17] Later, in early 1915, after the Ottoman government entered the war, Greeks in Thrace, along the Sea of Marmara, the Dardanelles, the Bosphorus, and the Black Sea coast, numbering several hundreds of thousands, were deported to the interior of Anatolia, but again they were not "subject to general massacre as were the Armenians."[18] Morgenthau's convincing explanation is that Istanbul did not want to antagonize the Greek government, then neutral and ruled by a pro-German king, by attacking its compatriots. The Greek deportations, then, were primarily strategic, a prophylactic measure in preparation for war, not unlike the actions taken toward foreign subjects in Istanbul and Jews in Palestine.

The Ottoman government was divided about the German alliance and the war. Talaat was not convinced that war was the best policy for the empire, and he told Morgenthau in late October 1914, that Turkey would join the war on Germany's side because he was convinced that Germany would win and take revenge on the Turks if they did not help.[19] "He analyzed the whole situation most dispassionately; he said that nations could not afford such emotions as gratitude, or hate, or affection; the only guide to action should be cold-blooded policy." "Russia is our greatest enemy," he continued, "and we are afraid of her. If now, while Germany is attacking Russia, we can give her a good strong kick, and so make her powerless to injure us for some time, it is Turkey's duty to administer that kick!"[20] Here Talaat's own realistic and strategic sense was paramount. That very evening "Turkish" ships, manned by Germans and perhaps without the full knowledge of the Young Turk leaders, attacked the Russian ship *Donets* in Odessa harbor, sank the French ship *Portugal*, and shelled the city. The Germans

---

[16] Ibid., p. 34.
[17] Ibid., p. 222.
[18] Ibid., p. 223.
[19] Ibid., pp. 85-86.
[20] Ibid., p. 87.

thus provoked Russia to declare war on the Ottoman Empire. Talaat seemed resigned: "Well, Wangenheim, Enver, and I prefer that war should come now."[21] The four non-ethnic Turks in the cabinet resigned in protest, among them the Armenian Oskan Effendi.

The Germans were also responsible for the closing of the Dardanelles, Ottoman policy toward the subjects of the Allied powers in Istanbul, and the policy of *jihad.* Wangenheim explained to Morgenthau the German strategy "to arouse the whole fanatical Moslem world against the Christians. Germany had planned a real 'holy war' as one means of destroying English and French influence in the world." "If we can stir the Mohammedans up against the English and Russians, we can force them to make peace."[22]

On November 13, 1914, the Sultan declared war, and the Sheik ul-Islam proclaimed a holy war against Russia, England, France, and their allies.

What about nationalism? Morgenthau reports that he observed no popular enthusiasm for the European war.[23] Patriotism, he repeats several times, was alien to "the Turk." [Note that he often uses "the Turk" in the singular to describe Turkish attitudes, mentalities, and emotions, further homogenizing, naturalizing, and essentializing nationality.] There was support for a war against Greece to win back the Aegean islands, and ordinary Turks subscribed to a fund to buy battleships from Britain to strengthen the Ottoman navy.[24] "The Turkish people have "little spontaneous patriotism," writes Morgenthau, "or any enthusiasm of any kind."[25]

The line between repelling foreign invasion and dealing with internal enemies was a very thin one in the minds of the Young Turk leaders. Morgenthau paraphrased Talaat's argument to him: "[T]hese different *blocs* in the Turkish Empire…had always conspired against Turkey; because of the hostility of these native populations, Turkey had lost province after province – Greece, Serbia, Rumania, Bulgaria, Bosnia, Herzegovina, Egypt, and Tripoli. In this way, the Turkish Empire had dwindled almost to the vanishing point. If what was left of Turkey was to survive,… he

---

[21] Ibid., p. 88.
[22] Ibid., pp. 111-112.
[23] Ibid., p. 43.
[24] Ibid., p. 53.
[25] Ibid., p. 155.

must get rid of these alien people."[26] Morgenthau goes on to interpret Talaat's "controlling idea" as "Turkey for the Turks."[27] It is unclear whether Talaat actually used those words. Indeed, it seems more likely from the text that this is Morgenthau's rendering of Talaat's ideas. Talaat talked about Turkifying Smyrna and the adjoining islands, and it seems that in his mind security was linked to the demographic homogeneity of the empire's borders. Ethnic Turks were simply believed to be more loyal to the regime than Armenians, Greeks, Kurds, Arabs, or even Jews.

Morgenthau was repeatedly appalled by the willingness of the Turks to resort to violence, which he related to their emotional volatility. When Talaat heard that the English had bombarded the Dardanelles and killed two Turks, he exploded to Morgenthau: "We intend to kill three Christians for every Moslem Killed."[28] Measuring Talaat's emotions and waiting for the right moment to make his requests, the ambassador noted "Talaat had shown several moods in this interview; he had been by turns sulky, good-natured, savage, and complaisant. There is one phase of the Turkish character, which Westerners do not comprehend and that is its keen sense of humour. Talaat himself greatly loved a joke and a funny story."[29] The ambassador, who in his own representation was the epitome of decorum, politesse, and civilization, felt that he was able to tame or manipulate the Turkish leader on many, but not all occasions.

For Morgenthau, it appears that violence is inscribed in Islam. He quotes at great length a secret pamphlet that followed the declaration of *jihad.* "Know ye that the blood of infidels in the Islamic lands may be shed with impunity – except those to whom the Moslem power has promised security and are allied with it [i.e., the Germans and Austrians].... The killing of infidels who rule over Islam has become a sacred duty, whether you do it secretly or openly, as the Koran has decreed."[30] The pamphlet mixed religion with anti-colonial nationalism, calling for "Turan for the Turanian Moslems, ... Caucasus for the Caucasian Moslems, and the Ottoman

[26] Ibid., p. 35.
[27] Ibid.
[28] Ibid., p. 100.
[29] Ibid., p. 101.
[30] Ibid., p. 11.

Empire for the Ottoman Turks and Arabs."[31] Morgenthau was convinced that the Germans had inspired this pamphlet, but their strategy in provoking anti-British and French violence through *jihad* "proved a failure."[32] On November 14, mobs attacked several foreign stores in Istanbul – the Bon Marché, an Austrian shop advertising "English clothes" for sale, and the Armenian-owned Tokatlian's, "the most important restaurant in Constantinople."[33] That was the extent of the "Holy War!" While the anti-colonialist uprising never occurred, Morgenthau ominously concludes, "Only one definite result did the Kaiser accomplish by spreading the inciting literature. It aroused in the Mohammedan soul all the intense animosity toward the Christian which is the fundamental fact in his strange, emotional nature, and thus started passions aflame that afterward spent themselves in the massacres of the Armenians and other subject peoples."[34] Emotion here is a kind of fire that consumes what it touches and then spends itself.

Morgenthau's text is replete with indelible characteristics of "the Turk." "Psychologically primitive," the Turk is essentially "a bully and a coward; he is brave as a lion when things are going his way, but cringing, abject, and nerveless when reverses are overwhelming him."[35] The Ottomans reverted in the war years to an older ancestral type: "the basic fact underlying the Turkish mentality is its utter contempt for all other races. A fairly insane pride is the element that largely explains this strange human species. The common term applied by the Turk to the Christian is 'dog,'...; he actually looks upon his European neighbor as far less worthy of consideration than his own domestic animals."[36] Yet there are also positive qualities. Besides a "keen sense of humour," "one of the most conspicuous traits in the Turkish character" is "its tendency to compromise and to bargain."[37] "So far as I can discover," he tells his readers, "the Ottoman Turks had only one great quality, that of military genius." But, less we forget their most essential qualities, Morgenthau goes

---

[31] Ibid.

[32] Ibid., p. 116.

[33] Ibid., p. 117.

[34] Ibid., p. 118.

[35] Ibid., pp. 164, 191.

[36] Ibid., p. 191.

[37] Ibid., pp. 101, 170.

on, "Such graces of civilization as the Turk has acquired in five centuries have practically all been taken from the subject peoples whom he so greatly despises."[38] The "innate attitude of the Moslem Turk to people not of his own race and religion [is] that they are not human beings with rights, but merely chattels, which may be permitted to live when they promote the interest of their masters, but which may be pitilessly destroyed when they have ceased to be useful. This attitude is intensified by a total disregard for human life and an intense delight in inflecting physical human suffering which are not unusually the qualities of primitive peoples."[39] The most primitive qualities of the Turk modified over centuries, but after the failure of the democratic revolution there was "an atavistic reversion to the original Turk."[40]

With the Turkish entry into the war, Djemal went off to Syria to direct the campaign against the British in Egypt and Enver directed the Caucasian front against Russia. Defeat quickly followed, and a general panic gripped Istanbul. It was feared that the city would fall to the Bulgarians who might join the war on the side of the Entente or to the British who were rumored to be about to break through the Dardanelles. Talaat "was the picture of desolation and defeat" in January 1915 as the thunder of the British guns at the straits seemed "to spell doom."[41] "The Turks," Morgenthau reminds us, "like most primitive peoples, wear their emotions on the surface, and with them the transition from exultation to despair is a rapid one."[42] There was fear of revolution in the city, and posters denounced Talaat. The Prefect of Police, Bedri Bey, rounded up unemployed young men and expelled them from the capital. Toward the end of the month Enver returned from the front, unsure of his reception by the public, after the devastating defeat at Sarikamish. The Young Turk leaders planned to burn down the city if the British broke through, a wanton act that shocked Morgenthau. "There are not six men in the Committee of Union and Progress," Talaat told him, "who care for anything that is old. We all like new things."[43]

---

[38] Ibid., pp. 192-193.
[39] Ibid., p. 194.
[40] Ibid., p. 196.
[41] Ibid., p. 135.
[42] Ibid.
[43] Ibid., p. 138.

The mood in Istanbul in the first months of the war needs to be carefully assessed, for many historians believe that it was precisely in this atmosphere that the Committee of Union and Progress took the decision to deal with the Armenians. Morgenthau tells us that the authority of the CUP at this time "throughout the empire was exceedingly tenuous." At the moment when the Allied fleet attacked the Dardanelles on March 18, the Ottoman state "was on the brink of dissolution." "Among the subject races the spirit of revolt was rapidly spreading. The Greeks and the Armenians would also have welcomed an opportunity to strengthen the hands of the Allies."[44] But the Allies did not break through; the Germans and Turks held them off, and the fleet pulled back. A month later the Allies landed troops at Gallipoli in another futile campaign. The Turks responded by rounding up foreigners to use as hostages placed among the Muslim villages in the Gallipoli region. The police even briefly arrested the prominent lawyer and commentator on Ottoman affairs, Sir Edwin Pears, a forty-year resident of the Ottoman capital. The panic subsided once Bulgaria joined the Central Powers, and the Ottomans gained a direct rail line to Germany while Russia's supply lines were cut off once the Allies withdrew from the Straits.[45]

Morgenthau elaborates a number of causes for the deportations and massacres of the Armenians, many of which have been foundational for Western and Armenian historiography of the Genocide. He begins with the nationalist perspective that the Young Turks were committed to a Turkified empire and adopted the policy of Abdul Hamid. "Their passion for Turkifying the nation seemed to demand logically the extermination of all Christians – Greeks, Syrians, and Armenians."[46] The error of past Muslim conquerors had been that they had not obliterated the Christians, "a fatal error of statesmanship" that "explained all the woes from which Turkey has suffered in modern times."[47] The war presented an opportunity, for Russia, France, and Britain could no longer stand in the way as they had during Abdul Hamid's reign. "Thus, for the first time in two centuries the Turks, in 1915, had their Christian populations utterly

---

[44] Ibid., p. 158.
[45] Ibid., pp. 176, 190-191.
[46] Ibid., p. 200.
[47] Ibid.

at their mercy. The time had finally come to make Turkey exclusively the country of the Turks."[48]

The Armenians, in Morgenthau's account, are innocent. While the fact "that the Armenians all over Turkey sympathized with the Entente was no secret," the Armenians acted with restraint. Their leaders urged them not to be provoked.[49] Rather than being primarily a matter of religious difference or conflict, the decision to carry out the deportations and massacres was a strategic choice. "Undoubtedly religious fanaticism was an impelling motive with the Turkish and Kurdish rabble who slew Armenians as a service to Allah, but the men who really conceived the crime had no such motive. Practically all of them were atheists, with no more respect for Mohammedanism than for Christianity, and with them the one motive was cold-blooded, calculating state policy."[50] In a sense they had become Germans.

Already in January and February 1915, "fragmentary reports began to filter in" to the American Embassy of killings of Armenians, "but the tendency was at first to regard these activities as mere manifestations of the disorders that had prevailed in the Armenian provinces for many years."[51] Talaat and Enver dismissed such reports "as wild exaggerations."[52] What the Armenians would later call "the defense of Van" was declared by officials "a mob uprising that they would soon have under control."[53] When prominent Armenians in the capital were arrested and Morgenthau broke the issue up to Talaat, the Young Turk leader said that the government was acting in self-defense, that the Armenians in Van "had already shown their abilities as revolutionists," and that Armenian leaders in Istanbul "were corresponding with the Russians, and he had every reason to fear that they would start an insurrection against the Central Government."[54]

Yet inseparable from their cool strategic calculation was the emotionally generated preference for the ends anticipated and the

---

[48] Ibid., p. 201.
[49] Ibid., pp. 203-204.
[50] Ibid., pp. 221-222.
[51] Ibid., p. 224.
[52] Ibid.
[53] Ibid.
[54] Ibid.

appropriate means to be used to achieve them. Talaat "went from one emotion to another as lightly as a child; I would find him fierce and unyielding one day, and uproariously good-natured and accommodating the next,"[55] When Morgenthau reported to Talaat that Armenians had been killed in Konya, Talaat asked, "Are *they* Americans?" "They are not to be trusted," he went on, "besides, what we do with them does not concern the United States." "As to your Armenians, we don't give a rap for the future! We live only in the present!"[56] He repeatedly asked for money earmarked by Americans for Armenian relief to be given to the Turks, who also needed aid "as badly as they do."[57] He requested that the insurance premiums due to Armenians from American companies be paid to the Turks, since the Armenians no longer had any need for them.[58]

Talaat explained to Morgenthau his reasoning for the Young Turks' treatment of the Armenians:

> These people…refused to disarm when we told them to. They opposed us at Van and at Zeitoun, and they helped the Russians. There is only one way in which we can defend ourselves against them in the future, and that is just to deport them.[59]

When Morgenthau protested that that was not a reason for "destroying a whole race" or "making innocent women and children suffer," Talaat simply added, "Those things are inevitable."[60] In a later, extended conversation – this one without Morgenthau's Armenian dragoman present – Talaat spoke most frankly:

> I have asked you to come today…so that I can explain our position on the whole Armenian subject. We base our objections to the Armenians on three distinct grounds. In the first place, they have enriched themselves at the expense of the Turks. In the second place, they are determined to domineer over us and to establish a separate state. In the third place, they have openly encouraged our enemies. They have assisted the Russians

[55] Ibid., p. 228.
[56] Ibid., p. 227.
[57] Ibid., p. 228.
[58] Ibid., p. 233.
[59] Ibid., p. 230.
[60] Ibid.

> in the Caucasus and our failure there is largely explained by their actions. We have therefore come to the irrevocable decision that we shall make them powerless before this war is ended.[61]

When Morgenthau attempted point by point to refute Talaat's argument, Talaat interrupted, "It is no use for you to argue,... we have already disposed of three quarters of the Armenians; there are none at all left in Bitlis, Van, and Erzeroum. The hatred between the Turks and the Armenians is now so intense that we have got to finish with them. If we don't, they will plan their revenge." He told Morgenthau that he had "asked you to come here so as to let you know that our Armenian policy is absolutely fixed and that nothing can change it. We will not have the Armenians anywhere in Anatolia. They can live in the desert but nowhere else."[62] In despair, Morgenthau told Talaat, "You are making a terrible mistake," repeating the phrase three times. "'Yes, we may make mistakes,' he replied, 'but' – and he firmly closed his lips and shook his head – 'we never regret.'"[63] Later he told Morgenthau, "No Armenian...can be our friend after what we have done to them."[64] On August 3, 1915, Morgenthau wrote in his diary of his meeting with Talaat: "He gave me the impression that Talaat is the one who desires to crush the poor Armenians."[65] Talaat reportedly told friends with pride, "I have accomplished more toward solving the Armenian problem in three months than Abdul Hamid accomplished in thirty years."[66]

As more and more evidence came into the American embassy that Armenians were being deported and murdered, Morgenthau requested a meeting with Enver, who was extraordinarily frank about what was happening:

> The Armenians had a fair warning...of what would happen to them in case they joined our enemies. Three months ago I sent for the Armenian Patriarch and I told him that if the Armenians attempted to start a revolution or to assist the Russians, I would be unable to prevent

---

[61] Ibid., p. 231.
[62] Ibid., p.232.
[63] Ibid.
[64] Ibid., p. 233.
[65] Ibid., p. 229.
[66] Ibid., p. 234.

> mischief from happening to them. My warning produced no effect and the Armenians started a revolution and helped the Russians. You know what happened at Van. They obtained control of the city, used bombs against government buildings, and killed a large number of Moslems. We knew that they were planning uprisings in other places. You must understand that we are now fighting for our lives at the Dardanelles and that we are sacrificing thousands of men. While we are engaged in such a struggle as this, we cannot permit people in our own country to attack us in the back. We have got to prevent this no matter what means we have to resort to. It is absolutely true that I am not opposed to the Armenians as a people. I have the greatest admiration for their intelligence and industry, and I would like nothing better than to see them become a real part of our nation. But if they ally themselves with our enemies, as they did in the Van district, they will have to be destroyed. I have taken pains to see that no injustice is done…[67]

Enver argued that European sympathy only encouraged the Armenians:

> I am sure that if these outside countries did not encourage them, they would give up their efforts to oppose the present government and become law-abiding citizens. We now have this country in our absolute control and we can easily revenge ourselves on any revolutionists.... The great trouble with the Armenians is that they are separatists. They are determined to have a kingdom of their own, and they have allowed themselves to be fooled by the Russians.... You must remember that when we started this revolution in Turkey there were only two hundred of us.... It is our experience with revolutions which makes us fear the Armenians. If two hundred Turks could overturn the Government, then a few hundred bright, educated Armenians could do the same thing. We have therefore deliberately adopted the plan of scattering them so that they can do us no harm.[68]

---

[67] Ibid., pp. 236.
[68] Ibid., pp. 236-238.

Morgenthau went on:

> In another talk with Enver I began by suggesting that the Central Government was probably not to blame for the massacres. I thought this would not be displeasing to him.
>
> "Of course. I know that the Cabinet would never order such terrible things as have taken place," I said. "You and Talaat and the rest of the Committee can hardly be held responsible. Undoubtedly your subordinates have gone much further than you have ever intended. I realize that it is not always easy to control your underlings."
>
> Enver straightened up at once. I saw that my remarks, far from smoothing the way to a quiet and friendly discussion, had greatly offended him. I had intimated that things could happen in Turkey for which he and his associates were not responsible.
>
> "You are greatly mistaken," he said. "We have this country absolutely under our control. I have no desire to shift the blame on to our underlings and I am entirely willing to accept the responsibility myself for everything that has taken place. The Cabinet itself has ordered the deportations. I am convinced that we are completely justified in doing this owing to the hostile attitude of the Armenians toward the Ottoman Government, but we are the real rulers of Turkey, and no underling would dare proceed in a matter of this kind without our orders."[69]

Morgenthau noted differences between Talaat and Enver. "Enver always asserted that he wished to treat the Armenians with justice – in this his attitude to me was quite different from that of Talaat, who openly acknowledged his determination to deport them."[70] He reported a conversation with the German naval attaché, Humann, who told the ambassador of Enver's hesitance about the deportation of the Armenians: "At first Enver wanted to treat the Armenians with the utmost moderation, and four months ago he insisted that they be given another opportunity to demonstrate their loyalty. But after what they did at Van, he had to yield to the army, which had been insisting all along that it should protect its rear. The

---

[69] Ibid., pp. 240-241.
[70] Ibid., p. 240.

Committee decided upon the deportations and Enver reluctantly agreed."[71]

But even with these differences, the attitudes toward the Armenians of most of the Young Turk leaders were quite similar. Foreign Minister Halil Bey "regarded the elimination of this race with utmost good humour" and defended the analysis of Enver.[72]

Morgenthau's account gives a compelling interpretation of the motivations of the principal Young Turk leaders. Fear was the driving emotion, insecurity compounded by the defeats in the winter of 1915 and the threats from Allied forces. Armenians were seen as a internal subversive force allied to the Russians. The war presented a unique opportunity to eliminate a long-term existential threat to the empire and the plans of the Young Turks for a more Turkified empire. Reason – strategic advantage – and emotion – fear, a sense of future danger, humiliation at the hands of Armenians, a sense of betrayal – conspired together to generate plans for mass deportation and massacre.

Morgenthau ends the book where he began, with the question of Germany's role in the war and the Armenian massacres. As he examines the German rhetoric and logic of their actions in Belgium, he finds similarities with the Turkish views on the Armenians. He argues that Turks had never deported Christians before, and their actions toward the Armenians were driven by a German idea based in *realpolitik*. To bolster his argument he quotes at length from Friedrich Naumann's *Mittel-Europa* (Berlin, 1915). Naumann (1860-1919) argued that German state interest required friendship with the Ottoman Empire and, consequently, a studied negligence of the Sultan's treatment of the Armenians.[73] Wangenheim reflected this view. He denounced the Armenians for the unprovoked rebellion in Van, considered them traitorous vermin, and declared "I will help the Zionists,... but I shall do nothing whatever for the Armenians."[74] "The Armenians," the German ambassador claimed, "have shown themselves in this war to be enemies of the Turks. It is quite apparent that the two peoples can never live together in the

---

[71] Ibid., p. 258.
[72] Ibid., p. 246.
[73] Ibid., pp. 252-254.
[74] Ibid., p. 254.

same country." Wangenheim sent a formal note of protest to the Porte on July 4, 1915, but refused to intervene further with the Turks. But he insisted to Morgenthau that "Germany is not responsible for this [the Armenian deportations and massacres]. Morgenthau told Wangenheim, "You are a Christian people and the time will come when Germans will realize that you have let a Mohammedan people destroy another Christian nation.... Crimes like these cry to heaven."[75] After Wangenheim's death, his successor, Graf Wolf-Metternich did intervene with Talaat and Enver, an action that his superior Foreign Minister Zimmerman considered a mistake.[76]

Morgenthau sees the German as complicit in the massacres, largely because of their unwillingness to act decisively to stop them, but he does not claim that the Germans ordered the deportations or approved of them. Rather their amoral *realpolitik* led them into this posture of indifference to human suffering. Nowhere does he argue that the Germans initiated or participated in the deportations and massacres.

Social science – at least political science and economics – has in the last decades moved away from affective explanations toward a model of human action directed by rational assessment of costs and benefits. Morgenthau's explanations seem quaint, for they depend on essentialized notions of national character and race and on instinctive emotional responses over which only civilized peoples have some control. Germans stand at the rational pole, while Turks are at the emotional pole. Yet by tacking back and forth between emotions and rationality in his depiction of the Turkish leaders, Morgenthau succeeds in giving us a subtle and convincing picture of their motivations, one that conforms to some of the most recent findings in the psychological literature on emotions and action.

Emotions are central to human beliefs, values, actions, group formation, and social relationships; therefore, must be incorporated into explanations of ethnic and national identification, ethnic, religious, and national conflict and violence. Neuropsychologists have demonstrated the intimate interconnection between decision-making and affect, and that making choices about the future require

[75] Ibid., p. 261.
[76] Ibid., p. 278.

preferences that are connected with the affective apparatus in the brain. There is no rational decision-making without emotion, and emotions, on the other hand, are in large part cognitive and can be understood as heuristics that guide our choices and drive our actions very often toward particular goals.

Among the most salient political emotions related to ethnic identification and conflict, national identity and nationalism are fear, anger, hatred, and resentment, but also, on the positive side, empathy, compassion, love, and pride. In Morgenthau's reports on the Young Turk leaders, fear is prevalent. The Armenians' role in Ottoman society, their successes at the expense of Turks, their lack of gratitude, and, in general, the reversal of traditional status relationships in which Muslims should be on top and Christians below all contributed to a generalized resentment of Turks toward Armenians. Anger is also expressed – anger at rebellion and the threat presented by the Armenians to the war effort and their relationship with the Russians. But anger is an emotion directed at what someone has done to you, while hatred is an even more powerful and destructive emotion directed at someone for what they are. For the Young Turks anger had turned into hatred of a group that was now conceived as an existential threat to their empire and their rulership.

Fear and anger, resentment and hatred are all found in the statements of Enver and Talaat to Ambassador Morgenthau. Given their strategic aim to preserve the empire, and their conceptualization of the Armenians as internal traitors threatening its existence, anger metastasized into hatred and made possible the choice to deport and murder the Armenians. Here was an ethnic cleansing combined with mass annihilation carried out, not by a nation-state, but by a decaying empire determined to save itself. That salvation required, in the minds of the Young Turks, and many of their German allies, the elimination of the Armenians.

The Young Turks carried out inhumane, monstrous acts. Some may think of them as monsters or madmen, but Morgenthau understood that they were both calculating and emotional actors, neither madmen nor monsters, but all too human. Once they embarked on the genocidal policy, they appealed to the affective understandings of ordinary Turks and Kurds about Armenians. The leaders found resonance in the "emotional disposition" of the population and were able to arouse feelings that led to murder, plunder, rape, and the most wanton cruelty. Still, it is the elites that bear the ultimate responsibility, for they initiated the policy, demanded compliance, played on the available popular emotional repertoire, and rationalized and legitimated activity that in most times and most places would have been beyond the law and norms of society.

34

Danish Reactions to the Armenian Genocide and Their Background

Henning Lehmann

What happened in Armenia and to the Armenians during the last quarter of the nineteenth century and the first quarter of the twentieth in many respects called for the same reactions in all parts of the civilized world, even if, at the same time it turned out that not all parts of the so-called "civilized world" were equally entitled to bear that name. However general the appeal to "civilization," human sympathy and compassion, each nation and each movement might have a line of its own, which it followed and which determined its mode of reaction.

Two prefatory remarks about the title of this paper might be appropriate. First, I shall make no attempt to present a collection of "reactions" in media or political circles. Thus, there is in this paper no "quantitative" report about how strong was the Danish reaction. It might very well be worthwhile to examine the matter on such premises. That, however, is not done here. Second, the word "background" of the title should be taken seriously – in the following direction: as far as time is concerned, there will be more about what was said and thought about the Armenians and their fate ten or twenty years before the genocide as such; and as far as patterns of reaction are concerned, there will be as much, or more, about nineteenth century cultural movements, as *background*, than about twentieth century political initiatives.

In particular, it is my intention to try to describe some of the elements in the backgrounds of two female figures who both played a role in the humanitarian assistance to Armenians during some of the hard years before and during World War I, and also in the attempts to save Armenian values (and, of course, Armenian refugees, not least children) in the wake of the War, i.e., Karen Jeppe and Maria Jacobsen. Some of these elements can best be understood when taking certain figures, movements and events in the Danish church of the nineteenth century into account.

In a brief survey, it might be reasonable to point to movements of revival as one of the most characteristic features of 19th century Denmark, as, indeed, it is in the history of other (European) countries of the time. The character – and name – of the first important movement of this kind is taken from Nicolai Frederik Severin Grundtvig (1783-1872), a very important figure in Danish history in general (he was a member of the assembly that formulated Denmark's first democratic constitution of 1849), in Danish literary and ecclesiastical history (among other things, he was a very prolific hymn writer); furthermore, he is considered the father of the Danish "folk high school," which has been a highly important element in Danish educational, and political, history of the nineteenth and twentieth centuries. The movement called by his name, even if building, thoroughly and explicitly, on the foundations of the Church, i.e., especially the 'Apostolic Creed,' in the context of the nineteenth and twentieth centuries had strong links with liberal movements, as have the folk high schools, still in the twenty-first century. It would take us too far, here, to delve deeper into Grundtvig's way of thinking. Only one element should be mentioned: his idea of assigning a specific role to each people in history. From the Bible and classical history we know about roles played by Jews, Greeks and Romans; but also a small people – such as, for example, the Danish – would have a role to play – as expressed through its own language, not least our "mother's tongue"; and it should understand, cultivate, and guard that role.

The second important movement of revival (formally inaugurated in the 1860s) in Danish bears the name *Indre Mission*. It is not a parallel to the German *Innere Mission* with its social activities. The idea of the name is that the official church of the time was thought to need missionary action within its own walls (*indre,* of course, means: internal, inside), and the action and inspiration needed is based on, what is generally assigned such terms as "pietist," "evangelical," and the like. The movement's demands on its members to turn their backs on the outside world may take different colours according to social circumstances, and so the *Indre*

Mission of poor people of Danish rural quarters is often considered to have a "darker" shade than that of the cities, not least Copenhagen, the capital. (The difference might not be entirely comparable to that of the Armenians of Istanbul and those of Anatolia at the same time, but the comparison suggests itself.) What is important in Danish circumstances, however, is that this movement (differently from its counterparts in the other Scandinavian countries), instead of forming a free church of its own, decided to remain within the Danish "evangelical-Lutheran" state church (or "folk church" [Danish: *folkekirke,* which is the word used in the Danish constitution]). It should be added that to the inspiration from German Pietism of the first generation of *Indre Mission* were added elements from English and Swedish revivalist traditions of the late nineteenth century.

Whereas Karen Jeppe had her background in the Grundtvigian movement, and Maria Jacobsen's principal supporters belonged to *Indre Mission,* mainly the city "branch," the environment of what was originally called the "Industrial Mission to Armenia" (which we shall touch upon a little later) was that of "rigorous" rural pietism.

It should be added, that Denmark of the late nineteenth and early twentieth centuries saw humanitarian figures, who found their inspiration in other circles and movements than those of the church, whether social or cultural, whether romantic or revolutionary, whether idealistic or realistic. One figure, in particular, should be mentioned in this context, that is Georg Brandes (1842-1927). He was born in a Jewish business family in Copenhagen, thus, belonging to the emancipated, liberal Jewish cultural environment, which was a fairly important element in nineteenth century Copenhagen. He was a very productive free-lance writer, inspired, not least, by the revolutionary ideas of the 1870s, and he became a very important source of inspiration for authors and literary critics and of politicians and radical anti-establishment activists, not only in Denmark, but throughout Europe. Friedrich Nietzsche, the German philosopher, e.g., called him "the good European and missionary of culture." It fits in very well with this picture of Georg Brandes, the European, that he was invited in 1903, to address, in Berlin, the "Union of Armenian Students in Europe."

Brandes' speech ("Armenia and Europe") was given in Berlin on February 2nd, 1903. It was published both in French and German, by the "Union des Étudiants Arméniens de l'Europe," and a Danish version is published in the periodical *Tilskueren* (i.e., *The Spectator*).

The first part of Brandes' speech recalls massacres of Armenians in 1894. This is done in a very dramatic way (and in a parenthesis, in the printed version, we are told that a number of ladies present at the Berlin meeting, got up and left the lecture hall crying). Brandes then gives a very vivid description of the country of Armenia and a number of highlights of Armenian history and literature, e.g., recalling, how Raffi, the Armenian writer, through his novel *Djalaleddin*, already gave a moving picture of Armenian sufferings of 1877. (I am sure that Brandes did not read Armenian; presumably he knew Raffi's novel from the French translation.) The principal message of Georg Brandes, giving his speech in Berlin, is that Germany, as the European friend of Turkey, tends to cover up the atrocities, and even to silence its own humanitarian relief workers, such as Dr. Johannes Lepsius, and as will be well-known, here he anticipates an element of the European political discussion after 1915, when once again Germany played the role of the friend of Turkey.

Before turning to Karen Jeppe and Maria Jacobsen, I should like to mention one further Danish personality, a Danish intellectual, who became an ardent spokesman of the Armenian cause. I am thinking of Åge Meyer Benedictsen (1866-1927). He was trained as a linguist with a very broad range of knowledge of languages – Slavonic as well as Persian, Finnish, Lithuanian, and Icelandic; (I am not quite sure, how deep was his knowledge of Armenian); however, he is characterized as a person who was more interested in the life and fate of the peoples than the theoretical approach to their languages. In 1901, he had travelled in Russia and Persia, and on his way back he passed through the city of Urfa, where the afore-mentioned Dr. Lepsius had his children's home. Before the German Orientmission had sent Dr. Lepsius to this place, there was an American station of mission and aid, headed by Miss Corinna Shattuck, whose relief work, too, was directed towards Armenian children, not least those who had become orphans during the 1890s.

Back in Denmark, in February 1902, Benedictsen gave a lecture on the problems and sufferings of the Armenians. One of those present in the lecture hall was Karen Jeppe, and this event was to be the inspiration of her life. I shall return to the biography of Karen

Jeppe. About Åge Meyer Benedictsen I shall only mention two further details: 1) He became the first author to publish a history of Armenia in Danish. It was published in 1925, and as can be guessed from this date, from what has already been said about the author, and from the title of the book: *Armenien - Et Folks Liv og Kamp gennem to Aartusinder* [Armenia - the life and struggle of a people through 2000 years], it was certainly not just a neutral textbook of history. 2) The book was published by the Danish Friends of Armenia (or literally: of the Armenians) [*De danske Armeniervenner*], the organization which supported Karen Jeppe, and had Benedictsen as its chairman for many years. So the book very much has the character of being a symbol of Danish solidarity towards and interest in the fate of the Armenians.

Åge Meyer Benedictsen's father was a Copenhagen merchant, his mother was an actress of the Royal Theatre, thus, belonging to city circles (as did Georg Brandes) – even metropolitan circles, as Denmark could offer at the time, whereas Karen Jeppe came from the countryside. (Maybe I should mention here, that Karen is a common, traditional girl's name in Danish. To the Armenian ear, a "Karen" would be a boy!) Karen Jeppe's father was a primary school teacher in the village of Gylling in East Jutland; and apart from her father, an important source of inspiration for Karen Jeppe was Otto Møller, pastor of the parish of Gylling, belonging to the Grundtvigian movement, described above.

Karen Jeppe was born in 1876, and when, 25 years old, she had heard Benedictsen's lecture, and, as she might have put it, had been hit by the message and felt herself obliged to go and help the Armenians; her father and the pastor advised her not to go. That may be very understandable for a number of reasons; among other things the young Karen didn't have a strong physical constitution. In the context of Danish church history, however, it might also be connected to, what might be called the reverse side of what was mentioned above about Grundtvig's idea of the particular identity and historical mission of each people and each nation, the argument that when Scripture says: "thou shalt love thy neighbour," the word "neighbour" should be taken literally, so that e.g., *in casu,* to a Danish girl of 1902, the Armenian, however great his sufferings, is not her "neighbour." (This is not necessarily an inhuman statement, when it is seen in its historical context of the late nineteenth and the early twentieth centuries). But Karen argued that she had heard the calling of her neighbour, the Armenian, through Mr. Benedictsen, and finally, she won, not only her father's and her spiritual adviser's acceptance, but their strong support for the years to follow; and this strongly contributed to the support gained in the Danish "folk high schools" towards the Danish "Friends of Armenia."

In other words, we are not only dealing with exceptional positions or individual acts, let alone accidental occurrences or singular events. To my mind, we have to do with factors and trends, significantly determining the Danish reaction to the events of 1915 and the following years and the level of information and interest for the Armenians. In particular, the support of Karen Jeppe from the environment of the Danish Grundtvigian folk high schools was, as emphasized already, an important – new – signal from that segment of the society of Denmark.

It may be added, that it is important to know about the activities of the first years of the twentieth century, in order also to understand what can be expected in our country, even today, concerning the attitude towards an understanding of what may be Armenian questions of the twenty-first century – and the Armenians' understanding of and expectations towards Denmark of today. It is, in fact, an extraordinary – even moving – experience to realize the established and honourable place, occupied by Maria Jacobsen and Karen Jeppe, in what one might call the treasury of modern Armenian legend (through which word I do not intend to remove the recollections from the realm of historical fact).

Three organizations were of particular interest in Denmark, when dealing with "the Armenian cause." *De danske Armeniervenner* [*Danish Friends of Armenia* (or: the Armenians)], the supporters of Karen Jeppe, have been mentioned already, and I have tried to argue that the constellation of Karen Jeppe, her father, and her pastor, and presumably the inspiring magic of Åge Meyer Benedictsen's rhetoric must have created a particular spiritual climate, which secured the support from the Danish folk high schools and the Grundtvig current. Not least through the personality of Åge Meyer Benedictsen support was also gained in academic, intellectual circles in Copenhagen, far from the countryside Grundtvigians. (Denmark, at the time, had only one university, that of Copenhagen, and Copenhagen, apart from being the seat of government and parliament, was also the city where the most important Danish newspapers and organizations had their headquarters.)

The name of the organization supporting Maria Jacobsen was *Kvindelige Missions Arbejdere* – usually abbreviated KMA (i.e., *Women Working for Mission*). This organization was founded in 1900, not as an independent society of missions, as the name might suggest, but as an organization with the aim of supporting, in particular, female missionaries sent by various societies of mission already in existence, and women active in humanitarian aid. The direct sources of inspiration and models for this organization seem to have been Swedish and English spiritual movements of the late nineteenth century, of a low church, evangelical, revivalist character. Both the first lady to be sent to the Armenian children's home in Mezreh not far from Harpoot, Christa Hammer, who was sent in 1901, and Maria Jacobsen, who went to Harpoot, were trained nurses, and, in fact, a great number of members of the KMA were nurses and female teachers. In addition to these groups it is interesting to notice in the Danish context, from the very names of board members and supporters, that many of them belonged to or had links to the Danish nobility, Danish landowners, and even the Danish Royal Court. For example, the first chairperson of KMA's branch for work among Armenians, Mrs. Wanda Oxholm, was married to the Lord Chamberlain of King Christian IX, and among leaders and members one meets with such names as *Vind, Collet,* and *Schaffalitzky* – and others belong to Danish noble families.

To my mind, it would be worthwhile in this connection to examine what might be called the conservative, idealistic philanthropists of the period. Apart from the names connected to the KMA, it could also be mentioned, that it seemed to be a matter of course, when Karen Jeppe needed travel money in order to go to Urfa, that one could count on a Danish landowner and philanthropist named Johannes Hage of Nivågård to pay the amount necessary. This landowner, Johannes Hage, by the way, financed a hospital for the local community of Nivå, a little town north of Copenhagen, and finally left his mansion house and his collection of paintings to become a museum open to the general public, thus, leaving the memory of a many-sided philanthropist. The cultural, spiritual, moral, and economic atmosphere of such circles were quite different from those of Karen Jeppe's Grundtvigian countryside, and in many ways, also of the pietistic background of many of the nurses and female teachers, who were the active elements in the movement behind KMA, and thus behind Maria Jacobsen, but their interest in the humanitarian activities of both ladies and their general openness to social, political and economic problems in Denmark as well as throughout Europe, should not be underestimated.

Maria Jacobsen was born in 1882 in very modest rural circumstances in Western Jutland. She was trained as a nurse in Copenhagen, and I think it might be true to say that the Copenhagen YWCA was the place where such girls as the young Maria would meet representatives of such circles as those described as initiators of the KMA. Maria Jacobsen was sent by the KMA to Harpoot in 1907, and her diary starts out with the preparations for her "mission," in particular the farewells and blessings of those who had inspired and prepared her for her new vocation. This diary was published by the Printing House of the Armenian Catholicossate of Antelias-Lebanon, in 1979. The book contains a facsimile edition of Maria Jacobsen's diary, written in Danish, for the years 1907-1919, to which is added an Armenian translation (and a certain amount of notes and explanations). As can be guessed from the years covered, there are many tales of hardship and tragedies caused by the events of 1915 and the following years - as strong as those told in the first part of Georg Brandes' speech of 1903, rendered above.

The place of origin of the third Danish organization, active among Armenians, *Dansk Industrimission i Armenien* [Danish Industry Mission in Armenia] seems to belong to parts of Danish society far away from the noble and royal circles just referred to, more related to Maria Jacobsen's original point of departure, that of rural pietism. The organization was founded in 1922, and its very name might compel us for a moment to consider the concepts used in Denmark and in the organizations mentioned, when confronted with problems, not only of Armenia, but also of the world at large.

Of course, the very word "mission" in this part of the world – indeed, not only in Denmark, primarily means "preaching the Gospel to people who have not yet heard it." Over the centuries, both in the Roman Catholic church, and in the great century of Missionary Societies of non-catholic churches of the Western world (that is the nineteenth century), the problem has occurred more than once, whether it was right and proper to preach and "proselytize" among members of other Christian churches. In later, ecumenical times, the use of the word "mission," in KMA, might have been felt to be slightly offensive. It would of course take me outside my topic here to pursue this matter much further. However, we have to understand, how the words were used at the time we are dealing with here. In this context, one further remark about a trend in the history of missions might be necessary. The term "industry mission" or "industrial mission" usually points towards the fact that pioneers and theoreticians of mission in the age of industrialization realized that missionary work would often have to be connected with social work, both in the third world and in the secularized environments of industrial cities of the Western world, where preaching the Gospel was felt to be as necessary as abroad (compare above about one argument for "indre" [internal] "mission").

I have not had the opportunity to study in detail the primary sources of the Danish *Industrimission i Armenien*, so I cannot demonstrate, how much of that kind of thinking lay behind the name, but it seems obvious that in addition to such points of view the founders were aware of the need of assisting the new, independent Armenia in building up its infrastructure, including its industries. However, before the Danish organization was formally founded – in 1922, Armenia had become a Soviet republic; and a Western, Christian organization would stand few chances of working in that Armenia. Therefore, they turned their attention to Armenian refugees in Greece, collecting money and sending people to support Armenian children and elderly people, and this was mainly done in cooperation with the Protestant Armenian church in Greece (in Thessaloniki and in Athens).

A couple of decades ago, it seemed that all three organizations had come to an end (at least as formal entities). The Karen Jeppe College of Aleppo, today, is purely Armenian, and the Bird's Nest in Lebanon was formally handed over to the Armenian Church quite a few years ago (and what remains of "follow-up"-activities to the KMA is, formally, in the hands of the organization of Danish Church Aid). It is interesting to notice, however, that today the *Industrimission* (now under the name of *Dansk Armeniermission* [Danish Mission to the Armenians]) is the only one of the three still (or rather, again) in existence, and that it seems to have found a good mode of cooperation, in Yerevan/Etchmiadzin, with the Armenian Church, among other things for educational purposes.

Even if a number of things have changed, such facts of modern times might be a good preparation for now rounding off this article through returning to the main features of the efforts made by Karen Jeppe and Maria Jacobsen in the second and following decade(s) of the twentieth century. These efforts may be summed up under three headings:

1. Their humanitarian and social work.

2. Their roles as eyewitnesses to massacres and on that background their contribution to informing directly or indirectly the Danish (and the international) public.

3. Their independent contributions to solving problems in the wake of the dramatic events of 1915.

The social, educational, and humanitarian work, of course, was the core of what they were sent to do. In both cases, they were sent to institutions already existing; in addition to what was, so to speak, a given fact of daily work in this respect, their colleagues and friends in the Middle East are often quoted for highly positive comments on their independent contribution to the relief work; e.g., Miss Corinna Shattuck, the American pioneer of the work in Urfa, is quoted for praising Karen Jeppe's pedagogic contribution to the training and education and rearing of the Armenian children.

About function no. 2: information about what happened, it might be important to recollect that both Karen Jeppe and Maria Jacobsen, of course, experienced extremely hard periods in their work to give elementary help to Armenian refugees in 1915, and the years before, and especially immediately after 1915, sometimes hiding refugees under the most difficult circumstances; and they both had to return to Denmark for a while after serious health problems, Karen Jeppe in 1918, and Maria Jacobsen in 1919. This was an element of the background for their international activities, Karen Jeppe mainly under the auspices of the League of Nations, where, persistently, she pointed out that the so-called "final solution" of the peace treaties after World War I contained no genuine solution at any rate no final, positive solution to the problems of the Armenians.

Maria Jacobsen, in 1920-21, went to the United States, where she contributed to the work done under the auspices of the American agency of "Near Eastern Relief," which, as is well-known, played a great role for Armenians and other displaced persons of the Near East after the great war.

Of course, two women placed in very hard circumstances, each in their humble place, will not, technically speaking, be able to testify to a "genocide," but they are, indeed, first-hand eyewitnesses to a number of examples of hardship and sufferings and murdering of individuals or families or groups. If it may be true to say, that Denmark was, during the 1920s, one of the places, where consciousness of the sufferings was kept alive, I am convinced that it was important that the three organizations mentioned had, in all strata of Danish society, their networks of spreading the information collected by the two women in the very heart of the areas of the drama, and, in fact, even in their convalescence periods Karen Jeppe and Maria Jacobsen gave a great number of lectures and talks about their experiences among the Armenians and their tyrants.

When I coined my third point as "their independent contributions to solving problems in the wake of the dramatic events of 1915," I had in mind what has been mentioned already, their efforts on the international scene.

Karen Jeppe's work, under the auspices of the League of Nations, took place in a subcommission under the commissioner for refugee work, the Norwegian Fridtjof Nansen. She had strong support from, among others, the Danish delegation to the League of Nations. Otherwise, the work was very hard and often discouraging. Up until 1927, however, she was the driving force in the work to secure, as she put it herself, "that the modest light, lit for the Armenians by the League of Nations should not be extinguished."

The other thing I had in mind, and presumably the most important thing was, that both Karen Jeppe and Maria Jacobsen returned again to the Middle East, not to Urfa and Harpoot, (that was impossible), but Karen Jeppe in, 1921, to Aleppo in what was now Syria under the French mandate, and Maria Jacobsen in 1922 to Lebanon, first to Zouk Michael, then to the Bird's Nest, first in Saida (Sidon), then in Jubayl.

Karen Jeppe was still quite weak in certain periods, and in 1925 she got a Danish assistant in Aleppo, Jenny Jensen, and Maria Jacobsen was joined by her sister Anna in the Bird's Nest in 1931. It was not only because of health problems, however, that Karen Jeppe asked for assistance, but also because she was, after 1923, active in a project, the intention of which was to found an agricultural colony east of River Euphrates, the Tell Armen (the Hill of the Armenians).

I shall not go into any further detail about the history of the institutions for Armenians in Lebanon and Syria, or in Greece and elsewhere, and their Danish connections. I shall only, by way of conclusion, point out one feature, which is often mentioned in order to characterize the fundamental values behind both Karen Jeppe's and Maria Jacobsen's work, the fact that they urged the Armenian women to take up again or pursue their traditional crafts and to teach their daughters these crafts and traditions. This, of course, is a very practical detail with two immediate purposes: for one thing to fill the daily life of the women, for another to produce goods that could be sold (in Denmark, as in other countries, where Armenian lace and embroidery were popular), in order to earn money for the work.

Beneath these practical purposes, however, to my mind, lies a deep respect for the Armenians as a people, and it is natural in the Danish context to connect this respect with the notion of "people" as used and elaborated by Grundtvig, the Danish theologian and pioneer in pedagogic matters, mentioned now a few times in my paper. To Grundtvig, as suggested above, a people had to understand itself as a people; it had "to become a people," as the individual had to become a true human being, before he or she or they could open themselves to the Christian message, and the process of becoming true human beings was a matter of the School, not of the Church; that is one of the fundamental axioms of the Grundtvigian tradition.

And so, in fact, I think that the basic strength of the work of Karen Jeppe and Maria Jacobsen lay in the fact that they were humble and modest enough to consider their own work as a preparatory work, a work of teaching and learning and supporting, aiming at assisting the Armenians in becoming Armenians or regaining their Armenianhood (and fortunately, in this respect I see certain parallels in the "Armeniermission" of the 1990s), and even if, in Denmark, as everywhere, cultural radicalism such as that of Georg Brandes, and ecclesiastical circles usually stand far apart, this way of thinking was a basis, that did not call for the usual tension between such opposite poles. In fact, viewed in the Danish context, some of those, who were active for "the Armenian cause" in the early days of the twentieth century, would have been surprised, if they had been, in other connections, met with the assumption that they stood on common ground.

The first thing for Karen Jeppe and Maria Jacobsen, and also for the pioneers of the Industry Mission, had been to help as many as possible survive. Now in the 1920s and later on, the task was a re-awakening into an Armenian existence, and however modest the Danish contribution may have been, measured in hard currency, even measured in the number of survivors, I think it might be true to say that the basic values of helping another people as laid out and practised by the two strong women, met a fairly qualified response in Denmark, and that this was to a great extent due to initiatives taken and networks created around the dawn of the twentieth century (the cruelties and humanitarian catastrophes, holocausts and genocides of which few people, or rather nobody, were able to foresee at the time).

Literature, Film, and Armenian Genocide Denial: The Case of Franz Werfel's *The Forty Days of Musa Dagh*

Vahram L. Shemmassian

In the Armenian genocide, several pockets of resistance existed. One such case involved Musa Dagh, a mountain situated to the southwest of the biblical town of Antioch (Antakya) and overlooking the Mediterranean Sea. This Armenian enclave consisted of six villages with a total population of more than 6,000 souls. On receiving deportation orders in late July 1915, their majority took up arms for self-defense,[1] a saga that captured the imagination of Franz Werfel in a novel entitled *The Forty Days of Musa Dagh*.[2] The following paper discusses the genesis of Werfel's bestseller and how its film project failed to materialize, thanks to a relentless campaign of obstruction and genocide denial by the Turkish government primarily through its embassy in Washington, D.C., with the solicited cooperation of the United States State Department.

The Novel

The Musa Dagh self-defense story, once its immediacy vanished, would probably have been relegated to oblivion had it not been for the pen of one man—Franz Werfel (1890-1945). Born in Prague to Jewish parents, Werfel resided in Vienna, where he was recognized

---

[1] For the history of Musa Dagh Armenians in the nineteenth century through the resistance of 1915, see Vahram L. Shemmassian, "The Armenian Villagers of Musa Dagh: A Historical-Ethnographic Study, 1840-1915," Ph.D. dissertation, University of California, Los Angeles, 1996.

[2] Franz Werfel, *The Forty Days of Musa Dagh*, translated from the German by Geoffrey Dunlop (New York: The Viking Press, 1934). The British edition (London: Jarrold Publishers, 1934) carries the abbreviated title of *The Forty Days*.

as an established author.[3] During World War I, he had learned about the Armenian atrocities through the European press and "promised myself that I would one day write a historical novel on the subject."[4] In 1929, he and his wife, Alma Mahler, took a fateful trip to the Middle East. The itinerary included a visit to Damascus, where the couple toured, among other places, a carpet-weaving factory. What the Werfels witnessed there left an indelible impression on them.[5] Wrote Alma in her memoirs:

> In passing the rows of looms we saw emaciated children with El Greco faces and enormous eyes roll around the floors, pick up spools and threads, and wield a broom now and then.
>
> "What strange children are these?" Franz Werfel asked the owner.
>
> "Those poor creatures? I pick them up in the street and give them ten piasters a day, so they won't starve. They're the children of the Armenians killed off by the Turks. If I don't take them in, they starve and nobody cares. They can't really work; they're too feeble."
>
> We walked out with daze. Nothing seemed important or beautiful any more. Shocked and wearied, we went to a coffeehouse, where Werfel was intrigued by the narghiles, the Turkish water pipes that were being smoked all around us. He bought a mouthpiece for one and started smoking pensively, unable to get the Armenian children out of his mind.[6]

---

[3] For a comprehensive bibliography of works by and on Franz Werfel, consult Jennifer E. Michaels, *Franz Werfel and the Critics* (Columbia, South Carolina: University of South Carolina Press, 1994), pp. 153-172.

[4] Franz Werfel, as cited in Peter Stephan Jungk, "Die vierzig Tage des Musa Dagh," in Lothar Huber, ed., *Franz Werfel: An Austrian Writer Reassessed* (Oxford, New York, Munich: Berg Publishers, 1989), p. 189, n. 3.

[5] Alma Mahler Werfel, *And the Bridge Is Love* (New York: Harcourt, Brace and Company, 1958), pp. 198-201. Although at the beginning of the book, *The Forty Days of Musa Dagh*, n. p. [v], Franz Werfel indicates 1929 as the year of his trip to the Middle East, Jungk, "Die vierzig Tage des Musa Dagh," p. 188, n. 1, disputes that date, offering instead the year 1930 as the correct time of the itinerary.

[6] Werfel, *And the Bridge Is Love*, p. 200. Franz Werfel himself wrote: "This book was conceived in March of 1929, in the course of a stay in Damascus. The miserable sight of some maimed and famished-looking

Werfel began to compile notes on the Armenian calamity while still on vacation. Back in Vienna, upon learning that pertinent documents existed in the French Ministry of War, he requested and obtained from his friend, Count Clauzel, the French ambassador to Austria, "the complete Armenian file from Paris..., with permission to keep and study the mass of facts for years."[7] The file included information on the Musa Dagh resistance, which Werfel chose as the subject of his novel.

The French dossier alone did not satisfy Werfel's quest for a thorough understanding of the intended subject. He accordingly visited the library of the Armenian Mekhitarist Order in Vienna to conduct further research beginning June 1930. There he familiarized himself with the reports of the German missionary, Dr. Johannes Lepsius, the eyewitness account of the Armenian Protestant pastor, Tigran Andreasian, and the geography of Musa Dagh.[8] He similarly interviewed a young celibate priest who, as a child, had witnessed the resistance.[9] Werfel even employed the services of a friend to study and advise him on "questions of Armenian administration and jurisdiction" and of a young journalist "to consult geographical volumes in the Vienna National Library in order to establish the nature of the climate in the summer of 1915 in Anatolia, the predominant winds and the amount of rainfall."[10] For the description

---

refugee children, working in a carpet factory, gave me the final impulse to snatch from the Hades of all that was, this incomprehensible destiny of the Armenian nation..." *The Forty Days of Musa Dagh*, "Note," n. p. [v].

[7] Werfel, *And the Bridge Is Love*, pp. 201-202. See also Jungk, "Die vierzig Tage des Musa Dagh," p. 176.

[8] Hans Wagener, *Understanding Franz Werfel* (Columbia, South Carolina: University of South Carolina Press, 1993), p. 117; George Schulz-Behrend, "Sources and Background of Werfel's Novel *Die Vierzig Tage Des Musa Dagh*," *The Germanic Review* XXVI: 2 (April, 1951): 111-123; Arshag Mahdesian, "A Probable Source of 'Forty Days of Musa Dagh'," *The Armenian Review* I:1 (Winter, 1948): 108-109; Jungk, "Die vierzig Tage des Musa Dagh," pp. 176-177.

[9] Tovmas Kajazn, "Frants Verfel inch'pēs grets' Musa Leran kaṙasun orerě" [How Franz Werfel Wrote 'The Forty Days of Musa Dagh'], in Martiros Gushagchian and Poghos Matuṙian, eds., *Hushamatean Musa Leran* [Memorial Book of Musa Dagh] (Beirut: Atlas Press, 1970), pp. 621-622.

[10] Jungk, "Die vierzig Tage des Musa Dagh," p. 179. See also idem, *Franz Werfel: A Life in Prague, Vienna, and Hollywood*, Anselm Hollo, trans.

of battle scenes, Werfel relied on his wartime experience and keen interest in and vast knowledge of military affairs.[11] In short, "Werfel's intensive study of the sources, carried on for two years, now proved its usefulness in even the smallest details:...children's games, handicraft, architecture, farming methods and Armenian costume were all integrated into the fabric of the novel."[12]

Werfel wrote the first draft of the Musa Dagh story in less than a year, from July 1932 through May 1933. This period coincided with the ascendancy of the Nazis to power in Germany, an ominous development that troubled Werfel deeply. As a result, in a state of spiritual exhaustion, he lost concentration, wrote with difficulty, and even contemplated changing the plot. Nevertheless, the work proceeded without interruption until November 1932, when he undertook a lecture tour in Germany to read a completed chapter devoted to a meeting between Dr. Lepsius and Enver Pasha, the Ottoman Minister of War. In his introductory remarks, Werfel explained to his audiences that the Armenian atrocities were carried out not in the distant past but rather during their own lifetime; that they involved people killing their fellow countrymen; and that the Christian Armenians fell victim to Turkish nationalism. Back in his writing routine, Werfel often reminded himself to be fair and to avoid categorizing all Turks under the same criminal rubric.[13] Be that as it may, when Werfel completed the final draft of his manuscript, "the whole house waited breathlessly for his descent from his study. It is a titanic achievement for a Jew to write a work like this at this time, exposed to such animosity. Both of us were unspeakably happy...," exclaimed his wife.[14]

(New York: Fromm International Publishing Corporation, 1991), p. 138; Wagener, *Understanding Franz Werfel*, p. 117.

[11] Jungk, "Die vierzig Tage des Musa Dagh," pp. 178-179; Wagener, *Understanding Franz Werfel*, p. 117.

[12] Jungk, "Die vierzig Tage des Musa Dagh," p. 178.

[13] Ibid., pp. 179-183; idem, *Franz Werfel*, pp. 139-140. Werfel, *The Forty Days of Musa Dagh*, "Note," n. p. [v], however, maintains that "the writing of the book followed between July 1932 and March 1933," and Alma Werfel, *And the Bridge Is Love*, p. 212, reiterates the nine-month period, "from July 1932 to March 1933."

[14] Werfel, *And the Bridge Is Love*, p. 217.

The Forty Days of Musa Dagh, as Werfel entitled his novel, revolves around a fictitious Gabriel Bagradian, a well-to-do man who has spent twenty-three years of his life in Paris, has married a French woman called Juliette, and has a son by the name of Stephan. Bagradian returns to his native Yoghunoluk (one of the six Armenian villages in Musa Dagh) to take care of some family business because of his brother's illness and eventual death. During their sojourn at Musa Dagh, World War I erupts, and the Bagradians are compelled to stay. While the entire Armenian population in the Ottoman Empire is subjected to deportations, exposure in deserts or concentration camps, and outright massacres amounting to genocide, the Armenians of Musa Dagh, led by one of their priests and Bagradian, choose to resist rather that be annihilated. The beleaguered highlanders succeed against all odds in repelling the Turkish assaults on their mountain fastness and are ultimately rescued by the French navy. Stephan Bagradian dies heroically in one of the battles and, as the rest sail to freedom, Gabriel loses his own life by an enemy bullet at his son's burial site.[15]

Shortly after the National Socialists secured more than 44 percent of the votes in the general elections for the German parliament on March 5, 1933, that is, before Werfel had completed his novel, members of the Prussian Academy of Arts, including Werfel, received a classified circular demanding abstinence from any form of opposition to the new regime should they wish to remain and serve in the Academy. Werfel elected to sign the declaration "in order to safeguard the future sales of his *Musa Dagh*." All the same, his published books, together with those of many other prominent Jewish authors, were publicly set on fire by German Nazi youths on May 10, and soon after he was expelled from the Academy. In this atmosphere of rampant anti-Semitism, Werfel legitimately feared, his publishers could either abandon or print a much-reduced version of *Musa Dagh*.[16] But surprisingly,

> *Die vierzig Tage des Musa Dagh* was published at the end of November 1933—in Austria and Switzerland the public reacted with almost unanimous approval. In Germany, however, the official reaction against the

---

[15] See Werfel, *The Forty Days of Musa Dagh.*

[16] Jungk, "Die vierzig Tage des Musa Dagh," pp. 180-185; idem, *Franz Werfel*, pp. 139-145.

> Armenian epic was a storm of criticism and abuse. Even the most insensitive reader could not have missed the parallels between the ideologies of the Young Turkish nationalism and National Socialism. Although no advertising for the novel was permitted within the Reich, German booksellers sold all the copies they had ordered. The fact that the work of 'des verbrannten Dichters' Werfel was allowed to be sold at all must be counted as one of the mysteries of the first months after Hitler's seizure of power.[17]

This enigmatic period of relative freedom was short lived. In February 1934, the novel was removed from the German market, the official explanation being that it "was liable to be a risk to public security and order." The conforming German press hailed the ban with high approval.[18] It must also have satisfied a Turkish journalist who, from the outset, had launched a campaign to have the book suppressed in Germany, Turkey's ally during World War I, for its defamatory portrayal of his native country.[19]

German censure notwithstanding, *Musa Dagh* received international recognition upon its rendition into numerous languages.[20] The English version appeared in London and New York in 1934. In either edition, the translator, Geoffrey Dunlop, to whose discretion was left the liberty of abridgement, had omitted 312 passages amounting to 1,062 lines or 11 percent of the original German text.[21] Even so, the book preserved much of its integrity and became an instant bestseller. Most critics lavished rave reviews.[22] Wrote Horace Gregory in the *Booklist*:

---

[17] Ibid., "Die vierzig Tage des Musa Dagh," p. 184.

[18] Ibid., p. 186.

[19] Ibid., p. 185; idem, *Franz Werfel*, p. 145.

[20] US National Archives (USNA), Record Group (RG) 59, File 811.4061, *Musa Dagh*, doc. 50, Warren A Chiljan to John H. Tolan, June 30, 1937.

[21] Haigaz Kazarian, "'The Forty Days of Musa Dagh' and Its English Translation," *The Armenian Review* XVI: 3-63 (Autumn, 1963): 18-22.

[22] For various lists of book reviews on *The Forty Days of Musa Dagh*, see Marion A. Knight, Mertice M. James, and Dorothy Brown, eds., *The Book Review Digest*, Thirtieth Annual Cumulation March 1934 to February 1935 Inclusive (New York: H.W. Wilson Company, 1935), p. 1,000; Evan Ira Farber, executive ed., *Combined Retrospective Index to Book Reviews in*

> I know of no contemporary novel where historical incident is given such complete reality. And in no other modern novel may we find a better interpretation of the motives behind mass movement, nor shall we find a better portrayal of a mass in action.... The Armenian nation has survived by that power which is obtained by minority and disenfranchised races throughout the world. It is from a knowledge of that power that Franz Werfel has written this remarkable novel and the many who will feel compelled to read it will gain the reward of an unforgettable experience.[23]

Similarly, the *New York Times* considered the novel "a very fine, powerfully written story,"[24] while William Saroyan commented in the *Saturday Review*: "Here, at last, is a contemporary novel full of the breath, the flesh and blood and bone and spirit, of life."[25] Indeed, maintained another reviewer, it "is a book to read, re-read and read again, and with every reading some new value will be found."[26] Even the harshest critics found room for praise. As Peter Quennell opined in the *New Outlook*, "The Forty Days is very far from being a masterpiece, but it is solider reading than most novels that tend to corpulence."[27]

The human drama so vividly portrayed in *Musa Dagh* captured the imagination of artists and intellectuals of different nationalities; their inspiration led to the creation of an opera, a symphony, a play,

---

Scholarly Journals, 1886-1974, vol. XII (Arlington, CA: Carrollton Press, 1982), p. 241; idem, *Combined Retrospective Index to Book Reviews in Humanities Journals, 1802-1974*, vol. 9 (Woodbridge, CT: Research Publications, Inc., 1983), p. 563.

[23] Horace Gregory in *Booklist* (December, 1934), as cited in Knight et al., *Book Review Digest*, p. 1,000.

[24] *New York Times* (December 2, 1934), as cited in Knight et al., *Book Review Digest*, p. 1,000.

[25] William Saroyan in *Saturday Review* (December 22, 1934), as cited in Knight et al, *Book Review Digest*, p. 1,000.

[26] J. W. M. in *Books* (December 2, 1934), as cited in Knight et al, *Book Review Digest*, p. 1,000.

[27] Peter Quennell in *New Outlook* (December, 1934), as cited in Knight et al, *Book Review Digest*, p. 1,000.

poetry, songs, and numerous other writings and studies.[28] Equally important, the powerful symbolism and message that the novel conveyed had a direct bearing on the lives of two peoples especially—the Armenian and Jewish. When Werfel arrived in the United States shortly after the book's American publication, Armenians hailed him as a hero, a non-Armenian who had embraced their cause by telling the world their forsaken story. Wherever the Werfels went, the Armenians followed them. As Alma Mahler reminisced, "the New York Armenian colony honored him [Werfel] at immense feasts with fiery speeches. On Christmas Eve they invited us to a catacomb banquet—very solemn, subterranean, and mysterious—and to services in an Armenian church. 'We were a nation,' said the priest in his sermon, 'but Franz Werfel gave us a soul.' And after the service the entire congregation filed past to shake hands with us."[29] Similar scenes of euphoria awaited the Werfels in Paris, where they were accorded a tumultuous reception befitting a "foreign potentate."[30]

The novel had had a tremendous impact also on Jews in Palestine and in Europe during the 1930s and 1940s. When the Hebrew version appeared in 1934, reviewers drew parallels between the fates of the Armenian and Jewish peoples, maintaining at the same time that this could have been an Israeli story simply by replacing the "Armenian" with a "Jew." Likewise, Gabriel Bagradian, the hero in the novel, was perceived as the embodiment of Zionism, as he was likened to Theodore Herzl as an estranged, alienated or assimilated son ultimately returning to and leading his

---

[28] Musa Ler Compatriotic Union of Armenia, *Im Musa Leṙ Ergaran* [My Musa Dagh Songbook] (Yerevan: Spyurk, 1994); Anne M. Avakian, *Armenia and the Armenians in Academic Dissertations: A Bibliography* (Berkeley, CA: Professional Press, 1974), pp. 8, 10, 18, 30; Rachel Kirby, *The Culturally Complex Individual: Franz Werfel's Reflections on Minority Identity and Historical Depiction in The Forty Days of Musa Dagh* (London: Associated University Presses, 1999); Michaels, *Franz Werfel*, pp. 153-172 passim; Gushagchian and Matuṙian, *Hushamatean*, pp. 602-716.

[29] Werfel, *And the Bridge Is Love*, p. 229. See also *Hayrenik* [Fatherland] (Boston) (November 30, 1935, and December 12, 1935).

[30] Werfel, *And the Bridge Is Love*, p. 230.

people. Hence the complaint that Werfel should have written about his own kind rather that advance the cause of others.[31]

During World War II, when Jews in Palestine felt threatened by the advance of German troops in Egypt, they devised a plan of resistance at Mount Carmel which, if activated, would have the resonance of other heroic stands, namely, Massada, Tobruk, and Musa Dagh. In fact, one of the designations given to the scheme was the "Musa Dagh Plan." In Europe, Musa Dagh was more emulated than Massada, because "for Jewish youth in the ghettos, Massada, as a symbol of suicide, was less relevant than Musa Dagh, which symbolized struggle and battle, which might have a chance and a faint hope for salvation." Faced with moral and existential dilemmas, leading proponents of the idea of converting the ghettoes into citadels of resistance had Musa Dagh as their model. So that, it became a must to read this "textbook," which circulated among many hands, both in Eastern and Western Europe. Dignified death on the altar of national honor now became a rationalized and internalized concept, better yet, the alternative being salvation.[32]

The Aborted Film Project

Concomitant with wide acclaim accorded to the novel, the motion picture industry in Hollywood showed keen interest in the story as a possible film project. Hopes for its realization increased when the movie giant, Metro-Goldwyn-Mayer (M-G-M), acquired the screen rights. But from the outset the producers realized the topic's sensitive nature as it related to Turkish national sentiments and interest. And indeed, Turkey soon began to exert pressure.[33] On November 16, 1934, the Turkish ambassador to the United States, Mehmet Münir Ertegun, visited Wallace Murray, chief of the Division of Near Eastern Affairs in the State Department, to express his concern regarding the reported filming of *Musa Dagh*. According to the ambassador, "Any such picture…could only give a

---

[31] Yair Auron, *The Banality of Indifference: Zionism & the Armenian Genocide* (New Brunswick, USA, and London, UK: Transaction Publishers, 2000), pp. 293-311.

[32] Ibid.

[33] Edward Minassian, "The Forty Years of Musa Dagh: The Film That Was Denied," *Journal of Armenian Studies* II: 2 (Fall/Winter, 1985-1986): 63-65.

distorted version of the alleged [Armenian] massacres and would almost certainly stir up anti-Turkish feeling in this country [USA]." Murray, after explaining that his government could not forestall the making of such a movie, "saw no objection" to referring the matter to the responsible filmmakers. After all, in the past motion picture companies had done their best to refrain from having friction with foreign governments respecting problematic movies, and this case could be handled the same way.[34] Murray accordingly contacted Will H. Hays, president of the Motion Pictures Producers and Distributors of America (MPPDA), to ask him to verify Ertegun's claim.[35]

Hays passed on the communiqué to Frederick L. Herron, Foreign Manager of MPPDA, who, having seen "the proposed scenario" prepared for M-G-M, assured Murray "That they [M-G-M] not only did not emphasize the Armenian massacre, but did not refer to it at all." At any rate, Herron promised to keep an eye on the matter, feeling confident that "there will be nothing in it that could offend the Turkish Ambassador or his countrymen."[36] Ertegun consequently thanked Murray for his "friendly action."[37] Meanwhile, Turkish Foreign Minister Tevfik Rustu Aras had approached G. Howland Shaw, counselor of the United States embassy in Istanbul, to lodge the same complaint. Like Murray, the latter explained that under the American system his government could not prevent a film from being produced. After his guest's departure, however, Shaw consulted with Asa Jennings of the American Friends of Turkey, who in turn promised to discuss the issue with the head of *Musa Dagh*'s production company in New York. All this information could prove useful in case Murray might be "able and think it wise to take some unofficial and informal action."[38]

Although Robert P. Skinner, United States Ambassador to Turkey, after being apprised of what had transpired between the State Department and the Turkish embassy in Washington, D.C., was

---

[34] USNA, RG 59, *Musa Dagh*, doc. 1, Wallace Murray memorandum to file, November 16, 1934.

[35] Ibid., doc. 2, Wallace Murray to Will H. Hays, November 19, 1934.

[36] Ibid., doc. 3, Frederick L. Herron to Wallace Murray, November 20, 1934; doc. 5, Wallace Murray to Mehmet Münir, November 26, 1934.

[37] Ibid., doc. 4, Mehmet Münir to Wallace Murray, December 6, 1934.

[38] Ibid., doc. 6, GHS to Wallace Murray, November 27, 1934.

pleased with "the successful efforts put forth informally" by the Division of Near Eastern Affairs,[39] a news item appearing in the *Washington Herald* on April 17, 1935, rekindled the issue. The item read:

> An extremely fascinating book is "Forty Days of Musa Dagh," the story of Christians who combined against the Turkish massacres in Armenia... Irving Thalberg, who has commissioned Carey Wilson to write the adaptation for it, has handed the direction to William Wellman, who recently signed a long-term contract with Metro-Goldwyn-Mayer. William Powell, who is Irving's choice, ought to be grand in the lead.[40]

Armed with this clipping, Ertegun advised Murray to draw Herron's attention, "before the film is released, ...to the interpretation given to the story by the press and to the fact that the production under such circumstances would be inopportune." Ertegun also wanted Murray to "appreciate how much importance I place on preventing the misleading of public opinion in America through erroneous features concerning the history of my country."[41] Apparently caught off guard by the snag, Herron offered his apologies: "I am sorry that this piece of publicity came out as it did and I am sure it is to be blamed on some over enthusiastic publicity man, whether connected with the studio or outside, I don't know. However, I will see that this type of interview is not repeated." "They [?] are—continued Herron—watching the production very closely in Hollywood and will continue to do so."[42]

Herron took a step further by paying a personal visit to Ertegun. The latter conveyed his strong opposition to the project, but Herron,

---

[39] Ibid., doc. 7, Paul Alling to G. Howland Shaw, December 18, 1934; doc. 8, PHA to the American Ambassador, Istanbul, December 19, 1934; doc. 9, Robert P. Skinner to Secretary of State, January 8, 1935.

[40] *Washington Herald* (April 17, 1935), as cited in USNA, RG 59, *Musa Dagh*, doc. 10.

[41] USNA, RG 59, *Musa Dagh*, doc. 10, Mehmet Münir to Wallace Murray, April 22, 1935.

[42] Ibid., doc. 13, Frederick L. Herron to Wallace Murray, April 29, 1935. See also doc. 11, Wallace Murray to Frederick L. Herron, April 27, 1935; docs. 12 and 14, Wallace Murray to Mehmet Münir, April 27, 1935, and May 1, 1935, respectively.

as before, assured his host that the finished draft of the script would contain no derogatory remarks respecting the Turkish government. The two also agreed that the completed scenario would be placed at Ertegun's disposal "for his perusal and approval." While approval would please M-G-M, disapproval might not necessarily halt production, in which case "the best course of action" would be considered. When Herron informed the State Department of his talks with the Turkish envoy, he was reminded that the film, like the novel itself, would in all probability be banned in Turkey and Germany, as well as in some Balkan countries having close relations with Turkey. Herron dismissed the Balkans as an important market. However, France, should it join the boycott in deference to its friendship with Turkey, could be problematic.[43]

In late May 1935, the Turkish press began to show interest in the *Musa Dagh* affair. A Turkish student in North Carolina, writing for the *Son Posta* [Latest Mail] of Istanbul, maintained that American public opinion, because of its "great naiveté" on Turkish society, was being exploited by "hostile propaganda" based on allegations of Armenian atrocities in Turkey during World War I.[44] Commenting along similar lines and lamenting the lack of countermeasures, the *Haber* (News) in turn hinted at a boycott in Turkey and friendly countries of all motion pictures produced by M-G-M, which "in the end...will be the loser."[45] The United States Commercial Attaché rushed to warn his Department of what might be in store, adding that the "revival [of the] Armenian Question can serve no useful purpose."[46]

Ambassador Skinner himself was less worried. Although the screening of the film would receive considerable coverage in the Turkish press, it was doubtful whether the government would go as far as boycotting all American movies and would probably distance itself from any responsibility should demonstrations take place. At any rate, most films in Turkey were German and French made, and the few American movies imported were neither new and of high

---

[43] Ibid., doc. 15, Wallace Murray memorandum to file, May 14, 1935.

[44] *Son Posta* (May 29, 1935), as cited in USNA, RG 59, *Musa Dagh*, doc. 17.

[45] *Haber* (May 30, 1935), as cited in USNA, RG 59, *Musa Dagh*, doc. 17.

[46] Gillespie, as cited in USNA, RG 59, *Musa Dagh*, doc 17, Robert P. Skinner to Secretary of State, June 4, 1935.

quality nor exhibited in the larger theaters. Besides, both newspapers alluded to above were of secondary importance and uninfluential. To be sure, Skinner wished that M-G-M would cancel the *Musa Dagh* project, which, if realized, could be detrimental to the Armenian remnants in Turkey. On a positive note, he went on to say that at least one Turk who had read the novel had come across "many passages...which were favorable to Turkey and the Turks, and that on the whole it charged the Government of the day as distinguished from the Turkish people with bringing about the deportation of the Armenians."[47]

All the same, a weary Ertegun called on Murray again, this time begging him to solicit the Secretary of State's direct involvement in obstructing the film's production. Murray, as before, took great pains in explaining the Federal Government's limitations when it came to freedom of expression as sanctioned by the Constitution. He would indeed be glad to draw the Secretary's attention to the controversy, but a satisfactory solution could come from M-G-M itself once it realized the seriousness of the repercussions associated with the production. Murray then "urged the Ambassador...not to take the matter too much to heart," but Ertegun regretted that the US was "not in a position to intervene," that is, directly.[48]

The intensity of the Turkish campaign perplexed M-G-M. Moreover, with a cancellation of the project, the company would forfeit what promised to be a lucrative deal given the novel's enormous popularity. Some insiders questioned the right of a foreign government to meddle in the business of an American company and the ramifications of such interference respecting future propositions. Whatever the prevalent apprehension, however, the M-G-M leadership, pressured by the State Department, adopted a strategy of dealing with the Turkish embassy in Washington, D.C., directly. Accordingly, the company commissioned Vice President J. Robert Rubin to meet with Ertegun.[49] The latter impressed upon his visitor

---

[47] USNA, RG 59, *Musa Dagh*, doc. 17, Robert P. Skinner to Secretary of State, June 4, 1935. See also doc. 18, Robert P. Skinner to Wallace Murray, June 6, 1935; doc. 19, Wallace Murray to Robert P. Skinner, June 20, 1935.

[48] Ibid., doc. 20, Wallace Murray memorandum to file, June 18, 1935. See also doc. 21, WMS to American Ambassador, Istanbul, June 21, 1935; doc. 22, Wallace Murray to Frederick L. Herron, June 21, 1935.

[49] Minassian, "The Forty Years of Musa Dagh," p. 66.

the unfairness of the story, calling it one-sided and injurious to "Turkish honor." He also spoke about the negative impact that the film would have on the existing warm bilateral relations between Turkey and the United States. Ertegun made no secret that not only the said movie, but all M-G-M productions would be blacklisted by his and other countries. Although Ertegun was reluctant to review an altered draft of the script because of the plot's inherent aversion to Turkish interests, Rubin "insisted that a trial examination of a draft scenario be made to ascertain the practicability of eventual suggestions. A copy was, therefore, prepared, submitted, and transmitted to the pertinent authorities in Turkey.[50]

Murray kept the pressure on Herron, who, having formed the strong impression that Ertegun was ready to renege on his promise to read the draft scenario for an official opinion, urged mutual understanding, but not acquiescence: "It would be much better for every one concerned if there would be cooperation in this rather than opposition. I am sure with the proper cooperation every one can be satisfied. If the script is not satisfactory that is another proposition, but I don't think in view of Mr. Rubin's visit to the Ambassador that the matter should be stopped now."[51] But Murray, apprehensive of the political complications that might arise should M-G-M fail to keep its part of the bargain not to make the film without prior Turkish approval, considered a contingency "disclaimer of any responsibility by the [State] Department…in preparation for any representations that the Turkish Ambassador would doubtless make…"[52]

The Turkish press turned on the heat in what appeared to be a calculated and concerted effort. During the week of September 3-10, 1935, several Istanbul newspapers, including *La République*, the French edition of the influential *Cumhuriyet* that boasted of 9,000 subscriptions, launched a vicious attack on Werfel and his novel, M-G-M, and the American media on the one hand and stressed the need for boycott and counterpropaganda to portray Turkey and the Turks

[50] USNA, RG 59, *Musa Dagh*, doc. 25, Mehmet Münir to Cordell Hull, September 5, 1935.
[51] Ibid., doc. 23, Frederick L. Herron to Wallace Murray, June 24, 1935.
[52] Ibid., doc. 30, [MSB] memorandum to file, September 12, 1935.

in a positive light before world public opinion on the other.[53] To begin with, Werfel, "a shameless Jew"[54] who had been "expelled by the German Government in a gentlemanly-like manner,"[55] unabashedly described the Turks as uncivilized, honorless, and murderous.[56] By doing so, Werfel "simply renews the vile accusations concocted by the Jew [Henry] Morgenthau," the United States ambassador to the Ottoman Empire during part of World War I, and his Armenian aide. If M-G-M, reflecting a desire on the part of the American people, wanted to torture humans in "the country of lynching," they would be better off by filming "the lynching of a few negroes, an event which under ridiculous pretexes occurs daily in New York, Chicago, and Texas. We would benefit therefrom…and learn what civilization is."[57] Unfortunately, it was difficult to dissuade M-G-M from producing *Musa Dagh* even if United States national interests were at stake, because the company "is an essentially Jewish concern with Jewish managers endowed with a different commercial mentality and that, therefore, it is doubtful that they shall act as would be the case with an entirely American concern."[58]

After thus casting doubt on Jewish loyalty to the United States and threatening a boycott of M-G-M, the Turkish press went on to warn "the other Jewish firms which maintain commercial relations with our country, for they also will suffer if they fail to stop this hostile propaganda." The media likewise called upon the Jewish people "to bring this Jewish company [M-G-M] to reason." Otherwise, the Turks would take matters into their own hands. In fact, the Jews owed it to Turkey given the hospitality and

[53] Ibid., doc. 35, G. Howland Shaw to Secretary of State, September 10, 1935.

[54] *La Republique* (September 9, 1935), as cited in USNA, RG 59, *Musa Dagh*, doc. 35.

[55] *Son Posta* (September 6, 1935), as cited in USNA, RG 59, *Musa Dagh*, doc. 35.

[56] *La Republique* (September 9, 1935), as cited in USNA, RG 59, *Musa Dagh*, doc. 35.

[57] *Son Posta* (September 6, 1935), as cited in USNA, RG 59, *Musa Dagh*, doc. 35.

[58] *La Republique* (September 6, 1935), as cited in USNA, RG 59, *Musa Dagh*, doc. 35.

benevolence that they enjoyed there without being subjected to persecutions, pressures, and anti-Semitism.[59] But Shaw, now the United States Chargé d'Affaires ad interim, did not fail to see the undercurrent of anti-Semitism in Turkey, even at some official level. For him, it was no coincidence that the German-trained Vedat Nedim Tör, head of the General Directorate of the Press, the propaganda branch in the Ministry of the Interior, had gone to Germany that summer to study "German Propaganda technique[s] under no less a master than Goebbels" and that the Turkish press had launched its attacks after his return.[60]

The Turkish papers also blamed the American media for disseminating "calumnies." One such target was the *Motion Picture Herald*, which, in its 119th issue, had carried "a large size advertisement" depicting the savagery of Turkish soldiers in the villages of Musa Dagh.[61] The August 18 literary supplement of the *New York Times* had "blacken[ed] our [Turkish] reputation before world public opinion even more" by declaring *Musa Dagh*, through its 100,000-strong Book of the Month Club, as the best novel in the US and pledging to send its subscribers some 50,000 copies. Given the fact that 170,000 copies had already been sold, the significant gratuities would add insult to injury.[62] Finally, commenting on a criticism leveled by the *New York Herald Tribune* at the US Government's cooperation with Turkey to censure the film, one Turkish counterpart dismissed "this nervousness" as "misplaced."[63]

While monitoring the situation via direct contact with M-G-M itself, the Ipekçi Brothers, exhibitors of M-G-M movies in Turkey, and the US embassy,[64] a defiant Turkish press went on the counteroffensive: "The enemy is spreading propaganda; we shall spread it also. To the book we will reply with a book; to the film

---

59 *Haber* (September 3, 1935), as cited in USNA, RG 59, *Musa Dagh*, doc. 35.

60 USNA, RG 59, *Musa Dagh*, doc. 35, G. Howland Shaw to Secretary of State, September 10, 1935.

61 *La Republique* (September 3, 1935), as cited in USNA, RG 59, *Musa Dagh*, doc. 35.

62 Ibid., (September 7, 1935).

63 Ibid., (September 8, 1935).

64 Ibid., (September 4-6 and 10, 1935).

with a film."[65] Having admittedly erred in the assumption that the stereotypical image of the Turk as a man with bloodthirsty eyes, carrying a sword, and entertaining a large harem had faded from Western memory, it was now proposed to manipulate motion pictures as the most effective weapon of modern propaganda to highlight Turkey's substantial accomplishments on the road to reform under Mustafa Kemal Atatürk.[66] While not opposed to any of this, the *Tan* [Dawn], *Cumhuriyet*'s main rival, tried to calm the "tempest in a tea pot" by reminding its readers that M-G-M had not yet produced the film and that it might abandon the project altogether. Therefore, "the matter can no longer stand journalistic exploitation."[67] Before too long the hoopla ebbed, and for a good reason.

Cognizant of the negative publicity directed against it, M-G-M decided to send a representative to Turkey in a bid "to obtain authorization for production," indeed an "unusual accommodation." But Fahir Epekji (Ipekçi), "Metro's man in Istanbul," found the maneuver a useless attempt.[68] At any rate, the Turkish response to the screenplay came on September 27, 1935: "It was not a question of cutting out a line here and page there — the whole thing was highly offensive to Turkey and the Turks" and revived the Armenian Question. In short, the script was categorically rejected.[69] Interestingly, even Greece, Turkey's traditional adversary, joined the chorus in opposing the film. Wavering between defiance to and acceptance of outside dictates, M-G-M finally buckled under pressure.[70] Its representative now agreed with Ertegun in a meeting at the Turkish embassy that the novel "could not but be harmful from every standpoint" and "that they would rather drop this scheme altogether." Ertegun transmitted "the satisfactory result" to his government without forgetting to thank the State Department and

---

[65] Ibid., (September 9, 1935).

[66] Ibid., (September 8-9, 1935); *Cumhuriyet* (September 10, 1935).

[67] *Tan* (September 8, 1935), as cited in USNA, RG 59, *Musa Dagh*, doc. 35.

[68] Minassian, "The Forty Years of Musa Dagh," pp. 67-68.

[69] USNA, RG 59, *Musa Dagh*, doc. 39, G. Howland Shaw to Secretary of State, September 27, 1935.

[70] Minassian, "The Forty Years of Musa Dagh," p. 69.

especially Murray for their indispensable contribution.[71] The *Motion Picture Herald* lashed out its anger against Turkey for her "selfish wish that a skeleton which has long reposed in the closet of a nation shall not be rattled."[72]

On December 12, the Turkish press reported that the film was still on M-G-M's production list.[73] After a speedy investigation, the United States authorities dismissed the sensationalistic rumor as a "false alarm."[74] Skinner even criticized the attitude of the government-run Turkish press Bureau as "somewhat irritating." And with the customs authorities holding the release, albeit temporarily, of other M-G-M films on no objectionable grounds,[75] it was not hard to recognize the extra pressure exerted to ensure the irrevocable shelving of *Musa Dagh.* In this, the Armenians of Istanbul were made pawns. Called upon by the Turkish media to show their opposition to Werfel's work and worried about the attention received due to their positive portrayal in the novel, on December 18, Armenian intellectuals and commoners assembled in their churchyard at Pangalti and burned Werfel's picture and book. After the choir and students sang the Turkish national anthem, Aram Aslan, a community leader, delivered a speech and, together with Asot (Ashot) Kecya, another intellectual, sent a similar telegram to

---

[71] USNA, RG 59, *Musa Dagh*, doc. 36, M. Münir Ertegun to Wallace Murray, October 4, 1935. See also doc. 37, Wallace Murray to Mehmet Münir Ertegun, October 9, 1935; doc. 38, WSM to American Ambassador, Istanbul, October 10, 1935; doc. 40, WSM to Secretary of Commerce, October 17, 1935; doc. 41, Robert P. Skinner to Secretary of State, October 5, 1935.

[72] *Motion Picture Herald* (December 7, 1935), as cited in USNA, RG 59, *Musa Dagh*, doc. 44.

[73] *La Republique* (December 12, 1935), as cited in USNA, RG 59, *Musa Dagh*, doc. 48.

[74] USNA, RG 59, *Musa Dagh*, doc. 43, Wallace Murray to Frederick L. Herron, December 14, 1935. See also doc. 44, Division of Near Eastern Affairs memorandum to file, December 17, 1935; doc. 45, Frederick L. Herron to Wallace Murray, December 17, 1935; doc. 45, Wallace Murray memorandum to Signing Officer, December 19, 1935; doc. 46, Hull telegram to Amembassy (sic), Istanbul, December 19, 1935; doc. 48, Robert P. Skinner to Secretary of State, December 12, 1935.

[75] Ibid., doc. 49, Robert P. Skinner to Secretary of State, December 24, 1935.

the Ministry of the Interior.[76] In this most "humiliating scene"[77] of coerced theatrics, Aslan declared:

> We wish to make it public to the world that the fate of those who try to create trouble among us is death, and this we did by burning the photo and the book, "Forty Days of Musa Dagh," by the cursed Franz Werfel, who has plotted against our sacred country. By this action, the Turkish Armenians have actually proved their hearty attachment to this glorious country, which has been turned into a paradise by Ataturk, our great President of the Republic and in which country they have lived a brotherly life for the first time in hundreds of years.[78]

The Armenians abroad were too disorganized and slow to be able to lobby effectively in favor of the movie. In June 1937, that is, two years after the heightened period of political football played around *Musa Dagh*, a certain Warren A. Chiljan, representing "many prominent Armenians" from the East Bay in the San Francisco area, solicited United States Congressman John H. Tolan's assistance in finding and passing on "the real facts" about the film's cancellation. First identifying the culpable "mysterious hands" as those of the Turkish government and France, Chiljan went on to blame the State Department for the "injustice" done to Armenians throughout America. What he wanted to know from Tolan was the degree of this implication, assuring him that "your efforts in this will not only be deeply appreciated by all of the Armenians throughout the world who are determined to follow it up, but the subject being very close to the Armenian heart, you will undoubtedly be idolized by each and every one of them."[79] Responding to Tolan's inquiry, Secretary of State Cordell Hull maintained that he was "not in a position to comment upon a privately concluded agreement [between M-G-M

---

[76] *Cumhuriyet* (December 19, 1935), as cited in USNA, RG 59, *Musa Dagh*, doc. 49.

[77] USNA, RG 59, *Musa Dagh*, doc. 49, Robert P. Skinner to Secretary of State, December 24, 1935.

[78] *Cumhuriyet* (December 19, 1935), as cited in USNA, RG 59, *Musa Dagh*, doc. 49.

[79] USNA, RG 59, *Musa Dagh*, doc. 50, Warren A. Chiljan to John H. Tolan, June 30, 1937. See also doc 50, John H. Tolan to Cordell Hull, July 2, 1937.

and the Turkish embassy] unless that agreement affects the interests of this Government."[80] Herron concurred with Hull's deliberate taciturnity: "I think...the less said about such things the better it is for everyone concerned and unless something further is desired from us I am going to bury the matter right where it stands."[81] The Armenians were thus hushed and staged no further challenge.

But the topic would not go away. On November 22, 1938, the *Boston Evening American* reported that, since the death of Turkish president Ataturk "has removed one of the greatest obstacles to the filming of '[The] Forty Days of Musa Dagh'," M-G-M was reconsidering the project.[82] Ertegun immediately notified the State Department, clarifying that "his Government's objections to the film have not changed in the least since the death of the late president."[83] Winds of change did in fact blow in terms of the motion picture industry's determination to "discard all scruples...with regard to making pictures which are objectionable to the dictatorial powers [and]...ridiculous sensitive governments."[84] But the State Department sought to exclude Turkey from the roster for political-economic expediency: "...Although the American film producers might be prepared to take their own losses resulting from disregard of foreign sensibilities, other American business (not to mention our foreign relations) might also suffer. Widespread anti-Americanism in Turkey, for instance, might result in losses to Socony-Vacuum, General Motors and Ford."[85] The director of the Motion Pictures Division, Bureau of Foreign and Domestic Commerce, begged to differ:

> He thought [that] that was a very weak argument, that each American business should stand on its own feet, that

---

[80] Ibid., doc. 51, Cordell Hull to John H. Tolan, July 10, 1937. See also doc. 52, Wallace Murray to Frederick L. Herron, July 10, 1937.

[81] Ibid., doc. 53, Frederick L. Herron to Wallace Murray, July 13, 1937.

[82] *The Boston Evening American* (November 22, 1938), as cited in USNA, RG 59, *Musa Dagh*, doc. 54.

[83] USNA, RG 59, *Musa Dagh*, doc. 55, Wallace Murray to Frederick L. Herron, December 17, 1938.

[84] Ibid., doc. 57, Memorandum of Conversation (telephone) between G.V. Allen and Golden, Director, Motion Pictures Division, Bureau of Foreign and Domestic Commerce, December 15, 1938.

[85] Ibid.

> the motion picture producers have cooperated with other American interests in the past certainly as fully as other American interests have cooperated with them, and that, if the shoe were on the other foot, he doubted that other American businesses would take any considerable steps to assist the American motion pictures business. He said that continual repression had brought the motion pictures pot to a boil and the producers were determined to take the lid off.[86]

Be that as it may, the State Department persuaded the director to refrain from any activity that would draw a wedge in US-Turkish amicable relations. Even so, since the Turkish ambassador might find it more difficult to obstruct the film this time around given the emergent defiant mood in Hollywood, the lack of convincing guarantees on the part of M-G-M, and the discernible rift between the company's Western and Eastern bureaus apropos of *Musa Dagh*, the State Department took no chances and consolidated its efforts with Herron again.[87] Such fears notwithstanding, *Musa Dagh* was shelved for over two decades. Beginning in 1961 M-G-M unsuccessfully attempted to resuscitate the project, ultimately losing the control of its rights in 1976.[88] Finally, in 1982, an independent Armenian filmmaker by the name of John Kurkjian was able to produce and exhibit the movie, indeed a modest realization that failed to garner international recognition.[89]

The *Musa Dagh* issue resurfaced in the Turkish campaign of denial of the Armenian genocide one more time, in 1990. That year,

---

[86] Ibid.

[87] Ibid., doc. 58, Wallace Murray to Welles and Messersmith, December 17, 1938; doc. 59, Frederick L. Herron to Wallace Murray, December 19, 1938; doc. 60, GSM to Wallace Murray and Burke, December 20, 1938; doc. 61, [GSM] to Frederick L. Herron, December 20, 1938; doc 62, Wallace Murray to Messersmith, December 21, 1938; doc. 63, Memo of conversation between Frederick L. Herron and Alling, January 11, 1939; doc. 64, [Secretary of State] to American Ambassador, Istanbul, February 3, 1939.

[88] Anthony Slide, comp., *Ravished Armenia and the Story of Aurora Mardiganian*, Filmmakers Series, no. 57 (Lanham, MD & London: The Scarecrow Press, Inc., 1997), p. 4.

[89] Minassian, "The Forty Years of Musa Dagh," p. 71.

Process Agency, located on Inkilap Sokak in Ankara, published a pamphlet entitled "The Truth about Musa Dagh" that included a "sworn statement" by a certain Albert J. Amateau, a 101 year-old French expatriate who was reportedly born in Talas, had studied in Izmir, Turkey, and had emigrated to the US in 1910.[90] The "facts" provided by Amateau were "submitted to oppose approval of resolution SJ 212, introduced by the Honorable Robert Dole, Senator and Republican Leader of the United States Senate, at the first session of the 101st Congress of the United States." That resolution sought "to designate April 24, 1990 as the 'National Day of Remembrance' of the 75th anniversary of the alleged Armenian genocide of 1915-1923 perpetrated by the government of the Ottoman Empire."[91]

Calling Franz Werfel "my friend," Amateau maintained that "the story was told him [Werfel] by his friend, the Armenian Bishop of Vienna and Werfel never doubted the Bishop's account. He did not investigate what he wrote. Years later, when the true facts about Mussa Dagh [sic] were established by the research of neutral investigators—which was never denied by the Armenians—Werfel discovered that he had been duped by his friend, the Bishop, with a concocted story. Werfel confessed to me [Amateau] his shame and remorse for having written the story, in which he had blamed the Ottomans as the aggressors and terrorists." Moving from the ludicrous to the preposterous, Amateau then told "the truth." According to him, Musa Dagh, with a population of 50,000 Armenians, was located in the Anatolian hinterland at Erzerum, that is, hundreds of kilometers to the northeast of its actual site near Antioch. Before taking up arms, the Armenian highlanders captured and mercilessly killed hundreds of their good Muslim and Jewish neighbors, simply because they belonged to different religions. The Armenians then attacked the rear of the Ottoman and German armies. By the time the "mystified" Turks had identified the insurgents' hideout, "the large [Armenian] army had disappeared down the other side of the mountain where they had found an exit to the Mediterranean." Only the rear guard, composed of "less than

---

[90] Process Agency, *The Truth about Musa Dagh* (Ankara, 1990), unpaginated pamphlet.

[91] Ibid.

500," surrendered to the Ottomans, the rest being rescued by the French and British navy and taken to Alexandria, Egypt.[92] Given Werfel's and my meticulous research respecting Musa Dagh, Amateau's account stands as a compilation of falsehoods serving Turkey's interest.

By focusing on Musa Dagh through Amateau, not only did Turkey attempt to deny the genocide but also recast the role of the victims as victimizers. Moreover, "even if 1.5 million Armenians lost their lives during the war, they died as soldiers, fighting a war of their own choosing against the Ottoman Empire which had treated them decently and benignly. They were the duped victims of the Russians, of the Allies, and of their own Armenian leaders." By painting such a distorted image of the Armenian calamity, Ankara aimed at playing on fears within the context of realpolitik in international relations: "It is not enough to say that they [US Senators] do not mean to hurt the Turks or Turkish/American relations. By entertaining the resolution [S.J. 212] without proof, they are actually going against the interests of Turkey and the safety of the United States and of NATO."[93] The tactic worked and the resolution was defeated. Morality, so fundamental to American politics, was put to the test in the venerable Congress and failed.[94]

---

[92] Ibid.

[93] Ibid.

[94] Vigen Guroian, "The Politics and Morality of Genocide," in Richard G. Hovannisian, ed., *The Armenian Genocide: History, Politics, Ethics* (New York: St. Martin's Press, 1992), pp. 327-336.

36

Denial of the Armenian Genocide as a Prototype

Richard Hovannisian

The year 2008 marks the ninety-third anniversary of the Armenian Genocide. That calamity completely altered the course of Armenian history as well as the geopolitical, economic, and ethnographic complexion of the Middle East. Today, the Armenian Genocide, like the genocides and genocidal massacres in Africa, Asia, and Europe, belongs to a past century and in the minds of many may not seem to have much relevance for current generations. Yet the lessons from those crimes remain compelling and need to be passed on. In the Armenian case, more than anything else it is the trauma that is especially enduring because of the refusal of the perpetrator regime or its successors to acknowledge the crime and to seek redemption. Instead of apologies and educational programs to face their history and themselves honestly, the Turkish government and most Turkish intellectuals continue along a path of self-righteous negation. In this dissimulation they are joined by sympathetic academics abroad, thereby only compounding the trauma of the victims. In fact, the case of the Armenian Genocide has become the prototype of denial of modern premeditated mass killing. It is not coincidental that, with one exception, there has been no ready admission of responsibility by any genocidal regime in the twentieth century.

It has been said that denial is the final phase of genocide. Following the physical destruction of a people and the foundations of their culture, memory is all that is left and is targeted as the last victim. Complete annihilation of a people requires the banishment of recollection and the suffocation of remembrance. Falsification, deception, and half-truths reduce what was to what may have been or perhaps what was not at all. Horrific terror gives way to reason, violence adapts to explanation, and history is reshaped to suit a contemporary agenda. By altering or erasing the past, a present is produced and a future is projected without concern for historical integrity.

Denial of the Armenian Genocide has become fully institutionalized. The strategies may change, but the objectives remain constant. Not sufficiently successful with unqualified denial, its practitioners have found that they can build a more plausible case through the tactics of rationalization and relativization. They strive to create doubt and to disguise blatant falsification by appealing to a sense of fair play and to the correctness of giving a hearing to the other side of a complex and misrepresented issue. Accusations against the purported perpetrator state, they maintain, are residues of historical prejudices and hostile wartime propaganda and the result of machinations of the alleged victims to enrich themselves personally and collectively at the expense of others. Emphasis is directed away from the planned, systematic process of mass murder, and genocide is explained in the context of general wartime civilian casualties, the numbers of victims are minimized, and doubt is cast on the reliability of eyewitness testimony and documents relating to the mass killings. Historical deception replaces absolute negation, but the goal is unchanged.

Deniers and rationalizers of the Armenian Genocide use the following arguments, many of which will be recognized by students of other mass killings:

1. Stories about alleged genocide are based on wartime propaganda;

2. Armenians in the Ottoman Empire were perceived as posing a very real security threat, and their actions demonstrated that these concerns were not imaginary;

3. There was no intent to annihilate the group, only to relocate it;

4. The Armenian deaths that occurred were primarily from the same causes that carried away far more Turks and Kurds;

5. The number of dead is much less than claimed, and most of the alleged victims actually ended up in other countries;

6. The myth of genocide was created for economic and/or political purposes;

7. Those who believe and promote the myth have been the willful or unwitting abettors of communism and Soviet expansion and the destabilization of the NATO alliance and the West;

8. The proponents of truth are struggling against powerful political lobbies to rectify negative stereotypes and historical misconceptions.[1]

The deniers manipulate statistics, history, and culture in order to minimize the significance of the Armenian presence in the area once called Armenia and now known as Eastern Anatolia. In this effort, it is necessary to obscure all evidence of that presence by changing place-names, destroying historical monuments, and making Armenians disappear from the written record. Proudly proclaiming a cultural heritage that includes ancient civilizations from the Hittites to the Romans and even the Byzantines, Turkish nationalist writers, buttressed by their foreign collaborators, have wiped away three millennia of Armenian history.[2] The elimination of a people has been followed by the destruction of thousands of its monuments of spiritual and material culture and now even a campaign to expunge its very memory. The arguments used by the negationists, rationalizers, and relativizers of the Armenian Genocide have universal application, and most examples below can easily be transferred to other mass killings of the twentieth century. Though this essay is far from comprehensive, for there are various shades and gradations of deniers and denial, the sources included here may be regarded as representative of the genre.

---

[1] See Richard G. Hovannisian, "The Armenian Genocide and Patterns of Denial," in *The Armenian Genocide in Perspective*, R. G. Hovannisian, ed. (New Brunswick, NJ, and Oxford: Transaction Books, 1986), pp. 111-134. For bibliographic essays on this subject, see Roger W. Smith, "Denial of the Armenian Genocide," in *Genocide: A Critical Bibliographic Review*, Israel W. Charny, ed., vol. 2 (London: Mansell, and New York: Facts on File, 1991), pp. 38-85.

[2] See, for example, Clive Foss, "The Turkish View of Armenian History: A Vanishing Nation," in *The Armenian Genocide: History, Politics, Ethics,* Richard G. Hovannisian, ed. (New York: St. Martin's Press, and London: MacMillan, 1992), pp. 250-279.

Wartime Propaganda

Stories about intentional mass killing, say the deniers, are founded on wartime propaganda for the purpose of turning public opinion against an enemy, which is made to seem so odious as to be worthy of merciless punishment. They point to the "myth of genocide" as Allied propaganda to demonize the other side and as a scheme to reap great sums of money as reparations. Former Turkish diplomat Kamuran Gürün complains about the organized propaganda campaign of the Armenians and shows the Turkish government to be the victim of its own lack of aggressiveness: "We can easily state that propaganda is one of the weakest points of Turks. This was so in the Ottoman Empire, as well as in the Turkish republic. The propaganda activity of Turks has been restricted to refuting articles and erroneous assertions; thus, it has been nothing more than a passive effort to defend the Turkish position. This attitude enabled the opposite side to act freely in portraying the Turks continuously as being guilty."[3]

American deniers, such as Stanford Shaw and Justin McCarthy, have labeled accounts of more than a million Armenian victims as the work of the "propaganda mills." McCarthy maintains that the prevailing prejudices in the West, the biased accounts of American missionaries, and the propaganda of the Allied Powers helped to perpetuate and intensify negative views of the Turks. In his manual for students and teachers, *Turks and Armenians*, McCarthy writes:

> The English propaganda machine churned out atrocity stories against both Germany and its ally Turkey to aid in its war effort both at home and abroad. Several European states coveted Ottoman territory, and the massacres and atrocities for which the Ottoman government was said to be responsible were used as the justification for breaking up the Ottoman Empire and for taking all or nearly all lands away from Ottoman rule. The Western nations needed to believe and promote Ottoman and Turkish atrocity stories in order to excuse their own plans to annex Ottoman lands.[4]

---

[3] Kamuran Gürün, *The Armenian File: The Myth of Innocence Exposed* (New York: St. Martin's Press, 1985), p. 36.

[4] Justin McCarthy and Carolyn McCarthy, *Turks and Armenians: A Manual on the Armenian Question* (Washington, D.C.: Assembly of Turkish-American Associations, 1989), pp. 85-86.

Although the propaganda against the Germans was subsequently exposed for what it was, this did not occur in the case of Turkey. "Instead, the deceptions and distortions of propaganda on the Turks and Armenians have survived, so the legacy of hatred and prejudice remains."[5] It has thus been the mission of McCarthy, Shaw, Heath Lowry, and others of like mind "to set the record straight."

Deniers are keen on discrediting survivor testimony. They insist that such accounts as are given by so-called survivors are full of inconsistencies and exaggerations and were intended to grab billions of dollars from the Turkish government. A Turkish denial booklet published in the 1980s asserts:

> Carefully coached by their Armenian nationalist interviewers, these aged Armenians relate tales of horror. . . in such detail as to astonish the imagination, considering that most of them already are aged eighty or more. Subjected to years of Armenian nationalist propaganda as well as the coaching of their interviewers, there is little doubt that their statements are of no use whatever for historical research.[6]

What underlies such a statement is the fear, in fact, that eye-witness accounts may have a great deal of use, even though it seems to be argued that eighty-year-old survivors cannot possibly retain a detailed memory of what occurred to them and those around them.

Provocation of the Alleged Victims

The deniers and rationalizers of genocide try to show that the alleged victims were not guiltless and the security measures taken by the state were no different from what other beleaguered governments have done before and after. The so-called Armenian victims were in most instances partisans, saboteurs, spies, and enemy collaborators – a virtual fifth column. Desperate acts of resistance, such as at Van, are offered as evidence of Armenian hostility, seriously jeopardizing the war effort by necessitating the diversion of regular armed forces to cope with the insurrections. Gürün explains:

---

[5] Ibid., p. 88.

[6] *Setting the Record Straight on Armenian Propaganda Against Turkey* (Washington, D.C.: Assembly of Turkish-American Associations, 1982), p. 11.

> The Armenians were forced to emigrate because they had joined the ranks of the enemy. The fact that they were civilians does not change the situation. Those who were killed in Hiroshima and Nagasaki during the Second World War were also civilians. Those who were killed during the First World War in France, Belgium, and Holland were also civilians. Those who died in London during the Battle of Britain were also civilians. . . . Turkey did not kill them [Armenians], but relocated them. As it was impossible to adopt a better solution under the circumstances, it cannot be accepted that those who died because they were unable to resist the hardships of the journey were killed by the Turks.[7]

Gürün has simply embellished the rationalization of a key architect of the Armenian Genocide, Minister of the Interior and Grand Vizier Talaat Pasha, who from his postwar place of hiding in Germany in 1919, wrote: "These preventive measures were taken in every country during the war, but, while the regrettable results were passed over in silence in the other countries, the echo of our acts was heard the world over, because everybody's eyes were upon us."[8] Decades later, a Turkish official in Washington tried to draw a parallel for Americans: "Turkish response to the Armenian excesses was comparable, I believe, to what might have been the American response, had the German-Americans of Minnesota or Wisconsin revolted on behalf of Hitler during World War II."[9] And Ambassador Şükrü Elekdag wrote in 1982: "What took place was a complex tragedy which claimed Turkish as well as Armenian lives. Indeed, it was a civil war within a global war stemming from an armed uprising of the Armenian minority at a time when the Ottoman state was fighting for survival during World War I. Many more Turks than Armenians perished."[10]

---

[7] Gürün, *The Armenian File*, p. 216.

[8] [Talaat], "Posthumous Memoirs of Talaat Pasha," *Current History*, 15 November 1921: 295.

[9] Altemur Kiliç, *Turkey and the World* (Washington, D.C.: Public Affairs Press, 1959), p. 18.

[10] United States Congress, 97th Congress, 2d session, *Congressional Record*, 128 (Washington, D.C.: Government Printing Office, 1982), pp. 1993-1994.

The rather transparent excuses for the Turkish deniers were refined by their Western collaborators. Years before he was challenged in the French courts in the 1990s for his denial of the Armenian Genocide, Professor Bernard Lewis cautiously advanced the cause of revisionism by couching the Armenian calamity in terms of mutual warfare threatening the very existence of the Turkish state: In *The Emergence of Modern Turkey*, published in 1961, Lewis explains:

> For the Turks, the Armenian [nationalist] movement was the deadliest of all threats. From the conquered lands of the Serbs, Bulgars, Albanians, and Greeks, they could, however reluctantly, withdraw, abandoning distant provinces and bringing the Imperial frontier nearer home. But the Armenians, stretching across Turkey-in-Asia from the Caucasian frontier to the Mediterranean coast, lay in the very heart of the Turkish homeland – and to renounce these lands would have meant not the truncation, but the dissolution of the Turkish state. Turkish and Armenian villages, inextricably mixed, had for centuries lived in a neighbourly association. Now a desperate struggle between them began – a struggle of two nations for the possession of a single homeland, that ended with the terrible holocaust of 1916 [sic], when a million and half Armenians perished.[11]

Stanford J. Shaw, in a volume co-authored with his wife and published by Cambridge University Press (*History of the Ottoman Empire and Modern Turkey*), presents many more deceptive arguments. He makes it seem, for instance, that in ordering the Armenian deportations the Turkish authorities were simply following a precedent already established by the Russians in clearing the border zones to be ready for battle. "Enver [Minister of War] followed this example to prepare the Ottoman side and to resist the expected Russian invasion. Armenian leaders in any case now declared their open support of the enemy, and there seemed no other alternative." Ascribing sinister motives to the Armenians, Shaw would have his readers believe that there was "no alternative" to deportation:

---

[11] Bernard Lewis, *The Emergence of Modern Turkey* (London, New York, Toronto: Oxford University Press, 1961), p. 350.

> It would be impossible to determine which of the Armenians would remain loyal and which would follow the appeals of their leaders. As soon as spring came, then, in mid-May 1915 orders were issued to evacuate the entire Armenian population from the provinces of Van, Bitlis, and Erzurum, to get them away from all areas where they might undermine the Ottoman campaigns, against Russia or against the British in Egypt.[12]

Concealing the fact that the Armenian population was deported and massacred throughout the width and breadth of Anatolia, Shaw claims that the Armenians were "evacuated" only from the war zone along the Russian frontier and from the Cilician countryside but not the cities in that region near the Mediterranean Sea.[13]

Justin McCarthy, a student of Stanford Shaw, tries to show himself to be more balanced, yet his underlying motives are as obvious as those of the most blatant deniers. He repeats Gürün's claim that Armenian rebellions flared all over Anatolia, requiring the diversion of entire army divisions to suppress the conspiratorial risings. McCarthy prides himself on being a demographer yet apparently does not see the untenable contradiction between his calculations minimizing the number of Armenians in the Ottoman Empire and his acceptance of Gürün's assertion that from the province of Sivas (Sebastia) alone there were 30,000 Armenian guerrillas. He allows himself to engage in wild exaggeration: "No one accurately counted the numbers, but unquestionably there were more than 100,000 Armenian guerrillas or other fighters from Anatolia or the Russian territories fighting in Anatolia."[14]

For McCarthy and all other deniers and rationalizers, the desperate efforts at self-defense in a few isolated places – Van, Shabin-Karahisar, Urfa, and Musa Dagh – are sufficient proof of Armenian disloyalty and conspiracy. Deportation became the

---

[12] Stanford J. Shaw, *History of the Ottoman Empire and Modern Turkey*, vol. 2, co-authored with Ezel Kural Shaw, *Reform, Revolution and Republic: The Rise of Modern Turkey, 1808-1975* (Cambridge, London, New York, Melbourne: Cambridge University Press, 1977), p. 315.

[13] Ibid.

[14] McCarthy, *Turks and Armenians*, p. 48; compare with Gürün, *The Armenian File*, p. 200.

Turkish government's response to the menace posed by the Armenians:

> The principle of the deportation was based on one of the few known ways to defeat a guerrilla insurgency and has been used from ancient up to modern times. Because guerrillas depend on local villages for supplies, support, and recruits, the guerrillas must be separated from the populace.... The Ottomans had for centuries deported groups who threatened civil order, including rebellious Turks.... Deportation of civilian populations because of real or imagined guerrilla threats has been practiced by many modern governments.[15]

McCarthy then leads the reader to the question of whether such seemingly extreme measures might actually have been the least of all possible evils: "Can one cause real suffering to deportees in order to ultimately save more lives by ending a war (an argument analogous to that of bombing of civilians in World War II)?"[16]

The Question of Intent: Rationalization and Relativization

It is imperative for deniers to make it seem that there was no intent to eliminate the targeted group. Intent underlies the United Nations Genocide Convention and widely accepted definitions of genocide. The horrors of war, they say, affect all elements of the population, not just one group. In fact, far more Turks and Kurds than Armenians died during World War I. It is meaningless to assign guilt, because war is evil as a phenomenon and creates universal suffering. Hence, differences in motivation and means of death are obscured in favor of the thesis of indiscriminate suffering during the general chaos and calamity of war, complicated further by civil strife and a certain breakdown of control. In time of such massive upheaval, differentiation between purported victim and perpetrator is not attainable. Pretending to engage in academic inquiry, deniers make quantitative comparisons in order to avoid qualitative ones, aiming to remove the specific features of systematic annihilation and to exonerate the guilty party.

---

[15] McCarthy, *Turks and Armenians*, p. 52.

[16] Ibid.

The disclaiming of intent once more has its prototype in the Armenian case. As early as 1919, Talaat Pasha, from his hiding place in Berlin, wrote: "I admit that we deported many Armenians from our eastern provinces, but we never acted in this matter upon a previously prepared scheme. The responsibility for these acts falls first of all upon the deported people themselves."[17] A publication of a Turkish governmental agency seven decades later repeats the argument that all humanity suffers during wartime and that no one group can be viewed as particular victim in periods of such universal affliction. "Certainly some lives were lost, as the result both of large scale military and bandit activities then going on in the areas through which they [the deportees] passed, as well as the general insecurity and blood feuds which some tribal forces sought to carry out as the caravans passed through their territories." The "tribal forces," of course, has reference to the Kurds, frequently the agents of death mobilized by the Young Turk regime's "Special Organization," but currently a serious problem for the Turkish government and therefore a convenient scapegoat for past excesses. Denying any intent of genocidal killings by the Turkish authorities, the publication admits that the problems of the relocated population were compounded by "severe shortage of fuel, food, medicine, and other supplies as well as large-scale plague and famine." It should be remembered, however, that "as many as three to four million Ottoman subjects of all religions died as a result of the same conditions that afflicted the deportees. How tragic and unfeeling it is, therefore, for Armenian nationalists to blame the undoubted suffering of the Armenians during the war to something more than the same anarchical conditions which afflicted all the Sultan's subjects."[18] Relativization neatly explains away the Armenian Genocide.

Turkish negationist Gürün, predictably seconded by American apologist McCarthy, maintains that the term "deportation" is incorrect, purposely misconstrued by the British and French for propaganda purposes. Actually, it was simply "changing one's location."[19] Gürün then makes an unusual plea, even for deniers and

[17] Talaat, "Posthumous Memoirs of Talaat Pasha," p. 294.

[18] *The Armenian Issue in Nine Questions and Answers* (Ankara: Foreign Policy Institute, 1982), p. 25.

[19] Gürün, *The Armenian File*, pp. 201-02. See also McCarthy, *Turks and Armenians*, p. 52.

apologists, to exclude from the count of Armenian victims the tens of thousands who perished during the "relocation."

> Various deaths occurred for various reasons during the relocation. Some of the deaths were due to epidemics, some were due to climatic factors, some were due to the hardships suffered during the journey, some were due to attacks, because officials did not protect them or because some officials engaged in illegal acts....
>
> Who are the ones who can be pointed to as "murdered" in these deaths? Certainly not the ones who were killed while fighting, nor those who died of epidemics of typhus, typhoid fever, cholera, and variola, which were then widespread in Turkey, or of famine. It cannot be claimed that they would not have died if they had stayed in their homes, because the epidemics spread to the areas of their residence and took hundreds of thousands of lives....
>
> Should we include in this group those who died because of climatic factors and the hardships of the journey during the emigration? We do not think so.[20]

Gürün conveniently ignores one of the five specific acts that constitute the crime of genocide according to the United Nations Convention: "deliberately inflicting on the group conditions of life calculated to bring about its physical destruction in whole or in part."[21]

Stanford Shaw pushed denial of the Armenian Genocide to new bounds in *History of Turkey and the Ottoman Empire*. After portraying the Armenians as long-time rebels and treacherous terrorists, he alleges that the orders for deportation involved only the actual or potential zones of war and that the Young Turk government acted in good faith in instructing that the Armenian exiles should not be harmed. He cites documents that were created for the record without giving even a hint that what happened in fact was the exact opposite of his description. Ignoring the overwhelming evidence of wholesale deportation and massacre, Shaw conceals the truth in stating that the Armenians were removed only from strategic war

---

[20] Gürün, *The Armenian File*, pp. 214-215.

[21] *Convention on the Prevention and Punishment of the Crime of Genocide*, Article II, United Nations, 9 December 1948.

zones and this with the utmost care for their safety and well-being. The government could not be more solicitous, even of this disloyal element, than the way he describes the deportation:

> Specific instructions were issued for the army to protect the Armenians against nomadic attacks and to provide them with sufficient food and other supplies to meet their needs during the march and after they were settled. Warnings were sent to the Ottoman military commanders to make certain that neither the Kurds nor any other Muslims used the situation to gain vengeance for the long years of Armenian terrorism. The Armenians were to be protected and cared for until they returned to their homes after the war. A supplementary law established a special commission to record the properties of some deportees and to sell them at auction at fair prices, with the revenues being held in trust until their return. Muslims wishing to occupy abandoned buildings could do so only as renters, with the revenues paid to the trust funds, and with the understanding that they would have to leave when the original owners returned. The deportees and their possessions were to be guarded by the army while in transit as well as in Iraq and Syria, and the government would provide for their return once the crisis was over.[22]

---

[22] Shaw, *History of the Ottoman Empire and Modern Turkey*, pp. 315-316. Several years after the publication of Shaw's volume, the Turkish Policy Institute copied this deceptive approach by publishing the following purported order of the Ottoman Council of Ministers:

> When those of the Armenians resident in the aforementioned towns and villages who have to be moved are transferred to their places of settlement and are on the road, their comfort must be assured and their lives and property protected; after their arrival their food should be paid for out of Refugees' Appropriations until they are definitively settled in their new homes. Property and land should be distributed to them in accordance with their previous financial situations as well as their current needs; and for those among them needing further help, the government should build houses, provide cultivators and artisans with seed, tools, and equipment.

Other passages read:

The fact that such nonsense appears in a volume published by one of the most reputable university presses is indicative of how deep the inroads of denial have reached.

In his student-teacher manual, Justin McCarthy, too, pleads the denier's case: "Orders were indeed sent from Istanbul ordering local administrators to protect lives and property of the deportees, and there was no reason to send out such orders if they were not meant to be enforced." The shortage of regular armed forces, he asserts, constrained the local governors to choose between protecting Muslim villages from Armenian bands or protecting Armenians from Muslims. "They chose to protect their own, as people usually will."[23] Advancing a favorite argument of the rationalization-relativization school of deniers, McCarthy suggests the following teaching objective. "The lesson of war in Eastern Anatolia is not that Turks massacred Armenians.... The lesson is that all the inhabitants of the Ottoman East suffered. They suffered such terrors that to try to choose whose torment was greater is absurd."[24] He offers the following caveat: "Genocide is a word of great power and vast value as propaganda. It is also a word with many imprecise definitions.... It would seem to be far better to study the history of the Armenians and the Turks as a great human loss, and to abandon propagandistic terms."[25]

The transformation of the small Soviet Armenian state into an independent republic in 1991 and the concerted attempts of its leaders to normalize relations with the Republic of Turkey created optimism that the intensity of the denial would wane and that perhaps a new era in Armenian-Turkish relations might eventually

---

> Make certain that indigent emigrants are given food and that their health is assured by daily visits by a doctor.... Sick people, poor people, women, and children should be sent by rail, and others on mules, in carts or on foot according to their power of endurance.... In cases where the emigrants are attacked, either in the camps or during the journey, all efforts should be taken to repel the attacks immediately.

See *The Armenian Issue in Nine Questions and Answers*, pp. 24-25.

[23] McCarthy, *Turks and Armenians*, p. 53.

[24] Ibid., p. 46.

[25] Ibid., p. 66.

lead to a Turkish admission of wrongdoing and at the very least a formal apology. But such hopes have been dashed by the unbending attitude of the Ankara government, as reflected in the publication in 1995, of a multi-volume work of the prime ministry's state archives entitled *Armenian Atrocities in the Caucasus and Anatolia According to Archival Documents*. The purpose of the publication is not only to reiterate all previous denials but also to demonstrate that it was in fact the Turkish people who were the victims of a genocide perpetrated by the Armenians. "These documents show that it was not the Turks who slaughtered Armenians, as the Armenians insist, but rather just the opposite, the Armenians slaughtered Turks, and this truth is shown clearly in the documents." Turkey, it is explained, had maintained an "honorable silence" for decades, but unfortunately that noble gesture has been interpreted by some as acceptance of guilt. What has to be made clear, therefore, is "that the truth is exactly the opposite of what is being said by Armenians and that it is time to put an end to the one-sided claims which have characterized this issue thus far."[26] With this development, the strategy of denial proceeds beyond the bounds of rationalization and relativization to a complete role reversal, making the victim the perpetrator.

Numbers

A common feature in the denial of genocide is the manipulation and questioning of statistics by the rationalizer-relativizers. Their skewed calculations are aimed at minimizing the numbers of potential victims inhabiting the areas controlled by the perpetrator side in order to diminish and relativize the gravity of the crime, and, if possible, to exonerate the accused entirely. As an example, the rationalizers, after juggling statistics to assert that there were far fewer Armenians in the affected regions than is generally accepted (the same tactic used by Holocaust deniers), insist that the Turkish authorities_simply wanted to relocate the untrustworthy elements. They challenge the reliability of the incriminating sources, in order to discredit the accuracy of the statistics, in order to dismiss the purported intent of the perpetrators, and in order to expose the so-called genocide as a myth.

---

[26] *Armenian Atrocities in the Caucasus and Anatolia According to Archival Documents* (Ankara: Prime Ministry State Archives, 1995), introduction.

Kamuran Gürün and other Turkish nationalist writers, using various formulas and scenarios, reach the conclusion that the total number of Armenians who died could not have been more than 300,000, and quite possibly no more than 100,000. "It is obvious that among these casualties the number of deaths which occurred for whatever reason during the emigration will be less than this figure, and the number of those who can be considered as having been killed will be even less."[27] It follows, therefore, that the number of Armenian victims was not disproportional to the losses of other elements during the war.

American authors Stanford Shaw, Justin McCarthy, and other denier-relativizers have refined the statistical manipulations to lower the number of Armenian victims almost out of sight. Shaw offers the following statistical contortions:

> The Entente propaganda mills and Armenian nationalists claimed that over a million Armenians were massacred during the war. But this was based on the assumption that the prewar Armenian population numbered about 2.5 million. The total number of Armenians in the empire before the war in fact came to at most 1,300,000, according to the Ottoman census. About half of these were resident in the affected areas, but, with the city dwellers allowed to remain, the number actually transported came to no more than 400,000, including some terrorists and agitators from the cities rounded up soon after the war began. In addition, approximately one-half million Armenians subsequently fled into the Caucasus and elsewhere during the remainder of the war. Since about 100,000 Armenians lived in the empire afterward, and about 150,000 to 200,000 immigrated to western Europe and the United States, one can assume that about 200,000 perished as a result not only of the transportation but also of the same conditions of famine, disease, and war action that carried away some 2 million Muslims at the same time.[28]

The inaccuracies contained in that paragraph have become institutionalized and are used repeatedly in various publications,

---

[27] Gürün, *The Armenian File*, p. 219.

[28] Shaw, *History of the Ottoman Empire and Modern Turkey*, pp. 315-316.

petitions, letters to the editor, and speeches in the United States Congress and other forums. Merciless deportation becomes "transportation" and the indiscriminate torment to death of men, women, and children becomes a relatively small loss caused by the "famine, disease, and war action" that afflicted the entire population. Planting reasonable doubt about intent and numbers through relativization of suffering is a potent weapon on which deniers rely.

The Trial of War Criminals

After both World War I and World War II, special tribunals gathered evidence and tried leaders of the defeated regimes for war crimes. A few high-ranking officials were brought before these tribunals as a symbolic process against the entire regime. Some of the accused did not deny the persecutions of the victim group but feigned ignorance or helplessness in the matter. These confessions are now damaging to the case of the deniers and therefore must be accounted for. The assertion is made that with the prevailing hysteria directed toward the defeated side, the postwar government in each case deemed it better to confess to the guilt of the predecessor regime in the hope of moderating somewhat the anticipated punishment. Hence, trials held in the courts of the victors or under their surveillance were invalid – a parody on true justice.

In the Armenian case, the postwar Turkish government created special military tribunals to try the Young Turk leaders for war crimes. All members of the central triumvirate – Enver, Talaat, Jemal – were sentenced to death, albeit *in absentia*, inasmuch as all had fled the country in the final days of the war. One district governor was actually hanged, but the process ended abruptly. The rise of the Turkish resistance movement led by Mustafa Kemal [Atatürk] had the effect of suspending the trials.[29] The British transferred many of the accused offenders to the island of Malta, but as the Allied Powers prepared to recognize and make their peace with Kemal, these men were released in a prisoner exchange. Nonetheless, a large corpus of incriminating material had been gathered and the proceedings of the

---

[29] See Vahakn N. Dadrian, *The History of the Armenian Genocide* (Providence and Oxford: Berghahn Books, 1995), pp. 303-343. See also Dadrian's bibliographic essay, "Documentation of the Armenian Genocide in Turkish Sources," in Charny, *Genocide,* pp. 86-138.

Turkish extraordinary tribunal were published as supplements of a semiofficial journal. While justice miscarried, the evidence remains. What was more, the Treaty of Sèvres between the Allied Powers and the official Turkish government in Constantinople (Istanbul) in August 1920 included provisions for the restoration of Armenian exiles, the rescue of Armenian women and children forcibly held in Muslim households, and the obligation of the Turkish government to cooperate in the gathering of evidence of war crimes and apprehending of accused criminals.[30]

The success of Mustafa Kemal's Turkish Nationalist movement and subsequent revision of the Treaty of Sèvres through the Lausanne treaties in 1923 did away with these provisions, but the relevant documents stand as reminders of the culpability of the Young Turk regime and require an explanation by deniers. They advance the same logic as those who dismiss the validity of the Nuremberg trials. Constantinople, they point out, was under Allied control, making the sultan's government nothing more than a helpless marionette. The release of most of the accused criminals by the British is offered as proof of their innocence.[31] The incriminating documents in the repositories of Germany, an ally of Turkey during World War I, are dismissed with the assertion that reports about purported Turkish plans to exterminate the Armenians were simply meant to divert attention away from Germany's own excesses against civilian populations. Deniers have an answer for everything when confronted with facts that contradict their arguments.

The Cold War and National Security

The subversion of memory, especially when associated with perceptions of security interests, has been applied to the portrayal of the past and has been exploited by individuals and governments alike. Terrence Des Pres has termed the creation of desired images at

---

[30] "Treaty of Peace between the British Empire and Allied Powers... Sèvres, August 10, 1920," in *British and Foreign State Papers*, vol. 113: 1920, Edward Parkes, ed., et al (London: His Majesty's Stationery Office, 1923), pp. 681-683, 706-707.

[31] See, for example, Gürün, *The Armenian File*, pp. 229-239; McCarthy, *Turks and Armenians,* pp. 87-94; *The Armenian Issue in Nine Questions and Answers* pp. 26-28.

the price of historical integrity as "the narrative of power."[32] Established power structures guide and ultimately determine accepted versions of the past. Deniers and rationalizers take advantage of these structures to advance their cause. Thus, throughout the existence of the Soviet Union and especially the years of the Cold War, any association with Russia or any information emanating from the Soviet Union was regarded with suspicion. It was not difficult for deniers in the West to extend this aversion by claiming that anyone who upheld the "myth" of an Armenian Genocide was a willful or naive abettor of the "evil empire," whose goal was the destabilization of the Western security system and especially key NATO partners such as the Republic of Turkey. Successive Turkish governments have used the geo-strategic position of the country in attempts to suppress memory. Pointing to its democratic, secularist, Western-oriented character and its long strategic border with the Soviet Union, Turkey has exerted inordinate political and economic pressures, sometimes entering into the realm of blackmail, to prevent official recognition and even discussion of the Armenian Genocide.

The strategy of Mustafa Kemal was to propagate the new image of Turkey and to avoid public discussion of the Armenian question. It was believed that with the passage of time the survivors and eyewitnesses would pass from the scene and their children would become acculturated in foreign countries, thereby resolving the problem without the need of any reparation, compensation, or even acknowledgment of wrongdoing. The Ankara government used diplomatic and economic channels to quash activities that might keep alive international memory of the Armenian tragedy. As an example, in the 1930s when Metro-Goldwyn-Mayer studios bought the film rights to Franz Werfel's celebrated novel, *The Forty Days of Musa Dagh*, depicting the struggle for survival of several Armenian villages near the Mediterranean Sea, the Turkish government protested to the Department of State, which interceded with the Motion Pictures Producers and Distributors of America to have MGM shelve the project. Quiet diplomatic and economic pressures

---

[32] Terrence Des Pres, "On Governing Narratives: The Turkish-Armenian Case," *Yale Review*, 2d ser., 75:4 (October, 1986): 517-531.

were sufficient to keep the film from the American and world public.[33]

By the outbreak of World War II, the Armenian Genocide had faded from the memory of most contemporaries, while many governments were quite willing to leave the issue in the closet in view of the failure of the world community to live up to the promises to repatriate and rehabilitate the Armenian survivors and to punish the guilty parties. With the Cold War evolving as soon as the world conflict ended and with the vaulting strategic significance of Turkey, pursuing the question of the Armenian Genocide would threaten the security interests of the West. Terrence Des Pres has noted that in the narrative of power, words such as "state security" and "national interest" are given exaggerated meaning and that "truth is at best a reckless element, a sort of wild card in a deck that otherwise is tightly stacked."[34]

It was not difficult to draw upon American academics sympathetic to Turkey, especially those engaged in Turkish studies or those who had lived in the country, to elevate denial and rationalization to the university level by placing the violent past into the perspective of current needs and the role of Turkey as a vital ally. Already in 1951, Princeton professor Lewis V. Thomas admitted that the Turks may have overreacted to any real Armenian threat and that much of the Armenian population had been "slain on the spot or converted to the Moslem faith and assimilated ... or expelled beyond the frontiers," adding, however, that the Turks did view the Armenians as an "active fifth column." He then draws the following chilling conclusions:

> By 1918, with the definitive excision of the total Armenian Christian population from Anatolia and the Straits area, except for a small and wholly insignificant enclave in Istanbul city, the hitherto largely peaceful processes of Turkification and Moslemization had been advanced in one great surge by the use of force.... Had

---

[33] See the Musa Dagh file in US National Archives, Record Group 59, General Records of the Department of State, File 861.4061. See also Hovannisian, "The Armenian Genocide and Patterns of Denial," pp. 120-121.

[34] Des Pres,"On Governing Narratives: The Turkish-Armenian Case," pp. 523, 527.

> Turkification and Moslemization not been accelerated there by the use of force, there certainly would not today exist a Turkish Republic, a Republic owing its strength and stability in no small measure to the homogeneity of its population, a state which is now a valued associate of the United States.[35]

Thomas began a process that was refined by a generation of his students, including Stanford Shaw, and the latter's students, Justin McCarthy, Heath Lowry, and others.

In efforts of the Armenian American community during the final decades of the twentieth century to have Congress adopt a commemorative resolution designating April 24 as a day to remember man's inhumanity to man, with particular reference to the Armenian Genocide but without casting any blame on the current Republic of Turkey, the Ankara government, its various agencies, its hired public relations firms, and its sundry supporters all played the security card once again. The Department of State, the Pentagon, and the National Security Council were pressured into lobbying against passage of the resolution. During the Senate debates, most opponents of the resolution voiced regret for past Armenian sufferings but now rose to emphasize the NATO connection, the affront to a critical ally, and the consideration of trade and business. But there were also a few who questioned the veracity of the Armenian Genocide, maintained that there are always two sides to every story, argued that Congress (which adopts hundreds of commemorative resolutions annually) should not make judgments on historical controversies, and warned that passage would encourage the forces wishing to destabilize the West. What was new about these statements resounding in the chambers of Congress was that they came straight out of the denial literature produced by the Turkish embassy, the Institute of Turkish Studies, which was funded by the Turkish government and established in Washington, D.C., and by the Association of Turkish American Associations.[36]

---

[35] Lewis V. Thomas and Richard N. Frye, *The United States and Turkey and Iran* (Cambridge, MA: Harvard University Press, 1951), pp. 60-61.

[36] On this issue, see Vigen Guroian, "The Politics and Morality of Genocide," in Hovannisian, *The Armenian Genocide: History, Politics, Ethics*, pp. 311-339.

The Institute of Turkish Studies and its director, Heath Lowry, were instrumental in securing the signature of sixty-nine academics in Turkish studies, many of whom had been awarded grants by the Institute, for an open letter published as an advertisement in the *New York Times* and the *Washington Post* and read more than once into the *Congressional Record.* The advertisement and its use by several Senators and Congressmen brought rationalization and relativization of the Armenian Genocide to the halls of Congress. The statement reads in part:

> As for the charge of "genocide": No signatory of this statement wishes to minimize the scope of Armenian suffering. We are likewise cognizant that it cannot be viewed as separate from the suffering experienced by the Muslim inhabitants of the region. The weight of the evidence so far uncovered points in the direction of serious inter-communal warfare (perpetrated by Muslim and Christian irregular forces), complicated by disease, famine, suffering and massacres in Anatolia and adjoining areas during the First World War.[37]

On one occasion, the decision of the Senate Judiciary Committee to report the commemorative resolution out to the full Senate for debate elicited an immediate response from the Turkish government. Aerial operations of American military in Turkey were curtailed and the threat was made of more drastic measures. Nearly every major firm doing business with Turkey or having signed contracts for the delivery of aircraft and other kinds of hardware was recruited into the campaign against the resolution.[38] In many public declarations, for example, deniers of the Armenian Genocide proclaim the reality and criminality of the Jewish Holocaust and make an appeal to keep

---

[37] *New York Times* and *Washington Post*, 19 May 1985. On the role of Heath Lowry and the Institute of Turkish Studies, see Roger W. Smith, Eric Markusen, and Robert Jay Lifton, "Professional Ethics and the Denial of the Armenian Genocide," *Holocaust and Genocide Studies*, 9:1 (1995): 1-22.

[38] See Richard G. Hovannisian, "The Armenian Diaspora and the Narrative of Power," in *Diasporas in World Politics*, Dimitri C. Constas and Athanassios G. Platias, eds. (London: MacMillan, 1993), pp. 192-197. For the Congressional debate in 1990, see 101st Congress, 2d session, *Congressional Record*, 136 (Washington, DC: Government Printing Office, 1990), pp. 1208-1236, 1312-1357, 1416-1488, 1692-1716, 1731-1732.

the memory of these "real" victims uncontaminated by confusing it in any way with the hoax of a so-called Armenian genocide. Such commingling, they caution Jewish audiences and policymakers would dishonor the memory of the innocent victims of the Holocaust and advance the designs of the Armenian deceivers. There has been repeated interference in trying to prevent examination of the Armenian Genocide even in scholarly conferences and forums.

Academic Freedom and the Warriors for Truth

A favorite ploy of deniers and rationalizers is to portray themselves as the champions of truth standing outside the established power structure but with the courage to challenge the influential forces that for decades have misrepresented the historical reality. They appeal to a sense of fair play and emphasize the importance and justice of learning about the other side of a legitimate debate. In fact, as soon as deniers manage to cast genocide into the category of a controversy, they have become successful, for from that position they can make even greater inroads through the processes of rationalization and relativization.

Freedom of speech is a cherished principle in many countries, and the deniers often seek cover under this ideal to propagate their falsehoods. What is disconcerting is that the champions of academic freedom often do not uphold the equally important principle of academic integrity based on reasonable inquiry and the use of standards of evidence and tolerate instead the gross violation of academic responsibility. The decision of a French court in 1995 holding Professor Bernard Lewis accountable for his denial in *Le Monde* of the Armenian Genocide elicited once again a chorus of complaints, some in major United States newspapers, including the *Wall Street Journal*.[39] Deniers of the Armenian Genocide try to show that they are engaged in an honest endeavor to reveal the truth and do away with distortions and myths that are barriers to peace and goodwill among peoples and nations. McCarthy appeals to teachers, scholars, and politicians to "ask themselves if it is fair to do other than present both sides of the story," noting that in the name of fairness educators have changed much of the "traditional wisdom"

---

[39] *Wall Street Journal*, 28 August 1995, p. A-11. See also responses to the editorial, 11 September 1995, p. A-21.

once taught to students regarding slavery, the treatment of native Americans, the White Man's Burden, and so forth. The time has come therefore to revise the "traditional wisdom" relating to the so-called Armenian Genocide.[40] Revisionism becomes fair and just, and the purveyors of deception hope to draw the uninformed into their web.

The New Practitioners

Practitioners of denial are still emerging. In recent years the names of Andrew Mango, Norman Stone, and Guenter Lewy have surfaced to find a place alongside those of Shaw, McCarthy, and Lowry. The most resourceful of them all is Lewy, who after having published books and articles to downplay the genocidal aspects of the treatment of the native Americans and of the Gypsies under the Nazi regime, has turned to the Armenian case in what he labels "A Disputed Genocide."[41] From a self-assumed lofty position of being non-Turk and non-Armenian, he tries to establish his credentials by chiding both Turks and Armenians for deception and exaggeration. He then proceeds to deconstruct the claims of the two sides. Herein lies the rub, for, in fact, what Lewy sets out to do is to disprove that there was a genocide, and, while affirming that many thousands of Armenians perished either through violence or as the result of the same terrible conditions that affected the entire Ottoman population, maintains that there is no solid evidence of premeditation, intent, or coordinated mass killing. It takes him more than 250 pages before he makes the following amazingly gullible or naive declaration: "I start with the assumption that the various decrees issued by the government in Constantinople dealing with the deportation and its implementation are genuine and were issued in good faith."[42]

Giving a new twist to rationalization and relativization, Lewy, after discussing the hardships endured by Ottoman army and Muslim population, explains: "A government as callous about the suffering of its own population as was the Young Turk regime could hardly be expected to be very concerned about the terrible human misery that

---

[40] McCarthy, *Turks and Armenians*, pp.100-101.

[41] Guenter Lewy, *The Armenian Massacres in Ottoman Turkey: A Disputed Genocide* (Salt Lake City: University of Utah Press, 2005).

[42] Ibid., p. 252.

would result from deporting its Armenian population, rightly or wrongly suspected of treason."[43] Thus, Guenter Lewy apparently has adopted the Young Turk position that the Armenians were alien, not a part of the empire's "own population." He pleads the case for disorganization and ill-preparedness rather than intent:

> We do not know how many Armenians perished as a result of starvation and disease and how many were killed by Kurds, seeking booty and women, or by fanatic Muslims, who regarded the Armenians as infidels and traitors. For all of these occurrences the incompetent Ottoman regime bears some indirect responsibility. But there is a difference between ineptness, even ineptness that has tragic and far-reaching consequences, and the premeditated murder of a people.... Even the fact that some fanatic Young Turk officials welcomed the death of large numbers of Armenians is not the same as intentionally seeking and causing such deaths.[44]

Elsewhere he reiterates: "Unfortunately and not surprisingly, the ability of the central government to influence events in the provinces remained limited."[45] This apology contradicts the multifaceted documentary and eyewitness evidence that the Young Turks carefully managed every aspect of the Armenian deportations and massacres.

To advance the thesis of mutual violence and to cast blame on the victims themselves (an echo of Talaat Pasha's self-vindication decades earlier), Lewy takes out of context passages from various cited reports and even introduces gross historical errors that may easily escape the scrutiny of all but specialists in the field. For example, to show that there was much civil strife and that the Armenians were not so innocent after all, he writes: "In January 1916 the Russians, led by advance guards of Armenian volunteers, took Diarbekir and then killed all Muslims unable to escape."[46] The problem with this account, of course, is that neither the Russian army nor Armenian volunteers ever occupied Diarbekir, which remained under firm Turkish control throughout World War I.

---

[43] Ibid., p. 61. See a similar statements on pp. 57, 255.

[44] Ibid., p. 256.

[45] Ibid., p. 208.

[46] Ibid., p. 118.

As a new champion of denial, Lewy also invokes United States General James G. Harbord, who, after having led a fact-finding military expedition to Anatolia and Armenia in the summer of 1919, submitted his findings to President Woodrow Wilson. From the extensive records of the Harbord mission, Lewy has discovered half a sentence to incriminate the Armenians "whose retaliatory cruelties unquestionably rivaled the Turks in their inhumanity."[47] Lewy picks a single disconnected clause to advance his thesis, and, as but one example of an oft-repeated selective cut-and-paste approach, has taken the quotation entirely out of context. In what cannot be accepted as plausible oversight, Guenter Lewy has omitted the first half of the sentence: "In the territory untouched by war from which Armenians were deported the ruined villages are undoubtedly due to Turkish deviltry...."[48] What is more, Lewy chooses to ignore, in the very same report, numerous passages that attest to the organized annihilation of the Armenians. Based on extensive evidence gathered and witnessed by his mission, General Harbord wrote:

> Massacres and deportations were organized in the spring of 1915 under a definite system. The soldiers going from town to town.... Young men were first summoned to the government building in each village and then marched out and killed. The women, the old men, and children were, after a few days, deported to what Talaat Pasha called "agricultural colonies," from the high, cool, breeze-swept plateau of Armenia to the malarial flats of the Euphrates and the burning sands of Syria and Arabia.[49]

Harbord concluded: "Mutilation, violation, torture, and death have left their haunting memories in a hundred beautiful Armenian valleys, and the traveler in that region is seldom free from the evidence of this most colossal crime of all the ages."[50] Yet, this "most colossal crime of all the ages" does not fit into Lewy's design

---

47 Ibid., p. 119.

48 U.S. Congress, 66th Cong., 2d sess., Senate Document no. 266, Major General James G. Harbord, *Conditions in the Near East: Report of the American Military Mission to Armenia* (Washington, D.C.: Government Printing Office, 1920), p. 9.

49 Ibid., p. 7.

50 Ibid.

to paint a scene of general tragedy affecting all elements of the population, thereby discounting genocidal intent or action.

One reviewer has aptly summarized Lewy's whitewash of Turkish policies as being simply a matter of "bad judgment, bad luck, bad planning, bad weather, bad local officials, and bad Kurds."[51] With such a convenient approach, it is no wonder that on the dust-jacket of Lewy's work, fellow rationalizers Norman Stone of Bilkent University in Ankara would write: "His book, which has Olympian fair-mindedness as well as thorough knowledge of the various sources, now replaces everything else," and Michael Gunter would add: "There is no other comparable work that so objectively, thoroughly, and meticulously reviews and analyzes so many different sources on both sides of this bitterly divisive issue." It makes little difference that Guenter Lewy's manuscript was bounced from press to press before the University of Utah Press published the volume as the first title in its Turkish and Islamic Studies series (a fact concealed in the initial printing but made public in subsequent ones), for, despite conceding that there was enormous loss of Armenian life, the volume has become something of a new testament in the arsenal of the negationists – an epistle distributed free of charge in quarters that still adhere to and promote the fixed and unyielding Turkish state narrative.[52]

Conclusion

It has been said that denial aims to reshape history, to rehabilitate the perpetrators, and to demonize the victims. Denial demonstrates the fragility of memory, truth, reason, and history. The process becomes increasingly sophisticated through rationalization and relativization. The deniers are more interested in justifying the present and shaping the future than they are in a conscientious portrayal of the past. By concealing the truth, they become exponents of and accomplices in the "Great Crime."

---

[51] Marc A. Mamigonian, *Journal of Armenian Studies*, 8:2 (Fall 2006), p. 74.

[52] The second title published in this series is *The Armenian Rebellion of Van* (2006), by Justin McCarthy, Esat Arslan, Cemalletin Taşkıran, and Ömer Turan.

Yet, there is hope. Growing numbers of teachers and students are becoming acquainted with the lessons and legacy of the Armenian Genocide. And many scholars are coming to understand the importance of facing and upholding the truth of this history. In the United States more than a hundred prominent scholars and noted literary figures have signed a petition deploring denial of the Armenian Genocide and calling for universal condemnation of the crime. "The Turkish government's denial of the Armenian Genocide encourages – by its very nature – the current programs that deny the Jewish Holocaust and the Cambodian genocide; it encourages genocidal episodes that are currently occurring in Africa, the Balkans, and elsewhere."[53] This expression of solidarity inspires guarded optimism in the ongoing struggle against the manipulators of truth.

There are also Turkish scholars, writers, and journalists, both inside and outside of Turkey, who have themselves begun to challenge the state's narrative of events. None has been more outspoken and critical than Taner Akçam, who with his latest publication, *A Shameful Act*, has brought together an impressive array of evidence that underscores the premeditated and ruthlessly implemented nature of the Armenian Genocide. In contrast to Guenter Lewy, he shows that the Young Turks were in fact highly organized and maintained direct control over operations in the interior provinces. It is inconceivable, Akçam concludes, that hundreds of thousands of people could have been deported and killed without the knowledge and approval of the central authorities. He marshals evidence from numerous sources to shatter the foundational arguments of the deniers.[54] There are hopeful indications that other Turkish scholars and writers are on the path to reaching equally unequivocal findings about the fate of the Ottoman Armenians and the culpability of the Young Turk officials and agents.

This survey is by no means exhaustive, but it should be sufficient to demonstrate how denial of the Armenian Genocide has become a prototype. The strategies of negationists, rationalizers, relativizers,

---

[53] *The Chronicle of Higher Education* (2 February 1996), p. A-30.

[54] Taner Akçam, *A Shameful Act: The Armenian Genocide and the Question of Turkish Responsibility* (New York: Henry Holt and Co., 2006).

and trivializers of modern genocides include the assertion that allegations of genocides were fabricated as politically-motivated propaganda; that the presumed victims were actually provocateurs and enemy collaborators; that legitimate preventive measures have been taken by all governments; that there never was the intent to victimize any specific group; that the numbers of dead have been grossly exaggerated and are in fact not out of proportion with the overall losses of the general population; that postwar trials of indicted organizers of the genocides were rigged and meant to take vengeance against the defeated side; that various attempts to exploit the genocide issue have in fact been aimed at destabilizing the NATO alliance and countries aligned with the "free world"; and that the very fundamental principle of academic freedom – the right to unfettered investigation and expression – is at stake and requires active resistance against those who cannot tolerate the view that there may be two sides to every story.

The arguments are spurious and contorted and their goal is to deceive and to confuse. Any success in raising doubt and uncertainty affords comfort, satisfaction, and encouragement to the deniers. The ongoing concerted campaign to suppress memory of the Armenian Genocide should be seen as a warning of things to come in relation to other crimes against humanity. The lesson is now being heeded by a growing legion of humanitarians and scholars who are insisting that academic and intellectual freedom must be matched by academic and intellectual integrity. How these issues will play out in the twenty-first century depends in large measure on whether there will be unflagging vigilance and strong and active commitment.

Armenian Studies
and
Armenian Literature

Archbishop Laud, Oxford, and Armenia

Christopher J. Walker

Between 1635 and 1639, Archbishop William Laud donated four Armenian manuscripts to the Bodleian Library, Oxford. They consisted of two psalters, of the fifteenth and sixteenth centuries, a sixteenth century prayer book, and a polyglot vocabulary, also of the sixteenth century.[1]

The collection is quite small and does not possess anything like the interest or significance of Laud's large bequests of Arabic, Persian and other eastern manuscripts, which together totaled about 250 items. Yet it shows an alertness to the importance of Armenian as an ancient culture and language. His manuscript bequests hint at a belief that the East contained one, or several, traditions of validity or pathways to understanding, which had hitherto remained obscure. A donation to the Bodleian represented the revelation to the world of something hitherto hidden. It was a secular epiphany.

Laud had become Chancellor of Oxford University in 1630, while still bishop of London. Arguably Oxford's greatest benefactor, he was not a scholar, but admired and promoted scholarship; and he saw the value of establishing a collection of manuscripts. He also energetically and enthusiastically collected oriental manuscripts, spending considerable sums of money in so doing. From 1634, a kind of manuscript tax was imposed on ships of the Levant Company, which meant principally those sailing to Constantinople or

---

[1] Sukias Baronian and F. C. Conybeare, *Catalogue of the Armenian Manuscripts in the Bodleian Library* (Oxford: Clarendon Press, 1918), p. vii.

to Alexandretta, the port for Aleppo.[2] The bishop formed a manuscript library, with the personal pride of a dedicated collector.

Laud's passion for the east undoubtedly fostered the flowering of oriental learning that continued in Oxford for thirty years after his appointment as Chancellor. We tend to think of Archbishop Laud today, if at all, as Charles I's enforcer, maybe a kind of tough grand vizier; a man who had grown close to the king since the death of Buckingham in 1628. He was less ferocious than the Earl of Strafford (who enforced the King's rule in Ireland), but like him was executed at the Tower of London. Aggressive in his promotion of a uniform church and a clergy with a high profile, he was among those who sought to impose the Prayer Book upon the Scots, and in England was at the heart of 'thorough', an authoritarian set of policies that principally meant strict implementation of the Act of Uniformity of 1559, which demanded that people worship according to only one type of ritual.[3] But there was another side to Laud's character, revealing an altogether more open and speculative outlook. He viewed the Anglican Church as not originating with Cranmer and Latimer, but deriving from St. Augustine of Canterbury in 597. He believed in the beauty of holiness.[4] He had an instinctive feeling for history, something that his opponents the Puritans (the forerunners of the Presbyterians and other Protestant groups) have almost always lacked. His manner of interpreting this search for roots principally meant a cautious opening of the Anglican Church towards the East. In order to escape the clogged Christianity of Roman Catholicism, with its garish and burdensome ceremonies, and the cold, severe and inartistic practices of the Puritans, he looked eastwards across the Mediterranean. The Greek Church was of great importance to Laud, and indeed other Eastern Churches were bracketed with that of Constantinople, as being the inheritors of valid and important Christian traditions, which might become allied to Anglicanism and which would thus elevate the Church of England from being a local reformed church into one of worldwide and well-

---

[2] G. J. Toomer, *Eastern Wisedome and Learning* (Oxford: Clarendon Press, 1996), pp. 105-111.

[3] Hugh Trevor-Roper, "Archbishop Laud in Retrospect," in *From Counter-Reformation to Glorious Revolution* (London: Pimlico, 1993), p. 144.

[4] Ibid., p. 141.

rooted significance.[5] Laud made it possible for Anglicans to take seriously the Eastern Churches, which included the Armenian Church.[6]

Although religious matters were of prime importance in the public and private discourse of the seventeenth century, they were not the only issues that created an awareness of Armenian matters in England at this time. John Cartwright's travel book of 1611, *The Preacher's Travels*, gives a reasonably informative view of the social and political condition of Armenia, divided between the Persian and Turkish empires. (A preacher in this sense was a chaplain attached to a trade mission.) Cartwright, who perceived the difference between Shia and Sunni rule, had probably made his journey in 1593.[7] Then, too, there was Edward Brerewood's *Enquiries touching the Diversities of Languages and Religions*, a pioneering work of comparative theology, anthropology and linguistics popular in the seventeenth century and going through five editions, first printed in 1614, the year after the author's death. Six pages concern the Armenians, covering such points as their capacity for trade, the two Catholicoses, as well as the author's view of Armenian theological issues. He listed such beliefs as that the Holy Ghost does not proceed from the Son, the true body of Christ is not present at the Eucharist, sacraments do not confer grace, and that the righteous will not enjoy blessedness until universal judgment. Brerewood declared that the Armenian alphabet had been invented by John Chrysostom, a claim that seems to have originated in print with Sixtus Senensis' 1593 *Bibliotheca*. Throughout, the text has been gleaned from other sources, but it is interesting to see the points placed together, and also to perceive their relevance to Protestant theology.[8] Thirdly, in Ephraim Pagitt's *Christianographie*, several pages are devoted to the Armenians, put together from information

---

[5] Ibid., pp. 136-137.

[6] Hugh Trevor-Roper, "The Church of England and the Greek Church in the Time of Charles I," in *From Counter-Reformation to Glorious Revolution*, p. 99.

[7] John Cartwright, *The Preacher's Travels*, London, 1611, quoted in Christopher J. Walker, *Visions of Ararat* (London: I.B. Tauris, 1997 and 2005), pp. 13-16.

[8] Edward Brerewood, *Enquiries Touching the Diversities of Languages and Religions*... (London: John Bill, 1614), pp. 170-174.

gathered from John Avediowites, an Armenian priest born in 'Parma' in Greater Armenia.[9] There is a passage here on the Armenians in India, and an account of Armenian ritual as observed in the city of Leopolis (i.e. Lvov or Lviv, today in Ukraine) by Andrew Lubelczik and set down by the Flemish humanist George Cassander. One finds also a reference to Ielphee [Julfa] and to Hodgee Nazar, an Armenian Prince, "who hath the sole government of the said citie, and that they live in as great security there, as the Persians do."[10] This constitutes an early reference to Armenian autonomy in Iran. Two points should be made about these works: one is that they were in English, and so were aimed not solely at a scholarly readership; and the second is that their intention was, despite the sometimes inaccurate information, primarily to inform and not to persuade.

However, it was through ecclesiastical politics rather than humanistic books that England had opened a window towards Eastern Churches and eastern peoples. William Laud was not the first Englishman to think creatively about the Eastern Churches. Already, at the time of King James I, a group of scholar-theologians had been busy translating the Greek fathers into Latin. The purpose was to bring these writings to the forefront, in order to sideline the writings of St. Augustine, whose doctrine of predestination had returned as a dominating feature in the harsh doctrines of Calvinism, and which had become part of the outlook of English Puritans.[11]

Against harshness: here we have another clue, admittedly an indirect one, for the study of Armenia and the East. One man was predominant in this context: Erasmus. Wherever there is enquiry, true research, or unbounded respect for scholarship in the sixteenth or seventeenth century, we find the spirit of Erasmus in the background. The intellectual heritage of Erasmus is complex, and his heirs might disagree with one another. But in their differing ways, they sought to soften the harsh outlines of religious belief, and to build bridges between the differing branches of Christianity. They were liberals, and proud of it, believing in consent, not war. In the

---

[9] Ephraim Pagitt, *Christianographie* (London: M. Costerden, 1635), pt. i. pp. 139ff. The pagination is faulty.

[10] Ibid., pt. i, p. 146.

[11] Hugh Trevor-Roper, "Hugo Grotius and England," in *From Counter-Reformation to Glorious Revolution,* p. 51.

movement for reuniting the differing parts of Christendom, they believed people should dispense with *adiaphora* – unnecessary items of belief, literally 'things indifferent' – and concentrate on the essence of the faith. And they held learning in high repute, believing that it should be wide and deep. Erasmus's main theological activity was the systematic examination of manuscripts of the New Testament. Textual criticism of the Bible was frowned upon by the Puritans, and sometimes considered to be sinful. To the sixteenth century Puritan biblical fundamentalist Thomas Cartwright, the Bible was neither dependent on the authority of the church nor to be interpreted by the reason of man, but, shining by its own light, it sought not enquiry, but humble submission to its laws.[12] John Owen, Oxford's Puritan vice-chancellor during the Commonwealth, would declare that the *kethibh* (the text as written) was the gift of providence, and the *qeri* (marginal corrections) man-made and therefore tainted with corruption, and would oppose the inclusion of vowel points in the Hebrew text.[13] There was little or no room for comparative studies and translations among Puritans. But wiser and more cultured spirits realized that the study of surrounding texts in various languages was essential to anyone who wanted to understand the origins of the faith, or to eliminate textual corruption from the text of the Bible. A better Bible meant studying, among others, the Armenian Bible.

Who was the spiritual offspring of Erasmus 100 years after his death? Undoubtedly, Hugo Grotius, the inventor of international law, and the friend of many scholars and learned men of the age. In 1617, in a lost moment in history, just before a bitter struggle consumed the Netherlands, he even envisaged a union of the reformed churches with the Greek Church and the Churches of Asia.[14] Sadly for this vision, the Calvinists triumphed at the Synod of Dort in 1618, crushing theological liberalism; the Netherlands were consumed in a complex struggle between Maurice of Nassau, the Stadtholder, and the Grand Pensionary Oldenbarnveldt. Grotius was

---

[12] John Hunt, *Religious Thought in England* (London: Strahan, 1870), vol. 1, p. 149.

[13] John Owen, *Works*, William H. Goold, ed. (London: Johnstone and Hunter, 1833), vol. 16, pp. 320, 393.

[14] Hugh Trevor-Roper, "Hugo Grotius and England," in *From Counter-Reformation to Glorious Revolution*, p. 55.

imprisoned in the fortress of Loewestein. At the same moment Europe imploded in the Thirty Years War, placing much of the Continent beyond scholarship.

Life in England in the seventeenth century was dominated by theological concerns, and Laud, with his high position under King Charles I, saw it as his job, above all, to enforce a uniform Anglicanism, and to crush Puritanism. All the decisions which he handed over, often with recommendations for severity, to the Courts of High Commission and Star Chamber related to matters of belief. Laud does not look at all Erasmian. But a small admixture of the Erasmian spirit is perceptible in him, and this was apparent in the context of learning. He showed an openness to knowledge that stood in contrast to his severe advice to the courts. He had the unrestricted attitude of a true patron of learning, in that he was prepared to see where an idea would travel. His choice of the great orientalist Edward Pococke in 1636, as the first holder of the Laudian chair of Arabic in Oxford, showed that he placed the growth of knowledge before theological correctitude, for Pococke mixed in speculative circles (as to some extent did Laud himself). He was the friend of Grotius, whose *De Veritate Religionis Christianae* (1627), which Pococke later was to translate into Arabic, demonstrated a distance from Calvinistic theology, since, by leaving out any reference to the Trinity, the text aimed to pare down Christianity to its essentials. This was the approach of Socinianism, the rational, tolerant, anti-metaphysical faith which welcomed common sense and the discoveries of science, and which was strong in Poland and Holland, and in England at Great Tew, but shunned by Puritans as the rotting agent of all religion. (Great Tew was the home of Lord Falkland, where in the 1630s and 40s religious questions were discussed with scholarship and freedom).[15] Socinianism had gained intellectual authority from its legacy of Italian humanism and its careful comparative approach to religious texts. Its moral authority had developed following the judicial murder of Michael Servetus at Geneva, burnt at the stake by the Calvinists in 1553, for disbelieving in the Athanasian Trinity, an event which gave a profound shock to all humane Reformers, even though the Geneva martyr was not

[15] Hugh Trevor-Roper, "The Great Tew Circle," in *Catholics, Anglicans and Puritans* (London: Secker and Warburg, and Chicago, Chicago University Press, 1987/1988), pp. 166-230.

himself a Socinian.[16] Now, if Anglicanism was to break out of its parochial shell, and establish good relations with the churches of the East, with their early and significant associations, it had to pare itself down, and to shed *adiaphora*. Almost imperceptibly, the Anglican Church, aiming to make connections with early (or 'primitive') Christianity, was in the first place opening a window to the East, and in the second making a moderate compact with what G.H. Williams has called the Radical Reformation, or Left Wing of the Reformation, where the index of devout faith was belief in the smallest number of things.[17] Laud himself was accused by his opponents of secret Socinianism.

Pococke was also a friend of the Parliamentary lawyer John Selden, a man not keen on church ceremonies of any sort, who became the member of Parliament for Oxford University under the Commonwealth, and to whom Pococke dedicated his most important book (1648-50), in which a small portion of historical text (by Gregory abul-Faraj) was heavily annotated by Pococke.[18] In 1663, the full text was published.[19] As regards Armenia, the latter contains reference to the Arsacid dynasty[20], to the conversion of Armenia[21], and to the Armenians' secession at the Council of Chalcedon, but only in reference to their alleged celebration of Christmas at Epiphany. Two Armenian manuscripts were bought by the Bodleian from the sale of Pococke's scholarly items in 1693.[22]

Pococke's appointment was in line with the view of the Anglican Church as an institution that valued scholarship. This was the Erasmian ideal. It was Edward Stillingfleet, a generation later, who said that the Anglican Church originated not in the writings and actions of Luther or Zwingli, but in Erasmus's translation of the New Testament, the *Novum Instrumentum*. Erasmus's mind was,

---

[16] E. M. Wilbur, *A History of Unitarianism: Socinianism and its Antecedents*, (Boston, Beacon Press, 1945), chapters 5, 9, 10-12.

[17] G. H. Williams, *The Radical Reformation* (London: Weidenfeld, 1962).

[18] Edward Pococke, *Specimen Historiae Arabum* (Oxford: Henry Hall, 1650/1648).

[19] Edward Pococke, trans. and ed., *Historia Compendiosa Dynastiarum* (Oxford: Henry Hall, 1633).

[20] Ibid., p. 63.

[21] Ibid., p. 85.

[22] Baronian and Conybeare, *Catalogue*, p. viii.

Stillingfleet contended, the most important element in the developing English church. The Dutch theologian stood for a religion at once rational and spiritual. Intelligence and piety supported each other. Pococke, Laud's choice, showed a clearly articulated inheritance from Erasmus: undogmatic, placing research above authority, and freely advancing learning for its own sake, which was the hallmark of Erasmus' method and which makes the Dutchman so pivotal. The freedom of belief and scholarship indicated by the pattern of Erasmus-Grotius-Laud-Pococke leads almost inevitably to a consideration of the Armenian Bible text – if only a sufficiently complete manuscript text could be found.

Laud's establishment of a tradition of learning, and of interest in the East led to the dispatch to Oxford of young men with an aptitude for Oriental languages. In 1639, a young Irishman, who had shown promise and ability at Trinity College, Dublin, (TCD), arrived at University College, Oxford. His name was Dudley Loftus, and his great-grandfather had been the first provost of TCD. Young Dudley did not stay long, since the countrywide Irish rebellion of 1641, necessitated his return home to defend Rathfarnham Castle. Politics, war and judicial matters thereafter took up much of his time, but in 1657 he was able to publish in Dublin *Logica Armeniaca in Latinam traducta*; also the *Liber psalmorum Davidis ex Armeniaco idiomate in Latinum traductus* in 1661.[23] These have a good claim to be the earliest works of scholarship using Armenian sources or the Armenian language to be translated within the British Isles. Some of the books from Loftus' library are still in Dublin, in Marsh's Library. They include a work by the Huguenot, and historian of Dr. Faustus, Pierre Victor Palma Cayet, *Paradigmata de quatuor linguis orientalibus, arabica, armena, syra, aethiopica* (Paris, 1596), and a 1636 book of the alphabets of eight oriental languages, including Armenian, also printed in Paris. It is possible, too, that Loftus learnt some of the language from Francesco Rivola's *Dictionarium Latino-Armenum*, printed in Milan in 1621, (reprinted in Paris in 1633), and from the same author's Armenian grammar (Paris, 1624). There does not appear to be much of an earlier date.

Dudley Loftus, like Edward Pococke, lived to a great age; indeed, the former married for the second time at the age of 76, and

[23] *Dictionary of National Biography*, "Dudley Loftus."

his general demeanour led the author in the old Dictionary of National Biography to describe him sniffily as noted for his levity, improvidence and indiscretion. Yet Loftus, like Pococke, remained dedicated to scholarship and learning to the end, not only after the Restoration of 1660, when interest in the orient sharply declined, but after the Glorious Revolution of 1688 too, when England delivered itself contentedly into rule by a Dutchman. In October 1690, when Pococke was 86 and Loftus 71, the Irishman wrote to the Laudian professor contesting a claim made in Sixtus Senensis' 1593 *Bibliotheca* that the entire last chapter of St. Mark's gospel was an addition. Loftus contended that that text was present in the Armenian version up to the eighth verse, and that this was so in every version he could locate.[24] The skepticism towards Sixtus is gratifying. Loftus adds a note on how he had spent his time in Ireland in the period of extreme disturbance leading up to the battle of the Boyne, which secured the rule of England's Protestant King in Ireland: he had been translating liturgies, eight Syriac and one Ethiopic, into Latin, and preparing an edition of the form of prayer used by the early church for the cure of disease.

Besides Laud, mention should be made of another Anglican archbishop, Laud's contemporary in Armagh, Ireland, Archbishop James Ussher, the ancestor of Clarence D. Ussher, the American humanitarian who was eye-witness to the self-defence of Van in 1915. Unlike Laud, James Ussher was a scholar; but, as a Protestant Irishman, his interest in church history was largely devoted to western Christendom, and to proving the persistence and superiority of the Protestant spirit over that of Rome. His interest in the age of mankind led him to study Hebrew, Syriac and Arabic, but there was no inner drive on his part to understand even part of the East, or to seek a valid connection with it. He referred to the Armenian liturgy in his *Answer to a Challenge Made by a Jesuit* of 1625. It is said that Ussher's *De Ecclesiarum Britannicarum Primordiis* used the Armenian fathers, but I have not seen the evidence of this.

Oriental learning had not ceased in England with the execution of the King and the establishment of the Commonwealth, a fact most clearly signified by the publication, supervised by the Royalist Brian

---

[24] Leonard Twells, *The Lives of Dr. Edward Pocock...* (London: Rivington, 1816), vol. 1, p. 338.

Walton, of the Polyglot Bible. This was an immense project, begun in 1652. It was to be a bigger and better response to the Paris Polyglot of 1645. Walton, a man from the Cambridge college of Peterhouse, was an upholder of Archbishop Laud's notions in matters of religious devotion, and had put up the backs of his largely Puritan parishioners by the formality of his church services. After clerical duty in London in 1641, and brief imprisonment as a delinquent for structuring his devotions according to the ritual prescribed by Laud, he moved to Oxford until it fell to Cromwell's New Model Army in 1646, whereupon he moved back to London. While at Oxford, he seems to have put in serious work at the study of oriental languages, and for his great project he gained the support of Selden and Ussher. The six folio volumes of the Polyglot appeared between 1652 and 1657; nine languages are represented, but regrettably not Armenian. In the Prolegomena, Walton mentions that he possessed an Armenian manuscript of the four Gospels, but it was in too poor a state to use as the basis for a printed text. 'Without a better copy, they [the Gospels] cannot be printed in type.' [25] Edward Pococke – involved, like every European oriental scholar of the time, in the project – wrote asking for an Armenian transcribed text to be sent from Rome, to be included in the last volume. His letter apparently went unanswered.[26] This was unfortunate, since to have included Armenian in this majestic publication (which actually made money) would have raised the profile of the Armenian language and culture. It is notable that in the *Introductio ad Lectionem linguarum orientalium* that Walton published in 1655, and which was a slim companion volume to the Polyglot, Armenian was included, and mentioned on the title page.[27] The Armenian language is given a couple of pages at the end, and the Armenian alphabet is printed, with corresponding Latin alphabet values. The letters are engraved in wood rather than set in metal type. This would appear to be the first printing of the Armenian alphabet in the British Isles. Perhaps its inclusion indicates that as late as 1655, Walton still had hopes of an Armenian text of the gospels in the great enterprise. Walton repeats

[25] Brian Walton, *Prolegomena...*, Francis Wrangham, ed. (Cambridge: Cambridge University Press, 1828), vol. 1, §5, vi, p. 310.

[26] Twells, *The Lives*, vol. 1, pp. 214-215.

[27] Brian Walton, *Introductio ad lectionem linguarum orientalium* (London, T. Roycroft, 1655).

the assertion of Sixtus Senensis found in Brerewood, that the Armenian alphabet had been devised by John Chrysostom. At least the error made a correction possible at a future date.

The publication of the Polyglot was, we can note in passing, a success for the Anglican Church when that church was officially banned; and a triumph for those Parliamentarian spirits, notably John Selden, whose love of learning overrode party allegiance. Even Cromwell himself exempted the imported paper from duty. Narrower spirits than Selden attacked the great achievement; the criticisms of Oxford's vice-chancellor John Owen have already been referred to, which echoed the complaint of dogmatic Puritans that a comparative study of the differing versions of the Bible was something in itself perverse, if not wrong. Puritans had and have difficulty in reconciling what they consider to be the providential nature of the scriptures with the confusions and forgetfulness of scribes; few appear to have given consideration the long section in the Book of Daniel in which an inattentive scribe, having shifted into Aramaic (which would have been more familiar to him), fails until rather too late to return to Hebrew.

Owen held that the principle underlying the publication of the Polyglot was that scripture might have been corrupted. This, he trumpeted, was the foundation of Islam, the principal prop of Popery, the pretence of fanatical anti-scripturists and the root of much hidden atheism in the world.[28] Today, we have Southern Baptists in the U.S. declaring that the King James Version is axiomatically unimprovable, and that biblical criticism is *ipso facto* wicked. The Vatican also put the Polyglot on the Index. Truly the Erasmian tradition of textual criticism was and is up against determined ideological opponents, proclaiming the fundamental, God-created (rather than man-written) nature of religious texts. To them textual corruption seems almost to represent divine incorruptibility. Walton dealt satisfactorily with Owen's criticisms, and his attitude to scholarship is summed up in his description of the Syriac manuscript: 'that noble, ancient, oriental treasure.'[29] Those words evoke Laudianism at its best: here was an expression of undogmatic feeling for the rich tilth of history, and of a cast of mind holding to

---

[28] John Owen, *Works*, vols. 16, 348.

[29] Brian Walton, *The Considerator Considered*, vol. 2 of Henry J. Todd, *Memoirs of Brian Walton* (London: Rivington, 1821), p. 185.

the idea that texts of faith were stronger and more significant for being contingent and chancy, rather than for being the legacy of a questionable providentiality. To Puritans, Walton's words were sins along the path of reprobation, showing that their Laudian opponents were fit only for damnation.

Marsh's Library is an attractive Queen Anne building in Dublin, just behind St. Patrick's Cathedral. It is the first public library in the British Isles, and its name commemorates a man who, though not born in Ireland, became identified with the country and eventually, in 1703, like James Ussher before him, was appointed Archbishop of Armagh. The career of Narcissus Marsh shows that there was some continuity in the study of oriental languages after 1660. He was a respecter of knowledge, and a buyer of manuscripts, most of which he acquired through an English intermediary in Aleppo. He aimed to emulate Laud as a benefactor. Marsh had already spent fifteen productive years at Exeter College, Oxford, before being appointed Provost of Trinity College Dublin and then being elevated to the archbishopric. In 1695, Marsh bought Dudley Loftus's Armenian manuscripts, and they figure among the eight bequeathed to the Bodleian on his own death in 1713.[30] Marsh also acquired Loftus's books and some of these at least, mentioned earlier, are still in the Library in Dublin named after him – e.g. Palma Cayet's 1596 *Paradigmata* and the 1636 volume of oriental alphabets. A 1636 edition of the Armenian liturgy printed by the Propaganda in Rome also figures there.

If Laud's project continued after 1660, in a somewhat half-hearted manner (in the case of Marsh) it also extended itself, under another identity and name. Although there was no new generation of scholars, nevertheless the initial impetus from the 1630s led to the publication of a book, in 1679, written by the English consul in Smyrna, Sir Paul Rycaut.[31] He had already gained repute as the continuer of Richard Knolles' 1603 *Historie of the Turkes*. Rycaut's book was entitled *The Present State of the Greek and Armenian Churches*, and the passages on the Armenian Church are derivative,

---

[30] Baronian and Conybeare, *Catalogue*, pp. vii-viii; *Dictionary of National Biography*, "Narcissus Marsh," G. J. Toomer, *Eastern Wisedome and Learning*, pp. 287-289.

[31] Paul Rycaut, *The Present State of the Greek and Armenian Churches*, (London: John Starkey, 1679).

semi-informative, often opinionated, and apt to be wrong. He appears not to have traveled beyond the Aegean coast, and though he interestingly identifies four Armenian Patriarchs (i.e. Catholicoses) – those of Etchmiadzin, Sis, Akht'amar and Gandzasar (spelt here "Canshahar") – he places Gandzasar geographically close to Sis. He does note the primacy of the Etchmiadzin See – an important point in subsequent disputes – but dismisses the Patriarchates of Constantinople and Jerusalem as creations of the Ottomans. Rycaut was writing, and gained such information as he demonstrates, before the rise of the careful Mekhitarists, and the book, a presentation of half-informed knowledge, represents an uncritical, pre-Mekhitarist view of the history of Armenian ecclesiastical institutions.

Over the next fifty years, Armenian studies gained a place in Continental Europe as a significant discipline. J. J. Schröder, professor of oriental languages at Marburg University, brought out an impressive Armenian thesaurus, which was printed in Amsterdam in 1711.[32] The Propaganda in Rome brought out a dictionary created by Jacques Villotte in 1714, which George Borrow found, and learnt from, in Norwich Public Library in the 1850s when he came to write *The Romany Rye*.[33] But arguably, the crowning work of this early period of Armenian work in the British Isles and Continental Europe, though printed in London, had its spiritual home in Cambridge.

By the fourth decade of the eighteenth century the two English universities were on the way to becoming failing institutions; the picture given by Edward Gibbon of his time at Magdalen College, Oxford – admittedly a decade or so later – of the dons' dull and deep potations cannot easily be forgotten. Yet, there was still intellectual vigour among some of the members, albeit sometimes of an eccentric kind. One of those was the successor to Isaac Newton as Lucasian Professor in Cambridge, William Whiston. Whiston did not, however, last long at his post; he was expelled from the university for his Arian (or moderate Unitarian) views. Newton had likewise been a disbeliever in the Trinity, of a more radical kind, but he had kept quiet about his faith. Whiston was a trusting soul, and believed he should be open about belief. He was a late adherent of the Radical

---

32 J. J. Schröder, *Grammatica sive Thesaurus Linguae Armenicae* (Amsterdam, 1711).

33 Jacques Villotte [Jacobus Villottius], *Dictionarium Novum Latino-Armenium* (Rome, 1714).

Reformation, seeking to return Christianity to its original pristine state. In this context his book *Primitive Christianity Revived* is perhaps his most important contribution. One contemporary said that he believed in everything except the Trinity.

In 1730, Whiston wrote a biography of his fellow Arian, Samuel Clarke, a man who some years earlier had been briefly tipped to be Archbishop of Canterbury, until the Queen was advised of the fact that Clarke was, as the Dictionary of National Biography puts it, not a Christian. At the end of his book, there is an advertisement for a forthcoming work and a request for subscribers. The text is as follows:

> As we had reason to think that the old Armenian language, though almost quite neglected by Europeans, and but very imperfectly known by the modern Armenians themselves, contained several ancient and curious works written in it, we have employed ourselves for some time to attain the knowledge of it, and have accordingly found our expectation proved true. For besides the Armenian version of the bible, it self highly valuable for its accuracy and antiquity as being made about AD 420, but not yet published in any Polyglott... there is this our author Mosis Chorenensis, who wrote a compendious History of Armenia in three books... This work seems very curious, as well upon account of the history it self, it being the only one that affords us any tolerable account of the ancient state of the Armenian nation, as of the authorities upon which it is founded... As the subject is entirely new we desire not to anticipate the judgement of the learned how far all these authorities are to be depended upon. This history was published by an Armenian archbishop in Amsterdam in the year 1695... we have translated it into Latin, and design to add short notes.[34]

Whiston here referred to himself and two of his able sons, who had taken it upon themselves to learn Armenian, and to re-publish (with textual variants) the 1695 Amsterdam edition of Khorenats'i edited by Thomas Vanandets'i, and give it a parallel Latin

[34] William Whiston, *Historical Memoirs of... Samuel Clarke* (London: John Whiston, 1730), sigg. N4r, N4v.

translation. The enterprise was admirable. It was finally offered to the public in 1736. In the preface, the brothers describe the almost chance chain of events by which they came to be interested in Armenians: William Whiston senior, in the course of his researches for *Primitive Christianity Revived*, received an Armenian manuscript in poor condition of two Pauline epistles not in the Western biblical canon. So he wrote to an English merchant living in Aleppo, to see if local Armenians could give him any information. He received a courteous reply – indeed more, since he was also sent a good manuscript, and a translation of the texts into Arabic.[35]

The first to publish an edition of these two epistles was David Wilkins, a talented linguist, originally a Prussian named Wilke, and at the time Lord Almoner's Professor of Arabic at Cambridge. Whiston then made contact with Schröder at Marburg University and Mathurin Veyssière de la Croze, of the Royal Library in Berlin, both of whom assisted in translation. Schröder appears to have sent a copy of his Armenian Grammar to the Whistons, and the sons embarked on the study of the language.[36] The result was the landmark edition of Khorenats'i, with the *Ashkharhats'uyts'* [Geography] and the two Pauline epistles printed at the end. With this production, Armenian studies had manifestly moved into the modern age.

English and Irish studies of Armenian had followed quite closely along the spiritual, ecclesiastical and political events of the turbulent times, all of which were interrelated. The impulse for study had emerged from Archbishop Laud's interest in the Greek Church, and within the context of a current of opinion that saw the idea of a link-up with the Eastern Churches as a counterweight to both Roman Catholicism and Puritan theology and ideology. The studies suffered during the English Civil War, but reemerged under the Commonwealth, with the probable first London printing of the Armenian alphabet in 1655, undertaken as a guide to the Polyglot Bible. Individual scholars explored Armenian topics in the years after 1660. And finally, with the arrival of a more objective attitude,

---

[35] Moses Chorenensis [Movsēs Khorenats'i], *Historiae Armeniae Libri III...* G. [i.e. W.] and G. Whiston, trans. and eds. (London: John Whiston, 1736), p. i.

[36] Ibid., p. xxii.

freed from ecclesiastical control, and from the interests of Laudians or the threats of Puritans, a good translation of Khorenats'i was issued in 1736.

The Beginnings of Armenian Studies in the United States: The *Armenian Quarterly*

Vartan Matiossian

Those who have followed Professor Dickran Kouymjian's long and distinguished career in the field of Armenian Studies will be able to notice at once the wide scope of his scholarly interests. He is one of the founders of the Society for Armenian Studies and an inquirer into the history and state of Armenology in the Diaspora. The present paper, devoted to the prehistory of Armenian Studies in the United States, could be fittingly included in this endeavor.[1]

The origins of Armenian scholarship in the United States have been tied to the names of the highly esteemed byzantinist Sirarpie Der Nersessian and the medievalist Robert Pierpont Blake.[2] Der Nersessian's *Armenia and the Byzantine Empire* (1945) became a sort of landmark for Armenian Studies in America.[3] Built upon a series of five lectures given at the Pierpont Morgan Library of New York in 1942, this book had been preceded by another series of fifteen lectures by the same author, a veritable course on Armenian illustrated manuscripts held at the same location in 1936, co-sponsored by the New York University, "le premier que sois jamais

[1] A preliminary result of this research constitutes a chapter of my book *Kostan Zariani shurj* [Around Kostan Zarian] (Antelias: Armenian Catholicosate of Cilicia, 1998), pp. 401-427.

[2] Nina Garsoian, "Armenovedeniye v SCHA," *Lraber Hasarakakan Gitutiunneri,* 10 (1971), pp. 23-24. See also Dickran Kouymjian, "Hayagitut'ean nerkan artasahmani mēj" [The Present of Armenian Studies Abroad], *Shirag* (October, 1972), p. 42.

[3] Sirarpie Der Nersessian, *Armenia and the Byzantine Empire* (Cambridge, Ma.: Harvard University Press, 1945) (reprinted in 1947).

donné aux Etats-Unis sur l'art arménien."[4] On the other hand, Blake and iranist Richard Frye published together in 1949 the English translation (in book form five years after) of the *History of the Nation of the Archers* ascribed to Grigor Aknerts'i, but actually written by Maghakia Abegha.[5] It is a well-known fact that the foundation of the NAASR (National Association for Armenian Studies and Research) was the catalyst for the creation of Armenian Studies chairs in various universities starting from the 1960s.

It has been frequently forgotten that, some two decades before the "chair movement," the first attempt at promoting Armenian Studies in the United States was led by an organization ad-hoc, the American-Armenian Cultural Association, which in 1946 published the two issues of the first Armenological journal in the United States, the *Armenian Quarterly*.[6] One of the leading forces of the Association and the journal was Constant (Kostan) Zarian (1885-1969), a foremost figure of twentieth century Armenian literature, who also was one of the pioneers in teaching Armenian Studies in the United States. His unpublished correspondence of this period gives an insight into the proto-history of the field.

The Association was organized on August 27, 1945, and obtained its legal recognition on September 4. Three highly regarded scholars were honorary presidents: Robert Blake, Henri Gregoire and Arthur Upham Pope. The president was Louis Gray; vice-president, Vahan H. Kalenderian; secretary, Constant Zarian; and treasurer, Edward Sahagian. Its headquarters were at the Iranian Institute (9 East 89th Street) in New York.[7]

According to the by-laws, the Board of Directors constituted the executive organ of the Association, which selected its officials from

---

4 *Archives Sirarpie Der Nersessian,* catalogue by Sylva Agémian, vol. I (Antelias: Armenian Catholicosate of Cilicia, 2003), p. 23. The complete chronology established by the compiler has, nevertheless, overlooked Der Nersessian's involvement in the editorial board of the *Armenian Quarterly.*

5 R. P. Blake and R. N. Frye, *History of the Nation of the Archers (the Mongols) by Grigor of Akanc'* (Cambridge, MA.: Harvard University Press, 1954).

6 See Levon Saryan, "An Index for the 'Armenian Quarterly' of 1946," *Armenian Review* (June, 1979), pp. 221-223.

7 "Announcements,'' *Armenian Quarterly*, 1 (1946), inside page to the back cover.

the membership (chairman, deputy chairman, secretary, and treasurer). The nine founding members were Wolfgang Born (Iranian Institute), Edward B. Redman, Henri Gregoire, Clarence Manning (Columbia University), Harry Hatch, Steven Bourgeois, Constant Zarian, John Gerig, and Vahan H. Kalenderian.

The Association was an organization "primarily devoted to the study of and research in the language, literature, art, history and culture of the Armenian people, and carrying on the noble work of institutions which have heretofore devoted and dedicated themselves to the study of the Armenian culture, now unable to function as a result of the devastating war, and thus bring to the attention of the world in general and American people in particular the rich treasures of Armenian culture which heretofore have been known only to a group of scholars."[8]

I have made some inroads into the origins of the Association, although more thorough archival inquiries could give us better answers to some questions.[9] For the time being, however, it seems unquestionable that this organization, exclusively cultural as it was, was born from a political decision. It enjoyed the moral and, most likely, material support of the Armenian National Committee (A.N.C.), the lobbying branch of the Armenian Revolutionary Federation, founded in New York at the end of 1944, by the U.S. Central Committee of the party, to have a role in the reawakening of the Armenian Cause at the aftermath of World War II.

The catalogue of the party press included in a memorial book on the sixtieth anniversary of the A. R. F. (1950) listed as such the *Armenian Quarterly*, giving the A.N.C. ("*Hay Dati Handznakhumb*") as publisher.[10] In his catalogue of the A.R.F. press published on the occasion of its centennial, the late Artashēs Tēr Khachaturian also included the *Armenian Quarterly,* with the Association as

---

[8] "Association By-Laws," *Armenian Quarterly,* 1 (1946), pp. 122-123.

[9] It is likely that some information about the Association and the Quarterly is to be found at the Armenian Revolutionary Federation archives located in Watertown (Massachusetts), which are not available to the public at this time.

[10] *Hushapatum H. H. Dashnaktsut'ean (1890-1950)* [Memorial of the A.R. Federation] (Boston: Hairenik Press, 1950), p. 573 (the catalogue was compiled by Sahak Tēr Tovmasian).

publisher.[11] Both entries contain factual mistakes, although Tēr Khachaturian seems to have seen the actual journal.

Lawyer Vahan Kalenderian, a founding member of the Association and vice-president, was a member of the party, the same as the treasurer, Edward Sahagian. Three other founding members (Zarian, Bourgeois and Hatch) had given the address of the A.N.C. (11 West 42nd Street) as theirs.[12]

A delegation sent by the Committee to the founding assembly of the United Nations in San Francisco (April-June 1945) had presented a memorandum on June 9, requesting the annexation of Western Armenia to Soviet Armenia and the return of Armenians to their ancestral lands.[13] According to Simon Vratzian, director of the Committee, Zarian had also been one of the members of that delegation,[14] although this is not completely sure.

That the A.N.C. had a hand in the publication of the *Quarterly* can be inferred from a letter from Vratzian to Zarian, who apparently had departed from New York, written on the Committee's letterhead on August 8, 1946:

> What has happened to you, son of God? I am worried. Has it been your health the reason you have not written a single word? Today finally I got your address; you hadn't even left your address.

---

[11] Ardashes Der Khatchadourian, *H. H. Dashnaktsut'ean 100amea mamulĕ (1890-1990)* [The 100-Year-Old Press of the A. R. Federation (1890-1990)] (Beirut: Hamazkayin, 1990), p. 75.

[12] "Association," p. 123. Harry Hovan Hatch (1886-1946), born in Armenia and emigrated to the United States before the Genocide, was an engineer who had been active in the community and served with the A.N.C. An article of his about the Armenian Question was published simultaneously in both Boston weeklies (Harry Hatch, "The Armenian Question," *Armenian Mirror-Spectator* [May 26 and June 2, 1945]; *Hairenik Weekly* [May 31, 1945]).

[13] "Parley Gets Armenian Plea. Group Demands Controversy With Armenians Be Settled," *San Francisco Examiner,* June 10, 1945, reprinted in *Hairenik Weekly* (June 21, 1945), p. 1. See the full text of the memorandum in *Hairenik Weekly* (June 28, 1945).

[14] Andranik Tsarukian, *Metserĕ ew... miusnerĕ* [The Great Ones and... the Others] (Beirut: Altapress, 1992), p. 266.

> There are no special news. Only Julian[15] often appears, nervous. And I'm not *au courant* to help him. At least you should have made some arrangements to ensure the publication of the 'Quarterly' in time. I'm afraid it will be late and will open the door to new chitchat. If your health is no good, write what's going on and what has to be done to put Julian's work to speed. [16]

To be fair, we have to mention that both the Association and its organ seem to have kept a non-political, non-partisan stance, at least in their public endeavors. The first mention of the *Quarterly* so far appears to be in Zarian's August 22, 1945 letter to Arshak Ch'ōpanian, the French-Armenian intellectual, asking for his contribution to the forthcoming journal.[17] Ch'ōpanian sent him a copy of his speech in French titled "La nation américaine et l'Arménie," pronounced at a funeral in honor to the late President Franklin Roosevelt on May 1945.[18] The answer is unknown; Zarian wrote again on January 14, 1946 to clarify the nature of the journal, since Ch'ōpanian seems to have been misled:

> It is going to be like 'La Revue des Et. Arméniennes' *[sic]*, fully scientific, without any political tendency. The studies will also not be written in a popular, propaganda fashion, but will be seriously devoted to those discoveries that scholars make in the field of our language and art. For these reasons the editorial board considered inappropriate to publish your so beautiful speech about Roosevelt (opinions differ here about that). I ask you to bear that in mind in your next writings. It would be excellent if you devoted a couple of articles to our Medieval poets, as you did in the past, or furnished critical information about new books on Armenian culture

---

[15] Reference to Giuliano Bonfante (see below).

[16] Museum of Literature and Art (MLA), Yerevan, Kostan Zarian's File (KZF), number 103 (in Armenian).

[17] MLA, Arshak Ch'ōpanian File (ACF), Section I, number 2165 (the letter is torn and is not entirely readable). Zarian's letters to Ch'ōpanian were written in Armenian.

[18] MLA, KZF, folder 83.

> in foreign languages. When you receive the first issue, you will see the nature of the journal.[19]

However, as the first series of the *Revue des Études Arméniennes* (1920-1934) had not been devoted exclusively to Armenian Studies, but also contained some articles about modern or current affairs, the first issue of the *Armenian Quarterly* printed an article written by the Soviet writer Marietta Shahinian, which later was part of her book *Journey through Soviet Armenia.*[20]

Zarian was the editor-in-chief of the *Armenian Quarterly*, with George P. Rice, Jr. (Columbia University) as assistant editor. Associate editors were Giuliano Bonfante (Princeton University), Louis Gray (Columbia), Henri Gregoire (École Libre des Hautes Études) and Sirarpie Der Nersessian (Wellesley College).[21] In the second issue Arthur Upham Pope (Iranian Institute) was included as an associate editor.[22]

The journal had two aims: to disseminate abroad the results of the studies by scholars in Armenia and gather together the efforts of Armenologists in Europe and America. Zarian explained the causes of its birth in the editorial of the inaugural issue:

> The war having almost entirely destroyed the European centers of the study of Armenian culture, it has been necessary to think of replacing them: an arduous task. In a world of upheavals, everything becomes displaced. At the last moment, several of the Armenian scholars, upon whose collaboration we counted, died; others have disappeared, and still others, driven away by the storm, have taken refuge in the United States. It was

[19] MLA, ACF, Section I, number 2166. Ch'ōpanian did not publish anything in the "Quarterly" and his name was not listed among the future contributors. The Armenian translation of this speech had already been published, see A. Ch'ōpanian, "Amerikean azgn u hay zhoghovurdě (chaŕ artasanuats P'arizi Hayots' yekeghetswuyn mēj, Mayis 6-in)" [The American Nation and the Armenian People (Speech at the Armenian Church of Paris, May 6)], *Hayastani Koch'nak* (June 30, 1945), p. 605-608.

[20] Marietta Shahinian, "Letters from Armenia," *Armenian Quarterly,* 1 (1946), p. 22-46 (probably reprinted from an unknown source with no mention of translator).

[21] *Armenian Quarterly,* 1 (1946), inside cover.

[22] *Armenian Quarterly,* 2 (1946), inside cover.

> natural that we should utilize their presence here, as well as to turn to good account the generous hospitality of this great country.[23]

Thus, the Institute de Philologie et d'Histoire Orientale et Slave, led by the Belgian byzantinist Henri Gregoire, had been forced to move out from Brussels after the German occupation and relocate to the École Libre des Hautes Études of New York, founded by Henri Focillon.

Two émigré scholars would be especially significant in the history of the *Quarterly*: Gregoire and the Italian linguist Giuliano Bonfante. Gregoire participated heavily in the organization of the first issue and, after his departure to Europe, Bonfante continued his association to the end.

The correspondence received by Zarian from these and other scholars offers an opportunity to reconstruct to some extent the origin and development of the first Armenological journal in the United States. Hopefully, some of Zarian's answers will turn up from different archives in the future.

In an undated letter in French, probably written at the beginning of September 1945, Gregoire communicated to Zarian in his rather embellished style that "because all poets are my masters and all Armenians are my friends, and I hope you won't see a constraint in this big creed of faith and confession of love, here is the (temporary) list of scholars whose I have asked (twice, in three cases) contributions to the first issue of the 'Armenian Quarterly' (which I'm literally dreaming with)."[24] The list included philologists Paul Peeters[25] and Maurice Leroy,[26] linguist George Dumezil,[27] turcologist

---

[23] "Introducing the Quarterly," *Armenian Quarterly*, 1 (1946), p. 1.

[24] MLA, KZF, number 3. The letter has been wrongly catalogued here, separately from other letters written by Gregoire.

[25] Peeters and Fr. Louis Maries were mentioned among contributors of future issues. Maries wrote to Gregoire on September 13, 1945, to inform that it would be impossible for him to contribute to the first issue, promising to do it so to the next issues (MLA, KZF, number 65). However, neither Peeters nor Maries published anything in the second issue.

[26] Maurice Leroy, "Arménien 'i miasin,'" *Armenian Quarterly*, 1 (1946), p. 98-100. Leroy, who had been Nicolas Adontz's student and his successor at the chair of Armenian Philology in the Université Libre of Brussels, wrote

Karl Menghes, Bonfante, Der Nersessian, and Blake. In the case of the last two, Gregoire had insisted on the need of having them as part of the editorial board and invited them to a meeting to be held two weeks later (September 19).

On September 12, Bonfante answered to Zarian:

> I thank you very much for your kind invitation for Sept. 19. My interest in Armenian things and my love for the unfortunate, noble and learned Armenian people has been unflinching for 30 years, and your invitation fulfil[l]s an old dream of mine. *Audivere dei mea iota...*
>
> But unfortunately I am tremendously busy this month, and not quite sure to attend your meeting. However, I will be glad to help in any way, and can take care of the linguistic section of your journal, *in part* or *in toto,* as far as the comparison with other Indo-European languages is concerned. As you probably know, I have several publication[s] on Armenian linguistics and have been consulted even recently by American journals concerning Armenian matters.
>
> I have a paper quite ready, *in French,* on *Greco-Armenian Isoglosses;* but it is long-hand, and it is unfortunately impossible for me to have it typewritten. If you want it, I can send it immediately.[28]

The first issue actually did not contain this article,[29] but Bonfante's influential study on the relations between the Armenian and the Phrygians.[30]

---

to Zarian on November 28, 1946 acknowledging the reception of the second issue and remarking he had not received either galley proofs of his article (he counted 44-45 errata, especially in the transliteration of Armenian words) or offprints (MLA, KZF, number 40).

[27] Dumezil was mentioned in the first issue among future contributors. On September 20, 1945 Gregoire informed Zarian that he was waiting for Dumezil's article any day (MLA, KZF, number 20).

[28] MLA, KZF, number 17. Bonfante wrote his first three letters in English and signed Julian H. Bonfante.

[29] It was, probably, the second part of G. Bonfante, "Les isoglosses gréco-arméniennes. I. Faits phonétiques," *Mélanges linguistiques offerts a M. Holger Pedersen* (= *Acta Jutlandica,* IX) (Aarhus, 1937), pp. 15-33. I have not been able to trace any reference to this second part, if ever published.

Sirarpie Der Nersessian, who after the publication of her book and several articles had became a leading voice of Armenian Studies in this country, on September 13, gave her consent to Zarian to become a member of the editorial board. She promised to write a fresh article about the iconoclastic controversy in Armenia,[31] despite being unable to attend the first editorial meeting.[32] In his September 19 answer to Zarian, Robert Blake expressed his interest about the new association and the project of the journal. He also accepted an honorary vice-presidency and membership on the editorial board, to whose first meeting confirmed his presence, "if this acceptance does not entail any active participation. I am at work on a large project which would keep me occupied to the exclusion of all other thoughts for the next two years at least. Hence, I cannot promise any contribution off-hand."[33]

One day later, Gregoire informed Zarian that he had ensured a contribution by Herbert Weissberger (the representation of the Last Judgment in Armenian painting) and insisted that he should write again to Der Nersessian about the abovementioned article and ask her about a reviewer's name for her book.[34]

On September 24, Bonfante suggested to Zarian to ask for a contribution from ethnologist Alexander Krappe (Princeton)[35] and added that "it was a great pleasure to meet you, and I want to

---

[30] Giuliano Bonfante, "Armenians and Phrygians," *Armenian Quarterly*, 1 (1946), pp. 82-97.

[31] Sirarpie Der Nersessian, "Image Worship in Armenia and Its Opponents," *Armenian Quarterly,* 1 (1946), pp. 67-81.

[32] MLA, KZF, number 105.

[33] MLA, KZF, number 16. Blake reported on October 5 that he would be unable to attend the October 20 symposium. His name is mentioned among future contributors, but he did not publish anything in the second issue.

[34] MLA, KZF, number 20. Weissberger's article was not published and his name was not mentioned at all in the journal. Der Nersessian's book was not reviewed, but instead, Gregoire's French preface was published in a quite awkward English version with no mention of the translator ("Of Books and Men," *Armenian Quarterly,* 1 [1946], pp. 108-110).

[35] Alexander Krappe's letters to Zarian, October 11, 1945 (in English) and October 6, 1946 (in French) (MLA, KZF, number 48). Cf. A. H. Krappe, "The Leucosyrians," *Armenian Quarterly,* 1 (1946), pp. 101-107. In his second letter, he had promised another article, of which we have no further reference.

reiterate how happy I am to be able to do something for the Armenian people."[36] It seems that it was decided at that meeting to hold a symposium devoted to Armenian culture at Columbia University on October 20. A second meeting of the editorial board took place on October 6.[37]

Some other well-known scholars were asked for their contributions: Jurgis Baltrusaitis,[38] Georges Cuendet,[39] Meyer Schapiro,[40] Harold W. Bailey,[41] and Philip K. Hitti.[42] Some of them promised to contribute in the future, although we do not know if they addressed any article to the journal. It had been announced at the symposium that some twenty American, French, Italian, and Belgian scholars would be among the contributors.[43]

Work on the first issue of the journal started in November[44] and was initially scheduled to end in December.[45] However, Zarian wrote to Ch'ōpanian on January 14 that "... everybody here is sick or about

---

[36] MLA, KZF, number 17.

[37] See Der Nersessian's letters to Zarian (October 4 and 10, 1945) (MLA, KZF, number 105).

[38] Letter to Zarian, Paris (August 31, 1945) (MLA, KZF, number 12).

[39] Letters to Zarian, Bougy-Val-Nyon (Switzerland) (October 17, 1945 and July 2, 1946) (MLA, KZF, number 47).

[40] Letter to Zarian, New York (October 3, 1945) (MLA, KZF, number 68).

[41] Letter to Zarian, Cambridge (England) (December 9, 1945) (MLA, KZF, number 15). He declined to contribute because he had little contact with Armenian Studies. However, his name was mentioned in the journal among future contributors.

[42] Letter to Zarian, Princeton (October 17, 1945) (MLA, KZF, number 54).

[43] "Cultural Association Begins Activity With New York Public Meeting,'' *Hairenik Weekly* (November 1, 1945), p. 1.

[44] November 24 and December 4, 1945 letters by Der Nersessian to Zarian deal with the proofs of her article. She wrote to Zarian on February 8, 1946 that she was departing to France until September and left to him the last proofreading (MLA, KZF, number 105). About Bonfante's article, see his letters to Zarian dated January 23 (in English) and March 1, 1946 (in Italian) (MLA, KZF, number 17).

[45] "Cultural Association," pp. 1-2; "Culture Association Presents Symposium," *Armenian Mirror-Spectator,* November 3, 1945, p. 3; "Amerika-Haykakan Mshakut'ayin Ěnkeraktsut'ean andranik handēsě" [The First Event of the American Armenian Cultural Association], *Armenia* (November 22, 1945), p. 4 (probably reprinted from *Hairenik* daily).

to get sick, and I also paid my duties to the epidemy myself, staying in bed for about 20 days. For this and other reasons the *Quarterly* was delayed and it will be published only by the end of this month... The second issue will be published in three months, but I would need to have the materials in my hands by the end of February."[46] Despite this assurance, the first issue (Spring) saw the light in April 1946.[47]

In the meantime, the one-day symposium at Columbia University had created a lively interest in a cross-section of the bitterly divided Armenian community.[48] The McMillin Academic Theater was packed with a thousand attendees from all sectors. Vahan Kalenderian presided over the session. After welcoming remarks on behalf of the university by Professor R. Fyfe from the German department, Clarence Manning offered an introductory speech. Papers were delivered by Der Nersessian ("A Phase of Armenian Culture"), Bonfante ("Armenians and Phrygians") and Gregoire ("The Epics of Armenia"). Finally, Zarian read a "superb speech in Armenian," according to one correspondent, about the American-Armenian Cultural Association and Armenian culture in general.[49] Bishop Tiran Nersoyan, newly-appointed head of the Armenian Prelacy of America, offered closing remarks.[50]

In his speech, which was promptly published, as well as its English translation, Zarian sought to dispel the notion of any partisanship behind the Association: "The sole aim of the American Armenian Cultural Association is to promote the research of Armenian culture, to acquaint the outsiders with the conquests of the

---

46 MLA, ACF, section I, number 2166.

47 Cf. "Cultural Ass'n Publishes New Quarterly," *Hairenik Weekly* (May 9, 1946), p. 1; "New Books and Magazines Received," *The Armenian Mirror-Spectator* (May 25, 1946), p. 3.

48 This symposium must have given room to the misleading idea that the *Armenian Quarterly* was founded at Columbia in 1945-1946 (Edward Alexander, "Gostan Zarian: An Appreciation," *Ararat* [Autumn 1999], p. 6)

49 T'ght'agits', "Amerika-Haykakan," pp. 3-4. See also Teghekatu, "Amerika-Haykakan Mshakut'ayin Ĕnkerakts'ut'ean aṙajin handēsĕ Kolumpiayi mēj" [The First Event of the American Armenian Cultural Association in Columbia], *Hayastani Koch'nak* (November 24, 1945), p. 1118; "Culture Association," p. 3.

50 At this time, the "Prelacy" had not changed its name to the current "Diocese."

Armenian genius, to enable the outside Armenologists to communicate to us the results of their researches, to synthesize the new discoveries pertaining to Armenian culture and to define the important place to which the Armenian genius is worthy in the general civilization of mankind".[51]

An editorial of the Boston-based *Hairenik* daily, the A.R.F. organ of the East Coast, after quoting these and other paragraphs from Zarian's speech, reflected at length on the foundation of the Association, probably also to counter some internal criticisms or misunderstandings:

> Being an organization exclusively devoted to culture, the American Armenian Cultural Association has done well, naturally, in setting herself on a *politically neutral* soil. As it has been declared in the first public assembly, her doors are widely open to all Armenians without any partisan or religious discrimination.
>
> It could not be in a different way. Armenian culture belongs to all Armenians and there is no cause or basis to have it appropriated by any political current or have it studied and presented to non-Armenians in a non-all-Armenian way.
>
> ... It is right that this new association is devoted to a work that has no immediate connection to Armenian current *political* demands or struggles. It is right that this association does not *directly* serve to the Armenian Cause, which is today the paramount interest of every single Armenian.
>
> However, there is no doubt that it will be also *indirectly* useful to the Armenian Cause.
>
> We do not have to forget that there is neither interest nor especial sympathy from non-Armenians towards Armenian territorial or political claims. But there is interest about Armenian cultural values. The American Armenian Cultural Association can create among non-Armenians *a warm atmosphere of interest and sympathy* in general towards the Armenian people, which cannot avoid to have a beneficial reflection on their response towards the Armenian political cause.

---

[51] Constant Zarian, "Cultural Association Says Doors Open to All," *Hairenik Weekly* (November 8, 1945), p. 1.

Afterwards, the editorial mentioned the potential impact of the Association on the Armenian-American new generation, which would help to attract more interest towards Armenian culture and political life.[52]

Hairenik Weekly (currently *The Armenian Weekly*), the English sister publication to the daily, also published an editorial aimed more to inbound self-criticism and asserted that the Association "should be hailed by all true American-Armenians as the outstanding achievement of the year in a torn community." And went on:

> We have tried to solve our troubles and to clear our misunderstandings by the method of direct combat against the forces of evil and we have failed to make progress in our efforts. We have failed to realize that the best method of combating evil is to direct our energies into channels of constructive and positive endeavors. The founding of the American Armenian Cultural Association is a deviation from the former methods, and is launching into a positive line of action. We should have started it years ago. Having failed to do so, it is now incumbent upon us to make up for lost time by doubling, and trebling our zeal, our resources, and our sacrifices for its success.
>
> … The American Armenian Cultural Association has an all-important mission – the task of restoring Armenia's cultural contribution to its rightful place in world civilization.[53]

Internal criticism by the rank-and-file of the party is not an unwarranted assumption. In a letter to Hagop Khashmanian, a prominent member of the A.R.F. in New York, Hamastegh, the noted Armenian-American writer and also a party member, wrote:

> Isn't it possible to make this 'Armenian Monthly' *[sic]* a little more lively and popular instead of making it accessible only to specialized professors? It looks like it is not going to come out of these boundaries. The important thing for us is that there is an Armenian generation with

---

[52] "Amerika-Haykakan Mshakut'ayin Ĕnkerakts'ut'iwnĕ" [The American Armenian Cultural Association], editorial, *Hairenik* (November 6, 1945), p. 4.

[53] "The Cultural Association," editorial, *Hairenik Weekly* (November 1, 1945), p. 2.

> new impulse coming into Armenian literature, some have already made big inroads, others have opened a way, and still others have all the requisites to build a road. We have to gather and warm up them around the 'Monthly,' instead of filling it with scholarly drab subjects. And once in a while we have to give that best samples from our literature in translation. What we have and who we are today; this is more important than 'Armenians and Phrygians' *[sic]*. That's more beneficial if we are pursuing something.[54]

In the aftermath of the symposium, one assistant, Dr. Arra Avakian, who would become one of the founders of NAASR a decade later and a lecturer of Armenian Studies at California State University, Fresno in the early 1970's, wrote a lengthy letter to the Association, outlining an extensive series of suggestions about the contents of the journal. It is interesting to quote his reflection on the future of the Armenian community as seen in those days:

> Many years ago (1936) in a public debate (sponsored by the Armenian Students' Association of America, Inc.) in New York pertaining to the outlook of the Armenian Community in America I maintained that in about 50 years the Armenian Community as we now know it would atrophy, but that there would emerge an intensive, concentrated cultural center, composed of scholars and savants, and supported by the Armenian Prelacy, by public institutions of learning (colleges and universities), by semi-cultural associations (Armenian Students' Association, Knights of Vardan *[sic]*, detached student groups), by political and charity organizations, and by individuals whose personal interest evokes it. As such, the cultural strength of the Armenian Community in America would become concentrated into a small body.
>
> With the establishment of the Association and its *Quarterly* I feel that we have taken the first step in that direction.[55]

---

[54] Hamastegh, *Namakani* [Correspondence] (Yerevan: Mughni Publishers, 2003), p. 136.

[55] Letter to the American Armenian Cultural Association, Detroit (October 24, 1945) (MLA, KZF, folder 123).

The first issue of the *Armenian Quarterly* justified Zarian's pretentions of turning it into an American version of the defunct *Revue des études arméniennes*. In fact, at that moment, World War II had disrupted scholarly activities in Europe: "All Armenological centers in Europe have been closed as result of the war. La Revue des Etudes Arminiennes [*sic*] is no longer published; the same is true of *Armeniaca* of Munich University and its successor *Caucasica*; the Mekhitarist monasteries have been obliged to contend with daily difficulties of their own; the higher institutions of learning are in an unenviable condition."[56]

Besides the already mentioned articles by Der Nersessian, Bonfante, Leroy, Krappe, and Shahinian, the issue had contributions by Gregoire and Gray.[57] There were reviews of Boris Piotrovsky's Russian monograph, *Urartu's History and Culture* (Kamilla Trever) and Leon Surmelian's autobiographical novel, *I Ask You, Ladies and Gentlemen* (Nona Balakian), as well as Hovhannes Zavrian's necrology (S. Asvatouroff).[58] Researchers have frequently quoted the articles by Gregoire, Der Nersessian, and Bonfante.

The transliteration key for the journal, although based on the phonetic values of Eastern Armenian, had adopted a popular way, with diacritical marks only for the letters *to, piur* and *ke* (t', p', k').[59] It seems to have been developed by Zarian and Gregoire; on July 10, 1946, Bonfante wrote to the former, "Since we are talking about the alphabet, I have to tell you that, as a linguist, I am a little amazed

---

[56] Zarian, "Cultural Association," p. 1. *Armeniaca* and *Caucasia* had been published in the late 1920's and early 1930's.

[57] Henri Gregoire, "An Armenian Dynasty on the Byzantine Throne," *Armenian Quarterly*, 1, 1946, pp. 4-21 (reprinted in *The Armenian Review,* 4, 1954, pp. 35-47); Louis H. Gray, "The Armenian Acts of the Martyrdom of S. Ignatius of Antioch," *Armenian Quarterly,* 1 (1946), pp. 47-66.

[58] "Of Books and Men," *Armenian Quarterly,* 1, 1946, pp. 110-116. Zavrian, a Paris-based scholar on pre-modern Armenian history and philology, had been invited to contribute a month before his death. Russian archaeologist Trever's review was probably translated from some unidentified Soviet source, but it is curious that nowhere was it mentioned that Piotrovsky's book was in Russian and the reviewer was hailing from the Soviet Union.

[59] "Transliteration of the Armenian Alphabet," *Armenian Quarterly*, 1 (1946), p. 117.

that at least no *advice* was asked from me about the *transliteration* of the Armenian alphabet."[60]

In his prefatory article, Zarian had singled out the remarkable importance of Soviet Armenia as a center of Armenian Studies and the growing efforts of the recently created (1943) Armenian Academy of Sciences as a hub of research, publication and organization. He also made reference to the fact that startling discoveries would make dramatic changes in current perceptions of Armenian history:

> Goethe, upon approaching the shores of Sicily, believed he had found the key to the mystery of civilizations. How many changes have taken place since then! The established frontiers of culture move, historical conceptions change, and often, but one stone, but one inscription is enough to make the whole edifice built upon these so-called irrefutable data and past studies, crumble away into dust.[61]

He went on to mention the excavations at Karmir Blur, which would soon shed important light on the civilization of Urartu; the hypothesis of an Urartian prototype for Greek temples; the revalorization of the Armenian role in the Byzantine Empire; the Armenian contribution to Iranian architecture in the twelfth and thirteenth centuries; the phenomenon of Sinan, the Ottoman architect of Armenian origin, in Islamic architecture, etcetera. This introduction concluded with a remark that had the characteristic imprint of Zarian's style:

> We have no wish to exaggerate. Each culture, no matter how great, is the result of intersecting currents. Each national dominance is born, takes form, and develops by using those pre-existing elements more suitable to its furtherance. The important thing is the intensity of its expression, the originality of its

---

[60] MLA, KZF, number 17 (italics in the Italian original). In the following lines, Bonfante summarized his remarks: "The traditional linguistic transliteration, that of Hübschmann, is mediocre, we know that, but the one you publish is even worse, and some things (like *tch*) are unintelligible. And what difference could it be between *tj* and *dj*? And between *tz* and *dz*? Besides, *j* is not right in my view (*z* is preferable). Instead, *dz* is good."

[61] "Introducing," p. 2.

> physiognomy, its inner sonority, and that fidelity to mother earth out of which it sprang, to be nourished with her life-blood, and imbued with her character. But once created, having taken on soul and substance, it behaves like a living organism: traversing frontiers, imposing itself upon its surroundings, inspiring and instigating other creations which will bear for a long time the imprint of its image.
>
> The study of cultures is the study of these occurrences, these reactions, and these transformations.[62]

Zarian, although not a published scholar in Armenian Studies,[63] was very interested in the scientific study of Armenian culture, and from his writings it is clear that he closely followed developments in the field and had done an ample amount of reading. Armenology in the proper sense of the word[64] was the focus of his interest during the 1940s and 1950s. During an interview held in 1955 he maintained that the main duty of the Diasporan intelligentsia was to devote herself to Armenian Studies and do research in areas that people in Armenia were not able to delve into:

> We have to solve the questions of our history ourselves and look into our past with our own eyes. Is our youth conscious of that? Of course, they are doing a lot of work in Armenia proper and we have to feel admiration for that. What do the thousands of Armenians living abroad do? There is plenty of material for research, plenty

[62] Ibid., p. 3.

[63] At the time, Zarian was doing research on the relation between Leonardo da Vinci and Armenia. He published an article on the subject in Yerevan in 1967. His main work, a history of art, was published posthumously (Kostan Zarian, *Depi Ararat* [Towards Ararat] (Yerevan: Sargis Khachents, 2001), pp. 25-226; see my review in *Journal of the Society for Armenian Studies*, vol. 14 [2005], pp. 217-220).

[64] We bear in mind the following definition by the late Karekin Sarkissian (Catholicos Karekin II of the Great House of Cilicia and Karekin I of All Armenians): "Armenology is the complex of scholarly studies whose aim is to bring under the light of human knowledge, with all possible clarity, precision and integrity, the past life of the Armenian people in all his aspects and phenomena, from prehistorical times to our current days" (Bishop Karekin Sarkissian, "Hayagitut'ean harts'ě Sp'iwṙk'i mēj [The Question of Armenian Studies in the Diaspora], *Pakin,* 1 [1967], p. 49).

> of sources, but nobody thinks about working in that direction.
>
> ... The study of the history of our painting is just starting. The frescoes found in Persia, Constantinople and other places have neither been studied nor photographed. We have hundreds of manuscripts in almost every country which have not been read yet. There are traces of Armenian architecture in Greece, the Balkans and France which still remain unknown. The Vatican archives are full of documents pertaining to the Armenians, left in darkness. Roman, Greco-Byzantine and Arab historians give hundreds of informations about Armenians and we do not do anything. Even the history of Cilicia has not been written yet. It is a beautiful career for the Armenian youth.[65]

In the mid-1940s, there were no outlets in English devoted to Armenian matters outside a few periodicals. The publication of the *Armenian Quarterly* was a significant leap of quality and, paradoxically, showed the existing void, because the level of the journal was not accessible to the middle reader. Nevertheless, it was a valuable effort to spread knowledge about Armenian culture in a highly scholarly way.[66] The level of scholarship was critical; Bonfante, for instance, reacted negatively to an article sent by Leon Arpee about the Armenian alphabet:

> The alphabet is not my own field and I think that Gregoire is much more competent than me, then I fully submit to his judgment. Personally, I do not think that it is

---

[65] Karo Polatian, *Zroyts'* [Conversation], vol. II (Cairo: Houssaper Press, 1961), p. 95, 101. This idea was inspired by a thought formulated by the Italian poet Giosue Carducci in the 1870s, shortly after Italian unification, and approximately quoted by Zarian thirty years before: "At this moment, Italy has to become a school, namely, to study all the experiences of the past to make new conclusions. If we are not conscientious of the values we have already created, we cannot create new ones. Let our youth study our language, our poems, architecture and painting, to be able to synthesize and go ahead" (Kostan Zarian, "Vardastan" [Rose Garden], *Nork,* vol. IV [1924], p. 286, reprinted in Idem, *Depi Ararat,* p. 282).

[66] In his letter of May 23, 1946, Bonfante told Zarian that he intended to submit the journal to the American Council of Learned Societies (MLA, KZF, number 17).

possible to cite as bibliography only the *Encyclopedia Britannica*; at least, it should have been a mention of works by Lepsius, Lagarde, Gardthausen, Müller, Taylor, Marquart and Junkier; among the most recent and important I will mention D. Diringer, *L'alfabeto nella storia della civiltà,* Firenze, 1932, pp. 456 ss.; 756 (contents) and P. Peeters, *Pour l'histoire des origines de l'alphabet arménien,* in *Revue des études arménienes,* 1929, pp. 203-37. *At least* Diringer's and Peeters's works should have been *discussed* a little. (It is incredible the criminal disregard they have about Italian books in these lands). Therefore, without knowing what Gregoire would say, I would publish it *on the condition* that the author cites and examines these works, especially the two last ones. This condition is *taxative* for me. [67]

Ultimately, the article was rejected and published elsewhere, seemingly with no changes.[68]

In his June 15, 1946 letter to Zarian, Leon Surmelian, his former student in Constantinople (1922), acknowledged the importance of a publication like the *Quarterly*:

I received the first issue of your impressive magazine of Armenology, *Armenian Quarterly*. This deserves the widest publicity and support at least among Armenian Americans, and if I can be of any service to you, please let me know. It should be immediately publicized in the entire Armenian press. You would need thousands of subscribers to keep a magazine like this going. I would suggest that you send the first issue to all prospective subscribers. I think that even those for whom this is heavy historical and literary stuff would treasure it, because there is no other magazine like it.

... Yet, the *Armenian Quarterly* is a valuable and wholly creditable undertaking, of which you may well be

---

[67] Ibid., (italics in the Italian original). Bonfante says to have attached to this letter a list of additional remarks regarding Arpee's article. The list has not been kept with the letter.

[68] See Leon Arpee, "The Riddle of the Armenian Alphabet," *The Armenian Mirror-Spectator* (October 26, 1946), p. 3. As said above, the only bibliographic reference is to the *Encyclopaedia Britannica* in regard to the discussion of demotic symbols in Egyptian writing.

> proud. I thank you for printing Nona Balakian's excellent review of my book, but my main purpose in writing this note is my eagerness to see this magazine's success in this crass commercial age, and you may be sure that I shall lose no opportunity to bring it to the attention of prospective readers.[69]

On April 26-28, 1946, the journal, together with other journals and institutions, sponsored an international conference of Byzantinists, Slavicists and Orientalists, held in New York, with twenty-five speakers. Bonfante, Gregoire, Pope, Manning, and Zarian were among the participants.[70]

Lectures on different aspects of Armenian culture were planned from April to June, with Gregoire, John Shapley, Bonfante, and Zarian as speakers. There is no indication in the press that they were actually held.[71]

Bonfante became Zarian's main collaborator. He helped to find new subscribers and contributors and also gave a hand in public relations. Through his efforts, Henry T. Rowell, editor of the *American Journal of Philology*, extensively reviewed the first issue of the *Quarterly*. Although quite favorable, the review warned about the "inadvisability of mixing the popular and the scholarly in the same journal," pointing out to Shahinian's travelogue and Balakian's review as examples of the former.[72]

While publishing the *Armenian Quarterly*, Zarian also taught history of Armenia culture at the Asia Institutes, in English, and at

---

[69] MLA, KZF, number 100. A few months before, Surmelian had published a memoir of his days in Constantinople, on the occasion of the passing away of his mentor, the poet Vahan Tekeyan (1878-1945) (Leon Zaven Surmelian, "With Vahan Tekeyan in Constantinople," *The Armenian Mirror-Spectator* [February 9, 1946], p. 3). The article was translated into Armenian (Lewon Zawēn Siwrmēlian, "Vahan Tēk'ēyani het-Polso mēj" [With Vahan Tekeyan in Constantinople], *Nor Kir* (Winter, 1946), pp. 229-233) and published together with the letters addressed to Surmelian by Tekeyan.

[70] "The First International Congress of Byzantine-Slavic and Oriental Scholars," *Armenian Quarterly*, 2 (1946), p. 209.

[71] See "Announcements," *Armenian Quarterly*, 1 (1946), inside back cover. It is repeated in the inside back cover of the second issue.

[72] *American Journal of Philology*, 4 (1946), p. 383.

the École Libre des Hautes Études, in French.[73] This information can be corroborated by his correspondence. However he did not teach Armenian Studies at Columbia University from 1944-1946, as mentioned by some biographical outlines.[74] This information, whose ultimate source I have been unable to locate, is completely unsubstantiated. The fact that the writer is listed on the editorial board of the Quarterly without any academic affiliation should suffice to correct this misunderstanding. Neither the directories of Columbia for those years, nor the faculty files kept at the university make any mention of Zarian.[75]

In June 1946, Zarian wrote to Bonfante about teaching a course of Armenian Studes at the École, as shown by the response from the

---

[73] "Zarian, dichter," *Elseviers Weekblad,* April 2, 1949, p. 24. Zarian made this statement to a Dutch weekly after his second visit to the Netherlands in 1949. He was probably the source for Hrachya Grigoryan's statement in this regard in his prologue to the bowdlerized 1963 edition of "The Ship on the Mountain"; see Kostan Zarian, *Navĕ leran vra* [The Ship on the Mountain] (Yerevan: Haypethrat, 1963), p. V. Cf. Gegham Sevan, *Sp'iuřk'ahay grakanut'ean patmut'ean urvagts'er* [Outlines of the History of Armenian Literature in the Diaspora], vol. I (Yerevan: Armenian Academy of Sciences Press, 1980), p. 235.

[74] Gh. Hayrapetyan, "Kostan Zarian," *Haykakan Sovetakan Hanragitaran*, vol. 3 (Yerevan: Armenian Encyclopedia, 1976), p. 670, reprinted verbatim, without mention of the author, in "Kostan Zarian," *Haykakan Hamaŕot Hanragitaran*, vol. 2 (Yerevan: Armenian Encyclopedia, 1995), p. 185; Hayk Khach'atryan, *Grakan Teghekatu* [Literary Guidebook] (Yerevani Sovetakan Grogh, 1986), p. 164. According to Armen Zarian, his father had taught "Armenian art and literature" at Columbia ("Mtk'i chambordĕ" [The Traveller of the Mind], interview with Armen Zarian, *Grakan Tert* [February 8, 1991], p. 3). Another biographer, T'oros T'oranian, wrote that Zarian taught there "world literature ... after World War II" (T'oros T'oranian, "Kostan Zarian [keankĕ ew gortsĕ]" [Kostan Zarian: Life and Work], *Nayiri*, March 15, 1970, p. 5). In the introduction to his translations, Ara Baliozian stated that Zarian had taught "Armenian culture." (Gostan Zarian, *The Traveller and His Road* [New York: Ashod Press, 1981], p. XII) or "History of the Armenian Culture" (Zarian, *Bancoop and the Bones of the Mammoth* [New York: Ashod Press, 1982], p. XIV), at Columbia.

[75] See Columbia University in the City of New York. Officers Directory Number for the Years 1944-1945, 1945-46, 1946-47, (New York, 1945, 1946, 1947), as well as Columbiana archives (Low Library), Columbia University.

Italian linguist on June 19: "P.S.: Yesterday it was not possible to talk about your course at the Ecole, because the agenda was overworked. But I will not forget about that. I think that the proposal should be presented to the *School of Literature* (where I belong) and not to the C[ouncil] of the Ecole."[76] On July 10 Bonfante gave a quite positive answer: "About your work (teaching at the Ecole) I did everything I could as a friend: now it depends on Gregoire and you (who both live in New York and may see each other easily) to define the details: the idea has been launched and *approved* by the Council of the Ecole per my proposition, as it is the rule".[77]

Despite the lack of further information, we are inclined to think that Zarian taught at the École des Hautes Études during the academic year 1946-1947 and, simultaneously, at the Asia Institutes (also called School for Asian Studies), where in 1946, according to its director Arthur U. Pope, Zarian would give "for the first time" in an American college, courses of Armenian language, literature and history.[78] Zarian continued his work until mid-1947, as shown by the June 13, 1947 letter in English from Czech Armenologist Jaromir Jedlika, sent to him with the address of the Asia Institutes:

> Just today we got the prospectus of your Institutes which was sent to the library of the Oriental Institute where I work now. I am lecturer of Armenian at the University of Prague and lecturer of Armenian and Georgian at the School of Oriental Languages which was established by the Oriental Institutes [sic] two years ago. But unfortunately our libraries here at the Institute as well at the University are very poor concerning the [sic] Armenian and Georgian literature. ... I think that there may be ideal conditions for scientifical [sic] work in your country. I should [sic] be very pleased if you could assure me that I am not mistaken. It is very strange that Caucasian Languages are not represented in your Courses and Lectures. Would there not be some chance of

[76] MLA, KZF, number 17.

[77] Ibid.

[78] "Asiatic Studies School, NYC, Offers Courses on Various Aspects", *New York Times,* September 22, 1946, p. 14 (reprinted as "Armenian Courses Added to Asiatic Studies," *The Armenian Mirror-Spectator,* 5 October 1946, p. 1 and "Armenian Courses Added to an Asiatic Program," *Hairenik Weekly* [November 14, 1946], p. 1).

> cooperation later on? ... I should like to hear about the [sic] Armenian studies in USA.[79]

Gregoire left to Paris in August 1946, after promising to send an article.[80]

The second and last issue of the journal (Summer) was published in September 1946,[81] containing articles by Zarian,[82] Pope,[83] Manning,[84] Hakob Manandian,[85] Levon Lisitzyan[86] and Dino

---

[79] MLA, KZF, number 18.

[80] See his letter dated "Thursday" (MLA, KZF, number 20), which from the context we assume it was written at the beginning of August, as well as Bonfante's August 26, 1946 letter to Zarian (MLA, KZF, number 17).

[81] See the ad for the second issue ("Off the Press!", *The Armenian Mirror-Spectator* [September 7, 1946], p. 4).

[82] Constant Zarian, "Cultural Renaissance of Armenia", *Armenian Quarterly*, 2, 1946, pp. 202-208. The article was almost immediately translated into Portuguese and reprinted in Sao Paulo (Brazil) (cf. Constant Zarian, "Renascimento Cultural da Armênia", *Revista Cultural Brasil-Armênia,* 1 [1947], pp. 8-11).

[83] Arthur Upham Pope, "Iranian and Armenian Contributions to the Beginnnings of Gothic Architecture," *Armenian Quarterly*, 2 [1946], pp. 125-172 (reprinted in *The Armenian Review,* 3, 1959, pp. 110-124, without photographs). It had been delivered as a paper at the Byzantino-Slavic conference organized by the Iranian Institute on May 18, 1946.

[84] Clarence A. Manning, "Nikolay Marr and Armenian Studies," *Armenian Quarterly,* 2 (1946), pp. 214-228 (reprinted in *The Armenian Review,* 3 [1954], pp. 128-132).

[85] Y. A. Manandian, "A Brief Survey of the History of Ancient Armenia," *Armenian Quarterly*, 2 (1946), pp. 186-201 (translated by Valentine Snow). The translation was done from the Russian original published in 1943 in Moscow-Leningrad (Manandian's Armenian translation was posthumously published in the journal *Etchmiadzin* in 1956-1957; cf. Hakob Manandian, *K'nnakan tesut'iwn hay zhoghovrdi patmut'ean* [Critical Outline of the History of the Armenian People], vol. II, materials for the second part, Yerevan: Armenian Academy of Sciences, 1960, pp. 50-73). A full translation of that text was published as a separate booklet, undated (*A Brief Survey of the History of Ancient Armenia*, New York, n. p., n.d.) and reprinted in 1950 (H. A. Manandian, "A Brief Survey of the History of Ancient Armenia," *The Armenian Review*, 3, 1950, p. 3-32) and 1975 (Hacob Manandian, *A Brief Survey of the History of Ancient Armenia* [New York: Diocese of the Armenian Church of America, 1975]; pages 52-56

Adamesteanu.[87] This issue, as it looks from its contents, was more "popular" than the first one. As an anonymous review in the *Hairenik Weekly* stated, "it is, at least in one respect, more attractive than the first issue, in that its contents are not so highly technical, although no less scholarly."[88]

The editorial work continued after the publication of this second issue. On May 23, Bonfante had told Zarian that he had a second linguistic article of around 50 pages, which was already typed and ready. This article, written in French, was actually sent during the second half of October. However, we do not know its subject.[89]

On February 1947, Georges Dumézil had sent "a small contribution of Armenian philology" after a request was made by Gregoire "last fall." The article, titled "Quelques adjectifs négatifs de l'arménien," was probably intended to appear in the third issue along Bonfante's study, since Dumézil asked to be informed if it would be

---

were written by Bedros Norehad). The booklet has no mention of translator, but the reprints were credited, mistakenly it seems, to Harry Shalian. None of these English editions are mentioned either in Manandian's bibliography (cf. L. Babayan and V. Hakobyan, *Hakob Manandian* [Yerevan: Yerevan State University, 1974], pp. 169-179) or in Armenag Salmaslian's *Bibliographie de l'Arménie* (Yerevan: Armenian Academy of Sciences, 1969), which only catalogued the articles by Pope, Manning, Lisitzyan, and Adamesteanu from the second issue of the *Armenian Quarterly*.

[86] Levon Lisitzyan, "Physiographic Armenia," *Armenian Quarterly*, 2 (1946), pp. 173-185 (translated by A. Mousayan, reprinted in *The Armenian Review,* 1, 1955, pp. 92-100). Lisitzyan (1892-1921) had been one of the main collaborators of the Austrian art historian Josef Strzygowski, together with T'oros T'oramanian. He was lecturer of historical geography and physical geography of Armenia at the People's University of Armenia from December 1920-February 1921, when he was killed during the anti-Bolshevik uprising that reestablished the independence of Armenia until April (L. Gharibjanian, *Yerevani petakan hamalsaranĕ* [1920-1930 tt.] [Yerevan State University [1920-1930 tt.] [Yerevan: Yerevan State University, 1965], p. 260). We have been unable to identify the original source of this translation.

[87] Dino Adamesteanu, "Nicholas Iorga and Armenian Studies," *Armenian Quarterly*, 2 (1946), pp. 210-213 (reprinted in *The Armenian Review,* 4 (1954), pp. 120-122).

[88] "Review. Armenian Quarterly," *Hairenik Weekly* (October 3, 1946), p. 2.

[89] See Bonfante's May 23, June 10, June 16, June 19, July 10, August 26 and October 30, 1946 letters in Italian to Zarian (MLA, KZF, number 17).

suitable and when it would be published.[90] The original typescript was kept in Zarian's files and, since it seemed not to have been published elsewhere, this writer printed it together with the original French letter exactly fifty years later.[91]

In January 1947, the philologist Ralph Marcus also contributed an article, devoted to the study of the Armenian text of Philo of Alexandria's "Quaestiones in Genesim," which he had promised by May 1946.[92]

A French-Armenian scholar of Armenian architecture, Armen Khachatrian, had also sent an article, as Der Nersessian wrote from Harvard on April 20, 1947: "Professor André Grabar, of the Collège de France, who has come over as a visiting scholar to Dumbarton Oaks this spring, has asked me to write to you in connection with the article sent to you by Mr. Khatchaturian. Mr. Khatchaturian is a student of his, and he had asked Mr. Grabar if he would look over the proofs of his articles before it goes to press. I hope it is not too late, and that you will be able to send a set of proofs to Mr. Grabar at the above address, at some time before the end of May."[93]

Noubar Maksoudian, a scholar from Nicosia (Cyprus), had also sent some articles on historical issues.[94]

However, despite this flow of contributions, the third issue was never published. At some point between April and May 1947, it seems, the journal closed shop. The reasons are unknown, although T'oros T'oranian has made allusion to "Armenian individuals belonging to certain circles [who] financially boycotted this periodical and were the cause for its demise."[95] Who were those "Armenian individuals"? We talked above about the Armenian National Committee being the umbrella organization for the

---

[90] MLA, KZF, number 27. Gregoire seems to have renovated his plea of 1945.

[91] Vartan Matiossian, "A Long-Lost Contribution to Armenian Linguistics by George Dumézil: 'Quelques adjectifs négatifs de l'arménien,'" *Annual of Armenian Linguistics,* vol. 18 (1997), pp. 1-5.

[92] See Ralph Marcus's letters to Zarian, May 24 and October 10, 1946, January 13 and February 17, 1947 (MLA, KZF, number 66).

[93] MLA, KZF, number 105, letter to Zarian dated April 20, 1947.

[94] MLA, KZF, number 62, letters to Zarian, November 23 and December 12, 1946 (in Armenian).

[95] T'oranian, "Kostan Zarian," p. 5.

Armenian-American Cultural Association. It is likely that, despite the purely academic work of the Association and its journal, this was the reason for friction and strife of political color. For instance, a correspondent writing about the Columbia symposium of October 1945 had pointed out that both the A.R.F. and the A.D.L (Armenian Democratic-Liberal Party) press, as well as the *Hayastani Koch'nak* weekly (neutral) had accepted to publish an advertisement, but the Progressive League's weekly organ, *Lraper*, had refused it, on the pretext that "it is a Dashnak job."[96] On the other hand, we might venture that some people could consider that it was not the best timing for a highly specialized Armenological journal and the financial means to be spent were not worthy of it. I hope that archival or press materials will turn up in the future and allow us to elaborate a more precise answer. In fact, one could say that the birth of *The Armenian Review* two years later, in Boston, as a semi-popular journal published by the Hairenik Association (a direct branch of the A.R.F. itself), was part of a deliberate strategy to fill the void left by the *Quarterly*, but with a publication far more politically charged and without purely scholarly pretensions, aimed at catering, first of all, to the needs of an educated Armenian-American public. Levon Saryan has noticed that "the early numbers of *The Armenian Review* owe much to the example set by the *Quarterly* in terms of overall quality, erudition, and format."[97]

In the fall of 1947, Zarian and his second wife, the American painter Frances Brooks, arrived in Europe.[98] His Armenological activities in the United States had come to an end and, with him, the first phase of the history of Armenian Studies in this country.[99]

---

[96] T'ght'agits', "Amerika-Haykakan," p. 3.

[97] Saryan, "An Index," p. 221.

[98] Tsarukian, *Metserĕ*, p. 288.

[99] However, in early 1949, David Marshall Lang wrote from London to Zarian's New York address asking for information on Armenological materials to be included in an annual bibliography called "The Oriental Year" (letter of January 4, 1949, kept in Zarian's private archive, Yerevan).

39

Genocide, Diaspora, and the Armenian Writer

Lorne Shirinian

For Armenian diaspora writers, the Genocide still appears to be the context and background for much of their work. It always seems to be there in diaspora texts either directly, as an allusion, as an image, or as an underlying metaphor. Loss, exile, dislocation, alienation, ethnic marginality, disempowerment, and continuing trauma are just some of the central themes of this literature. Perhaps in time this will change as the Armenian diaspora reconceptualizes itself. It may develop new elements of its identity that will not place genocide, loss, exile, and trauma, as they are now felt and understood, as the key components of its identity. That will be a key moment in Armenian diaspora history.

Today, many in their twenties and older actively research the diaspora and Genocide out of personal conviction as they seek to understand how they came to know them. They feel the need to confront the events of their heritage in order to see to what extent they can accept them as part of their own lives. So much of contemporary artistic and scholarly activity continues to revolve around memory and identity after the Genocide. These cultural productions are not at all abstract, but rather are immediately relevant to lived reality in the diaspora. While many artists acknowledge the diaspora as their community, others exclude it, not accepting it as part of their identity or not wanting to deal with it. Thus, one of the first choices the Armenian diaspora writer or artist must make is where to position himself or herself in relation to the Genocide. This is where the artistic challenge begins. How is it possible for literature, for example, to impose form on that which had a structure, but was formless, to impose an artistic construct on atrocity and the social sanctioning of annihilation? Genocide is the complete denial of the creative instinct, of any aesthetic. How is it possible to find an appropriate language? This has been a major challenge for Armenian artists.

There is, however, the experience of having survived genocide, and many of the survivors, without any adequate analogue in their human experience or any pre-existing literary models, have been able to struggle in acquired languages such as English and French to convey, if only partially, what their experience was. These memoirs are part artistic and part historical.[1] The compulsion, the absolute necessity to write, is clear in these texts, as Terrence Des Pres noted:

> When men and women are forced to endure terrible things at the hands of others—whenever, that is, extremity involves moral issues—the need to remember becomes a general response. Spontaneously they make it their business to record the evil forced upon them.... Here and in similar situations, survival and bearing witness become reciprocal acts.[2]

Armenian survivor memoirs force us to contemplate the relationship among the acts of witnessing, testifying, writing and reading and among history, narrative, memory, identity, and art.

One of the consequences of the Armenian Genocide not being universally recognized, although this is changing, has been that most survivor memoirs remain unknown and unread. They were published in private editions with small runs and distributed locally through churches and cultural organizations almost exclusively. These important texts were never considered by the mainstream literary machine that could have reviewed them and introduced them to a larger readership. In their way, many Armenian diaspora writers of succeeding generations bear witness for the witnesses. I have been very aware of doing this and have accepted it as a conscious act in my writing.

In Armenian diaspora literature, there is a correlation between witnessing and imaginative fiction. The survivor-witness's testimony is a discursive act and a speech act—a vow to tell, an offering of

---

[1] See Lorne Shirinian, *Survivor Memoirs of the Armenian Genocide* (Reading, England: Taderon Press, 1999).

[2] Terrence Des Pres, *The Survivor: An Anatomy of Life in the Death Camps* (New York: Oxford University Press, 1980), p. 31.

one's own speech as material proof, a validation of truth. Testifying, then, is more than making a statement. This necessity to speak out is recalled in Borges' story, "The Witness," "...and yet one thing, or an infinite number of things, dies with every man's or woman's death, unless the universe itself has a memory.... What will die with me the day I die?"[3] The story each survivor tells is history that will be lost, and thus deserves to be heard. At the same time, one must be careful not to misread survivor memoirs of the Armenian Genocide as resistance to oppression and assimilation. To do so would be a displacement of the narrative of atrocity with alternative models. The challenge is how to incorporate the Genocide and its testimony into our institutions. Without a broadly accepted controlling narrative to explain the Genocide, it passes through our lives without any means of anchoring it socially and artistically. We should be wary of words like *survival* that can lead to a verbal fairy tale of a life reborn in the new world in the diaspora in which the deportations, mass slaughter, as well as every individual death, horror, and exile are masked. As much as we would like to see each survivor and her testimony as a victory over death, we need to find a more complex version of memory and the self.

The ideas in this paper are based on several key beliefs. The first is that a people is as strong as its cultural integrity and vitality. Second, when a catastrophe happens to a national group like the Armenians, recovery can occur through an awareness of and a confrontation with the truth of the disaster and the inherent suffering. Third, in great part, the profession of writers, artists, and scholars involves the work of remembering in order to give voice to the victims. This is essential despite the fact that every society has its own "regime of truth" as Foucault writes; these consist of mechanisms through which and by which the various types of acceptable discourses are constructed that are sanctioned as being capable of producing the *truth*.

I have wanted to focus on the necessity of narrative in the recovery and exploration of memory. As survivors of the Genocide pass away without any meaningful resolution regarding the issue of official international recognition and all that it implies before the

---

[3] Jose Luis Borges, *Collected Fictions*, Andrew Hurley, trans. (New York: Viking, 1999), p. 311.

states of the world, those of my generation are living out the emotional needs of our parents and grandparents. No doubt the anguish and the impact will increase with time rather than lessen as the indifference over the years has been exacerbated by the fact that many states continue to collude with Turkish governments, which have consistently denied that the Genocide took place. Faced with this, the necessity of narratives becomes crucial. Individuals create a sense of what is important and how they should behave by referring to the stories they have learned. Alasdair MacIntyre, the moral philosopher, writes in *After Virtue* that one can only respond to the question, what am I to do by asking what stories am I a part of?[4]

As the son of two orphan-survivors of the Armenian Genocide, I have accepted the responsibility to confront the Genocide as part of my heritage, as terrible as that sounds; yet it was something my parents were never completely able to do. In some respects, the urge to create characters and the need to complete a poem, story, novel, play, or film is my search to recreate those lost: grandfathers, grandmothers, uncles, aunts, cousins, my father, my mother. If being traumatized means, in part, to be possessed by an image or event that remains unresolved, then the trauma of the Genocide is repeated as it is passed on to succeeding generations. There may be no solution other than to fight despair and to seek justice.

As a diaspora writer who is compelled to write about the Genocide, all I can do is portray my mediated experiences of memory of the events. In other words, I can recall and understand the Genocide only through the ways it has come down to me. I live a vicarious past through the memory of a witness's memory. Perhaps a strong element in my work is the representation of this vicariousness. This is the difference between lived history and the post-memory of the events. Marianne Hirsch defines the term, post-memory, in the following manner:

> Postmemory most specifically describes the relationship of children of survivors of cultural or collective trauma to the experiences of their parents, experiences that they "remember" only as the narratives and images with which they grew up, but that are so

---

[4] Alasdair MacIntyre quoted in Robert Fulford, *The Triumph of Narrative: Storytelling in the Age of Mass Culture* (Toronto: Anansi, 1999), p. 33.

> powerful, so monumental, as to constitute memories in their own right.[5]

Portraying the Genocide as a vicarious past imposes a distinction between my work and the testimony of my parents, for example. Consequently, my post-memory of the Genocide cannot be a way to provide final answers to the great questions raised by the Genocide. I have to accept that my art cannot be an instrument of redemption. I reject the notion that the suffering during the Genocide and the resulting trauma immediately after and into the diaspora might in some way be redeemed and even compensated by art in the large sense. In this context, art resists closure and accepts uncertainty.

In a great measure, the way the Genocide has come to me and how it has formed my inner life are central elements in my work. If Genocide survivors have left oral and written testimony as to their experiences, I, in my turn, give testimony to my Genocide experience, which has come to me through histories, survivor memoirs, photographs, novels, poems, plays, artwork, and films and which I pass on through my creations.

There are, however, certain dangers in the process as the Genocide as subject matter can become displaced by the artist who confuses aesthetic pleasure with very stylized postmodern representations. Such cultural products such as body art, for example, can focus more on the process of stimulation rather than on an exploration of the events and their relationship to the artist. The power of the Genocide could be used as a source to energize and regenerate such stylized forms. Whereas this in itself could be significant, it risks being facile, vulgar, and injurious.

Years from now, should an historian care to know the social and cultural history of the Armenian diaspora in North America, she will have to study its art and literature and how the artists of the time understood the events around them. The historian will need to know how history was being mediated and left for the next generation.

It is essential that in the post-Armenian Genocide world in the diaspora, artists represent their experience of memory work ethically.

---

[5] Marianne Hirsch, "Surviving Images: Holocaust Photographs and the Work of Postmemory," in *Visual Culture and the Holocaust*, Barbie Zelizer, ed. (New Brunswick, New Jersey: Rutgers University Press, 2001), pp. 218-219.

Through the imagination, they make meaning out of the memory of events they never experienced directly. The haunting question in all of this is whether collectively, after the last Genocide survivor has passed away, there will remain the residue of a deep memory of the Armenian Genocide. And if there is, will anyone be able to give it meaning?

40

Unfinished Business: Exorcism and Catharsis in Contemporary Armenian Drama of the Nineties

S. Peter Cowe

It is quite significant that in a decade marked by broader novelistic treatments of the impact of the Genocide on Armenian immigration to America and the transformation of traditional Armenian family life in this country, such as Carol Edgarian's *Rise the Euphrates* (1994), Peter Balakian's *Black Dog of Fate* (1997) and Nancy Kricorian's *Zabelle* (1998), that no less than four plays in English were produced on the same thematic nexus.[1] Whereas the novelist enjoys the leisure of tracing the story through all its meanderings and tergiversations over 200-300 pages, evoking ambience by a wealth of local color, and frequently uncovering the characters' psyche to explore subtleties of mood, thought, and unconscious play of symbols, and the film director may enhance the medium's expressiveness by appeal to location, musical score, and photographic sleight of hand, not to mention a barrage of special effects, the playwright's possibilities, in contrast, are pared down to the essentials of action and dialogue within the relatively brief expanse of dramatic time.[2]

---

[1] Subsequently, the novelistic treatment of the theme has significantly expanded. In this connection, among others, one might mention Micheline Aharonian Marcom, *Three Apples Fell from Heaven* (New York: Riverhead Books, 2001) and Elif Shafak, *The Bastard of Istanbul* (New York: Viking, 2007). New plays also continue to appear, such as Lorne Shirinian, *Exile in the Cradle* (Kingston, Ont., Canada: Blue Heron Press, 2003).

[2] These means were applied to powerful effect by Frunze Dovlat'yan in his final film *Karot* [Nostalgia] (1990), which also deals with the theme of Genocide, its aftermath, and contemporary ramifications with regard to the

Like the novels just mentioned, all the plays under consideration were written in English and hence are directed at a more inclusive audience and readership, reaching beyond the confines of the Armenian ethnic group to which all the main characters belong. Indeed, the recognition that there is little Genocide awareness outside the Armenian community and the desire to raise popular consciousness about the issue is a significant factor in their genesis.[3] Herand Markarian's *Mirrors* (1996), loosely based on his mother's struggles, was conceived as a work for his daughter Yeraz to direct as part of her senior thesis at Barnard College, New York. Nshan Parlakian's *Grandma, Pray for Me* (1990) seems to emerge out of the background to the Columbus Countdown 1992 in illumining immigrant life in the United States through the prism of the Armenian experience. The arresting title *Beast on the Moon*, of the only play by a non-Armenian Richard Kalinoski (1995), relates to an eclipse of the moon in 1893 on the occasion of which Ottoman troops fired at what to their pre-modern perception appeared to be a huge beast in the sky obscuring the moon. Two years later, however, the target of their bullets was not a space monster, but their own Armenian neighbors, as the massacres in various regions foreshadowed the more appalling atrocities of 1915-1922/3.[4] However, perhaps the most striking statement of this disquieting situation is found in the mouth of Ani, the heroine of Leslie Ayvazian's playwrighting debut *Nine Armenians* (1997). Turning the eulogy at her grandfather's funeral into a personal confessional she concludes:

> He waited to tell his Armenian grandchildren in American schools, playing on teams in American sports. I

Karabagh question and the current mass movement agitating for secession from the Soviet Union. Atom Egoyan's more controversial film *Ararat* (2002) also deals with the Genocide's continuing impact on the Armenian community from a more oblique perspective.

[3] Since then various factors have conspired to transform the present international climate of opinion as we move toward the centennial commemoration of the Genocide's inception.

[4] Richard Hovannisian, "The Armenian Question in the Ottoman Empire 1876-1914" in Richard Hovannisian, ed., *The Armenian People from Ancient to Modern Times*, vol. 2 (New York: St. Martin's Press, 1997), pp. 222-226.

> knew he was waiting and I didn't want to hear. My friends didn't know about the Armenians. Pam Hansen didn't know that my grandfather's family was forced to walk across a desert without food or water, until they dropped dead. My American friends who became more important to me than school. Or grades. Or Papa. And now again the Armenians are starving. And no one knows.[5]

Also in keeping with the novels, the four plays display a powerful autobiographical and genealogical impulse and center on the interpersonal relationships in families, which have been problematized and rendered dysfunctional to various degrees as a result of the Genocide's bitter legacy. Varteny Ross (alias Bedrossian) in *Mirrors* has never married in the United States because her sweetheart was killed by gendarmes in the old country along with most of her family. Imagining her surviving brother also to be dead, she falls unconscious and sustains cranial concussion on receiving a note from him out of the blue, which triggers the release of so many painful repressed memories.[6] Aram Tomassian in *Beast on the Moon* is deprived of his family under similar circumstances at a tender age and grows up an orphan. Consequently, his efforts to start a family of his own in Racine, Wisconsin, are hampered by his pronounced individualism and lack of social skills.[7] Although the parents of John and Louise in *Nine Armenians* were able to escape to the New World, they transferred some of their psychological trauma to their children. John becomes extremely protective of his daughter Ani, whom we have already met, while Louise develops into a hypochondriac, constantly worried about her heart and, even by Armenian standards, unnaturally preoccupied with food, hardly a scene passing without her making an appearance with a tray of *boreg*

---

[5] Leslie Ayvazian, "Nine Armenians," in *Contemporary Armenian American Drama: an Anthology of Ancestral Voices*, N. Parlakian, ed. (New York: Columbia University Press), pp. 194-195.

[6] Herand Markarian, "Mirrors," in *Contemporary Armenian American Drama: an Anthology of Ancestral Voices*, N. Parlakian, ed. (New York: Columbia University Press, 2004), pp. 243, 274.

[7] Richard Kalinoski, "Beast on the Moon," in *Humana Festival '95*, (Plays for Actors) (Lyme, NH: Smith and Kraus, 1995), pp. 143-145.

or container of *kat'nabur*.[8] Meanwhile, Deacon in *Grandma, Pray for Me*, has conducted a ménage à trois for years, maintaining a 'spiritual' rapport with the widowed Agate who lives upstairs, to whom he was betrothed in the old country, while being married to Diamond, a girl he had met in the States after losing contact with Agate's family in the aftermath of the Genocide.[9]

Each of the family cases depicted has scars and a lot of unfinished business in coming to terms with the psychological impact of the events that unfolded at the turn of the twentieth century, even at one or two generations remove from the incidents in question. Although very different in tone and treatment, as will already have become apparent, all the plays indicate the possibility of emerging from this pathology, if not by finding meaning in the memory, at least by gaining a certain release from its stranglehold and thereby achieving renewed hope and ultimately a sense of closure. The latter is by no means automatic, but rather demands a great deal of effort by the parties involved to face and exorcise the demons from the past in order to treat the wounds and attain healing and catharsis of spirit. This is the fundamental axis around which their diverse plot lines revolve. It is also particularly appropriate for dramatic handling, since recent psychological investigation has revealed the extent to which identity is formed and reformed through negotiation in interpersonal exchange. In the following analysis, I will briefly review how the plays approach this central issue, starting with the two that focus on the survivor generation and also happen to be simpler in construction and comprise fewer characters.

I will begin with Kalinoski's *Beast on the Moon*, which traces Aram Tomassian's emotional and intellectual development from the early twenties in Act One to 1933 in the second. This harrowing play

---

[8] E.g. Ayvazian, "Nine Armenians," pp. 202, 220. Food and its rituals are developed as a multifaceted sub-theme foregrounding the role of table fellowship to cement ties in the extended family, contrasting the current affluent lifestyle in America with the starvation of the Genocide deportations and post-earthquake Republic of Armenia, and adding local color through the mesmerizing mantra of dishes unfamiliar to the main English-speaking audience.

[9] Nishan Parlakian, "Grandma, Pray for Me," in *Contemporary Armenian American Drama: An Anthology of Ancestral Voices*, Nishan Parlakian, ed. (New York: Columbia University Press), p. 97.

reveals the internal dichotomy in this temperamental artist between his professional and personal life. It is lightened only by the interjections of a narrator located in the present and momentary infusions of humor, until the final climax. A successful photographer like his father before him, Aram had bribed his way to the States by selling pieces from his father's stamp collection.[10] Once established there, he is keen to achieve a name for himself and gain recognition. When he wins a large contract to photograph company executives because of his meticulous craftsmanship, his acceptance by the higher echelons means more to him than payment for the job.[11] As proof of his acceptance of American consumerism and belief in technological progress, he celebrates the occasion by buying his wife a new Westinghouse electric iron.[12]

His fascination with providing an objective reminder of events carries over into his private life, in which he insistently captures memorable moments on film.[13] Moreover, he had picked his bride from a photograph of Armenian orphans in Istanbul, or so he thought.[14] When the girl in her late teens arrives, she confesses that the one he selected had died and the administrators had decided to send her instead so that at least one of their charges should survive. To his chagrin, he later learns that Seta is barren, as a result of malnourishment in her youth, and is desolated at this cruel news which robs him of his most cherished hope. He had blown up his family portrait from the old country, framed it and hung it on the

---

[10] Photography has been an important profession for Armenians in the Middle East, as in other parts of the world, up to the present, combining the elements of art and technology, for which Armenians have demonstrated a particular penchant. The role of the Abdullah brothers in Constantinople and Antoine Sevrugin in Tehran in the later nineteenth century are especially noteworthy.

[11] Kalinoski, "Beast on the Moon," p. 131.

[12] Ibid., p. 132.

[13] Ibid., pp. 106-107, to celebrate Seta's arrival in the United States and pp. 146-147, at the conclusion in recognition of the greater bonding that has developed between the couple and Vincent, an Italian orphan, whom they adopt.

[14] Ibid., pp. 104-105. On the practice such arranged marriages, see Isabel Kaprielian-Churchill, "Armenian Refugee Women: the Picture Brides," *Ararat*, 42 (Spring, 2001).

wall. However, it was no ordinary image and so upset Seta that she covered it with a sweater when her husband was not around. Aram had cut off all the heads and substituted his own for that of his father and his wife's in place of his mother. His plan had been to redeem the loss of the four children by having four of his own, as Varteny's brother Armenag did in *Mirrors*.[15] But now that possibility had been removed by a woman, with whom he shared little apart from being orphaned. His naïve, one-sided and rather mechanical approach to marriage and family had been called into question by reality.

In fact, the couple are contrasted very much like the bride Aruseak and her in-laws in Zabēl Asatur's play *Harsĕ* [The Bride].[16] Seta comes from an upper middle class background in the city, with her father a lawyer and general, and her mother a teacher, and has a penchant for singing.[17] Aram, in contrast, seems to hail from a small town background, and tries to defend his conservative view of women's subservient role and unobtrusive modesty by reference to scripture, only to find that there too Seta can more than hold her own.[18] Thwarted and disgruntled, he falls into a deep depression, venting passive aggression against his wife, as the cause of his disappointment, by refusing to talk to her. Only when she finally

[15] Markarian, "Mirrors," p. 272. In this connection, we note Oshagan's comments regarding the Armenian community to the effect that sexual relations have been traditionally perceived as being a duty to raise children. See Vahe Oshagan, "Otsum" [Unction] in *T'akardin Shurj* [Round the Snare] (New York: Oskedar), pp. 60-88.

[16] This play from early twentieth century Constantinople highlights the generational and class disconnect between a mother and daughter from a village background, who have recently moved to the Ottoman capital and their new bride, an elegant artistic young woman from a wealthy family in Smyrna, the empire's second city and an important center of international trade. In juxtaposing these two contrastive lifestyles the author seeks to underscore the narrow-mindedness and restrictions of the traditional model of women's socially constructed role and encourage the wider acceptance of her more emancipated modern counterpart, who emerges as a veritable paragon of virtue. See Zabēl Asatur, *The Bride*, N. Parlakian, trans. (Whitestone, NY: Griffin House Publications, 1987).

[17] Kalinoski, "Beast on the Moon," pp. 109-110, 120.

[18] Ibid., pp. 108-111, 115-116, 143-144.

resorts to the same treatment does he comprehend the enormity of what he has done.[19]

As a woman, Seta is more in tune with her emotions than her husband and is quicker to establish a network of contacts, such as Mrs. Benetti, the owner of a store where she spends more time than Aram is comfortable with.[20] One day she brings home a street urchin who had tried to steal bread from the shop. His father is dead, his mother is in hospital, and he has just run away from a Catholic orphanage after being abused by a priest.[21] Since it is cold, Seta plans to give Vincent an old coat of Aram's before sending him off. Suddenly Aram bursts in and becomes inordinately angry at his wife's action and sends the boy packing. The sight of Vincent wearing his coat acts as a catalyst for some buried memories to resurface. At his wife's coaching, Aram finally agrees to tell his story. He is outraged at the sacrilege of his 'relic', since his father's coat provided cover for him while the troops rounded up the rest of his family during the Genocide. When he finally ventured out from under it, the first thing he saw was his family members' heads suspended from the clothesline.[22] This was the awful presence, which brooded over the picture on their wall. Aram's outing of his deepest secret brings about an expurgation of spirit through an objectification of the event and achieving a psychological distancing from it. Moreover, sharing it with his wife is a sign of the trust he has developed in her and the first real indication of the reciprocity and bonding, which has been taking place between them.[23]

---

[19] To contextualize Aram's repression of his feelings against the background of a similar response on the part of one sub-group of Genocide survivors, see Donald E. Miller and Lorna Touryan-Miller, *Survivors: An Oral History of the Armenian Genocide* (Berkeley, CA: University of California Press., 1993), pp. 158, 163-164.

[20] On the general finding of immigrant women's greater facility in making a swifter, more successful transition to the host culture through the easy establishment of enabling networks, see Anny P. Bakalian, *Armenian-Americans: From Being to Feeling Armenian* (New Brunswick, NJ: Transaction Publishers), p. 174.

[21] Kalinoski, "Beast on the Moon," p. 144.

[22] Ibid., p. 145.

[23] This process is assisted by his wife's reenacting her mother's crucifixion for refusing to renounce her faith. Though Aram at first seeks to discount

Progressively freed from the shackles of his past, Aram is increasingly empowered to take initiative. Where one image had violently separated him from the orphan Vincent, another unexpectedly draws them together, if more contrivedly. The boy proudly displays the one coin he has left from his father, while Aram shows him the single stamp remaining from his father's collection.[24] Ultimately, the once unthinkable occurs when Aram acquiesces to his wife's request to adopt the boy. Aram's personal life has gained a maturity and wholeness to balance his career success. The moment is symbolically celebrated by Aram's buying Vincent a new jacket and exploiting his technical skill to slip in front of the lens for his first family portrait on automatic release. This pose underscores his full participation in the scene rather than exclusion from it by maintaining a professional distance. A microcosm of the ethnic melting pot, these three isolated individuals have come together to realize the American dream as represented by the middle-aged Vincent of the frame narrative who brings the work to a close.

As Markarian states in the introduction, his play *Mirrors* highlights the paradigmatic way in which an encounter between three persons illuminates their evolving exploration of selfhood as they realize the extent to which each reflects and contrasts their understanding of who they are in the present in the light of their problematized past.[25] As mentioned above, the main character is an elderly Genocide survivor Varteny Bedrossian. On arrival in the United States she had curtailed her surname to Ross, probably not so much in an effort to assimilate to her new surroundings, since apart from church she lived the life of a recluse, but rather in order to distance herself from her traumatic experiences in an Anatolian village. Later we hear of the atrocities perpetrated on her family. Her father was strapped to a mill wheel until he drowned, her pregnant aunt had her womb ripped open to satisfy a bet on the sex of the child she was carrying, while the rest of the adults were shot and the village set on fire.[26] As in real survivors' testimony, it is likely that

---

the 'play' as a form of witchcraft, it then becomes a catalyst for him to unburden himself of his deepest secret regarding the atrocities perpetrated against his family.

[24] Ibid. p. 145.

[25] Markarian, "Mirrors," p. 237.

[26] Ibid., p. 268.

she was continually haunted by these memories. However, receiving a letter from her long-lost brother Armenag plunged her into a state the psychiatrists at the clinic she is admitted to term anterograde amnesia: she has lost all present cognizance.

In her hospital ward she gradually relives her teenage romance, her memories acted out expressionistically on stage by her sweetheart Garo, a shepherd *fedayee*, and her younger self with whom she talks intermittently. The scene is vividly evoked by the use of symbolically color-coded light sequences and the playing of the love song *Dele Yaman.*[27] Finally, she acknowledges her block to the doctor: "The Gendarme has me in a web." To which he replies, "You can get out of the web if you let me."[28] Her exorcism involves the administration of a drug, which apparently heightens her sensations and draws her deeply suppressed experience into the open conscious realm. Here the realization is facilitated by the use of mime by the doctor and nurse as a play-within-a-play. And indeed the whole scene is a powerful metaphor for the dramatist's physick and the curative properties of the stage for the audience's moral and psychological health.[29] The gendarme accosts Varteny in attempted rape, provoking her to stab him fatally to protect her honor with the scissors she used to cut tarragon for her mother.

The role of the psychiatrist, Dr. Brown, is developed to reveal his own quest for identity. He knows nothing about his natural parents and virtually nothing about his first adoptive parents, who died in a fire, which destroyed their house and papers. His past basically begins with his second adoptive parents who were missionaries and brought him to the United States from a foreign orphanage. His personal search inspired his scientific and professional career, lending him something of an absent-minded professor-ish air, which borders on the obsessive, as he devotes his

---

[27] Ibid., pp. 267-270. The phenomenon parallels that of the main character in Henrik Malyan's film *Nahapet* (1977) on the basis of a short story by Hrach'ya K'och'ar, who continues to relive the painful memory of having to witness his family's execution somewhere in the eastern provinces of the Ottoman Empire until after being finally persuaded to remarry in what has become Soviet Armenia, he relives the joy of fatherhood and rediscovers his purpose in life. There, too, the folksong *Dele Yaman* is a leitmotif.

[28] Ibid., p. 270.

[29] Ibid., pp. 270-271.

full time and attention to sleuthing out Varteny's case background, even to the point of neglecting his home and family for three straight days. In response to a query by another patient Mary, Brown enunciates the play's crux as follows:

> What an intricate, pathetic trio: Teny is living in her past, Mary has forgotten her existing past, and I... am searching for my non-existent past. When will this labyrinthine search for tranquility come to an end?[30]

Mary is much less developed as a character. She appears to be suffering from a form of senile dementia, and yet displays an unusual array of symptoms. She cannot recall early memories, but has reasonable retention of her interaction with Varteny, while yet querying the identity of the woman who regularly visits her and claims to be her sister. It seems that her primary role is rhetorical, in light of the above citation.

While the extended exposition and violent climax are handled well, the aftermath comes across as less convincing because of the immediacy and completeness of Varteny's recovery. Resting in her wheelchair later the same day, she remarks chirpily to Dr. Brown, "I killed him, Doc... No more nightmares. The Gendarme can't hurt me anymore."[31] Brown's own situation seems more compelling in that although he has come to accept his genealogy as beginning with his adoptive parents, a status which offers a faint light and new hope, nevertheless, his involvement with patients like Varteny prevents him from, as he says, "pulling the trigger that would kill my non-existent past," i.e. the possibility of discovering more about his pre-history and early life, in consideration of which he feels he could construct a more complete self image.[32] Although family ties impinge less intensely in this play than in the previous and the two that follow, Varteny's desire to reconnect with her brother and visit him, suggests the sides of the wound coming together in healing and foreshadows the fuller, richer life that awaits her.[33]

Grandma, Pray for Me is a reflective, poetic, understated portrayal of the tensions of life in an ethnic Armenian neighborhood

---

[30] Ibid., p. 267.
[31] Ibid., pp. 271-272.
[32] Ibid., p. 259.
[33] Ibid., p. 272.

in the center of a large city like New York in the inter-war years.[34] Like *Beast on the Moon*, it contains a frame narrative spoken by the grandson Mickey, who currently muses on that vanished society, which epitomizes his innocent youth as "a prayerful pause between one holocaust and another."[35] Mickey's epilogue reveals his total immersion in the major trends of American life, which is prefigured by his tentative entry into the workforce in the central part of the play.[36] Having undergone the leveling experience of serving in the military, he fulfils the American dream by going to college and embarking on a successful corporate career, which catapults his family from the deteriorating fabric of the inner city out to the suburbs.[37]

Whereas *Beast on the Moon* offers a panoramic development over about a decade, though this play amply suggests that longer-term processes are at work, it telescopes the action into a single day on the eve of the Second World War, already pregnant with intimations of the new order.[38] Grandma, the matriarch of an extended family, suffers a stroke, and her impending death symbolizes the end of an era, as the other family members split and reform in nuclear groups.[39] Despite the fact that Grandma's husband as well as one son and two daughters were victims of the Genocide and she reminisces briefly about her relatively well-off status in the old country, she seems to have been able to come to terms with her

---

[34] Parlakian, "Grandma, Pray for Me," pp. 121-122.

[35] Ibid., p. 136.

[36] Ibid., pp. 104, 115-119.

[37] Ibid., p. 121. Mickey's trajectory is characteristic of the American mainstream in the post-war years. The topic is discussed in Peter Balakian, *Black Dog of Fate: An American Son Discovers his Armenian Past* (New York: Basic Books, 1987), pp. 5, 35-38, with regard to the author's own family that moved out of New York city to settle in the commuter towns of Teaneck and Tenafly, New Jersey. Earlier, it was broached in Peter Najarian, *Voyages* (New York: Pantheon Books, 1971), pp. 97-100, where the narrator highlights his older brother Yero's deep desire for acceptance by American majority culture and the impact on him in this connection of serving in WWII, marrying, and moving to the suburbs, in contrast to his own more rebellious tendencies toward the counter-culture of the sixties.

[38] Parlakian, "Grandma, Pray for Me," p. 121.

[39] Ibid., pp. 119-120.

past and its losses.[40] Indeed she stands out as a figure of great serenity and wisdom about the cycle of life and death as well as of a homespun pragmatism about making the most of the present opportunity.[41] With her continual attitude of prayer, she embodies a mystical Armenian spirit of survival, which is at its most tangible in Mickey's birth. As he says, "I was born here out of a need—how shall I put it—it was a need for the decimated Armenian people to live on after the holocaust of 1915. God tossed them to the far corners of the earth. My people came to America."[42] In this play, it is the aftermath of the Genocide in causing the upheaval of the diaspora with its attendant culture shock and clash of values, which is foregrounded.

Whereas Grandma continues to function according to Old World rhythms, the brunt of straddling the two cultures has fallen on her son, Deacon, who is thus caught in a series of dichotomies, which are objectified in his "spiritual bigamy." Betrothed to Agate, he had lost contact with her for many years during which he married Diamond. Agate, too, had married, and then convinced her husband to take the upstairs apartment where she still lives as a widow with her daughter Pearl. In flirting with Agate, Deacon tries to tap into his carefree youth before he was burdened with responsibilities as breadwinner on his father's death.[43] Possessed of a poetic and philosophic bent, he considers he should have been a monk, and freely admits he has been an unwilling father.[44] Diamond, he states, deprived him of his loneliness and represents reality, whereas Agate holds out youthful hope.[45]

While Deacon extends Diamond "autumnal love," which seems to imply a platonic caring but unphysical relationship, she intimates she cannot subsist vicariously on TV soap operas for ever, and hints darkly that she cannot say where her unfulfilled yearning for warmth

---

[40] Ibid., p. 94. The play associates this with her prayer and religious devotion.

[41] Ibid., p. 115.

[42] Ibid., p. 89.

[43] Ibid., pp. 97-103.

[44] Ibid., pp. 117-118. His name Deacon, a term for the ecclesiastical order immediately below that of priest, already suggests something of his inner struggle to balance the demands of the spiritual and material realms.

[45] Ibid., p. 102.

and romance will take her once Mickey is off their hands.[46] Agate, too, is frustrated by this rather incestuous condition until she is present at a humorous interlude marked by a visit to Grandma by two physicians, an oculist and a podiatrist, at Mickey's instigation. Their names, Cyclops and Achilles, perhaps suggest the debate between the philosopher and the poet to be the teacher of Greece, since the former delights in measuring, while the latter specializes in theatre and the arts.[47] Finally, Cyclops has to admit his instruments only apply to the physical realm of sight, not the broader mental and spiritual dimension of vision.[48] Not only is Achilles more adept in the latter sphere, but more direct and tactile, and hence, by gently soothing Agate's foot, he begins to soften her bitterness, persuading her to come for a longer session at his office. This arousal in turn emboldens her to seek a "divorce" from Deacon, whose impending loss of his mother's stabilizing presence provides him with a flash of realism to grasp that there is no point in pondering what life could have been like when this one can be so fulfilling.[49] Consequently, he even takes his parental responsibilities more seriously by buying Mickey a coat for his new job, symbolically seeking to prepare him to leave the warmth of his adolescent home environment to face the rigors of the outside world.[50] The resolution of the conflicts between body and soul, work and leisure, family and self, Armenian and American in the older generation, pave the way for the smoother transition experienced by Mickey, whose path to marrying Agate's daughter Pearl is now clear, thereby realizing his parents' hopes and ensuring the survival and successful thriving of their line, living the American dream, the success of an Armenian making it in the American mainstream, and rising up the corporate ladder.

---

[46] Ibid., pp. 102-103, 113.

[47] Ibid., pp. 106-111. Thus, in Plato's *Symposium*, Socrates is hailed triumphant first against Agathon, the youthful tragedian, and then the more mature figures of Euripides and Aristophanes, who remonstrate against the possibility of a tragedian writing comedy and vice-versa, implying that such arts do not qualify as a *tekhnē*, a skill capable of being learned by anyone with the necessary aptitude.

[48] Ibid., p. 107.

[49] Ibid., pp. 111-112.

[50] Ibid., p. 119. The significance of a coat as symbol of comfort and protection recurs in several of the plays under discussion.

The final play, *Nine Armenians,* set in 1992, focuses more emphatically on the contribution of the third generation and hence on a reawakened sense of Armenian ethnic identity in the wake of the collapse of the Soviet Union, the rise of the Karabagh movement and subsequent war with Azerbaijan and the proclamation of an independent Armenian Republic, a major new development in terms of its potential as a homeland with which to identify.[51] Whereas in *Grandma* the cyclical structure alluded to is the universal one of one generation succeeding another, here the parallel cited in Ani's speech between the starving Armenians of the First World War and those suffering from the devastating earthquake of 1988 paves the way for a return to the homeland for the granddaughter, as part of a team bearing relief supplies, carrying with her an urn containing her grandfather's ashes to find their resting place in the native soil.[52] Inspired by Vartan's example of witnessing to the atrocities of the Genocide, Ani, who already has a heightened social conscience, is

---

[51] Ayvazian, "Nine Armenians," pp. 38-39, 45-56, 105-108,121-126. One may compare the theme of return to that of Mel Divan (alias Mels Divanyan), the main character in Vigen Chaldranyan's film *Symphony of Silence* (2001), who after a shady past associated with bank robbery, goes back to the Armenian Republic initially for a visit, but then decides to stay to play a role in the multifaceted project of reconstruction. At the same time, several recent plays from Yerevan concentrate on the opposite phenomenon of the continuing exodus from the homeland, which marks the plot of Chaldranyan's earlier work *Kyrie Eleyson* (1995).

[52] Ayvazian, "Nine Armenians," pp. 195-196. Here we meet the theme of return in terms of the grandfather going back where he came from, though in this case he started life in Kayseri (Caesarea) in central Anatolia and is now being flown back to Yerevan in the Armenian Republic. The yearning of Armenian immigrants in America to return to their home region recurs frequently in literature. One of the most poignant is that of Baghdasar Margosian (Uncle Baghdo), who had wanted to go to Armenia all his life, even to the point of being buried there at least (Antranig Antreassian, *The Cup of Bitterness and Other Stories*, J. Antreassian, trans. [New York: Ashod Press, 1979], p. 66). It is also found in writing representative of the new wave of immigration ensuing on the downfall of the Soviet Union in works such as Khoren Aramouni, *Harut' Pap* [Grandpa Harut'] (Glendale, CA: Ayb Ben Publishing, 1997), in which the main character feels himself so alienated that he determines to go back, leaving the rest of his family in California.

overcome by a zeal to offer the victims and their families at least moral support, even if unable to be of much practical help.[53] At the same time, in a highly charged scene where an old man (played by the same actor as her grandfather) knocks on her door at the Hotel Armenia asking for help, she rises to the occasion in the difficult conditions without heat and light by giving the man her coat.[54]

On her return, she states she had received more than she gave and displays evidence of greater Armenian acculturation in dance and fluency in the language than before.[55] The grandparents' and parents' rather weak response to her accusation of their dereliction in this regard is that they were waiting for her to ask them about such things. Her retort is that Armenian had been employed as a medium to exclude them and discuss matters she was not supposed to hear.[56] The full impact of this situation is patent in her younger brother Raffi, a regular all-American kid, who gives Ani pops as a parting gift at the airport and shows the middle sibling Virginia how to dance on roller blades. When asked by his grandfather what he is drawing, he replies, "aliens," and when further primed on drawing landscapes with a mountain, he completely misses the old man's hint and responds blandly, "not usually."[57] However, later he cutely sends Ani a sketch of Mt. Ararat, asking her to correct it against the real thing. Moreover, the underlying current of hope, which permeates the piece, is symbolized by the rather obvious leitmotif of birds building a nest in a tree near the grandparents' house, who successfully rear a clutch of young as the winter of the opening scene revolves into a summer finale.[58]

---

[53] Ibid., pp. 200-202.

[54] Ibid., pp. 218-219.

[55] Ibid., pp. 220-224, 229.

[56] Ibid., pp. 199, 221. The practice was widespread in the Armenian community of America, the first generation tending to emphasize the importance of English for their offspring in order to facilitate their entry into the mainstream. In diasporas of the Middle East like Syria and Lebanon where Armenian language became standard in the communities through the medium of schools, periodical press, etc., Turkish was often employed by the older generation as a medium for discussing matters from which children were to be excluded.

[57] Ibid., p. 188.

[58] Ibid., pp. 183, 185-86, 227, 229-230.

However, on the whole, the male characters are less important than their female counterparts. Both the grandfather and Uncle Garo die in the course of the drama and we have already alluded to some of the problems of Ani's father John. The latter bears a western name, is alienated from the homeland (being gripped by fear at the enormity of the genocide), from his neurotic sister Louise, and increasingly from the rest of the family. This is particularly in evidence during the long final scene when he is reduced to sitting reading the papers in the car as he waits for the others to finish their goodbyes and negotiations about the amount of food they are to take home from the communal Sunday lunch at grandma's.[59] Ani had already posed the conflict of authority in the altercation at the airport in which she had stated that her father could take back the money for her airfare, but she would go eventually. "Your family escaped and you'll never go back. But I can go, Dad." Moreover, when pressed by Louise, he confesses to being miserable.

Over against this, we are struck by the strength of character and initiative displayed by the women of the family who emerge as significant tradents of Armenian culture and the creators of continuity in home and family life. Ani's grandmother tells her of the selfless heroism and solidarity exhibited at the Genocide by her mother-in-law. Being transported to become mistress to a Turkish officer, she ordered the carriage to halt and joined the lines of women being deported into the desert.[60] Similarly, the grandmother has the candor to admit she loved her children more than her husband because the marriage was arranged.[61] She is also responsible for organizing her husband's cremation and Ani's carrying his ashes to Armenia, while having a casket of logs interred in the local cemetery so as not to offend the sensibilities of the rest of the family. As a result of Ani's pioneering visit, her mother determines to go to Yerevan for a month to help in the orphanages and networks with the

---

[59] Ibid., pp. 226-232. With this we might compare the rich, evocative description of this ethnic ritual in Balakian, *Black Dog of Fate*, pp. 6-7, 17, 35-37.

[60] Ayvazian, "Nine Armenians," p. 222.

[61] Ibid., p. 221. In that traditional context the primary relationship was often that between the mother and her eldest son, who would provide for her and protect her after her husband's death, granted the lower life expectancy among men.

other women of the family about the household chores a full week before she informs her husband of the decision.[62] Their openness and bonding are manifest in the keening or hand-wringing episode[63] and then over a dance spontaneously initiated by Ani in the final scene, which is successively joined by the other women as a triumphant statement of the continuity of Armenian culture in the unity of the different generations and the re-created sisterhood of the diaspora and the homeland.[64]

In conclusion, it emerges that although all four plays treat the theme of survival and resolving the social and psychological issues raised by the Genocide for Armenian family life in America, there is a significant divergence among them in terms of focus and voice. While *Mirrors* attempts to illumine the universal role of the past in the individual's construction of the self, *Beast on the Moon* and *Grandma, Pray for Me* are integrationist models of the successful acculturation of immigrant groups. Parlakian posits a poetic unquantifiable "spirit of survival," which grants Armenians the ability to endure. However, one wonders whether Mickey's children in the suburbs do not resemble the third generation of *Nine Armenians* as portrayed by Ayvazian. Written from a woman's perspective against the backdrop of the earthquake of December 7, 1988, and in the immediate euphoria of Armenia's independence, and with an exuberance characteristic of the voluntarism of the third generation re-establishing contact with its roots, the work highlights the central role rapport with the Armenian Republic can play in re-integrating Armenian culture in the diaspora.[65]

---

[62] Ibid., pp. 224-225.

[63] Ibid., pp. 222-224.

[64] Ibid., p. 229. The significance of the Armenian earthquake of 1988 as the pivotal moment in altering Armenian diasporic attitudes toward the homeland, as yet still under Soviet control, is well illustrated in Lucine Kasbarian, *Armenia: A Rugged Land, an Enduring People* (Parsippany, NJ: Dillon Press., 1998), pp. 70-73. This succinct overview of Armenian history and culture devotes an unexpectedly large amount of space to the event.

[65] Although traditionally few Armenian women wrote plays, this facet of women's empowerment is also a feature of the 1990s, both in the Armenian Republic, as witnessed by Anahit Aghasaryan, "Madmen of the World, Unite!" in N. Parlakian and S. P. Cowe, eds., *Modern Armenian Drama: An Anthology* (New York: Columbia University Press, 2001), pp. 388-444;

Karine Khodikyan, *Piesner* [Plays] (Yerevan: Apolon, 1997) and *Khaghi zhamanakĕ* [Play Time] (Yerevan: HGM Hratarakch'ut'iwn, 2004); and the recent anthology Herand Markarian, *Armenian Drama*, H. Markarian, ed. (Yerevan: Writers' Union of Armenia, 2006), as well as figures like Bianca Bagatourian in the United States.

William Saroyan

41

Willliam Saroyan: The Writer

Barlow Der Mugrdechian[1]

William Saroyan became a nationally known writer with his first published work, *The Daring Young Man on the Flying Trapeze*, in 1934, and remained an important part of the American literary scene until his death in 1981. During his lengthy career he produced an enormous body of work, thousands of pages, much of which however, has remained critically unexamined until today. He explored virtually every literary genre, from the short story, to plays, novels, and autobiography, but he is perhaps best remembered for his short stories, which reflect his own unique view of the world and of his art.

Saroyan's world-view was based on his love of life, of every experience and feeling of life, and it was through his art, through his expressive writing, which encompassed that love, that he sought to uncover the secret of life, the spiritual core of humankind.

William Saroyan, born to Armenak and Takoohi Saroyan, an immigrant Armenian family from Bitlis, in Fresno in 1908, had a strong sense of his own identity, both as an Armenian and as an American. His own powerful sense of self-identity informed his later works as well. His stories explored the many facets of identity, both from an Armenian and non-Armenian perspective. His humble beginnings would have given little inkling that he would emerge to become one of the most authentic of American literary voices, one whose impact would be felt on many generations of writers.

---

[1] This article is dedicated to my friend and colleague Dickran Kouymjian, who has studied William Saroyan and his work for many years, and has often taught courses about Saroyan at Fresno State and at other universities. Kouymjian has written and spoken frequently about his friend Saroyan, and has contributed greatly to keeping Saroyan's memory alive.

Saroyan burst forth on the American writing scene during the American depression, with his insuppressible good humor and unique vision of everyday life. Saroyan's works are filled with optimism, an optimism which belies the difficult life that the young Saroyan experienced, losing his father at age three, and spending five difficult years in an orphanage in Oakland, California, separated, except for infrequent visits, from his mother. His youth was also spent in poverty, in Fresno, where he had returned with his sisters and brother in 1916. The ten years of his life spent in Fresno, from 1916-1926, established Saroyan's core values. He said in one of his journals, "During those ten solid years of living in Fresno I made my life, I forged my soul...I recognized and accepted my character and I made my decision about the kind of life I was going to live, or at any rate try to live. And therefore those ten years were surely as important as any other ten years of my life and possibly the most important."[2] The hard lessons of life were deeply impressed on Saroyan.

As Nona Balakian says in her book, *The World of William Saroyan*:

> ...the future seemed to hold little certainty for an educated grade-school dropout, somewhat foreign-looking, living in a small, inland region in California and striving for national recognition.[3]

Who would have guessed that the young Saroyan would someday become the darling of Broadway and America and whose larger than life presence would be part of the literary scene for forty-seven years, until his death in 1981?

But his early life shaped his approach to life and literature, between which there was no separation. He admired the work of Walt Whitman, Sherwood Anderson, and Emerson, and their outlook on life. Based on the experience of life, he expressed his deepest inner thoughts through his writing.

Saroyan embraced a form of writing which eschewed the use of form in his literary work, rather utilizing an often stream of

---

[2] *William Saroyan: An Armenian Trilogy*, Dickran Kouymjian, ed. (Fresno: The Press at California State University, Fresno, 1986), p. 4.

[3] Nona Balakian, *The World of William Saroyan* (Lewisburg: Bucknell University Press, 1998), p. 28.

consciousness style in his writing. This style, placed him among such American writers as D. H. Lawrence and Walt Whitman, and in contrast to writers such as Henry James and T.S. Eliot, whose works reflected more distance between writer and work.

Saroyan's choice of style often put him at odds with the critics, who valued a more structured form to writing. It was the New Critics especially who wanted to separate the writer from his text, and to consider the text as a separate unit. This tension between Saroyan and the critics grew, and one example of it was Saroyan's rejection of the Pulitzer Prize, in 1940. Later in the 1940s and 1950s, Saroyan continued to lose favor among with the critics, and reading Saroyan lost favor in the academy, and in universities. But Saroyan never bowed to the critics, always feeling that his way was the right way.

As Balakian commented:

> To understand the true nature of Saroyan's art and grasp the foundation on which his art is based one must bear in mind that from the beginning of his career he held the belief (which he never abandoned) that experiment was a necessary component of creativity, and creativity itself the greatest part of "what is loosely called art.'"[4]

It was this love of creativity that was a hallmark of his work, which ranged, as earlier mentioned, among a wide variety of genres.

It is the quest for meaning in life that is the underlying basis of Saroyan's work. And it was the poverty from which he came that impelled his writing.

> I took to writing at an early age to escape from meaninglessness, uselessness, unimportance, insignificance, poverty, enslavement, ill health, despair, madness, and all manner of other unattractive, natural and inevitable things. I have managed to conceal my madness fairly effectively.[5]

It was that madness which reappeared frequently as a theme in Saroyan's works, in the often eccentric characters which people his stories and novels.

---

[4] Ibid., p. 30.

[5] David Stephen Calonne, *William Saroyan: My Real Work is Being* (Chapel Hill and London: University of North Carolina Press, 1983), p. 6.

Saroyan was able to straddle the line between reality (the world around him) and the world of his characters. Saroyan's approach in his work was an existential way to make sense of the world. He knew that the world as it was, the real world, was uninhabitable, and that it must be remade through art. And it was this struggle to constantly create, which Saroyan followed as his muse in his writing.

Saroyan's long career can be divided into several phases, each giving an insight into both the writer and the man. David Stephen Calonne has astutely divided Saroyan's literary career into five parts: Part 1-from 1934-1939, he wrote short stories, such as *The Daring Young Man on the Flying Trapeze, Inhale and Exhale,* and *Three Times Three*; from 1939-1943 he wrote plays, *My Heart is in the Highlands* and *The Time of Your Life*; from 1943 to 1951, he wrote his first two novels as well as short stories, among which is *The Human Comedy*; from 1951-1964, he wrote novels dealing with marriage and family, *Rock Wagram, The Laughing Matter, Boys and Girls Together, One Day in the Afternoon of the World*; and from 1964 until his death in 1981, he primarily delved into his own life through his autobiographical works such as *Days of Life and Death and Escape to the Moon* and *Obituaries*.[6] For the last twenty years of his life, Saroyan lived both in Paris and in Fresno, continuing his prodigious creative writing. In Fresno, he lived and worked in two tract homes, one that he lived in, the other next door, where he worked. And he almost never varied from a rigorous schedule of writing, which called for hours a day of writing. All of this was documented by his discipline of dating his works. In his last twenty years, he also had the opportunity to try and affirm his own legacy. He did this through self-contemplation and through the genre of the autobiography.

Saroyan's stories are full of children – children who live as only children can – full of wonder at the world, living in the timeless moments of discovery, and as Calonne says, "it is their un-self conscious faith in the miraculous nature of experience which he [Saroyan] celebrates."[7]

A look at just a few of his works will illustrate this leitmotiv of Saroyan. In the *Human Comedy*, the story takes place in a mythical

---

[6] Calonne, *William Saroyan*, pp. 12-13.
[7] Ibid., p. 58.

town of Ithaca, California, which is everytown USA. Saroyan writes of the Macauley family, a family that represents all families – it could be Armenian, or Irish, or Italian, or any of the many ethnic groups who lived in Fresno and who inhabited his literary world. Saroyan, at his core, believed in the equality of man, and that all people were truly created equal. That was reflected in his own work. The unity of mankind was constantly part of his search for truth in art. In Calonne's words:

> With John Donne, Saroyan believed that every man's death diminishes me, for he envisions humanity as a vast organic, interconnected body of sacred life.
>
> ... The driving impulse behind his vision of life is the conviction that we are all tied together by the bonds of common humanity-within each human breast beats the same cosmic energy."[8]

The naming of the three Macauley children after Greek heroes such as Marcus, Homer, and Ulysses, puts the story into the universal, outside of the specific experience. In the series of short vignettes, Saroyan unfolds a story of everyday life, but told through the eyes of the children. In is through Homer Macauley's interaction as a postal delivery boy that the larger issues of the world come into view. *The Human Comedy* was originally a screenplay before being published in 1943. World War II is only a background in the story, but one that eventually intrudes into the story. The threat eventually invades Ithaca, when Homer must see death for the first time when he delivers a post-card to a mother whose son is lost in the war.

Saroyan wants to introduce the reader to the world of everyday mysteries and he succeeds through the series of childhood experiences, which Homer and Ulysses have. Everthing is new for them, everything is a cause for wonder. Thus, it is through life that the reader sees the larger issues of life and humanity. The eyes of the child are open to the wonders of life.

It is part of the maturing process when Homer must deliver the death message post-cards, which intrude on the peaceful life in Ithaca. The stories are inhabited with children and adults, who have all of the characteristics of the people who Saroyan loved to write about.

---

[8] Ibid., p. 99.

A second work, *My Heart's in the Highlands*, takes place in 1914 Fresno. Here Saroyan use the roles of a poet, his son, and the elderly Jasper McGregor, to explore the world of poetry and art. The poor poet, who can barely make a living, represents man's inner drive to remake the world in his own image. The poet is the creative element, which tries to make sense out of the chaos of the world. The world is full of uncertainty, and it is through the writer's conscious efforts that he can reintegrate himself. *My Heart's in the Highlands* represents the metaphorical homeland of Armenia, where the poet's heart remains – it is the longing and separation, which Saroyan knew well. Saroyan believed that it was through art that reintegration would take place.

Saroyan was always proud of his Armenian heritage, always proud to defend himself against anyone who would disparage that heritage. But this pride was never chauvinistic, but rather his view was that all people shared a common bond. In fact it was not until the last phase in his writing career, the last twenty years, when he consciously began to explore the Armenian part of himself, in his continuous quest for self.

In a series of plays, published after his death, *William Saroyan: An Armenian Trilogy*,[9] Saroyan takes the often painful step of self examination, to delve into the deepest parts of his psyche. In three plays, "Armenians," "Bitlis," and "Haratch," Saroyan deals with the questions which faced the Armenians who lived in the Diaspora – in "Armenians," he discusses the early Armenian community of Fresno and how the Armenians faced the issue of coming to terms with a permanent separation from their homeland. Again, Saroyan was only too painfully aware of separation, because of the death of his own father. Three priests take different roles, with different voices and the interplay between characters becomes an existential exploration of identity.

In "Bitlis," Saroyan makes his first visit back to the place of his forefathers, back to Bitlis. Here Saroyan's views on the universality of man are explored, especially when he finds that Bitlis is inhabited by Armenians no more, but by Kurds. How does he reconcile his own preconceptions about Bitlis, with the real world, with what he

---

[9] *William Saroyan: An Armenian Trilogy*, Dickran Kouymjian, ed. (Fresno: The Press at California State University, Fresno, 1986).

actually finds? He learns that being Armenian is a matter of choice, and that his affirmation of Armenianness is what makes him Armenian.

In "Haratch" the final play, the action takes place in the offices of the *Haratch* newspaper in Paris, France. A group of Armenians, intellectuals, clergy, and others are involved in a dense and complex argument about the ultimate fate of the Armenians. Can Armenians survive in the Diaspora? How do the Armenians deal with the pain of assimilation? What is an Armenian? It is with these three stories that Saroyan explores the Armenian identity. In these last stories, Saroyan conducts the ultimate inner search, to make sense of his own world.

Saroyan, the writer, has been the subject of biographies and critical essays, which attempt to place the writer in the context of his life and times. It was Saroyan's zest for life, his life-long search for self-realization through his work that makes William Saroyan among the best of American literature.

As Calonne observed:

> His [Saroyan's] primary emphasis had always been on the quest for individual identity, purpose and meaning, and ultimately he sought the brotherhood of man, the spiritual realization of all humanity. His work attempts to define man's state of spiritual exile and fragmentation, to record his anguished yearning for completion and inner fulfillment.[10]
>
> ...Saroyan always knew what he was "after," that nameless awful and beautiful mystery at the heart of life. His genius lay in his ability successfully to evoke and celebrate it through art.[11]

Saroyan, the writer, balanced life as it was with the best possibilities of life: despair and hope, separation and integration. As one reads William Saroyan's work, one can feel the universal search for integration in a fragmented world, his search for the spiritual core of man. This, then, is Saroyan the writer, one whose life and work was devoted to a search, which he could not entirely complete, but a

---

[10] Calonne, *William Saroyan*, p. 145.

[11] Ibid., p. 149.

writer whose work was always thought provoking, entertaining, and full of the exuberance that he himself exhibited throughout his life.

42

William Saroyan on Madness, Genius, and Inspiration

David Stephen Calonne

William Saroyan wrote incessantly on the themes of madness, creativity, and inspiration. The relation between apparent "insanity" and inspiration was explored in antiquity by Plato in his dialogues *Ion* and *Phaedrus*, and from the nineteenth century Romantic period in particular, we have inherited the notion of some possible link between genius and madness, or in modern psychoanalytic parlance – "neurosis." If one thinks of the great nineteenth century figures – Beethoven, Blake, Dostoyevsky, Nietzsche, Rimbaud, Van Gogh, Poe – the picture which emerges is clear: to be a genius is to be eccentric, different, odd, perhaps genuinely mad, but certainly "abnormal."

All of these themes appear in the work of William Saroyan, the Armenian American writer who came to fame in the 1930s with the publication of *The Daring Young Man on the Flying Trapeze* (1934), won the Pulitzer Prize (which he refused) for his absurdist vaudeville play *The Time of Your Life* (1939), and reached a large American audience with his best-selling novel of World War II, *The Human Comedy* (1943). Madness, genius, creativity, inspiration, the purpose of art, the question of writing as "therapy" and its connection to psychoanalysis, the relationship between suffering and being of Armenian descent – all were obsessive themes for Saroyan.

In psychoanalytic terms, the "traumata" in Saroyan's early life were multiple: the death of his father Armenak when Saroyan was just three years old; his subsequent terrible years in the Fred Finch Orphanage and separation from his mother; and the poverty he faced during his childhood in Fresno. In his autobiography *Here Comes, There Goes, You Know Who*, Saroyan wrote: "I took to writing at an early age to escape from meaninglessness, uselessness, unimportance, poverty, enslavement, ill health, despair, madness, and all manner of other unattractive, natural, and inevitable things. I have managed to conceal my madness rather effectively."[1] The passage is significant, for Saroyan here couples madness and writing and declares that writing is his "escape" from – among other difficult aspects of life – madness. He has been, is and will continue to be "mad," but in typical subtly ironic Saroyan fashion he adds: "I have managed to conceal my madness fairly effectively."

He makes the connection between writing and self-strengthening even more explicit in the preface to his play *Don't Go Away Mad*. Saroyan asserts that he needed to write "because I hate to believe I'm sick or half-dead; because I want to get better; because writing is my therapy."[2] This is a frequent comment by both creative artists and scientists: that their work is a kind of "therapy" which heals their sense of self-division. Here Saroyan agrees exactly with D.H. Lawrence: "One sheds one's sicknesses in books – repeats and presents again one's emotions to be master of them."

Yet the idea of madness poses a kind of paradox for Saroyan, for he knows he cannot ever completely "escape" from this madness and he would agree with George Bernard Shaw that the insane thing is to adapt yourself to an insane world. And he would agree with Henry Miller, who in his *Hamlet* letters considered the "normal": "And the normal is a monstrous thing, if it is regarded frankly. But that is only to say that human life itself is a monstrous affair. In the sight of God, that is. In the sight of God the normal is the abnormal. Nothing must horrify God more, assuming He could be horrified, than the sight of the normal man."[3]

Saroyan's conception of madness is complex, and he struggles with its multiple meanings throughout his work. In *Days of Life and*

---

[1] William Saroyan, *Here Comes, There Goes, You Know Who* (New York: Simon and Schuster, 1960), pp. 2-3.

[2] Saroyan, "Preface" to *Don't Go Away Mad and Two Other Plays* (New York: Harcourt Brace, 1949), xv. Compare Graham Greene: "Writing is a form of therapy; sometimes I wonder how all those who do not write, compose or paint can manage to escape the madness, the melancholia, the panic fear which is inherent in the human situation." Quoted in Anthony Storr, *Solitude: A Return to the Self* (New York: Ballantine, 1988), p. 123.

[3] Henry Miller, *Hamlet Letters*, Michael Hargraves, ed. (Santa Barbara: Capra Press), p. 145.

Death and Escape to the Moon, a journal kept in Paris/1967 and Fresno/1968 and published in 1970, he writes: "Madness, is anything of man's without it? Nothing in the universe may be said to be – all of it is sensible. But man *is* a madness, and everything he does is mad."[4] He also inverts the categories of sane and insane in his powerful preface "A Writer's Declaration" *in The Whole Voyald and Other Stories*: "[The writer] is also mad, measurably so, but saner than all others, with the best sanity, the only sanity worth bothering about – the living, creative, vulnerable, valorous, unintimidated and arrogant sanity of a free man."[5] The writer is mad but free; "normal" men are sane and horribly trapped, leading as Thoreau declared, "lives of quiet desperation."

In *Letters from 74 rue Taitbout*, Saroyan addressed one "letter" to "Dr. Freud, Dr. Jung, and Dr. Adler" and continued to explore the question of sanity and "adjustment": "Now, of course all his life everybody adjusts, from the minute he's out in the open to the minute he rolls back into the closed. He adjusts…himself into a total incapacity to find out who he is and what he might do about it. He is not himself, he is his adjustments, he is a product manufactured by his government."[6] For Saroyan, finding one's identity is the primary purpose of every human life and a life completely "adjusted" to the requirements of society is non-existence.

In *Short Drive, Sweet Chariot*, Saroyan writes in Chapter 10 of meeting on a boat on Lake Michigan a St. Louis Police Department psychologist. Saroyan says to him: "I am interested in madness. I believe it is the biggest thing in the human race, and the most constant. How do you take away from a man his madness without

---

[4] Saroyan, *Days of Life and Death and Escape to the Moon* (New York: Dial Press, 1970), p. 120.

[5] Saroyan, "Preface," *The Whole Voyald and Other Stories* (Boston: Little Brown, 1956), p. 14. Saroyan also wrote about his fellow absurdist dramatists Beckett and Ionesco in an essay entitled "Ionesco" published in *Theatre Arts*, July, 1958: "Beckett and Ionesco are not mad. They have discovered the means by which to reveal, in acceptable and deeply moving terms, that the human race is mad, and that the world has been in an uncharted and unknown dimension of hopeless lunacy—if not criminality—for centuries and is now away off in this dimension," pp. 26-27.

[6] William Saroyan, *Letters from 74 rue Taitbout* (New York: World Publishing, 1969), p. 17.

also taking away his identity? Are we sure it is desirable for a man's spirit not to be at war with itself, or that it is better to be serene and ready to go to dinner than to excited and unwilling to stop for a cup of coffee, even?"[7] Saroyan echoes here Rainer Maria Rilke's famous statement regarding psychoanalysis: that if he were to throw out his demons (i.e., undergo analysis), he might cast away his angels as well – "How do you take away from a man his madness without also taking away his identity?" And Saroyan goes on to describe the "madness" he observed in London during World War II: "Man's madness is man, himself. If man becomes too much for himself, if his madness becomes too much to put up with, to wait with, alone, what is the good of running to Freud instead of to God? Instead of running to the source of the whole thing, the source of the man himself, and the madness itself?"[8]

Thus like Henry Miller, it follows that his attitude towards psychoanalysis was that he did not need it because he accepted his madness on one level as having some necessary connection to his genius and, in any case, he was doing his own psychoanalysis by his constant exploration of his memories of childhood. Writing for Saroyan, as for Marcel Proust, is looking for lost time, as he remarked in *Here Comes, There Goes, You Know Who*: "I have so far mainly considered the earliest times, not especially intending to do so, but falling into it, as it were, perhaps because when the nature of your work is to remember, you tend to start at or near the beginning, and then to go back again and again, expecting most likely to find out a little more fully why you have become estranged, why you are one place and the world another, as the Armenian saying is."[9] The task of self-integration, then, is for Saroyan the task

---

[7] William Saroyan, *Short Drive, Sweet Chariot* (New York: Phaedra, 1966), p. 94.

[8] Ibid., p. 95. Saroyan returns to Freud in *Births* (Berkeley: Creative Arts, 1983), pp. 51-52. And in *Freud on Broadway: A History of Psychoanalysis and the American Drama* (New York: Hermitage House, 1955), David Sievers attempted to read Saroyan psychoanalytically: "The work of Saroyan remains of particular interest for the psychoanalytic-minded, with its recurring leitmotifs of child-like passive-dependency, naïve wish-fulfillment for a better world, hostility toward money, oral regression, free associational dream distortion…," p. 254.

[9] Saroyan, *Here Comes*, p. 142-43.

of the artist, rather that of the psychoanalyst. His memoir *Not Dying* is dedicated "to the psychiatrist in the sky" – apparently the only one he ever consulted.

Thus, madness for Saroyan has two aspects: there is the real suffering he experienced and which makes him "mad" and there is the madness which seems linked to his literary gift, to his inborn genius – in ancient Greek his "daimon" – and with this presence he does not want to tamper. And he proudly reserves the right to suffer and to learn from suffering and from this acceptance achieve wisdom. As we shall see, it is this aspect which may be said to be his Near Eastern, Armenian understanding of madness.

It is complexities such as these which have so exercised modern psychologists and students of creativity.[10] Being crazy does not make one a genius: the genetic stuff that makes a Bach or Nietzsche or Van Gogh remains a mystery. The fact that an artist is relatively balanced or unbalanced is not the *source* of his creativity. As Lionel Trilling observed: "Granting that the poet is uniquely neurotic, what is surely not neurotic, what indeed suggests nothing but health, is his power of using his neuroticism... It is wrong to find the root of the artist's power and the source of his genius in neurosis."[11]

The seeming oddness of the person of genius is partially due to his fierce dedication to spiritual goals in a materialistic world. In this respect, Saroyan's example also mirrors the philosophy of the Romantics, for it was in the nineteenth century that the notion emerged of the artist as a kind of substitute religious figure. His creativity, the spark of inspiration, is "divine" for he appears to make something *ex nihilo*. The old orthodoxies were no longer cohering, and it was left to the great composer, artist, philosopher, or writer to

---

[10] There is a large literature on creativity, as well as its connections with madness and genius. See *The Creativity Question*, Albert Rothenberg and Carl R. Hausman, eds. (Durham: Duke University Press, 1976); Denise Shekerjian, *Uncommon Genius: How Great Ideas are Born* (New York: Viking, 1990); Silvano Arieti, *Creativity: The Magic Synthesis* (New York: Basic Books, 1976); Vera John-Steiner, *Notebooks of the Mind: Explorations of Thinking* (New York: Harper and Row, 1985); Kay Redfield Jamison, *Touched with Fire: Manic-Depressive Illness and the Artistic Temperament* (New York: Free Press, 1993).

[11] Lionel Trilling, "Art and Neurosis" in *The Liberal Imagination: Essays on Literature and Society* (New York: Harcourt Brace, 1978), p. 165.

take up the burden of spiritual illumination – a notion we see achieve its climax in a work such as Friedrich Nietzsche's *Also Sprach Zarathustra* (1883-1885). The insistency on art's essentially healing "sacred" purpose recurs throughout Saroyan's oeuvre.

But the artist is not some special creature deserving idolization. On the contrary, as Saroyan wrote in a book of essays by himself, Henry Miller and Hilaire Hiler entitled *Why Abstract?:* "The artist is not a freak. He is simply the isolation and extension of those good qualities which are in all men...All the elements of art were always there, waiting for a perception in one man to reveal these elements to all men."[12] Art is a "superactual world [which] can allow no accident in things. At the same time it can permit no reality which at its core is not miraculous. The surprise of art is not shock, but wonder."[13] The artist creates wonder in the place of horror; the work of art is a creation of order and wholeness in the face of despair and chaos.

In this regard, Saroyan again recalls Henry Miller who asserted: "The artist's dream of the impossible, the miraculous, is simply a result of his inability to adapt himself to what is vulgarly called 'reality.' He creates, therefore, a reality of his own, in the poem, a reality which is suitable to him, a reality in which he can live out his unconscious desires, wishes, dreams."[14] So too Saroyan's traumatic childhood, what he calls his "paranoia" in *Here Comes, There Goes, You Know Who*, is transformed by his art; his need to remake the world according to the heart's desires. Writing and imagination are reparative; things may not work out in life, but you can make them come out right on paper, on music sheets, on canvas.

Frequently, the theme of madness occurs in relation to Saroyan's Armenian heritage. Armenians are *khent* (mad) and being Armenian and being crazy often amount to the same thing. Armenians are Don Quixotes, impractical dreamers who plant pomegranate trees in the desert and are disappointed when they do not bloom. Saroyan charts his own Armenian genealogy of insanity in his autobiography: "It was early said of the fourth child and second son of Armenak and Takoohi Saroyan that he was the inheritor of the nature and spirit of

---

[12] Hilaire Hiler, Henry Miller, William Saroyan, *Why Abstract*? (London: The Falcon Press, 1948), p. 34.

[13] William Saroyan, *Razzle-Dazzle* (New York: Harcourt, Brace, 1942), p. 505.

[14] Henry Miller, *Hamlet*, p. 63.

a man called *Khent Baro*, which is the Armenian way of saying Mad Baro, whose proper name was Barunak Saroyan…And Lucy, soon after I became established in the family after the years at the orphanage, remarked again and again, 'he is Mad Baro all over again…In any case, like it or not, the theory was that it had come to me to preserve and extend the qualities of this man Barunak Saroyan. This jokester, prankster, upstart, cut-up, loud-mouth, and hooligan, who was irritable, short-tempered, unreasonable, demanding, and surely at least a little mad."[15] It will be noted in this passage Saroyan's finely modulated, contained, yet outrageous humor; the best comedians are of course completely mad.

In *Not Dying*, the theme of madness and depression recurs. Saroyan says to his son Aram in a kind of warning of the pitfalls of being from the Saroyan clan: "Now, I must make known to you that there is a very powerful and yet not entirely accountable order of sorrow in my family, which is surely in yourself, too, which you must recognize, accept, understand, and seek to control, for this sorrow, while not entirely useless, can be deeply troublesome, and in the end actually killing. Everyone has it, most likely, in one degree or another, but my family has it excessively."[16] Again, one notes the almost courtly style here; each phrase is again carefully controlled. I am reminded of Yevgeny Yevtushenko's comment that Hemingway's refined, restrained style was that of a man who was clenching his teeth to prevent himself from crying out in pain.

Again, in his memoir *Days of Life and Death and Escape to the Moon*, Saroyan returns to his familial history: "Lunacy runs straight down the middle of every branch of my family. We have nobody who is not some kind of nut."[17] To be an Armenian, and worse to be a Saroyan Armenian, it appears, is to have, perhaps, more than the usually share of a sorrow which seems close to clinical depression.

In a late story, "Madness in the Family," Saroyan again connects madness with the essential nature of being Armenian:

> Going mad was a specialty of the family. Until a man had gone mad, it was understood he was still a boy. If he never did, he was not the equal of those who had. Only a few reached the age of thirty unseized, and, over a period

---

[15] Saroyan, *Here Comes,* pp. 108, 110.
[16] William Saroyan, *Not Dying* (New York: Harcourt, 1963), p. 183.
[17] William Saroyan, *Days of Life and Death and Escape to the Moon*, p. 52.

> of a century, only two or three members of the family went the whole distance unseized. More than a few took the trip several times, after which they were considered wise men, or perhaps even holy men, as if they had made the pilgrimage to Jersualem, as, in a sense, they had.
>
> With the women it was another matter, although most of them took the trip too; but with the help of the other women in the family, their journeying was fairly well concealed. Women on the trip tended to reject their children, their brothers and sisters, their parents, their parents' parents, and themselves. Their madness was justified and reasonable, which may have made its concealment a relatively simple matter. The demands on women for diplomatic behavior were so severe and so taken for granted by the men that madness was upon the women practically all of the time.
>
> With the men the madness took several traditional forms, including a repudiation of God, or rather Jesus and Christianity, since nothing but trouble had come of the Father, the Son, the Holy Ghost, and the Church. Another common form of the madness was a total rejection of the human race, based upon ancient and contemporary evidence that the human race was criminal and contemptible...In Bitlis, my father, Manak, [Saroyan's father's name was Armenak] was considered wise and worthy because he had made the trip to madness before he was twelve, which was uncommon....[18]

Although this is phrased in the inimitable, subtle, marvelous, ironic, comic Saroyan manner, there are serous truths as well. For example, the shaman is often seized in adolescence with madness, which makes him the wise figure in many tribal societies. As Saroyan remarks, after the "trip" they were considered "wise men or perhaps even holy men." Here again madness can be a kind of catharsis, a cleansing ritual for the psyche. Other Armenian characters in Saroyan's fiction, such as Arak Vagramian in the novel *Rock Wagram* (1952), also go "mad" in a kind of spiritual crisis which has one of its sources in their Armenian identity. The narrator of *Rock Wagram* tells us "there is no experience, winked or not, that

---

[18] William Saroyan, "Madness in the Family" in *Madness in the Family*, Leo Hamalian, ed. (New York: New Directions, 1988), pp. 1-2.

is without madness from the time a man is born to the time he dies, and the madness of every man is enormous."[19]

Mircea Eliade, in his masterful *Shamanism: Archaic Techniques of Ecstasy*, describes the shaman's characteristics: "Sometimes there is not exactly an illness but rather a progressive change in behavior. The candidate becomes meditative, seeks solitude, sleeps a great deal, becomes absent-minded, has prophetic dreams and sometimes seizures. All these symptoms are only the prelude to the new life that waits the unwitting candidate. His behavior, we may add, suggests the first signs of a mystical vocation, which are the same in all religions and are too well known to dwell upon."[20] It is noteworthy that Saroyan has chosen the same term – seized" – to describe the transformation his characters undergo that Eliade uses to describe the shamanic vision.

Thus, the question of Saroyan's attitude towards madness can be seen in relation to his Armenian heritage: the Armenians were mad, but it was a life-giving madness, a mystical initiation into ecstatic truth, rather like the madness Kazantzakis celebrates in *Zorba the Greek*. Americans – White Anglo-Saxon Protestants – on the other hand, often lacked madness and therefore lacked vitality, passion, and meaning. Saroyan possessed too much Armenian Bitlists'i peasant instinctive strength to be very patient with the whining of pampered Americans. The Armenians, an ancient people with thousands of years of history, a written language and magnificent literature and an elaborate and refined culture had also experienced continual suffering from the depredations of conquering armies (in antiquity trapped between the warring powers of Rome and Parthia), culminating in the Genocide of 1915. The Armenians knew about *real* suffering.

This theme appears in "The Time Before" – a tribute to Saroyan's mother and a description of his own birth. Towards the end of the story, Saroyan contrasts his Armenian mother to women in America: "While she was with child my mother journeyed in a chair car across the American continent; kept house, cooked, baked

---

[19] William Saroyan, *Rock Wagram* (New York: Doubleday, 1951), pp. 77-78.

[20] Mircea Eliade, *Shamanism: Archaic Techniques of Ecstasy* (Princeton: Bollingen, 1964), p. 35

bread, washed and ironed clothes, made and mended clothes for her children, took care of her sick husband, and worked in a cannery in order to earn money with which to pay rent and buy food. She is eager that I put all this down in this account and suggests that I quote her as saying there are women and women. She is contemptuous of women she sees in movies going around being melodramatic about phony emotional problems which she thinks are a lot of crap, as she says in Armenian. These women are very ugly, she says."[21] The passage is noteworthy, for Saroyan calls what many spoiled Americans consider to be difficulties "phony emotional problems." One of Saroyan's early fans, J.D. Salinger, drew a portrait of a famous teenager who also saw a great deal of "phoniness" in American life and who struggled with real spiritual suffering and madness.

In *The Time of Your Life*, the madness of the world has paralyzed the main character Joe's will. The other characters are also aware of the lunacy in themselves and the world, as we see when Krupp the waterfront cop says: "I think we're all crazy. It came to me while I was on my way to Pier 27. All of a sudden it hit me like a ton of bricks. A thing like that never happened to me before. Here we are in this wonderful world, full of all the wonderful things – here we are – all of us, and look at us. Just look at us. We're crazy. We're nuts. We've got everything, but we feel lousy and dissatisfied just the same." When Nick mentions the fact that the sad Arab is the "nicest guy in the world," Krupp responds: "But crazy. Just like all the rest of us. Stark raving mad."[22] Saroyan sees madness as endemic to modern life, a madness the Arab (i.e., *the Armenian*: "no foundation, all the way down the line") correctly diagnoses.

Yet, I do not want to suggest that Saroyan only considered the "abstract existential" madness of the world and never struggled with his own quite literal madness, for of course he did. In "Runaway Walter Winchell and Robinson Jeffers" in *Sons Come and Go But Mothers Hang in Forever*, he wrote:

> I had long known that there was something about me that was either violent or frightening for some reason. In

---

[21] *The Booster: September 1937-Easter 1939* (New York: Johnson Reprint Corporation, 1968), p. 26.

[22] William Saroyan, *The Time of Your Life* (New York: Harcourt, Brace), p. 141.

> certain three-sided clothing store mirrors, I had for some years come upon the reflected triple images of myself with shock and disbelief, regret and shame, disappointment and despair, for I was indeed clearly violent, mad, and ugly, all because of something in me that had always been there—an intensity of some kind, a tension, an obsession with getting everything that was there to be got, a passion, an insanity, whatever might be the proper word or series of words for it.
>
> And for hours after such an assault out of the three-sided mirror upon the illusion of myself, about my appearance, about my reality, which I wanted to believe was kindly, courteous, thoughtful, and handsome, I would be in despair about this revelation, this truth, and I would try to imagine how I might cast out the demon that was in me, or at the very least how I might keep it quiet and not so terribly noticeable.[23]

Thus again, we have Rilke's demons (yet also the ancient Greek "daimon" or creative indwelling genius and spirit – Socrates spoke of his "daimon" telling him the proper course of action) and the struggle of the artist to cope with the inner tensions the "daimon" creates.

Perhaps the darkest night of the soul for Saroyan was in the early 1950s. *In Not Dying,* Saroyan describes the time following his divorce when he felt he was "mad" yet through sheer force of will sat in front of his fireplace in his San Francisco house and began to compose three books – *Rock Wagram, The Laughing Matter* and *Tracy's Tiger*: "I was not about to go berserk, I had already gone, I had been there, I was there, I *was* berserk, but I was also intact, I was in my own study, and I had my own fire."[24] Saroyan remarks that he

---

[23] William Saroyan, *Sons Come and Go, Mothers Hang in Forever* (New York: McGraw-Hill, 1976), p. 89.

[24] Saroyan, *Not Dying*, 100. James Tashjian quotes Saroyan: "I've done many mad things in my life, but something in me drives me to do such things. I regret my *having* to do them. It isn't easy for me to be me. I have always been in full rebellion against the world, *and* myself…I've never understood myself, so how could anyone else understand me?" "Which Saroyan Visited Filene's" in Leo Hamalian, ed., *William Saroyan: The Man and the Writer Remembered* (London and Toronto: Associated University Presses), p. 103.

"knew the arrogant loneliness of the writer at work, the old writer in the old fight, the lone man in the great contest with time and mystery. If I was mad, I was also free to heal the madness. The madness was private, my own, not public, and I was free to find out how best to banish it, and to become restored."[25] It is writing which saves him, the act of creation which begins to heal his fragmented self.

Saroyan wanted to confront the dark night of the soul directly, fearlessly, and to learn wisdom from the encounter: in a dark time the eyes begin to see, as Theodore Roethke declared. In *Here Comes, There Goes, You Know Who*, Saroyan wrote: "And I don't believe I am afraid of madness, because madness is also myself, I have always had it, I don't think I would give up my paranoia for anything in the world, I understand it too well, and I'm not sure the specialists understand paranoia in general as well as I understand mine in particular. All children are paranoid. It might be a good idea for the specialists to look into that."[26]

As I have suggested above, the artist seeks to redeem this paranoia through the creative act and through the blessedness of inspiration. The person of genius has the gift of transformation: he can take the chaos of experience and through his imagination make us take wings up and out of the chaos. Saroyan sensed this genius in himself from an early age, and he also sensed the liabilities of the gift.

Perhaps the notions of genius, madness and inspiration are linked because the artist, Jekyll and Hyde-like, has two selves which all of us have but which are more pronounced in their characters than in "normal" people. To be a genius is to be both more active and more passive than is usual and to be in thrall to a sometimes overwhelming force: daimon, god, unconscious – which seeks expression. The genius is both more full of energy, demanding to be shaped into artistic form, and more forced to lie in wait. As Igor Stravinsky once said in referring to his waiting for inspiration to compose: "I can wait as an insect waits."

The pleasure of writing for Saroyan clearly derived not only from a kind of therapy in which the broken self can be reassembled.

---

[25] Saroyan, *Not Dying*, p. 102.
[26] Saroyan, *Here Comes*, pp. 147-148.

There is also the possibility of an even more intense pleasure: that of inspiration. Inspiration, as the ancients knew, cannot be forced. The day-to-day life of the writer is prosaic and hard work: letters to editors, revision of drafts, pestering notes to publishers who have not made payment. But when inspiration comes, ecstasy also comes. As Emily Dickinson said: you know it's poetry if you feel as if the top of your head is being blown off.

Perhaps the greatest book on poetic inspiration is E.R. Dodds' *The Greeks and the Irrational*. Dodds points out that "the first writer whom we know to have talked about poetic ecstasy is Democritus, who held that the finest poems were composed *met enthousiasmou kai hierou pneumatos*," "with inspiration and a holy breath," and denied that anyone could be a great poet *sine furore*."[27] Plato linked the ecstasy of inspiration with madness in his *Phaedrus* in which Socrates asserts: "*ta megista toun agathon emin gignetai dia manias*: "our greatest blessings come to us by way of madness" [Phaedrus 244A]. And Plato adds: *theia mentoi dosei didomenes*": "provided the madness is given us by divine gift."[28]

So also Saroyan describes inspiration as a revelatory even in which the very essence of the self is altered in a kind of magic alchemy. The act of writing itself, when inspired, takes the writer out of chaos and into sacred cosmos, transforming his vulnerable flesh briefly into an oceanic feeling of deeply pleasurable sensation. In *Not Dying*, Saroyan observed:

> I used to believe my face was coarse, for instance, but after I had finished writing something, I noticed that my face was suddenly no longer coarse. The work had changed me so powerfully inside that you could see it in my face, which was still the same face, but no longer coarse...when you work at the making of a new piece of writing you gradually put away from yourself a lot of trash that is in your nature. You concentrate so intensely that in a sense you leave your body entirely, although it's there all the time. Your spirit, or *the* spirit, takes over – not for long, the spirit doesn't need a lot of time, it

---

[27] E.R. Dodds, *The Greeks and the Irrational* (Berkeley: University of California Press, 1964), p. 82. See also the excellent historical survey by Penelope Murry, *Genius: The History of an Idea* (Oxford: Blackwell, 1989).
[28] Dodds, *The Greeks and the Irrational*, p. 64.

> certainly doesn't need forever. It operates entirely in the instant, now, canceling time as we understand it. Afterwards, a writer notices that he has worked three hours, for instance, of perhaps only thirty minutes, abut now and then six or seven hours, which he hadn't noticed as minutes or hours, or as time at all.[29]

It is instructive to read this passage in connection with the text quoted above in which Saroyan experiences his face as ugly and violent in the three-way mirror: here the mirror reveals the loveliness seen in the face purified by dross in the act of creation.

And in a book in which authors describe their experiences with the art of writing entitled *On Being A Writer*, Saroyan remarks: "After you've taken your chair and have written a while – perhaps an hour or so – it comes along, and you start to move ahead strongly. Psychiatrists say you're drawing on the collective memory in the Jungian sense. It's like a prize-fighter who crosses himself before a fight. It isn't he who will win, it's something else through him. Same goes for writing."[30] Saroyan invokes Jung's concept of archetypes – the universal unconscious "collective memory" – which in a way is rather like the Internet. In the act of writing, the artist opens his self into a cosmic Internet and if he is lucky this infinite realm will put him in contact with the archaic, universal symbolic source of divine poetic creation.

This source is, of course, the Muse, and Saroyan echoes the Romantic conception of the artist as a kind of instrument through which the energy of divine creativity is expressed. The pleasure derives from being a conduit through which a kind of elemental energy passes into the body electric. The "therapeutic" aspect derives from the fact that writing puts together, or composes the self: *componere* is Latin for "to put together" from which we get the word "composition." So too for Saroyan writing is a way of making sense of experience which otherwise would remain inchoate.

It is striking how many writers report the same facts when describing the rituals of writing or what is sometimes called "the creative process." Jorge Luis Borges reports in a 1968 interview:

---

[29] Saroyan, *Not Dying*, p. 102.

[30] *On Being A Writer,* Bill Strickland, ed. (Cincinnati: Writer's Digest Books, 1989), p. 102.

"When I feel I'm going to write something, then I just am quiet and I try to listen. Then something comes through. And I do what I can in order not to tamper with it. And then, when I begin to hear what's coming through, I write it down."[31] Borges also adds: "So I try to interfere as little as possible with the revelation, I believe, no? I believe the author is actually one who receives. The idea of the muse…Of course, I'm not saying anything new."[32]

Borges also declares: "I can only say that when I am writing, I feel I am being led somewhere by something. I can't go beyond that. I don't think I should talk in terms of the Muse or the Holy Ghost or the unconscious. I know that when I am writing, I am merely a tool, but as to the real name of the tool, I know nothing whatever. So that would be inspiration."[33] Virtually all accounts I have read speak of the essential "passivity" of the experience of inspiration. Henry Miller speaks of taking "dictation" as the voice speaks to him and tells him what to write.

One of the best recent studies on the relation between madness, creativity and inspiration is Anthony Storr's *Solitude: A Return to the Self* (1988). Many of his insights apply directly to Saroyan and his complex artistic sensibility. Storr posits that the creative person finds in his work the sustenance that most "normal" people seek in relationships. Beethoven, Henry James, Goya, Wittgenstein found in solitude the opportunity to explore and *create themselves* through music, art, philosophy, literature. This solitude was in fact absolutely necessary, for without it we would not have their magnificent works. Storr thus argues with psychoanalytic theory's emphasis on relationships as primary – that the desire for solitude necessarily springs from a failure in human relationship and art from "neurosis."

The creative person does in fact live with greater inner tension than the average person, but his self-division acts as a catalyst to make something out of the discomfort. As Storr writes: "The greater the disharmony within, the sharper the spur to seek harmony, or if one has the gifts, to *create* harmony."[34] Thus, most human beings

---

[31] Jorge Luis Borges, *Conversations*, Richard Burgin, ed. (Jackson: University of Mississippi Press, 1998), p. 77.

[32] Ibid., p. 235.

[33] Ibid., p. 128.

[34] Anthony Storr, *Solitude: A Return to Self* (New York: Ballantine, 1988), p. 132.

suffer similar disappointments, losses, tragedies and reversals, yet the creative artist or scientist is able to transform these dissonances into harmony through the act of creation.

In great acts of creativity, true utterance happens. Madness may be partially due to the hypersensitivity of the artist: artists have a skin less than normal, but this also allows deeper feeling and perception. Madness also implies a break in normal functioning, a divergence from one's usual "social role." But it is precisely this break ("break on through to the other side" as Jim Morrison and The Doors sang) which allows fresh awareness and magic to happen.

Arthur Sainer describes this well in his essay "The Saroyan Self Remembered:" "The fanciful in the Saroyan narrative is exemplified by the serendipitous manner in which people and events suddenly materialize, often without discernible cause, engage our attention for a moment, and then disappear...And in the Saroyan narrative, suddenly materializing beings and events seem to impel themselves inward, as if breaking through a sky light into the interior structure of the story. Beings and events manifest themselves for nothing more nor less than the ongoing delight of the universe."[35]

This is the source of the sense of magic in Saroyan and the link to inspiration and genius. This sense of alchemical transformation, of taking the simple events of daily life and revealing their fantastic qualities; of interrupting our usual sense of "cause and effect"; of being able to suddenly see the loveliness in things usually ignored. These are the qualities we associate with the dream and with childhood. The artist is driven to try to recapture the sense of sacral wonder he had as a child: thus the frequent seeming childlikeness of persons of genius. Those who knew Saroyan attested to his abundant sense of fun and lack of inhibition and repression, his joy, vitality and capacity for constant renewal. These are all characteristics we associate with very intelligent children: energy, delight (energy is eternal delight, said William Blake), religious awe.

The religious function of art and the drive towards wholeness which the act of creation incarnates is admirably summed up by Abraham Maslow: "the creative person, in the inspirational phase of the creative furor, loses his pasts and his future and lives only in the

---

[35] Arthur Sainer, "The Saroyan Self Remembered," in Leo Hamalian, ed., *William Saroyan*, p. 198.

moment. He is all there, totally immersed, fascinated and absorbed in the present, in the current situation, in the here-now, with the matter-in-hand...This ability to become 'lost in the present' seems to be a *sine qua non* for creativeness of any kind. Also certain prerequisites of creativeness – in whatever realm – somehow have something to do with this ability to become timeless, selfless, outside of space, of society, of history. It has begun to appear strongly that this phenomenon is a diluted, more secular, more frequent version of the mystical experience that has been described so often as to have become what Huxley called *The Perennial Philosophy*."[36]

For Saroyan it was in the ecstatic "peak experiences" of creative exaltation as well as the small daily pleasure of eating a peach (his children complained he would spray the juice all over himself in his eagerness to savor the taste of the peach) that madness was redeemed in the art of life and the life of art. Vladimir Nabokov once said in an interview published in *Strong Opinions*: "looking at it objectively, I have never seen a more lucid, more lonely, better balanced mad mind than mine."[37] Nabokov catches marvelous and wittily here the fact that having his kind of "mad" mind is actually the sign of a highly "lucid" and "balanced" individual.

This was true of Saroyan as well. The genius, the artist, the creative person, far from being an eccentric abnormal person is rather the summit of health. The artist incarnates the struggles of his time: he is in fact a type of the higher man and the reason he seems odd is simply because he is a precursor or a sign pointing towards a higher form of evolutionary human possibility. In overcoming his inner conflicts through the making of art (if only momentarily) he actualizes the potentialities within all humans. Artists, said Ezra Pound, are the antennae of the race.

We, thus, need to distinguish between qualities of the artist's work itself and the myths that have grown up around the question of creativity largely since the Romantic period. And these have to do with the presumed personal characteristics of persons of genius – what we now call his "lifestyle": solitary, lonely, isolated, obsessed

---

[36] Abraham Maslow, *The Farther Reaches of Human Nature* (New York: Penguin, 1976), p. 59.

[37] Vladimir Nabokov, *Strong Opinions* (New York: McGraw-Hill, 1973), p. 129.

with work to exclusion of relationships, slovenly, addicted to alcohol or drugs. All this, of course, is strictly irrelevant to the question of genius.[38]

Creativity is the triumph of self – both over the limits of aloneness and the influence of others. Artistic or scientific activity thus constitutes the principle way out of madness for the creative individual. The expression of self through imaginative activity is simultaneously the effacement of self and the highest exaltation of self. Subjectivity achieves a kind of objectification through symbolic, imaginative action and the inchoate self is made whole. "Neurosis" is the conflict between the way things are and the way they should be.

The gulf between one's dream and reality gives rise to a tension which creates the symbol or Jung's archetype. When we are powerfully moved by a symbol in Saroyan – the egg in *The Human Comedy*, the mice in *The Beautiful People*, the trapeze in "The Daring Young Man on the Flying Trapeze", the toys in *The Time of Your Life*, the trumpet music in *My Heart's in the Highlands* – it is because the mad dreamer poet has through his imagination created a vision of that inspirational world which his genius heart loves.

---

[38] One reason why the film *Amadeus* was so popular, I believe, was due to the "romanticizing" of Mozart—eccentricity, childlikeness, joyous rebelliousness, narcissism, humor, ribald extravagance, effortless creativity, a life spent making beauty.

William Saroyan's Letters to Rouben Mamoulian

Artsvi Bakhchinyan

In December 2003, during my visit to Washington D.C., I had a chance to conduct research on the newly received archive of the eminent American filmmaker Rouben Mamoulian (1898–1987) in the Library of Congress. Among a number of interesting materials, there were six letters and one telegram by William Saroyan (1908–1981) addressed to Mamoulian.

Mamoulian and Saroyan were not close friends, but were always friendly with each other and mutually appreciated each other's works. In 1928, when Saroyan was twenty years old, he traveled from California to New York for the first time, to get closer to literary and cultural circles. On Broadway, Saroyan watched the *Congai* drama, directed by Mamoulian.[1] Later Saroyan sent a letter to Mamoulian appreciating his film *We Live Again* (1934). As Mamoulian recalled during his meetings in Armenia: "Once I received a delightful letter about one of my films. It was signed: "William Saroyan." That made me glad: "Gee, he is my compatriot… and he wrote so well!"[2] Shortly after this meeting Saroyan and Mamoulian met in Hollywood. This means they became acquainted in 1934 or 1935. Later in his book *Sons Come and Go, Mothers Hang in Forever* Saroyan described one of his meetings with Mamoulian in the short-story "Rouben Mamoulian Directing Miriam Hopkins in *Becky Sharp* for Me."[3] According to actor Suren

---

[1] Lawrence Lee and Barry Gifford, *Saroyan: A Biography* (New York, 1984), p. 260.

[2] Gharib Hayrapetyan, *Kinoyi hancharĕ* [The Genius of Film], *Kamk' hayrenyats'* (October, 1997), no. 13.

[3] William Saroyan, *Sons Come and Go, Mothers Hand in Forever* (New York, 1976), pp. 91-93.

Abeghian, who lived in the United States, when the Metro Goldwin Meyer Hollywood studio planned to shoot Franz Werfel's novel, *Forty Days of Musa Dagh* in 1935, under Mamoulian's direction, Saroyan suggested his contribution.[4] (The shooting of this novel was stopped by demand of the Turkish government).

William Saroyan, keenly interested in film art, tried to make a career in Hollywood, thus collaboration with his well-known compatriot Mamoulian seemed to be logical. However, nothing happened, moreover, Saroyan was disappointed in the film industry. But for many years they cherished the idea of making projects together. In 1964, at the Cannes Film Festival, Mamoulian said that he would like to shoot a film with Armenian art professionals: the scriptwriter can be William Saroyan, the composer – Aram Khachatourian, designer – Martiros Saryan, and Charles Aznavour will star.[5]

In 1971, during his visit to Armenia, Mamoulian said about Saroyan: "I call him Bill as many others. We speak Armenian: I with my Armenian, he – with his Moush dialect (actually it was Bitlis dialect – A. B.). …Once he… came and suggested to me to take a trip to Armenia together, saying, that they waited for him for a long time. My mother burst in out joy telling me to take that chance. But later Saroyan realized his journey alone."[6]

The letters are written from 1935 to 1948. The value of all the letters go beyond the historical as they bear Saroyan's style of writing. They demonstrate the ideas that those two outstanding American-Armenians had for a collaboration that never happened. The first letter is of special interest since it deals with William Saroyan's impressions from his first visit to Soviet Armenia. All letters, except of the last one, are typewritten with Saroyan's corrections, and only his signature is handwritten. The first letter was translated into Armenian by me and published in *Azg* daily of Yerevan (Artsvi Bakhchinyan, "Mi chshtum Ruben Mamulyani veraberyal" [A Correction About Rouben Mamoulian], *Azg*, 9 April 2005, p. 5).

---

[4] Souren Abeghian's writing was provided me by his widow, the now deceased Rouzan Abeghian and now is in my personal file.

[5] *Hayastan* (June 6, 1963).

[6] *Sovetakan arvest* (1968), no 11, p. 47.

On the occasion of publishing these letters, I would like to express my gratitude to Mrs. Alice Lotvin Birney, literary manuscript specialist of the Library of Congress, for facilitating my job with Mamoulian's archive, as well as Mr. Robert Setrakian, President of the William Saroyan Foundation, for his kind permission to publish these letters of Saroyan's.

–1–

New Moscow Hotel.
Moscow, USSR.
July 5, 1935.

Dear Mr. Mamoulian:

I have just come to Moscow from Erivan where I spent several days. In Erivan there is great industrial and agricultural activity, but not much cultural. I went to a theater and had to leave after the first act. The play was altogether unreal and the acting was too obviously acting. The opera Anoush, however, was very fine.[7] There is a young tenor in Erivan named Sharatelian[8] (sic) who is a first-rate artist. His voice is completely Armenian. I met an actress in Erivan who asked me to send greetings to your mother.[9] I am sorry I have forgotten her name. Everybody in Erivan hopes you will go there some day and make an Armenian picture.

I have ever seen a place so delightful to the eye as Moscow. Red Square with Lenin's Tomb is very impressive, but I like most of all St. Basil's Cathedral. In America all our buildings are shaped like

---

[7] The edited version of Armen Tigranyan's (1878–1950) opera, "Anoush," was directed in the Yerevan Opera and Ballet Theatre in 1935.

[8] Shara Talyan (1893–1965), Armenian singer.

[9] Saroyan perhaps means actress Arous Voskanyan (1889–1943), who knew Rouben Mamoulian's mother, amateur actress Vergine Mamoulian (1876–1972). Some letters by Vergine Mamoulian addressed to Voskanyan (see documents no. 343-344) are kept in Arous Voskanyan's personal file, in the State Museum of Literature and Art in Yerevan. Rouben Mamoulian was familiar with Arous Voskanyan's art and he wrote a review about her in the Russian periodical *Slovo* in Tiflis, in 1919 or 1920.

boxes. In Moscow it is not yet so, although two American type buildings are now being constructed. They don't look very Russian to me.

The new subway, or Metro, is an excellent job of engineering. The underground canyons are broad and spacious and the air is very cool and clean. Each station has a different style of architecture and is made of different stone. Everybody in Moscow is very proud of the subway. It is better than the subways in Berlin, Paris, London and New York. Everything in Russia is better. And they smile proudly. The coffee is terrible. The trains are uninhabitable. There is no water. (On the trains). And so on.

Moscow should be the scene of a great motion picture. The idea I mentioned, Laughter, would fit in very nicely here. The kind of laughter in Czarist Russia, and the kinds in New Russia. I think it would be a good picture.

I wrote a play while I was in New York called Subway Circus. The Theater Guild asked my agent to let them see any play I might do, so I hurried and wrote this play in six days, and then took the Berengeria to Europe. I think it is a very fine play, with exceptionally broad creative opportunities for the director, but I am afraid the Guild will not accept it because it may seem expensive to produce. Actually, though, although there are many players and many simple scenes, it ought not to be at all expensive to produce.

If you would like to take a look at the play, you may obtain it (unless it has been accepted by the Guild[10] or some other producer) from my agent, Ann Watkins, Inc., 210 Madison Avenue, New York. Harold Matson[11] or Pat Duggan[12] will know about it.

I must warn you that it isn't much of a play to read. It isn't intended for reading. it is intended for the theatre. Parts of the play need to be improved: I went at the job too swiftly, having bought my steamship ticket and wishing to hand in the play before any defects if

---

[10] Theater in New York.

[11] Harold (Hal) Matson (1917–1986), theater and film producer.

[12] Pat Duggan (1910–1987), theater and film producer.

you like the general idea. (This of course sounds like the usual story).

Maybe the play is lousy. I think it is not only good, but important as a development (spelling) in the theatre, but I am probably wrong: until, I mean, it is produced and proved to me good.

The idea of this note was primarily this: to tell you how much I like Moscow and to say that I am sending you a pictorial street map of the city. I look forward to returning to my native land (America this time). George Gershwin[13] played portions of his music for Porgy at Bennett Cerf's[14] one evening. It is swell music. I think the opera will be a tremendous success.

From Moscow (I can hardly believe it) I send you and your father and mother sincere good wishes:

William Saroyan

–2–

348 Carl Street.
San Francisco
November 22, 1937.

Dear Rouben:

Are you in Europe? Are you in New York? Are you home for Thanksgiving? Will you be home for Christmas? How are you? I got your card from Rome[15] and was very glad and surprised. I was glad

---

[13] George Gershwin (1898–1937), American composer, author of the popular opera *Porgy and Bess*.

[14] Bennett Cerf (1898–1971), humorist and publisher, one of the founding editors of Random House Inc., later president of the New York-based publishing firm.

[15] In September, 1937 Rouben Mamoulian traveled in Italy. In Venice he visited the Mekhitarist congregation on San Lazzaro island. In Rome he met

to hear from you and surprised that you were so far from home. I read in one of the New York American-Armenian newspapers of your visit to the Young Armenian Club of London. That young man Khatchadouring (I think that's his name) is (Khatchadourian)[16] a great admirer of yours and asked me when I was in London in 1935 to speak to you about him when I saw you again. I was kind of afraid o do so because I didn't know how to tell you he hoped to get a job with you. So I didn't say anything. Do you know of any young Armenian (or any infant, child, youth, middle-aged, or old) Armenian who wouldn't like to get a job with you? Are we a race of artists? I should say we are. Remember the rug merchant? They're all that way too. Their getting into that business is easily understood: art, with a profit; and easy work; and a chance to talk extravagantly. The funniest thing of all was when he said, Them cocci (for cock-eyed) Armenians in Fladelphia (for Philadelphia). A great guy, though. Well, I hope I hear from you soon, wherever you are. (I have made two more books of stories accepted, making six before I shall be thirty years old.)

Best regards:
Bill.

–3–

348 Carl Street.
San Francisco
December 29, 1937.

Dear Rouben:

I hear you got attacked by a volcano, so Happy New Year. After an experience like that any new year is bound to be a happy one. I feel almost that lucky myself. I am going to make 1938 a banner year for me, as the saying is. A banner year, I think, is one in which you

---

Prime Minister (Duce) Mussolini, who suggested to him to direct a movie in Italy (*Arevelk* [December 15, 1937])

[16] (I'll get it right yet: Khatchadourian.)

win or buy a banner. If I don't win one, I'm going to buy one. As I've said in the enclosed letter, misaddressed, unopened, and returned, I have two new books scheduled for publication in 1938. The first one, in case I didn't say so in the unopened letter, is called Love, Here Is My Hat: Modern Age Books, May 1938, 50,000 copies first edition, 25 c a copy. The second one is called The Trouble With Tigers: Harcourt, Brace, September or October 1938, $2.50 a copy. This means that all my work is done for 1938 so I can devote the year to tennis, music, conversation, and loafing. No agent in Hollywood can get me a job, even though I've publicly bragged that I won't take one.

How are you? I was in Hollywood a couple of days before Xmas. I thought I'd see you but heard you were still in N.Y. I hear the theatrical season is kind of exciting: Of Mice and Men; Wonder Boy; and so on. (I plan to write me a great play someday before I die. I have written a great one act one: The Hungerers.) Do you ever look at The One Act Play magazine? I am to have another one act play in that magazine, as well as a play in the form of an essay called Death and Syncopation. The play is only my story The Man With the Heart in the Highlands. I have a story in the February number of The Atlantic Monthly. It is so good it is practically out of this world.[17] Did you have a great adventure traveling all over Europe? I read in the N.Y. Times that you are coming to Hollywood early in 1938. I'd like to get down there and play you three fast sets of tennis some day before you get real busy with your next picture.

With a late Merry Xmas and best wishes for 1938.

Yours truly:

Bill.

–4–

[March 1938]

FA 149 44 NL XU = SAN FRANCISCO CALIF 7
ROUBEN MAMOULIAN
710 North Palm Dr. Beverly Hills California

---

[17] "The Pomegranate Trees."

Dear Rouben. Can't wait to get started. Look forward with great pleasure to work with you. Before I leave town, however, believe I should have a contract. Please urge Feldman to arrange. Can report for work immediately. Wire or telephone overload 7884.

Best regards

Bill Saroyan.[18]

–5–

348 Carl Street.
San Francisco
March 27, 1938.

Dear Rouben:

Thank you very much for your kind letter and please forgive me for taking this long to acknowledge it. It was delightful to be spending a little time with you again, in spite of an inevitable bad luck we had with the story and in spite of the matter of compensation, a thing involving personally neither yourself nor myself and at the most a matter of business routine. I have treated it at such in my relations with Mr. Feldman whose activities are exclusively business. As I told you, I feel that I was entitled to some reasonable compensation from Columbia: nothing from Feldman. I feel that this would apply to any writer. A writer's time and talent have some tangible value when they are used for purposes not his own. I was willing to forget whole thing when I left Hollywood. I wouldn't care for $50. from Feldman.; his secretary returned the Western Union money order for $20. which I had sent Feldman, endorsed by him; and I returned it to him, insomuch, as that money doesn't belong to me. I have seen few movies since my return to San Francisco and have decided that writers ought look at movies, not to write them. I doubt very much if I shall return again to Hollywood

[18] Mamoulian sent a reply telegram to Saroyan, dated March 7, 1938, keeping it in the same file, where he wrote the following: "Will you come immediately to work with me at Columbia. Your previous salary. Feldman handling. Greetings, Rouben Mamoulian."

for a job. And I doubt very much if it will over be possible for me to accomplish anything, except alone, as always. I am working again, except that it does not seem like work, which is the only kind of work I am pleased to do for any length of time[19]. The Atlantic Monthly for April, out in a day or two, will contain the story I mentioned, The Journey to Hanford, and the editor has asked me for more. I have written a new one and sent it to him, and am not arranging the table of contents of my new book, The Trouble With Tigers. I don't know whether I'll be doing a play or not. A year is such a long time, and a day is too, that I forget to be ambitious or industrious when I am in San Francisco and let the accomplishment of the year happen as it will. The first thing I feel for some reason, when I am in Hollywood is that a lot of time is going by, being lost, and so on, which isn't actually the case at all. Anyhow, I seem to have a feeling of being inwardly suspended while time is going by at a terrific pace when I am in Hollywood. So it appears that if I am ever to get ahead of the game a few dollars, it is going to have to be through a miracle. And I believe in them; the greatest of them all to me will always be the publication of my first story; by all rights it should have been rejected; but it wasn't. And then after it was published it should gone unnoticed, but it didn't; something like that is bound to happen again in a year or two. In the meantime, maybe like in the song, I'm not lazy, I'm dreaming. Thanks again for writing, for the pleasant times when I was down there; and all good wishes.

Yours truly: Bill.

–6–

348 Carl Street.
San Francisco
June 7, 1938.

Dear Rouben:

Thanks very much for your note of June 3rd. I'm pleased that you're not going to do "Murder in Massachusetts," inasmuch as I

---

[19] As for instance, a lifetime.

have always felt that that was a sterile story and altogether unworthy of your talent.

About an idea for a picture:

I still feel that my suggested substitute for "Murder in Massachusetts" --- Columbia's Gems of 1938--- is worthy of consideration. The sketches I wrote for this idea are somewhere in my room, but are misplaced. I believe I might be able to find them if I looked real hard. The reasons I feel this sort of picture should be done by Columbia are several: (a) Almost every other major studio profitably produces at least one picture of this sort each year; (b) such a picture enables a studio to put to work, profitably, a great amount of its idle acting talent; (c) the movie fan truly enjoys a picture of great variety, a picture which in a certain sense is an approximation of the old big-time vaudeville show, a show combining all the forms of entertainment: the play, the dance, the song, the variety act, the skit, the orchestra, etcetera, etcetera; and (d) the very making of such a picture is more likely to be a pleasure for those involved than the making of the more pretentious sort of picture --- and of course when a thing is done with pleasure, it is more apt to give pleasure. I think my basic story for Columbia's Gems of 1938 is potentially sufficient to enable the studio to put a writer or two to work and in about a month's time produce a shooting script. I myself would not care to work on the story, inasmuch as that would necessitate going to Hollywood, which I would rather not do.

If you feel there would be no harm in offering this story idea to Columbia, I will be glad to try my best to find the manuscript and offer it to the studio through my agent James J. Geller[20] of the William Morris Agency.[21] This would be necessary, insomuch as I am financially in debt and morally obligated to this agent and agency and have given my word to try to pay my debt at the first opportunity, by allowing Mr. Geller to represent me in Hollywood.

---

[20] James J. Geller (1893–1963).

[21] William Morris Agency, talent and literary agency, founded in 1898 in New York City.

Since my last visit to Hollywood I have done quite a little work, including a play: My Heart's in the Highlands, which my New York agent is now offering to producers. I feel optimistic about its chances of being produced, but so far it has not been formally accepted. I think it is a remarkable play: very simple and completely untheatrical. If it is accepted I plan to drop everything else for the time being and see what luck I'll have with another play. If it is not accepted, I believe I will go to Dublin, Ireland for four or five weeks.

I have another idea for a picture which I hesitate to describe because I am afraid no one but myself will think it is a good idea. Technically, I feel this idea, if fulfilled, will be of great significance to the art of the motion picture. The idea is this: to film from six to ten short stories, each with its title, each complete in itself, and all of them together making a whole work of art. I apologize that I cannot think of any other writer's stories but my own, specifically, the stories in my fourth book, Little Children.[22] This year appears to be the most experimental the theatre has known in many many years, and I believe any studio daring enough to risk a little money on an experiment of this sort has an excellent chance of gaining prestige as well as making a good profit.

As to out and out movie stories, I am afraid I will never be able to invent one.

I want to thank you sincerely for the kind words you said about me recently in Fresno. With kindest regards to you and your parents.[23]

Yours truly: Bill.

-7-

41 West 58 Plaza 5-4769
December 12, 1948

---

[22] Saroyan's book, published in 1937.

[23] Zakaria Mamoulian (1866–1966), former militarist and banker.

Dear Rouben:

I know you are at work and I look forward keenly to the opening of your play; I had the typing company send you a copy of one of play "Don't Go Away Mad" and I am wondering if I could have it back, as I am now all out of good copies. You could leave it at the desk and I could pick it up.

Carol[24] joins me in sending Azadia[25] and you our warm regards.

Yours
Bill

---

[24] Carol Marcus (1926–2003), William Saroyan's wife from 1942 to 1950 and from 1950 to 1952.

[25] Azadia Newman (died in 2001), Rouben Mamoulian's wife, an artist.

44

William Saroyan and Aram Kevorkian: A Friendship

Harry Keyishian

In April 1961 a thirty-one year old Armenian-American attorney just hired by the firm of Coudert Fréres in Paris was introduced to one of their celebrity clients, the author William Saroyan. Aram Jack Kevorkian instantly endeared himself to Saroyan by announcing, "My name is Aram…and, what's more, my son's name is Aram."[1] Thus began a friendship that lasted twenty years – years that marked Saroyan's declining literary fortunes but that brought success for the attorney, who not only prospered professionally but also became author of an influential monthly newsletter subscribed to on-line by readers in 55 nations. It was a friendship marked by deep commitment on the part of Kevorkian, who provided Saroyan legal service and personal loyalty through trying personal times and circumstances.

When Kevorkian died suddenly on December 20, 2003, he was mourned by many as a keen intellect and a shrewd, often caustic observer of French politics and the human condition in general. But he was also known as a cordial man ready to appreciate beauty in all forms, whether of ideas, art, conversation, or music. For Saroyan, who could be the most difficult of men, he had an infinity of patience and affection.

Born in Philadelphia in 1928, Aram Kevorkian had a family legacy of Armenian patriotism and letters. His father Karnig, who had left the village of Chunkoush in 1912 to settle in America, was so outraged by the massacres of 1915, in which his family and 10,000 other residents of the village had been slaughtered, that he

---

[1] Aram J. Kevorkian, *Confessions of a Francophile and other essays from The Kevorkian Newsletter, 1980-2000* (Reading, Berks [UK]: Taderon Press, 2002), p. 313.

enlisted in the Armenian Volunteer Movement, composed of dedicated young men like himself, and made his way to Russia in hopes of joining the war against the Turks. Hostilities ended before they saw any action, however, and Karnig returned to the United States to settle in Philadelphia where, in 1919, at the age of 24, he started the Armenian language weekly newspaper *Groong*. He edited the paper until 1962.[2]

One of the most dramatic stories covered in *Groong* was that of Soghomon Tehlirian, the young Armenian who in 1921, in Germany, assassinated Talaat Bey, the Turkish Interior Minister responsible in large measure for organizing the deportations and massacres of Armenians. Tehlirian turned himself in to the authorities, openly confessed and justified his deed, and stood trial before a German court, which eventually acquitted him. Among others reporting on international reaction to the sensational trial was Hripcimée Hovaguimian, a gifted young writer living in Marseilles, who contributed many pieces to *Groong* about responses to the trial. Collaboration and collegiality led to romance. In 1926, she became Kevorkian's wife and moved to Philadelphia.

Their sons were eventually enlisted to help publish *Groong* and to make this Armenian enterprise part of their permanent identities. Kevorkian writes:

> My brother Andrew and I were born into a thoroughly Armenian family in Philadelphia, carrying the torch of Armenian survival. The *Groong* was our life and our livelihood, our home and our language were Armenian, and only the public schools and the streets of Philadelphia made Americans of my brother and me.

From those public schools, Aram went on to The University of Pennsylvania and Harvard Law School. In 1953, he was awarded a Fulbright scholarship that took him to Paris for a year. After a year back in the United States, he returned to Paris in 1955 as a United States army officer with the Judge Advocate General's Corps and served for thirty months. He, thereafter, joined a Wall Street law

---

[2] Aram J. Kevorkian, "Chunkoush," *The Kevorkian Newsletter*. The Groong is, in Armenian lore, a migratory messenger bird. Karnik and Hripcimée Kevorkian's *Groong* is not to be confused with the current on-line news journal of that name, begun in 1988.

firm, but was convinced by his wife Eve, who was French, to settle in Paris in 1961, with the happy collateral results of a great legal career and his friendship with Saroyan.

The *Kevorkian Newletter*, which brought him fame (and was prominently cited in his *New York Times* obituary), began in 1978 as a limited service to clients, informing them of current changes in the French legal climate that could affect their business dealings. By 1980, the *Newsletter* began to include personal reflections and philosophic pieces on a wide range of topics. Kevorkian was urbane, widely read, witty, and pragmatic, with a deep appreciation of irony wherever he saw it — in his native America as well as in France. Like his favorite philosopher, Michel de Montaigne, Kevorkian was a skeptic with ideals. A keen analyst, he could cast a satiric eye on all manifestations of corruption and stupidity, whether found in individuals or nations, in a writing style that ranged from learned to colloquial, as required by his topic.

Though Kevorkian characterized himself as a "Francophile," he was frequently critical of the foibles of what he termed "the functionary-political class that has taken control of the Fifth Republic."[3]

> When my eldest son was in the *lycée*, we were talking one day about science, and he told me: "*The French are the best scientists.*" Astounded, I asked, "*Where did you learn that?*" He replied, "*From my physics teacher.*" I told him, "*The fool, instead of teaching you physics, he's teaching you chauvinism*!"[4]

In general, he was pained by the banality and mediocrity of those who had risen to high position in France because of an exclusionary educational system.

One of his most impressive abilities was to draw clarifying distinctions. In his essay of October 1993, entitled "Montaigne and Descartes,"[5] he distinguished between those who truly subject their ideas to interrogation and proof and those who abuse reason to avoid testing their ideas. The latter he identified with the followers of Descartes, who dominated French thought. Calling them

---

[3] Aram J. Kevorkian, *Confessions*, p. 19.
[4] Ibid., p. 64.
[5] Ibid., pp. 121-126.

representatives of a "lazy" strain in French thought, he felt that their "retreat" to reason had created a facile reconciliation between faith and modernity that, in the end, produced a false ethics and justified chauvinism, elitism, and authoritarian thinking. (Indeed, "Cartesianism" and its negative effects are his pretty constant themes.) In his July 1996 *Newsletter* "Catholic and Protestant Justice",[6] he contrasted American justice, with its presumption of innocence and its reliance on evidence, with the French assumption that the "deep-seated convictions"[7] of judges was sufficient grounds to affirm guilt or innocence. Whatever impinged on or substituted itself for a genuine search for truth was anathema to his spirit.

Kevorkian wrote on Armenian issues with the same keenness of mind. Invited to Armenia in 1991 to give advice on their constitution, he consulted with government leaders on such issues as economics, trade, the development of stock and commodity exchanges, and other national concerns. His most meaningful conversations, however, were with a waiter who served his table at his hotel. The man described the morally demeaning conditions forced upon him by the Soviet system and the shady practices he and others were forced to adopt in order to survive economically. He expresses pity not only for the waiter but "also for all the decent people who aspire[d] to honest lives in the Soviet Union":

> The Turks often destroyed the bodies of Armenians, but when Armenians managed to stay alive, their basic values — religion, family, integrity, and hard work — were left intact. Both my parents came to America honest and remained honest all their lives. The Soviet system attacks the mind and soul of individuals by its absurd pretense of improving human nature; its failure to face reality made liars and tyrants of its leaders, and forced ordinary, honest people to become thieves and crooks. This is the unpardonable crime of Communism.[8]

For Kevorkian, Communism's assault on personal integrity invalidated whatever other claim to good it boasted.

---

[6] Ibid., pp. 213-218.
[7] Ibid., p. 215.
[8] Ibid., p. 79.

Kevorkian cast an often critical but mainly loving eye on America. He admired its more broadly realized democracy, its tolerance, its genuine effort to do justice in its courts and its cheerful, spirited character. On the other hand, he condemned the internment of Japanese during World War II ("a permanent blot on President Roosevelt's record and that of the United States Supreme Court,"[9] the neglect of public transportation in America and the havoc wrought on the American environment by its breakdown. He deplored the "total subservience to money"[10] that has come to dominate American politics, and which he felt to be no improvement on the oligarchical tendencies of French politics. He despised President Bill Clinton for his moral failings and his personal irresponsibility, dismissing the defense by Clinton supporters that he was a good president in other ways. (He did acknowledge, however, that "had he been born Guillaiume Clinton in Brittany, he surely would have become... President of France, with fewer headaches than he has now."[11] He was no better pleased with Clinton's successor, whom he enjoyed calling "a-boush," which Armenians will recognize as "fool."

While the formally educated, deeply read Kevorkian and the more intuitive, impressionistic Saroyan would not seem a natural pair, they became close on both professional and personal matters. Kevorkian's first legal service to Saroyan was to help settle his huge tax bill with the U.S. government, which had been the cause of much bitterness and motivated his move to France. In 1961, Kevorkian arranged the purchase of the sixth floor flat at 74 rue Taitbout which famously was to be Saroyan's Paris residence for twenty years (and which provided the title of one of his books). In 1966, Kevorkian did the legal work to set up the Saroyan Foundation, through which the author intended to control his literary and financial legacy.[12]

In personal terms, Saroyan borrowed money from Kevorkian, called him when he feared he was having a heart attack, asked him to

---

[9] Ibid., p. 283.

[10] Ibid., p. 372.

[11] Ibid., p. 307.

[12] John Leggett, *A Daring Young Man: A Biography of William Saroyan* (New York: Knopf, 2002), pp. 325, 350, 360.

make arrangements to renovate 74 rue Taitbout when Lucy and Aram Saroyan stayed there in 1968.[13]

Both were very much in the process of "finding themselves" and Kevorkian reported back to Saroyan on their activities. In a position to observe the unfortunate family dynamics of the clan.[14] Kevorkian also understood the personal qualities that magnified his children's faults in Saroyan's mind:

> [Saroyan] was an old-fashioned Fresno Armenian who thought a child should get married and not fool around and have boyfriends and be free and easy, and the man—if he had a manchild—the man should get a job, or work, or do something.[15]
>
> Kevorkian was also in a position to see beneath the surface of Saroyan's public persona and to understand that "with strangers he had a sort of natural braggadocio and seemingly thick skin, but obviously he was very, very sensitive and he was living in a different world underneath that.[16]

These encounters did not prevent the inevitable quarrels that Saroyan had with all his friends, associates, and benefactors (copiously documented in John Leggett's biography of Saroyan). In 1974, Kevorkian and his wife Eve, who had many theatrical connections, tried to arrange a Paris production of *The Time of Your Life*. Saroyan was pleased at the possibility, but unhappy with the financial terms he was being offered by the actors, and he accused Kevorkian of not representing him with sufficient vigor. For his part, Kevorkian felt that the terms Saroyan was asking were unrealistic, considering the limited resources of the theater group.[17] Saroyan assailed his friend for siding with actors rather than with him:

> As he stood there in my office roaring with rage, I sat there smiling and said, "That's O.K. Bill, nothing you say

---

[13] Ibid., pp. 342, 355, 360.

[14] Ibid.

[15] Lawrence Lee and Barry Gifford, *Saroyan: A Biography* (New York: Harper & Row, 1984), p. 284.

[16] Ibid., p. 272.

[17] Ibid., pp. 407-408.

> or do can possibly get me mad at you." This made him even angrier and he stormed out.[18]

Thus began a breach that lasted six years until Saroyan, then dying, called Kevorkian out of the blue and asked him to visit Fresno. There, the attorney for the first time saw the city that, as a reader of Saroyan's stories, he had come to feel was the ideal place for a boyhood.

Years earlier, when Kevorkian contemplated leaving the law firm for which he was working and striking out on his own, Saroyan gave him sage advice: "Aram, there is no need to be anxious. When the time comes to make the move, go with joy in your heart." These words gave Kevorkian both the courage to take up the challenge with spirit and exhilaration. In his last letter to Saroyan, when the author was near death, Kevorkian repeated these words: "go with joy in your heart." On the day before he died, Saroyan replied with a handwritten note: "With deepest thanks and love."[19] Those may have been the last words he wrote.

I met Aram Kevorkian at the University of California, Berkeley, in 1996 at the registration desk for the conference "Saroyan Plus Fifteen," which had been organized by Dickran Kouymjian, when he was visiting professor there. After checking in and making rooming arrangements, Aram and I fell in with each other and walked around the campus, enjoying the atmosphere and talking about a thousand things, beginning, naturally enough, with our mutual interest in Saroyan and then effortlessly branching out into many topics that gave me a taste of his wide knowledge and his broad range of enthusiasms. He was my favorite kind of companion: one I could enjoy listening to for hours, but who insisted also on knowing all about my interests and passions.

He truly seemed to have acquired the secret of the good life, one filled with meaningful delights and pleasures in all realms of activity—ideas, foods, sights, sounds, stories, and sensations. We discovered a mutual passion for the philosopher Montaigne, that great ironist, in whose sanity, clarity of vision, and skepticism we had both found a steady anchor.

---

[18] Kevorkian, *Confessions*, p. 23.
[19] Ibid., p. 24.

But the best came last, when we made our way back to the guest residence after dinner and Aram, spotting a piano in a hall, said that he needed to play Bach before turning in or he would have trouble sleeping. Would I mind listening? No, I would not. And so I was treated to thirty or forty minutes of extraordinary music, with loving commentary on the qualities of each piece.

The next day we made our conference presentations and mingled with the other speakers and the audience. I told David Stephen Calonne, author of a study of Saroyan, "Hey, hang out with us tonight. Aram Kevorkian plays Bach on the piano before turning in." David said that would be great: he also played Bach. So that evening, the two took turns showing off for each other: dueling Bach. David's approach was energetic and percussive: Bach with a beat. Aram's Bach flowed with a lyric line, it hovered and shimmered. Either way, I was in Bach heaven.

When I got home to New Jersey, I told my wife that I had made a great discovery on my trip: that we had been living our lives along entirely false lines. (We are well suited for each other in a bad way: we pretty consistently let our duties and obligations get the better of our pleasures.) "There is another way to live," I announced. We don't have to live this way, I told her, and I have proof. I met a delightful, distinguished man who knows the secret of how to live a life full of curiosity, graciousness, delight in life, and gratitude for existence.

After that, I stayed in contact via e-mail and became a faithful reader of the *Newsletter*, spreading the wealth by forwarding selected issues to selected friends, who in turn became admirers and subscribers. In 2002, my wife and I were in England for a conference and I insisted that we take in Paris as well, so that she could meet the person about whom I'd been speaking so incessantly. We had dinner two nights with Aram and Eve, visited his office and apartment, were treated to wonderful conversation and hospitality, tremendous views of Paris, and of course Bach, including an impromptu but very learned discussion, with musical examples, of Bach's influence on Chopin. My wife too was converted.

My next-to-last exchange with Kevorkian concerned a news item I had read about an association of French towns with scatological names. On the one hand, I suspected that the piece might be a hoax. On the other hand — what do Frenchmen make of the "Grand

Tetons" of the American west! I shared the message with other e-mail correspondents who fancied themselves experts in detecting urban legends. Aram jumped right into this trivia fest, researching and affirming the existence of this association — another example of his catholic taste — and of course coming up with some additional hilarious town names on his own.

Our final exchange concerned John Leggett's biography of William Saroyan, which I had been assigned to review for the magazine *Ararat*. I asked him for background information that I needed and of course he responded quickly and informatively. He added a warning, however, not to take too much stock in negative appraisals of Saroyan who, whatever his personal faults, was a man who knew how to enjoy life and was fun to be with. He wrote, on December 7, "I've detected a sourness in your own appraisal of Bill, and would like to get to the bottom of it. Bill had his paranoid moments, which reached its peak when he was drafted, but he was also, more often, a gloriously vivacious torrent of humanity and good humor." I assured him that I was still working out my assessment and meant to be thoughtful, and that I would certainly try the review out on him before sending it off to be published. I don't know whether he received the message. I miss terribly the chance to continue the conversation, on this and many, many other matters.

Having the Time of Your Life: William Saroyan's Challenge to the Culture Industry

Micah Jendian

> Nobody alive in the world is not an actor. (He said it. I mean Shakespeare. But let's go into it in detail.) Almost everybody alive, though, is a very pathetic actor. Every man has one character to play, himself. That is no easy thing. Before a man can give a good performance of himself he must spend many years rehearsing. It takes the average man almost a whole lifetime to be able to learn to speak like himself, to walk like himself, and to laugh like himself. It takes many men many generations to be able to *be* themselves.[1]

In William Saroyan's image of the world as theater, man is the only player, and "growth" the only act.[2] Achieving authentic selfhood, being oneself, is one of his major concerns. Humanity's performance, though, is "a *bad* bad play," Saroyan appraises, "with unmitigated lousy players."[3] What disrupts rehearsal and impedes the process of becoming oneself? How can those impediments be countered and a good performance inspired? These questions were central to Saroyan's life and art.

Saroyan's fiction suggests an answer. In "The Fifty-Yard Dash," twelve-year-old Aram Garoghlanian is intrigued by an advertisement in *Argosy All-Story Magazine*. Promoting his strength program, Lionel Strongfort is clad in "nothing but a little bit of leopard skin"

---

[1] William Saroyan, "The Two Theatres," *The Time of Your Life* (New York: Harcourt, Brace and Co., 1939), p. 210.

[2] Ibid., p. 208.

[3] Ibid., p. 212.

and "loaded all over with muscle."[4] Awestruck by this image, Aram enthusiastically decides to become "the most powerful man" in his neighborhood .[5] Having no money of his own, Aram asks his Uncle Gyko for three dollars to purchase the secrets to great strength. Reluctantly, Gyko gives Aram the money, advising that Strongfort is a fraud and that the secret of greatness is "the releasing within one's self of those mysterious and vital forces which are in all men."[6]

The secrets of Lionel Strongfort arrive, instructing Aram to "get up early in the morning and for an hour or so do various kinds of acrobatic exercises, which [are] illustrated. Also to drink plenty of water, get plenty of fresh air, eat good wholesome food, and keep it up until you [are] a giant."[7] He follows Strongfort's rules for four straight days, feeling "more powerful every day,"[8] and has the opportunity to show his increased strength at his school's track meet. Certain that he has left the other runners far behind in the fifty-yard dash, Aram opens his eyes to see that he is in last place. He loses by ten yards and goes home feeling sick.

Aram is eager to be someone that he is not and rehearses for that role until it becomes painfully apparent to him that he is not the most powerful young man in his neighborhood. His unrealistic notion of himself surfaces with his reading of Strongfort's letter, the only purpose of which is to make a sale. Typical of advertisements and motivated by profit, Strongfort's letter encourages a fantasy which his product promises to make a reality. Aram subsequently becomes a "pathetic actor," directing his thoughts and actions toward the fulfillment of another character's role. In contrast to Aram's acceptance of popular commercial culture, his old-country uncle advocates a quest for authentic selfhood. Gyko encourages Aram to tap his own "mysterious and vital forces." "The Fifty-Yard Dash," like many Saroyan stories, exposes the stratagem of consumer culture, our susceptibility to its allure, and its ultimate spuriousness.

Saroyan was keenly aware of the impact of popular commercial culture on the lives of Americans and recognized its potential to

---

[4] William Saroyan, "The Fifty Yard Dash," *My Name is Aram* (New York: Harcourt, Brace & World, 1940), p. 68.

[5] Ibid., p. 67.

[6] Ibid., p. 69.

[7] Ibid., p. 74.

[8] Ibid., p. 75.

hinder autonomous development. Motion pictures, radio, television, advertisements, and the commercial culture at large, Saroyan knew, are threats to authentic selfhood because they offer false notions of reality; project fantastic images, personalities, and lifestyles for emulation; generate diversions from the self; blunt awareness and imagination; and promote individuality while actually inculcating homogeneity. These confusing stage directions and dialogue lead to our poorly staged performances of ourselves and explain why it "takes many men many generations to be able to *be* themselves." Saroyan's recognition of this phenomenon came during the early stages of the consumer culture's development and anticipated the first substantial cultural critique by over a decade. With this awareness, Saroyan was committed to countering these effects through his work and envisioned that his fiction would aid in the process of being one's self. For these reasons, Saroyan's perception of the pernicious effects of the consumer culture as early as the thirties is especially noteworthy.

Although today these effects are more widely understood, the first critical and penetrating analyses of mass culture emerged in the mid-forties, after technological progress and a booming post-World War II economy accelerated the expansion of American consumer culture. The most significant contributions to this critical discourse were provided by the members of the Frankfurt School – Theodor Adorno, Max Horkheimer, Herbert Marcuse, Leo Lowenthal, Erich Fromm, Freidrich Pollock, and Walter Benjamin. These interdisciplinary scholars sought to "penetrate the world of things to show the underlying relations between persons"[9] and were committed to "liberation from all forms of domination."[10]

Adorno and Horkeimer's seminal work *Dialectic of Enlightenment* was published in German in 1944 and in English in 1947. Adorno's chapter "The Culture Industry: Enlightenment as Mass Deception" contains the crux of their argument. Adorno contends that the manufacturers of culture view people primarily, if

---

[9] Max Horkheimer, *Critical Theory: Selected Essays*, trans. Matthew J. O'Connell, et al. (New York: Herder, 1972), p. 171.

[10] Patrick Bratlinger, *Bread and Circuses: Theories of Mass Culture as Social Decay* (Ithaca: Cornell Univ. Press, 1983), p. 228.

not solely, as consumers,[11] produce consumers' "needs,"[12] and make "technology into psychotechnology, into a procedure for manipulating men."[13] Adorno and Horkheimer used the term "culture industry" to point out that this "culture" does not arise "spontaneously from the masses themselves," but is imposed from above: "The culture industry intentionally integrates its customers from above. . . . [T]he masses are not primary, but secondary, they are an object of calculation; an appendage of the machinery. The customer is not king, as the culture industry would like to have us believe, not its subject but its object."[14] Deborah Cook concurs that American culture is "[f]ar from being a culture by and for the masses--as the older folk and popular cultures once were."[15] Cook further explains that the culture industry "is geared to profit-making, controlled by centralized interlocking corporations, and staffed with marketing and financial experts, management and production teams, technicians, 'star' reporters, writers, actors, musicians, and other creative talent."[16]

Despite subtleties of thought among members of the Frankfurt School regarding the "specific mechanisms" of the culture industry,[17] R. B. Kershner contends that each subscribed to Adorno's thesis that:

> The total effect of the culture industry is one of anti-enlightenment, in which, as Horkheimer and I have noted, enlightenment, that is the progressive technical domination of nature, becomes mass deception and is turned into a means for fettering consciousness. *It impedes the development of autonomous, independent individuals who judge and decide consciously for themselves.*[18](emphasis added)

---

[11] Theodor Adorno and Max Horkheimer, *Dialectic of Enlightenment* 1944, trans. John Cumming (New York: Herder, 1972), p. 147.
[12] Ibid., p. 144.
[13] Ibid., p. 163.
[14] Theodor Adorno, "Culture Industry Reconsidered," *New German Critique* 6 (1975), p. 12.
[15] Deborah Cook, *The Culture Industry Revisited: Theodor W. Adorno on Mass Culture*, (Lanham: Rowman, 1996), p. X.
[16] Ibid.
[17] R. B. Kershner, "Introduction," *Joyce and Popular Culture*. By Kershner, p. 2.
[18] Adorno, "Culture Industry Reconsidered," pp. 18-19.

Nevertheless, Adorno and other members of the Frankfurt School believed in the emancipatory potential of autonomous and authentic art. In his *Aesthetic Theory*, Adorno explains that "by the inherent tendency of art to cast different lights on the familiar, artworks correspond to the objective need for a transformation of consciousness that could become a transformation of reality". [19]

Culture critic Marshall McLuhan explains that "[t]he artist picks up the message of cultural and technological challenge decades before its transforming impact occurs."[20] This was certainly true in the case of Saroyan. As early as 1921, Saroyan was aware of the ambiguous effects of advancing technology. This awareness resulted from his perception of the adverse relationship between the phonograph and his own imagination. Saroyan recounts that as a thirteen-year-old boy he heard with an "internal ear" "many great symphonies which no composer ever put to paper and no orchestra ever performed."[21] This changed when he purchased a phonograph with money he had earned selling newspapers. His observations of its effects are poignant: "[A]s I listened more and more to the music of the phonograph I heard my own music less and less. If the external ear is surfeited with music, the internal ear tends to become deaf."[22] Saroyan recognized that not only phonographs but other forms of technologies could deafen the individual's "music" as well. In his writing, he seeks to make that "internal" music be heard. As he states in his first collection of stories, published in 1934, "I want to restore man to himself. . .. I want him to be himself."[23] From the outset, Saroyan was dedicated to this objective:

> In 1934 I believed in writing. I believed it could do everything—anything—but I had in mind that it could bring love, and therefore meaning and balance, order and equity, to the human race. I had in mind that writing

---

[19] Theodor Adorno, *Aesthetic Theory*. Robert Hullot-Kentor, trans., Gretal Adorno and Rolf Tiedemann, eds. (Minneapolis: Univ. of Minnesota Press, 1997), p. 243.

[20] Marshall McLuhan, *Understanding Media: The Extensions of Man* (New York: McGraw, 1964), p. 110.

[21] William Saroyan, *The Bicycle Rider in Beverly Hills* (New York: Scribner's, 1952), p. 12.

[22] Ibid., p. 22.

[23] William Saroyan, "Myself Upon the Earth," *The Daring Young Man on the Flying Trapeze* (New York: Random, 1934), p. 54.

> could improve the very nature of man. I believed this because I believed that all aspects of possibility are in all men, and that the desired aspects may come to dominate the others by means of awareness—as when a man begins to think and choose—and I believed that nothing moves a man swifter to awareness—to thinking and choosing—than the reading of a good piece of writing.... I believed that writing was going to play a very important role in the survival and enlargement of the human being.[24]

This artistic vision parallels Adorno's belief in the transformative possibilities of emancipatory art. Since "all aspects of possibility" exist in everyone, Saroyan, like his character Gyko, sought to encourage "the releasing within one's self of those mysterious and vital forces." Even though our rehearsal is often undermined by the culture industry and our performance of ourselves is "a *bad* bad play," Saroyan's optimism reigns: "We all hope it will some day turn out to be a *good* good play."[25] He not only carried this hope but actively worked toward its realization through his fiction.

In his 1936 short story "The Whistle," Saroyan cautions that we are rehearsing for the "wrong" roles and summons us to live more autonomous and authentic lives: "Everybody seems to be getting away from themselves, as if themselves were nothing at all, and they seem to be throwing themselves into fantastic configurations of other personalities.... This is wrong.... After you are born you yourself are supposed to be the inhabitant of the earth and you yourself are supposed to do your living."[26]

Daily, advertisements are seen, movies attended, stars idolized, lyrics sung, programs watched, fashions studied, and products purchased. Even deliberate attempts to side-step the culture industry are not complete. The culture industry is ubiquitous and our exposure to it virtually unavoidable. Regardless of the extent of our interaction with the culture industry, our participation is largely unreflective; we "just do it." Without realizing it, our "personal"

---

[24] William Saroyan, *After Thirty Years: The Daring Young Man on the Flying Trapeze* (New York: Harcourt, 1964), pp. 27-28.
[25] Ibid., p. 212.
[26] William Saroyan "The Whistle," *Inhale and Exhale* (New York: Random, 1936), p. 424.

mannerisms, style, desires, and aspirations are mass-produced by the culture industry. Saroyan's declaration that "you yourself are supposed to do your living" speaks to this phenomenon. Our prospects for mitigating these effects and giving a "good performance" of ourselves reside in our heightened awareness of the culture industry's threat to authentic selfhood.

Throughout his fiction, Saroyan presents a number of characters whose self-identity is either lost or challenged by their participation in the culture industry. These portrayals provide us with an opportunity to reflect on our own interactions with the culture industry. Saroyan's character Charlie in "I Could Say Bella Bella,"[27] for example, has trouble being himself. His reliance on the lyrics from the song "Bei Mir Bist Du Schön" to communicate with others prevents him from finding and using his own voice. In 1937, Songwriters Hall of Fame member Sammy Cahn wrote the English lyrics for the song. Recorded by the Andrew Sisters, it became an instant hit, selling over a million records and earning the first gold record by a female group. "Bei Mir Bist Du Schön" was enormously popular--number one on *Your Hit Parade* for two weeks, the number three sheet music seller of 1938, and sung by Priscilla Lane in the Warner Film *Love, Honour and Behave*.[28] The heart of the song's lyrics is:

Until I first met you I was lonesome
And when you came in sight, dear, my heart grew light
And this old world seemed new to me

You're really swell, I have to admit, you
Deserve expressions that really fit you
And so I've racked my brain, hoping to explain
All the things that you do to me

Bei mir bist du schön, please let me explain
Bei mir bist du schön means you're grand
Bei mir bist du schön, again I'll explain
It means you're the fairest in the land
I could say bella, bella, or even say wunderbar

---

[27] William Saroyan, "I Could Say Bella Bella," *The Trouble with Tigers* (New York: Harcourt, Brace, and Company, 1938).
[28] Don Taylor, *Hit Parade 1920-1955: An Encyclopedia of the Top Songs of the Jazz, Depression, Swing, and Sing Eras* (New York: Quill, 1985), p. 92.

Each language only helps me tell you how grand you are
I've tried to explain, bei mir bist du schön
So kiss me, and say you understand

Saroyan notes that when *New Yorker* published this story in its May 14, 1938 issue, "everybody in America was singing those words, or hearing somebody else sing them."[29]

The story begins with the main character, Charlie, drunkenly introducing himself to a young woman. He is glad that he is drunk, for he knows he wouldn't have the courage to speak with her if he were sober. Charlie sings, "I could say bella bella."[30] Suddenly becoming completely sober, Charlie is unable to continue his performance, he is at a loss for words: "He knew the play was over, and shouldn't be."[31] Though initially charmed, she feels the same way, thinking, "Why did he have to change all of a sudden and become ordinary, making her ordinary too, spoiling everything."[32] As Charlie walks off, she remembers his singing, "I could say bella bella," and feels ridiculous.[33] "[A]s if to end the foolish song," she, too, walks away.[34]

Artworks which aid in the process of autonomous development, Adorno attests, "hint at what life would be like were it emancipated from imposed identity."[35] "I Could Say Bella Bella" does just this. Charlie's dependence on the lyrics of the song suggests that any sense of identity that he has is not his own, but borrowed from the culture industry. His character is a perfect example of Adorno and Horkheimer's observation that "the effort to achieve individuation has at last been replaced by the effort to imitate."[36] "I Could Say Bella Bella" exposes the failure of an imposed identity to establish genuine connections with others and, therefore, implicitly advocates

---

[29] Introduction, William Saroyan, *Thirty-Four More Great Stories* (New York: Avon, 1944).
[30] Saroyan, "I Could Say Bella," p. 58
[31] Ibid., p. 60.
[32] Ibid.
[33] Ibid.
[34] Ibid.
[35] Quoted in Deborah Cook, *The Culture Industry Revisited: Theodor W. Adorno on Mass Culture* (Lanham: Rowman, 1996), p. 122.
[36] Theodor Adorno and Max Horkheimer, *Dialectic of Enlightenment* (1944) trans. John Cumming (New York: Herder, 1972), p. 156.

a striving for autonomous development apart from the culture industry. As this song played on the radio, Saroyan thought these lyrics would diminish listeners' own voices. This story immediately responded to its threat to authentic selfhood. In other stories, Saroyan exposes and critiques ideologies disseminated through the culture industry.

"[B]etter dead than blind and living" judges the chorus in Sophocles's *Oedipus the King*.[37] Jesus teaches that the eye is "the lamp of the body" (Matt. 6:22). In "The Allegory of the Cave," Plato asserts that "the bewilderments of the eyes" are obstacles to a life worth living.[38] Keen vision and perception, indeed, have long been valued in mythology, lore, and religion. The culture industry, though, has emerged as the "modern replacement for religion and mythology."[39] This supplantation points to the significant role that the culture industry plays in providing a set of beliefs about the world – how it operates and how it is to be understood, as well as our purpose in it – which govern all aspects of our lives. As Adorno and Horkheimer postulate, "The whole world is made to pass through the filter of the culture industry."[40] Richard Pells concurs, noting that already in the thirties "few forces were more potent in shaping the way men saw the world than the newsreel, the picture magazine, the radio program, and the Hollywood film."[41] The culture industry's challenge to authentic selfhood, indeed, goes beyond effects on one's appearance, mannerisms, and behavior. The ideology it advances, when internalized, becomes the very lens through which individuals perceive, and subsequently understand, the world. Adorno worries that "people may not only lose true insight into reality, but ultimately their very capacity for life experience may be dulled by the constant

---

[37] Sophocles, *Oedipus the King*, David Grene, trans., *The Complete Greek Tragedies*, David Grene and Richard Lattimore, eds. (Chicago: Univ. of Chicago Press, 1959), p. 1369.

[38] Plato, *The Republic*, Benjamin Jowett, trans. (New York: Modern Library, 1941), p. 258.

[39] Patrick Brantlinger, *Bread and Circuses: Theories of Mass Culture as Social Decay* (Ithaca: Cornell Univ. Press, 1983), p. 100.

[40] Adorno and Horkheimer, *Dialectic of Enlightenment*, p. 126.

[41] Richard Pells, *Radical Visions and American Dreams: Culture and Social Thought in the Depression Years* (New York: Harper, 1973), p. 263.

wearing of blue and pink spectacles."[42] Saroyan, too, expresses disgust over the illusions that the culture industry generates. Its ideology, he insists, functions as "rose-colored glasses," preventing an accurate perception of reality.[43] In his fiction, Saroyan seeks to expose the culture industry's attempt to replace mythology and religion, and thereby mitigates its power to shape our world view.

Introducing his story "Public Speech," Saroyan proposes, "The masses aren't ready, I'm afraid, for the shock of genuine knowing, and not spiritually equipped to face the inward tragedy which occurs with genuine knowing."[44] This passage illuminates the appeal of the culture industry's ideology, which simplifies reality, imposes order on experience, and thus shields against the complexity of life. Adorno affirms this contention:

> The phrase, the world wants to be deceived, has become truer than had ever been intended. People are not only, as the saying goes, falling for the swindle; if it guarantees them even the most fleeting gratification they desire a deception which is nonetheless transparent to them. They force their eyes shut and voice approval, in a kind of self-loathing for what is meted out to them, knowing fully the purpose for which it is manufactured. Without admitting it they sense that their lives would be completely intolerable as soon as they no longer clung to the satisfactions which are none at all.[45]

What Adorno labels "deception" in this passage, advocates of the culture industry call "an ordering factor."[46] This classification, Adorno explains, serves as the culture industry's "most ambitious defense": "In a supposedly chaotic world it [the ideology of the culture industry] provides human beings with something like

---

[42] Theodore Adorno, "How to Look at Television," *The Culture Industry: Selected Essays on Mass Culture,* J. M. Bernstein, ed., (London: Routledge, 1991), p. 147.

[43] William Saroyan, "Solo for Tin Gazoo," *Inhale and Exhale* (New York: Random, 1936), p. 182.

[44] William Saroyan, "Public Speech," *Three Times Three* (Los Angeles: The Conference Press, 1936), p. 70.

[45] Adorno, "The Culture Industry Revisited," p. 70.

[46] Ibid., p. 16.

standards for orientation."[47] For both Saroyan and Adorno, this line of defense is none at all. Their concern with "genuine knowing" and "true insight into reality" explains their opposition to the culture industry's ideology.

Art fails, Saroyan claims, "if it does not improve optics, intelligence and humanity, for by this improvement exists art's only chance to improve the world, the world's behavior, the relations of man toward man, and the relations of man toward God."[48] Saroyan's stories succeed, exposing the untruths and delusiveness of the dominant myths propagated by the culture industry – primarily the myths of individualism and materialism.

The most prevalent myth in America is that individuals have control over their lives. Although a part of the American psyche since the early history of the nation, this myth deepened during the turbulent years of the thirties. Belief in one's own omnipotence instilled necessary confidence amid the general despair and hopelessness brought on by the Depression. To this day, this myth has laudably inspired many to assume more control over their lives. Nonetheless, belief in rugged individualism has its deficiencies, namely its use to "defen[d] inequality by perpetuating the myth that achievement is earned, and that those who have wealth and power (and those who don't) deserve their station in life."[49] and to affirm that "problems can be solved without radical change of basic assumptions and social structures."[50] Proceeding fundamentally from depictions of "heroic" characters who embody the individualist myth in movies, television, and songs, this ideology creates a society which is neither reflective nor self-critical.

According to Herbert Marcuse, the myth of individualism "systematically promoted" by the culture industry also contributes to

---

[47] Ibid.

[48] William Saroyan, "Curtain," *Razzle-Dazzle* (New York: Harcourt, Brace, 1940), p. 505.

[49] James Combs, *Polpop: Politics and Popular Culture in America* (Bowling Green: Bowling Green State Univ. Popular Press, 1984), p. 246.

[50] Eric Mottram, "Living Mythically: The Thirties," *Journal of American Studies* 6.3 (1972): pp. 267-87.

"one-dimensional thought" and "pervades, distorts, and shapes" the larger culture.[51]

Without the capacity for critical thought, these "one-dimensional being[s]" perceive the world superficially, and true knowledge of the world and self are thwarted.

One multi-dimensional aspect of American culture which more genuinely portrays life is the circus. Pointing to the fullness of the circus – its simultaneous celebration and parody of human achievement – John Culhane appreciates the circus as a metaphor for human existence. He writes:

> From the beginning, it was the contrast between the achievements of the human beings and trained animals in the acts and the foibles and failures of the clowns that made the circus for me. . . . From the circus--in, around, above the ring that has always symbolized for man his ultimate wholeness--we learn to reconcile the basic conflicts in human nature, between what we are and what we aspire to be. . . . For over two hundred years in this country, *it has mirrored the American dream of boundless aspiration while burlesquing the idea of constant success.* But we clowns do have a history of overcoming our conceits and self-delusions just in time to catch each other before we fall. And that is why the circus is a truly happy dream, and its history a valuable comment on the human comedy[52]. (emphasis added)

The clowns brings us down to earth, helping us to maintain a balanced vision. Without them, the wholeness of the circus is lost.

For Saroyan, too, the circus was an "artful, theatrical history of life on earth."[53] Like Culhane, Saroyan acknowledged the circus's whole and balanced vision of life: "The circus is not a thing of fragments. It is a whole work. All of its parts combine to form a play which is the most democratic of all plays, the most universal in appeal, and the most varied and broad in its significance. ... *a*

---

[51] Herbert Marcuse, *One-Dimensional Man: Studies in the Ideology of Advanced Industrial Society* (Boston: Beacon, 1968), p. 380.

[52] John Culhane, *The American Circus: An Illustrated History* (New York: Holt, 1990), pp. xxi-xxii.

[53] Introduction to William Saroyan, "Subway Circus," *Razzle-Dazzle*, p. 462.

parody, on the one hand, of human effort, and on the other a glorification of human accomplishment."[54] (emphasis added)

What Saroyan and Culhane value most about the circus, the culture industry shunned. The balanced vision of the circus was corrupted through movies, songs, and newspapers. With its influence, the culture industry catapulted trapeze artists and wild animal trainers to mythic status. By celebrating these individual circus actors apart from the rest of the performers, who comprised the whole of the circus in popular songs and the fifteen circus-themed movies produced between 1928 and 1934,[55] young boys across the nation dreamed of being like them, and adults internalized the ideology they embodied. As a consequence, these one-dimensional representations contributed to the myth of individualism.

Such stories about wild animal trainers also propagated the myth of individualism. Their control over dangerous animals implies that individuals can rule the forces of nature which threaten their existence. In 1932, however, lion tamer Clyde Beatty was bitten by a lion, infected, and faced the likelihood of his death. Beatty's misfortune challenged the myth of rugged individualism. The culture industry, via the radio and newspapers, kept the nation informed. Beatty soon announced that he would return to the cage of the circus and did so within the year. John Culhane acknowledges the implications of Beatty's triumph over the attack, remarking that Beatty "burst on the American scene as a symbol of winning out against great odds"[56] and "became a symbol of recovery."[57] He exemplified "the belief that an American boy could overcome the 'Law of the Jungle.'"[58] Even though we may be bitten by nature, so the message went, we can still overcome it and establish our dominance. The myth of individualism, though momentarily challenged, remained intact. The culture industry celebrated and disseminated the lessons that Beatty embodied – *Time Magazine* featured Clyde Beatty on the cover of the March 29, 1937 issue.

---

[54] Ibid., pp. 460-461.

[55] Tom Ogden, *Two Hundred Years of the American Circus* (New York: Facts, 1993), pp. 143-150.

[56] Culhane, *The American Circus*, p. 208.

[57] Ibid., p. 209.

[58] Ibid., p. 210.

In 1936, Saroyan's second collection of short stories, *Inhale and Exhale*, included "The Barber Whose Uncle Had His Head Bitten Off by a Circus Tiger." This story critically responds to the media's advancement of the myth of individualism through the Beatty incident. The story begins with the eleven-year-old narrator being badgered by his teacher and family and community members to cut his terrific mane of hair. After a bird attempts to build a nest in his hair, the boy decides to visit an Armenian barber named Aram. During the leisurely haircut, they sip coffee and laugh, while Aram recounts the story of his uncle Misak. Once a professional wrestler, Misak is now poor. Tired of being laughed at for squandering his money, he looks for work with no success. One day, a clown asks Misak to join the circus. The day before, the clown explains, the man who used to place his head into a yawning tiger's mouth was killed during a performance. A lover of "the wild beasts of the jungle," Misak agrees to be the replacement. When performing, though, the tiger, "full of the ugliness of things living on earth," clamps its jaws on Misak's head and Misak too dies.[59]

Misak's fate sharply contrasts with Clyde Beatty's and works to undermine the myth of individualism. Whereas the myth insists that individuals can command their environment, Saroyan's story acknowledges that there are forces present in the world – "the ugliness of things living on earth"[60] – which are indeed outside of one's ability to control. The tale's implicit ideology may help the young boy from having to learn the hard way of the myth of individualism's falseness. He does not need to have his head taken off by a circus tiger, only his hair clipped by a wise barber. For readers, too, Saroyan's story is a trip to the barber-shop.

The barber, Aram, also recognizes the threat that the modern world poses against being oneself and authentic living. Learning from the boy that he has been pressured to get a haircut, Aram tells the boy: "That is the way with the world.... Always telling you what to do. What's wrong with a little hair? Why do they do it?" "Earn money, they say," he continues, expressing his own frustrations, "Buy a farm. This. That. Ah, they are against letting a man live a quiet life."[61] Aram, the young boy knows, "wasn't a barber anyway.

---

[59] William Saroyan, *Inhale and Exhale* (New York: Random, 1936), p. 169.
[60] Ibid.
[61] Ibid., p. 166.

He was just pretending to be a barber, so his wife wouldn't bother him too much. He was just doing that to satisfy the world."[62] Though the barber-shop is always empty, Aram contentedly reads the Armenian newspapers and watches and talks to people all day. He does not want to lose himself in pursuit of money and wants to remain fully human, imaginatively alive and genuinely connected with others: "All he wanted to do was read and talk to decent people. He had five children, three boys and two girls, but they were all like his wife, and he couldn't talk to them. All they wanted to know was how much was he making."[63] Aram's family's values demonstrate the influence of the culture industry. Not only does this story undermine those values, it also offers other, more humane values, to take their place. Saroyan exalts Aram as a new hero, worthy of emulation.

Philosophers have long contemplated the question "What is the good life?" The culture industry has not only derived an answer but has convinced millions of its truth – materialism, "a doctrine that the only or the highest values or objectives lie in material well-being and in the furtherance of material progress."[64] Conveniently for the culture industry, this doctrine profits them greatly. To suggest that the "good life" is "to know and be thyself" would bankrupt the industry. Despite its cost, subscription to the myth of materialism is extensive. Guided by the belief that fulfillment comes through material objects, many devotees to the myth have sacrificed everything to achieve this end, including their own personal development and genuine connections with others. Convinced of the falseness of this myth and its threat to authentic selfhood, Adorno and Horkheimer deplore that "the deceived masses are today captivated by the myth...even more than the successful are. Immovably, they insist on the very ideology which enslaves them."[65] Again, Adorno and Horkheimer look to art to inspire liberation from this enslavement. Saroyan sought to deflate the myth of materialism and reorient his readers to humane values.

Saroyan's story "Harry" from *The Daring Young Man* is a notable example of one such effort. The story begins by introducing

---

[62] Ibid., p. 167.
[63] Ibid.
[64] "Materialism," *Webster's New Collegiate Dictionary* (1980 ed.).
[65] Adorno and Horkheimer, *Dialectic of Enlightenment*, p. 133.

Harry: "This boy was a worldbeater. Everything he touched turned to money."[66] By the age of fourteen, he already has saved over six hundred dollars, all earned on his own. A born salesman, Harry achieves enormous success regardless of what he sells. He has the walls of all the houses in the foreign district mounted with the color religious pictures. In less than two months, he has over sixty married women subscribed to *True Stories Magazine*. He frequently buys six used cars at a time, gives them a nice paint job, and sells them for three or four times the price he pays. He sells electric refrigerators, vacuum cleaners, earthquake and life insurance, and jumps at every opportunity to amass profits.

His quest for profits, though, makes him insensitive to the repercussions of his sales. After the housewives begin reading *True Stories Magazine*, "a lot of unconventional things began to happen."[67] Secret love affairs are initiated, women send away "for eye-lash beautifiers, bath salts, cold creams, and things of that sort," and "[a]ll the ladies beg[i]n to rouge their lips and powder their faces and wear silk stockings and tight sweaters."[68] Harry introduces these women to the empty enticements of the culture industry, and according to form, they emulate the adventurous lives of those presented to them. Through his representation of these effects, Saroyan implicitly cautions against following the models of the culture industry. His admonitions, in this context, especially apply to the myth of materialism.

Harry's determination to make money is steadfast. By age seventeen, he earns "a small fortune," but no one understands why he wanted so much money. When asked, "Harry would look confused a moment, as if he himself didn't know, and then he would come out and say: 'I want to get a hold of a half million dollars so I can retire.'"[69] Harry's hesitation is telling. He lacks the self-knowledge which accompanies devotion to values not fashioned by himself. Already thinking of retiring at eighteen, Harry talks about possibly traveling around the world. Any notion of living life is always delayed. The day for him to truly live, though, never comes. Harry gets sick. His plans are thwarted, and his money in the bank is of no

[66] William Saroyan, *The Daring Young Man*, p. 179.
[67] Ibid. p. 180.
[68] Ibid.
[69] Ibid., p. 184.

help. Even though confined to his bed, he continues trying to sell life insurance to his visitors. Saroyan explains that "it wasn't that Harry really wanted more money; it was simply that he couldn't open his mouth unless it was to make a sales talk. He couldn't carry on an ordinary conversation because he didn't know the first thing about anything that didn't have something to do with insurance, or automobiles, or real estate."[70] Over the years, Harry's compulsion to make money led him to objectify others solely as consumers. Consumed by the materialist myth, Harry has forgotten how to be a person and treat others as people as well.

Harry dies before he is twenty-two. His demise unmistakably reveals the fallacy of the materialist myth. Ironically, though, his town preserves the myth. Following Harry's death, the local newspaper runs a story about his life, celebrating him as a smart and ambitious man. The townspeople, too, talk to children about Harry "in order to make them ambitious."[71] Saroyan's story, however, makes plain that Harry is a poor role model. Nothing should take precedence, Saroyan intimates, over authentic selfhood and recognition of others as human beings. These relationships, with oneself and others, make life worth living.

Unlike Harry, Saroyan "felt the need to be only a writer, a writer writing, and not a success of any kind."[72] He was convinced that it was "worth while to want to make man aware of himself, aware of the greatness that is within him, if he will only stop being timid, if he will only stop letting things bully him; at least to *want* to."[73] The myths of individualism and materialism propagated by the culture industry "bully" humanity into disregarding humane values. Helping others to achieve self-awareness, Saroyan believed, "is essentially the job of every man who writes, and that anything else any of us do is irrelevant."

Saroyan, though, was not exclusively the hopeful optimist that many consider him. He experienced the "inner tragedy" that accompanies "genuine knowing." When these somber emotions

---

[70] Ibid., p. 185.
[71] Ibid., p. 187.
[72] William Saroyan, "A Writer's Declaration," *The Whole Voyald* (Boston: Little, Brown, 1956), p. 5.
[73] William Saroyan, "Panorama Unmerciful," *Inhale and Exhale,* (New York: Random, 1936), p. 242.

arose, Saroyan would go outdoors and "try to look at things clearly."[74] This process yielded a clarity which informed his work:

> The earth is good and the living is good, only they have gotten us into such a mess with their arrangement that we forget to focus our vision on the splendid things and we lose track of our proper function here. We forget that it is pretty fine merely to be able to draw breath, to have energy and motion, clean senses and clear vision, to sit at a table and eat humbly, to walk and talk and read and sleep and be alive. The competitiveness of our time oppresses us and we forget all the essential things.[75]

Our participation in this competitiveness can be largely attributed to the myths of individualism and materialism that the culture industry advances. As a result, vision is impaired and self-realization thwarted. Saroyan's effort to help others "look at things clearly" entailed a critique of these myths. As the preceding analysis demonstrates, Saroyan's stories help to dissolve the ideology of the culture industry and make "genuine knowing" possible. His readers will not need "many generations to be able to *be* themselves."

In Saroyan's "The Poor and Burning Arab," Aram Garoghlanian's Uncle Khosrove befriends a man named Khalil. Khosrove and Khalil meet, Aram presumes, at the Arax Coffee House, a place frequented mostly by Armenians, but also by all those who long for the old country. Throughout the story, these men, an Armenian and an Arab, often sit in silence in the Garoghlanian family parlour for hours at a time. Young Aram cannot understand why the men are so quiet. During one of their silent visits, Aram sits at the dining room table and turns the pages of an old copy of the *Saturday Evening Post* that he "knew by heart – especially the pictures: Jello, very architectural; automobiles, with high-toned people standing around; flashlights flashing into dark places; tables set with bowls of soup steaming; young men in fancy ready-made suits and coats; and all sorts of other pictures."[76] "Quiet, boy, quiet,"

---

[74] Ibid.

[75] Ibid.

[76] William Saroyan, "The Poor and Burning Arab," *My Name Is Aram,* (New York: Harcourt, Brace and World, 1940), p. 201.

his Uncle Khosrove roars. Aram assumes that he had "turned the pages a little too quickly."[77]

In the silence, each man communes with his authentic self, and in understanding himself is able to understand and communicate with the other. Aram, the young American, is unable to either experience or understand this phenomenon. Saroyan's emphasis on the boy's familiarity with the advertisements of the *Saturday Evening Post* implicates the culture industry in Aram's ignorance. McLuhan's explanation of the dynamic of advertisements clarifies this association: "Ads seem to work on the very advanced principle that a small pellet or pattern in a noisy, redundant barrage of repetition will gradually assert itself. Ads push the principle of noise all the way to the plateau of persuasion."[78] The "noise" generated by the advertisements stands in sharp contrast to the silence that Khosrove and Khalil enjoy. Just as Saroyan's acquisition of a phonograph for a time made him deaf to his "own music" when he was a boy,[79] so in this story does the clamour of America's commercial culture damage a young boy's "internal ear." Since that experience and the publication of Saroyan's stories which critique the culture industry, the "noise" of the culture industry has amplified significantly.

Years before his death, Saroyan reflected on the "laundered and ironed flour sack" that housed the papers of his failed poet father, who died when Saroyan was age three. Considering the disposition of his own manuscripts, Saroyan did not "like the idea of leaving them anywhere" and concluded that he had to find a suitable home for his life work.[80] In 1996, Stanford University acquired Saroyan's archives, and head librarian Michael Keller has stressed, "He's an under-appreciated writer now, but that will change."[81]

William Saroyan's contributions to twentieth century American literature and to a more general critique of commercial culture have indeed been "under-appreciated." Prior to the post-World War II

---

[77] Ibid.

[78] McCluhan, *Understanding Media*, p. 227.

[79] William Saroyan, *The Bicycle Rider in Beverly Hills* (New York: Scribner's, 1952), p. 22.

[80] Willliam Saroyan, *Here Comes, There Goes, You Know Who* (New York: Simon, 1961), p. 239.

[81] Mark A. Arax, "Collection's Fate Adds New Chapter to Saroyan Legend," *Los Angeles Times* (May 22, 1996): A1+.

escalation of the culture industry and the critique of its effects which followed, he had already examined its threat to "the survival and enlargement of the human being." In response, he sought to undo the culture industry's damage. He would improve impaired vision, heighten dulled self-awareness, and revitalize blunted imagination. Saroyan wanted to "restore man to himself" so that our performances of ourselves would "some day turn out to be a *good* good play."

At age fifty-six, Saroyan reflected on his thirty years as a writer. He recounted his anticipation at the dawn of his career, assessed his position in the literary world, and offered a prophecy concerning the future acknowledgment of his work:

> The big thing about 1934 was the adventure, the fact that I didn't know how the whole literary aspect of my identity was going to turn out, although my confidence was enormous, and it was inconceivable to me that I would not become one of the greatest writers of all time, forthwith. That is the truth, that is how it was, it would be wrong of me not to say so. It doesn't matter what kind of writer I have in fact turned out to be-so far. I'm not finished yet, perhaps not by a long shot.[82]

Indeed, Saroyan is "not finished yet," "not by a long shot." William Saroyan's work is relevant today more than ever.

---

[82] William Saroyan, *After Thirty Years* (New York: Harcourt, Brace and World, 1964), p. 28.

46

William Saroyan: Performance Machine

H. Aram Veeser

"Mr. Saroyan is a writer. He is also an act." Thus, Lewis Garnet. "Saroyan is more fascinated by the road than the route," thus, Patrick McGilligan.[1] Everyone agrees that Saroyan loved to perform – he was a performance machine. And once that was said, discussion ended. His frenzied work schedule, his tendency to take on his critics, his increasing self-isolation, and even his loud voice – he was a performance machine – critics assumed that Saroyan performed in the way that neurotics acted out. Saroyan "was a mere *jongleur*, an off-the-wall Armenian starved for publicity, a passing phenomenon whose luck had run out in the Big Apple, along with his minor talent." Thus, James Tashjian's acid paraphrase of this line of thinking.

Of all the critics who have tried to grasp this surprisingly difficult and complex writer, only Dickran Kouymjian has grasped the pithy coherence that defines Saroyan's life and work. To do so, Kouymjian had to annul the vacuous story of a young romantic flower writer who lost his touch and declined into fuddled embitterment and sad delusions. In place of this popularly supposed American primitive and romantic humanist, Kouymjian's acute readings of Saroyan, especially of the late plays, establish Saroyan as an Adornian late-stylist who, like third-period Beethoven, outgrew the harmonies he had mastered so thoroughly and consciously defied the humanistic core of his earlier, more palatable work. Saroyan, just

---

[1] Patrick McGilligan, "Mr. Saroyan's Thoroughly American Movie," *The Modern Novel and the Movies*, Gerald Peary and Roger Shotzkin, eds. (New York: Frederick Ungar, 1978), in Alice K. Barter, "Introduction: Saroyan and His Critics," *Critical Essays on William Saroyan*, Harry Keyishian, ed. (New York: G. K. Hall & Co., 1995), pp. 1-31.

as relentlessly as Adorno's Beethoven, denies faith in even the possibility of human fulfillment and instead pours all his energies into exploring the machineries that were once able to produce the illusion of humanity.

One wonders why Saroyan has failed to attract the enormous sophistication that goes into analysis of almost any other comparable third-world exile, or post-colonial writer, the terrific subtlety of Spivak on Mahasweta Devi, or Barbara Harlow on Mahmoud Darwish, or Tim Brennan on Salman Rushdie, or Anthony Appiah on Wole Soyinka, and on and on.[2] The Saroyan enthusiast must feel slightly hurt. Why should these critics shun Saroyan? Is it that Saroyan is too simple? Or is it that those critics are too lazy? A bid to reclaim Saroyan for pure criticism might begin with "performance" and "machine."

It is easy enough to place Saroyan with Jackson Pollack and the brilliant circle of artists that Clement Greenberg called "action painters." Kouymjian shows how eagerly Saroyan recorded and invited attention to the mechanical conditions of writing, from hymns to his typewriter to elaborate, precise logs of time spent typing, performance data that he affixed to his finished manuscripts. But performance and performativity mean something more complex nowadays, and since Greenberg, we have come to associate performance art with a certain kind of self-display. Thus, the *jongleur*, the vaudevillian, the neurotic. The "performative" in ordinary language philosophy had already expunged any clear dividing line supposedly marking deeds off from words. "I bet," "I confess," and "I do" were actions; they changed one's marital or financial or legal status.[3] Derrida and de Man got hold of this old

[2] Anthony Appiah, *In My Father's House: Africa in the Philosophy of Culture* (New York: Oxford University Press, 1992); Homi K. Bhabha, *The Location of Culture*, (London and New York: Routledge, 1994); Timothy Brennan, *Salman Rushdie and the Third World: Myths of the Nation* (New York: St. Martin's Press, 1989); Barbara Harlow, *Resistance Literature* (New York: Methuen, 1987); and Gayatri Chakravorty Spivak, "Translator's Preface" and "Afterword," Devi Mahasweta, *Imaginary Maps: Three Stories by Mahasweta Devi*, Gayatri Chakravorty Spivak, trans. (New York: Routledge and Calcutta: Thema, 1995).

[3] J. L. Austin, *How To Do Things With Words* (Cambridge: Harvard University Press, 1962).

idea. They argued that every statement and not just bets, promises, and marriage vows, performed an action, created a new world or confirmed an old one. "Performative" in this philosophical and linguistic sense challenged the assumption that "to do" is the opposite of "to say." Saying something can be doing something. The speech-act Saroyan has a corresponding rise in status. Big talkers now become world creators, founders of discourse.

A further redefining of performance comes from queer theorists. "One's gender identity is a performative accomplishment."[4] One *must* choose among fixed roles. "Those who fail to do their gender right are regularly punished."[5] Performance seen from this angle takes on a certain political interest. The politics of performance art also has radical political overtones. "Performance is non-reproductive" and thus is "the runt of the litter" among the arts.[6] "Performance clogs the smooth machinery of reproductive representation necessary to the circulation of capital."[7] Angelika Festa stands beside the road with a mirror on her face: she performs female disappearance.[8] Can the performance be reproduced? No--videotape it, and it becomes something else, a document. Can it be sold? Debatable. Eric Bogosian has sold out the hall for many of his performance pieces. "Performance honors the idea that a limited number of people in a specific time/space frame can have an experience which leaves no visible trace afterwards."[9] Saroyan attacked his daily writing ferociously. Was he creating a product? No, he was a performer staging his own disappearance.

Yet a third group of contemporary critics has redefined performance yet another way: postcolonial critics have worked out a third kind of performance theories of postcolonial mimicry. Colonized person sees and mimics, and is in turn seen and surveilled. India fashioned the distinctive qualities of English civilization. In

---

4 Judith Butler, *Gender Trouble: Feminism and the Subversion of Identity* (New York and London: Routledge, 1990), p. 271.

5 Ibid., p. 273.

6 Peggy Phelan, *Unmarked: The Politics of Performance* (London: Routledge, 1993), p. 148.

7 Ibid.

8 Peggy Phelan and Lynda Hart, *Acting Out: Feminist Performances* (Ann Arbor: University of Michigan Press, 1993), p. 28.

9 Phelan, *Unmarked: The Politics of Performance*, p. 149.

many ways it acted as a disturbing force, a magnetic power placed at the periphery tending to destroy the natural development of Britain's character.[10] Performances by a French-Canadian or an Armenian might thus shape an America to which they are wholly peripheral. One also learns from postcolonials that the production of the post-colony rests on the nation as narration part of that consists in a repetitious, recursive strategy that asserts nationalist of every turn.[11] We exist because we say we do. The speech-act defines nationalism. Like gender, the post-colonial nation must be performed in order to exist.

Why introduce these barbarous and difficult redefinitions of performative? Because these three versions of performativity finally provide a vocabulary equal to the challenge of Saroyan's performances. Now a fuller adequation of word and referent is possible (as a postcolonial critic might say). Reviewers tended to assume that Saroyan's relentless labors reflected his desperate wish to make a lasting name for himself. Performers ranked lower than artists. Actors and musicians played second fiddle to playwrights and composers. "Not marble statues nor the monuments of princes shall outlive this powerful rhyme." The assumption that Saroyan had fixed his eye on posterity resolved a number of problems. It explained his attempts to outwit death: with his books *Not Dead Yet* and *Obituaries*, his distribution of his own pre-emptive death notices to newspapers, and most of all his relentless 7-day-a-week typewriting regimen.[12] He was, it would appear, scrambling to pile up accomplishments before the final buzzer, to be marking out his niche – as one critic puts it – in the American literary canon.

These assumptions make Saroyan into a pathetic, bean-counting compulsive, a prostrate victim to all sorts of market driven assumptions about good art being art that lasts, assumptions consistent with a five-year-old's emotions and a sales-clerk's philosophy of cultural value. Cut off critical debate. Saroyan becomes easily understood, not to say transparent. A writer upon whom critical reflection would be wasted effort. He is for Joseph

---

[10] Eric Stokes, *The English Utilitarians and India* (Oxford: Clarendon Press, 1959), p. 3.

[11] Homi K. Bhabha, "DissemiNation," *Nation and Narration* (London and New York: Routledge, 1990), p. 297.

[12] William Saroyan, *Obituaries* (Berkeley, CA.: Creative Arts Press, 1979).

Remenyi, "A romanticist…impressed with his own histrionic emotionalism. ...Sentimental, generous, genial, warm, whimsical, amused and amusing"; for James Thurber, "sloppy, mushy, a proletarian writer," and for William Fisher, "a man incapable of facing his dilemma frankly or of articulating it meaningfully."[13] In short, an Armenian starved for publicity.

This same mushy character reappears in so ostensibly sympathetic a figure as Michael Arlen, who flies across the country so Saroyan can bless Arlen's own pilgrimage to Armenia. Arlen on Saroyan: "J.D. Salinger must have heard that voice, and Richard Brautigan, and Jack Kerouac, and all those writers of the personal sound, the flower writers, the writers of our modern Era of Feeling."[14] Touchingly determined to leave his mark, Saroyan was succeeded. Even so hip a critic of Saroyan as Kouymjian lapses into these almost unavoidable assumptions. An example from Kouymjian's introduction to *An Armenian Trilogy*:

> Saroyan wrote his plays for posterity, as he said many times, perhaps nowhere more concisely that in a letter of March 7, 1975, to Gerald Pollinger, his London agent:
>
> I write at least one new large play a year and quite a few shorter plays. I send them nowhere because it is a waste of time, with the situation what it is in the theatre--Broadway is in the real estate and high finance business, off-Broadway is a lot of cliques, the university theatres are kids who can't do anything with half the skill required, and so I let the new plays accumulate. [15]

As I read the quotation, I kept waiting for Saroyan's assertion – an assertion made "nowhere more concisely" – that he wrote his plays for posterity. He does not say so. He says only that he writes a

[13] Joseph Remenyi, "William Saroyan: A Portrait," *College English* 6 (November, 1944), pp. 95-96, in Barter 7; William Fisher, "Whatever Became of Saroyan" *College English* 16 (Spring, 1958) p. 339, in Barter, 10.

[14] Michael J. Arlen, *Passage to Ararat* (New York: Farrar, Strauss & Giroux, 1975), p. 48.

[15] Dickran Kouymjian, *William Saroyan: An Armenian Trilogy*, with an introductory essay by Dickran Kouymjian, ed. (Fresno, CA.: The Press at California State University, Fresno, 1986), p. 3.

lot of them. Why he writes them – that question he leaves completely untouched. "I let the new plays accumulate." Very helpful!

But elsewhere Saroyan has commented on writing for posterity. He says he does not do it.

> William Saroyan: For me, I tried to tell myself long ago: "Remember hieroglyphics and words chiseled in stone, the Rosetta Stone for instance, and when you write, thing that it must go into stone, and then you will say something." It can paralyze you, if you insist that this is going to go into stone. You might not say anything for a long time.
>
> Interviewer: You have memory as well as imagination.
>
> WS: Where is the question?
>
> Interviewer: It's a statement.[16]

In this rather funny example of stunned incomprehension, Saroyan renounces all claims on performance posterity, and lasting achievement. Nothing he writes is written in stone. If you try to write for posterity, it can "paralyze you," "you might not say anything," Saroyan casually says. Garig Basmajian blurts out a flummoxed non sequitur, and the interview grinds to a halt.

All Saroyan's comments on posterity confirm that he has no interest in it. "I began to write the book so that the writing of it could take the place of dying, or my own literal death," he tells Keyishian.[17] "Most of all, though, I have liked *the play*. That is, the granted *unreality*, as when children say *Play like*."[18] Basmadjian starts asking how many unpublished novels, stories, plays, and Saroyan replies, carelessly:

> Everything. You see, that's none of my business. That's the business of whoever is a scholar or whoever wants to. My business is to live. Writing is living. . .[19]

---

[16] Garig Basmadjian and William Saroyan, "Interview," *Ararat* (Spring, 1984), pp. 36-37.

[17] Harry Keyishian, *Ararat* (Spring, 1984), p. 42.

[18] Quoted by David S. Calonne, *William Saroyan: My Real Work is Being* (Chapel Hill: University of North Carolina Press, 1983), p. 72.

[19] Basmadjian and Saroyan, "Interview," p. 38.

Posterity, he explains, as if to a little boy, "is none of my business." Some scholar can edit and publish his work – "or whoever (else) wants to." It's unimportant. "Writing is living," he affirms; writing is not posthumous reputation.

In order to make Saroyan a fit object for sophisticated critical attention, let us reconsider the assumption that Saroyan is writing for posterity. He is not. The energies fueling his creative achievement have little to do with the hereafter. They arise and discharge themselves in the now.

Second, let us consider Saroyan not a man, but rather a machine. His attachment to his Royal 2000 typewriter, to his bicycle, to the *Hairenik* printing press was more durable than his attachment to Carol, Aram, Lucy, or any mere human being. Play? This machine worked. In Saroyan's case, to detranscendatilize art production.

A writer may not be his own most truthful or accurate analyst. But Saroyan's practice confirms all that I have argued: performativity installs reality, never outlasts its moment, and builds a nation – a nation, in his case, of Armenians. No one captures Saroyan the machine better than Kouymjian:

> There werc no outlines or synopses, always a single typed draft, which was edited with pen if it was latei sent for publication or production. But since the major portion of the writing of his late years was never sent to publishers, it is preserved exactly as it was first typed.
>
> ...Whatever the subject or literary form, all were written at nearly the same pace: between 2,000 and 2,500 words an hour, usually in half-hour sessions on consecutive days until finished. Not uncommonly, several works were written at the same time... standing at the typewriter composing...[20] ...The ritual was unvarying; Saroyan never skipped a day, and never spent more than twenty to thirty minutes on a page. He composed at the typewriter without benefit of drafts, outlines, or notes. The intensity of his creation was aided only by reflection. ... The first draft was always the final one, and none was rewritten."... [21]

---

[20] Dickran Kouymjian, *Warsaw Visitor*, with an introductory essay by Dickran Kouymjian, ed. (Fresno, CA.: The Press at California State University, Fresno, 1986), pp. 4-5.

[21] Kouymjian, *William Saroyan: An Armenian Trilogy*, pp. 9-10.

The Roman poet Horace advised newcomers to spend ten years licking each poem into shape, and Ben Jonson agreed: only thus could one be not for an age but for all time. Saroyan is not interested. He noted his starting time – to the minute – atop each page. The exact moment he stopped appeared at the bottom. He raced the clock.

Steve Redgrave, a four-time Olympic sculling gold medalist, "works out six hours a day, seven days a week – all this for perhaps ten six-and-a-half-minute races a year."[22] "From the beginning I wanted to excel," Saroyan writes. Kouymjian understands the athletic nature of Saroyan's achievement: "Why did [the play] *Bitlis* need eleven years of gestation before it could be spat out whole in less than 'four hours?'"[23] He had an athlete's superstitions. "These things need luck," Saroyan remarks about Arlen. Saroyan, no less than Steve Redgrave, was a performance machine. Lest we mistake this for a habit of his dotage, recall that his Pulitzer-winning play, the "Time of Your Life," took six days to write. Foster correctly notes that the gimmicks that gave rise to Saroyan's topics and titles were "Little more than an excuse for writing."

"I did my best, and let me urge you to do your best, too"; that was the substance of his philosophy, easily translating to the performative ethos, may the best man/woman win. Like a boat racer, once he moves on to a new work, the past is forgotten.

Every performance was final and soon forgotten. Lucy: "Everything he was working on was always his best one. That work would be his favorite. He would say, 'This is better. Better!' I've never seen anyone work that hard."[24] In the words of another great performer, James Brown, "I do not care about the past; I just want our love to last."

Saroyan's machine-like quality extended to a love of machines themselves. A character in Saroyan's "Armenians" remarks, "Whenever I am confused about who I am I go in the back and look at the four different black printing presses. I just look at them. What great faces and bodies they have, and what glorious work they are able to do."[25] Saroyan's debt to the bicycle is (forgive me) a moving

---

[22] "Putting In His Oar," *The New Yorker* (July 22, 1996), p. 34.

[23] Kouymjian, *William Saroyan: An Armenian Trilogy*, p. 14.

[24] Lucy Saroyan, Harry Keyishian, *Ararat* (Spring, 1984), p. 77.

[25] Kouymjian, *William Saroyan: An Armenian Trilogy*, p. 165.

one: "Moving the legs evenly and steadily soon brings to the rider a valuable knowledge of pace and rhythm... I learned [my style] from things on which I moved, and as writing is a thing that moves I think I was lucky to learn as I did."[26] Writing required Saroyan to become half-human. What Gilles Deleuze and Felix Guattari call a machinic assemblage. Such assemblages "the stirrup, the horse, two armed riders..." mark turning points in history.[27] The merely athletic drive to excel would have interest. Rather the second and third qualities of performativity, the qualities of mimicry and mockery in an oppressive situation, and the nation-narrating, reality-creating power of performative speech. Again, Kouymjian: "genocide – one nearly forgotten and even denied by its perpetrators... motivated Saroyan to demand of himself some clarifications of this confounding experience, clarifications articulated through art."[28]

From Budd Schulberg: "Every word he put down was a holy miracle to him, the son of an immigrant Armenian grape-grower who could not only talk the adopted language, but use the words to make beautiful American sentences."[29] That Saroyan mimickry had an edge. In *Chance Meetings*, (a late memoir)[30]: "the human experience...can be made tolerable only by mockery in one form or another...including (or especially) in all those things which are ordinarily, even, to the comedians, plainly sacred." This is moreover a post-colonial, oppressed-race sort of mockery: "Go ahead, destroy this race. Destroy Armenia...Send them from their homes into the desert. Let them have neither bread nor water... See if the race will not live again when two of them meet in a beer parlor twenty years after, and laugh...See if you can stop them from mocking the big

---

[26] Ibid.

[27] Gilles Deleuze and Félix Guattari, *A Thousand Plateaus: Capitalism and Schizophrenia* (Minneapolis and Oxford: University of Minnesota Press, 1987).

[28] Kouymjian, *William Saroyan: An Armenian Trilogy*, p. 28.

[29] Budd Schulberg, "Saroyan: Ease and Unease on the Flying Trapeze," *Esquire* (October, 1960), p. 85, in Barter, 13.

[30] David S. Calonne, *William Saroyan: My Real Work is Being* (Chapel Hill: University of North Carolina Press, 1983), p. 83.

ideas of the world, you sons of bitches, a couple of Armenians talking in the world, go ahead and try to destroy them."[31]

Saroyan felt that the repeated performance of the self could alone create the self. He included "Saroyan," the character as a leading figure in his later plays *Bitlis* and *Haratch*, in a play entitled *An Imaginary Character Named Saroyan*. In *Warsaw Visitor* he takes it to the limit-all three characters-Mustache, Saroyan, the Devil. But more important he understands the Armenian "nation" as a narration. Armenia – a fact – if it is to be a fact-solely of verbal iteration. Language's nation-building power springs out of Saroyan fully formed, 30 years before Homi Bhabha, Arjun Appadurai, and the postcolonial critics: "who is an Armenian?" demands Zulal, a character in *Haratch*. "An Armenian is a Turk who says, I am an 'Armenian'..."[32]

But is Saroyan not the principal advocate of essential Armenianness, the tireless promulgator of theses about the nature of uniquely Armenian characteristics? Who but Saroyan comes to the American mind when prompted to name "a famous Armenian"? Jack Kevorkian, Doctor Death, or Kirk Kerkorian are incidentally Armenian, but Saroyan is fundamentally so, for the condition of being Armenian is the content of all his work. Yet it appears that Saroyan was finally agnostic, at best, about the very existence of something called "Armenian identity."

He joins the other misunderstood American middle-easterner, Edward Said. Both men are known principally as defenders and epitomes of ethnic identity, Armenian and Palestinian. But both prove, upon examination, to be decidedly circumspect about the very possibility of ethnic identity. Readers of Edward Said will recognize the preference for affiliation over filiation, for voluntary and invented bonds rather than genetic, inherited ones. According to Said, dispossessed Palestinians can afford to demand full territorial repatriation no longer. "To affirm a prior belonging, a long historical patriation, has involved for us a prolonged denial of what we have now become, disinherited outsiders."[33] He ridiculed the simplistic

[31] William Saroyan, *Inhale & Exhale* (New York: Modern Library, 1936), p. 438.

[32] Kouymjian, *William Saroyan: An Armenian Trilogy*, pp. 153-154.

[33] Edward W. Said, *After the Last Sky: Palestinian Lives* (New York: Pantheon, 1985).

version of the Palestinian quest for repatriation, and dismissed as silly and racist the longing to restore a purely Palestinian society.[34] Instead of patriation, filiation, and blood-ties, Said recommends affiliation, loyalty to ideas and goals. Saroyan clearly neglected his filial ties. This drive towards intellectual not blood amity, operated at the personal level. David Kherdian, the poet: "He was like a father to his father, and to his son a stranger. It was not his destiny to be either – he was a writer. So I realized then that it was because of this that there had been room in his life for me, his life, a willingness to impact and encourage and advance someone not of his bloodline but of that other line that was closer to his heart."[35] Saroyan's capacity for warmth and bonding was lavished on the machinery that went into producing Armenian identity, and while part of that machinery was flesh and blood – Kherdian, Michael Arlen, Jr., and others he nourished and reinforced, it was also institutional (*Hairenik Weekly*) and mechanical (the Royal typewriter, the *Haratch* printing presses). It was for these that he felt sincere affection. And because Saroyan decided for the machine over life, the personal became the political. His tireless self-production was a matter of physical manufacturing, as little glamorous and as physically taxing as factory assembly line work. Early on, Saroyan reports saying to himself, "Hell, you've made a beginning, but you have put forward a bragging character and that may not be a good thing. It may be something you will have to live down."[36]

Many have dismissed this performed identity as a *debased* performance of course. Edward Foster does. "While he later became mostly an entertainer, his early work was a real contribution to the literature of freedom."[37] This story of declining powers is both too easy and profoundly mistaken. Saroyan matured into what has been called "late style," a condition of intransigent mastery and sharpened

---

[34] In Edward W. Said, *The Question of Palestine* (New York: Times Books, 1979).

[35] *Ararat* (Spring, 1984), p. 64.

[36] Alice K. Barter, "Introduction: Saroyan and His Critics," *Critical Essays on William Saroyan*, Harry Keyishian, ed. (New York: G. K. Hall & Co., 1995), p. 17.

[37] Ibid., p. 22.

alienation.[38] We should rather experience Saroyan as a figure whose early sentimentality and humanism ripened into a spiny antihumanism, a recognition that nothing works, a love of discipline, solitude, and the well-executed workday. His career can be taken as a whole, as a single performance that in its impressive scope "dramatizes new relations between the traditionally timeless work of art and the transient generation, the publics, that are addressed by it."[39] As members of his publics, finally it is this radically complex performer we would be more interested to read about. Saroyan is a human bridge from a gently romantic and nostalgic vision to another, tougher, hard-nosed late style. He is a bridge, in other words, from the genocide to a place beyond it, a fiercer place that has yet to be fully surveyed much less mapped, domesticated, and colonized. Over that bridge walked Michael Arlen, Dickran Kouymjian, Anahid Kassabian, and David Kherdian. New journals, such as *The Armenian Review* and *Armenian Forum*, fall to the task of explaining this moment to itself. There was Armenian writing before Saroyan, such writing after him. And they are not the same.

---

[38] Theodor W. Adorno, *Beethoven: The Philosophy of Music* (Stanford: Stanford University Press, 1998), pp. 123-138; Rose Subotnik, *Developing Variations: Style and Ideology in Western Music* (Minneapolis and Oxford: University of Minneapolis Press, 1991), pp. 3-42; and Edward Said, *Late Style: Music and Literature Against the Grain* (New York: Pantheon, 2006).

[39] W. J. T. Mitchell, *Picture Theory: Essays on Verbal and Visual Representation* (Chicago: University of Chicago Press, 1994).

CONTRIBUTORS

ROUBEN PAUL ADALIAN is the Director of the Armenian National Institute (ANI) in Washington, D.C. He is a specialist on the Caucasus and the Middle East, and has taught at a number of universities, including Georgetown and Johns Hopkins. He is the associate editor and resource editor on the Armenian Genocide, of the award-winning *Encyclopedia of Genocide* (1999), and has contributed to a number of publications including *Genocide: Essays Toward Understanding, Early-Warning, and Prevention* (1999) and *America and the Armenian Genocide* (2003). He received his Ph.D. in history from the University of California at Los Angeles (UCLA).

JOSEPH M. ALEXANIAN graduated from Wheaton College, Wheaton, Illinois, with a B.A. in Greek, from Fuller Theological Seminary, Pasadena, California, with an M. Div. in Pastoral Studies, and from the University of Chicago with a Ph.D. in New Testament and Early Christian Literature. In 1973, he joined the faculty of Trinity International University, Deerfield, Illinois, and taught in the Department of Biblical Studies until his retirement in 1995. His research area is New Testament textual criticism and he is the coordinator of the Armenian Version for the International Project on the Text of Acts.

SEBOUH ASLANIAN recently defended with distinction his dissertation entitled "From the Indian Ocean to the Mediterranean: Circulation and the Global Trade Network of Armenian Merchants from New Julfa, Isfahan, 1605-1747" at Columbia University. His research interests include historical sociology, world history, and the interface between economic and cultural history in the early modern period. He has taught World and Middle Eastern history at Claremont McKenna College and the University of California at

Irvine and is currently visiting Assistant Professor of Middle Eastern and Indian Ocean history at Whitman College in Washington State.

ARTSVI BAKHCHINYAN is a Yerevan-based freelance researcher in Armenian studies. He is author of seven books on various aspects of Armenian reality as well as articles in Armenian, Russian, and English. His last major work was the voluminous *Study of Armenians in World Cinema* (2004). Bakhchinyan is also involved in film research, as Vice-President of the Armenian Association of Film Critics and Cinema Journalists.

PETER BALAKIAN is Donald M. and Constance H. Rebar Professor of the Humanities at Colgate University. He holds a Ph.D. in American Civilization from Brown University, is a prize-winning poet, and author of *Black Dog of Fate: An American Son Uncovers His Armenian Past* (1997) and *The Burning Tigris: The Armenian Genocide and America's Response* (2003). He is the recipient of the Anahid Literary Prize (1990), a Guggenheim Fellowship (1999), and the Raphael Lemkin prize for best book in English on the subject of human rights and genocide (2005).

GEORGE A. BOURNOUTIAN has taught Armenian, Iranian, and Russian history at Glendale Community College, UCLA, Tufts University, Ramapo College, Columbia University, New York University, and the University of Connecticut. He is Senior Professor of Middle Eastern and East European History at Iona College in New York. He is the author of fifteen books, including *Armenians and Russians, (1626-1796)* (2001), *A Concise History of the Armenian People* (2003), *The History of Vardapet Arak'el of Tabriz* (2005), and numerous articles in scholarly journals and encyclopedias.

AZAT BOZOYAN studied in the faculty of history at Yerevan State University and graduated in 1978. He received his Ph.D. in Byzantine Studies at the Academy of Sciences of the Republic of Armenia in 1979. Since 1982, he has been working at the Academy and in 1999 he was appointed head of the section on the "Christian East." He is a professor at Yerevan State University, at the Khach'atur Abovian Pedagogical Institute, the Gevorkian Theological Seminary, and at the Pastoral Seminary in Yerevan.

Since 2001, he has been the head of the Karekin I Armenological and Theological Center in the Mother See of Holy Etchmiadzin.

MARCO G. BRAMBILLA is a practicing architect specializing in the preservation of historic architectural monuments. He has lectured on the "History of Islamic and Armenian Architecture" and "Restoration of Historic Architectural Monuments," in Italy, Iran, and the United States. Over the last thirty years, he was the project architect of several historical buildings, from major monuments of Islamic architecture in Iran, to Armenian churches and historic architectural monuments in Europe and in the United States. He has offices in California, Italy, and Armenia.

HELMUT BUSCHHAUSEN attended the University of Münster and studied art history, archaeology, oriental languages, and church history. He has been professor at the Institut für Kunstgeschichte and the Institut für Byzantinistik, University of Vienna. An eminent European art historian, he specializes in the paleo-Christian and Byzantine periods. Separately and with Heide Lenzen Buschhausen he has published numerous studies on Armenian, in addition to those on Greek, Coptic or Syriac manuscripts. Among their most important works on Armenian art are: *The Illuminated Armenian Manuscripts of the Mekhitarist Congregation in Vienna* (1977) and a facsimile edition of the Etchmiadzin Gospels (1999).

DAVID STEPHEN CALONNE, was born in Los Angeles, and received his B.A. from the University of California at Los Angeles and his Ph.D. from the University of Texas at Austin. He has taught at the University of Texas at Austin, the University of Michigan, and presently teaches at Eastern Michigan University. He has published essays in *Ararat*, the *Armenian Review*, the *Journal of the Society for Armenian Studies*, *Armenian Forum*, and is the author of *William Saroyan: My Real Work is Being* (1983); *The Colossus of Armenia: G.I. Gurdjieff and Henry Miller* (1997); and most recently *Charles Bukowski: Sunlight Here I Am/Interviews and Encounters, 1963-1993* (2003).

LEVON CHOOKASZIAN is UNESCO Chair of Armenian Art History at Yerevan State University. He is the author of numerous articles and a monograph on Armenian miniature and modern painting. He has written biographies of numerous Armenian artists and his articles have been published in Armenian, Russian, Polish, English, French, German, and Norwegian scholarly journals. Furthermore, he has contributed numerous entries on Armenian art to encyclopedias and has written a monograph on the famous thirteenth century Armenian painter T'oros Ṙoslin, which is being translated into English for publication.

JAMES CLACKSON is Senior Lecturer in the Faculty of Classics at Cambridge University and Fellow and Director of Studies at Jesus College Cambridge. He studied Armenian with Professor Charles Dowsett of Oxford. He is the author of *The Linguistic Relationship between Armenian and Greek* (1994), *Indo-European Linguistics: An Introduction* (2007), and a major analysis of the unique Armeno-Greek papyrus in the Bibliothèque nationale de France.

S. PETER COWE is Professor of Armenian Language and Culture at the University of California at Los Angeles. He is a founding member of the Association internationale des études arméniennes (1983). He received an M.A. in Armenology and subsidiary Theology from the University of Oxford, Mansfield College, and in 1983 a Ph.D. in Armenology from the Hebrew University of Jerusalem. In 1996, he became Professor of Armenian Studies at UCLA, where in 2000, he was appointed as the holder of the Grigor Narekatsi Chair in Armenian Language and Culture. He is the author of several books, including *Modern Armenian Drama: An Anthology* (2001).

CLAUDE COX holds a Ph.D. in Septuagint Studies from the University of Toronto. During his graduate studies he spent a year in Yerevan, working at the Matenadaran. His doctoral thesis produced an edition of the book of Deuteronomy in classical Armenian. He has taught at a number of Canadian universities and colleges, aside from serving as a church minister and chaplain. He is currently Adjunct Associate Professor of Old Testament and Hebrew at McMaster Divinity College, Hamilton, Ontario. He and his family live in Barrie, Ontario, just north of Toronto.

YOLANDE CROWE is an independent scholar who is licenciée ès-lettres from the Sorbonne, Paris. She received a Ph.D. in Islamic Art and Archaeology from the School of Oriental and African Studies, London, where her thesis was on "The Great Mosque in Divrigi." She has made regular contributions and publications for congresses of Turkish, Persian, and South Asian Arts since 1973. She has published *Les Arts de l'Islam, Musées Royaux d'Art et d'Histoire* (1976) and *Persia and China, Safavid Blue and White Ceramics in the Victoria and Albert Museum, 1501-1738* (2002).

GÉRARD DÉDÉYAN graduated from the prestigious École normale supérieure and then studied history, publishing his first doctoral thesis, *La Chronique attribuée au Connétable Smbat* (1980) and then a second doctoral thesis *Les Arméniens entre Grecs, Musulmans et Croisés... (1068-1150)*, 2 vols. (2003), which was awarded the Schlumberger Prize of the Académie des Inscriptions et Belles-Lettres. He has been teaching at the Université Paul Valéry–Montpellier III, since 1968. Since 1994, he has been the co-director of the Jewish, Armenian, and Oriental Christian Research Center. In 2003, he was elected Corresponding Member of the Armenian Academy of Sciences.

BARLOW DER MUGRDECHIAN graduated from the University of California at Los Angeles with an M.A. (1983) and C. Phil. (1985) in Armenian Language and Literature. He has taught Armenian language, literature, history, art, and culture courses for the past twenty-three years in the Armenian Studies Program at California State University, Fresno. He served as President of the Society for Armenian Studies for four years (2001-2004). In 1996, he received the Provost's Award for Excellence in Teaching and in 2000, he was awarded an honorary doctorate degree from Yerevan State University.

ROBERTA ERVINE is Associate Professor of Armenian Studies at St. Nersess Armenian Seminary in New Rochelle, New York. Prior to taking that position, she lived for more than twenty years in Jerusalem's Armenian Monastery of the Sts. James. While there she studied with Archbishop Norayr Bogharian, curator of manuscripts for the monastery, and Bishop Guregh Kapikian, Armenian

Supervisor of the Status Quo in the Holy Places. She also taught for a number of institutions, including the Holy Translators School and the Hebrew University of Jerusalem.

ERIC P. HAMP received his Ph.D. from Harvard University and since then has taught at the University of Chicago, where he is Robert Maynard Hutchins Distinguished Service Professor Emeritus, Departments of Linguistics, Slavic Languages and Literatures, Psychology (Cognition and Communication) and the Committee on the Ancient Mediterranean World. His field is Indo-European linguistics, particularly Celtic languages and Albanian. He served for many years as editor of the *International Journal of American Linguistics* and did field work on Quileute, Ojibwa, and Ainu.

RICHARD G. HOVANNISIAN is holder of the Armenian Educational Foundation Chair in Modern Armenian History at the University of California at Los Angeles. His publications include *Armenia on the Road to Independence* (1967), the four-volume *Republic of Armenia* (1971-1996), five volumes on the Armenian Genocide, seven volumes in the UCLA series, Historic Armenian Cities and Provinces, and sixty research articles relating to Armenian, Caucasian, Middle Eastern, and Islamic studies. He was elected Academician of the National Academy of Sciences of Armenia in 1990 and has been awarded honorary doctoral degrees by Yerevan State University and Artsakh State University.

MICAH JENDIAN was born and raised in Fresno, California, and earned a B.A. in Philosophy from the University of California at Los Angeles. He continued his education at San Diego State University as a Dolores Zohrab Liebmann Fellow, earning a M.A. in English in 1999. His article has been excerpted from his Master's thesis "Falling From the Trapeze: William Saroyan's Challenge to the Culture Industry." He also has presented numerous papers on Saroyan's work at academic conferences. He currently teaches in the Department of English at Grossmont College in San Diego.

HARRY KEYISHIAN is Professor of English at Fairleigh Dickinson University in Madison, New Jersey, where he teaches courses in literature, drama, film, and communications. He holds a Ph.D. from

New York University. His published books are *Michael Arlen* (1976), a study of the English novelist; *Critical Essays on William Saroyan* (1996), on the American author; *The Shapes of Revenge: Victimization, Vengeance, and Vindictiveness in Shakespeare* (also 1996); and *Screening Politics* (2003), a study of American movies about politicians and political campaigns. He is Director of Fairleigh Dickinson University Press.

MICHAEL KOVACS received his B.A. in English from the University of California at Berkeley, and his M.A. in English with an emphasis in American literature at Stanford University. He has taught English and writing at the University of Nevada, Las Vegas, and City College of San Francisco. Currently, he is the head of marketing and public relations for a Fortune 200 company in Silicon Valley, and also teaches English and writing part-time at Gavilan College in Gilroy, California.

HENNING LEHMANN received a Master of Theology (cand. theol., Aarhus University, 1960), a degree in Patristic and Armenian Studies (Heidelberg, Bonn, Paris, London/Cambridge, 1961-64), and Dr. Phil. (Copenhagen, 1975). He is Associate Professor in Patristic/Church history (Aarhus, 1960-1983), President of Aarhus University (1983-2002) and Professor, History of Eastern Churches (2002 until his retirement in 2003). He has published a number of articles on Patristic and Armenian subjects, including *Per Piscatores. Studies in the Armenian version of a collection of homilies by Eusebius of Emesa and Severian of Gabala* (1975) and *Armenierne-kultur og historie* (in Danish, 1984). He was co-editor of the *Album of Armenian Paleography* (2002).

CHRISTINA MARANCI is Associate Professor of Medieval Art at the University of Wisconsin-Milwaukee. She is the author of *Medieval Armenian Architecture: Constructions of Race and Nation* (2001), and articles in *Revue des études arméniennes*, *Gesta*, *The Journal for the Society of Architectural Historians*, and *The Art Bulletin*. She focuses on the art and architecture of the medieval Caucasus and cross-cultural encounters. Her forthcoming book, *The Geometry of Power*, explores the role of the Armenian church building and issues of epigraphy, relief sculpture, and ceremonial on the seventh century eastern frontier.

MARIELLE MARTINIANI-REBER is a native of Lyon where she completed her studies, including a doctorate from the University of Lyon II in 1984. She taught Byzantine art from 1978-1982 at the University of Lyon II, and then between 1984 and 1988 at the University of Lausanne. Since 1984, she has worked at the Museum of Art and History in Geneva, as a scientific research assistant, and since 1995, as chief conservator of the department of applied art. She is a world-renowned expert in Oriental and Byzantine textiles and has published numerous books, articles, and exhibition catalogues in the field of Byzantine art and Oriental textiles, and mounted dozens of major museum exhibitions.

VARTAN MATIOSSIAN teaches at the Hovnanian School, New Jersey, and is affiliated with the School of Oriental Studies, University del Salvador, Buenos Aires, where he previously taught Armenian subjects. He has written extensively about Armenian history and literature in numerous publications in Armenian, Spanish, and English. He is the author of three books in Armenian: *Kostan Zariani shurj* [About Kostan Zarian] (1998); *Haravayin koghmn ashkharhi. Hayerĕ Latin Amerikayi mēj skizbēn minch'ew 1950* [The Southern Side of the Earth: Armenians in Latin America from the Beginnings to 1950] (2005); and *Anverj veradardz. Hayastani chanaparhnerĕ (1989-2004)* [Everlasting Return: The Roads to Armenia, 1989-2004] (2005).

BARBARA J. MERGUERIAN directs the Women's Information Center of the Armenian International Women's Association in Boston, Massachusetts. A graduate of Brown University, she earned her doctorate in Modern European history from Harvard University. She has been a visiting professor at Tufts University, Yerevan State University in Armenia, and California State University, Fresno. The former editor of the *Armenian Mirror-Spectator* newspaper and of the *Journal of Armenian Studies*, she is the editor or co-editor of several books, including *Armenian Women in a Changing World.* Her articles deal with United States foreign policy and the programs of the American missionaries among the Armenians in the Ottoman Empire in the nineteenth and early twentieth centuries.

CLAUDE MUTAFIAN is the son of parents born on the Black Sea shore, who survived the Genocide. From 1980 on he became more and more interested in history and began to write books and articles about Cilician Armenia, the Crusades, and the Mongols, as well as about other topics in Armenian history. He has been curator of several exhibitions, *Le royaume arménien de Cilicie* (Chapel of the Sorbonne, Paris, 1993), *Roma-Armenia* (Sixtine Hall, Vatican, 1999), and *Arménie. La magie de l'écrit* (Marseille, April 27-July 22, 2007). In 2002, he became Doctor in History at "Paris-I-Panthéon-Sorbonne" University, with a thesis on "The Diplomacy of Cilician Armenia."

MIKAËL NICHANIAN received his Ph.D. at Paris University with a thesis on "Byzantine Aristocracy and Imperial Power (7th-9th c.)" in 2004. He was appointed curator of Armenian books and manuscripts at the Bibliothèque nationale de France in 2007. A former student of the École normale supérieure, he has taught medieval history at the universities of Lyon and Paris. He is a member of the "Centre de recherches d'histoire et civilisation de Byzance" (CNRS-Collège de France) since 2000. He has published a number of articles on Byzantine and Armenian subjects and is the author of *Le monde byzantin, économie et société : du 8e siècle à 1204* (2006).

HILARY RICHARDSON, M.A. (Cantab.), M.A (N.U.I.), read Archaeology and Anthropology at Cambridge University, and History of Art at University College Dublin (UCD), also studying at the National College of Art, Dublin. A former lecturer in the Department of Archaeology at UCD, she concentrated on teaching Irish and early Christian art and its background. She has spoken at conferences in Armenia, Austria, Britain, and has published many papers in the field of Celtic art and early Christian art, and *An Introduction to Irish High Crosses* (1990), and "Visual Arts and Society," Chap. xix, in *A New History of Ireland*, vol. I (2005).

VAHRAM SHEMMASSIAN is Assistant Professor and Director of Armenian Studies in the Department of Modern and Classical

Languages and Literatures at California State University, Northridge. He holds a Ph.D. in History from the University of California at Los Angeles. He has conducted extensive research in numerous governmental and non-governmental archives in the United States, Europe, the Middle East, and Armenia, gathering data on the Armenians of Musa Dagh, as well as Armenian Genocide survivors in the Middle East at the end of World War I. He has published several scholarly articles, delivered lectures at community events and in universities, and participated in symposia and conferences.

LORNE SHIRINIAN is a professor of English and Comparative Literature at the Royal Military College of Canada and head of the Department of English. He received his Ph.D. in Comparative Literature from the Université de Montréal. He is also a poet, playwright, and writer of fiction. His most recent works of fiction are *Memory's Orphans* (2002) and his collection of stories, *When Darkness Falls Upon Us* (2005). His area of research is the way the Armenian Genocide has affected the development of Armenian diaspora culture. He is the author of twenty books of poetry, fiction, drama, and cultural criticism.

MICHAEL STONE received his B.A. (Hons.) degree in 1960 from the University of Melbourne and his Ph.D. from Harvard in 1965. In 1985, he earned the senior doctoral degree, D.Litt., from the University of Melbourne. He was appointed to the Hebrew University of Jerusalem in 1966 and, eventually, became Professor of Armenian Studies and Gail Levin de Nur Professor of Religious Studies in 1980. He was editor-in-chief of the *Album of Armenian Paleography* (2004), with co-editors Dickran Kouymjian and Henning Lehmann. He was founder and President for twenty years, and now Honorary Life President of the Association internationale des études arméniennes.

RONALD GRIGOR SUNY is Charles Tilly Collegiate Professor of Social and Political History at the University of Michigan and Professor Emeritus of Political Science and History at the University of Chicago. He was the first holder of the Alex Manoogian Chair in Modern Armenian history at the University of Michigan, Ann Arbor (1981-1995). He is the author of *Armenian in the Twentieth Century*

(1983), *Looking Toward Ararat: Armenia in Modern History* (1993) and *The Soviet Experiment: Russia, the USSR, and the Successor States* (1998). He is currently working on a biography of Stalin.

YVES TERNON received his doctorate in history from the University of Paris (IV-Sorbonne) after a career as an eminent surgeon. A recognized and distinguish authority on genocide studies, he is the author of major works on the subject, in particular the Armenian Genocide and the Holocaust. He is an activist against negationism in all its forms. His first books (1969, 1971, 1973) discussed the role of doctors and medicine within the Nazi regime. His most recent works are the fifth edition of *1915. Le génocide des Arméniens*, with Gérard Chaliand (2006) and *Guerres et génocides au XXe siècle* (2007).

ROBERT W. THOMSON received his Ph.D. at Cambridge University with a thesis on Armenian and Syriac versions of works by Athanasius of Alexandria. He was appointed the first Mashtots Professor of Armenian Studies at Harvard University in 1969. From 1984 to 1989 he served as Director of Dumbarton Oaks in Washington, D.C., and, in 1992, was appointed Calouste Gulbenkian Professor of Armenian Studies at Oxford University. He has translated important historical, philosophical, and theological works written in Armenian, Syriac, and Georgian. Since retiring in 2001 he has devoted particular attention to Armenian biblical commentaries.

GIUSTO TRAINA is Professor of Greek History at the University of Rouen (France). He also teaches Classical Armenian at the Université catholique de Louvain. He is a member of the Board of the Association internationale des études arméniennes. He is author of several publications on Armenian history and philology and he recently published and translated the Venice Manuscript of Ps. Callisthenes' *Life of Alexander the Macedonian*. In his latest book *428 dopo Cristo. Storia di un anno* (2007) he analyzes the global repercussions on the late Roman world of the fall of the last Armenian king.

GABRIELLA ULUHOGIAN had been teaching for thirty-two years as Professor of Armenian Language and Literature in the Faculty of

Arts of Bologna University. Though interested in the development of Armenian language and literature through the centuries, her education and deepest interests led her to devote herself in particular to the study of the relations between Classical and Armenian culture. She published various documents, the most remarkable of which is *Un'antica mappa della Chiesa armena* (2000). She has authored a number of scientific articles in Italian and in Armenian.

EDDA VARDANYAN graduated in 1988 from the Art Institute of Yerevan. From 1996-2001 she taught in the Department of Art History at Yerevan State University. She received her doctorate from the Sorbonne (École practique des hautes études) and is a senior scientist at the Mesrop Mashtots‘ Matenadaran in Yerevan. She is member of the "Centre de recherches d'histoire et civilisation de Byzance" (CNRS, Collège de France). She has participated in international conferences, has published numerous articles, and most recently a book (with Tim Greenwood), on Hakob Jughayets‘i, *Hakob's Gospels: The Life and Work of an Armenian Artist of the Sixteenth Century* (2006).

BERT VAUX is University Lecturer in Phonology and Morphology at the University of Cambridge and a fellow of King's College. He is the author of *The Phonology of Armenian* (1998) and editor of the *Annual of Armenian Linguistics* (1999-present). His research focuses on phonological theory and Armenian dialectology. Author of dozens of articles on phonology and dialectology, in 1998, he formulated a theory on voiceless fricatives, which has now become known as Vaux's Law in linguistic theory.

H. ARAM VEESER is an Associate Professor of English at The City College of New York. He is the editor of *The New Historicism* (1989), *The New Historicism Reader* (1994), *The Confessions of the Critics* (1996), and *The Stanley Fish Reader* (1999). He is co-author of *Ken Aptekar: Painting Between the Lines, 1990-2000* (2001). His book, *The Influence of Edward Said* is forthcoming in the Fall of 2008. He has written for a number of journals including the *Nation Magazine*, *The Minnesota Review*, *The Journal of Armenian Studies*, *Armenian Forum*, and *Ararat*.

CHRISTOPHER J. WALKER is the author of *Armenia: The Survival of a Nation* (1980), and of *Visions of Ararat: Writings on Armenia* (1997), as well as a number of articles on Armenian history. He is the co-author (along with the late David Marshall Lang) of *The Armenians* (1987). He briefly studied under the late Professor Dowsett of Oxford. His recent books include a biography of Oliver Baldwin, and a study of Islam and the West. He is currently working on Socinianism in England in the 1690s.

JOS J. S. WEITENBERG is Professor of Armenian Studies at Leiden University. His main interest is the study of the interaction of linguistic data with cultural and historical developments. Specifically he works on the historical growth of Armenian dialects. He is interested in the manufacture of computerized holdings of Classical Armenian texts. His most recent project is the *Leiden Armenian Lexical Textbase*, an interconnected set of texts, textual analyses, and dictionaries of Classical Armenian. He is currently preparing a descriptive grammar of Classical Armenian.

CHRISTOPHER YOUNG is a distinguished English judge, now in part-time retirement; like the famous traveler Henry Finnis Blosse Lynch, he is a member of the Athenaeum. He has traveled widely in the Eastern provinces of Turkey and published articles and read conference papers on late Byzantine history. Formerly a post-graduate student of London University, he is now preparing a doctoral thesis on H. F. B. Lynch at Oxford University.

BOGHOS LEVON VARDAPET ZEKIYAN heads the Chair of Armenian Studies at Ca' Foscari University of Venice, Italy, and is Professor of Institutions of the Armenian Church at the Pontifical Oriental Institute of Rome. Besides Armenian studies, his main scholarly interests include philosophy and theology. A member from abroad of the National Academy of Sciences of Armenia and active member of the Venetian Academy, he is the author of thirteen volumes and of more than 160 scholarly papers. Among his works is *The Armenian Way to Modernity: Armenian Identity between Tradition and Innovation, Specificity and Universality* (1997).